W9-AYE-443

Fundamentals of Management

5th Edition

Fundamentals of Management

Ricky W. Griffin
Texas A & M University

Houghton Mifflin Company   Boston   New York

In memory of my grandfather,
Andrew Allen Robinson

Vice-President and Executive Publisher: George Hoffman
Executive Editor: Lisé Johnson
Senior Marketing Manager: Nicole Hamm
Development Editor: Julia Perez
Senior Project Editor: Fred Burns
Art and Design Manager: Jill Haber Atkins
Cover Design Director: Tony Saizon
Senior Composition Buyer: Chuck Dutton
New Title Project Manager: James Lonergan
Editorial Assistant: Katilyn Crowley
Editorial Assistant: Jill Clark

Cover credit: Newton's Cradle, Close Up. The Riser Collection © Jon Feingersh, Getty Images.

Photo credits may be found on page 529.

Copyright © 2008 by Houghton Mifflin Company. All rights reserved.

No part of this work may be reproduced or transmitted in any form or by any means, electronic or mechanical, including photocopying and recording, or by any information storage or retrieval system without the prior written permission of Houghton Mifflin Company unless such copying is expressly permitted by federal copyright law. Address inquiries to College Permissions, Houghton Mifflin Company, 222 Berkeley Street, Boston, MA 02116-3764.

Printed in the U.S.A.

Library of Congress Control Number: 2007931306

ISBN-13: 978-0-618-91707-5
ISBN-10: 0-618-91707-1

1 2 3 4 5 6 7 8 9—DOW—11 10 09 08 07

Brief Contents

Contents

PART 2 Planning

5 Entrepreneurship and New Venture Management   121

7   Organization Change and Innovation

8   Managing Human Resources in Organizations

PART

4 Leading

9 Basic Elements of Individual Behavior in Organizations 258

10 Managing Employee Motivation and Performance 290

11 Leadership and Influence Processes

12 Communication in Organizations

13 Managing Work Groups and Teams 383

PART 5 Controlling

14 Basic Elements of Control 415

15 Managing Operations, Quality, and Productivity 447

Appendix

Preface

Over the last five decades, hundreds of books have been written for introductory management courses. As the body of material comprising the theory, research, and practice of management has grown and expanded, textbook authors have continued to mirror this expansion of material in their books. Writers have understood the importance of adding new material pertinent to traditional topics, such as planning and organizing, while simultaneously adding coverage of emerging new topics, such as diversity and information technology. As a by-product of this trend, our textbooks have grown longer and longer, making it increasingly difficult to cover all the material in one course.

Another emerging trend in management education is a new focus on teaching in a broader context. That is, introductory management courses are increasingly being taught with less emphasis on theory alone and more emphasis on application of concepts. Teaching students how to apply management concepts successfully often involves focusing more on skills development and the human side of the organization. This trend requires that textbooks cover theoretical concepts within a flexible framework that enables instructors to make use of interactive tools such as case studies, exercises, and projects.

This textbook represents a synthesis of these trends toward a more manageable and practical approach. By combining concise text discussion, standard pedagogical tools, lively and current content, an emphasis on organizational behavior, and exciting skills-development materials, *Fundamentals of Management* answers the need for a new approach to management education. This book provides almost limitless flexibility, a solid foundation of knowledge-based material, and an action oriented learning dimension that is unique in the field. Indeed, well over 150,000 students were introduced to the field of management using the first four editions of this book. This fifth edition builds solidly on the successes of the earlier editions.

Organization of the Book

Most management instructors today organize their course around the traditional management functions of planning, organizing, leading, and controlling. *Fundamentals of Management* uses these functions as its organizing framework. The book consists of five parts, with fifteen chapters and one appendix.

Part One introduces management through two chapters. Chapter 1 provides a basic overview of the management process in organizations, and Chapter 2 introduces students to the environment of management. Part Two covers the first basic management function, planning. Chapter 3 introduces the fundamental concepts of planning and discusses strategic management. Managerial decision making is the topic of Chapter 4. Finally, Chapter 5 covers entrepreneurship and the management of new ventures.

The second basic management function, organizing, is the subject of Part Three. In Chapter 6 the fundamental concepts of organization structure and design are introduced and discussed. Chapter 7 explores organization change and organizational innovation. Chapter 8 is devoted to the management of human resources.

Many instructors and managers believe that the third basic management function, leading, is especially important in contemporary organizations. Thus Part Four consists of five chapters devoted to this management function. Basic concepts and processes associated with individual behavior are introduced and discussed in Chapter 9. Employee motivation is the subject of Chapter 10. Chapter 11 examines leadership and influence processes in organizations. Communication in organizations is the topic of Chapter 12. The management of groups and teams is covered in Chapter 13.

The fourth management function, controlling, is the subject of Part Five. Chapter 14 introduces the fundamental concepts and issues associated with management of the control process. A special area of control today, managing for total quality, is discussed in Chapter 15.

Finally, the Appendix provides interpretations of the Skills Self-Assessment Instruments found at the end of each chapter.

Skills-Focused Pedagogical Features

With this text, it has been possible to address new dimensions of management education without creating a book so long that it is unwieldy. Specifically, each chapter is followed by an exciting set of skills-based exercises. These resources were created to bring an active and behavioral orientation to management education by requiring students to solve problems, make decisions, respond to situations, and work in groups. In short, these materials simulate many of the day-to-day challenges and opportunities that real managers face.

Among these skills-based exercises are three different *Building Effective Skills* organized around the set of basic management skills introduced in Chapter 1 of the text. The *Skills Self-Assessment Instrument* exercise helps readers learn something about their own approach to management. Finally, an *Experiential Exercise* provides additional action-oriented learning opportunities, usually in a group setting.

New to the fifth edition, each chapter also contains boxed features entitled *Managing in Times of Change* and *Eye on Management*. The *Managing in Times of Change* boxes are intended to depart briefly from the flow of the chapter to highlight issues related to today's ever-evolving management field. The *Eye on Management* boxes highlight management topics as they relate to contemporary businesses and organizations. A video segment is tied to each box and appears on the accompanying DVD.

Another new feature in the fifth edition is an end-of-chapter exercise that ties back to the chapter opening incident. This feature, *You Make the Call*, ask students to put themselves in the role of a consultant, a senior manager, or someone else hypothetically connected with the organization featured in the chapter opening incident. In this role they are then prompted to provide suggestions, forecast future events, and/or similar activities.

The fifth edition also retains the popular end-of-chapter *Test Prepper* feature. Students can take these short true/false and multiple-choice quizzes to gauge their retention and comprehension of chapter material. The answers can be found at the end of the text.

In addition to the end-of-chapter exercises, every chapter includes important standard pedagogy: learning objectives, a chapter outline, an opening incident, boldface key terms, a summary of key points, questions for review, questions for analysis, and an end-of-chapter case with questions.

Acknowledgments

I would like to acknowledge the many contributions that others have made to this book. My faculty colleagues at Texas A&M University have contributed enormously both to this book and to my thinking about management education. At Houghton Mifflin, an outstanding team of professionals, including Julia Perez, Lisé Johnson, and Fred Burns, have made more contributions to this book than I could even begin to list. Many reviewers helped shape the content and form of the materials in this book, though any and all errors are of course my own responsibility.

I want to extend special thanks to Jim Allyn (Moorpark College), Sally Alkazin (Linfield College), Robert Ash (Santiago Canyon College), Sherryl Berg-Ridenour (DeVry College—Pomona), Maynard Bledsoe (Meredith College), Alain Broder (Touro College), Murray Brunton (Central Ohio Tech), Sam Chapman (Diablo Valley College), Elizabeth Anne Christo-Baker (Terra Community College), Gary Corona (Florida Community College—Jacksonville), Dr. Anne Cowden (California State University), Carol Cumber (South Dakota State University), Thomas DeLaughter (University of Florida), Anita Dickson (Northampton Community College), Joe Dobson (Western Illinois University), Michael Dutch (University of Houston), Renee Eaton (University of Portland), Norb Elbert (Eastern Kentucky University), Teri Elkins-Longacre (University of Houston), Anne Fiedler (Barry University), William Furrell (Moorpark College),Eugene Garaventa (College of Staten Island), Bonnie Garson (Reinhardt College), Phillip Gonsher (Johnson Community College), Patricia Green (Nassau Community College), Joseph S. Hooker, Jr. (North Greenville College), David Hudson (Spalding University), George W. Jacobs (Middle Tennessee State University), Aaron Kelley (Ohio University), David Nemi (Niagara Community College), Judy Nixon (University of Tennessee—Chattanooga), James O'Neil (Keene State College), Thomas Paczkowski (Cayuga Community College), Ranjna Patel (Bethune–Cookman College), Lisa Reed (University of Portland), Dr. Joan Rivera (Angelo State University), Roberta B. Slater (Pennsylvania College of Technology), Robert Smoot (Hazard Community College), Sheryl A. Stanley (Newman University), Gary Taylor (South Dakota State University), Abraham Tawil (Baruch College), Barry Van Hook (Arizona State University), Ruth Weatherly (Simpson College), and Mary Williams (Community College of Nevada).

I would also like to thank Margaret Hill. Margaret has become an integral part of this project, as well as of my other Houghton Mifflin textbooks. I sincerely appreciate the high level of professionalism that she brings to her work.

My wife, Glenda, and our children, Dustin, Ashley, and Matt, are, of course, due the greatest thanks. Their love, care, interest, and enthusiasm help sustain me in all that I do.

I enthusiastically invite your feedback on this book. If you have any questions, suggestions, or issues to discuss, please feel free to contact me. The most efficient way to reach me is through e-mail. My address is rgriffin@tamu.edu.

R.W.G.

Fundamentals of Management

Understanding the Manager's Job

FIRST THINGS FIRST

Marissa Mayer: Google's Top Designer

"I'm the gatekeeper. I have to say no to a lot of people."

—MELISSA MAYER, VICE PRESIDENT, GOOGLE

At the ripe old age of thirty, Marissa Mayer is one of the top twenty managers at Google and its vice president of "Search Products and User Experience." Mayer rose to the top through a combination of intelligence, ambition, and talent. She was a high school valedictorian, debate leader, and pompom squad captain. She earned a Stanford bachelor's and a master's in artificial intelligence, and she patented several of her ideas. Her first task at Google was user interface design, so she read many psychology books to understand perception. While working full time at Google, Mayer teaches programming to Stanford undergraduates and has won several teaching awards.

Mayer has a strong vision for the website's appearance and function. The simplicity of Google's site is deceptive. Every Google search ranks 8 billion Web pages after solving an equation with over 500 million variables. But Google also offers images, interactive maps, foreign-language translation, and more. It is Mayer's job to make sure that users can quickly and easily find what they want, while at the same time providing enough features. Mayer says, "Google has the functionality of a really complicated Swiss Army knife, but the home page is our

The talents of executives like Marissa Ann Mayer have helped Google become one of the best known firms in the world.

LEARNING OBJECTIVES

After studying this chapter, you should be able to:

- Define management, describe the kinds of managers found in organizations, identify and explain the four basic management functions, describe the fundamental management skills, and comment on management as science and as art.

- Justify the importance of history and theory to managers and explain the evolution of management thought through the classical, behavioral, and quantitative perspectives.

- Identify and discuss key contemporary management perspectives represented by the systems and contingency perspectives and identify the major challenges and opportunities faced by managers today.

way of approaching [the knife] closed. It's simple, it's elegant, you can slip it in your pocket, but it's got the great doodad when you need it."

She is the one who gives the thumbs-up or thumbs-down to any new design idea. Mayer's stringent rule is that any new service must receive millions of page views each day, or it doesn't get added to the home page. She wants the home to remain uncluttered so that Google's site looks different from Yahoo!'s and Microsoft's. The two competitors each have approximately 60 services, 140 links, and numerous advertisements. By comparison, Google's site offers 6 services, 17 links (up from 11 in 2001), and no ads. "[Our site] gives you what you want, when you want it, rather than everything you could ever want, even when you don't," says Mayer. She does not let worry get in the way of innovation, saying, "Customers remember your average over time. That philosophy frees you from fear."

Mayer focuses on the 87 percent of people who rate ease of use as their top priority. To maintain simplicity, lots of good ideas simply don't make the cut. "I'm the gatekeeper," Mayer states. "I have to say no to a lot of people." She is concerned that, once more features are added, they will be impossible to remove. At the same time, she is sensitive to the demands of both engineers and users for more elements. Google now offers a customized website that allows additional complexity. (Try it out by clicking on the "Personalized Home" button on the upper right portion of the Google main home page, at www.google.com.)

Although Mayer may be uncompromising in her approach to design, she maintains good relationships with her staff. Two or three times a week, she holds informal "office hours" at Google, a technique she learned from her college professors. "I keep my ears open," she says. "I work at building a reputation for being receptive." Monthly brainstorming sessions for 100 engineers are another one of Mayer's tools for eliciting creativity.

During her tenure at Google, Mayer has overseen expansion of the site into 100 languages and helped to add 100 specialized features. Her colleagues must be doing something right too. The company has grown from a dozen employees in 1998 to 5,000 in 2006. Today, Google controls 60 percent of the search market, up from 45 percent at the end of 2004. (Yahoo! controls 30 percent and MSN just 6 percent.) After a year in which revenues are expected to top $3.5 billion, Google stock is hot. Google went public in August 2004, selling shares for about $100. Eighteen months later, the shares traded for $450. With managers like Mayer leading the firm, Google seems poised to continue this success into the future.

This book is about managers like Melissa Mayer and the work she does. In Chapter 1, we examine the general nature of management, its dimensions, and its challenges. We explain the concepts of management and managers, discuss the management process, and summarize the origins of contemporary management thought. We conclude by introducing critical challenges and issues that managers are facing now and will continue to encounter in the future.

An Introduction to Management

An **organization** is a group of people working together in a structured and coordinated fashion to achieve a set of goals. The goals may include profit (Starbucks Corporation), the discovery of knowledge (Iowa State University), national defense (the U.S. Army), coordination of various local charities (United Way of America), or social satisfaction (a sorority).

Managers are responsible for using the organization's resources to help achieve its goals. More precisely, **management** can be defined as a set of activities (including planning and decision making, organizing, leading, and controlling) directed at an organization's resources (human, financial, physical, and information), with the aim of achieving organizational goals in an efficient and effective manner. By **efficient**, we mean using resources wisely and in a cost-effective way. By **effective**, we mean making the right decisions and successfully implementing them. In general, successful organizations are both efficient and effective.[1]

Today's managers face a variety of interesting and challenging situations. The average executive works 60 hours a week, has enormous demands placed on his or her time, and faces increased complexities posed by globalization, domestic competition, government regulation, shareholder pressure, and Internet-related uncertainties. The job is complicated even more by rapid changes, unexpected disruptions, and both minor and major crises. The manager's job is unpredictable and fraught with challenges, but it is also filled with opportunities to make a difference. Good managers can propel an organization into unprecedented realms of success, whereas poor managers can devastate even the strongest of organizations.[2]

Kinds of Managers

Many different kinds of managers work in organizations today. Figure 1.1 shows how various kinds of managers within an organization can be differentiated by level and by area.

Levels of Management   One way to classify managers is in terms of their level in the organization. **Top managers** make up the relatively small group of executives who manage the overall organization. Titles found in this group include president, vice president, and chief executive officer (CEO). Top managers create the organization's goals, overall strategy, and operating policies. They also officially represent the organization to the external environment by meeting with government officials, executives of other organizations, and so forth.

Howard Schultz, CEO of Starbucks, is a top manager, as is Deidra Wager, the firm's executive vice president. The job of a top manager is likely to be complex and varied. Top managers make decisions about such activities as acquiring other companies, investing in research and development, entering or abandoning various markets, and building new plants and office facilities. They often work long hours and spend much of their time in meetings, on the telephone, or dealing with email. In most cases, top managers are also very well paid. In fact, the elite top managers of very large firms sometimes make several million dollars a year in salary, bonuses, and stock.[3]

Middle management is probably the largest group of managers in most organizations. Common middle-management titles include plant manager, operations manager, and division head. **Middle managers** are responsible primarily for

---

organization
A group of people working together in structured and coordinated fashion to achieve a set of goals

management
A set of activities (including planning and decision making, organizing, leading, and controlling) directed at an organization's resources (human, financial, physical, and information), with the aim of achieving organizational goals in an efficient and effective manner

efficient
Using resources wisely and in a cost-effective way

effective
Making the right decisions and successfully implementing them

top managers
The relatively small group of senior executives who manage the overall organization

middle managers
The relatively large set of managers responsible for implementing the policies and plans developed by top managers and for supervising and coordinating the activities of lower-level managers

Figure 1.1
KINDS OF MANAGERS BY LEVEL AND AREA

Organizations generally have three levels of management, represented by top managers, middle managers, and first-line managers. Regardless of level, managers are also usually associated with a specific area within the organization, such as marketing, finance, operations, human resources, administration, or some other area.

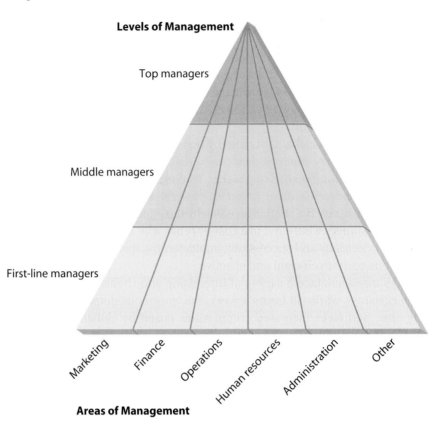

implementing the policies and plans developed by top managers and for supervising and coordinating the activities of lower-level managers.[4] Plant managers, for example, handle inventory management, quality control, equipment failures, and minor union problems. They also coordinate the work of supervisors within the plant. Jason Hernandez, a regional manager at Starbucks responsible for the firm's operations in three eastern states, is a middle manager.

First-line managers supervise and coordinate the activities of operating employees. Common titles for first-line managers are supervisor, coordinator, and office manager. Positions like these are often the first held by employees who enter management from the ranks of operating personnel. Wayne Maxwell and Jenny Wagner, managers of Starbucks coffee shops in Texas, are first-line managers. They oversee the day-to-day operations of their respective stores, hire operating employees to staff them, and handle other routine administrative duties required of them by the parent corporation. In contrast to top and middle managers, first-line managers typically spend a large proportion of their time supervising the work of subordinates.

first-line managers
Managers who supervise and coordinate the activities of operating employees

Managing in Different Areas of the Organization   Regardless of their level, managers may work in various areas within an organization. In any given firm, for example, these may include marketing, financial, operations, human resources, administrative, and other areas.

Marketing managers work in areas related to the marketing function—getting consumers and clients to buy the organization's products or services (be they Motorola digital cell phones, Ford automobiles, *Newsweek* magazines, Associated Press news reports, flights on Southwest Airlines, or cups of latte at Starbucks).

These areas include new-product development, promotion, and distribution. Given the importance of marketing for virtually all organizations, developing good managers in this area can be critical.

Financial managers deal primarily with an organization's financial resources. They are responsible for such activities as accounting, cash management, and investments. In some businesses, such as banking and insurance, financial managers are found in especially large numbers.

Operations managers are concerned with building and managing the systems that create an organization's products and services. Typical responsibilities of operations managers include production control, inventory control, quality control, plant layout, and site selection.

Human resource managers are responsible for hiring and developing employees. They are typically involved in human resource planning, recruiting and selecting employees, training and development, designing compensation and benefit systems, formulating performance appraisal systems, and discharging low-performing and problem employees.

Administrative, or general, managers are not associated with any particular management specialty. Probably the best example of an administrative management position is that of a hospital or clinic administrator. Administrative managers tend to be generalists; they have some basic familiarity with all functional areas of management rather than specialized training in any one area.[5]

Many organizations have specialized management positions in addition to those already described. Public relations managers, for example, deal with the public and media for firms like Altria Group, Inc. and the Dow Chemical Company to protect and enhance the image of the organization. Research and development (R&D) managers coordinate the activities of scientists and engineers working on scientific projects in organizations such as Monsanto Company, NASA, and Merck & Company. Internal consultants are used in organizations such as Prudential Insurance to provide specialized expert advice to operating managers. International operations are often coordinated by specialized managers in organizations like Eli Lilly and Rockwell International. The number, nature, and importance of these specialized managers vary tremendously from one organization to another. As contemporary organizations continue to grow in complexity and size, the number and importance of such managers are also likely to increase.

Basic Management Functions

Regardless of level or area, management involves the four basic functions of planning and decision making, organizing, leading, and controlling. This book is organized around these basic functions, as shown in Figure 1.2.

Planning and Decision Making   In its simplest form, *planning* means setting an organization's goals and deciding how best to achieve them. *Decision making*, a part of the planning process, involves selecting a course of action from a set of alternatives. Planning and decision making help maintain managerial effectiveness by serving as guides for future activities. In other words, the organization's goals and plans clearly help managers know how to allocate their time and resources. Part Two of this text is devoted to planning and decision-making activities and concepts.

planning
Setting an organization's goals and deciding how best to achieve them

decision making
Part of the planning process that involves selecting a course of action from a set of alternatives

Figure 1.2
THE MANAGEMENT PROCESS

Management involves four basic activities—planning and decision making, organizing, leading, and controlling. Although there is a basic logic for describing these activities in this sequence (as indicated by the solid arrows), most managers engage in more than one activity at a time and often move back and forth between the activities in unpredictable ways (as shown by the dotted arrows).

Planning and Decision Making
Setting the organization's goals and deciding how best to achieve them

Organizing
Determining how best to group activities and resources

Controlling
Monitoring and correcting ongoing activities to facilitate goal attainment

Leading
Motivating members of the organization to work in the best interests of the organization

organizing
Determining how activities and resources are to be grouped

leading
The set of processes used to get members of the organization to work together to further the interests of the organization

controlling
Monitoring organizational progress toward goal attainment

technical skills
The skills necessary to accomplish or understand the specific kind of work being done in an organization

Organizing Once a manager has set goals and developed a workable plan, the next management function is to organize people and the other resources necessary to carry out the plan. Specifically, *organizing* involves determining how activities and resources are to be grouped. Although some people equate this function with the creation of an organization chart, we will see in Part Three that it is actually much more.

Leading The third basic managerial function is leading. Some people consider leading to be both the most important and the most challenging of all managerial activities. *Leading* is the set of processes used to get members of the organization to work together to further the interests of the organization. We cover the leading function in detail in Part Four.

Controlling The final phase of the management process is *controlling*, or monitoring the organization's progress toward its goals. As the organization moves toward its goals, managers must monitor progress to ensure that it is performing in such a way as to arrive at its "destination" at the appointed time. Part Five explores the control function.

Fundamental Management Skills

To carry out these management functions most effectively, managers rely on a number of specific skills. The most fundamental management skills are technical, interpersonal, conceptual, diagnostic, communication, decision-making, and time-management skills.[6]

Technical Skills *Technical skills* are the skills necessary to accomplish or understand the specific kind of work being done in an organization. Technical skills are especially important for first-line managers. These managers spend much of their time training subordinates and answering questions about work-related problems.

Eye on Management

Managing for "Absolutely, Positively, Outrageous Customer Service" at Southwest Airlines

Southwest Airlines is one of the most consistently profitable and effective companies in the United States. The passenger air carrier was the first in the United States to offer no-frills, point-to-point flights at discounted rates. Passengers are willing to give up amenities such as reserved seating and meals in order to keep prices low. Other cost-cutting initiatives include Southwest's leadership in ticketless travel, online booking, nonunion labor force, and use of smaller, regional airports. Yet Southwest hasn't sacrificed quality as it cuts costs. The airline regularly sets safety and passenger satisfaction records and enjoys one of the best corporate reputations of any American firm.

Southwest is known for its loyal and motivated workforce. Wages at Southwest Airlines are only about industry average, but the employees quickly become immersed in the Southwest culture and most seem willing to put extra time, effort, and energy into their jobs. Southwest Airlines seems to do it all, satisfying customers, employees, and stockholders alike.

The video shows Ms. Sand, a first-line manager at Southwest, describing the nature of her job. She lists her job duties and also tells about some of the challenges she faces. View the video and then answer the following questions.

1. Discuss how Ms. Sand, a first-line manager, engages in the management functions of planning, organizing, leading, and controlling.

2. Discuss how Ms. Sand, a first-line manager, uses the various management skills identified in this chapter.

3. How is the job of Ms. Sand, a first-line manager, similar to the jobs of top and middle managers, in terms of management functions and skills?

They must know how to perform the tasks assigned to those they supervise if they are to be effective managers.

Interpersonal Skills   Managers spend considerable time interacting with people both inside and outside the organization. For obvious reasons, then, the manager also needs ***interpersonal skills***—the ability to communicate with, understand, and motivate both individuals and groups. As a manager climbs the organizational ladder, he or she must be able to get along with subordinates, peers, and those at higher levels of the organization. Because of the multitude of roles managers must fulfill, a manager must also be able to work with suppliers, customers, investors, and others outside of the organization.

> *interpersonal skills*
> The ability to communicate with, understand, and motivate both individuals and groups

Conceptual Skills   ***Conceptual skills*** depend on the manager's ability to think in the abstract. Managers need the mental capacity to understand the overall workings of the organization and its environment, to grasp how all the parts of the organization fit together, and to view the organization in a holistic manner. This allows managers to think strategically, to see the "big picture," and to make broad-based decisions that serve the overall organization.

> *conceptual skills*
> The manager's ability to think in the abstract

Diagnostic Skills   Successful managers also possess ***diagnostic skills***, or skills that enable a manager to visualize the most appropriate response to a situation. A physician diagnoses a patient's illness by analyzing symptoms and determining their probable cause. Similarly, a manager can diagnose and analyze a problem in the organization by studying its symptoms and then developing a solution.

> *diagnostic skills*
> The manager's ability to visualize the most appropriate response to a situation

communication skills
The manager's abilities both to effectively convey ideas and information to others and to effectively receive ideas and information from others

Communication Skills *Communication skills* refer to the manager's abilities both to effectively convey ideas and information to others and to effectively receive ideas and information from others. These skills enable a manager to transmit ideas to subordinates so that they know what is expected, to coordinate work with peers and colleagues so that they work well together, and to keep higher-level managers informed about what is going on. In addition, communication skills help the manager listen to what others say and to understand the real meaning behind letters, reports, and other written communication.

decision-making skills
The manager's ability to correctly recognize and define problems and opportunities and to then select an appropriate course of action to solve problems and capitalize on opportunities

Decision-Making Skills Effective managers also have good decision-making skills. *Decision-making skills* refer to the manager's ability to correctly recognize and define problems and opportunities and to then select an appropriate course of action to solve problems and capitalize on opportunities. No manager makes the right decision *all* the time. However, effective managers make good decisions *most* of the time. And, when they do make a bad decision, they usually recognize their mistake quickly and then make good decisions to recover with as little cost or damage to their organization as possible.

time-management skills
The manager's ability to prioritize work, to work efficiently, and to delegate appropriately

Time-Management Skills Finally, effective managers usually have good time-management skills. *Time-management skills* refer to the manager's ability to prioritize work, to work efficiently, and to delegate appropriately. As already noted, managers face many different pressures and challenges. It is too easy for a manager to get bogged down doing work that can easily be postponed or delegated to others.[7] When this happens, unfortunately, more pressing and higher-priority work may get neglected.[8]

The Science and the Art of Management

Given the complexity inherent in the manager's job, a reasonable question relates to whether management is a science or an art. In fact, effective management is a

Time management skills include the manager's ability to prioritize work, to work efficiently, and to delegate appropriately. Most effective managers have good time management skills. Those who don't, such as this manager, often find themselves behind schedule and don't get their work done.

I'M AFRAID WE HAD TO CANCEL THE 'PERFECT PLANNING' SEMINAR. WE FORGOT TO BOOK THE HOTEL UNTIL IT WAS TO LATE AND THE SPEAKER WE'D HOPED TO USE DIED IN 1958

www.CartoonStock.com

blend of both science and art. And successful executives recognize the importance of combining both the science and the art of management as they practice their craft.[9]

The Science of Management   Many management problems and issues can be approached in ways that are rational, logical, objective, and systematic. Managers can gather data, facts, and objective information. They can use quantitative models and decision-making techniques to arrive at "correct" decisions. And they need to take such a scientific approach to solving problems whenever possible, especially when they are dealing with relatively routine and straightforward issues. When Starbucks considers entering a new market, its managers look closely at a wide variety of objective details as they formulate their plans. Technical, diagnostic, and decision-making skills are especially important when practicing the science of management.

The Art of Management   Even though managers may try to be scientific as often as possible, they must frequently make decisions and solve problems on the basis of intuition, experience, instinct, and personal insights. Relying heavily on conceptual, communication, interpersonal, and time-management skills, for example, a manager may have to decide among multiple courses of action that look equally attractive. And even "objective facts" may prove to be wrong. When Starbucks was planning its first store in New York City, market research clearly showed that New Yorkers preferred drip coffee to more exotic espresso-style coffees. After first installing more drip coffeemakers and fewer espresso makers than in their other stores, managers had to backtrack when the New Yorkers lined up clamoring for espresso. Starbucks now introduces a standard menu and layout in all its stores, regardless of presumed market differences, and then makes necessary adjustments later. Thus, managers must blend an element of intuition and personal insight with hard data and objective facts.[10]

The Evolution of Management

Most managers today recognize the importance of history and theory in their work. For instance, knowing the origins of their organization and the kinds of practices that have led to success—or failure—can be an indispensable tool in managing the contemporary organization. Thus, in our next section, we briefly trace the history of management thought. Then we move forward to the present day by introducing contemporary management issues and challenges.

The Importance of History and Theory

Some people question the value of history and theory. Their arguments are usually based on the assumptions that history has no relevance to contemporary society and that theory is abstract and of no practical use. In reality, however, both theory and history are important to all managers today.

A *theory* is simply a conceptual framework for organizing knowledge and providing a blueprint for action.[11] Although some theories may seem abstract and irrelevant, many others are actually very simple and practical. Most management theories that are used to build organizations and guide them toward their goals are grounded in reality.[12] In addition, most managers develop and refine their own beliefs—or theories—about how they should run their organization and manage their employees.

theory
A conceptual framework for organizing knowledge and providing a blueprint for action

Awareness and understanding of important historical developments are also important to contemporary managers.[13] Understanding the historical context of management provides a sense of heritage and can help managers avoid the mistakes of others. Most courses in U.S. history devote time to business and economic developments in this country, including the Industrial Revolution, the early labor movement, and the Great Depression, and to such captains of U.S. industry as Cornelius Vanderbilt (railroads), John D. Rockefeller (oil), and Andrew Carnegie (steel). The contributions of those and other industrialists left a profound imprint on contemporary culture.[14]

Many managers are also realizing that they can benefit from a greater understanding of history in general. For example, Ian M. Ross of AT&T's Bell Laboratories cites *The Second World War* by Winston Churchill as a major influence on his approach to leadership. Other books that are often mentioned by managers for their relevance to today's business problems include such classics as Plato's *Republic*, Homer's *Iliad*, and Machiavelli's *The Prince*.[15] And, in recent years, new business history books are directed more at women managers and the lessons they can learn from the past.[16]

Managers at Wells Fargo clearly recognize the value of history. For example, the company maintains an extensive archival library of its old banking documents and records and even employs a full-time corporate historian. As part of their orientation and training, new managers at Wells Fargo take courses to become acquainted with the bank's history.[17] And the firm's logo is an old-fashioned stage coach.

The Historical Context of Management

The practice of management can be traced back thousands of years. The Egyptians used the management functions of planning, organizing, and controlling when they constructed the pyramids. Alexander the Great employed a staff organization to coordinate activities during his military campaigns. The Roman Empire developed a well-defined organizational structure that greatly facilitated communication and control. Socrates discussed management practices and concepts in 400 B.C., Plato described job specialization in 350 B.C., and Alfarabi listed several leadership traits in A.D. 900.[18]

In spite of this history, the serious study of management did not begin until the nineteenth century. Two of its first pioneers were Robert Owen and Charles Babbage. Owen (1771–1858), a British industrialist and reformer, was one of the first managers to recognize the importance of an organization's human resources and to express concern for the personal welfare of his workers. Babbage (1792–1871), an English mathematician, focused his attention on efficiencies of production. He placed great faith in the division of labor and advocated the application of mathematics to such problems as the efficient use of facilities and materials.

The Classical Management Perspective

classical management perspective
Consists of two distinct branches—scientific management and administrative management

At the dawn of the twentieth century, the preliminary ideas and writings of these and other managers and theorists converged with the emergence and evolution of large-scale businesses and management practices to create interest and focus attention on how businesses should be operated. The first important ideas to emerge are now called the ***classical management perspective***. This perspective actually includes two different viewpoints: scientific management and administrative management.

Scientific Management   Productivity emerged as a serious business problem during the first few years of this century. Business was expanding and capital was readily available, but labor was in short supply. Hence, managers began to search for ways to use existing labor more efficiently. In response to this need, experts began to focus on ways to improve the performance of individual workers. Their work led to the development of ***scientific management***. Some of the earliest advocates of scientific management included Frederick W. Taylor (1856–1915), Frank Gilbreth (1868–1924), and Lillian Gilbreth (1878–1972).[19] Taylor played the dominant role.

One of Taylor's first jobs was as a foreman at the Midvale Steel Company in Philadelphia. It was there that he observed what he called ***soldiering***—employees deliberately working at a pace slower than their capabilities. Taylor studied and timed each element of the steelworkers' jobs. He determined what each worker should be producing, and then he designed the most efficient way of doing each part of the overall task. Next he implemented a piecework pay system. Rather than paying all employees the same wage, he began increasing the pay of each worker who met and exceeded the target level of output set for his or her job.

After Taylor left Midvale, he worked as a consultant for several companies, including Simonds Rolling Machine Company and Bethlehem Steel. At Simonds he studied and redesigned jobs, introduced rest periods to reduce fatigue, and implemented a piecework pay system. The results were higher quality and quantity of output, and improved morale. At Bethlehem Steel, Taylor studied efficient ways of loading and unloading railcars and applied his conclusions with equally impressive results. During these experiences, he formulated the basic ideas that he called "scientific management." Figure 1.3 illustrates the basic steps Taylor suggested. He believed that managers who followed his guidelines would improve the efficiency of their workers.[20]

Taylor's work had a major impact on U.S. industry. By applying his principles, many organizations achieved major gains in efficiency. Taylor was not without his detractors, however. Labor argued that scientific management was just a device to get more work from each employee and to reduce the total number of workers needed by a firm. There was a congressional investigation into Taylor's ideas, and evidence suggests that he falsified some of his findings.[21] Nevertheless, Taylor's work left a lasting imprint on business.[22]

Frank and Lillian Gilbreth, contemporaries of Taylor, were a husband-and-wife team of industrial engineers. One of Frank Gilbreth's most interesting contributions was to the craft of bricklaying. After studying bricklayers at work, he developed

> *scientific management*
> Concerned with improving the performance of individual workers

> *soldiering*
> Employees deliberately working at a slow pace

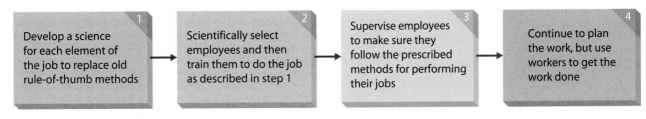

Figure 1.3
STEPS IN SCIENTIFIC MANAGEMENT

Frederick Taylor developed this system of scientific management, which he believed would lead to a more efficient and productive workforce. Bethlehem Steel was among the first organizations to profit from scientific management and still practices some parts of it today.

several procedures for doing the job more efficiently. For example, he specified standard materials and techniques, including the positioning of the bricklayer, the bricks, and the mortar at different levels. The results of these changes were a reduction from 18 separate physical movements to 5 and an increase in output of about 200 percent. Lillian Gilbreth made equally important contributions to several different areas of work, helped shape the field of industrial psychology, and made substantive contributions to the field of personnel management. Working individually and together, the Gilbreths developed numerous techniques and strategies for eliminating inefficiency. They applied many of their ideas to their family and documented their experiences raising 12 children in the book and original movie *Cheaper by the Dozen.*

Administrative Management   Whereas scientific management deals with the jobs of individual employees, **administrative management** focuses on managing the total organization. The primary contributors to administrative management were Henri Fayol (1841–1925), Lyndall Urwick (1891–1983), and Max Weber (1864–1920).

administrative management Focuses on managing the total organization

Henri Fayol was administrative management's most articulate spokesperson. A French industrialist, Fayol was unknown to U.S. managers and scholars until his most important work, *General and Industrial Management*, was translated into English in 1930.[23] Drawing on his own managerial experience, he attempted to systematize the practice of management to provide guidance and direction to other managers. Fayol also was the first to identify the specific managerial functions of planning, organizing, leading, and controlling. He believed that these functions accurately reflect the core of the management process. Most contemporary management books (including this one) still use this framework, and practicing managers agree that these functions are a critical part of their jobs.

After a career as a British army officer, Lyndall Urwick became a noted management theorist and consultant. He integrated scientific management with the work of Fayol and other administrative management theorists. He also advanced modern thinking about the functions of planning, organizing, and controlling. Like Fayol, he developed a list of guidelines for improving managerial effectiveness. Urwick is noted not so much for his own contributions as for his synthesis and integration of the work of others.

Although Max Weber lived and worked at the same time as Fayol and Taylor, his contributions were not recognized until some years had passed. Weber was a German sociologist, and his most important work was not translated into English until 1947.[24] Weber's work on bureaucracy laid the foundation for contemporary organization theory, discussed in detail in Chapter 6. The concept of bureaucracy, as we discuss later, is based on a rational set of guidelines for structuring organizations in the most efficient manner.

The Classical Management Perspective Today   The classical management perspective provides many techniques and approaches to management that are still relevant today. For example, thoroughly understanding the nature of the work being performed, selecting the right people for that work, and approaching decisions rationally are all useful ideas—and each was developed during this period. Similarly, some of the core concepts from Weber's bureaucratic model can still be used in the design of modern organizations, as long as their limitations are recognized. Managers should recognize that efficiency and productivity can indeed be measured and controlled in many situations. Recent advances in areas such as business-to-business (B2B) commerce also have efficiency as their primary goal. On the other hand, managers must remember the limitations of the classical perspective and avoid its narrow focus on efficiency to the exclusion of other important perspectives.

The Behavioral Management Perspective

Early advocates of the classical management perspective viewed organizations and jobs from an essentially mechanistic point of view; that is, they sought to conceptualize organizations as machines and workers as cogs within those machines. Even though many early writers recognized the role of individuals, their focus tended to be on how managers could control and standardize the behavior of their employees. In contrast, the **behavioral management perspective** placed much more emphasis on individual attitudes and behaviors and on group processes, and recognized the importance of behavioral processes in the workplace.

> *behavioral management perspective*
> Emphasizes individual attitudes and behaviors and group processes

The behavioral management perspective was stimulated by a number of writers and theoretical movements. One of those movements was *industrial psychology*, the practice of applying psychological concepts to industrial settings. Hugo Munsterberg (1863–1916), a noted German psychologist, is recognized as the father of industrial psychology. He established a psychological laboratory at Harvard in 1892, and his pioneering book, *Psychology and Industrial Efficiency*, was translated into English in 1913.[25] Munsterberg suggested that psychologists could make valuable contributions to managers in the areas of employee selection and motivation. Industrial psychology is still a major course of study at many colleges and universities. Another early advocate of the behavioral approach to management was Mary Parker Follett (1868–1933).[26] Follett worked during the scientific management era, but quickly came to recognize the human element in the workplace. Indeed, her work clearly anticipated the behavioral management perspective, and she appreciated the need to understand the role of behavior in organizations.

The Hawthorne Studies   Although Munsterberg and Follett made major contributions to the development of the behavioral approach to management, its primary catalyst was a series of studies conducted near Chicago at Western Electric's Hawthorne plant between 1927 and 1932. The research, originally sponsored by General Electric, was conducted by Elton Mayo and his associates.[27] Mayo was a faculty member and consultant at Harvard. The first study involved manipulating illumination for one group of workers and comparing their subsequent productivity with the productivity of another group whose illumination was not changed. Surprisingly, when illumination was increased for the experimental group, productivity went up in both groups. Productivity continued to increase in both groups, even when the lighting for the experimental group was decreased. Not until the lighting was reduced to the level of moonlight did productivity begin to decline (and General Electric withdrew its sponsorship).

Another experiment established a piecework incentive pay plan for a group of nine men assembling terminal banks for telephone exchanges. Scientific management would have predicted that each man would try to maximize his pay by producing as many units as possible. Mayo and his associates, however, found that the

The Hawthorne studies were a series of early experiments that focused on behavior in the workplace. In one experiment involving this group of workers, for example, researchers monitored how productivity changed as a result of changes in working conditions. The Hawthorne studies and subsequent experiments led scientists to the conclusion that the human element is very important in the workplace.

group itself informally established an acceptable level of output for its members. Workers who overproduced were branded "rate busters," and underproducers were labeled "chiselers." To be accepted by the group, workers produced at the accepted level. As they approached this acceptable level of output, workers slacked off to avoid overproducing.

Other studies, including an interview program involving several thousand workers, led Mayo and his associates to conclude that human behavior was much more important in the workplace than had been previously believed. In the lighting experiment, for example, the results were attributed to the fact that both groups received special attention and sympathetic supervision for perhaps the first time. The incentive pay plans did not work because wage incentives were less important to the individual workers than was social acceptance in determining output. In short, individual and social processes played major roles in shaping worker attitudes and behavior.

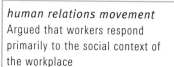

human relations movement
Argued that workers respond primarily to the social context of the workplace

The Human Relations Movement   The ***human relations movement***, which grew from the Hawthorne studies and was a popular approach to management for many years, proposed that workers respond primarily to the social context of the workplace, including social conditioning, group norms, and interpersonal dynamics. A basic assumption of the human relations movement was that the manager's concern for workers would lead to increased satisfaction, which would in turn result in improved performance. Two writers who helped advance the human relations movement were Abraham Maslow (1908–1970) and Douglas McGregor (1906–1964).

In 1943 Maslow advanced a theory suggesting that people are motivated by a hierarchy of needs, including monetary incentives and social acceptance.[28] Maslow's hierarchy, perhaps the best-known human relations theory, is described in detail in Chapter 10. Meanwhile, Douglas McGregor's Theory X and Theory Y model

Theory X Assumptions	1. People do not like work and try to avoid it.
	2. People do not like work, so managers have to control, direct, coerce, and threaten employees to get them to work toward organizational goals.
	3. People prefer to be directed, to avoid responsibility, and to want security; they have little ambition.
Theory Y Assumptions	1. People do not naturally dislike work; work is a natural part of their lives.
	2. People are internally motivated to reach objectives to which they are committed.
	3. People are committed to goals to the degree that they receive personal rewards when they reach their objectives.
	4. People will both seek and accept responsibility under favorable conditions.
	5. People have the capacity to be innovative in solving organizational problems.
	6. People are bright, but under most organizational conditions their potential is underutilized.

Table 1.1
THEORY X AND THEORY Y

Douglas McGregor developed Theory X and Theory Y. He argued that Theory X best represented the views of scientific management and Theory Y represented the human relations approach. McGregor believed that Theory Y was the best philosophy for all managers.

Source: D. McGregor and W. Bennis, *The Human Side Enterprise: 25th Anniversary Printing*, 1960, Copyright © 1960 The McGraw-Hill Companies, Inc. Reprinted with permission.

best represents the essence of the human relations movement (see Table 1.1).[29] According to McGregor, Theory X and Theory Y reflect two extreme belief sets that different managers have about their workers. ***Theory X*** is a relatively pessimistic and negative view of workers and is consistent with the views of scientific management. ***Theory Y*** is more positive and represents the assumptions that human relations advocates make. In McGregor's view, Theory Y was a more appropriate philosophy for managers to adhere to. Both Maslow and McGregor notably influenced the thinking of many practicing managers.

Contemporary Behavioral Science in Management Munsterberg, Mayo, Maslow, McGregor, and others have made valuable contributions to management. Contemporary theorists, however, have noted that many assertions of the human relationists were simplistic and provided inadequate descriptions of work behavior. Current behavioral perspectives on management, known as ***organizational behavior***, acknowledge that human behavior in organizations is much more complex than the human relationists realized. The field of organizational behavior draws from a broad, interdisciplinary base of psychology, sociology, anthropology, economics, and medicine. Organizational behavior takes a holistic view of behavior and addresses individual, group, and organization processes. These processes are major elements in contemporary management theory.[30] Important topics in this field include job satisfaction, stress, motivation, leadership, group dynamics, organizational politics, interpersonal conflict, and the structure and design of organizations.[31] A contingency orientation also characterizes the field (discussed more fully later in this chapter). Our discussions of organizing (Chapters 6–8) and leading (Chapters 9–13) are heavily influenced by organizational behavior. And, finally, managers need a solid understanding of human behavior as they address such diversity-related issues as ethnicity and religion in the workplace. Indeed, all of these topics are useful to help managers

Theory X
A pessimistic and negative view of workers consistent with the views of scientific management

Theory Y
A positive view of workers; it represents the assumptions that human relations advocates make

organizational behavior
Contemporary field focusing on behavioral perspectives on management

better deal with fallout from the consequences of layoffs and job cuts and to motivate today's workers.

The Behavioral Management Perspective Today   The primary contributions of this approach are related to ways in which it has changed managerial thinking. Managers are now more likely to recognize the importance of behavioral processes and to view employees as valuable resources instead of mere tools. On the other hand, organizational behavior is still relatively imprecise in its ability to predict behavior, especially the behavior of a specific individual. It is not always accepted or understood by practicing managers. Hence the contributions of the behavioral school are just beginning to be fully realized.

The Quantitative Management Perspective

The third major school of management thought began to emerge during World War II. During the war, government officials and scientists in England and the United States worked to help the military deploy its resources more efficiently and effectively. These groups took some of the mathematical approaches to management developed decades earlier by Taylor and Gantt and applied them to logistical problems during the war.[32] They learned that problems regarding troop, equipment, and submarine deployment, for example, could all be solved through mathematical analysis. After the war, companies such as DuPont and General Electric began to use the same techniques for deploying employees, choosing plant locations, and planning warehouses. Basically, then, this perspective is concerned with applying quantitative techniques to management. More specifically, the **quantitative management perspective** focuses on decision making, economic effectiveness, mathematical models, and the use of computers. There are two branches of the quantitative approach: management science and operations management.

> **quantitative management perspective**
> Applies quantitative techniques to management

Management Science   Unfortunately, the term *management science* appears to be related to scientific management, the approach developed by Taylor and others early in the twentieth century. But the two have little in common and should not be confused. **Management science** focuses specifically on the development of mathematical models. A mathematical model is a simplified representation of a system, process, or relationship.

> **management science**
> Focuses specifically on the development of mathematical models

At its most basic level, management science focuses on models, equations, and similar representations of reality. For example, managers at Detroit Edison use mathematical models to determine how best to route repair crews during blackouts. Citizens Bank of New England uses models to figure out how many tellers need to be on duty at each location at various times throughout the day. In recent years, paralleling the advent of the personal computer, management science techniques have become increasingly sophisticated. For example, automobile manufacturers DaimlerChrysler and General Motors use realistic computer simulations to study collision damage to cars. These simulations give them precise information and avoid the costs of crashing so many test cars.

> **operations management**
> Concerned with helping the organization more efficiently produce its products or services

Operations Management   Operations management is somewhat less mathematical and statistically less sophisticated than management science and can be applied more directly to managerial situations. Indeed, we can think of **operations management** as a form of applied management science. Operations management techniques are generally concerned with helping the organization produce its products or services more efficiently and can be applied to a wide range of problems.

For example, Rubbermaid and Home Depot each use operations management techniques to manage their inventories. (Inventory management is concerned with specific inventory problems, such as balancing carrying costs and ordering costs, and determining the optimal order quantity.) Linear programming (which involves computing simultaneous solutions to a set of linear equations) helps United Airlines plan its flight schedules, Consolidated Freightways develop its shipping routes, and General Instrument Corporation plan what instruments to produce at various times. Other operations management techniques include queuing theory, break-even analysis, and simulation. All of these techniques and procedures apply directly to operations, but they are also helpful in such areas as finance, marketing, and human resource management.[33]

The Quantitative Management Perspective Today   Like the other management perspectives, the quantitative management perspective has made important contributions and has certain limitations. It has provided managers with an abundance of decision-making tools and techniques and has increased understanding of overall organizational processes. It has been particularly useful in the areas of planning and controlling. Relatively new management concepts such as supply chain management and new techniques such as enterprise resource planning, both discussed later in this book, also evolved from the quantitative management perspective. Even more recently, mathematicians are using tools and techniques from the quantitative perspective to develop models that might be helpful in the war against terrorism.[34] On the other hand, mathematical models cannot fully account for individual behaviors and attitudes. Some believe that the time needed to develop competence in quantitative techniques retards the development of other managerial skills. Finally, mathematical models typically require a set of assumptions that may not be realistic.

Contemporary Management Perspectives

It is important to recognize that the classical, behavioral, and quantitative approaches to management are not necessarily contradictory or mutually exclusive. Even though each of the three perspectives makes very different assumptions and predictions, each can also complement the others. Indeed, a complete understanding of management requires an appreciation of all three perspectives. The systems and contingency perspectives can help us integrate the earlier approaches and enlarge our understanding of all three.

The Systems Perspective

The systems perspective is one important contemporary management perspective. A *system* is an interrelated set of elements functioning as a whole.[35] As shown in Figure 1.4, by viewing an organization as a system, we can identify four basic elements: inputs, transformation processes, outputs, and feedback. First, inputs are the material, human, financial, and information resources the organization gets from its environment. Next, through technological and managerial processes, inputs are transformed into outputs. Outputs include products, services, or both

system
An interrelated set of elements functioning as a whole

Figure 1.4

THE SYSTEMS PERSPECTIVE OF ORGANIZATIONS

By viewing organizations as systems, managers can better understand the importance of their environment and the level of interdependence among subsystems within the organization. Managers must also understand how their decisions affect and are affected by other subsystems within the organization.

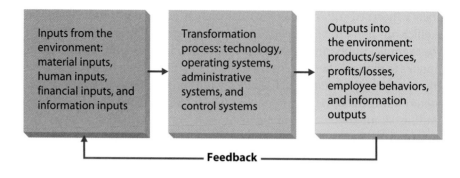

open system
A system that interacts with its environment

closed system
A system that does not interact with its environment

subsystem
A system within another system

synergy
Two or more subsystems working together to produce more than the total of what they might produce working alone

entropy
A normal process leading to system decline

(tangible and intangible); profits, losses, or both (even not-for-profit organizations must operate within their budgets); employee behaviors; and information. Finally, the environment reacts to these outputs and provides feedback to the system.

Thinking of organizations as systems provides us with a variety of important viewpoints on organizations, such as the concepts of open systems, subsystems, synergy, and entropy. **Open systems** are systems that interact with their environment, whereas **closed systems** do not interact with their environment. Although organizations are open systems, some make the mistake of ignoring their environment and behaving as though their environment were not important.

The systems perspective also stresses the importance of **subsystems**—systems within a broader system. For example, while the marketing, production, and finance functions within Mattel are systems in their own right, they are also subsystems within the overall organization. Because they are interdependent, a change in one subsystem can affect other subsystems as well. If the production department at Mattel lowers the quality of the toys being made (by buying lower-quality materials, for example), the effects are felt in finance (improved cash flow in the short run owing to lower costs) and marketing (decreased sales in the long run because of customer dissatisfaction). Managers must therefore remember that although organizational subsystems can be managed with some degree of autonomy, their interdependence should not be overlooked.

Synergy suggests that organizational units (or subsystems) may often be more successful working together than working alone. The Walt Disney Company, for example, benefits greatly from synergy. The company's movies, theme parks, television programs, and merchandise-licensing programs all benefit one another. Children who enjoy a Disney movie like *Cars* want to go to Disney World, see the *Cars* attractions there, and buy stuffed toys and action figures of the film's characters. Music from the film generates additional revenues for the firm, as do computer games and other licensing arrangements for lunchboxes, clothing, and so forth. Synergy was also the major objective of Procter & Gamble's recent decision to buy Gillette—the firm decided it could use its own retailing presence and international distribution networks to substantially increase Gillette's sales. And Gillette's products are natural complements to P&G's existing line of grooming products.[36] Synergy is an important concept for managers because it emphasizes the importance of working together in a cooperative and coordinated fashion.[37]

Finally, **entropy** is a normal process that leads to system decline. When an organization does not monitor feedback from its environment and make appropriate adjustments, it may fail. For example, witness the problems of Studebaker (an automobile manufacturer) and Montgomery Ward (a major retailer). Each of these organizations went bankrupt and closed its doors because it failed to revitalize itself and keep pace with changes in its environment. A primary objective of management, from a systems perspective, is to continually re-energize the organization to avoid entropy.

The Contingency Perspective

Another noteworthy recent addition to management thinking is the contingency perspective. The classical, behavioral, and quantitative approaches are considered **universal perspectives** because they try to identify the "one best way" to manage organizations. The **contingency perspective**, in contrast, suggests that universal theories cannot be applied to organizations because each organization is unique. Instead, the contingency perspective suggests that appropriate managerial behavior in a given situation depends on, or is contingent on, unique elements in that situation.[38]

Stated differently, effective managerial behavior in one situation cannot always be generalized to other situations. Recall, for example, that Frederick Taylor assumed that all workers would generate the highest possible level of output to maximize their own personal economic gain. We can imagine some people being motivated primarily by money—but we can just as easily imagine other people being motivated by the desire for leisure time, status, social acceptance, or any combination of these (as Mayo found at the Hawthorne plant). Leslie Wexner, founder and CEO of the Limited, used one managerial style when his firm was small and rapidly growing, but that style did not match as well when the Limited became a huge, mature enterprise. Thus Wexner had to alter his style at that point to better fit the changing needs of his business.

> **universal perspective**
> An attempt to identify the one best way to do something

> **contingency perspective**
> Suggests that appropriate managerial behavior in a given situation depends on, or is contingent on, a wide variety of elements

Contemporary Management Challenges and Opportunities

Interest in management theory and practice has heightened in recent years as new issues and challenges have emerged. No new paradigm has been formulated that replaces the traditional views, but managers continue to strive toward a better understanding of how they can better compete and lead their organizations toward improved effectiveness.

Contemporary Applied Perspectives   In recent years, books written for the popular press have also had a major impact on both the field of organizational behavior and the practice of management. This trend first became noticeable in the early 1980s with the success of such classics as William Ouchi's *Theory Z* and Thomas Peters and Robert Waterman's *In Search of Excellence*. Each of these books spent time on the *New York Times* best-seller list and was required reading for any manager wanting to at least appear informed. Biographies of executives such as Lee Iacocca and Donald Trump also have received widespread attention. And bidding for the publishing rights to Jack Welch's memoirs, published when he retired as CEO from General Electric, exceeded $7 million.[39]

Other applied authors have greatly influenced management theory and practice. Among the most popular applied authors today are Peter Senge, Stephen Covey, Tom Peters, Jim Collins, Michael Porter, John Kotter, and Gary Hamel.[40] Their books highlight the management practices of successful firms such as Shell, Ford, IBM, and others, or outline conceptual or theoretical models or frameworks to guide managers as they formulate strategies or motivate their employees. Scott Adams, creator of the popular comic strip *Dilbert*, is also immensely popular today. Adams is a former communications industry worker who developed his strip to illustrate some of the absurdities that occasionally afflict contemporary organizational life. The daily strip is routinely posted outside office doors, above copy machines, and beside water coolers in hundreds of offices.

Contemporary Management Challenges Managers today also face an imposing set of challenges as they guide and direct the fortunes of their companies. Coverage of each of these is thoroughly integrated throughout this book. In addition, many of them are highlighted or given focused coverage in one or more special ways.

Globalization is one significant contemporary challenge faced by all managers. Managing in a global economy poses many different challenges and opportunities. For example, at a macro level, property ownership arrangements vary widely. So does the availability of natural resources and components of the infrastructure, as well as the role of government in business. Moreover, behavioral processes vary widely across cultural and national boundaries. For example, values, symbols, and beliefs differ sharply among cultures. Different work norms and the role that work plays in a person's life, for example, influence patterns of both work-related behavior and attitudes toward work. They also affect the nature of supervisory relationships, decision-making styles and processes, and organizational configurations.

Another management challenge that has taken on renewed importance is ethics and social responsibility and their relationship to corporate governance. Unfortunately, business scandals involving unethical conduct have become almost commonplace today. From a social responsibility perspective, increasing attention has been focused on pollution and business's obligation to help clean up our environment, business contributions to social causes, and so forth. The proper

Globalization is one of the greatest opportunities and challenges facing managers today. This McDonald's restaurant near Shanghai, China, provides a vivid illustration. As with a comparable restaurant in the United States, owners must deal with customers, suppliers, competitors, and government officials. But the nature of its relationship with each of these groups is very different from those relationships in the United States. And both are different when compared to McDonald's in England, South Africa, Australia, or any of the other 100 countries where McDonald's does business.

framework for corporate governance is often at the center of these debates and discussions.

Quality also continues to pose an important management challenge today. Quality is an important issue for several reasons. First, more and more organizations are using quality as a basis for competition. Continental Airlines, for example, stresses its high rankings in the J. D. Power survey of customer satisfaction in its print advertising. Second, improving quality tends to increase productivity because making higher-quality products generally results in less waste and rework. Third, enhancing quality lowers costs. Managers at Whistler Corporation once realized that the firm was using 100 of its 250 employees to repair defective radar detectors that had been built incorrectly in the first place.

The shift toward a service economy also continues to be important. Traditionally, most businesses were manufacturers—they used tangible resources like raw materials and machinery to create tangible products like automobiles and steel. In the last few decades, however, the service sector of the economy has become much more important. Indeed, services now account for well over half of the gross domestic product in the United States and play a similarly important role in many other industrialized nations. Service technology involves the use of both tangible resources (such as machinery) and intangible resources (such as intellectual property) to create intangible services (such as a haircut, insurance protection, or transportation between two cities). Although there are obviously many similarities between managing in a manufacturing and a service organization, there are also many fundamental differences.

Managers must also contend with the changing nature of the workforce. During the 1980s, many people entering the workforce were what came to be called yuppies, slang for "young urban professionals." These individuals were highly motivated by career prospects, sought employment with big corporations, and often were willing to make work their highest priority. But younger people entering the workforce in the 1990s were frequently quite different from their predecessors. Sometimes called Generation X-ers, these workers were less devoted to long-term career prospects and less willing to adapt to a corporate mind-set that stresses conformity and uniformity. Instead, they often sought work in smaller, more entrepreneurial firms that allowed flexibility and individuality. They also placed a premium on lifestyle considerations, often putting location high on their list of priorities when selecting an employer. And, of course, new workers entering the workforce today are different from their counterparts in the 1980s and those in the 1990s.

Thus managers are increasingly faced with the challenge of first creating an environment that will be attractive to today's worker. Second, managers must address the challenge of providing new and different incentives to keep people motivated and interested in their work. Finally, they must build enough flexibility into the organization to accommodate an ever-changing set of lifestyles and preferences.

Numerous other challenges and opportunities also continue to emerge. One of these is an erratic economy and a dynamic business environment that make it difficult to plan. Another important challenge is the management of diversity. Yet another is employee privacy. A related issue has to do with the increased capabilities that technology provides for people to work at places other than their offices. The appropriate role of the Internet in business strategy is also a complex arena for managers.

Summary of Key Points

1. Define management, describe the kinds of managers found in organizations, identify and explain the four basic management functions, describe the fundamental management skills, and comment on management as science and as art.

   • Management is a set of activities (planning and decision making, organizing, leading, and controlling) directed at using an organization's resources (human, financial, physical, and information) to achieve organizational goals in an efficient and effective manner.

   • A manager is someone whose primary responsibility is to carry out the management process within an organization.

   • Managers can be classified in terms of level: top managers, middle managers, and first-line managers.

   • Managers can also be classified in terms of area: marketing, finances, operations, human resources, administration, and specialized.

   • The basic activities of the management process include planning and decision making (determining courses of action), organizing (coordinating activities and resources), leading (motivating and managing people), and controlling (monitoring and evaluating activities).

   • Effective managers tend to have the following skills: technical, interpersonal, conceptual, diagnostic, communication, decision-making, and time-management.

   • The effective practice of management requires a synthesis of science and art; that is, it calls for a blend of rational objectivity and intuitive insight.

2. Justify the importance of history and theory to managers and explain the evolution of management thought through the classical, behavioral, and quantitative perspectives.

   • Understanding the historical context and precursors of management and organizations provides a sense of heritage and can also help managers avoid repeating the mistakes of others.

   • The classical management perspective, which paid little attention to the role of workers, had two major branches: scientific management (concerned with improving efficiency and work methods for individual workers) and administrative management (concerned with how organizations themselves should be structured and arranged for efficient operations).

   • The behavioral management perspective, characterized by a concern for individual and group behavior, emerged primarily as a result of the Hawthorne studies. The human relations movement recognized the importance and potential of behavioral processes in organizations but made many overly simplistic assumptions about those processes. Organizational behavior, a more realistic outgrowth of the behavioral perspective, is of interest to many contemporary managers.

   • The quantitative management perspective, which attempts to apply quantitative techniques to decision making and problem solving, has two components: management science and operations management. These areas are also of considerable importance to contemporary managers. Their contributions have been facilitated by the tremendous increase in the use of personal computers and integrated information networks.

3. Identify and discuss key contemporary management perspectives represented by the systems and contingency perspectives and identify the major challenges and opportunities faced by managers today.

   • There are two relatively recent additions to management theory that can serve as frameworks for integrating the other perspectives: the systems perspective and the contingency perspective.

   • The important issues and challenges that contemporary managers face include globalization, economic instability, diversity, privacy, outsourcing, ethics and social responsibility, corporate governance, and the new workplace.

Discussion Questions

Questions for Review

1. What are the four basic functions that make up the management process? How are they related to one another?

2. What are the most common designations for management levels within an organization? How precise or arbitrary are these classifications?

3. Identify several of the important skills that help managers succeed. Give an example of each.

4. Briefly describe the principles of scientific management and administrative management. What assumptions do these perspectives make about workers?

5. Describe the systems perspective. Why is a business organization considered an open system?

Questions for Analysis

1. Recall a recent group project or task in which you have participated. Explain how members of the group displayed each of the managerial skills.

2. The text notes that management is both a science and an art. Recall an interaction you have had with a superior (manager, teacher, group leader, or the like). In that interaction, how did the superior use science? If he or she did not use science, what could have been done to use science? In that interaction, how did the superior use art? If she or he did not use art, what could have been done to use art?

3. Watch a movie that involves an organization of some type. *Harry Potter, Training Day, Star Wars,* and *Minority Report* would all be good choices. Identify as many management activities and skills as you can.

4. Young, innovative, or high-tech firms often adopt the strategy of ignoring history or attempting to do something radically new. In what ways will this strategy help them? In what ways will this strategy hinder their efforts?

5. Can a manager use tools and techniques from several different perspectives at the same time? For example, can a manager use both classical and behavioral perspectives? Give an example of a time when a manager did this and explain how it enabled him or her to be effective.

Building Effective Time-Management Skills

Exercise Overview

Time-management skills refer to the manager's ability to prioritize work, to work efficiently, and to delegate appropriately. This exercise allows you to assess your current time-management skills and to gain suggestions for how you can improve in this area.

Exercise Background

As described in this chapter, effective managers must be prepared to switch between the four basic activities in the management process. Managers must also be able to fulfill a number of different roles in their organizations, and they must employ many different managerial skills as they do so. In addition, managers' schedules are busy and full of complex, unpredictable, and brief tasks, requiring managers to "switch gears" frequently throughout a workday.

Franklin Covey, management consultant and author of *The 7 Habits of Highly Effective People* and other best-selling books, has developed a way of prioritizing tasks. He uses the terms *urgent* and *important* to characterize tasks. "Urgent" refers to tasks that must be done right away, such as tasks that have an approaching deadline. "Important" tasks are those that are critical; that is, tasks that have a big impact on key areas of one's life.

Thus, according to Covey, tasks fall into one of four quadrants: tasks that are both urgent and important, urgent but not important, important but not urgent, or neither urgent nor important.

Covey claims that most people spend too much time on tasks that are urgent, when they should instead give high priority to tasks that are important. He asserts that workers who concentrate on urgent tasks meet their deadlines, but they may neglect critical areas such as long-term planning, and they may also neglect critical areas of their personal life. Effective managers can balance the demands of their urgent tasks with an understanding of the need to spend an appropriate amount of time on those that are important.

Exercise Task

1. Draw a 2-by-2 cell matrix that reflects Covey's ideas about time management. The matrix should look like this:

	Urgent	**Not Urgent**
Important	Quadrant 1 "The Quadrant of Necessity"	Quadrant 2 "The Quadrant of Leadership"
Not Important	Quadrant 3 "The Quadrant of Deception"	Quadrant 4 "The Quadrant of Waste"

2. In each cell of the matrix, list some of your activities over the last day or several days. In quadrant 1, the quadrant of necessity, list any items such as emergencies, work crises, problems, tasks with near deadlines, and last-minute tasks. In quadrant 2, the quadrant of leadership, list any activities you engaged in that were aimed at accomplishment of long-term goals or prevention of problems. For example, exercise prevents future health problems, while time spent building important family relationships or friendships accomplishes a key long-term goal. Other examples include planning, preparation, getting a start on tasks with far-off deadlines, recreation and stress relief, and exploring new opportunities and ideas. In quadrant 3, the quadrant of deception, list tasks that had urgent deadlines but in fact did not help you to accomplish important goals. Common quadrant 3 activities include time spent on other people's problems, routine meetings and reports, and interruptions. Parties, social activities, and anything you feel "pressured" to do may also fit in quadrant 3. Quadrant 4, the quadrant of waste, is also sometimes called the quadrant of default because people tend to default to quadrant 4 activities to avoid activities in other quadrants. In quadrant 4, list time spent watching television, surfing the web or instant messaging, chatting aimlessly, or reading junk mail. Anything done to excess can be put in quadrant 4. What proportion of your time did you spend in each quadrant?

3. In *The 7 Habits of Highly Effective People,* Covey claims that those who spend most of their time in quadrant 1 may be meeting their deadlines but aren't making good long-term use of time. Over time, people who stay in quadrant 1 most of the time will become increasingly consumed by problems. If you spend a large proportion of time in quadrant 1, you are likely to experience stress, which may lead you to escape by engaging in quadrant 4 activities. Minimize time spent in this quadrant. Instead, spend some time in quadrant 2 to get ahead of your problems through better planning and preparation.

Folks who spend much of their time in quadrant 2 tend to be effective in their personal and professional lives. They are proactive, focused on opportunities rather than problems. They often make profound and positive changes in the people and organizations around them. It's virtually impossible to spend too much time in this quadrant. If you spend a high proportion of your time here, you are in control, balanced, disciplined, experience few crises, and remain focused on your long-term vision. Move into this quadrant as much as you can.

A person who spends a lot of time in quadrant 3 feels and is busy, but looking back, little has been accomplished. Folks may enjoy pleasing others and being needed, but it's important that they also spend time on their own long-term goals. Too much time spent in quadrant 3 can leave you feeling frustrated or even victimized, as you try to meet the expectations of others. Other results of quadrant 3 activities can include feeling out of touch with your own feelings or goals, feeling worthless, and experiencing shallow relationships. Engage in some quadrant 3 activities, but be sure to balance that time with time spent in quadrant 2.

Quadrant 4 is perhaps the most dangerous quadrant. People who spend too much time in quadrant 4 are irresponsible, neglecting themselves and others. If quadrant 4 activities account for a very large proportion of your time, you likely have broken relationships, are dependent on others for basic support, and have difficulty completing courses or holding a job. A moderately large amount of time spent in quadrant 4 provides a great opportunity to improve your time management skills. Minimize quadrant 4 activities and spend the time in quadrant 2 if possible.

If you do engage in some trivial activities, make sure that you truly enjoy them and limit the time spent.

4. What is one thing that you can do today to make better use of your time? Try it and see if your time management improves.

Building Effective Conceptual Skills

Exercise Overview

Conceptual skills form the manager's ability to think in the abstract. This exercise will help you extend your conceptual skills by identifying potential generalizations of management functions and skills for different kinds of organizations.

Exercise Background

This introductory chapter discusses four basic management functions and seven vital management skills. The chapter also notes that management is applicable across many different kinds of organizations.

Identify one large business, one small business, one educational organization, one healthcare organization, and one government organization. These might be organizations about which you have some personal knowledge or simply organizations that you recognize. Now imagine yourself in the position of a top manager in each organization.

Write the names of the five organizations across the top of a sheet of paper. List the four functions and seven skills down the left side of the paper. Now think of a situation, problem, or opportunity relevant to the intersection of each row and column on the paper. For example, how might a manager in a government organization engage in planning and need diagnostic skills? Similarly, how might a manager in a small business carry out the organizing function and need conceptual skills?

Exercise Task

1. What meaningful similarities can you identify across the five columns?

2. What meaningful differences can you identify across the five columns?

3. Based on your assessment of the similarities and differences as identified in Exercise Tasks 1 and 2, how easy or difficult do you think it might be for a manager to move from one type of organization to another?

Building Effective Decision-Making Skills

Exercise Overview

Decision-making skills refer to a manager's ability to recognize and define problems and opportunities correctly and then to select an appropriate course of action to solve those problems and capitalize on the opportunities.

This exercise will help you develop your own decision-making skills while also helping you to better understand the importance of subsystem interdependencies in organizations.

Exercise Background

Assume you are the vice president of a large American company that designs and manufactures sunglasses. Because of the rise in consumer demand, the firm has grown substantially in recent years. At the same time, this growth has not gone unnoticed, and several competitors

have entered the market in the last two years. Your CEO has instructed you to find a way to cut costs by 10 percent so that prices can be cut by the same amount. She feels that this tactic is necessary to retain your market share in the face of new competition.

You have looked closely at the situation and have decided that there are three different ways you can accomplish this cost reduction. One option is to begin buying slightly lower-grade materials, such as plastic and glass. Another option is to lay off a portion of your workforce and then pressure the remaining workers to work harder. As part of this same option, future growth in manufacturing capacity will be outsourced to developing countries. The overseas workers will be paid a lower wage than U.S. workers. The third option is to replace your existing manufacturing equipment with newer, more efficient equipment. Although this will require a substantial up-front investment, you are certain that lower production costs can be achieved.

Exercise Task

With this background in mind, respond to the following:

1. Carefully examine each of the three alternatives under consideration. In what ways might each alternative affect other parts of the organization?

2. Which is the most costly option (in terms of impact on other parts of the organization, not absolute dollars)? Which is the least costly?

3. What are the primary obstacles that you might face regarding each of the three alternatives?

4. Can you think of other alternatives that might accomplish the cost-reduction goal?

Skills Self-Assessment Instrument

Self-Awareness

Introduction: Self-awareness is an important skill for effective management. This assessment is designed to help you evaluate your level of self-awareness.

Instructions: Please respond to the following statements by writing a number from the following rating scale in the column. Your answers should reflect your attitudes and behavior as they are *now*, not as you would *like* them to be. Be honest. This instrument is designed to help you discover how self-aware you are so that you can tailor your learning to your specific needs.

Rating Scale

6 Strongly agree

5 Agree

4 Slightly agree

3 Slightly disagree

2 Disagree

1 Strongly disagree

_____ 1. I seek information about my strengths and weaknesses from others as a basis for self-improvement.

_____ 2. When I receive negative feedback about myself from others, I do not get angry or defensive.

_____ 3. In order to improve, I am willing to be self-disclosing to others (that is, to share my beliefs and feelings).

_____ 4. I am very much aware of my personal style of gathering information and making decisions about it.

_____ 5. I am very much aware of my own interpersonal needs when it comes to forming relationships with other people.

_____ 6. I have a good sense of how I cope with situations that are ambiguous and uncertain.

_____ 7. I have a well-developed set of personal standards and principles that guide my behavior.

_____ 8. I feel very much in charge of what happens to me, good and bad.

_____ 9. I seldom, if ever, feel angry, depressed, or anxious without knowing why.

_____ 10. I am conscious of the areas in which conflict and friction most frequently arise in my interactions with others.

_____ 11. I have a close relationship with at least one other person with whom I can share personal information and personal feelings.

Source: *Developing Management Skills,* 2nd ed., by Whetten, Cameron, © 1991. Reprinted with permission of Pearson Education, Inc., Upper Saddle River, NJ. For interpretation, see Interpretations of Skills Self-Assessment Instruments in the appendix near the end of this text.

Experiential Exercise

Johari Window

Purpose: This exercise has two purposes: to encourage you to analyze yourself more accurately and to start you working on small-group cohesiveness. This exercise encourages you to share data about yourself and then to assimilate and process feedback. Small groups are typically more trusting and work better together, as you will be able to see after this exercise has been completed. The Johari Window is a particularly good model for understanding the perceptual process in interpersonal relationships.

This skill builder focuses on the *human resources model* and will help you develop your *mentor role*. One of the skills of a mentor is self-awareness.

Introduction: Each individual has four sets of personality characteristics. One set, which includes such characteristics as working hard, is well known to the individual and to others. A second set is unknown to the individual but obvious to others. For example, in a working situation, a peer group might observe that your jumping in

to get the group moving off dead center is appropriate. At other times, you jump in when the group is not really finished, and you seem to interrupt. A third set of personality characteristics is known to the individual but not to others. These are situations that you have elected not to share, perhaps because of a lack of trust. Finally, there is a fourth set, which is not known to the individual or to others, such as why you are uncomfortable at office parties.

Instructions: Look at the Johari Window below. In quadrant 1, list three things that you know about yourself that you think others know also. List three things in quadrant 3 that others do not know about you. Finally, in quadrant 2, list three things that you did not know about yourself last semester that you learned from others.

Sources: Adapted from Joseph Luft, *Group Processes: An Introduction to Group Dynamics* (Palo Alto, CA: Mayfield, 1970), pp. 10–11; William C. Morris and Marshall Sashkin, *Organizational Behavior in Action* (St. Paul, MN: West, 1976), p. 56.

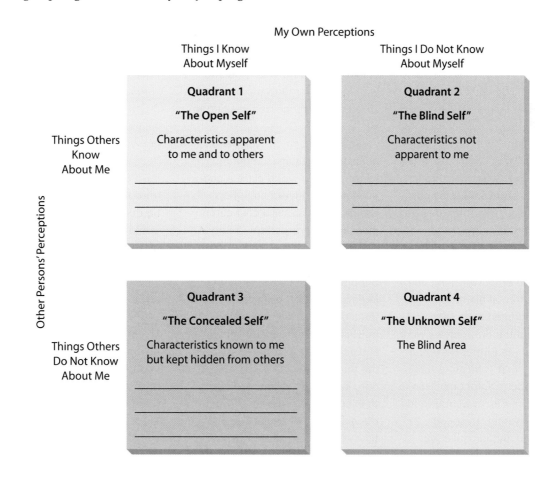

My Own Perceptions

	Things I Know About Myself	Things I Do Not Know About Myself
Things Others Know About Me	**Quadrant 1** **"The Open Self"** Characteristics apparent to me and to others	**Quadrant 2** **"The Blind Self"** Characteristics not apparent to me
Things Others Do Not Know About Me	**Quadrant 3** **"The Concealed Self"** Characteristics known to me but kept hidden from others	**Quadrant 4** **"The Unknown Self"** The Blind Area

Other Persons' Perceptions

CHAPTER CLOSING CASE

HOME DEPOT'S FAILED MANAGER

Home Depot is second only to Wal-Mart in U.S. retail sales. Yet, like its rival, that very success has made it difficult for the company to continue to grow and innovate. So from 2000 to 2006, former CEO Bob Nardelli made tremendous changes in the organization. He hoped to reduce costs, increase profit margins, and raise stock price. When Nardelli accomplished his financial goals but share price failed to rise, he was abruptly forced to resign. Insiders and outside observers were shocked that a successful corporate leader could fall so far, so fast.

One concern was Nardelli's management approach, characterized as "command-and-control." This centralized structure gave high-level managers a great deal of authority to make decisions for lower-level managers and workers. Nardelli also emphasized militaristic discipline and obedience, increased the formal management hierarchy, and required others to implement stringent plans to a high standard. Command-and-control was widely popular throughout the 1950s and 60s but fell out of favor by the 1970s. It ignored or even contradicted many of today's management trends, including teamwork and collaboration, experimentation, employee empowerment, and reducing the formal hierarchy.

Nardelli adopted command-and-control to help the firm recover from problems with its former decentralized structure that gave store managers tremendous autonomy. Home Depot founders Bernie Marcus and Arthur Blank wanted to encourage innovation and initiative, but

instead, the company "grew so fast the wheels were starting to come off," says Edward Lawler, a business professor at USC.

Nardelli learned this approach at General Electric (GE), where he worked for 29 years and rose to be a senior vice president. GE's managers are known for the success of their rigorous financial discipline and ruthless style. Yet Nardelli's approach came at a cost. Midlevel and store managers resented taking direction from above. "This retail organization never really embraced [Nardelli's] leadership style," said Matthew Fassler, an analyst who studies Home Depot. Nardelli eliminated underperforming managers, replacing 98 percent of top managers during his tenure as CEO. Fifty-six percent of the new managers were recruited from outside and were unfamiliar with the company's systems and processes, leading to waste.

Another concern was the decline in customer service, changing a store that was world class a decade ago into a lackluster shopping experience. Nardelli's cost-cutting measures decreased the number of customer-service employees in the stores, frustrating customers. Shoppers often had a hard time finding a knowledgeable salesperson at the store. Customer satisfaction ratings slipped lower than rival Lowe's and sales slipped over 5 percent in the third quarter of 2006. In addition, loss of autonomy and ability to experiment led to lower worker morale. Many of Home Depot's long-time employees quit in frustration.

One former manager complained that Nardelli was more concerned about how he measured good customer service than he was about inspiring it. The manager says, "The mechanics are there. The soul isn't." Critics claimed Nardelli turned a flexible, entrepreneurial employer into "a factory." While founders Marcus and Blank had a friendly, approachable, entrepreneurial style, Nardelli was seen as arrogant and numbers-obsessed. Kenneth Langone, the third co-founder of Home Depot, says Nardelli was "maniacal about goals, objectivity, accomplishments." In fact, when Nardelli was accused of being more interested in finances than in people, he would reply, "Facts are friendly."

A third concern is the lack of increase in Home Depot's share price. The total market value of Home Depot shares outstanding dropped 40 percent over the last six years. Total return to shareholders was down 13 percent for 2005. Yet sales have increased, costs have dropped, and profit margins improved. The low share price may be due to lack of investor confidence in the company's—and Nardelli's—performance. While Nardelli achieved his financial objectives, he was perceived as deficient in long-term strategy and vision for the firm.

For example, under Nardelli's leadership, Home Depot spent billions of dollars to repurchase some of its own stock. This action raises stock price by reducing the number of shares outstanding. Yet shareholders would rather see the firm invest capital in projects that support long-term growth and innovation. Stock repurchase is a signal that company executives cannot think of a better use for the stockholders' money. Nardelli also failed to assure stockholders about the company's ability to compete effectively against Lowe's, its closest challenger.

Nardelli leaves with an eye-popping $210 million in separation compensation, although he did not raise share price. Or did he? On the day his resignation was announced, the value of Home Depot stock rose 3 percent.

CASE QUESTIONS

1. Give examples from the case of times when Bob Nardelli was planning, organizing, leading, and controlling.

2. What types of managerial roles did Nardelli fulfill? What managerial skills did he use?

3. In your opinion, did Nardelli tend to place more emphasis on the science of management or the art of management? What were the advantages and disadvantages of his approach?

REFERENCES

Geoff Colvin, "Nardelli's Downfall: It's All About the Stock," *Fortune*, January 3, 2007, www.fortune.com on January 16, 2007; Brian Grow, "Out at Home Depot," *BusinessWeek*, January 15, 2007, pp. 56–62; Brian Grow, "Renovating Home Depot," *BusinessWeek*, March 6, 2006, pp. 50–58; "How Nardelli Finally Helped the Stock," *BusinessWeek*, January 3, 2007, www.businessweek.com on January 16, 2007; Jennifer Reingold, "Bob Nardelli Is Watching," *Fast Company*, December 2005, www.fastcompany.com on March 1, 2006; Harry R. Weber, "Analysts: Home Depot Needs Makeover," *BusinessWeek*, January 6, 2007, www.businessweek.com on January 16, 2007.

YOU MAKE THE CALL

Marissa Mayer: Google's Top Designer

1. Do you think Google employees enjoy working for Mayer? Describe some of the benefits and some of the challenges of working for her.

2. What do you think are Marissa Mayer's principal strengths as a manager? What are her weaknesses?

3. Consider your assessment of Mayer's strengths and weaknesses as a manager. If you were her superior, what kinds of managerial positions would you recommend she attempt? What types of positions would *not* be suitable for her?

4. Would you like to work for Mayer or would you rather have her work for you? Explain.

Test Prepper

ACE self-test

college.hmco.com/pic/griffinfund5e

You've read the chapter, studied the key terms, and the exam is any day now. Think you're ready to ace it? Take this sample test to gauge your comprehension of chapter material. You can check your answers at the back of the book. Want more test questions? Visit the student website at http://college.hmco.com/pic/griffinfund5e/ and take the ACE quizzes for more practice.

1. T   F   Arne Sorenson, senior vice president for finance at Marriott, is a middle manager.

2. T   F   When a manager forms a team with members from each functional area, she is engaged in organizing.

3. T   F   Scientific management focuses on jobs of individual employees.

4. T   F   Classical, behavioral, and quantitative approaches make different assumptions and predictions. They are contradictory and mutually exclusive.

5. T   F   Shannon believes there is one best way to do everything. She has a universal perspective.

6. As an operations manager for Cintas, Dave Warns is responsible for motivating subordinates. To accomplish that he must primarily use which skill?
   a. Technical
   b. Conceptual
   c. Decision-making
   d. Interpersonal
   e. Time-management

7. Mark prefers to make decisions based on "gut feeling" and experience. He is most likely to describe management as _____.)
   a. science
   b. art
   c. theory Z

   d. theory Y
   e. theory X

8. When employees deliberately work at a slower pace it is called _____.
   a. bureaucracy
   b. the Hawthorne effect
   c. soldiering
   d. theory Y behavior
   e. synergy

9. A system that does not interact with its environment is best described as a(n) _____ system.
   a. closed
   b. sub-
   c. operating
   d. open
   e. transformation

10. Which of the following is NOT a contemporary management challenge faced by managers in the United States?
    a. Stagnant work environment
    b. Quality
    c. Globalization
    d. Shift away from manufacturing economy
    e. Ethics and social responsibility

The Environments of Organizations and Managers

chapter 2

FIRST THINGS FIRST

Leading Lenovo: China's Foremost Global Capitalist

"We have roots in both China and the West. We have a Chinese chairman and an American CEO."

— YANG YUANQING, CHAIRMAN, LENOVO

It was a very big gamble when Chinese PC maker Lenovo, headed by 42-year-old Yang Yuanqing, bought the personal computer business unit of IBM for $1.75 billion in May 2005. The manufacturer had annual sales of $3 billion but was attempting to take over a $10 billion firm. IBM was exiting the PC business due to declining profits. If a competitive company thought the prospects were poor, how could a smaller, less experienced firm succeed? Lenovo faces numerous obstacles in its environment but it also enjoys some advantages.

Global business competition is ever-present and consumers are more accepting of items manufactured overseas, an important opportunity for Lenovo. Although the company has a 35 percent market share in China, their global share is a mere 4.7 percent, so most of their growth will come from foreign sales. Global business

Lenovo, led by Yang Yuanqing, is dealing with numerous environmental forces in its quest to become a global computer giant.

LEARNING OBJECTIVES

After studying this chapter you should be able to:

- Discuss the nature of an organization's environments and identify the components of its general, task, and internal environments.

- Describe the ethical and social environment of management, including individual ethics, the concept of social responsibility, and how organizations can manage social responsibility.

- Discuss the international environment of management, including trends in international business, levels of international business activities, and the context of international business.

- Describe the importance and determinants of an organization's culture, as well as how organization culture can be managed.

has a downside, too, as Lenovo learned when it sold 14,000 PCs to the U.S. State Department. Concerned about the possibility of snooping by the Chinese government, Congress limited use of Lenovo PCs to projects where security was not a concern.

The personal computer industry is intensely competitive. The IBM acquisition thrust Lenovo into third place, behind rivals Dell and Hewlett-Packard. Yet with Dell's investment of $16 billion in China in 2006, Lenovo is in a precarious position. The competition lowers profitability for all participants. In 2006, Lenovo profited $22 million on sales of $13 billion, in part because of the expense of the IBM purchase. On a positive note, analysts expect income of over $100 million in 2007 and over $300 million in 2008.

Internally, Lenovo has mastered several key skills, including low-cost, efficient manufacturing and supply chain management. Most of the firm's facilities are located in China, where labor and other costs are low. Notebook computers will continue to be made in China but some desktop manufacturing facilities will be located elsewhere. Yang says, "You don't want to stick [desktops] on a boat, because a PC's value drops each week anywhere from half-a-percent to a percent and a half."

Lenovo is laboring under an unusual and complex management structure. The company is 27 percent owned by the Chinese Academy of Sciences, a state-run association. IBM owns 10 percent, 15 percent is owned by employees, 10 percent by private investors, and 35 percent by public shareholders. The firm's board of directors includes representatives from several of these groups. Yang sees the diversity as an advantage. "We have roots in both China and the West," he says. "We have a Chinese chairman and an American CEO. In every country, our country leader is local."

Another challenge for Lenovo is the full integration of IBM. Blending two corporate cultures can be difficult, especially when differing national cultures must also be accommodated. For example, in China, where capitalism was only recently adopted, many companies are cautious and fail to innovate. Chinese firms are known for using seniority-based rewards, as well as highly central-ized and formalized decision making. In contrast, Yang is adopting a more Westernized management style, requiring everyone to be addressed by first names, implementing a merit-based promotion system, and firing low-performing employees.

The purchase of IBM helped Lenovo to cope with its complex environment. Overnight, the company gained market share and credibility in developed nations. It also grew larger, an opportunity for better economies of scale. Another coping mechanism was the hiring of former Dell executive William Amelio as CEO. Amelio, former head of Dell's Asian operations, has replaced most of the top team with a hand-picked leadership team from Dell.

To continue its development, Lenovo will adopt several strategies for the next five years. On Yang's to-do list: increase marketing efforts outside of China, improve efficiency at IBM's former facilities, gradually phase out the IBM brand,

and strengthen relationships with key suppliers. Despite doubts and challenges, Lenovo is maintaining its position in a tough environment. Can Lenovo learn to compete and dominate on a global scale?

The business world operates in what can appear to be mysterious ways. Sometimes competition hurts, but sometimes it helps. When Starbucks opens a new store, its closest competitors often benefit. Ford and General Motors compete with each other for consumer dollars but work together to promote the interests of the U.S. auto industry. And CEOs face growing pressure to cut costs and curb their own salaries as they grow their businesses. Clearly, the environmental context of business today is changing in unprecedented ways.

The Organization's Environments

The **external environment** is everything outside an organization's boundaries that might affect it. There are actually two separate external environments: the **general environment** and the **task environment**. An organization's **internal environment** consists of conditions and forces within the organization.

The General Environment

Each of the following dimensions embodies conditions and events that have the potential to influence the organization in important ways.

The Economic Dimension   The **economic dimension** of an organization's general environment is the overall health and vitality of the economic system in which the organization operates.[1] Particularly important economic factors for business are general economic growth, inflation, interest rates, and unemployment. McDonald's U.S. operation is functioning in an economy currently characterized by moderate growth, low unemployment, and low inflation.[2] These conditions breed paradoxical problems. Low unemployment means that more people can eat out, but McDonald's also has to pay higher wages to attract new employees.[3] Similarly, low inflation means that the prices McDonald's must pay for its supplies remain relatively constant, but the company also is somewhat constrained from increasing the prices it charges consumers for a hamburger or milkshake. The economic dimension is also important to nonbusiness organizations. For example, during weak economic conditions, funding for state universities may drop, and charitable organizations such as the Salvation Army are asked to provide greater assistance at the same time that their own incoming contributions dwindle. Similarly, hospitals are affected by the availability of government grants and by the number of low-income patients they must treat free of charge.

The Technological Dimension   The **technological dimension** of the general environment is made up of the methods available for converting resources into products or services. Although technology is applied within the organization, the forms and availability of that technology come from the general environment. Computer-assisted manufacturing and design techniques, for example, allow Boeing to simulate the more than three miles of hydraulic tubing that will run through its 787 aircraft currently under development. The results include decreased warehouse

---

external environment
Everything outside an organization's boundaries that might affect it

general environment
The set of broad dimensions and forces in an organization's surroundings that determines its overall context

task environment
Specific organizations or groups that affect the organization

internal environment
The conditions and forces within an organization

economic dimension
The overall health and vitality of the economic system in which the organization operates

technological dimension
The methods available for converting resources into products or services

needs, higher-quality tube fittings, fewer employees, and major time savings. Although some people associate technology with manufacturing firms, it is also relevant in the service sector. For example, just as an automobile follows a predetermined path along an assembly line as it is built, a hamburger at McDonald's follows a predefined path as the meat is cooked, the burger assembled, and the finished product wrapped and bagged for a customer. The rapid infusion of the Internet into all areas of business is also a reflection of the technological dimension. Another recent advancement is the rapid growth of integrated business software systems.

> *political-legal dimension*
> The government regulation of business and the relationship between business and government

The Political-Legal Dimension The ***political-legal dimension*** of the general environment consists of government regulation of business and the relationship between business and government. This dimension is important for three basic reasons. First, the legal system partially defines what an organization can and cannot do. Although the United States is basically a free market economy, there is still significant regulation of business activity. McDonald's, for example, is subject to a variety of political and legal forces, including food preparation standards and local zoning requirements.

Second, pro- or antibusiness sentiment in government influences business activity. For example, during periods of probusiness sentiment, firms find it easier to compete and have fewer concerns about antitrust issues. On the other hand, during a period of antibusiness sentiment, firms may find their competitive strategies more restricted and may have fewer opportunities for mergers and acquisitions because of antitrust concerns.

Finally, political stability has ramifications for planning. No business wants to set up shop in another country unless trade relationships with that country are relatively well defined and stable. Hence U.S. firms are more likely to do business with England, Mexico, and Canada than with Haiti and Afghanistan. Similar issues are relevant to businesses' assessments of local and state governments. A new mayor or governor can affect many organizations, especially small firms that do business in only one location and are susceptible to deed and zoning restrictions, property and school taxes, and the like.

The Task Environment

Because the impact of the general environment is often vague, imprecise, and long term, most organizations tend to focus their attention on their task environment. This environment includes competitors, customers, suppliers, strategic partners, and regulators. Although the task environment is also quite complex, it provides useful information more readily than the general environment, because the manager can identify environmental factors of specific interest to the organization, rather than having to deal with the more abstract dimensions of the general environment.[4] Figure 2.1 depicts the task environment of McDonald's.

> *competitor*
> An organization that competes with other organizations for resources

Competitors An organization's ***competitors*** are other organizations that compete with it for resources. The most obvious resources that competitors vie for are customer dollars. Reebok, Adidas, and Nike are competitors, as are Albertson's, Safeway, and Kroger. McDonald's competes with other fast-food operations, such as Burger King, Wendy's, Subway, and Dairy Queen. But competition also occurs between substitute products. Thus Ford competes with Yamaha (motorcycles) and Schwinn (bicycles) for your transportation dollars; and Walt Disney World and

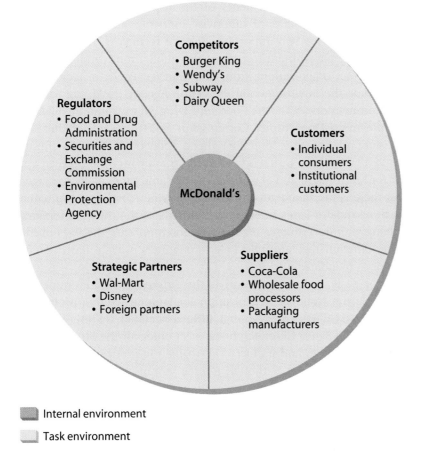

Figure 2.1
MCDONALD'S TASK ENVIRONMENT

An organization's task environment includes its competitors, customers, suppliers, strategic partners, and regulators. This figure clearly highlights how managers at McDonald's can use this framework to identify and understand their key constituents.

■ Internal environment

□ Task environment

Carnival Cruise Lines compete for your vacation dollars. Nor is competition limited to business firms. Universities compete with trade schools, the military, other universities, and the external labor market to attract good students; and art galleries compete with each other to attract the best exhibits.

Customers   A second dimension of the task environment is **customers**, or whoever pays money to acquire an organization's products or services. Most McDonald's customers are individuals who walk into a restaurant to buy food. But customers need not be individuals. Schools, hospitals, government agencies, wholesalers, retailers, and manufacturers are just a few of the many kinds of organizations that may be major customers of other organizations. Some institutional customers, such as schools, prisons, and hospitals, also buy food in bulk from restaurants like McDonald's.

> *customer*
> Whoever pays money to acquire an organization's products or services

Suppliers   ***Suppliers*** are organizations that provide resources for other organizations. McDonald's buys soft drink products from Coca-Cola; individually packaged servings of ketchup from Heinz; ingredients from wholesale food processors; and napkins, sacks, and wrappers from packaging manufacturers. Besides material resources such as these, businesses also rely on suppliers for information (such as economic statistics), labor (in the form of employment agencies), and capital (from lenders such as banks). Some businesses strive to avoid depending exclusively on particular suppliers. Others, however, find it beneficial to create strong relationships with single suppliers.

> *supplier*
> An organization that provides resources for other organizations

regulator
A body that has the potential to control, legislate, or otherwise influence the organization's policies and practices

regulatory agency
An agency created by the government to regulate business activities

interest group
A group organized by its members to attempt to influence organizations

Regulators   *Regulators* are elements of the task environment that have the potential to control, legislate, or otherwise influence an organization's policies and practices. There are two important kinds of regulators. *Regulatory agencies* are created by the government to protect the public from certain business practices or to protect organizations from one another. Powerful federal regulatory agencies include the Environmental Protection Agency (EPA), the Securities and Exchange Commission (SEC), the Food and Drug Administration (FDA), and the Equal Employment Opportunity Commission (EEOC). Many of these agencies play important roles in protecting the rights of individuals. The FDA, for example, helps ensure that the food we eat is free from contaminants; thus, it is an important regulator for McDonald's and Starbucks. At the same time, many managers complain that there is too much government regulation. Most large companies must dedicate thousands of labor hours and hundreds of thousands of dollars a year to complying with government regulations. To complicate the lives of managers even more, different regulatory agencies sometimes provide inconsistent—even contradictory—mandates.

The other basic form of regulator is the ***interest group.*** Prominent interest groups include the National Organization for Women (NOW), Mothers Against Drunk Driving (MADD), the National Rifle Association (NRA), the League of Women Voters, the Sierra Club, Ralph Nader's Center for the Study of Responsive Law, Consumers Union, and industry self-regulation groups such as the Council of Better Business Bureaus. Although interest groups lack the official power of government agencies, they can exert considerable influence by using the media to call attention to their positions. MADD, for example, puts considerable pressure on alcoholic-beverage producers (to put warning labels on their products), automobile companies (to make it more difficult for intoxicated people to start their cars), local governments (to stiffen drinking ordinances), and bars and restaurants (to refuse to sell alcohol to people who are drinking too much).

strategic partner (or strategic ally)
An organization working together with one or more other organizations in a joint venture or similar arrangement

Strategic Partners   Another dimension of the task environment is ***strategic partners*** (also called strategic allies)—two or more companies that work together in joint ventures or other partnerships.[5] As shown in Figure 2.1, McDonald's has several strategic partners. For example, it has one arrangement with Wal-Mart whereby small McDonald's restaurants are built in many Wal-Mart stores. The firm also has a long-term deal with Disney: McDonald's will promote Disney movies in its stores, and Disney will build McDonald's restaurants or kiosks in its theme parks. And many of the firm's foreign stores are built in collaboration with local investors. Strategic partnerships help companies get from other companies the expertise they lack. They also help spread risk and open new market opportunities. Indeed, most strategic partnerships are actually among international firms. For example, Ford has strategic partnerships with Volkswagen (sharing a distribution and service center in South America) and Nissan (building minivans in the United States).

The Internal Environment

Organizations also have an internal environment that consists of their owners, board of directors, employees, and the physical work environment. (Another especially important part of the internal environment is the organization's culture, discussed separately later in this chapter.)

Owners   The *owners* of a business are, of course, the people who have legal property rights to that business. Owners can be a single individual who establishes and runs a small business, partners who jointly own the business, individual investors who buy stock in a corporation, or other organizations. McDonald's has 700 million shares of stock, each of which represents one unit of ownership in the firm. The family of McDonald's founder Ray Kroc stills owns a large block of this stock, as do several large institutional investors. In addition, there are thousands of individuals who own just a few shares each. McDonald's, in turn, owns other businesses. For example, it owns several large regional bakeries that supply its restaurants with buns. Each of these is incorporated as a separate legal entity and managed as a wholly owned subsidiary by the parent company. At various times McDonald's also has had a substantial ownership position in Chipolte Mexican Grill, Boston Market, and Pret-A-Manger.

> **owners**
> Whoever can claim property rights to an organization

Board of Directors   A corporate **board of directors** is a governing body elected by the stockholders and charged with overseeing the general management of the firm to ensure that it is being run in a way that best serves the stockholders' interests. Some boards are relatively passive. They perform a general oversight function but seldom get actively involved in how the company is really being run. But this trend is changing, as more and more boards are carefully scrutinizing the firms they oversee and exerting more influence over how they are being managed. This trend has been accelerated by numerous recent business scandals. In some cases, board members have been accused of wrongdoing. In other cases, boards have been found negligent for failing to monitor the actions of the firm's executives.[6] At issue is the concept of *corporate governance*—who is responsible for governing the actions of a business. We discuss corporate governance more fully later.

> **board of directors**
> Governing body elected by a corporation's stockholders and charged with overseeing the general management of the firm to ensure that it is being run in a way that best serves the stockholders' interests

Employees   An organization's employees are also a major element of its internal environment. Of particular interest to managers today is the changing nature of the workforce, as it becomes increasingly more diverse in terms of gender, ethnicity, age, and other dimensions. Workers are also calling for more job ownership—either partial ownership in the company or at least more say in how they perform their jobs.[7] Another trend in many firms is increased reliance on temporary workers—individuals hired for short periods of time with no expectation of permanent employment. Employers often prefer to use "temps" because they provide greater flexibility, earn lower wages, and often do not participate in benefits programs. But these managers also have to deal with what often amounts to a two-class workforce and with a growing number of employees who have no loyalty to the organization where they work, because they may be working for a different one tomorrow.[8]

Physical Work Environment   A final part of the internal environment is the actual physical environment of the organization and the work that people do. Some firms have their facilities in downtown skyscrapers, usually spread across several floors. Others locate in suburban or rural settings and may have facilities more closely resembling a college campus. Some facilities have long halls lined with traditional offices. Others have modular cubicles with partial walls and no doors. The top hundred managers at Mars, makers of Snickers and Milky Way, all work in a single vast room. Two co-presidents are located in the very center of the room, and the other managers are arrayed in concentric circles around them. Increasingly, newer facilities have an even more open arrangement, where people work in large rooms, moving among different tables to interact with different people on different projects. Freestanding computer workstations are available for those who need them, and a few small rooms may be available off to the side for private business.[9]

The Ethical and Social Environment of Management

The ethical and social environment has become an especially important area for managers in the last few years. In this section we first explore the concept of individual ethics and then describe social responsibility.

Individual Ethics in Organizations

ethics An individual's personal beliefs about whether a behavior, action, or decision is right or wrong

We define **ethics** as an individual's personal beliefs about whether a behavior, action, or decision is right or wrong.[10] Note that we define ethics in the context of the individual—people have ethics; organizations do not. Likewise, what constitutes ethical behavior varies from one person to another.[11] For example, one person who finds a twenty-dollar bill on the floor of an empty room believes that it is okay to keep it, whereas another feels compelled to turn it in to the lost-and-found department. Further, although **ethical behavior** is in the eye of the beholder, the term usually refers to behavior that conforms to generally accepted social norms. **Unethical behavior**, then, is behavior that does not conform to generally accepted social norms.

ethical behavior Behavior that conforms to generally accepted social norms

unethical behavior Behavior that does not conform to generally accepted social norms

Managerial Ethics   **Managerial ethics** consists of the standards of behavior that guide individual managers in their work.[12] One important area of managerial ethics is the treatment of employees by the organization. It includes, for example, hiring and firing, wages and working conditions, and employee privacy and respect. An example of how different managers might approach this area involves minimum

Ethics scandals have become alarmingly commonplace. Enron, WorldCom, Ken Lay, and Martha Stewart are just a few of the businesses and people who have been tarnished by these scandals. More recently, scrutiny has been focused on potential over-billing by Halliburton, a major U.S. contractor helping rebuild Iraq. Former Army Corps of Engineers employee Bunnatine Greenhouse is shown here testifying at a congressional inquiry into Halliburton's business practices.

wages. While the U.S. government sets a minimum hourly wage, this amount is often not enough to live above the poverty level in high-cost areas such as New York and San Francisco. Some managers might say that paying only the legal minimum is the right business practice, while others might be inclined to pay a wage more attuned to local conditions.

> *managerial ethics*
> Standards of behavior that guide individual managers in their work

Numerous ethical issues stem from how employees treat the organization, especially in regard to conflicts of interest, secrecy and confidentiality, and honesty. A *conflict of interest* occurs when an employee's decision potentially benefits the individual to the possible detriment of the organization. To guard against such practices, most companies have policies that forbid their buyers from accepting gifts from suppliers. Divulging company secrets is also clearly unethical. Employees who work for businesses in highly competitive industries—electronics, software, and fashion apparel, for example—might be tempted to sell information about company plans to competitors. A third area of concern is honesty in general. Relatively common problems in this area include such activities as using a business telephone to make personal long-distance calls, surfing the Internet at work, stealing supplies, and padding expense accounts. Although most employees are inherently honest, organizations must nevertheless be vigilant to avoid problems with such behaviors.

Managerial ethics also comes into play in the relationship of the firm and its employees with other economic agents. The primary agents of interest include customers, competitors, stockholders, suppliers, dealers, and unions. The behaviors between the organization and these agents that may be subject to ethical ambiguity include advertising and promotions, financial disclosures, ordering and purchasing, shipping and solicitations, bargaining and negotiation, and other business relationships.

For example, businesses in the pharmaceuticals industry have been under growing fire because of the rapid escalation of the prices they charge for many of their drugs. These firms counter that they must invest heavily in research and development programs to develop new drugs and that they need to charge higher prices to cover these costs. The key in situations like this, then, is to find the right balance between reasonable pricing and price gouging. And, as in so many other questions involving ethics, there are significant differences of opinion.[13]

Another area of concern in recent years involves financial reporting by various e-commerce firms. Because of the complexities inherent in valuing the assets and revenues of these firms, some of them have been very aggressive in presenting their financial position in a highly positive light. And at least a few firms have substantially overstated their earnings projections to entice more investment. Moreover, some of today's accounting scandals in traditional firms have stemmed from similarly questionable practices.[14]

Managing Ethical Behavior   Spurred partially by increased awareness of ethics scandals in business and partially by a sense of enhanced corporate consciousness about the distinction between ethical and unethical behaviors, many organizations have reemphasized ethical behavior on the part of employees. This emphasis takes many forms, but any effort to enhance ethical behavior must begin with top management. It is top managers, for example, who establish the organization's culture and define what will and what will not be acceptable behavior. Some companies have also started offering employees training in how to cope with ethical dilemmas.

At Boeing, for example, line managers lead training sessions for other employees, and the company has an ethics committee that reports directly to the board of directors. The training sessions involve discussions of different ethical dilemmas that employees might face and how managers might handle those dilemmas. Chemical Bank and Xerox also have ethics training programs for their managers.

Organizations are also going to greater lengths to formalize their ethical standards. Some, such as General Mills and Johnson & Johnson, have prepared guidelines that detail how employees are to treat suppliers, customers, competitors, and other constituents. Others, such as Whirlpool, Texas Instruments, and Hewlett-Packard, have developed formal ***codes of ethics***—written statements of the values and ethical standards that guide the firms' actions. Of course, firms must adhere to such codes if they are to be of value. In one now-infamous case, Enron's board of directors voted to set aside the firm's code of ethics in order to implement a business plan that was in violation of that code.[15]

Of course, no code, guideline, or training program can truly substitute for the quality of an individual's personal judgment about what is right behavior and what is wrong behavior in a particular situation. Such devices may prescribe what people should do, but they often fail to help people understand and live with the consequences of their choices. Making ethical choices may lead to very unpleasant outcomes—firing, rejection by colleagues, and the forfeiture of monetary gain, to name a few. Thus managers must be prepared to confront their own conscience and weigh the options available when making difficult ethical decisions.

Emerging Ethical Issues   Ethical scandals have become almost commonplace in today's world. Ranging from business and sports to politics and the entertainment industry, these scandals have rocked stakeholder confidence and called into question the moral integrity of our society. At the same time, most women and men today conduct themselves and their affairs in accordance with high ethical standards. Hence, as we summarize several emerging ethical issues in organizations, it is important to remember that one cannot judge everyone by the transgressions of a few.

Ethical Leadership   In recent years the media have been rife with stories about unscrupulous corporate leaders. For every unethical senior manager, of course, there are many highly ethical ones. But the actions of such high-profile deposed executives as Dennis Kozlowski (Tyco), Kenneth Lay (Enron), and Bernard Ebbers (WorldCom) have substantially increased the scrutiny directed at all executives. As a direct result, executives everywhere are being expected to exhibit nothing but the strongest ethical conduct. This leadership, in turn, is expected to help set the tone for the rest of the organization and to establish both norms and a culture that reinforce the importance of ethical behavior.[16]

The basic premise behind ethical leadership is that because leaders serve as role models for others, their every action is subject to scrutiny. If a senior executive exercises questionable judgment, this sends a signal to others that such actions are acceptable. This signal may, in turn, be remembered by others when they face similar situations. As a result, CEOs such as Aramark's Joseph Neubauer and Costco's James Sinegal are now being held up as the standard against which others are being measured. The basic premise is that CEOs must set their company's moral tone by being honest and straightforward and by taking responsibility for any shortcomings that are identified. To support this view, Congress passed the ***Sarbanes-Oxley Act,***

---

codes of ethics
A formal, written statement of the values and ethical standards that guide a firm's actions

Sarbanes-Oxley Act of 2002
A law that requires CEOs and CFOs to vouch personally for the truthfulness and fairness of their firms' financial disclosures and imposes tough new measures to deter and punish corporate and accounting fraud and corruption

requiring CEOs and CFOs to vouch personally for the truthfulness and fairness of their firms' financial disclosures. The law also imposes tough new measures to deter and punish corporate and accounting fraud and corruption.

Corporate Governance   A related area of emerging concern is ethical issues in corporate governance. As discussed earlier, the board of directors of a public corporation is expected to ensure that the business is being properly managed and that the decisions made by its senior management are in the best interests of shareholders and other stakeholders. But many of the recent ethical scandals that we have mentioned have actually started with a breakdown in the corporate governance structure. For instance, WorldCom's board approved a personal loan to the firm's then-CEO, Bernard Ebbers, for $366 million, when there was little evidence that he could repay it. And Tyco's board approved a $20 million bonus for one of its own members for helping with the acquisition of another firm. Boards of directors are also criticized when they are seen as not being sufficiently independent of senior management.[17]

Ethics and Information Technology   A final set of issues that has emerged in recent times involves information technology. Among the specific focal points in this area are individual rights to privacy and the potential abuse of information technology by individuals. Indeed, online privacy has become a hot topic, as companies sort out the related ethical and management issues. DoubleClick, an online advertising network, is one of the firms at the eye of the privacy storm. The company has collected data on the habits of millions of Web surfers, recording which sites they visit and which ads they click on. DoubleClick insists that the profiles are anonymous and are used simply to match surfers with appropriate ads. However, after the company announced a plan to add names and addresses to its database, it was forced to back down because of public concerns over invasion of online privacy.

One way in which management can address these concerns is to post a privacy policy on the company website. The policy should explain exactly what data the company collects and who gets to see the data. It should also allow people a choice about having their information shared with others and indicate how people can opt out of data collection. Disney, IBM, and other companies support this position by refusing to advertise on websites that have no posted privacy policies.

In addition, companies can offer Web surfers the opportunity to review and correct information that has been collected, especially medical and financial data. In the offline world, consumers are legally allowed to inspect their own credit and medical records. In the online world, this kind of access can be costly and cumbersome, because data are often spread across several computer systems. Despite the technical difficulties, government agencies are already working on Internet privacy guidelines, which means that companies will need internal guidelines, training, and leadership to ensure that they are in compliance.

Social Responsibility in Organizations

As we have seen, ethics are associated with individuals and their decisions and behaviors. Organizations themselves do not have ethics, but they relate to their environments in ways that often involve ethical dilemmas and decisions. These situations are generally referred to within the context of the organization's *social responsibility*. Specifically, social responsibility is the set of obligations an

social responsibility
The set of obligations an organization has to protect and enhance the societal context in which it functions

organization has to protect and enhance the societal context in which it functions. Some of the more salient arguments on both sides of this contemporary debate are summarized in Figure 2.2 and further explained in the following sections.

Arguments for Social Responsibility   People who argue in favor of social responsibility claim that, because organizations create many of the problems that need to be addressed, such as air and water pollution, resource depletion, and global warming, organizations should play a major role in solving them. They also argue that, because corporations are legally defined entities with most of the same privileges as private citizens, businesses should not try to avoid their obligations as citizens. Advocates of social responsibility point out that, whereas governmental organizations have stretched their budgets to the limit, many large businesses often have surplus revenues that could be used to help solve social problems. For example, Dell donates surplus computers to schools, and many restaurants give leftover food to homeless shelters.

Arguments Against Social Responsibility   Some people, however, including the famous economist Milton Friedman, argue that widening the interpretation of social responsibility will undermine the U.S. economy by detracting from the basic mission of business: to earn profits for owners. For example, money that Chevron or General Electric contributes to social causes or charities is money that could otherwise be distributed to owners in the form of dividends. A few years ago, shareholders of Ben & Jerry's Homemade Holdings expressed outrage when the firm refused to accept a lucrative exporting deal to Japan simply because the Japanese distributor did not have a strong social agenda.[18]

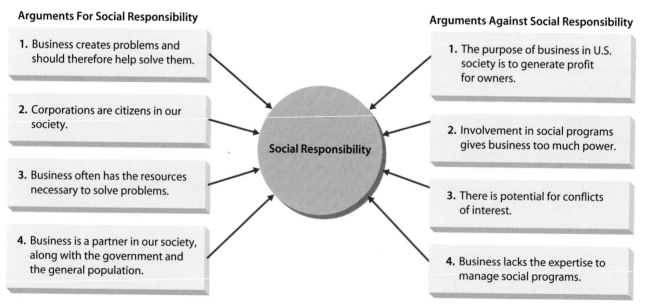

Arguments For Social Responsibility

1. Business creates problems and should therefore help solve them.

2. Corporations are citizens in our society.

3. Business often has the resources necessary to solve problems.

4. Business is a partner in our society, along with the government and the general population.

Social Responsibility

Arguments Against Social Responsibility

1. The purpose of business in U.S. society is to generate profit for owners.

2. Involvement in social programs gives business too much power.

3. There is potential for conflicts of interest.

4. Business lacks the expertise to manage social programs.

Figure 2.2
ARGUMENTS FOR AND AGAINST SOCIAL RESPONSIBILITY

Although many people want everyone to see social responsibility as a desirable aim, there are in fact several strong arguments that can be advanced both for and against social responsibility. Hence organizations and their managers should carefully assess their own values, beliefs, and priorities when deciding which stance and approach to take regarding social responsibility.

Environmentalism is becoming increasingly important as people, governments, and businesses begin to address global warming and other concerns about the quality of our natural environment. As new technologies replace older ones, dealing with electronic waste and other byproducts is taking on greater importance. Hewlett-Packard is helping do its part by operating a large-scale computer recycling program. An HP employee, Raj Winder-Kaur, is shown here dismantling and sorting parts from old personal computers.

Another objection to increasing the social responsibility of businesses reflects the position that corporations already wield enormous power and that involvement in social programs gives them even more power. Still another argument against social responsibility focuses on the potential for conflicts of interest. Suppose, for example, that one manager is in charge of deciding which local social program or charity will receive a large grant from her business. The local civic opera company (a not-for-profit organization that relies on contributions for its existence) might offer her front-row tickets for the upcoming season in exchange for her support. If opera is her favorite form of music, she may be tempted to direct the money toward the local company, when it might actually be needed more in other areas.[19]

Finally, critics argue that organizations lack the expertise to understand how to assess and make decisions about worthy social programs. How can a company truly know, they ask, which cause or program is most deserving of its support or how money might best be spent?

Managing Social Responsibility

The demands for social responsibility placed on contemporary organizations by an increasingly sophisticated and educated public are probably stronger than ever. Indeed, as the challenges and issues associated with growing concerns about global warming escalate, businesses must increasingly consider environmental factors in both their strategic thinking as well as their everyday business practices.[20] As we have seen, there are pitfalls for managers who fail to adhere to high ethical standards and for companies that try to circumvent their legal obligations. Organizations therefore need to fashion an approach to social responsibility in the same way that they develop any other business strategy. In other words, they should view social responsibility as a major challenge that requires careful planning, decision making, consideration, and evaluation. They may accomplish this through both formal and informal dimensions of managing social responsibility.

Formal Organizational Dimensions Some dimensions of managing social responsibility are a formal and planned activity on the part of the organization. The formal organizational dimensions through which businesses can manage social responsibility include legal compliance, ethical compliance, and philanthropic giving.

Legal compliance is the extent to which the organization conforms to local, state, federal, and international laws. The task of managing legal compliance is generally assigned to the appropriate functional managers. For example, the organization's top human resources executive is responsible for ensuring compliance with regulations concerning hiring, pay, and workplace safety and health. Likewise, the top finance executive generally oversees compliance with securities and banking regulations. The organization's legal department is likely to contribute to this effort by providing general oversight and answering queries from managers about the appropriate interpretation of laws and regulations. Unfortunately, though, legal compliance may not be enough—in some cases, for instance, perfectly legal accounting practices have still resulted in deception and other problems.[21]

Ethical compliance is the extent to which the members of the organization follow basic ethical (and legal) standards of behavior. We noted earlier that organizations have increased their efforts in this area—providing training in ethics and developing guidelines and codes of conduct, for example. These activities serve as vehicles for enhancing ethical compliance. Many organizations also establish formal ethics committees, which may be asked to review proposals for new projects, to help evaluate new hiring strategies, or to assess a new environmental protection plan. They might also serve as a peer review panel to evaluate alleged ethical misconduct by an employee.[22]

Finally, *philanthropic giving* is the awarding of funds or gifts to charities or other worthy causes. Target routinely gives a share of its pretax income to charity and social programs. Giving across national boundaries is also becoming more common. For example, Alcoa gave $112,000 to a small town in Brazil to build a sewage treatment plant. And Japanese firms such as Sony and Mitsubishi make contributions to a number of social programs in the United States. However, in the current climate of cutbacks, many corporations have also had to limit their charitable gifts over the past several years as they continue to trim their own budgets.[23] And many firms that continue to make contributions are increasingly targeting them to programs or areas where the firm will get something in return. For example, firms today are more likely than they were a few years ago to give money to job training programs rather than to the arts. The logic is that they get a more direct payoff from the former type of contribution—in this instance, a better-trained workforce from which to hire new employees.[24]

Informal Organizational Dimensions In addition to these formal dimensions of managing social responsibility, there are also informal ones. Leadership, organization culture, and how the organization responds to whistle blowers all help shape and define people's perceptions of the organization's stance on social responsibility.

legal compliance
The extent to which an organization complies with local, state, federal, and international laws

ethical compliance
The extent to which an organization and its members follow basic ethical standards of behavior

philanthropic giving
Awarding funds or gifts to charities or other worthy causes

Leadership practices and organization culture can go a long way toward defining the social responsibility stance an organization and its members will adopt.[25] As described earlier, for example, ethical leadership often sets the tone for the entire organization. For example, Johnson & Johnson executives for years provided a consistent message to employees that customers, employees, communities where the company did business, and shareholders were all important—and primarily in that order. Thus, when packages of poisoned Tylenol showed up on store shelves, Johnson & Johnson employees did not need to wait for orders from headquarters to know what to do: they immediately pulled all the packages from shelves before any other customers could buy them.[26]

Whistle-blowing is the disclosure, by an employee, of illegal or unethical conduct on the part of others within the organization.[27] How an organization responds to this practice often indicates its values as they relate to social responsibility. Whistle blowers may have to proceed through a number of channels to be heard, and they may even get fired for their efforts.[28] Many organizations, however, welcome their contributions. A person who observes questionable behavior typically first reports the incident to his or her boss. If nothing is done, the whistle blower may then inform higher-level managers or an ethics committee, if one exists. Eventually, the person may have to go to a regulatory agency or even the media to be heard. For example, Charles W. Robinson Jr. worked as a director of a SmithKline lab in San Antonio. One day he noticed a suspicious billing pattern that the firm was using to collect lab fees from Medicare: The bills were considerably higher than the firm's normal charges for those same tests. He pointed out the problem to higher-level managers, but his concerns were ignored. He subsequently took his findings to the U.S. government, which sued SmithKline and eventually reached a settlement of $325 million.[29]

> *whistle-blowing*
> The disclosure, by an employee, of illegal or unethical conduct on the part of others within the organization

The International Environment of Management

Another important competitive issue for managers today is the international environment. After describing recent trends in international business, we examine levels of internationalization and the international context of business.

Trends in International Business

The stage for today's international business environment was set at the end of World War II. Businesses in war-torn countries such as Germany and Japan had no choice but to rebuild from scratch. Consequently, they had to rethink every facet of their operations, including technology, production, finance, and marketing. Although it took many years for these countries to recover, they eventually did so, and their economic systems were subsequently poised for growth. During the same era, many U.S. companies grew somewhat complacent. Their customer base was growing rapidly. Increased population, spurred by the baby boom, and increased affluence resulting from the postwar economic boom greatly raised the average person's standard of living and expectations. The U.S. public continually wanted new and better products and services. Many U.S. companies profited greatly from this pattern, but most were also guilty of taking it for granted.

U.S. firms are no longer isolated from global competition or the global market. A few simple numbers help tell the full story of international trade and industry.

First of all, the volume of international trade increased more than 3,000 percent between 1960 and 2000. Further, although 176 of the world's largest corporations are headquartered in the United States, there are also 81 in Japan, 39 in France, 37 in Germany, and 35 in Britain.[30] Within certain industries, the preeminence of non-U.S. firms is even more striking. For example, only three each of the world's ten largest banks and ten largest electronics companies are based in the United States. Only two of the ten largest chemical companies are U.S. firms. On the other hand, U.S. firms account for six of the eight largest aerospace companies, three of the seven largest airlines, four of the nine largest computer companies, four of the five largest diversified financial companies, and six of the ten largest retailers.[31]

U.S. firms are also finding that international operations are an increasingly important element of their sales and profits. For example, in 2005 Exxon Corporation realized 97 percent of its revenues and 72 percent of its profits abroad. For Avon, these percentages were 98 percent and 68 percent, respectively.[32] From any perspective, then, it is clear that we live in a truly global economy. Virtually all businesses today must be concerned with the competitive situations they face in lands far from home and with how companies from distant countries are competing in their homeland.

Levels of International Business Activity

Firms can choose various levels of international business activity as they seek to gain a competitive advantage in other countries. The general levels are exporting and importing, licensing, strategic alliances, and direct investment. Table 2.1 summarizes the advantages and disadvantages of each approach.

Exporting and Importing   Importing or exporting (or both) is usually the first type of international business in which a firm gets involved. *Exporting,* or making a product in the firm's domestic marketplace and selling it in another country, can involve both merchandise and services. *Importing* is bringing a good, service, or capital into the home country from abroad. For example, automobiles (Mazda, Ford, Volkswagen, Mercedes-Benz, Ferrari) and stereo equipment

---

> **exporting**
> Making a product in the firm's domestic marketplace and selling it in another country

---

Table 2.1

ADVANTAGES AND DISADVANTAGES OF DIFFERENT APPROACHES TO INTERNATIONALIZATION

When organizations decide to increase their level of internationalization, they can adopt several strategies. Each strategy is a matter of degree, as opposed to being a discrete and mutually exclusive category. And each has unique advantages and disadvantages that must be considered.

Approach to Internationalization	Advantages	Disadvantages
Importing or Exporting	1. Small cash outlay	1. Tariffs and taxes
	2. Little risk	2. High transportation costs
	3. No adaptation necessary	3. Government restrictions
Licensing	1. Increased profitability	1. Inflexibility
	2. Extended profitability	2. Competition
Strategic Alliances or Joint Ventures	1. Quick market entry	Shared ownership (limits control and profits)
	2. Access to materials and technology	
Direct Investment	1. Enhanced control	1. Complexity
	2. Existing infrastructure	2. Greater economic and political risk
		3. Greater uncertainty

(Sony, Bang & Olufsen, Sanyo) are routinely exported by their manufacturers to other countries. Likewise, many wine distributors buy products from vineyards in France, Italy, or California and import them into their own country for resale. U.S. sports brands, such as team jerseys and logo caps, have become one of the latest hot exports.[33]

Licensing A company may prefer to arrange for a foreign company to manufacture or market its products under a licensing agreement. Factors that may lead to this decision include excessive transportation costs, government regulations, and home production costs. *Licensing* is an arrangement whereby a firm allows another company to use its brand name, trademark, technology, patent, copyright, or other assets. In return, the licensee pays a royalty, usually based on sales. Franchising, a special form of licensing, is also widely used in international business. Kirin Brewery, Japan's largest producer of beer, wanted to expand its international operations but feared that the time involved in shipping it from Japan would cause the beer to lose its freshness. Thus it has entered into a number of licensing arrangements with breweries in other markets. These brewers make beer according to strict guidelines provided by the Japanese firm and then package and market it as Kirin Beer. They pay a royalty to Kirin for each case sold. Molson produces Kirin in Canada under such an agreement, and the Charles Wells Brewery does the same in England.[34]

Strategic Alliances In a *strategic alliance,* two or more firms jointly cooperate for mutual gain.[35] For example, Kodak and Fuji, along with three other major Japanese camera manufacturers, collaborated on the development of a new film cartridge. This collaboration allowed Kodak and Fuji to share development costs, prevented the advertising war that might have raged if they had developed different cartridges, and made it easier for new cameras to be introduced at the same time as the new film cartridges. A *joint venture* is a special type of strategic alliance in which the partners actually share ownership of a new enterprise. Strategic alliances have enjoyed a tremendous upsurge in the past few years.

Direct Investment Another level of commitment to internationalization is direct investment. *Direct investment* occurs when a firm headquartered in one country builds or purchases operating facilities or subsidiaries in a foreign country. The foreign operations then become wholly owned subsidiaries of the firm. Examples include Ford's acquisitions of Jaguar, Volvo, and Kia, as well as British Petroleum's acquisition of Amoco. Dell Computer's new factory in China is also a direct investment, as is the new Disney theme park in Hong Kong. And Coca-Cola recently committed $150 million to build a new bottling and distribution network in India.[36] Many U.S. firms are using maquiladoras for the same purpose. *Maquiladoras* are light assembly plants built in northern Mexico close to the U.S. border. The plants are given special tax breaks by the Mexican government, and the area is populated with workers willing to work for very low wages.

The Context of International Business

Managers involved in international business should also be aware of the cultural environment, controls on international trade, the importance of economic communities, and the role of the GATT and WTO.

---

importing
Bringing a good, service, or capital into the home country from abroad

licensing
An arrangement whereby one company allows another company to use its brand name, trademark, technology, patent, copyright, or other assets in exchange for a royalty based on sales

strategic alliance
A cooperative arrangement between two or more firms for mutual gain

joint venture
A special type of strategic alliance in which the partners share in the ownership of an operation on an equity basis

direct investment
A firm's building or purchasing operating facilities or subsidiaries in a different country from the one where it has its headquarters

maquiladoras
Light assembly plants that are built in northern Mexico close to the U.S. border and are given special tax breaks by the Mexican government

DILBERT: © Scott Adams/Dist. by United Feature Syndicate, Inc.

Dealing with people from other cultures can be a rewarding experience and it can also be a challenge. Language barriers, for example, pose major obstacles. Interestingly, some people believe that if they talk more slowly or raise their voices, people who do not speak their language will somehow have a better understanding of what is being said. As illustrated in this cartoon, this flawed logic can even extend to electronic communication.

The Cultural Environment One significant contextual challenge for the international manager is the cultural environment and how it affects business. A country's culture includes all the values, symbols, beliefs, and language that guide behavior. Cultural values and beliefs are often unspoken; they may even be taken for granted by those who live in a particular country. Cultural factors do not necessarily cause problems for managers when the cultures of two countries are similar. Difficulties can arise, however, when there is little overlap between the home culture of a manager and the culture of the country in which business is to be conducted. For example, most U.S. managers find the culture and traditions of England relatively familiar. The people of both countries speak the same language and share strong historical roots, and there is a history of strong commerce between the two countries. When U.S. managers begin operations in Vietnam or the People's Republic of China, however, many of those commonalities disappear.

Cultural differences between countries can have a direct impact on business practice. For example, the religion of Islam teaches that people should not make a living by exploiting the misfortune of others; as a result, charging interest is seen as immoral. This means that in Saudi Arabia, there are few businesses that provide auto-wrecking services to tow stalled cars to the garage (doing so would be capitalizing on misfortune), and in the Sudan, banks cannot pay or charge interest. Given these cultural and religious constraints, those two businesses—automobile towing and banking—seem to hold little promise for international managers in those particular countries!

Some cultural differences between countries can be even more subtle and yet have a major impact on business activities. For example, in the United States most managers clearly agree about the value of time. Most U.S. managers schedule their activities very tightly and then try hard to adhere to their schedules. Other cultures do not put such a premium on time. In the Middle East, managers do not like to set appointments, and they rarely keep appointments set too far into the future. U.S. managers interacting with managers from the Middle East might misinterpret the late arrival of a potential business partner as a negotiation ploy or an insult, when it is merely a simple reflection of different views of time and its value.[37]

Eye on Management

Global Competition at Subway

Subway is the second-largest restaurant chain in the world (behind number one McDonald's), with 27,189 restaurants in 85 countries, including over 6,000 international stores. Every year it adds more than 500 restaurants to the chain.

Many firms believe in customizing their products, but Subway requires each franchisee, regardless of location, to include the same items. Local stores are allowed a mere six "local" items on the menu. Ingredients such as meats, cheeses, and breads are standardized. Exceptions are made only in the case of strict cultural or religious requirements. For example, many Subway locations in India do not offer beef sandwiches, while those in predominantly Muslim countries do not offer pork.

Although these restrictions might seem harsh, in many ways Subway is ahead of its competitors in encouraging and supporting international franchisees. For example, the company's website features investment information in French, German, and Spanish, in addition to English. Subway's international development agents assist the company and potential investors in developing stores in a certain geographic location. These efforts and others ensure that Subway doesn't lose touch with its local markets. The firm has developed a winning international strategy, combining standardization and customization.

The video describes Subway's approach to internationalization, including the company's history of global expansion. View the video and then answer the following questions.

1. Subway uses franchising, a form of licensing, to enter foreign markets. How does this choice help Subway to expand its international business? What are some of the potential problems with this choice?

2. Subway has operations in 85 countries. What do you think the impact of cultural or religious differences might be? What might be the impact of economic differences?

3. List some of the management challenges Subway faces as it expands globally. Include challenges in planning, organizing, leading, and controlling.

Language itself can be an important factor. Beyond the obvious and clear barriers posed when people speak different languages, subtle differences in meaning can also play a major role. For example, Imperial Oil of Canada markets gasoline under the brand name Esso. When the firm tried to sell its gasoline in Japan, it learned that Esso means "stalled car" in Japanese. Likewise, when Chevrolet first introduced a U.S. model called the Nova in Latin America, General Motors executives could not understand why the car sold poorly. They eventually learned, though, that, in Spanish, *no va* means "it doesn't go." The color green is used extensively in Moslem countries, but it signifies death in some other lands. The color associated with femininity in the United States is pink, but in many other countries yellow is the most feminine color.

Controls on International Trade   Another element of the international context that managers need to consider is the extent to which there are controls on international trade. These controls include tariffs, quotas, export restraint agreements, and "buy national" laws. A *tariff* is a tax collected on goods shipped across national boundaries. Tariffs can be collected by the exporting country, by countries through which goods pass, or by the importing country. Import tariffs, which are the most common, can be levied to protect domestic companies by increasing the cost of foreign goods. Japan charges U.S. tobacco producers a tariff on cigarettes imported into Japan as a way to keep their prices higher than the prices charged by domestic

> *tariff*
> A tax collected on goods shipped across national boundaries

firms. Tariffs can also be levied, usually by less-developed countries, to raise money for the government.

Quotas are the most common form of trade restriction. A *quota* is a limit on the number or value of goods that can be traded. The quota amount is typically designed to ensure that domestic competitors will be able to maintain a certain market share. Honda is allowed to import 425,000 autos each year into the United States. This quota is one reason why Honda opened manufacturing facilities here. The quota applies to cars imported into the United States, but the company can produce as many other cars within our borders as it wants; such cars are not considered imports. *Export restraint agreements* are designed to convince other governments to limit voluntarily the volume or value of goods exported to or imported from a particular country. They are, in effect, export quotas. Japanese steel producers voluntarily limit the amount of steel they send to the United States each year.

"Buy national" legislation gives preference to domestic producers through content or price restrictions. Several countries have this type of legislation. Brazil requires that Brazilian companies purchase only Brazilian-made computers. The United States requires that the Department of Defense purchase only military uniforms manufactured in the United States, even though the price of foreign uniforms would be only half as much. Mexico requires that 50 percent of the parts of cars sold in Mexico be manufactured inside its own borders.

Economic Communities   Just as government policies can either increase or decrease the political risk that international managers face, trade relations between countries can either help or hinder international business. Relations dictated by quotas, tariffs, and so forth can hurt international trade. There is currently a strong movement around the world to reduce many of these barriers. This movement takes its most obvious form in international economic communities.

An international *economic community* is a set of countries that agree to markedly reduce or eliminate trade barriers among member nations. The first (and in many ways still the most important) of these economic communities is the European Union. The *European Union* (or EU, as it is often called) can be traced to 1957 when Belgium, France, Luxembourg, Germany, Italy, and the Netherlands signed the Treaty of Rome to promote economic integration. Between 1973 and 1986 these countries were joined by Denmark, Ireland, the United Kingdom, Greece, Spain, and Portugal, and the group became known first as the European Committee and then as the European Union. More recently, Austria, Finland, and Sweden joined the EU in 1995; twelve additional countries (mostly from the formerly Communist-controlled eastern European region joined between 2004 and 2007, bringing the EU's membership to 27 countries. For years these countries have followed a basic plan that led to the systematic elimination of most trade barriers. The new market system achieved significantly more potential when most of the EU members eliminated their home currencies (such as French francs and Italian lira) beginning on January 1, 2002, and adopted a new common currency call the euro.

Another important economic community encompasses the United States, Canada, and Mexico. These countries have long been major trading partners with one another; more than 70 percent of Mexico's exports go to the United States, and more than 65 percent of what Mexico imports comes from the United States. During the last several years, these countries have negotiated a variety of agreements to

quota
A limit on the number or value of goods that can be traded

export restraint agreements
Accords reached by governments in which countries voluntarily limit the volume or value of goods they export to or import from one another

economic community
A set of countries that agree to markedly reduce or eliminate trade barriers among member nations (a formalized market system)

European Union
The first and most important international market system

make trade even easier. The most important of these, the **North American Free Trade Agreement, or NAFTA,** eliminates many of the trade barriers—quotas and tariffs, for example—that existed previously.[38]

The Role of the GATT and WTO   The context of international business is also increasingly being influenced by the **General Agreement on Tariffs and Trade (GATT)** and the World Trade Organization (WTO). The General Agreement on Tariffs and Trade was first negotiated following World War II in an effort to avoid trade wars that would benefit rich nations and harm poorer ones. Essentially, the GATT is a trade agreement intended to promote international trade by reducing trade barriers and making it easier for all nations to compete in international markets. The GATT was a major stimulus to international trade after it was first ratified in 1948 by 23 countries; by 1994 a total of 117 countries had signed the agreement.

One key component of the GATT was identification of the so-called *most favored nation* (MFN) principle. This provision stipulates that if a country extends preferential treatment to any other nation that has signed the agreement, then that preferential treatment must be extended to all signatories to the agreement. Members can extend such treatment to nonsignatories as well, but they are not required to do so.

The **World Trade Organization, or WTO**, came into existence on January 1, 1995. The WTO replaced the GATT and absorbed its mission. The WTO is headquartered in Geneva, Switzerland, and currently includes 140 member nations and 32 observer countries. Members are required to open their markets to international trade and to follow WTO rules. The WTO has three basic goals:

1. To promote trade flows by encouraging nations to adopt nondiscriminatory and predictable trade policies

2. To reduce remaining trade barriers through multilateral negotiations

3. To establish impartial procedures for resolving trade disputes among its members

The World Trade Organization is certain to continue to play a major role in the evolution of the global economy. At the same time, it has also become a lightning rod for protesters and other activists, who argue that the WTO focuses too narrowly on globalization issues to the detriment of human rights and the environment.

The Organization's Culture

As we noted earlier, an especially important part of the internal environment of an organization is its culture. **Organization culture** is the set of values, beliefs, behaviors, customs, and attitudes that helps the members of the organization understand what it stands for, how it does things, and what it considers important.[39]

The Importance of Organization Culture

Culture determines the "feel" of the organization. A strong and clear culture can play an important role in the competitiveness of a business. At the same time, though, there is no universal culture that will help all organizations. The

---

North American Free Trade Agreement, or NAFTA
An agreement between the United States, Canada, and Mexico to promote trade with one another

General Agreement on Tariffs and Trade (GATT)
A trade agreement intended to promote international trade by reducing trade barriers and making it easier for all nations to compete in international markets

World Trade Organization, or WTO
An organization, which currently includes 140 member nations and 32 observer countries, that requires members to open their markets to international trade and to follow WTO rules

organization culture
The set of values, beliefs, behaviors, customs, and attitudes that helps the members of the organization understand what it stands for, how it does things, and what it considers important

stereotypic image of Microsoft, for example, is that of a workplace where people dress very casually and work very long hours. In contrast, the image of Bank of America for some observers is that of a formal setting with rigid work rules and people dressed in conservative business attire. And Texas Instruments likes to talk about its "shirtsleeve" culture, in which ties are avoided and few managers ever wear jackets. Southwest Airlines maintains a culture that stresses fun and excitement.

Of course, the same culture is not necessarily found throughout an entire organization. For example, the sales and marketing department may have a culture quite different from that of the operations and manufacturing department. Regardless of its nature, however, culture is a powerful force in organizations, one that can shape the firm's overall effectiveness and long-term success. Companies that can develop and maintain a strong culture, such as Starbucks and Procter & Gamble, tend to be more effective than companies that have trouble developing and maintaining a strong culture, such as Kmart.[40]

Determinants of Organization Culture

Where does an organization's culture come from? Typically, it develops and blossoms over a long period of time. Its starting point is often the organization's founder. For example, James Cash Penney believed in treating employees and customers with respect and dignity. Employees at JCPenney are still called "associates" rather than "employees" (to reflect partnership), and customer satisfaction is of paramount importance. The impact of Sam Walton, Ross Perot, and Walt Disney is still felt in the organizations they founded.[41] As an organization grows, its culture is modified, shaped, and refined by symbols, stories, heroes, slogans, and ceremonies. And many decisions at Walt Disney Company today are still framed by asking, "What would Walt have done?"

Corporate success and shared experiences also shape culture. For example, Hallmark Cards has a strong culture derived from its years of success in the greeting card industry. Employees speak of "the Hallmark family" and care deeply about the company; many of them have worked there for years. At Kmart, in contrast, the culture is quite weak, the management team changes rapidly, and few people sense any direction or purpose in the company. The differences in culture at Hallmark and Kmart are in part attributable to past successes and shared experiences.

Managing Organization Culture

How can managers deal with culture, given its clear importance but intangible nature? Essentially, the manager must understand the current culture and then decide whether it should be maintained or changed. By understanding the organization's current culture, managers can take appropriate actions. Culture can also be maintained by rewarding and promoting people whose behaviors are consistent with the existing culture and by articulating the culture through slogans, ceremonies, and so forth.

But managers must walk a fine line between maintaining a culture that still works effectively and changing a culture that has become dysfunctional. For example, many of the firms already noted, as well as numerous others, take pride in perpetuating their culture. Shell Oil, for example, has an elaborate display in the lobby of its Houston headquarters that tells the story of the firm's past. But other companies may face situations in which their culture is no longer a strength. For example, some critics feel that the organization culture at General Motors places too much emphasis on product development and internal competition among divisions, and not enough on marketing and competition with other firms.

Culture problems sometimes arise from mergers or from the growth of rival factions within an organization. Wells Fargo, which relies heavily on flashy technology and automated banking services, acquired another large bank, First Interstate, which had focused more attention on personal services and customer satisfaction. Blending these two disparate organization cultures was difficult for the firm, as managers argued over how best to serve customers and operate the new enterprise.[42]

To change culture, managers must have a clear idea of what they want to create. When Continental Airlines "reinvented" itself a few years ago, employees were invited outside the corporate headquarters in Houston to watch the firm's old policies and procedures manuals set afire. The firm's new strategic direction is known throughout Continental as the "Go Forward" plan, intentionally named to avoid reminding people about the firm's troubled past and to focus on the future instead.

Summary of Key Points

1. Discuss the nature of an organization's environments and identify the components of its general, task, and internal environments.
   - Managers need to have a thorough understanding of the environment in which they operate and compete. The general environment consists of the economy, technology, and the political-legal climate. The task environment consists of competitors, customers, suppliers, strategic partners, and regulators.
   - The internal environment consists of the organization's owners, board of directors, employees, physical environment, and culture. Owners are those who have claims on the property rights of the organization. The board of directors, elected by stockholders, is responsible for overseeing a firm's top managers. Individual employees are other important parts of the internal environment. The physical environment, yet another part of the internal environment, varies greatly across organizations.

2. Describe the ethical and social environment of management, including individual ethics, the concept of social responsibility, and how organizations can manage social responsibility.

   - The ethical and social environment of management is also quite important. Understanding the differences between ethical and unethical behavior, as well as appreciating the special nature of managerial ethics, can help guide effective decision making. Understanding the meaning of and arguments for and against social responsibility can help a manager effectively address both the formal and the informal dimensions of social responsibility.

3. Discuss the international environment of management, including trends in international business, levels of international business activities, and the context of international business.

   - The international environment of management can be a crucial one. Current trends have resulted in the increasing globalization of markets, industries, and businesses. Organizations seeking to become more international can rely on importing, exporting, licensing (including franchising), strategic alliances, and direct investment to do so. National culture, controls on international trade, economic communities, and the WTO combine to determine the context of international business.

4. Describe the importance and determinants of an organization's culture, as well as how organization culture can be managed.

   • Organization culture is the set of values, beliefs, behaviors, customs, and attitudes that helps the members of the organization understand what it stands for, how it does things, and what it considers important. Organization culture is an important environmental concern for managers. Managers must understand that culture is a key determinant of how well their organization will perform. Culture can be assessed and managed in a number of different ways.

Discussion Questions

Questions for Review

1. Identify and discuss each major dimension of the general environment and the task environment.

2. Do organizations have ethics? Why or why not?

3. What are the arguments for and against social responsibility on the part of businesses? In your opinion, which set of arguments is more compelling?

4. Describe the basic levels of international business involvement. Why might a firm use more than one level at the same time?

5. Describe various barriers to international trade.

Questions for Analysis

1. Can you think of dimensions of the task environment that are not discussed in the text? Indicate their linkages to those that are discussed.

2. What is the relationship between the law and ethical behavior? Can a behavior be ethical but illegal at the same time?

3. What is your opinion of whistle-blowing? If you were aware of criminal activity in your organization but knew that reporting it would probably cost you your job, what would you do?

4. What industries do you think will feel the greatest impact of international business in the future? Are there industries that will remain relatively unaffected by globalization? If so, which ones? If not, explain why not.

5. What is the culture of your college or university? How clear is it? What are its most positive and its most negative characteristics?

Building Effective Diagnostic and Decision-Making Skills

Exercise Overview

Diagnostic skills are the skills that enable a manager to visualize the most appropriate response to a situation. Effective diagnosis of a situation then provides a foundation for effective decision making. Decision-making skills draw on the manager's ability to recognize and define problems and opportunities correctly and then to select an appropriate course of action to solve problems and capitalize on opportunities. This exercise will help you develop your diagnostic and decision-making skills by applying them to an ethical business dilemma.

Exercise Background

As businesses, industries, societies, and technologies become more complex, ethical dilemmas become more puzzling. Consider the ethical dilemmas related to the online publication of music. The growth of file-sharing programs and fast Internet connections, the desire of many businesses and customers to bypass intermediaries, and changing societal definitions of "theft" all contributed to the difficult situation.

In 2001, Napster, then the most popular file-sharing program, was shut down by a lawsuit from the Recording Industry Association of America, which represented music publishers and distributors. After Napster's demise, many legal music distribution sites came online, including iTunes, buy.com, and MP3.com. However, there are still many distributors that spread mainly illegal content, including Grokster, KaZaA, and others.

Exercise Task

1. Consider each of the stakeholders in the online music publishing industry. These would include recording artists, recording companies, and consumers. It would also include online file-sharing companies such as Grokster and legitimate websites such as iTunes. From the point of view of each party, what are the ethical problems within the online music industry today?

2. What would be the "best" outcome for each of the parties?

Use the Internet to investigate up-to-date information about online music publishing, and then answer the following questions.

3. Is there any way to satisfy the needs of all the stakeholders? If yes, tell how this can be accomplished. If no, explain why a mutually beneficial solution will not be possible.

4. What impact did your personal ethics have on your answer to Question 3?

Building Effective Interpersonal Skills

Exercise Overview

Interpersonal skills reflect the manager's ability to communicate with, understand, and motivate individuals and groups. Managers in international organizations must understand how cultural manners and norms affect communication with people in different areas of the world. This exercise will help you evaluate your current level of cultural awareness and develop insights into areas where you can improve.

Exercise Background

As firms become increasingly globalized, they look for managers with international experience or skills. Yet many American college graduates do not have strong skills in foreign languages, global history, or international cultures.

Exercise Task

Take the International Culture Quiz that follows. Then, on the basis of your score, answer the question at the end. In order to make the quiz more relevant, choose your answers from one or more of the ten largest countries in the world. In order, these are China, India, the United States, Indonesia, Brazil, Pakistan, Bangladesh, Russia, Nigeria, and Japan.

The International Culture Quiz

1. Name the major religion practiced in each of the ten largest countries.

2. When greeting a business associate, in which country or countries is it proper to shake hands? to bow? to hug or kiss?

3. In which country or countries should you avoid wearing the color purple?

4. In which country or countries would smiling be considered suspicious?

5. In which country or countries are laughter and smiling often used as a way of covering up feelings of embarrassment or displeasure?

6. Which part of someone else's body should you never touch in Indonesia? in India? Which part of your own body should you never touch in China?

7. In which country or countries would a server or small-business person require that a tip be paid before the service is rendered?

8. In which country or countries would it be an insult to address someone in Spanish?

9. In which country or countries is whistling considered bad luck?

10. In which country or countries is it important to give printed business cards to all business associates?

11. In which country or countries might you be asked your family size or income upon first meeting with a new business associate?

12. In which country or countries should gum not be chewed at work?

Your instructor will provide the answers. Was your score high or low? What does your score tell you about your cultural awareness?

What do you think you could do to improve your score? Share your ideas with the class.

(Reprinted by permission of the author Margaret Hill.)

Building Effective Communication Skills

Exercise Overview

Communication skills consist of a manager's ability to receive information and ideas from others effectively and to convey information and ideas effectively to others. This exercise will help you develop your communication skills, while also helping you to understand the importance of clarity and tact while communicating about sensitive subjects, such as ethical issues.

Exercise Background

Scenario 1: Assume that, following two years' experience in corporate marketing with a national cell phone provider, you are hired by a competing firm. Shortly after you begin your new job, your new boss, the marketing vice president, asks you to provide specific details about your former employer's customers. He intends to use that information to attempt to "steal" those customers, for example, by offering them a lower price. You signed a nondisclosure agreement with your first employer that forbids you to reveal that information. In addition, you have strong ethical concerns. When you questioned your boss, he replied, "Don't worry about it. Everyone does it and it's no big deal." You want to keep this job, but feel compelled to respond.

Scenario 2: Assume that, following two years' experience in corporate marketing with a national cell phone provider, you are hired by a competing firm. Shortly after you begin your new job, your new boss, the marketing vice president, asks you to contact some of your former colleagues. He intends to use your personal friendships and knowledge to "steal" those employees, for example, by offering them a higher salary. As far as you know, there are no legal concerns with this request, but you are unsure about the ethical implications. When you questioned your boss, he replied, "Don't worry about it. Everyone does it and it's no big deal." You want to keep this job, but feel compelled to respond.

Exercise Task

1. With Scenario 1 in mind, compose a written response for your boss, outlining your position. While you may mention legal consequences, be sure to emphasize ethical issues. To persuade your boss to change his mind, you will need to address his statement and also the underlying reasons for his request.

2. With Scenario 2 in mind, compose a written response for your boss, outlining your position. To persuade your boss to change his mind, you will need to address his statement and also the underlying reasons for his request.

3. What do you think the likely outcome would be for each scenario? What would the ultimate consequences be for you, your boss, and your company?

4. While Scenarios 1 and 2 are similar, there is an important difference—the certainty that an action is unethical versus uncertainty about an action's ethical implications. How does that difference affect your communication?

Skills Self-Assessment Instrument

Global Awareness

Introduction: As we have noted, the environment of business is becoming more global. The following assessment is designed to help you assess your readiness to respond to managing in a global context.

Instructions: You will agree with some of the following statements and disagree with others. In some cases you may find it difficult to make a decision, but you should force yourself to make a choice. Record your answers next to each statement according to the following scale:

   4 Strongly agree

   3 Somewhat agree

   2 Somewhat disagree

   1 Strongly disagree

_____ 1. In Japan, loudly slurping your soup is considered to be a sign that you like the soup.

_____ 2. In Korea, business leaders tend to encourage competition among subordinates.

_____ 3. In China, the status of every business negotiation is private, and details are not discussed publicly.

_____ 4. In Thailand, it is rude for men and women to walk together in public.

_____ 5. In Latin America, business people touch each other more than North Americans do under similar circumstances.

_____ 6. In some South American countries, it is considered normal and acceptable to show up for an appointment one to two hours late.

_____ 7. In Mexico, when rewarding a Mexican worker for a job well done, it is best *not* to praise him or her publicly.

_____ 8. American managers tend to base evaluations of their subordinates on job performance, whereas in Iran, managers are more likely to base their evaluations on friendship.

_____ 9. The doors in German offices and homes are generally kept tightly shut to preserve privacy and personal space.

_____ 10. In West Germany, leaders who display charisma are *not* among the most desired.

For interpretation, see Interpretations of Skills Self-Assessment Instruments in the appendix near the end of this text.

Experiential Exercise

Assessing Organization Culture

Purpose: While organization culture is intangible, it is not difficult to observe. This activity will help to improve your skills in observing and interpreting organization culture, which can help to make you a more effective participant and leader in organizations.

Introduction: Clues to organization culture may be found by observing details that relate to member behavior, traditions or customs, stories, attitudes, values, communication patterns, organization structure, employee dress and appearance, and even office space arrangements. Do members address each other by first names? Are office doors left open or closed? What do members wear? How are achievements recognized? Does the workplace feel energized or laid-back? Do members smile and laugh often? Does seniority or expertise earn more respect?

Instructions: First, observe clues to organization behavior at your school, college, or university. To the extent possible, observe a diversity of members including students, teaching faculty, and nonteaching staff. Write down specific examples. For example, students typically wear blue jeans while instructors usually wear suits. In the cafeteria, freshmen sit mainly with other freshmen. A professor may be referred to as "Doctor" by staff, while she may refer to staff by their first name.

Second, interpret the facts. Use your observations to describe the organization's core values. What does it value most? How did you come to that conclusion?

Third, with the class or in small groups, discuss your facts and interpretations. Focus especially on areas of disagreement. Where individuals disagree about the culture, try to understand why the disagreement occurs. If the facts differ, perhaps the individuals observed two different groups. For example, students majoring in business may be different than students in engineering or education. Or perhaps the organization culture tolerates or encourages lots of differences. If there is agreement on facts but interpretations differ, then perhaps the individuals making the interpretations can explore their differing perceptions.

CHAPTER CLOSING CASE

COFFEE, CAFÉ, KAFFEE, OR COPI—STARBUCKS SPANS THE GLOBE

Whether its customers are ordering in English, Spanish, German, or phonetic Chinese, Starbucks is known around the world for its coffeehouses. The first U.S. stores were opened in 1984 and internationalization started in 1995, with shops in Japan and Singapore. Starbucks expanded rapidly in Pacific Rim countries and had outlets in Thailand, Australia, the Philippines, and more by 2000. China's first locations were opened in 1999 in Beijing. The Middle East was the next region that Starbucks entered, and the first European outlets were opened in 2001. Latin America's first stores opened in Puerto Rico and Mexico in 2002. Over the last five years, the company has expanded the number of international stores and added countries.

Today, Starbucks has over 3,600 international stores in 36 countries. How does Starbucks choose international expansion targets? Size of the market can be important but it's not used alone. For example, Starbucks has already entered most European countries and all of the developed economies in Asia. However, among the ten largest countries by population, Starbucks does business in just four, including China, Indonesia, Japan, and the United States. The other six—Bangladesh, Brazil, India, Nigeria, Pakistan, and Russia—have yet to see a Starbucks outlet. Other variables include the local standard of living and the similarity of the business environment to that in the United States. Countries with a different business climate or with many low-income individuals are not attractive targets. Starbucks also avoids countries with high levels of anti-American sentiment.

In addition to choosing good candidate countries for global expansion, Starbucks also has to decide whether to use direct investment or enter into strategic alliances with local partners. In the United States, about two-thirds of locations are company owned. Starbucks does not franchise, but it does have strategic alliances with vendors servicing bookstores, hotels, college campuses, and airports. Outside of the United States, however, Starbucks has adopted a slightly different policy. There, only about one-third of locations are company owned and the rest are alliances. This system allows the firm to gain local expertise, while reducing its own investment and risk exposure.

Starbucks's power and brand recognition make it easy for the firm to find local partners. However, in some regions and countries, the company's reputation creates challenges. The Indian government decided in January 2007 to delay the company's plans to expand there. India only began allowing foreign investment in retail stores in 2006, and it still excludes some foreign competitors, such as Wal-Mart, in hopes of protecting local businesses.

Another set of decisions concern cultural adaptation, which involves finding the optimal mix between standardization and customization for local tastes. For ease and efficiency in operations, as well as to ensure high quality, Starbucks would prefer standardization. However, they have made changes when required by law or custom in overseas locations. "We remain highly respectful of the culture and traditions of the countries in which we do business," says founder Howard Schultz. "We recognize that our success is not an entitlement, and we must continue to earn the trust and respect of customers every day." Typically, the beverages remain the same but the snacks are customized to suit local preferences. Green tea beverages, popular in many Asian countries, were offered by Starbucks to compete with local teahouses. In the Middle East, there are men-only and family areas in the shops. Sometimes the company refuses to change. It does not allow smoking even in smoking cultures, saying it interferes with the coffee aroma. Starbucks always insists on lots of space, even in crowded Tokyo.

Wherever it goes, Starbucks finds itself educating its customers about the very American experience it offers. When the company first entered China for example, many consumers were unfamiliar with coffee. The drink had been unpopular there, perhaps because the proportions of coffee, milk, and sugar were often wrong. Starbucks employees provided information and taste samples to demonstrate the proper mixture. Starbucks should not find it hard to teach foreign customers to enjoy an "American" drink. After all, when the company was first founded, its goal was to introduce coffee drinkers in the United States to the Italian-style beverages Schultz enjoyed on his European vacations. Today, Starbucks may become the "first taste" of America for many individuals.

CASE QUESTIONS

1. What factors in the external environment influence Starbucks as it does business outside of the United States? Give some specific examples from each dimension.
2. What are the advantages and disadvantages of Starbucks's choices regarding levels of international business activity?
3. How can Starbucks be respectful of local culture and laws while still remaining true to its own organization culture as a very "American" firm? List some actions the firm can take in its international stores.

REFERENCES

"2005 Annual Report," Company Fact Sheet, "Company Timeline," Starbucks Coffee International, (quote) Starbucks website, www.starbucks.com on March 5, 2006; The Associated Press, "India Puts Starbucks Retail Plan on Hold," *BusinessWeek*, January 10, 2007, www.businessweek.com on January 11, 2007; Randall Frost, "Global Packaging: The Reality," *BusinessWeek*, January 23, 2006, www.businessweek.com on March 5, 2006; John Pastier, "Starbucks: Selling the American Bean," *BusinessWeek*, December 1, 2005, www.businessweek.com on March 5, 2006; Gianfranco Zaccai, "Global or Local? Make It Both," *BusinessWeek*, August 22, 2005, www.businessweek.com on March 5, 2006.

YOU MAKE THE CALL

Leading Lenovo: China's Foremost Global Capitalist

1. Assume you are a management consultant. How would you rate Lenovo's strategies for the future? Will the strategies help the firm to address its strengths, weaknesses, opportunities, and threats? Why or why not?
2. If you were a manager at Lenovo, what other actions would you take to avoid threats and take advantages of opportunities in its environment?
3. If you were a manager at Dell, how would you respond to Lenovo's strategies?
4. As a user of personal computers, how do you think the rivalry in the PC industry will affect you?

Test Prepper

college.hmco.com/pic/griffinfund5e

You've read the chapter, studied the key terms, and the exam is any day now. Think you're ready to ace it? Take this sample test to gauge your comprehension of chapter material. You can check your answers at the back of the book. Want more test questions? Visit the student website at http://college.hmco.com/pic/griffinfund5e/ and take the ACE quizzes for more practice.

1. T F The consumer price index (CPI) rose by 1.9 percent for all of 2003. This is an example of the political-legal dimension of the general environment of the United States.

2. T F If you buy stock in a company, you are an owner.

3. T F The most effective board of directors consists of people who do business with the firm and are personally acquainted with the CEO.

4. T F Gerber bought a company producing baby food in Poland. This is an example of a direct investment.

5. T F The set of values, beliefs, customs, and attitudes that helps members of an organization determine how that organization does things and what it stands for is its code of ethics.

6. JCPenney, Sears, and Macy's represent which part of the task environment to one another?

    a. Competitors

    b. Customers

    c. Suppliers

    d. Regulators

    e. Strategic partners

7. Who is responsible for corporate governance?

    a. Owners

    b. The board of directors

    c. Employees

    d. Shareholders

    e. Regulators

8. Awarding funds to charities or worthy causes is called _____.

    a. legal compliance

    b. ethical compliance

    c. philanthropic giving

    d. social responsibility

    e. corporate privilege

9. Mexico requires less tax from companies that build assembly plants along the U.S./Mexico border. In this arrangement, the U.S. firms are using _____.

    a. tariffs

    b. quotas

    c. an economic community

    d. maquiladoras

    e. construction subsidies

10. The advantages of importing and exporting include all EXCEPT which of the following?

    a. Small cash outlay

    b. Little risk

    c. No adaptation necessary

    d. Relatively straightforward

    e. Enhanced control

Planning and Strategic Management

chapter 3

FIRST THINGS FIRST

The Video Game Wars

"We think gamers will be spending most of their time...playing with others and with characters that they care about."

—HOWARD MARKS, CEO, VIDEO GAME MAKER ACCLAIM

Video games often portray war-fighting action, but there are also many different kinds of war. One example today is the strategic war for dominance in the video game industry. As the industry matures, the number of competitors gets smaller because larger firms absorb smaller ones. Those remaining are more powerful, yet competition is more intense. Electronic Arts and Sony are the largest players in this industry and each has adopted a different strategy for success.

Electronic Arts (EA) is the number one video game producer, making games for just about every game console, handheld game, PC, PDA, and mobile phone. Until this year, the company's strategy has been to develop games around popular movies or sports, such as *Lord of the Rings* and *Madden NFL*. EA's strategy

Video games like these have helped make Electronic Arts one of the leading firms in the industry.

LEARNING OBJECTIVES

After studying this chapter, you should be able to:

- Summarize the planning process and describe organizational goals.
- Discuss the components of strategy and the types of strategic alternatives.
- Describe how to use SWOT analysis in formulating strategy.
- Identify and describe various alternative approaches to business-level strategy formulation.
- Identify and describe various alternative approaches to corporate-level strategy formulation.
- Discuss how tactical plans are developed and implemented.
- Describe the basic types of operational plans used by organizations.

minimizes the huge risk of creating a video game. It takes dozens of staff, millions of dollars, and 12 to 18 months to produce one new game. Sales revenues are unpredictable and some expensive games have fizzled.

EA, under pressure from entrepreneurial rivals, must increase innovation, shifting to more internal development. However, developers are rotated freely among projects, helping out wherever they are needed. This increases productivity but hurts teamwork. In contrast, the teams at many small studios work on one game from start to finish. Small companies created many of gaming's biggest successes, including *Grand Theft Auto* and *Halo*. EA is switching to dedicated teams that can more readily improve just one segment of programming, for example, how weapons fire or how characters show emotions.

Sony is the number two video game producer and makes games solely for its PlayStation platforms. Video game hardware, not the games themselves, has always been their priority. Sony's approach is not focused on blockbusters. Instead, the company tries to manage the risky video game production process by investing less, which has led to lower expenses but also to fewer of the cutting-edge effects and graphics that video game fans love. Some of their top-selling games include *The Da Vinci Code*, *Field Commander*, and *Untold Legends*.

While both EA's new strategy and Sony's strategy could lead to success, EA's seems to be more in tune with industry changes. One important development is the growing popularity of massive multiplayer online games, known as MMOs. These games network thousands of players into an online community, where members interact through a role-playing scenario. One of the most widely known MMOs is *World of Warcraft.* This game allows individual play, group play, and individual or group play with online members. Writing MMO games is more difficult than writing games for individuals or small groups. EA's new emphasis on innovative concepts and increased use of teams should make it easier for them to develop MMOs, while Sony's emphasis on value will not help it do so.

Which strategy is superior? It may be neither, because new strategies are evolving. Small studio Acclaim is developing high-quality games that it gives away for free. Product endorsement fees for items highlighted within the game cover the cost. Acclaim hopes that users will understand that the ads pay for the game, much as TV advertising pays for broadcasts. Acclaim also sells virtual items, for real money. The users can resell the items when they are finished using them in the game. Acclaim's games are primarily MMOs. "We think gamers will be spending most of their time . . . playing with others and with characters that they care about," says Acclaim CEO Howard Marks. Instead of relying on medieval Dungeons and Dragons settings, the company offers games for all ages and with a wide variety of settings. Finally, Acclaim's games are available as online downloads. The games work on any platform that enables downloaded games. Thus far, only the Microsoft Xbox does so, but Acclaim hopes other game console makers will follow suit.

In a rapidly changing and complex environment, with competitors who have very different resources and weaknesses, using a technology that is still evolving, there are a number of possible strategic responses. Only time will tell which company adopted the correct approach.[1]

The video game market reflects two of the most critical concerns for an organization, managing strategy and strategic planning. One dominant company, Electronic Arts, has flourished by pursuing one strategy, while another dominant company, Sony, has found success with a very different strategy. Yet each firm must also continue to be vigilant to new strategic models being developed by other firms seeking a share of the lucrative video game market. If either EA or Sony stumbles, it stands to lose millions of dollars in revenues. But those firms that most effectively manage their strategies are virtually certain to reap huge rewards.

This chapter is the first of three that explore strategic management and the planning process in more detail. We begin by examining the nature of planning and organizational goals. We then discuss strategic management, including its components and alternatives, and describe the kinds of analysis needed for firms to formulate their strategies. Finally, we examine how strategies are implemented through tactical and operational planning.

Planning and Organizational Goals

The planning process itself can best be thought of as a generic activity. All organizations engage in planning activities, but no two organizations plan in exactly the same fashion. Figure 3.1 is a general representation of the planning process that many organizations attempt to follow. But although most firms follow this general framework, each also has its own nuances and variations.[2]

As Figure 3.1 shows, all planning occurs within an environmental context. If managers do not understand this context, they are unable to develop effective plans. Thus understanding the environment is essentially the first step in planning. The previous chapter covers many of the basic environmental issues that affect organizations and how they plan. With this understanding as a foundation, managers must then establish the organization's mission. The mission outlines the organization's purpose, premises, values, and directions. Flowing from the mission are parallel streams of goals and plans. Directly following the mission are strategic goals. These goals and the mission help determine strategic plans. Strategic goals and plans are primary inputs for developing tactical goals. Tactical goals and the original strategic plans help shape tactical plans. Tactical plans, in turn, combine with the tactical goals to shape operational goals. These goals and the appropriate tactical plans determine operational plans. Finally, goals and plans at each level can also be used as input for future activities at all levels.

Organizational Goals

Goals are critical to organizational effectiveness, and they serve a number of purposes. Organizations can also have several different kinds of goals, all of which must be appropriately managed. And a number of different kinds of managers must be involved in setting goals.

Figure 3.1
THE PLANNING PROCESS

The planning process takes place within an environmental context. Managers must develop a complete and thorough understanding of this context to determine the organization's mission and to develop its strategic, tactical, and operational goals and plans.

The Environmental Context

The organization's mission
• Purpose   • Premises   • Values   • Directions

Strategic goals → Strategic plans

Tactical goals → Tactical plans

Operational goals → Operational plans

Purposes of Goals Goals serve four important purposes.[3] First, they provide guidance and a unified direction for people in the organization. Goals can help everyone understand where the organization is going and why getting there is important.[4] Top managers at General Electric have long had a goal that every business owned by the firm will be either number one or number two in its industry. This goal helps set the tone for decisions made by GE managers as it competes with other firms like Whirlpool and Electrolux.[5] Likewise, Starbucks's goal of increasing the number of its retail stores from 10,000 to 30,000 helps everyone in the firm recognize the strong emphasis on growth and expansion that is driving the firm.[6]

Second, goal-setting practices strongly affect other aspects of planning. Effective goal setting promotes good planning, and good planning facilitates future goal setting. For example, Starbucks's ambitious growth goals demonstrate how setting goals and developing plans to reach them should be seen as complementary activities. The strong growth goal should encourage managers to plan for expansion by looking for new market opportunities. Similarly, they must also always be alert for competitive threats and new ideas that will help facilitate future expansion.

Third, goals can serve as a source of motivation for employees of the organization. Goals that are specific and moderately difficult can motivate people to work harder, especially if attaining the goal is likely to result in rewards.[7] The Italian furniture manufacturer Industrie Natuzzi SpA uses goals to motivate its workers. Each craftsperson has a goal for how long it should take to perform her or his job, such as sewing leather sheets together to make a sofa cushion or building wooden frames for chair arms. At the completion of assigned tasks, workers enter their ID numbers and job numbers into the firm's computer system. If they get a job done faster than their goal, a bonus is automatically added to their paycheck.[8] Starbucks's employees know that additional growth may open up new career opportunities for them.

Finally, goals provide an effective mechanism for evaluation and control. This means that performance can be assessed in the future in terms of how successfully today's goals are accomplished. For example, suppose that officials of the United

Way of America set a goal of collecting $250,000 from a particular small community. If, midway through the campaign, they have raised only $50,000, they know that they need to change or intensify their efforts. If they raise only $100,000 by the end of their drive, they will need to carefully study why they did not reach their goal and what they need to do differently next year. On the other hand, if they succeed in raising $265,000, evaluations of their efforts will take on an entirely different character.

Kinds of Goals   Goals are set for and by different levels within an organization. The four basic levels of goals are the mission and strategic, tactical, and operational goals. An organization's *mission* is a statement of its "fundamental, unique purpose that sets a business apart from other firms of its type and identifies the scope of the business's operations in product and market terms."[9] For instance, Starbucks's mission statement is to be "the premier purveyor of the finest coffee in the world while maintaining our uncompromising principles while we grow." This statement helps managers at Starbucks make decisions and direct resources in clear and specific ways. *Strategic goals* are goals set by and for top management of the organization. They focus on broad, general issues. For example, Starbucks's goal of 30,000 retail outlets is a strategic goal. *Tactical goals* are set by and for middle managers. Their focus is on how to operationalize actions necessary to achieve the strategic goals. To achieve Starbucks's goal of tripling its number of retail outlets, managers are working on tactical goals related to company-owned versus licensed stores and the global distribution of stores in different countries. *Operational goals* are set by and for lower-level managers. Their concern is with shorter-term issues associated with the tactical goals. An operational goal for Starbucks might be a target number of new stores to open in each of the next five years. (Some managers use the words *objective* and *goal* interchangeably. When they are differentiated, however, the term *objective* is usually used instead of *operational goal*.)

> **mission**
> A statement of an organization's fundamental purpose

> **strategic goal**
> A goal set by and for top management of the organization

> **tactical goal**
> A goal set by and for middle managers of the organization

> **operational goal**
> A goal set by and for lower-level managers of the organization

Kinds of Organizational Plans

Organizations establish many different kinds of plans. At a general level, these include strategic, tactical, and operational plans.

Strategic Plans   Strategic plans are the plans developed to achieve strategic goals. More precisely, a *strategic plan* is a general plan outlining decisions of resource allocation, priorities, and action steps necessary to reach strategic goals.[10] These plans are set by the board of directors and top management, generally have an extended time horizon, and address questions of scope, resource deployment, competitive advantage, and synergy. We discuss strategic planning further in the next major section.

> **strategic plan**
> A general plan outlining decisions about resource allocation, priorities, and action steps necessary to reach strategic goals

Tactical Plans   A *tactical plan*, aimed at achieving tactical goals, is developed to implement specific parts of a strategic plan. Tactical plans typically involve upper and middle management and, compared with strategic plans, have a somewhat shorter time horizon and a more specific and concrete focus. Thus tactical plans are concerned more with actually getting things done than with deciding what to do. Tactical planning is covered after our discussion of strategic planning.

> **tactical plan**
> A plan aimed at achieving tactical goals and developed to implement parts of a strategic plan

Operational Plans   An *operational plan* focuses on carrying out tactical plans to achieve operational goals. Developed by middle and lower-level managers, operational plans have a short-term focus and are relatively narrow in scope. Each one

> **operational plan**
> Focuses on carrying out tactical plans to achieve operational goals

deals with a fairly small set of activities. We cover operational planning in the last section of this chapter.

The Nature of Strategic Management

A ***strategy*** is a comprehensive plan for accomplishing an organization's goals. ***Strategic management***, in turn, is a way of approaching business opportunities and challenges—it is a comprehensive and ongoing management process aimed at formulating and implementing effective strategies. Finally, ***effective strategies*** are those that promote a superior alignment between the organization and its environment and the achievement of strategic goals.[11]

The Components of Strategy

In general, a well-conceived strategy addresses three areas: distinctive competence, scope, and resource deployment. A ***distinctive competence*** is something the organization does exceptionally well. (We discuss distinctive competencies more fully later.) A distinctive competence of Limited Brands is speed in moving inventory. It tracks consumer preferences daily with point-of-sale computers, electronically transmits orders to suppliers in Hong Kong, charters 747s to fly products to the United States, and has products in stores 48 hours later. Because other retailers take weeks or sometimes months to accomplish the same things, the Limited uses this distinctive competence to remain competitive.[12]

The ***scope*** of a strategy specifies the range of markets in which an organization will compete. Hershey Foods has essentially restricted its scope to the confectionery business, with a few related activities in other food-processing areas. In contrast, its biggest competitor, Mars, has adopted a broader scope by competing in the pet food business and the electronics industry, among others. Some organizations, called conglomerates, compete in dozens or even hundreds of markets.

A strategy should also include an outline of the organization's projected ***resource deployment***—how it will distribute its resources across the areas in which it competes. General Electric, for example, has been using profits from its highly successful U.S. operations to invest heavily in new businesses in Europe and Asia. Alternatively, the firm might have chosen to invest in different industries in its domestic market or to invest more heavily in Latin America. The choices it makes as to where and how much to invest reflect issues of resource deployment.

Types of Strategic Alternatives

Most businesses today also develop strategies at two distinct levels. These levels provide a rich combination of strategic alternatives for organizations. The two general levels are business-level strategies and corporate-level strategies. ***Business-level strategy*** is the set of strategic alternatives from which an organization chooses as it conducts business in a particular industry or market. Such alternatives help the organization focus its competitive efforts for each industry or market in a targeted and focused manner.

Corporate-level strategy is the set of strategic alternatives from which an organization chooses as it manages its operations simultaneously across several industries and several markets.[13] As we discuss later, most large companies today

---

strategy
A comprehensive plan for accomplishing an organization's goals

strategic management
A comprehensive and ongoing management process aimed at formulating and implementing effective strategies; a way of approaching business opportunities and challenges

effective strategy
A strategy that promotes a superior alignment between the organization and its environment and the achievement of strategic goals

distinctive competence
An organizational strength possessed by only a small number of competing firms

scope
When applied to strategy, it specifies the range of markets in which an organization will compete

resource deployment
How an organization distributes its resources across the areas in which it competes

business-level strategy
The set of strategic alternatives from which an organization chooses as it conducts business in a particular industry or market

compete in a variety of industries and markets. Thus, although they develop business-level strategies for each industry or market, they also develop an overall strategy that helps define the mix of industries and markets that are of interest to the firm.

Drawing a distinction between strategy formulation and strategy implementation is also instructive. ***Strategy formulation*** is the set of processes involved in creating or determining the strategies of the organization, whereas ***strategy implementation*** are the methods by which strategies are operationalized or executed within the organization. The primary distinction is along the lines of content versus process: the formulation stage determines what the strategy is, and the implementation stage focuses on how the strategy is achieved.

Using SWOT Analysis to Formulate Strategy

The starting point in formulating strategy is usually SWOT analysis. ***SWOT*** is an acronym that stands for strengths, weaknesses, opportunities, and threats. As shown in Figure 3.2, SWOT analysis is a careful evaluation of an organization's internal strengths and weaknesses as well as its environmental opportunities and threats. In SWOT analysis, the best strategies accomplish an organization's mission by (1) exploiting an organization's opportunities and strengths while (2) neutralizing its threats and (3) avoiding (or correcting) its weaknesses.

Evaluating an Organization's Strengths

Organizational strengths are skills and capabilities that enable an organization to conceive of and implement its strategies. Sears, for example, has a nationwide

corporate-level strategy
The set of strategic alternatives from which an organization chooses as it manages its operations simultaneously across several industries and several markets

strategy formulation
The set of processes involved in creating or determining the strategies of the organization; it focuses on the content of strategies

strategy implementation
The methods by which strategies are operationalized or executed within the organization; it focuses on the processes through which strategies are achieved

SWOT
An acronym that stands for strengths, weaknesses, opportunities, and threats

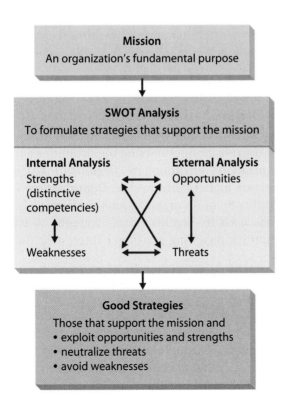

Figure 3.2
SWOT ANALYSIS

SWOT analysis is one of the most important steps in formulating strategy. Using the organization's mission as a context, managers assess internal strengths (distinctive competencies) and weaknesses as well as external opportunities and threats. The goal is then to develop good strategies that exploit opportunities and strengths, neutralize threats, and avoid weaknesses.

organizational strength
A skill or capability that enables an organization to conceive of and implement its strategies

network of trained service employees who repair Sears appliances. Jane Thompson, a Sears executive, conceived of a plan to consolidate repair and home improvement services nationwide under the well-known Sears brand name and to promote them as a general repair operation for all appliances, not just those purchased from Sears. Thus the firm capitalized on existing capabilities and the strength of its name to launch a new operation.[14]

A *distinctive competence* is a strength possessed by only a small number of competing firms. Distinctive competencies are rare among a set of competitors. Peter Jackson's Weta Digital special effects company, for example, has elevated the cinematic art of special effects to new heights. Industrial Lights & Magic (ILM), owned by George Lucas, is Weta's only real competitor. However, Weta has some copyrighted and patented methods, while ILM has others. So, the two firms share a general distinctive competence but also have their own unique ones as well. Organizations that exploit their distinctive competencies often obtain a *competitive advantage* and attain above-normal economic performance.[15]

Evaluating an Organization's Weaknesses

organizational weaknesses
A skill or capability that does not enable an organization to choose and implement strategies that support its mission

Organizational weaknesses are skills and capabilities that hinder or do not enable an organization to choose and implement strategies that support its mission. An organization has essentially two ways of addressing weaknesses. First, it may need to make investments to obtain the strengths required to implement strategies that support its mission. Second, it may need to modify its mission so that it can be accomplished with the skills and capabilities that the organization already possesses.

In practice, organizations have a difficult time focusing on weaknesses, in part because organization members are often reluctant to admit that they do not possess all the skills and capabilities needed. Evaluating weaknesses also calls into question the judgment of managers who chose the organization's mission in the first place and who failed to invest in the skills and capabilities needed to accomplish it.

Evaluating an Organization's Opportunities and Threats

organizational opportunity
An area in the environment that, if exploited, may generate higher performance

organizational threat
An area that increases the difficulty of an organization's performing at a high level

Whereas evaluating strengths and weaknesses focuses attention on the internal workings of an organization, evaluating opportunities and threats requires analyzing an organization's environment. **Organizational opportunities** are areas that may generate higher performance. **Organizational threats** are areas that increase the difficulty of an organization's performing at a high level. For instance, Toyota has used its organizational strengths to capitalize on environmental opportunities regarding consumer interest in fuel-efficient hybrid automobiles.

Formulating Business-Level Strategies

A number of frameworks have been developed for identifying the major strategic alternatives that organizations should consider when choosing their business-level strategies. Two important classification schemes are Porter's generic strategies and strategies based on the product life cycle.

Porter's Generic Strategies

According to Michael Porter, organizations may pursue a differentiation, overall cost leadership, or focus strategy at the business level.[16] An organization that pursues a ***differentiation strategy*** seeks to distinguish itself from competitors through the quality of its products or services. Firms that successfully implement a differentiation strategy are able to charge more than competitors because customers are willing to pay more to obtain the extra value they perceive.[17] Rolex pursues a differentiation strategy. Rolex watches are handmade of precious metals like gold or platinum and stainless steel and are subjected to strenuous tests of quality and reliability. The firm's reputation enables it to charge thousands of dollars for its watches. Coca-Cola and Pepsi compete in the market for bottled water on the basis of differentiation. Coke touts its Dasani brand on the basis of its fresh taste, whereas Pepsi promotes its Aquafina brand on the basis of its purity.[18] Other firms that use differentiation strategies are Lexus, Nikon, Mont Blanc, and Ralph Lauren.

An organization implementing an ***overall cost leadership strategy*** attempts to gain a competitive advantage by reducing its costs below the costs of competing firms. By keeping costs low, the organization is able to sell its products at low prices and still make a profit. Timex uses an overall cost leadership strategy. For decades, this firm has specialized in manufacturing relatively simple, low-cost watches for the mass market. The price of Timex watches, starting around $39.95, is low because of the company's efficient high-volume manufacturing capacity. Poland Springs and Crystal Geyser bottled waters are promoted on the basis of their relative low cost. Other firms that implement overall cost leadership strategies are Hyundai, Eastman Kodak, BIC, and Old Navy.

A firm pursuing a ***focus strategy*** concentrates on a specific regional market, product line, or group of buyers. This strategy may have either a differentiation focus, whereby the firm differentiates its products in the focus market, or an overall cost

> *differentiation strategy*
> A strategy in which an organization seeks to distinguish itself from competitors through the quality of its products or services

> *overall cost leadership strategy*
> A strategy in which an organization attempts to gain a competitive advantage by reducing its costs below the costs of competing firms

> *focus strategy*
> A strategy in which an organization concentrates on a specific regional market, product line, or group of buyers

A focus strategy concentrates on a specific market, product line, or group of buyers. As airlines continually adjust their requirements for what passengers are allowed to carry onboard commercial flights, some businesses have generated extra profits by helping passengers more efficiently meet these requirements. For instance, this Body Shop store in Atlanta's Hartsfield Jackson International airport sells small bags of toiletries prepackaged in accordance with current regulations.

Managing in Times of Change

PlayStation 2 Plays On

It's common wisdom: customers pay high prices to get the latest and greatest video games. It was true throughout the 1980s and 1990s, as buyers shelled out hundreds of dollars for each new game technology. Yet when competition exists among digital formats, consumers eventually come to prefer one system. While convergence on a single standard has already happened for the DVD video format and the MP3 music format, the home video game industry still retains three formats, one from each of the three largest competitors.

Sony's PlayStation2 (PS2) is expected to sell more consoles in 2007 than Nintendo's top-rated Wii, last year's bestseller, Xbox 360 from Microsoft, or even Sony's new PS3. Could this be Sony's year to finally dominate the industry?

One reason that Sony's strategy of prolonging sales of the PS2 is working so well is related to costs. Sony's experience and economies of scale reduce manufacturing costs. Sony makes about $8 profit on every $130 PS2 it sells and loses about $250 on every $700 PS3. Low-cost production, which accounts for about one-fifth of the cost of the newer machines, supports low pricing for consumers. Reliance on a single standard simplifies software purchases and sharing, reducing consumers' costs.

Another factor supporting the strategy is the wide availability of games for the PS2. Game developers concentrate resources on the PS2 when sales remain strong. For example, Rockstar Games announced in February 2007 that their hottest new title, *Grand Theft Auto: Vice City Stories*, would appear in PS2 format. Game developers' long experience with the PS2 reduces their costs.

The PS2's long-life strategy is also supported by the overwhelming number of consoles and games already in use. The PS2 is the most popular game console of all time, with 103 million machines worldwide and the console's dominance is likely to continue. Projected sales of consoles for 2007 are 6 million units for the Wii and PS3, 10 million for the Xbox 360, and 11 million for the PS2. More top-selling games were developed for the PS2 than for other consoles.

Competition in the industry is cutthroat. Will Sony's PS2 be the last video game format standing?

References: Kenji Hall, "The Golden Oldie of Gaming," *BusinessWeek*, January 8, 2007, p. 42; Kevin Ohannessian, "Sony's Risky Game," *Fast Company*, November 2006, www.fastcompany.com on January 18, 2007; Tor Thorsen, "It's Official: GTA:VCS Is PS2-Bound," *GameSpot*, February 7, 2007, www.gamespot.com on February 10, 2007; "Wii Beats PlayStation 3 in Sales, but Xbox 360 Beats Them Both," *Reuters*, January 12, 2007, www.foxnews.com on January 18, 2007.

leadership focus, whereby the firm manufactures and sells its products at low cost in the focus market. In the watch industry, Tag Heuer follows a focus differentiation strategy by specializing in rugged waterproof watches aimed at active consumers. Fiat follows a focus cost leadership strategy by selling its automobiles only in Italy and in selected regions of Europe; Alfa Romeo uses focus differentiation to sell its high-performance cars in these same markets. Fisher-Price uses focus differentiation to sell electronic calculators with large, brightly colored buttons to the parents of preschoolers; stockbroker Edward Jones focuses on small-town settings. General Mills has been focusing new-product development on consumers who eat meals while driving—the watchword is "Can we make it 'one-handed'?" so that drivers can safely eat or drink it.

Strategies Based on the Product Life Cycle

product life cycle
A model that portrays how sales volume for products changes over the life of products

The *product life cycle* is a model that shows how sales volume changes over the life of products. Understanding the four stages in the product life cycle helps managers recognize that strategies need to evolve over time. As Figure 3.3 shows, the cycle begins when a new product or technology is first introduced. In this

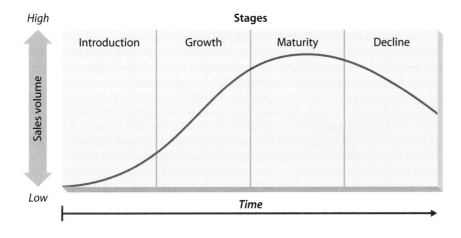

Figure 3.3
THE PRODUCT LIFE CYCLE

Managers can use the framework of the product life cycle—introduction, growth, maturity, and decline—to plot strategy. For example, management may decide on a differentiation strategy for a product in the introduction stage and a prospector approach for a product in the growth stage. By understanding this cycle and where a particular product falls within it, managers can develop more effective strategies for extending product life.

introduction stage, demand may be very high and sometimes outpaces the firm's ability to supply the product. At this stage, managers need to focus their efforts on "getting product out the door" without sacrificing quality. Managing growth by hiring new employees and managing inventories and cash flow are also concerns during this stage.

During the *growth stage,* more firms begin producing the product, and sales continue to grow. Important management issues include ensuring quality and delivery and beginning to differentiate an organization's product from competitors' products. Entry into the industry during the growth stage may threaten an organization's competitive advantage; thus strategies to slow the entry of competitors are important.

After a period of growth, products enter a third phase. During this *maturity stage,* overall demand growth for a product begins to slow down, and the number of new firms producing the product begins to decline. The number of established firms producing the product may also begin to decline. This period of maturity is essential if an organization is going to survive in the long run. Product differentiation concerns are still important during this stage, but keeping costs low and beginning the search for new products or services are also important strategic considerations.

In the *decline stage,* demand for the product or technology decreases, the number of organizations producing the product drops, and total sales drop. Demand often declines because all those who were interested in purchasing a particular product have already done so. Organizations that fail to anticipate the decline stage in earlier stages of the life cycle may go out of business. Those that differentiate their product, keep their costs low, or develop new products or services may do well during this stage.

Formulating Corporate-Level Strategies

Most large organizations are engaged in several businesses, industries, and markets. Each business or set of businesses within such an organization is frequently referred to as a *strategic business unit,* or *SBU.* An organization such as General Electric operates hundreds of different businesses, making and selling products as diverse as jet engines, nuclear power plants, and light bulbs. GE organizes these businesses into approximately 20 SBUs. Even organizations that sell only one product may operate in several distinct markets.

Decisions about which businesses, industries, and markets an organization will enter, and how to manage these different businesses, are based on an organization's corporate strategy. The most important strategic issue at the corporate level concerns the extent and nature of organizational diversification. **Diversification** describes the number of different businesses that an organization is engaged in and the extent to which these businesses are related to one another. There are three types of diversification strategies: single-product strategy, related diversification, and unrelated diversification.[19]

> *diversification*
> The number of different businesses that an organization is engaged in and the extent to which these businesses are related to one another

---

Single-Product Strategy

An organization that pursues a **single-product strategy** manufactures just one product or service and sells it in a single geographic market. The WD-40 Company, for example, essentially manufactures only a single product, WD-40 spray lubricant, and for years sold it in just one market, North America. WD-40 has started selling its lubricant in Europe and Asia, but it continues to center all manufacturing, sales, and marketing efforts on one product.

> *single-product strategy*
> A strategy in which an organization manufactures just one product or service and sells it in a single geographic market

---

The single-product strategy has one major strength and one major weakness. By concentrating its efforts so completely on one product and market, a firm is likely to be very successful in manufacturing and marketing the product. Because it has staked its survival on a single product, the organization works very hard to make sure that the product is a success. Of course, if the product is not accepted by the market or is replaced by a new one, the firm will suffer. This happened to slide-rule manufacturers when electronic calculators became widely available and to companies that manufactured only black-and-white televisions when low-priced color televisions were first mass-marketed. Similarly, Wrigley has long practiced what amounts to a single-product strategy with its line of chewing gums. But, because younger consumers are buying less gum than earlier generations, Wrigley is facing declining revenues and lower profits.[20]

Related Diversification

Given the disadvantage of the single-product strategy, most large businesses today operate in several different businesses, industries, or markets.[21] If the businesses are somehow linked, that organization is implementing a strategy of **related diversification**. Virtually all larger businesses in the United States use related diversification.

> *related diversification*
> A strategy in which an organization operates in several businesses that are somehow linked with one another

---

Pursuing a strategy of related diversification has three primary advantages. First, it reduces an organization's dependence on any one of its business activities and thus reduces economic risk. Even if one or two of a firm's businesses lose money, the organization as a whole may still survive because the healthy businesses will generate enough cash to support the others.[22] At Limited Brands, sales declines by the firm's Limited division may be offset by sales increases by its Express division.

Second, by managing several businesses at the same time, an organization can reduce the overhead costs associated with managing any one business. In other words, if the normal administrative costs required to operate any business, such as legal services and accounting, can be spread over a large number of businesses, then the overhead costs *per business* will be lower than they would be if each business had to absorb all costs itself. Thus the overhead costs of businesses in a firm that pursues related diversification are usually lower than those of similar businesses that are not part of a larger corporation.[23]

Third, related diversification allows an organization to exploit its strengths and capabilities in more than one business. When organizations do this successfully, they capitalize on synergies, which are complementary effects that exist among their businesses. *Synergy* exists among a set of businesses when the businesses' economic value together is greater than their economic value separately. McDonald's is using synergy as it diversifies into other restaurant and food businesses. For example, its McCafe premium coffee stands in some McDonald's restaurants and investments in Donatos Pizza, Chipolte Mexican Grill, and Pret A Manger each allow the firm to create new revenue opportunities while using the firm's existing strengths in food-product purchasing and distribution.[24]

Unrelated Diversification

Firms that implement a strategy of **unrelated diversification** operate multiple businesses that are not logically associated with one another. At one time, for example, Quaker Oats owned clothing chains, toy companies, and a restaurant business. Unrelated diversification was a very popular strategy in the 1970s. During that time, several conglomerates like ITT and Transamerica grew by acquiring literally hundreds of other organizations and then running these numerous businesses as independent entities. Even if there are important potential synergies among their different businesses, organizations implementing a strategy of unrelated diversification do not attempt to exploit them.

> **unrelated diversification**
> A strategy in which an organization operates multiple businesses that are not logically associated with one another

In theory, unrelated diversification has two advantages. First, a business that uses this strategy should have stable performance over time. During any given period, if some businesses owned by the organization are in a cycle of decline, others may be in a cycle of growth. Unrelated diversification is also thought to have resource allocation advantages. Every year, when a corporation allocates capital, people, and other resources among its various businesses, it must evaluate information about the future of those businesses so that it can place its resources where they have the highest potential for return. Given that it owns the businesses in question and thus has full access to information about the future of those businesses, a firm implementing unrelated diversification should be able to allocate capital to maximize corporate performance.

Despite these presumed advantages, research suggests that unrelated diversification usually does not lead to high performance. First, corporate-level managers in such a company usually do not know enough about the unrelated businesses to provide helpful strategic guidance or to allocate capital appropriately. To make strategic decisions, managers must have complete and subtle understanding of a business and its environment. Because corporate managers often have difficulty fully evaluating the economic importance of investments for all the businesses under their wing, they tend to concentrate only on a business's current performance. This narrow attention at the expense of broader planning eventually hobbles the entire organization.

Second, because organizations that implement unrelated diversification fail to exploit important synergies, they are at a competitive disadvantage compared to organizations that use related diversification. Universal Studios has been at a competitive disadvantage relative to Disney because its theme parks, movie studios, and licensing divisions are less integrated and therefore achieve less synergy.

For these reasons, almost all organizations have abandoned unrelated diversification as a corporate-level strategy. Transamerica has sold off numerous businesses and now concentrates on a core set of related businesses and markets. Large corporations that have not concentrated on a core set of businesses have eventually been acquired by other companies and then broken up. Research suggests that these organizations are actually worth more when broken up into smaller pieces than when joined.[25]

Managing Diversification However an organization implements diversification—whether through internal development, vertical integration, or mergers and acquisitions—it must monitor and manage its strategy. ***Portfolio management techniques*** are methods that diversified organizations use to determine which businesses to engage in and how to manage these businesses to maximize corporate performance. Two important portfolio management techniques are the BCG matrix and the GE Business Screen.

BCG Matrix The ***BCG*** (for Boston Consulting Group) ***matrix*** provides a framework for evaluating the relative performance of businesses in which a diversified organization operates. It also prescribes the preferred distribution of cash and other resources among these businesses.[26] The BCG matrix uses two factors to evaluate an organization's set of businesses: the growth rate of a particular market and the organization's share of that market. The matrix suggests that fast-growing markets in which an organization has the highest market share are more attractive business opportunities than slow-growing markets in which an organization has small market share. Dividing market growth and market share into two categories (low and high) creates the simple matrix shown in Figure 3.4.

The matrix classifies the types of businesses in which a diversified organization can engage as dogs, cash cows, question marks, and stars. *Dogs* are businesses that have a very small share of a market that is not expected to grow. Because these businesses do not hold much economic promise, the BCG matrix suggests that organizations either should not invest in them or should consider selling them as soon as possible. *Cash cows* are businesses that have a large

---

portfolio management techniques
Methods that diversified organizations use to determine which businesses to engage in and how to manage these businesses to maximize corporate performance

BCG matrix
A framework for evaluating businesses relative to the growth rate of their market and the organization's share of the market

Figure 3.4
THE BCG MATRIX

The BCG matrix helps managers develop a better understanding of how different strategic business units contribute to the overall organization. By assessing each SBU on the basis of its market growth rate and relative market share, managers can make decisions about whether to commit further financial resources to the SBU or to sell or liquidate it.

Source: *Perspectives*, No. 66, "The Product Portfolio." Adapted by permission from The Boston Consulting Group, Inc., 1970.

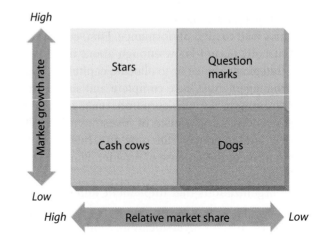

share of a market that is not expected to grow substantially. These businesses characteristically generate high profits that the organization should use to support question marks and stars. (Cash cows are "milked" for cash to support businesses in markets that have greater growth potential.) *Question marks* are businesses that have only a small share of a quickly growing market. The future performance of these businesses is uncertain. A question mark that is able to capture increasing amounts of this growing market may be very profitable. On the other hand, a question mark unable to keep up with market growth is likely to have low profits. The BCG matrix suggests that organizations should invest carefully in question marks. If their performance does not live up to expectations, question marks should be reclassified as dogs and divested. *Stars* are businesses that have the largest share of a rapidly growing market. Cash generated by cash cows should be invested in stars to ensure their preeminent position. For example, when BMW bought Rover a few years ago, experts thought its products would help the German auto maker reach new consumers. But the company was not able to capitalize on this opportunity, so it ended up selling Rover's car business to a British firm and Land Rover to Ford.[27]

GE Business Screen   Because the BCG matrix is relatively narrow and overly simplistic, General Electric (GE) developed the ***GE Business Screen***, a more sophisticated approach to managing diversified business units. The GE Business Screen is a portfolio management technique that can also be represented in the form of a matrix. Rather than focusing solely on market growth and market share, however, the GE Business Screen considers industry attractiveness and competitive position. These two factors are divided into three categories, to make the nine-cell matrix shown in Figure 3.5.[28] These cells, in turn, classify business units as winners, losers, question marks, average businesses, or profit producers.

As Figure 3.5 shows, both market growth and market share appear in a broad list of factors that determine the overall attractiveness of an industry and the overall

> **GE Business Screen**
> A method of evaluating businesses along two dimensions: (1) industry attractiveness and (2) competitive position; in general, the more attractive the industry and the more competitive the position, the more an organization should invest in a business

Figure 3.5
THE GE BUSINESS SCREEN

The GE Business Screen is a more sophisticated approach to portfolio management than the BCG matrix. As shown here, several factors combine to determine a business's competitive position and the attractiveness of its industry. These two dimensions, in turn, can be used to classify businesses as winners, question marks, average businesses, losers, or profit producers. Such a classification enables managers to allocate the organization's resources more effectively across various business opportunities.

Source: From *Strategy Formulation: Analytical Concepts*, 1st edition, by Charles W. Hofer and Dan Schendel. Copyright © 1978. Reprinted with permission of South-Western, a division of Thomson Learning: www.thomson-rights.com. Fax 800-730-2215.

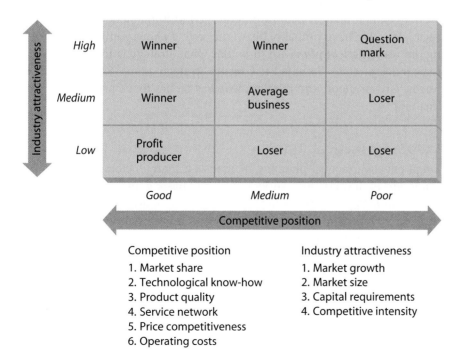

Competitive position
1. Market share
2. Technological know-how
3. Product quality
4. Service network
5. Price competitiveness
6. Operating costs

Industry attractiveness
1. Market growth
2. Market size
3. Capital requirements
4. Competitive intensity

quality of a firm's competitive position. Other determinants of an industry's attractiveness (in addition to market growth) include market size, capital requirements, and competitive intensity. In general, the greater the market growth, the larger the market, the smaller the capital requirements, and the less the competitive intensity, the more attractive an industry will be. Other determinants of an organization's competitive position in an industry (besides market share) include technological know-how, product quality, service network, price competitiveness, and operating costs. In general, businesses with large market share, technological know-how, high product quality, a quality service network, competitive prices, and low operating costs are in a favorable competitive position.

Think of the GE Business Screen as a way of applying SWOT analysis to the implementation and management of a diversification strategy. The determinants of industry attractiveness are similar to the environmental opportunities and threats in SWOT analysis, and the determinants of competitive position are similar to organizational strengths and weaknesses. By conducting this type of SWOT analysis across several businesses, a diversified organization can decide how to invest its resources to maximize corporate performance. In general, organizations should invest in winners and in question marks (where industry attractiveness and competitive position are both favorable); should maintain the market position of average businesses and profit producers (where industry attractiveness and competitive position are average); and should sell losers. For example, Unilever recently assessed its business portfolio using a similar framework and, as a result, decided to sell off several specialty chemical units that were not contributing to the firm's profitability as much as other businesses. The firm then used the revenues from these divestitures and bought more related businesses such as Ben & Jerry's Homemade and Slim-Fast.[29]

Tactical Planning

As we note earlier, tactical plans are developed to implement specific parts of a strategic plan. You have probably heard the saying about winning the battle but losing the war. ***Tactical plans*** are to battles what strategy is to a war: an organized sequence of steps designed to execute strategic plans. Strategy focuses on resources, environment, and mission, whereas tactics focus primarily on people and action.[30]

Developing Tactical Plans

Although effective tactical planning depends on many factors, which vary from one situation to another, we can identify some basic guidelines. First, the manager needs to recognize that tactical planning must address a number of tactical goals derived from a broader strategic goal.[31] An occasional situation may call for a stand-alone tactical plan, but most of the time tactical plans flow from and must be consistent with a strategic plan.

For example, top managers at Coca-Cola developed a strategic plan for reestablishing the firm's dominance of the soft-drink industry. As part of developing the plan, they identified a critical environmental threat—considerable unrest and uncertainty among the independent bottlers that packaged and distributed Coca-Cola's products. To simultaneously counter this threat and strengthen the

tactical plan
A plan aimed at achieving tactical goals and developed to implement parts of a strategic plan; an organized sequence of steps designed to execute strategic plans

company's position, Coca-Cola bought several large independent bottlers and combined them into one new organization called "Coca-Cola Enterprises." Selling half of the new company's stock reaped millions in profits while effectively keeping control of the enterprise in Coca-Cola's hands. Thus the creation of the new business was a tactical plan developed to contribute to the achievement of an overarching strategic goal.[32]

Second, although strategies are often stated in general terms, tactics must specify resources and time frames. A strategy can call for being number one in a particular market or industry, but a tactical plan must specify precisely what activities will be undertaken to achieve that goal. Consider the Coca-Cola example again. Another element of its strategic plan involves increased worldwide market share. To expand sales in Europe, managers developed tactical plans for building a new plant in the south of France to make soft-drink concentrate and for building another canning plant in Dunkirk. The firm has also invested heavily in India.[33] Building these plants represents a concrete action involving measurable resources (funds to build the plants) and a clear time horizon (a target date for completion).

Finally, tactical planning requires the use of human resources. Managers involved in tactical planning spend a great deal of time working with other people. They must be in a position to receive information from others within and outside the organization, process that information in the most effective way, and then pass it on to others who might make use of it. Coca-Cola executives have been intensively involved in planning the new plants, setting up the new bottling venture noted earlier, and exploring a joint venture with Cadbury Schweppes in the United Kingdom. Each activity has required considerable time and effort from dozens of managers. One manager, for example, crossed the Atlantic 12 times while negotiating the Cadbury deal.

Executing Tactical Plans

Regardless of how well a tactical plan is formulated, its ultimate success depends on the way it is carried out. Successful implementation, in turn, depends on the astute use of resources, effective decision making, and insightful steps to ensure that the right things are done at the right times and in the right ways. A manager can see an absolutely brilliant idea fail because of improper execution.

Proper execution depends on a number of important factors. First, the manager needs to evaluate every possible course of action in light of the goal it is intended to reach. Next, he or she needs to make sure that each decision maker has the information and resources necessary to get the job done. Vertical and horizontal communication and integration of activities must be present to minimize conflict and inconsistent activities. And, finally, the manager must monitor ongoing activities derived from the plan to make sure they are achieving the desired results. This monitoring typically takes place within the context of the organization's ongoing control systems.

Operational Planning

Another critical element in effective organizational planning is the development and implementation of operational plans. Operational plans are derived from

Table 3.1

TYPES OF OPERATIONAL PLANS

Plan	Description
Single-use plan	Developed to carry out a course of action not likely to be repeated in the future
Program	Single-use plan for a large set of activities
Project	Single-use plan of less scope and complexity than a program
Standing plan	Developed for activities that recur regularly over a period of time
Policy	Standing plan specifying the organization's general response to a designated problem or situation
Standard operating procedure	Standing plan outlining steps to be followed in particular circumstances
Rules and regulations	Standing plans describing exactly how specific activities are to be carried out

tactical plans and are aimed at achieving operational goals. Thus operational plans tend to be narrowly focused, have relatively short time horizons, and involve lower-level managers. The two most basic forms of operational plans and specific types of each are summarized in Table 3.1.

Single-Use Plans

A ***single-use plan*** is developed to carry out a course of action that is not likely to be repeated in the future. As Disney planned its newest theme park in Hong Kong, it developed numerous single-use plans for individual rides, attractions, and hotels. The two most common forms of single-use plans are programs and projects.

Programs   A ***program*** is a single-use plan for a large set of activities. It might consist of identifying procedures for introducing a new product line, opening a new facility, or changing the organization's mission. As part of its own strategic plans for growth, Black & Decker bought General Electric's small-appliance business. The deal involved the largest brand-name switch in history: 150 products were converted from the GE to the Black & Decker label. Each product was carefully studied, redesigned, and reintroduced with an extended warranty. A total of 140 steps were used for each product. It took three years to convert all 150 products over to Black & Decker. The total conversion of the product line was a program.

Projects   A ***project*** is similar to a program but is generally of less scope and complexity. A project may be a part of a broader program, or it may be a self-contained single-use plan. For Black & Decker, the conversion of each of the 150 products was a separate project in its own right. Each product had its own manager, its own schedule, and so forth. Projects are also used to introduce a new product within an existing product line or to add a new benefit option to an existing salary package.

Standing Plans

Whereas single-use plans are developed for nonrecurring situations, a ***standing plan*** is used for activities that recur regularly over a period of time. Standing plans can greatly enhance efficiency by making decision-making routine. Policies, standard operating procedures, and rules and regulations are three kinds of standing plans.

---

single-use plan
Developed to carry out a course of action that is not likely to be repeated in the future

program
A single-use plan for a large set of activities

project
A single use plan of less scope and complexity than a program

standing plan
Developed for activities that recur regularly over a period of time

Policies As a general guide for action, a policy is the most general form of standing plan. A ***policy*** specifies the organization's general response to a designated problem or situation. For example, McDonald's has a policy that it will not grant a franchise to an individual who already owns another fast-food restaurant. Similarly, Starbucks has a policy that it will not franchise at all, instead retaining ownership of all Starbucks coffee shops. Likewise, a university admissions office might establish a policy that admission will be granted only to applicants with a minimum SAT score of 1200 and a ranking in the top quarter of their high school class. Admissions officers may routinely deny admission to applicants who fail to reach these minimums. A policy is also likely to describe how exceptions are to be handled. The university's policy statement, for example, might create an admissions appeals committee to evaluate applicants who do not meet minimum requirements but may warrant special consideration.

> **policy**
> A standing plan that specifies the organization's general response to a designated problem or situation

Standard Operating Procedures Another type of standing plan is the ***standard operating procedure***, or ***SOP***. An SOP is more specific than a policy, in that it outlines the steps to be followed in particular circumstances. The admissions clerk at the university, for example, might be told that, when an application is received, he or she should (1) set up an electronic file for the applicant; (2) merge test-score records, transcripts, and letters of reference to the electronic file as they are received; and (3) forward the electronic file to the appropriate admissions director when it is complete. Gallo Vineyards in California has a 300-page manual of SOPs. This planning manual is credited with making Gallo one of the most efficient wine operations in the United States. McDonald's has SOPs explaining exactly how Big Macs are to be cooked, how long they can stay in the warming rack, and so forth.

> **standard operating procedure (SOP)**
> A standard plan that outlines the steps to be followed in particular circumstances

Rules and Regulations The narrowest of the standing plans, ***rules and regulations***, describe exactly how specific activities are to be carried out. Rather than guiding decision making, rules and regulations actually take the place of decision

> **rules and regulations**
> Describe exactly how specific activities are to be carried out

THANK YOU FOR NOT USING ME FOR PERSONAL BUSINESS

www.CartoonStock.com

Organizations often establish standing plans that describe how specific activities are to be carried out. They are also used to define what employees can and cannot do. In recent years many businesses have adopted rules that govern employee usage of business computers, email networks, and so forth.

making in various situations. Each McDonald's restaurant has a rule prohibiting customers from using its telephones, for example. The university admissions office might have a rule stipulating that if an applicant's file is not complete two months before the beginning of a semester, the student cannot be admitted until the next semester. Of course, in most organizations a manager at a higher level can suspend or bend the rules. If the high school transcript of the child of a prominent university alumnus and donor arrives a few days late, the director of admissions might waive the two-month rule. Indeed, rules and regulations can become problematic if they are excessive or enforced too rigidly.

Rules and regulations and SOPs are similar in many ways. They are both relatively narrow in scope, and each can serve as a substitute for decision making. An SOP typically describes a sequence of activities, however, whereas rules and regulations focus on one activity. Recall our examples: the admissions SOP consisted of three activities, whereas the two-month rule related to only one activity. In an industrial setting, the SOP for orienting a new employee could involve enrolling the person in various benefit options, introducing him or her to coworkers and supervisors, and providing a tour of the facilities. A pertinent rule for the new employee might involve when to come to work each day.

Contingency Planning and Crisis Management

contingency planning
The determination of alternative courses of action to be taken if an intended plan is unexpectedly disrupted or rendered inappropriate

Another important type of planning is ***contingency planning*** (illustrated in Figure 3.6), or the determination of alternative courses of action to be taken if an intended plan of action is unexpectedly disrupted or rendered inappropriate.[34] ***Crisis management***, a related concept, is the set of procedures the organization

crisis management
The set of procedures the organization uses in the event of a disaster or other unexpected calamity

Crisis management has taken on increased importance over the past several years. Julie Gerberding and Mitchell Cohen both work for the Centers for Disease Control and Prevention. They are shown here discussing a large-scale exercise to see how well the CDC would react to a global pandemic flu outbreak, an event predicted by many leading scientists.

uses in the event of a disaster or other unexpected calamity. Some elements of crisis management may be orderly and systematic, whereas others may be more ad hoc and develop as events unfold.

An excellent example of widespread contingency planning occurred during the late 1990s in anticipation of what was popularly known as the "Y2K bug." Concerns about the impact of technical glitches in computers stemming from their internal clocks' changing from 1999 to 2000 resulted in contingency planning for most organizations. Many banks and hospitals, for example, had extra staff available; some organizations created backup computer systems; and some even stockpiled inventory in case they could not purchase new products or materials.[35]

The devastating hurricanes that hit the Gulf Coast in 2005—Katrina and Rita—dramatically underscored the importance of effective crisis management. For example, inadequate and ineffective responses by the Federal Emergency Management Agency (FEMA) illustrated to many people that organization's weaknesses in coping with crisis situations. On the other hand, some organizations responded much more effectively. Wal-Mart began ramping up its emergency preparedness on the same day that Katrina was upgraded from a tropical depression to a tropical storm. In the days before the storm struck, Wal-Mart stores in the region were supplied with powerful generators and large supplies of dry ice so they could reopen as quickly as possible after the storm had passed. In neighboring states, the firm also had scores of trucks standing by crammed with both emergency-related inventory for its stores and emergency supplies it was prepared to donate—bottled water, medical supplies, and so forth. And Wal-Mart often beat FEMA by several days in getting those supplies delivered.[36]

Seeing the consequences of poor crisis management after the terrorist attacks of September 11, 2001, and the 2005 hurricanes, many firms today are actively working to create new and better crisis management plans and procedures. For example, both Reliant Energy and Duke Energy rely on computer trading centers where trading managers actively buy and sell energy-related commodities. If a terrorist attack or natural disaster such as a hurricane were to strike their trading

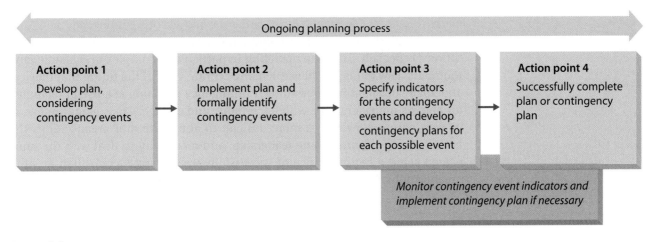

Figure 3.6
CONTINGENCY PLANNING

Most organizations develop contingency plans. These plans specify alternative courses of action to be taken if an intended plan is unexpectedly disrupted or rendered inappropriate.

centers, they would essentially be out of business. Prior to September 11, each firm had relatively vague and superficial crisis plans. But now they and most other companies have much more detailed and comprehensive plans in the event of another crisis. Both Reliant and Duke, for example, have created secondary trading centers at other locations. In the event of a shutdown at their main trading centers, these firms can quickly transfer virtually all their core trading activities to their secondary centers within 30 minutes or less.[37] Unfortunately, however, because it is impossible to forecast the future precisely, no organization can ever be perfectly prepared for all crises.

The mechanics of contingency planning are shown in Figure 3.6. In relation to an organization's other plans, contingency planning comes into play at four action points. At action point 1, management develops the basic plans of the organization. These may include strategic, tactical, and operational plans. As part of this development process, managers usually consider various contingency events. Some management groups even assign someone the role of devil's advocate to ask, "But what if . . ." about each course of action. A variety of contingencies is usually considered.

At action point 2, the plan that management chooses is put into effect. The most important contingency events are also defined. Only the events that are likely to occur and whose effects will have a substantial impact on the organization are used in the contingency-planning process. Next, at action point 3, the company specifies certain indicators or signs that suggest that a contingency event is about to take place. A bank might decide that a 2 percent drop in interest rates should be considered a contingency event. An indicator might be two consecutive months with a drop of .5 percent in each. As indicators of contingency events are being defined, the contingency plans themselves should also be developed. Examples of various situations for which contingency plans are appropriate include delaying plant construction, developing a new manufacturing process, and cutting prices.

After this stage, the managers of the organization monitor the indicators identified at action point 3. If the situation dictates, a contingency plan is implemented. Otherwise, the primary plan of action continues in force. Finally, action point 4 marks the successful completion of either the original or a contingency plan.

Contingency planning is becoming increasingly important for most organizations, especially for those operating in particularly complex or dynamic environments. Few managers have such an accurate view of the future that they can anticipate and plan for everything. Contingency planning is a useful technique for helping managers cope with uncertainty and change. Crisis management, by its very nature, however, is more difficult to anticipate. But organizations that have a strong culture, strong leadership, and a capacity to deal with the unexpected stand a better chance of successfully weathering a crisis than do other organizations.[38]

Summary of Key Points

1. Summarize the planning process and describe organizational goals.
   - The planning process includes understanding the environment, formulating a mission, and creating goals and plans.
   - Goals serve four purposes: they provide guidance, facilitate planning, motivate employees, and facilitate evaluation and control.
   - By understanding the environmental context, managers develop a number of different types of goals and plans, including strategic plans, tactical plans, and operational plans.

2. Discuss the components of strategy and the types of strategic alternatives.
   - A strategy is a comprehensive plan for accomplishing the organization's goals.
   - Effective strategies, including business-level and corporate-level strategies, address three organizational issues: distinctive competence, scope, and resource deployment.

3. Describe how to use SWOT analysis in formulating strategy.
   - SWOT analysis considers an organization's strengths, weaknesses, opportunities, and threats.
   - Using SWOT analysis, an organization chooses strategies that support its mission and exploit its opportunities and strengths, neutralize its threats, and avoid its weaknesses.

4. Identify and describe various alternative approaches to business-level strategy formulation.
   - A business-level strategy is the plan an organization uses to conduct business in a particular industry or market.
   - Porter suggests that businesses may formulate a differentiation strategy, an overall cost leadership strategy, or a focus strategy at this level.
   - Strategies may also be based on the four stages of the product life cycle: introduction, growth, maturity, and decline.

5. Identify and describe various alternative approaches to corporate-level strategy formulation.
   - A corporate-level strategy is the plan an organization uses to manage its operations across several businesses.

- A firm that does not diversify is implementing a single-product strategy.
- An organization pursues a strategy of related diversification when it operates a set of businesses that are somehow linked.
- Related diversification reduces the financial risk associated with any particular product, decreases the overhead costs of each business, and enables the organization to create and exploit synergy.
- An organization pursues a strategy of unrelated diversification when it operates a set of businesses that are not logically associated with one another.
- Organizations manage diversification through the organization structure that they adopt and through portfolio management techniques. The BCG matrix classifies an organization's diversified businesses as dogs, cash cows, question marks, or stars according to their market share and market growth rate. The GE Business Screen classifies businesses as winners, losers, question marks, average businesses, or profit producers according to their industry attractiveness and competitive position.

6. Discuss how tactical plans are developed and executed.
   - Tactical plans are formulated at the middle of the organization and have an intermediate time horizon and moderate scope.
   - Tactical plans are developed to implement specific parts of a strategic plan and must flow from strategy, specify resource and time issues, and commit human resources.
   - Execution of tactical plans depends on evaluation, dissemination of information and resources, and monitoring.

7. Describe the basic types of operational plans used by organizations.
   - Operational plans, derived from a tactical plan and aimed at achieving one or more operational goals, are carried out at the lower levels of the organization, have a shorter time horizon, and are narrower in scope.
   - There are two major types of operational plans. Single-use plans are designed to carry out a course of action that is not likely to be repeated in the

future, including programs and projects. Standing plans are designed to carry out a course of action that is likely to be repeated several times, including policies, standard operating procedures, and rules and regulations.

- Contingency planning and crisis management are also emerging as very important forms of operational planning

Discussion Questions

Questions for Review

1. Describe the purposes of organizational goals. Be certain to note how the purpose varies for different kinds of goals.
2. Identify and describe Porter's generic strategies.
3. What are the basic differences among a single-product strategy, a strategy based on related diversification, and a strategy based on unrelated diversification?

4. What is tactical planning? What is operational planning? What are the similarities and differences among them?
5. What is contingency planning? How is it similar to, and how is it different from, crisis management?

Questions for Analysis

6. Suppose an organization does not have an identifiable distinctive competence. Assuming that the organization's managers can determine how to develop one, how long is it likely to remain unique? Why?
7. Suppose a firm decides to move from a single-product strategy to a strategy based on related diversification. How might managers use SWOT analysis to select attributes of its current business to serve as bases of relatedness among the potential businesses it may acquire or launch?
8. For decades Procter & Gamble promoted its Ivory soap brand as being "99 and 44/100 percent pure."

The firm also refuses to use deodorants, perfumes, or colors in Ivory, and it packages the soap in plain paper wrappers with no foil or fancy printing. Is Ivory using a product differentiation strategy, a low-cost strategy, or a focus strategy? Or is it using some combination? Explain your answer.

9. Which kind of plan—tactical or operational—should be developed first? Why? Does the order really matter? Why or why not?
10. Cite examples of each type of operational plan that you have used or encountered at work, at school, or in your personal life.

Building Effective Decision-Making Skills

Exercise Overview

Decision-making skills reflect the manager's ability to recognize and define problems and opportunities correctly and then to select an appropriate course of action to solve problems and capitalize on opportunities. As noted in the chapter, many organizations use SWOT analysis as part of the process of strategy formulation. This exercise will help you better understand how managers obtain the information they need to perform such an analysis and use it as a framework for making decisions.

Exercise Background

SWOT is an acronym for strengths, weaknesses, opportunities, and threats. Good strategies are those that exploit an organization's opportunities and strengths, while neutralizing threats and avoiding or correcting weaknesses.

Assume that you have just been hired to run a medium-size manufacturing company. The firm has been manufacturing electric motors, circuit breakers, and similar electronic components for industrial use. In recent years, the firm's financial performance has gradually eroded. You have been hired to turn things around.

Meetings with both current and former top managers of the firm have led you to believe that a new strategy is needed. In earlier times the firm was successful in part because its products were of top quality, which enabled the company to charge premium prices for them.

Recently, however, various cost-cutting measures have resulted in a decrease in quality. Competition has also increased. As a result, your firm no longer has a reputation for top-quality products, but your manufacturing costs are still relatively high. The next thing you want to do is to conduct a SWOT analysis.

Exercise Task

With the situation described above as context, do the following:

1. List the sources you will use to obtain information about the firm's strengths, weaknesses, opportunities, and threats. If you are using the Internet, give specific websites or URLs.

2. For what types of information are data readily available on the Internet? What categories of data are difficult or impossible to find on the Internet?

3. Rate each source in terms of its probable reliability.

4. How confident should you be in making decisions based on the information obtained?

Building Effective Conceptual Skills

Exercise Overview

Conceptual skills consist of the manager's ability to think in the abstract. Strategic management is often thought of in terms of competition. For example, metaphors involving war or sports are often invoked by strategists. However, cooperation is another viable strategic alternative to competition. Cooperation has been a popular strategy in many countries for years, and the importance of cooperative strategic alliances and joint ventures is rising in the United States. This game will provide you with an illustration of the advantages of a cooperative strategy in comparison with a competitive strategy.

Exercise Background

Competitive and cooperative strategies are quite complex when implemented in organizations. However, a simple and clear illustration of the principles underlying competition and cooperation can be given through the use of a game.

This game illustrates a "prisoner's dilemma" situation. The prisoner's dilemma is a classic situation used to demonstrate concepts related to game theory. In the original prisoner's dilemma, two criminals are suspected in a crime but there is not enough evidence to convict either of them. The two criminals are separated and each is told that if he will "rat" on the other one, he will go free. Of course, if neither rats, both go free. If both rat, then both go to prison. The optimal outcome (for the prisoners!) occurs when neither rats on the other. However, in real situations, the most common outcome is just the opposite—that both "rat" and both go to jail.

The prisoner's dilemma case has been used by game theorists to describe how people make decisions about whether to act cooperatively or competitively. Although there are cases in which cooperation would be the most beneficial for both parties, human nature frequently causes the parties to choose competition instead, a scenario that often leads to the worst outcomes. In the game you are about to play, you will see how choices about competition versus cooperation affect outcomes.

The main message of this game is: "It's nice to be nice, to the nice." You will find that competition is the preferred mode when rivals are behaving competitively but cooperation is preferred in situations where rivals are willing to be cooperative. In a mixed case, faced with some rivals that are cooperative and some that are competitive, the cooperative firms can band together and effectively compete against the competitive firms, by using their combined power.

Exercise Task

You should form groups of four to play the board game *Trouble* by Milton Bradley, *Sorry* by Parker Brothers, or a generic equivalent of those games. In the game, four players move pieces around a board in an attempt to complete the course first. When players land on an occupied space, they choose whether to send their opponent's piece back to the start.

It's best to have one game for each four students. If that's not possible, the next-best alternative is to have at least four games and form the students into four groups, so that students can closely watch each strategy being played out. However, it's possible to play the game with just one set, if volunteers come forward to play the game in front of the entire class. This can also be effective if the class is small.

There are four different rule sets, which can be played simultaneously or sequentially.

For all rule sets: Four players per game. Each player uses only two pieces, not four (in order to make the game play faster). Players start moving pieces on their first roll of the dice, rather than waiting for a specific number (again, for speed). In addition, the following rules apply.

Rule Set 1: This is the purely cooperative game. Players should try not to land on an occupied space and they may never send any of their opponent's pieces back to the start. If they must land on an occupied space, the player should put their piece in the next free spot, not displacing his or her opponent.

Rule Set 2: This is the purely competitive game. Players must land on occupied spaces if possible and they must always send their opponent's piece back to the start when they do.

Rule Set 3: This is the mixed case, "wolf among the sheep" game. One player is chosen at the start to be the competitive one (the wolf) and the group (the sheep) is informed. During play, the wolf plays by Rule Set 2, sending his or her opponent's pieces back to the start whenever possible. The three sheep play by Rule Set 1. That is, they may never send any opponent's pieces back to the start.

Rule Set 4: This is the mixed case, "retaliation" game. One player is chosen at the start to be the competitive one (the wolf) and the group (the sheep) is informed. During play, the wolf plays by Rule Set 2, sending his or her opponent's pieces back to the start whenever possible. The three sheep play by Rule Set 1 when they are facing another sheep. That is, they should try not to send any sheep's pieces back to the start. However, the three sheep play by Rule Set 2 when they are facing the wolf. That is, the sheep should try to send the wolf's pieces back to the start whenever possible.

After the four games have been played and the results noted, discuss the outcomes. In the mixed case games, who won—the sheep or the wolf? Which game finished most quickly? Which took the longest? Which game was most fun and which was most dull? Explain why.

Interpretation

You will likely find that the cooperative game (Rule Set 1) goes quickly and smoothly. All players do about equally well, except for the random nature of the dice roll. This game may seem boring.

You will likely find that the competitive game (Rule Set 2) takes the longest, as players must constantly start over. All players do about equally poorly.

You will likely find that the "wolf among the sheep" game (Rule Set 3) seems very unfair, as the wolf has a strong advantage. This is the case that prevails when some competitors compete aggressively and others do not. It's also analogous to the situation where one student cheats on an exam, when all the others are honest.

You will likely find that the retaliation game (Rule Set 4) seems to be fair because the wolf often does not win. This is the situation in which some rivals cooperate for mutual benefit with other trusted rivals, while aggressively competitive rivals find that the others "gang up" and use their combined power to squash any competitive tactics. This is analogous to the situation where the honest students study together to help each other, excluding the cheating student from the study group.

You may prefer the fun game over the boring one. However, you might feel differently if it was a real business competition rather than a trivial board game. While boring is undesirable in a board game, it might be very desirable in real companies, because in real life, intense competition can be damaging and expensive. "Losing" might mean loss of jobs or bankruptcy for the company.

In conclusion, cooperation with trusted others can be more effective than competition, and it can also be very effective at thwarting those who compete too aggressively.

Illegal acts such as collusion between competitors should obviously be avoided. However, managers should look for opportunities for productive, legal cooperation, such as joint alliances, shared resources, or business partnerships.

Reprinted by permission of the author Margaret Hill.

Building Effective Diagnostic Skills

Exercise Overview

Diagnostic skills are the skills that enable a manager to visualize the most appropriate response to a situation. As rivalry increases in an industry, competitors develop similar capabilities, making it more difficult to achieve differentiation. In such an industry, price becomes the primary competitive weapon. (The soft-drink, fast-food, airline, and retail industries, for example, are suffering from this problem today.) This in-class demonstration will show you the difficulties of developing an effective competitive response in such a situation.

Exercise Background

Assume that you are the owner of a small business, such as a gas station or fast-food outlet, that is located directly across the street from a rival firm. Your products are not differentiated, and you cannot make them so. Customers prefer the less expensive product, and they switch on the basis of the price difference between the products—the larger the difference, the more customers will switch. Customer switching behavior is shown in Table 3.2.

Further, the following conditions apply to both you and your competitor:

1. You both have a $1.00 cost of production per unit. This number cannot be changed.

2. At the beginning of the game, you are both charging a price of $1.10, for a per-unit profit of $.10.

3. The market consists of exactly 100 customers per period. This number cannot be changed.

Therefore, at the beginning period, you and your rival are charging the same price (0 cents difference) and thus are splitting the market 50/50, or selling 50 units per period. Both you and your rival have per-period profits of $5.00 (50 units × $.10).

For the demonstration, two teams of students, representing your firm and your rival, will separately and independently make a decision about price for the upcoming period. Price is the only variable you can control. Each team will write down its price, and then your professor will disclose the resulting market share and profits for each team. The demonstration will continue for several periods, the exact number of which is not known to the teams. The objective is to be profitable.

Exercise Task

1. Consider volunteering to be part of one of the groups involved in demonstrating this concept in front of the class.

2. Play out the scenario (participants) and observe (class).

3. Did each of the teams choose a strategy that made profit maximization possible? Were the strategies equally profitable? Why or why not?

Table 3.2

When the price difference is . . .	The market share split is . . .
0 cents	50/50
1 cent	60/40
2 cents	70/30
3 cents	80/20
4 cents	90/10
5 cents	100/0

4. Competing firms are prohibited by law from fixing prices—that is, from jointly deciding on a price. However, price signaling, in which firms do not directly conspire but instead send subtle messages, is legal. Could the two teams in this demonstration use price signaling? What conditions are necessary to make price signaling an effective strategy?

5. What does this demonstration tell you about competitive dynamics in an industry where products are undifferentiated?

Reprinted by permission of the author Margaret Hill

Skills Self-Assessment Instrument

Self-Assessment

Your Work Life Strengths and Weaknesses

Introduction: The Strengths, Weaknesses, Opportunities, Threats (SWOT) analysis helps organizations identify their internal capabilities and limitations, as well as significant events and trends from the external environment. The SWOT technique can also be useful in understanding your own personal strengths and weaknesses. The following assessment will help you better understand the SWOT analysis process as well as identify areas for improvement in your readiness for a current or future career.

Instructions: Create two lists, one of your strengths and one of your weaknesses. Judge items as strengths and weaknesses by thinking of them in relation to your current or anticipated future career. For example, creativity may be more valued in a career in marketing, while empathy might be more valued in human resources management. If you are having trouble thinking of items or deciding how to classify them, speak to a friend, fellow student, or someone who knows you well. Their insights can be useful.

List the following as strengths:
- Work experience in a similar or related field.
- Formal and informal education. This should include degrees earned or expected, as well as non-credit courses and other types of training.
- Technical skills or knowledge related to your career. This could include, for example, an IT worker's command of programming languages or an accountant's knowledge of audit procedures.
- Generalized skills. Skills that are valued in just about any job would include leadership, teamwork, communication, and more. Refer to the list of fundamental management skills in Chapter 1 for more ideas.
- Personal characteristics. Again, most careers call for positive personal characteristics such as initiative, creativity, confidence, optimism, self-discipline, energy, ability to handle stress, and so on.
- Job-seeking skills. The ability to present a professional appearance, to network, to mentor others or be mentored, among others, are job-seeking skills that could be an asset in your career.

List the following as weaknesses:
- Lack of any of the above; for example, no work experience or no degree.
- Areas that are weak or undesirable relative to other job-seekers, such as low GPA or unrelated major, weak skills, little technical knowledge, or negative personal characteristics, i.e., poor self-control or an inability to handle criticism.

For interpretation, see Interpretations of Skills Self-Assessment Instruments in the appendix near the end of this text.

Experiential Exercise

The SWOT Analysis

Purpose: SWOT analysis provides the manager with a cognitive model of the organization and its environmental forces. By developing the ability to conduct such an analysis, the manager builds both process knowledge and a conceptual skill. This skill-builder focuses on the *administrative management model*. It will help you develop the *coordinator role* of the administrative management model. One of the skills of the coordinator is the ability to plan.

Introduction: This exercise helps you understand the complex interrelationships between environmental opportunities and threats and organizational strengths and weaknesses. Strategy formulation is facilitated by a SWOT analysis. First, the organization should study its internal operations in order to identify its strengths and weaknesses. Next, the organization should scan the environment to identify existing and future opportunities and threats. Then the organization should identify the relationships that exist among these strengths, weaknesses, opportunities, and threats. Finally, major business strategies usually result from matching an organization's strengths with appropriate opportunities or from matching the threats it faces with weaknesses that have been identified.

Instructions: First, read the short narrative of the Trek Bicycle Corporation's external and internal environments, found below.

Second, divide into small group and conduct a SWOT (strengths, weaknesses, opportunities, threats) analysis for Trek, based on the short narrative. You may also use your general knowledge and any information you have about Trek or the bicycle manufacturing industry. Then prepare a group response to the discussion questions.

Third, as a class, discuss both the SWOT analysis and the groups' responses to the discussion questions.

Discussion Questions:

1. What was the most difficult part of the SWOT analysis?

2. Why do most firms not develop major strategies for matches between threats and strengths?

3. Under what conditions might a firm develop a major strategy around a match between an opportunity and a weakness?

Trek's External and Internal Environments

Today in the United States, inflation, cost of materials, and unemployment are fairly low and are not increasing. Emerging economies are growing more rapidly than the U.S. economy in general. Foreign trade is relatively open, so manufacturers face intense international and local competition, with pressure to keep prices low, and also to have the opportunity to utilize low-cost labor and raw materials from around the world. New manufacturing technologies, futuristic materials, and e-commerce are becoming more prevalent and affordable. The political-legal climate is favorable to business in the United States and most developing nations, while regulation is higher in the E.U. The standard of living is stable, the population is aging, and ethnic diversity is increasing.

Today in the bicycle manufacturing industry, manufacturers must invest very heavily in research and development (R&D) to compete effectively on a global scale. Domestically, the bicycle manufacturing industry is fragmented, with the largest firm, Trek, controlling just 24 percent of sales. The industry's customers are primarily local, independent bike retailers, a very fragmented group. The Internet, and eBay in particular, provide alternate channels for new and used bike sales. Bike riders, the ultimate purchasers, are interested in style, comfort, and high-tech features, as well as environmental and health issues. Suppliers of many bike components are small, local manufacturers located in developing countries. However, a few suppliers are more powerful, such as Shimano, an internationally known maker of bicycle components and cycling gear. Regulators are not a significant force for bicycle manufacturers, but Trek and others have numerous joint ventures. In one example, Trek teamed with AMD, Nike, and other companies to produce the high-performance cycle used by Lance Armstrong in the Tour de France and other races.

Trek has excellent R&D capability and effectively utilizes low-cost manufacturers in producing the more affordable products in its broad line of bikes. However, its Wisconsin factory produces its high-end lines and can customize a bike to a customer's exact specifications. Trek is beginning to push to improve the customer bike-buying experience. The company will limit the number of retailers it uses and requires retailers to stock a higher percentage of Trek products. In return, it will provide training and funds to improve in-store marketing and increase customer loyalty.

Trek Bicycle Corporation SWOT Analysis Sheet

Environmental Analysis   **Organizational Analysis**

Opportunities
_____
_____
_____
_____
_____
_____
_____
_____
_____
_____
_____
_____
_____

Strengths
_____
_____
_____
_____
_____
_____
_____
_____
_____
_____

Threats
_____
_____
_____
_____
_____
_____
_____
_____
_____
_____
_____
_____

Weaknesses
_____
_____
_____
_____
_____
_____
_____
_____
_____
_____
_____
_____
_____
_____

Relationships Between
Opportunities and Strengths
1. _____
2. _____
3. _____

Relationships Between
Opportunities and Weaknesses
1. _____
2. _____
3. _____

Relationships Between
Threats and Strengths
1. _____
2. _____
3. _____

Relationships Between
Threats and Weaknesses
1. _____
2. _____
3. _____

Major Strategies Matching
Opportunities with Strengths
1. _____
2. _____
3. _____

Major Strategies Matching
Threats with Weaknesses
1. _____
2. _____
3. _____

CHAPTER CLOSING CASE

FEMA'S DISASTROUS RESPONSE TO HURRICANE KATRINA

A $150 billion estimated cost of recovery, 2.5 million persons displaced from their homes, 1,100 deaths, thousands hospitalized, and, as of January 2006, 3,600 individuals still missing. U.S. annual GDP may drop 1 percent, reflecting the $130 billion in annual contributions made by the region. Over 100,000 jobs lost in two months in Louisiana alone. A quarter of a million of homes destroyed. An estimated 372,000 elementary and secondary students without schools and eleven universities temporarily closed.

The force of a Category 5 hurricane is one of the most destructive natural events. Hurricane Katrina, which hit the Gulf Coast on August 29, 2005, was the costliest natural disaster in American history and led to vast human suffering. Yet human errors were responsible for much of the economic, physical, and emotional damage, as many individuals, organizations, and governmental bodies failed to respond appropriately. Blame has been placed on everyone from the citizens to President Bush, but none has received more blame than the Federal Emergency Management Agency, or FEMA.

One factor in the fiasco is FEMA chief Michael Brown's lack of leadership. His emails of August 29 discuss rolling up his shirtsleeves to impress television viewers and whining to his deputy director, "Can I quit now? Can I go home?" An employee emailed him on August 31, saying New Orleans was "past critical" and mentioning deaths and water shortages. Brown wrote back only: "Thanks for the update. Anything

specific I need to do or tweak?" (Amid controversy and shock, Brown resigned on September 12.)

Yet lack of planning was, surprisingly, not one of the causes of FEMA's disastrously inadequate response. The agency was well aware of the possibility of a Katrina-like disaster. In July 2004, FEMA staged "Hurricane Pam," a disaster simulation focused on New Orleans. The exercise hypothesized mass evacuations and levee destruction. In 2005, Brown's superior, Director of Homeland Security Michael Chertoff, introduced a National Preparedness Plan. The plan included scenario-based planning for 15 disaster scenarios, including a flu pandemic, major earthquake, and terrorist attack—and a major hurricane.

Although the possible extent of the damage was known, as was the responsibility for various actions, there was a lack of clear communication and a failure to coordinate the actions of different organizations and governments. Although Governor Blanco asked FEMA for aid and New Orleans ordered evacuation, FEMA failed to provide the necessary support. The U.S. Army was prepared to drop food and water via helicopter as early as August 30 but was never asked to do so. Yet city and state officials claim their organizations were overwhelmed and unable to request the help. One *BusinessWeek* editor sums up the situation, saying, "There is no clear strategy for dealing with extraordinary disaster scenarios that can easily overwhelm local officials. And the lack of such unambiguous procedures can lead to

chaos." One Louisiana state official commented, "If you do not know what your needs are, you can't request to FEMA what you need."

What can be done to help authorities respond more effectively? One scholar attributes the problems to a failure of imagination. Dr. Lee Clarke, a Rutgers University professor, claims planners neglected to consider worst-case scenarios. "The usual or recommended way of looking at risk . . . is probabilistic thinking," says Clarke. "Probability says it is highly unlikely that a nuclear power plant will melt down. Possibilism wonders what happens if a nuclear power plant has a particularly bad day. . . . [It] is worst case thinking." Clarke's theory would call for emergency responders to plan for worst-case, as well as most-likely-case, scenarios.

Another approach would focus on grass-roots planning efforts. During Katrina, for example, many groups and individuals took heroic actions to help victims. The U.S. Coast Guard, helped by hundreds of privately owned watercraft, rescued 22,000 stranded individuals, more than the USCG rescued in the previous half century. Businesses donated millions and families opened their homes to victims. In this approach, planning for future Katrinas could be improved by building on local knowledge and resources. The process should include those who are not included in the current system, such as the disabled, the elderly, and individuals without transportation.

Anderson Cooper, a CNN correspondent, reflected that the lesson learned in Katrina is, "we are not as ready as we can be." Whatever it takes, we need to improve our planning processes and be ready, because there will surely be a next time. For, as Stanford professor Scott Sagan says, "Things that have never happened before happen all the time."

CASE QUESTIONS

1. In your opinion, were the problems experienced by agencies coping with Hurricane Katrina occurring at the strategic, tactical, or operational level? Explain.
2. Should FEMA handle planning for hurricanes and other natural disasters with a single-use plan or a standing plan? What would be the advantages of each approach?
3. How would worst-case planning have helped emergency responders react more effectively to Hurricane Katrina?

CASE REFERENCES

"Brown Defends FEMA Response," *Fox News*, September 28, 2005, www.foxnews.com on January 15, 2006; "'Can I Quit Now?' FEMA Chief Wrote as Katrina Raged," *CNN*, November 3, 2005, www.cnn.com on January 15, 2006; Lee Clarke, "Worst Case Katrina," *Understanding Katrina: Perspectives from the Social Sciences*, September 12, 2005, The Social Sciences Research Council website, www.ssrc.org on January 15, 2006; "FEMA Director Brown Resigns," *CNN*, September 12, 2005, www.cnn.com on January 15, 2006; "If Katrina Teaches Us Nothing Else. . . " *BusinessWeek*, October 10, 2005, www.businessweek.com on January 15, 2006; "Labor Market Statistics for Areas Affected by Hurricanes Katrina and Rita," Bureau of Labor Statistics, www.bls.gov on January 15, 2006; Andrew Lakoff, "From Disaster to Catastrophe: The Limits of Preparedness," *Understanding Katrina: Perspectives from the Social Sciences*, September 30, 2005, The Social Sciences Research Council website, www.ssrc.org on January 15, 2006; "Reported Locations of Katrina/Rita Applicants," January 20, 2006, FEMA website, www.fema.gov on January 22, 2006; Tricia Wachtendorf and James M. Kendra, "Improvising Disaster in the City of Jazz: Organizational Response to Hurricane Katrina," *Understanding Katrina: Perspectives from the Social Sciences*, September 21, 2005, The Social Sciences Research Council website, www.ssrc.org on January 15, 2006.

YOU MAKE THE CALL

The Video Game Wars

1. If you ran Electronic Arts, what changes, if any, would you make in the firm's strategy?
2. If you ran Sony's video game business, what changes, if any, would you make in the firm's strategy?
3. If you ran a smaller video game start-up like Acclaim, how might you go about developing a strategy to more effectively compete with EA and Sony?
4. If you play video games now, what aspects of the strategies used by EA, Sony, and Acclaim tend to cause you to play more or fewer of each company's games?
5. If you do not currently play video games, what strategies, if any, might EA, Sony, and Acclaim adopt to increase your interest in playing?

Test Prepper

ACE self-test

college.hmco.com/pic/griffinfund5e

You've read the chapter, studied the key terms, and the exam is any day now. Think you're ready to ace it? Take this sample test to gauge your comprehension of chapter material. You can check your answers at the back of the book. Want more test questions? Visit the student website at http://college.hmco.com/pic/griffinfund5e/ and take the ACE quizzes for more practice.

1. T F A goal set by and for lower-level managers of the organization is a tactical goal.

2. T F Chelsea Milling Company, maker of Jiffy Mixes, has never spent one cent on advertising. Jiffy mixes sell for one-third to one-half as much as their competitors. Chelsea Milling Company uses an overall cost leadership strategy.

3. T F In the maturity stage of the product life cycle, demand for the product levels off.

4. T F Nike sells shoes, athletic apparel, and athletic equipment. In so doing, it uses unrelated diversification.

5. T F Portfolio management techniques help top executives decide what businesses to engage in.

6. Which of the following is NOT a purpose of goals?

   a. Provide guidance and a unified direction for people in the organization

   b. Promote good planning

   c. Serve as a source of motivation for employees

   d. State an organization's fundamental purpose

   e. Provide an effective mechanism for evaluation and control

7. Newspapers have identified decreasing readership by the 18–34 age group as a long-term

   a. strength.

   b. weakness.

   c. opportunity.

   d. threat.

   e. None of the above

8. Radio stations in the United States have begun using radio data systems (RDS). RDS enables stations to transmit a small amount of print information to radios equipped to receive it—information such as station identification, song title, and traffic information. Stations that currently use RDS are using which strategy?

   a. Differentiation

   b. Cost leadership

   c. Focus

   d. Product life cycle

   e. None of the above

9. The Morning News began publishing a free tabloid-size daily newspaper called *Quick*, designed for readers 18–34. The Morning News is willing to take a short-term loss because it considers the potential advertising revenue to be great. *Quick* is a

   a. star.

   b. question mark.

   c. cash cow.

   d. dog.

   e. None of the above

10. Opaque websites such as Priceline and Hotwire do not let customers know where they will be staying until they have already paid for their hotel room. This is an example of which of the following?

    a. Program

    b. Project

    c. Policy

    d. Regulation

    e. Planning

chapter **4**

Managing Decision Making

FIRST THINGS FIRST

Making Tough Choices at Wal-Mart

"[Managers at Wal-Mart] would rather have a painkiller [than] take the vitamin of change."
—JULIE ROEHM, FORMER SENIOR V.P. OF MARKETING
COMMUNICATIONS, WAL-MART

After years of phenomenal growth, high profitability, and the admiration of Wall Street, Wal-Mart today is suffering from a variety of problems and disappointments. It seems obvious that the firm is stagnating and a complete overhaul will be necessary. The company's leaders, headed by CEO Lee Scott, are facing what could be their most important decision—what changes to make to improve results at the world's largest retailer. Observers are questioning whether Wal-Mart's decision-making process could be a part of the problem.

In 2006, several key executives left the firm. Overseas expansion plans fizzled, costing the company almost $1 billion. Sales declined or remained flat at many locations. About 5 percent of former shoppers now refuse to buy from Wal-Mart, due to the unfashionable merchandise, dated and crowded stores, unfavorable publicity, and lack of customer service. Sam's Club profitability was hurt due to company restrictions against head-to-head competition with Wal-Marts. The firm lost a class-action labor suit that alleged unpaid overtime. Even worse, more class-action suits are pending, so the firm will face years' of lawsuits. Share price has fallen 22 percent since 2000, costing shareholders $90 billion in value. Everyone is unhappy. Meanwhile, rivals Target and JCPenney are going strong.

To improve performance, Wal-Mart tried something new and hired a number of outside managers. The managers came from companies with strong marketing departments, such as McDonald's, Frito-Lay, and Chrysler. They were expected to bring provocative and fresh sensibilities to the staid and conservative firm. These managers developed new initiatives, such as launching a more stylish line of clothing and home furnishings in 2005. Unfortunately, customers interested in chic goods were not impressed. Efforts to upgrade electronics, for example flat-screen TVs, have fared better, but customers demand more service for these more complex and pricey goods.

Most critically, merchandisers, the managers who work with suppliers to determine the product mix, did not appreciate the need to change. Everything the new marketing managers attempted was undermined by the merchandisers, who are considered the most powerful group in the company. When Julie Roehm, the recently hired head of marketing communications, tried to create a new ad campaign to showcase style, the merchandisers insisted on creating in-store displays that continued to focus on price. "I spent so much time on signs in the stores, it was mind-boggling," says Roehm. She created a slightly racy ad to showcase the company's lingerie to air during *Desperate Housewives*, but it was canceled when one viewer complained. Roehm was horrified that such a large company would switch direction and overrule a manager on such slight feedback. "You are never going to satisfy 100% of the people," she states.

Roehm might have been a little too edgy for Wal-Mart. When she painted her new, gray office a cheerier yellow green, her colleagues reacted with shock. She misread the organization culture, for example by allowing business travel to keep her from the office on Fridays, when CEO Scott held top-level meetings. More experienced Wal-Mart executives were "super-nice," Roehm says, but they didn't come forward to help her adjust. She describes Wal-Mart's culture as passive-aggressive and highly resistant to outside influence. "The importance of culture can't be underestimated," she says. "[Managers at Wal-Mart] would rather have a painkiller [than] take the vitamin of change."

It's understandable that Wal-Mart is cautious. After all, their business model has been incredibly successful and much copied. Wal-Mart's impact, as an employer of 1.3 million workers and serving as the largest buyer for many manufacturers, is huge. An organization that large doesn't change easily. Yet the firm must open itself more, especially to hired outsiders knowledgeable about best practices.

Unfortunately, that change is still unlikely. In February 2007, at its annual meeting, Wal-Mart managers acknowledged the problems. But instead of opening up

LEARNING OBJECTIVES

After studying this chapter, you should be able to:

- Define decision making and discuss types of decisions and decision-making conditions.
- Discuss rational perspectives on decision making, including the steps in rational decision making.
- Describe the behavioral aspects of decision making.
- Discuss group and team decision making, including the advantages and disadvantages of group and team decision making and how it can be more effectively managed.

Despite its recent problems Wal-Mart remains one of the world's most successful businesses.

a dialogue with customers and investors, the firm made no major announcements and did not even allow the media to attend, stifling sources of feedback.

If current trends continue, disgruntled investors may pressure the company to change its processes. For the sake of the suppliers, customers, employees, and investors, let's hope so.[1]

Wal-Mart managers and their critics provide clear examples that illustrate the complexities of decision making, as well as its pervasiveness throughout the management process. Indeed, some experts believe that decision making is the most basic and fundamental of all managerial activities.[2] Thus we discuss it here, in the context of the first management function, planning. Keep in mind, however, that although decision making is perhaps most closely linked to the planning function, it is also part of organizing, leading, and controlling.

We begin our discussion by exploring the nature of decision making. We then describe rational perspectives on decision making. Behavioral aspects of decision making are then introduced and described. We conclude with a discussion of group and team decision making.

The Nature of Decision Making

Managers at Disney recently made the decision to buy Pixar Animation for $7.4 billion.[3] At about the same time, the general manager of the Ford dealership in Bryan, Texas, made a decision to sponsor a local youth soccer team for $200. Each of these examples reflects a decision, but the decisions differ in many ways. Thus, as a starting point in understanding decision making, we must first explore the meaning of decision making as well as types of decisions and conditions under which decisions are made.[4]

Decision Making Defined

decision making
The act of choosing one alternative from among a set of alternatives

Decision making can refer to either a specific act or a general process. **Decision making** per se is the act of choosing one alternative from among a set of alternatives. The decision-making process, however, is much more than this. One step of the process, for example, is that the person making the decision must both recognize that a decision is necessary and identify the set of feasible alternatives before selecting one. Hence, the **decision-making process** includes recognizing and defining the nature of a decision situation, identifying alternatives, choosing the "best" alternative, and putting it into practice.[5]

decision-making process
Recognizing and defining the nature of a decision situation, identifying alternatives, choosing the "best" alternative, and putting it into practice

The word *best*, of course, implies effectiveness. Effective decision making requires that the decision maker understand the situation driving the decision. Most people would consider an effective decision to be one that optimizes some set of factors, such as profits, sales, employee welfare, and market share. In some situations, though, an effective decision may be one that minimizes loss, expenses, or employee turnover. It may even mean selecting the best method for going out of business, laying off employees, or terminating a strategic alliance.

We should also note that managers make decisions about both problems and opportunities. For example, making decisions about how to cut costs by 10 percent reflects a problem—an undesirable situation that requires a solution. But decisions

Decision making is the act of choosing one alternative from among a set of alternatives. Most decisions take place under conditions of certainty, risk, or uncertainty. Consider, for instance, the decision that confronted Nebraska farmer Bob Roberts during a recent drought. One option was to grow corn, which he could sell for cash. The other was to grow alfalfa to feed his cows. And clearly, each option had a degree of risk.

are also necessary in situations of opportunity. Learning that the firm is earning higher-than-projected profits, for example, requires a subsequent decision. Should the extra funds be used to increase shareholder dividends, reinvest in current operations, or expand into new markets?

Of course, it may take a long time before a manager can know if the right decision was made. For example, the top management team at Eastman Kodak has made several major decisions that will affect the company for decades. Among other things, for example, it sold off several chemical- and health-related businesses (reducing the firm's debt by $7 billion in the process), launched a major new line of advanced cameras and film called Advantix, made major new investments in digital photography, and continued to invest heavily in emerging technologies. But analysts believe that the payoffs from these decisions will not be known for several years.[6]

Types of Decisions

Managers must make many different types of decisions. In general, however, most decisions fall into one of two categories: programmed and nonprogrammed.[7] A ***programmed decision*** is one that is relatively structured or recurs with some frequency (or both). Starbucks uses programmed decisions to purchase new supplies of coffee beans, cups, and napkins, and Starbucks employees are trained in exact procedures for brewing coffee. Likewise, the Bryan Ford dealer made a decision that he will sponsor a youth soccer team each year. Thus, when the soccer club president calls, the dealer already knows what he will do. Many decisions regarding basic operating systems and procedures and standard organizational transactions are of this variety and can therefore be programmed.[8]

Nonprogrammed decisions, on the other hand, are relatively unstructured and occur much less often. Disney's decision to buy Pixar was a nonprogrammed decision. Managers faced with such decisions must treat each one as unique, investing enormous amounts of time, energy, and resources into exploring the situation from

programmed decision
A decision that is fairly structured or recurs with some frequency (or both)

nonprogrammed decision
A decision that is relatively unstructured and occurs much less often than a programmed decision

all perspectives. Intuition and experience are major factors in nonprogrammed decisions. Most of the decisions made by top managers involving strategy (including mergers, acquisitions, and takeovers) and organization design are nonprogrammed. So are decisions about new facilities, new products, labor contracts, and legal issues.

Decision-Making Conditions

Just as there are different kinds of decisions, there are also different conditions in which decisions must be made. Managers sometimes have an almost perfect understanding of conditions surrounding a decision, but at other times they have few clues about those conditions. In general, as shown in Figure 4.1, the circumstances that exist for the decision maker are conditions of certainty, risk, or uncertainty.[9]

Decision Making Under Certainty When the decision maker knows with reasonable certainty what the alternatives are and what conditions are associated with each alternative, a ***state of certainty*** exists. Suppose, for example, that managers at Singapore Airlines make a decision to buy five new jumbo jets. Their next decision is from whom to buy them. Because there are only two companies in the world that make jumbo jets, Boeing and Airbus, Singapore Airlines knows its options exactly. Each has proven products and will guarantee prices and delivery dates. The airline thus knows the alternative conditions associated with each. There is little ambiguity and relatively little chance of making a bad decision.

Few organizational decisions, however, are made under conditions of true certainty. The complexity and turbulence of the contemporary business world make such situations rare. Even the airplane purchase decision we just considered has less certainty than it appears. The aircraft companies may not be able to really guarantee delivery dates, so they may write cost-increase or inflation clauses into contracts. Thus the airline may be only partially certain of the conditions surrounding each alternative.

Decision Making Under Risk A more common decision-making condition is a state of risk. Under a ***state of risk***, the availability of each alternative and its potential payoffs and costs are all associated with probability estimates. Suppose, for example, that a labor contract negotiator for a company receives a "final" offer from the union right before a strike deadline. The negotiator has

> **state of certainty**
> A condition in which the decision maker knows with reasonable certainty what the alternatives are and what conditions are associated with each alternative

> **state of risk**
> A condition in which the availability of each alternative and its potential payoffs and costs are all associated with probability estimates

Figure 4.1
DECISION-MAKING CONDITIONS

Most major decisions in organizations today are made under a state of uncertainty. Managers making decisions in these circumstances must be sure to learn as much as possible about the situation and approach the decision from a logical and rational perspective.

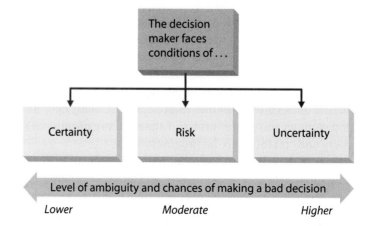

two alternatives: to accept or to reject the offer. The risk centers on whether the union representatives are bluffing. If the company negotiator accepts the offer, she avoids a strike but commits to a relatively costly labor contract. If she rejects the contract, she may get a more favorable contract if the union is bluffing, but she may provoke a strike if it is not.

On the basis of past experiences, relevant information, the advice of others, and her own judgment, she may conclude that there is about a 75 percent chance that union representatives are bluffing and about a 25 percent chance that they will back up their threats. Thus she can base a calculated decision on the two alternatives (accept or reject the contract demands) and the probable consequences of each. When making decisions under a state of risk, managers must reasonably estimate the probabilities associated with each alternative. For example, if the union negotiators are committed to a strike if their demands are not met, and the company negotiator rejects their demands because she guesses they will not strike, her miscalculation will prove costly. As indicated in Figure 4.1, decision making under conditions of risk is accompanied by moderate ambiguity and chances of a bad decision. Executives at Porsche have made several recent decisions under conditions of risk, starting with the question of whether the firm should join most of the world's other auto makers and build sport-utility vehicles (and potentially earn higher revenues) or maintain its focus on high-performance sports cars. Although the additional revenue is almost certain, the true risk in the firm's ultimate decision to build its Cayenne SUV is that the brand may lose some of its cachet among its existing customers. And now the firm is facing additional risky decisions regarding potential new products, including a four-door coupe, a smaller SUV, and even a minivan.[10]

Decision Making Under Uncertainty   Most of the major decision making in contemporary organizations is done under a ***state of uncertainty***. The decision maker does not know all the alternatives, the risks associated with each, or the likely consequences of each alternative. This uncertainty stems from the complexity and dynamism of contemporary organizations and their environments. The emergence of the Internet as a significant force in today's competitive environment has served to increase both revenue potential and uncertainty for most managers.

To make effective decisions in these circumstances, managers must acquire as much relevant information as possible and approach the situation from a logical and rational perspective. Intuition, judgment, and experience always play major roles in the decision-making process under conditions of uncertainty. Even so, uncertainty is the most ambiguous condition for managers and the one most prone to error.[11] Indeed, many of the problems associated with the downfall of Arthur Andersen resulted from the firm's apparent difficulties in responding to ambiguous and uncertain decision parameters regarding the firm's moral, ethical, and legal responsibilities.[12]

> **state of uncertainty**
> A condition in which the decision maker does not know all the alternatives, the risks associated with each, or the consequences each alternative is likely to have

Rational Perspectives on Decision Making

Most managers like to think of themselves as rational decision makers. And, indeed, many experts argue that managers should try to be as rational as possible in making decisions.[13] This section highlights the fundamental and rational perspectives on decision making.

A state of uncertainty exists when the decision maker does not know all the alternatives, the risks associated with each, or the consequences each alternatively is likely to have. When faced with uncertainty, a decision maker should acquire as much information as possible and approach the situation with logic and rationality. Of course, if all else fails, there is always the option shown here!

"Hurry it up, Solomon Brothers are waiting for my decision."

www.CartoonStock.com

The Classical Model of Decision Making

classical decision model
A prescriptive approach to decision making that tells managers how they should make decisions; assumes that managers are logical and rational and that their decisions will be in the best interests of the organization

The ***classical decision model*** is a prescriptive approach that tells managers how they should make decisions. It rests on the assumptions that managers are logical and rational and that they make decisions that are in the best interests of the organization. Figure 4.2 shows how the classical model views the decision-making process.

1. Decision makers have complete information about the decision situation and possible alternatives.

2. They can effectively eliminate uncertainty to achieve a decision condition of certainty.

3. They evaluate all aspects of the decision situation logically and rationally.

   As we see later, these conditions rarely, if ever, actually exist.

Steps in Rational Decision Making

A manager who really wants to approach a decision rationally and logically should try to follow the ***steps in rational decision making***, listed in Table 4.1. These steps

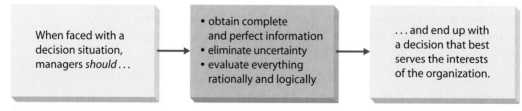

Figure 4.2
THE CLASSICAL MODEL OF DECISION MAKING
The classical model of decision making assumes that managers are rational and logical. It attempts to prescribe how managers should approach decision situations.

Table 4.1

Step	Detail	Example
1. Recognizing and defining the decision situation	Some stimulus indicates that a decision must be made. The stimulus may be positive or negative.	A plant manager sees that employee turnover has increased by 5 percent.
2. Identifying alternatives	Both obvious and creative alternatives are desired. In general, the more important the decision, the more alternatives should be generated.	The plant manager can increase wages, increase benefits, or change hiring standards.
3. Evaluating alternatives	Each alternative is evaluated to determine its feasibility, its satisfactoriness, and its consequences.	Increasing benefits may not be feasible. Increasing wages and changing hiring standards may satisfy all conditions.
4. Selecting the best alternative	Consider all situational factors and choose the alternative that best fits the manager's situation.	Changing hiring standards will take an extended period of time to cut turnover, so increase wages.
5. Implementing the chosen alternative	The chosen alternative is implemented into the organizational system.	The plant manager may need permission from corporate headquarters. The human resources department establishes a new wage structure.
6. Following up and evaluating the results	At some time in the future, the manager should ascertain the extent to which the alternative chosen in step 4 and implemented in step 5 has worked.	The plant manager notes that, six months later, turnover dropped to its previous level.

STEPS IN THE RATIONAL DECISION-MAKING PROCESS

Although the presumptions of the classical decision model rarely exist, managers can still approach decision making with rationality. By following the steps of rational decision making, managers ensure that they are learning as much as possible about the decision situation and its alternatives.

in rational decision making help keep the decision maker focused on facts and logic and help guard against inappropriate assumptions and pitfalls.

Recognizing and Defining the Decision Situation The first step in rational decision making is recognizing that a decision is necessary—that is, there must be some stimulus or spark to initiate the process. For many decisions and problem situations, the stimulus may occur without any prior warning. When equipment malfunctions, the manager must decide whether to repair or replace it. Or, when a major crisis erupts, as described in Chapter 3, the manager must quickly decide how to deal with it. As we already note, the stimulus for a decision may be either positive or negative. A manager who must decide how to invest surplus funds, for example, faces a positive decision situation. A negative financial stimulus could involve having to trim budgets because of cost overruns.

Inherent in problem recognition is the need to define precisely what the problem is. The manager must develop a complete understanding of the problem, its causes, and its relationship to other factors. This understanding comes from careful analysis and thoughtful consideration of the situation. Consider the situation currently being faced in the international air travel industry. Because of the

steps in rational decision making
Recognize and define the decision situation; identify appropriate alternatives; evaluate each alternative in terms of its feasibility, satisfactoriness, and consequences; select the best alternative; implement the chosen alternative; follow up and evaluate the results of the chosen alternative

growth of international travel related to business, education, and tourism, global carriers like Singapore Airlines, KLM, JAL, British Airways, American Airlines, and others need to increase their capacity for international travel. Because most major international airports are already operating at or near capacity, adding a significant number of new flights to existing schedules is not feasible. As a result, the most logical alternative is to increase capacity on existing flights. Thus Boeing and Airbus, the world's only manufacturers of large commercial aircraft, have recognized an important opportunity and have defined their decision situation as how to best respond to the need for increased global travel capacity.[14]

Identifying Alternatives Once the decision situation has been recognized and defined, the second step is to identify alternative courses of effective action. Developing both obvious, standard alternatives and creative, innovative alternatives is generally useful. In general, the more important the decision, the more attention is directed to developing alternatives.[15] If the decision involves a multimillion-dollar relocation, a great deal of time and expertise will be devoted to identifying the best locations. JCPenney once spent two years searching before selecting the Dallas–Fort Worth area for its new corporate headquarters. If the problem is to choose a color for the company softball team uniforms, less time and expertise will be brought to bear.

Although managers should seek creative solutions, they must also recognize that various constraints often limit their alternatives. Common constraints include legal restrictions, moral and ethical norms, authority constraints, and constraints imposed by the power and authority of the manager, available technology, economic considerations, and unofficial social norms. Boeing and Airbus identified three different alternatives to address the decision situation of increasing international airline travel capacity: they could independently develop new large planes, they could collaborate in a joint venture to create a single new large plane, or they could modify their largest existing planes to increase their capacity.

Evaluating Alternatives The third step in the decision-making process is evaluating each of the alternatives. Figure 4.3 presents a decision tree that can be used to judge different alternatives. The figure suggests that each alternative be evaluated

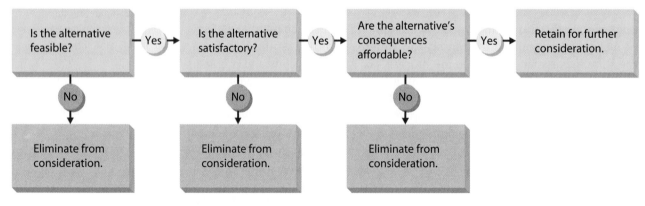

Figure 4.3
EVALUATING ALTERNATIVES IN THE DECISION-MAKING PROCESS
Managers must thoroughly evaluate all the alternatives, which increases the chances that the alternative finally chosen will be successful. Failure to evaluate an alternative's feasibility, satisfactoriness, and consequences can lead to a wrong decision.

in terms of its *feasibility*, its *satisfactoriness*, and its *consequences*. The first question to ask is whether an alternative is feasible. Is it within the realm of probability and practicality? For a small, struggling firm, an alternative requiring a huge financial outlay is probably out of the question. Other alternatives may not be feasible because of legal barriers. And limited human, material, and information resources may make other alternatives impractical.

When an alternative has passed the test of feasibility, it must next be examined to see how well it satisfies the conditions of the decision situation. For example, a manager searching for ways to double production capacity might initially consider purchasing an existing plant from another company. If more detailed analysis reveals that the new plant would increase production capacity by only 35 percent, this alternative may not be satisfactory. Finally, when an alternative has proven both feasible and satisfactory, its probable consequences must still be assessed. To what extent will a particular alternative influence other parts of the organization? What financial and nonfinancial costs will be associated with such influences? For example, a plan to boost sales by cutting prices may disrupt cash flows, require a new advertising program, and alter the behavior of sales representatives because it requires a different commission structure. The manager, then, must put "price tags" on the consequences of each alternative. Even an alternative that is both feasible and satisfactory must be eliminated if its consequences are too expensive for the total system. Airbus felt it would be at a disadvantage if it tried to simply enlarge its existing planes, because the Boeing 747 is already the largest aircraft being made and could readily be expanded to remain the largest. Boeing, meanwhile, was seriously concerned about the risk inherent in building a new and even larger plane, even if it shared the risk with Airbus as a joint venture.

Selecting an Alternative   Even though many alternatives fail to pass the triple tests of feasibility, satisfactoriness, and affordable consequences, two or more alternatives may remain. Choosing the best of these is the real crux of decision making. One approach is to choose the alternative with the optimal combination of feasibility, satisfactoriness, and affordable consequences. Even though most situations do not lend themselves to objective, mathematical analysis, the manager can often develop subjective estimates and weights for choosing an alternative.

Optimization is also a frequent goal. Because a decision is likely to affect several individuals or units, any feasible alternative will probably not maximize all of the relevant goals. Suppose that the manager of the Kansas City Royals needs to select a new outfielder for the upcoming baseball season. Bill hits .350 but has difficulty catching fly balls; Joe hits only .175 but is outstanding in the field; and Sam hits .290 and is a solid but not outstanding fielder. The manager probably would select Sam because of the optimal balance of hitting and fielding. Decision makers should also remember that finding multiple acceptable alternatives may be possible; selecting just one alternative and rejecting all the others might not be necessary. For example, the Royals's manager might decide that Sam will start each game, Bill will be retained as a pinch hitter, and Joe will be retained as a defensive substitute. In many hiring decisions, the candidates remaining after evaluation are ranked. If the top candidate rejects the offer, it may be automatically extended to the number-two candidate and, if necessary, to the remaining candidates in order. For the reasons noted earlier, Airbus proposed a joint venture with Boeing. Boeing, meanwhile, decided that its best course of action was to modify its existing 747 to increase its capacity. As a result, Airbus then decided to proceed on its own to develop and manufacture a new jumbo jet. Boeing, however, also decided that in addition to modifying its 747 it would also develop a new plane to offer as an alternative, albeit one not as large as the 747 or the proposed Airbus plane.

Implementing the Chosen Alternative After an alternative has been selected, the manager must put it into effect. In some decision situations, implementation is fairly easy; in others, it is more difficult. In the case of an acquisition, for example, managers must decide how to integrate all the activities of the new business, including purchasing, human resources practices, and distribution, into an ongoing organizational framework. For example, when Hewlett-Packard announced its acquisition of Compaq, managers also acknowledged that it would take at least a year to integrate the two firms into a single one. Operational plans, which we discussed in Chapter 3, are useful in implementing alternatives.

Managers must also consider people's resistance to change when implementing decisions. The reasons for such resistance include insecurity, inconvenience, and fear of the unknown. When JCPenney decided to move its headquarters from New York to Texas, many employees resigned rather than relocate. Managers should anticipate potential resistance at various stages of the implementation process. (Resistance to change is covered in Chapter 7.) Managers should also recognize that even when all alternatives have been evaluated as precisely as possible and the consequences of each alternative weighed, unanticipated consequences are still likely. Any number of factors—unexpected cost increases, a less-than-perfect fit with existing organizational subsystems, or unpredicted effects on cash flow or operating expenses, for example—could develop after implementation has begun. Boeing has set its engineers to work expanding the capacity of its 747 from today's 416 passengers to as many as 520 passengers by adding 30 feet to the plane's body. The company has also been developing its new plane intended for international travel, the 787. Airbus engineers, meanwhile, have been developing and constructing its new jumbo jet equipped with escalators and elevators, and capable of carrying 655 passengers. Airbus's development costs alone are estimated to be more than $12 billion.

Following Up and Evaluating the Results The final step in the decision-making process requires that managers evaluate the effectiveness of their decision—that is, they should make sure that the chosen alternative has served its original purpose. If an implemented alternative appears not to be working, the manager can respond in several ways. Another previously identified alternative (the original second or third choice, for instance) could be adopted. Or the manager might recognize that the situation was not correctly defined to begin with and start the process all over again. Finally, the manager might decide that the original alternative is in fact appropriate but has not yet had time to work or should be implemented in a different way.[16]

Failure to evaluate decision effectiveness may have serious consequences. The Pentagon once spent $1.8 billion and eight years developing the Sergeant York antiaircraft gun. From the beginning, tests revealed major problems with the weapon system, but not until it was in its final stages, when it was demonstrated that the gun was completely ineffective, was the project scrapped.

At this point, both Boeing and Airbus are nearing the crucial period when they will learn whether they made good decisions. Airbus's A380 is scheduled to make its

Behavioral forces often play a major role in how decisions get made. Take Truett Cathy, for example. Mr. Cathy founded and still runs Chick-Fil-A, a successful fast-food chain. Unlike virtually all of its competitors, though, Chick-Fil-A restaurants are closed on Sunday even though sales and profits would undoubtedly increase if the firm's restaurants opened everyday. The decision to maintain this policy reflects Cathy's view that people come before profits. Mr. Cathy is shown here speaking to a group of school kids touring the firm's headquarters in Georgia.

first commercial flight in 2007. Its final design allows seating for up to 850 people, and major airports around the world have been building new runways and terminal areas to accommodate the behemoth. Boeing's expanded 747 should be in service around the same time. Meanwhile, though, it appears that Boeing's secondary initiative for designing the new 787 may prove to be the best decision of all. A key element of the new plane is that it is much more fuel-efficient than other international airplanes. Given the dramatic surge in fuel costs in recent years, a fuel-efficient option like the 787 is apt to be an enormous success. However, the 787 will not be available for passenger service until 2009, so its real impact will not be known for a few more years.[17]

Behavioral Aspects of Decision Making

If all decision situations were approached as logically as described in the previous section, more decisions might prove to be successful. Yet decisions are often made with little consideration for logic and rationality. Some experts have estimated that U.S. companies use rational decision-making techniques less than 20 percent of the time.[18] And, even when organizations try to be logical, they sometimes fail. For example, when Starbucks opened its first coffee shops in New York, it relied on scientific marketing research, taste tests, and rational deliberation in making a decision to emphasize drip over espresso coffee. However, that decision still proved wrong, as New Yorkers strongly preferred the same espresso-style coffees that were Starbucks's mainstays in the West. Hence, the firm had to hastily reconfigure its stores to better meet customer preferences.

On the other hand, sometimes when a decision is made with little regard for logic, it can still turn out to be correct.[19] An important ingredient in how these forces work is the behavioral aspect of decision making. The administrative model better reflects these subjective considerations. Other behavioral aspects include political forces, intuition and escalation of commitment, risk propensity, and ethics.

The Administrative Model

Herbert A. Simon was one of the first experts to recognize that decisions are not always made with rationality and logic.[20] Simon was subsequently awarded the Nobel Prize in economics. Rather than prescribing how decisions should be made, his view of decision making, now called the ***administrative model***, describes how decisions often actually are made. As illustrated in Figure 4.4, the model holds that managers (1) use incomplete and imperfect information, (2) are constrained by bounded rationality, and (3) tend to "satisfice" when making decisions.

administrative model
A decision-making model that argues that decision makers (1) use incomplete and imperfect information, (2) are constrained by bounded rationality, and (3) tend to "satisfice" when making decisions

bounded rationality
A concept suggesting that decision makers are limited by their values and unconscious reflexes, skills, and habits

satisficing
The tendency to search for alternatives only until one is found that meets some minimum standard of sufficiency

Bounded rationality suggests that decision makers are limited by their values and unconscious reflexes, skills, and habits. They are also limited by less-than-complete information and knowledge. Bounded rationality partially explains how U.S. auto executives allowed Japanese auto makers to get such a strong foothold in the U.S. domestic market. For years, executives at GM, Ford, and Chrysler compared their companies' performance only to one another's and ignored foreign imports. The foreign "threat" was not acknowledged until the domestic auto market had been changed forever. If managers had gathered complete information from the beginning, they might have been better able to thwart foreign competitors. Essentially, then, the concept of bounded rationality suggests that although people try to be rational decision makers, their rationality has limits.

Another important part of the administrative model is ***satisficing***. This concept suggests that rather than conducting an exhaustive search for the best possible alternative, decision makers tend to search only until they identify an alternative that meets some minimum standard of sufficiency. A manager looking for a site for a new plant, for example, may select the first site she finds that meets basic requirements for transportation, utilities, and price, even though further search might yield a better location. People satisfice for a variety of reasons. Managers may simply be unwilling to ignore their own motives (such as reluctance to spend time making a decision) and therefore not be able to continue searching after a minimally acceptable alternative is identified. The decision maker may be unable to weigh and evaluate large numbers of alternatives and criteria. Also, subjective and personal considerations often intervene in decision situations.

Because of the inherent imperfection of information, bounded rationality, and satisficing, the decisions made by a manager may or may not actually be in the best interests of the organization. A manager may choose a particular location for the new plant because it offers the lowest price and best availability of utilities and transportation. Or she may choose the location because it is located in a community where she wants to live.

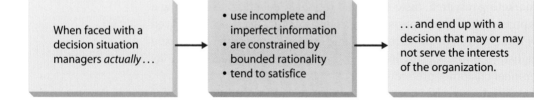

When faced with a decision situation managers *actually* . . .

- use incomplete and imperfect information
- are constrained by bounded rationality
- tend to satisfice

. . . and end up with a decision that may or may not serve the interests of the organization.

Figure 4.4

THE ADMINISTRATIVE MODEL OF DECISION MAKING

The administrative model is based on behavioral processes that affect how managers make decisions. Rather than prescribing how decisions should be made, it focuses more on describing how they are made.

In summary, then, the classical and administrative models paint quite different pictures of decision making. Which is more correct? Actually, each can be used to better understand how managers make decisions. The classical model is prescriptive: it explains how managers can at least attempt to be more rational and logical in their approaches to decisions. The administrative model can be used by managers to develop a better understanding of their inherent biases and limitations.[21] In the following sections, we describe more fully other behavioral forces that can influence decisions.

Political Forces in Decision Making

Political forces are another major element that contributes to the behavioral nature of decision making. Organizational politics is covered in Chapter 11, but one major element of politics, coalitions, is especially relevant to decision making. A **coalition** is an informal alliance of individuals or groups formed to achieve a common goal. This common goal is often a preferred decision alternative. For example, coalitions of stockholders frequently band together to force a board of directors to make a certain decision.

> **coalition**
> An informal alliance of individuals or groups formed to achieve a common goal

The impact of coalitions can be either positive or negative. They can help astute managers get the organization on a path toward effectiveness and profitability, or they can strangle well-conceived strategies and decisions. Managers must recognize when to use coalitions, how to assess whether coalitions are acting in the best interests of the organization, and how to constrain their dysfunctional effects.[22]

Intuition and Escalation of Commitment

Two other important decision processes that go beyond logic and rationality are intuition and escalation of commitment to a chosen course of action.

Intuition *Intuition* is an innate belief about something, without conscious consideration. Managers sometimes decide to do something because it "feels right" or they have a "hunch." This feeling usually is not arbitrary, however. Rather, it is based on years of experience and practice in making decisions in similar situations.[23] An inner sense may help managers make an occasional decision without going through a full-blown rational sequence of steps. For example, the New York Yankees once contacted three major athletic shoe manufacturers—Nike, Reebok, and Adidas—and informed them that they were looking to make a sponsorship deal. While Nike and Reebok were carefully and rationally assessing the possibilities, managers at Adidas quickly realized that a partnership with the Yankees made a lot of sense for them. They responded very quickly to the idea and ended up hammering out a contract while the competitors were still analyzing details.[24] Of course, all managers, but most especially inexperienced ones, should be careful not to rely too heavily on intuition. If rationality and logic are continually flouted for "what feels right," the odds are that disaster will strike one day.

> **intuition**
> An innate belief about something, without conscious consideration

Escalation of Commitment Another important behavioral process that influences decision making is **escalation of commitment** to a chosen course of action. In particular, decision makers sometimes make decisions and then become so committed to the courses of action suggested by those decisions that they stay with them, even when the decisions appear to have been wrong.[25] For example, when people buy stock in a company, they sometimes refuse to sell it even after repeated

> **escalation of commitment**
> A decision maker's staying with a decision even when it appears to be wrong

drops in price. They choose a course of action—buying the stock in anticipation of making a profit—and then stay with it even in the face of increasing losses. Moreover, after the value drops, they rationalize that they can't sell now because they will lose money.

For years Pan American World Airways ruled the skies and used its profits to diversify into real estate and other businesses. But, with the advent of deregulation, Pan Am began to struggle and lose market share to other carriers. When Pan Am managers finally realized how ineffective their airline operations had become, experts today point out that the "rational" decision would have been to sell off the remaining airline operations and concentrate on the firm's more profitable businesses. But because they still saw the company as being first and foremost an airline, they instead began to slowly sell off the firm's profitable holdings to keep the airline flying. Eventually, the company was left with nothing but an ineffective and inefficient airline, and then had to sell off its more profitable routes before eventually being taken over by Delta. Had Pan Am managers made the more rational decision years earlier, chances are the firm could still be a profitable enterprise today, albeit one with no involvement in the airline industry.[26]

Thus decision makers must walk a fine line. On the one hand, they must guard against sticking too long with an incorrect decision. To do so can bring about financial decline. On the other hand, managers should not bail out of a seemingly incorrect decision too soon, as Adidas once did. Adidas had dominated the market for professional athletic shoes. It subsequently entered the market for amateur sports shoes and did well there also. But managers interpreted a sales slowdown as a sign that the boom in athletic shoes was over. They thought that they had made the wrong decision and ordered drastic cutbacks. The market took off again with Nike at the head of the pack, and Adidas never recovered. Fortunately, a new management team has changed the way Adidas makes decisions, and the firm is again on its way to becoming a force in the athletic shoe and apparel markets.

Risk Propensity and Decision Making

risk propensity
The extent to which a decision maker is willing to gamble when making a decision

The behavioral element of **risk propensity** is the extent to which a decision maker is willing to gamble when making a decision. Some managers are cautious about every decision they make. They try to adhere to the rational model and are extremely conservative in what they do. Such managers are more likely to avoid mistakes, and they infrequently make decisions that lead to big losses. Other managers are extremely aggressive in making decisions and are willing to take risks.[27] They rely heavily on intuition, reach decisions quickly, and often risk big investments on their decisions. As in gambling, these managers are more likely than their conservative counterparts to achieve big successes with their decisions; they are also more likely to incur greater losses.[28] The organization's culture is a prime ingredient in fostering different levels of risk propensity.

Ethics and Decision Making

As we introduce in Chapter 4, individual ethics are personal beliefs about right and wrong behavior. Ethics are clearly related to decision making in a number of ways. For example, suppose that, after careful analysis, a manager realizes that his company could save money by closing his department and subcontracting with a supplier for the same services. But to recommend this course of action would result in the loss of several jobs, including his own. His own ethical standards will clearly shape how he proceeds.[29] Indeed, each component of managerial ethics (relationships of the firm to its employees, of employees to the firm, and of the firm to other economic agents) involves a wide variety of decisions, all of which are likely to have an ethical component. A manager must remember, then, that, just as behavioral processes such as politics and risk propensity affect the decisions she makes, so, too, do her ethical beliefs.

Group and Team Decision Making in Organizations

In more and more organizations today, important decisions are made by groups and teams rather than by individuals. Examples include the executive committee of General Motors, product design teams at Texas Instruments, and marketing planning groups at Dell Computer. Managers can typically choose whether to have individuals or groups and teams make a particular decision. Thus knowing about forms of group and team decision making and their advantages and disadvantages is important.[30]

Forms of Group and Team Decision Making

The most common methods of group and team decision making are interacting groups, Delphi groups, and nominal groups. Increasingly, these methods of group decision making are being conducted online.[31]

Interacting Groups and Teams *Interacting groups and teams* are the most common form of decision-making group. The format is simple—either an existing or a newly designated group or team is asked to make a decision. Existing groups or teams might be functional departments, regular work teams, or standing committees. Newly designated groups or teams can be ad hoc committees, task forces, or newly constituted work teams. The group or team members talk among themselves, argue, agree, argue some more, form internal coalitions, and so forth. Finally, after some period of deliberation, the group or team makes its decision. An advantage of this method is that the interaction among people often sparks new ideas and promotes understanding. A major disadvantage, though, is that political processes can play too big a role.

> *interacting group or team*
> A decision-making group or team in which members openly discuss, argue about, and agree on the best alternative

Delphi Groups A *Delphi group* is sometimes used to develop a consensus of expert opinion. Developed by the Rand Corporation, the Delphi procedure solicits input from a panel of experts who contribute individually. Their opinions are combined and, in effect, averaged. Assume, for example, that the problem is to establish an expected date for a major technological breakthrough in converting coal into usable energy. The first step in using the Delphi procedure is to obtain the cooperation of a panel of experts. For this situation, experts might include various research scientists, university researchers, and executives in a relevant energy industry. At first, the experts are asked to anonymously predict a time frame for the expected breakthrough. The persons coordinating the Delphi group collect the responses, average them, and ask the experts for another prediction. In this round, the experts who provided unusual or extreme predictions may be asked to justify them. These explanations may then be relayed to the other experts. When the predictions stabilize, the average prediction is taken to represent the decision of the group of experts. The time, expense, and logistics of the Delphi technique

> *Delphi group*
> A form of group decision making in which a group is used to achieve a consensus of expert opinion

rule out its use for routine, everyday decisions, but it has been successfully used for forecasting technological breakthroughs at Boeing, market potential for new products at General Motors, research and development patterns at Eli Lilly, and future economic conditions by the U.S. government.[32]

Nominal Groups   Another useful group and team decision-making technique that is occasionally used is the **nominal group**. Unlike the Delphi method, in which group members do not see one another, nominal group members are brought together in a face-to-face setting. The members represent a group in name only, however; they do not talk to one another freely like the members of interacting groups. Nominal groups are used most often to generate creative and innovative alternatives or ideas. To begin, the manager assembles a group of knowledgeable experts and outlines the problem to them. The group members are then asked to individually write down as many alternatives as they can think of. The members then take turns stating their ideas, which are recorded on a flip chart or board at the front of the room. Discussion is limited to simple clarification. After all alternatives have been listed, more open discussion takes place. Group members then vote, usually by rank-ordering the various alternatives. The highest-ranking alternative represents the decision of the group. Of course, the manager in charge may retain the authority to accept or reject the group decision.

> **nominal group**
> A structured technique used to generate creative and innovative alternatives or ideas

Advantages of Group and Team Decision Making

The advantages and disadvantages of group and team decision making relative to individual decision making are summarized in Table 4.2. One advantage is simply that more information is available in a group or team setting—as suggested by the old axiom "Two heads are better than one." A group or team represents a variety of

---

Eye on Management

Team Decision Making at the Riverwood Clinic

This seven-minute video shows three employees of the Riverwood Clinic debating the relative merits of two different locations for an important fund-raising event. Much of the discussion presents varying perceptions of each of the choices. Some of the information presented is factual and would support a rational decision-making process. Behavioral aspects of decision making also play an important part in this discussion.

View the video and then answer the following questions individually or as a class.

1. In what ways is this decision process rational? In what ways does this video reflect behavioral aspects of the decision process?

2. How should this decision be made—on a rational basis or with consideration of behavioral elements? Or should the process be some combination of both? Explain why you think so.

3. Consider the male employee, who appears to be in charge of the meeting. At one point in the video, he repeats the two women's points and seems about to reach a conclusion. Instead, he sums up with, "Oh, I don't know." Do you think he genuinely didn't know his opinion, or was he making that comment as a tactic? If it was a tactic, what was he trying to accomplish? Did he succeed?

4. Do you think the ultimate decision was the "best" one? Why or why not? You can consider both rational and behavioral elements in your answer.

5. How did the use of teams impact the effectiveness of the ultimate decision? How would the ultimate decision have differed if this decision had been made by just one individual?

Advantages	Disadvantages
1. More information and knowledge are available.	1. The process takes longer than individual decision making, so it is costlier.
2. More alternatives are likely to be generated.	2. Compromise decisions resulting from indecisiveness may emerge.
3. More acceptance of the final decision is likely.	3. One person may dominate the group.
4. Enhanced communication of the decision may result.	4. Groupthink may occur.
5. Better decisions generally emerge.	

Table 4.2

ADVANTAGES AND DISADVANTAGES OF GROUP AND TEAM DECISION MAKING

To increase the chances that a group or team decision will be successful, managers must learn how to manage the process of group and team decision making. Federal Express and IBM are increasingly using groups and teams in the decision-making process.

education, experience, and perspective. Partly as a result of this increased information, groups and teams typically can identify and evaluate more alternatives than can one person.[33] The people involved in a group or team decision understand the logic and rationale behind it, are more likely to accept it, and are equipped to communicate the decision to their work group or department.[34] Finally, research evidence suggests that groups may make better decisions than individuals.[35]

Disadvantages of Group and Team Decision Making

Perhaps the biggest drawback of group and team decision making is the additional time and hence the greater expense entailed. The increased time stems from interaction and discussion among group or team members. If a given manager's time is worth $50 an hour, and if the manager spends two hours making a decision, the decision "costs" the organization $100. For the same decision, a group of five managers might require three hours of time. At the same $50-an-hour rate, the decision "costs" the organization $750. Assuming the group or team decision is better, the additional expense may be justified, but the fact remains that group and team decision making is more costly.

Group or team decisions may also represent undesirable compromises.[36] For example, hiring a compromise top manager may be a bad decision in the long run because he or she may not be able to respond adequately to various subunits in the organization nor have everyone's complete support. Sometimes one individual dominates the group process to the point where others cannot make a full contribution. This dominance may stem from a desire for power or from a naturally dominant personality. The problem is that what appears to emerge as a group decision may actually be the decision of one person.

Finally, a group or team may succumb to a phenomenon known as "groupthink." **Groupthink** occurs when the desire for consensus and cohesiveness overwhelms the goal of reaching the best possible decision.[37] Under the influence of groupthink, the group may arrive at decisions that are made not in the best interests of either the group or the organization, but rather to avoid conflict among group members. One of the most clearly documented examples of groupthink involved the space shuttle *Challenger* disaster. As NASA was preparing to launch the shuttle, numerous problems and questions arose. At each step of the way, however, decision makers argued that there was no reason to delay and that everything would be fine. Shortly after its launch, the shuttle exploded, killing all seven crew members.

groupthink
A situation that occurs when a group or team's desire for consensus and cohesiveness overwhelms its desire to reach the best possible decision

Managing Group and Team Decision-Making Processes

Managers can do several things to help promote the effectiveness of group and team decision making. One is simply being aware of the pros and cons of having a group or team make a decision to start with. Time and cost can be managed by setting a deadline by which the decision must be made final. Dominance can be at least partially avoided if a special group is formed just to make the decision. An astute manager, for example, should know who in the organization may try to dominate and can either avoid putting that person in the group or put several strong-willed people together.

To avoid groupthink, each member of the group or team should critically evaluate all alternatives. So that members present divergent viewpoints, the leader should not make his or her own position known too early. At least one member of the group or team might be assigned the role of devil's advocate. And, after reaching a preliminary decision, the group or team should hold a follow-up meeting wherein divergent viewpoints can be raised again if any group members wish to do so.[38] Gould Paper Corporation used these methods by assigning managers to two different teams. The teams then spent an entire day in a structured debate presenting the pros and cons of each side of an issue to ensure the best possible decision. Sun Microsystems makes most of its major decisions using this same approach.

Summary of Key Points

1. Define decision making and discuss types of decisions and decision-making conditions.
   - Decision making is the act of choosing one alternative from among a set of alternatives.
   - The decision-making process includes recognizing and defining the nature of a decision situation, identifying alternatives, choosing the "best" alternative, and putting it into practice.
   - Two common types of decisions are programmed and nonprogrammed.
   - Decisions may be made under states of certainty, risk, or uncertainty.

2. Discuss rational perspectives on decision making, including the steps in rational decision making.
   - Rational perspectives on decision making rest on the classical model.
   - This model assumes that managers have complete information and that they will behave rationally. The primary steps in rational decision making are
     - recognizing and defining the situation
     - identifying alternatives
     - evaluating alternatives
     - selecting the best alternative
     - implementing the chosen alternative

   - following up and evaluating the effectiveness of the alternative after it is implemented

3. Describe the behavioral aspects of decision making.
   - Behavioral aspects of decision making rely on the administrative model.
   - This model recognizes that managers use incomplete information and that they do not always behave rationally.
   - The administrative model also recognizes the concepts of bounded rationality and satisficing.
   - Political activities by coalitions, managerial intuition, and the tendency to become increasingly committed to a chosen course of action are all important.
   - Risk propensity is another important behavioral perspective on decision making.
   - Ethics also affect how managers make decisions.

4. Discuss group and team decision making, including the advantages and disadvantages of group and team decision making and how it can be more effectively managed.
   - To help enhance decision-making effectiveness, managers often use interacting, Delphi, or nominal groups or teams.

- Group and team decision making in general has several advantages as well as disadvantages relative to individual decision making.

- Managers can adopt a number of strategies to help groups and teams make better decisions.

Discussion Questions

Questions for Review

1. Describe the difference between programmed and nonprogrammed decisions. What are the implications of these differences for decision makers?

2. What are the different conditions under which decisions are made?

3. Describe the behavioral nature of decision making. Be certain to provide some detail about political forces, risk propensity, ethics, and commitment in your description.

4. What is meant by the term *escalation of commitment?* In your opinion, under what conditions is escalation of commitment likely to occur?

5. Explain the differences between three common methods of group decision making—interacting groups, Delphi groups, and nominal groups.

Questions for Analysis

6. Was your decision about what college or university to attend a rational decision? Did you go through each step in rational decision making? If not, why not?

7. Most business decisions are made under conditions of either risk or uncertainty. In your opinion, is it easier to make a decision under a condition of risk or a condition of uncertainty? Why?

8. Recall a decision that you recently made that had ethical implications. Did these implications make the decision easier or harder?

9. In what ways are escalation of commitment and decision making under conditions of risk closely related to one another?

10. Consider the following list of business decisions. Which decisions would be handled most effectively by group or team decision making? Which would be handled most effectively by individual decision making? Explain your answers.
- A decision about switching pencil suppliers
- A decision about hiring a new CEO
- A decision about firing an employee for stealing
- A decision about calling 911 to report a fire in the warehouse
- A decision about introducing a brand-new product

Building Effective Conceptual Skills

Exercise Overview

Conceptual skills reflect the manager's ability to think in the abstract. This exercise will help you understand the effect that nonrational biases and risk propensity can have on decision making.

Exercise Background

Two psychologists, Amos Tversky and Daniel Kahneman, conducted much of the research that led to our knowledge of decision-making biases. Tversky and Kahneman found that they could understand individuals' real-life choices by presenting experimental subjects with simulated decisions in a laboratory setting. They developed a theory they called "prospect theory," which uses behavioral psychology to explain why individuals are nonrational when making economic decisions. Their work has contributed a great deal to the developing discipline of behavioral economics. In fact, in 2002 Kahneman won the Nobel Prize in economics for development of these concepts. (Tversky could not share in the award because the Nobel Prize cannot be given posthumously.)

Tversky and Kahneman's most important finding was that an individual's *perception* of gain or loss in a situation is more important than an objective measure of gain or loss. Thus individuals are nonrational; that is, they do not make decisions purely on the basis of rational criteria. Related to this conclusion, Tversky and Kahneman found that humans think differently about gains from the way they think about losses. This is called "framing." Another finding is that people allow their perceptions to be skewed positively or negatively, depending on what information they receive first. Later, when new information becomes available, people have a hard time letting go of their initial perceptions, even if the new information contradicts their original impression. This effect is referred to as "anchoring and adjustment."

In order to answer the questions that follow, you must be able to calculate an expected value. To calculate an expected value, multiply each possible outcome value by the probability of its occurrence, and then sum all the results. Here is a simple example: You have a 50 percent chance of earning 80 points on an exam and a 50 percent chance of earning 70 points. The expected value can be calculated as $(.5 \times 80) + (.5 \times 70)$, or a .5 chance of 80 points (equal to 40 points) plus a .5 chance of 70 points (equal to 35 points). Therefore, the expected value of your exam is 75 points.

Exercise Task

This exercise must be done during class time. Your professor will pass out the list of questions during class.

Answer the list of brief questions that your professor will provide to you. No answer is correct or incorrect; simply choose your most likely response. Then, when the professor asks, share your answers with the class.

1. Discuss the answers given by the class. Why do students' answers differ?

2. What have you learned about decision-making biases and risk propensity from these experiments?

(Reprinted by permission of the author Margaret Hill.)

Building Effective Decision-Making Skills

Exercise Overview

Decision-making skills reflect the manager's ability to recognize and define problems and opportunities correctly and then to select an appropriate course of action for solving problems and capitalizing on opportunities.

This exercise will enable you to compare individual decision making with decision making conducted through the use of nominal groups.

Exercise Background

Individual decision making has some advantages—for example, speed, simplicity, and lack of conflict. However, there are times when these advantages are outweighed by other considerations. Innovation, in particular, is lower when one person makes a decision alone. A group decision is preferable when innovation is required, because more input from more diverse individuals can generate more varied alternative courses of action.

Nominal groups are especially well suited for fostering creativity. Nominal groups give individuals the freedom to list as many creative alternatives as they can, without worrying about criticism or political pressure. Nominal groups also pool input from many individuals and allow creative responses to the pooled input. Thus nominal groups foster creativity by combining techniques for improving both individual and group innovation.

Exercise Task

1. Assume that your class represents the top administrators of a state-run university with about 15,000 students. The university is currently facing a problem. Over the last three years, there have been an increasing number of applicants to the school. However, the university's staff and physical facilities have remained at the same level. The school is under pressure from students and their families to admit more applicants. The state legislature, which provides over half of the university's funds, is responding to this pressure by

asking the university to increase enrollment by at least 3,000 students. However, they are unwilling to increase funding at all to help pay for the expansion.

2. Individually, write down as many creative responses to the problem as you can. Do not worry about whether the alternatives you are generating are practical. In fact, try to list as many different, even "far-out," responses as you can.

3. Share your list with the class.

4. Ask other students questions about their suggestions only for purposes of clarification. Do not, under any circumstances, reveal whether you think any idea is "good" or "bad."

5. After all the individual ideas are listed and clarified, add to the list any other ideas you have developed.

6. As a class, vote on the list. Choose the three actions that you think are most likely to resolve the problem to the satisfaction of the interested parties.

7. Did the nominal group technique generate alternatives that are more creative than those you generated on your own?

8. In your opinion, are the alternatives chosen by the class vote "better" solutions than those you thought of on your own? Explain your answer.

9. Give some suggestions about what types of decisions in organizations could be effectively made through nominal-group decision making. When should it *not* be used?

Building Effective Technical Skills

Exercise Overview

Technical skills are the skills necessary to accomplish or understand the specific kind of work being done in an organization. This exercise will enable you to practice technical skills in using the Internet to obtain information for making a decision.

Exercise Background

Assume that you are a business owner seeking a location for a new factory. Your company makes products that are relatively "clean"—that is, they do not pollute the environment, nor will your factory produce any dangerous waste products. Thus most communities would welcome your plant.

You are seeking a place that has a stable and well-educated workforce, as well as ample affordable housing, access to quality health care, and a good educational system. You have narrowed your choice to the following towns.

1. Santa Cruz, California

2. Madison, Wisconsin

3. Manhattan, Kansas

4. College Station, Texas

5. Amherst, Massachusetts

6. Athens, Georgia

Exercise Task

With this background information as context, do the following:

1. Use the Internet to research each of these cities.

2. Rank-order the cities on the basis of the criteria noted.

3. Select the best city for your new factory.

Skills Self-Assessment Instrument

Decision-Making Styles

Introduction: Decision making is clearly important. However, individuals differ in their decision-making style, or the way they approach decisions. The following assessment is designed to help you understand your decision-making style.

Instructions: Respond to the following statements by indicating the extent to which they describe you. Circle the response that best represents your self-evaluation.

1. Overall, I'm _____ to act.

    1. quick   2. moderately fast   3. slow

2. I spend _____ amount of time making important decisions as/than I do making less important ones.

    1. about the same   2. a greater   3. a much greater

3. When making decisions, I _____ go with my first thought.

    1. usually   2. occasionally   3. rarely

4. When making decisions, I'm _____ concerned about making errors.

    1. rarely   2. occasionally   3. often

5. When making decisions, I _____ recheck my work more than once.

    1. rarely   2. occasionally   3. usually

6. When making decisions, I gather _____ information.

    1. little   2. some   3. lots of

7. When making decisions, I consider _____ alternatives.

    1. few   2. some   3. lots of

8. I usually make decisions _____ before the deadline.

    1. way   2. somewhat   3. just

9. After making a decision, I _____ look for other alternatives, wishing I had waited.

    1. rarely   2. occasionally   3. usually

10. I _____ regret having made a decision.

    1. rarely   2. occasionally   3. often

Source: Adapted from Lussier, Robert N., *Supervision: A Skill-Building Approach*, Second Edition, pp. 122–123, copyright © 1994 by Richard D. Irwin, Inc. Reproduced with permission of The McGraw-Hill Companies. For interpretation, see Interpretations of Skills Self-Assessment Instruments in the appendix near the end of this text.

Experiential Exercise

Decision Making with Journaling and Affinity Diagrams

Purpose: This exercise gives you practice in using both journaling and affinity diagrams, both of which are tools for effective decision making. These techniques can be used to help expand and improve your decision making in many areas of your life, both personal and professional.

Introduction: The chemist Linus Pauling, winner of Nobel Prizes in both Chemistry and Peace, said, "The best way to have a good idea is to have a lot of ideas." Journaling is one technique to increase the quantity of ideas generated in response to a decision situation. Affinity diagrams can be used alone or in conjunction with journaling or other idea-generation techniques. Affinity diagrams help you to interpret and organize a quantity of diverse ideas. The diagrams are particularly useful in decision situations that involve lots of ideas, where the ideas are very different from each other and the relationships between the ideas are not well understood, and where the underlying questions seem overwhelming or too complex to analyze rationally.

Instructions:

1. Have on hand a number of index cards or sticky notes, at least 50. Or use several sheets of paper cut into at least 50 smaller slips. Set aside 30 minutes or so of quiet time. Assume that graduation day is approaching and you are faced with the decision about where to live. Assume that your options are broad and that the decision will be for at least five years but would not necessarily commit you for the rest of your life. You could choose to live in an urban, suburban, or rural community. You could choose a large or small community, various regions of the country or world, and many different types of social and economic settings.

2. Think about the qualities you desire for your future hometown. Briefly jot qualities that you desire, putting one quality on each piece of paper. Relax and visualize your ideal community, and then commit the ideas to paper. For example, your ideas might include "ethnic diversity" or "upscale suburb." Or something quite different might be important to you. Allow the answers to just "come to" you. Don't try to force your

thinking along any one path. Don't edit yourself or criticize your thoughts at this point in the process. It's OK to have some ideas that don't seem rational, that are duplicates, or even some ideas that seem meaningless.

If you can, work quickly and without interruption. Try to generate at least 25 ideas. If that number comes easily to you, generate some more. Stop when you feel that you've exhausted your supply of ideas. This process is one way to use the technique known as "journaling."

3. Lay out the slips of paper so you can see all of them and then read them. Begin to move the slips of paper into groups of ideas that are similar to each other. Gradually, as you rearrange the slips, patterns of ideas will emerge. Again, don't try to be critical or rational at this point, simply consider the relationships between the ideas. Keep moving the slips into different combinations until you find a set of groups that "feels right."

Then assign each of these groups a theme that identifies the common element. For example, you might group the ideas "green housing," "good public transportation," and "vegetarian restaurants" into a theme called "environmentally conscious." Or you might group "good public transportation," "short commute to work," and "walk to restaurants and stores" into a theme called "convenience." The finished project, a grouping of a diverse set of ideas into related themes, is called an "affinity diagram."

Follow-up Questions:

1. Did the techniques of journaling and affinity diagramming help you generate more ideas and better see the connections between ideas? If so, explain how. If not, what technique(s) would have worked better?

2. Note that both of these techniques explicitly encourage the behavioral aspects of decision making, especially intuition. Do you think this is appropriate when making this type of decision? Or would a more rational approach be more effective?

3. How might a manager use these techniques at work? What situations would not be appropriate for the use of these techniques?

CHAPTER CLOSING CASE

THE DECISION-MAKING MIND OF MICROSOFT

There was a time when Microsoft seemed unbeatable. Early dominance in the operating systems industry gave the company the resources to relentlessly upgrade their products, copy popular features from other software companies, and acquire competitors with promising ideas. Every year, Microsoft seemed to increase in size and power. Today that has changed. While many in the industry still respect the company's preeminent position, Microsoft now displays a vulnerability—in online applications.

Microsoft employs some of the top minds in the industry, has extensive industry experience, and is flush with cash. At first glance, it seems that if any company can adapt and thrive as the industry shifts focus to online applications, Microsoft would be the one. But the company is losing ground. It's losing the online battle to Google, and it's trailing Sony and Nintendo in video games, Apple in music players, and IBM in business applications. While Microsoft earned revenues greater than $44 billion in 2006, less than 10 percent of that was from online ventures. Old-line programs MS Office and Windows contributed 80 percent of profits. To regain its former position, Microsoft must make the right decisions.

CEO Steve Ballmer leads with his positive attitude and drive. "You've got to be very realistic about where you are, but very optimistic about where you can be. You have to believe," he says. "If we don't get it right at first, we'll just keep coming and coming and coming and

coming." Yet in spite of his leadership, and that of chairman and founder Bill Gates, in the past Microsoft has been slow to recognize the need to change. In the 1980 when networking was a relatively new field, Microsoft hesitated because the business was so different from the market for desktop PC software. Competitor Novell stepped into the void and it took Microsoft years to catch up. Microsoft also divested some online services in the 1990s, when they were slow to catch on. Ballmer admits his timidity was a mistake.

Today Ballmer tries to be an advocate for creativity and broad-minded thinking. He says, "Focus is an essential thing, but you sort of want to focus short-term and be expansive long-term." He is building alliances with other high-tech manufacturers, such as the company's partnership with EMC, which makes data storage products. From these alliances, Microsoft not only augments its power and splits venture costs but also gains access to the firms' specialized knowledge. Ballmer gives about 120 speeches each year to industry associations. At these meetings, he also holds a dozen or more smaller meetings, each focused on a particular subset of the industry, problem, or technology. Again, he comes away with specific information.

However, Ballmer excels most at internal, intense meetings to hash out strategic direction. In 2000, the company's top leaders met to discuss the controversial topic of video gaming. Ballmer told everyone, even

Gates, that they couldn't leave the room until the issues were decided. The result was the Xbox. In 2005, Ballmer took top executives on a retreat to determine Microsoft's response to competition in Internet services. After 14 hours during which employees vented about past mistakes and brainstormed new ideas, the group emerged with a plan for bringing the Internet into every application. One great resource is industry veteran Ray Ozzie, newly hired by Microsoft. Ozzie, the creator of Lotus Notes, has become the strategic visionary and voice for the online revolution at Microsoft. He listens to even the lowliest programmer and drafts comprehensive statements that capture Microsoft's strategies and culture in unique ways.

Another new hire is Gary Flake, former head of research at Yahoo!, who turned down an offer from Google after he observed Microsoft managers in action. "[I was] stunned at how open the company was to change, how self-critical the culture was," Flake observes. "Microsoft, more than the others, is redefining itself." How exactly will that be accomplished? Microsoft won't say. The company announced that 2007 spending would be $2 billion greater than in 2006, but gave no further details.

One possibility is a rumored new product that puts basic Office technology on the Internet for free. That could help Microsoft compete with Google, which already offers a similar service. On the other hand, it may cannibalize sales of Microsoft's top-selling, lucrative software. Whatever the answer is, hopefully that spending will create some new businesses to drive future growth. To quote one analyst's advice, Microsoft should "[b]e aggressive. . . . Come out swinging. Embrace the new model."

CASE QUESTIONS

1. Use the rational decision-making model to explain why Microsoft can make better decisions when it has more complete and diverse sources of information.

2. Use the behavioral decision-making model to explain why Microsoft can make better decisions when it has more complete and diverse sources of information.

3. What form of group decision making does Microsoft use? Does Microsoft appear to suffer from any of the potential drawbacks of that form? Explain.

REFERENCES

Jay Greene, "Microsoft Brings the Work Online," *BusinessWeek*, September 14, 2006, www.businessweek.com on January 20, 2007; Jay Greene, "Microsoft's Strange Spending Splurge," *BusinessWeek*, April 28, 2006, www.businessweek.com on January 20, 2007; Catherine Holahan, "Can Microsoft Out-Google Google? *BusinessWeek*, September 13, 2006, www.businessweek.com on January 20, 2007; David Kirkpatrick, "Microsoft's New Brain," *Fortune*, April 18, 2006, www.fortune.com on May 15, 2006; Steve Lohr, "Preaching from the Ballmer Pulpit, *New York Times*, January 28 2007, pp. BU1, 8, 9.

YOU MAKE THE CALL

Making Tough Choices at Wal-Mart

1. Would you like to work as a marketing manager at Wal-Mart? Would you like to be hired as a new marketing manager at Wal-Mart? Why or why not?

2. If you were in charge of Wal-Mart's marketing, how would you encourage the old and new managers to make decisions as a team?

3. Would you like to invest in Wal-Mart? Why or why not?

4. Do you shop at Wal-Mart? If not, what could the company do to attract you as a customer?

5. Are there any companies that you do not support because of moral or ethical concerns? What are those concerns?

6. Why do you think Target and JCPenney are not as publicly disliked as Wal-Mart? Is there a lesson for Wal-Mart?

Test Prepper

college.hmco.com/pic/griffinfund5e

You've read the chapter, studied the key terms, and the exam is any day now. Think you're ready to ace it? Take this sample test to gauge your comprehension of chapter material. You can check your answers at the back of the book. Want more test questions? Visit the student website at http://college.hmco.com/pic/griffinfund5e/ and take the ACE quizzes for more practice.

1. T   F   The word *best* implies optimization.

2. T   F   Pranali plans to buy a new car. She has good information on price, reliability, service, and insurance cost. From a financial standpoint, she is making her decision in a state of risk.

3. T   F   When one is identifying alternatives, developing obvious standard alternatives and creative innovative alternatives is generally useful.

4. T   F   Satisficing is part of the rational decision-making model.

5. T   F   During the first episode of *The Apprentice*, two teams were challenged to make the most money selling lemonade. One team chose to sell outside the fish market. It turned out to be a bad choice, but team members were reluctant to challenge the decision until it was too late. This is an example of groupthink.

6. The decision-making process includes defining the situation, identifying alternatives, choosing the "best" alternative, and
    a. getting feedback.
    b. putting it into practice.
    c. getting another opinion.
    d. presenting it to the group.
    e. All of the above

7. Which decision-making condition is the most ambiguous?
    a. Certainty
    b. Uncertainty
    c. Risk

    d. Programmed
    e. Nonprogrammed

8. When Kraft Foods monitors its sales of beef-related products, it is in which stage of the rational decision-making process?
    a. Identifying alternatives
    b. Evaluating alternatives
    c. Selecting alternatives
    d. Implementing chosen alternatives
    e. Evaluating results

9. Tonisha evaluated alternative prices for her financial consulting business. She determined that one alternative had to be eliminated because she did not have the human resources and capital necessary to accomplish it. She evaluated the alternatives for
    a. feasibility.
    b. satisfactoriness.
    c. probable outcomes.
    d. consequences.
    e. optimization.

10. Which of the following is NOT an advantage of group decision making?
    a. More knowledge is available.
    b. Groupthink can occur.
    c. General acceptance of the final decision is more likely.
    d. Better decisions are generally made.
    e. Communication is enhanced.

Entrepreneurship and New Venture Management

chapter 5

FIRST THINGS FIRST

"We're not doing this to cash in. We're doing this to build something cool."

—MARK ZUCKERBERG, FOUNDER, FACEBOOK

Do you Facebook? Your answer is probably yes. Facebook was started by Mark Zuckerberg, a college sophomore, in February 2004. Zuckerberg was a computer prodigy who turned down a $1 million job offer at Microsoft after high school graduation, choosing Harvard instead. At Harvard, he noted that each residence hall had a directory, but there was no collegewide listing, which hampered socializing. According to Zuckerberg, "I've always enjoyed building things and puttering around with computer code, so I sat down and in about a week I had produced the basic workings of the site."

As the site grew, more universities were added based on the recommendations of Harvard undergraduates. Within six months of launch, the site had 1 million users. By February 2007, membership included 17 million members at 47,000 schools worldwide. Facebook.com is the sixth-most visited Internet site and the second among college students, behind number-one Google. Altogether, about 85 percent of eligible U.S. college students belong to Facebook.

Mark Zuckerberg, founder of Facebook, has seen his social networking business grow into a business valued at $2 billion.

LEARNING OBJECTIVES

After studying this chapter, you should be able to:

- Discuss the nature of entrepreneurship.
- Describe the role of entrepreneurship in society.
- Understand the major issues involved in choosing strategies for small firms and the role of international management in entrepreneurship.
- Discuss the structural challenges unique to entrepreneurial firms.
- Understand the determinants of the performance of small firms.

Facebook began as a noncommercial enterprise, but as its popularity grew, so did its need for funds. Venture capitalists were generous in exchange for ownership shares. Another source of funding is advertising. Facebook allows its users to post online flyers for a flat fee of as little as $5 for 10,000 posts. Corporate online advertising is also available and constitutes a major source of income, which is rumored to be over $70 million per week.

Anyone with an email address ending in the .edu suffix may register for free at Facebook. The Facebook system allows users to exchange photos and messages, as well as post personal information and view others' information. Facebook restricts access to students, granting a certain amount of security to users. In addition, users can only contact others through approved mechanisms, such as through the lists of mutual friends, through school affiliation, or by joining one of thousands of user-defined groups.

Facebook's college-oriented appeal is obvious to anyone who enters the site. On the one hand, that generates a high level of comfort and interest with the site's content. On the other hand, some disapprove of Facebook for glamorizing a "party" lifestyle. As *Rolling Stone* writer David Kushner says, "Surfing the site can feel like wandering through a giant dorm where every door is open and every kid is swilling Jack Daniel's." Facebook has a policy of not censoring users' posts, but that has led to criticism for including photos and descriptions of drug-taking, nudity, obscenity, and hate speech.

There are other drawbacks related to revealing too much information. Third-party advertisers can place "cookies" on users' computers, allowing the company to gather information about the user without permission. Some worry that Facebook facilitates identity theft or even worse, stalking. Facebook warns users not to reveal too much personal information or to block access to a limited number of known individuals, but some scary incidents have occurred.

Some colleges discipline students when their Facebook pages reveal evidence of underage drinking or sexual misconduct. At one evangelical university, students who admit to being gay in their Facebook profiles are expelled. In addition, many employers and university admission committees routinely examine Facebook profiles. Workers who reveal company information or a boss's incompetence have been caught in the act and fired. Facebook is even becoming an important tool for the police and has allowed the identification of several criminals on U.S. campuses. "[Facebook] is like putting stuff on the six o'clock news," says employment lawyer Garry Mathiason, who urges Facebook members to be discreet. "Once you've opened the drapes, people can see everything."

Facebook's increasing popularity with an important demographic segment shows no sign of slowing down. It comes as no surprise, then, that Facebook may be the target of a corporate acquisition. After MySpace.com was purchased by media giant News Corporation for $580 million, there was speculation that Facebook would be next. But no, Zuckerberg turned down an offer of $750 million in early 2006, and is apparently holding out for $2 billion. Viacom, which owns

MTV and Comedy Central, is one possible buyer, as is Google, which also owns YouTube.

From a dorm-living Harvard sophomore to CEO of a firm valued at $2 billion, Zuckerberg has had an amazing three years. He insists, "We're not doing this to cash in. We're doing this to build something cool." Facebook is very cool, and it's also very hot.

Just like Mark Zuckerberg, thousands of people all over the world start new businesses each year. And, like Facebook, some of these businesses succeed, while unfortunately, many others fail. Some of the people who fail in a new business try again, and sometimes it takes two or more failures before a successful business gets under way. Henry Ford, for example, went bankrupt twice before succeeding with Ford Motor Company.

This process of starting a new business, sometimes failing and sometimes succeeding, is part of what is called "entrepreneurship," the subject of this chapter. We begin by exploring the nature of entrepreneurship. We then examine the role of entrepreneurship in the business world and discuss strategies for entrepreneurial organizations. We then describe the structure and performance of entrepreneurial organizations.

The Nature of Entrepreneurship

Entrepreneurship is the process of planning, organizing, operating, and assuming the risk of a business venture. An *entrepreneur*, in turn, is someone who engages in entrepreneurship. Mark Zuckerberg, as highlighted in our opening case, fits this description. He put his own resources on the line and took a personal stake in the success or failure of Facebook. Business owners who hire professional managers to run their businesses and then turn their attention to other interests are not true entrepreneurs. Although they are assuming the risk of the venture, they are not actively involved in organizing or operating it. Likewise, professional managers whose job is running someone else's business are not entrepreneurs, for they assume less-than-total personal risk for the success or failure of the business.

Entrepreneurs start new businesses. We define a *small business* as one that is privately owned by one individual or a small group of individuals and has sales and assets that are not large enough to influence its environment. A small, two-person software development company with annual sales of $100,000 would clearly be a small business, whereas Microsoft Corporation is just as clearly a large business. But the boundaries are not always this clear-cut. For example, a regional retailing chain with 20 stores and annual revenues of $30 million may sound large but is really very small when compared to such giants as Wal-Mart and Sears.

entrepreneurship
The process of planning, organizing, operating, and assuming the risk of a business venture

entrepreneur
Someone who engages in entrepreneurship

small business
A business that is privately owned by one individual or a small group of individuals and has sales and assets that are not large enough to influence its environment

The Role of Entrepreneurship in Society

The history of entrepreneurship and of the development of new businesses is in many ways the history of great wealth and of great failure. Some entrepreneurs have been very successful and have accumulated vast fortunes from their entrepreneurial efforts. For example, when Microsoft Corporation first sold its stock to the public in 1986, Bill Gates, then just 30 years old, received $350 million for his share of Microsoft.[1] Today his holdings—valued at over $60 billion—make him the richest person in the United States and one of the richest in the world.[2] Many more entrepreneurs, however, have lost a great deal of money. Research suggests that the majority of new businesses fail within the first few years of founding.[3] Many that last longer do so only because the entrepreneurs themselves work long hours for very little income.

As Figure 5.1 shows, most U.S. businesses employ fewer than 100 people, and most U.S. workers are employed by small firms. For example, Figure 5.1(a) shows that approximately 90 percent of all U.S. businesses employ 20 or fewer people; another 8 percent employ between 20 and 99 people. In contrast, only about 1 percent employs 1,000 or more workers. Figure 5.1(b) shows that 25.6 percent of all U.S. workers are employed by firms with fewer than 20 people; another 29.1 percent work in firms that employ between 20 and 99 people. The vast majority of these companies are owner operated.[4] Figure 5.1(b) also shows that 12.7 percent of U.S. workers are employed by firms with 1,000 or more total employees.

On the basis of numbers alone, then, small business is a strong presence in the economy, which is also true in virtually all of the world's mature economies. In Germany, for example, companies with fewer than 500 employees produce two-thirds of the nation's gross national product, train nine of ten apprentices, and employ four of every five workers. Small businesses also play major roles in the economies of Italy, France, and Brazil. In addition, experts agree that small businesses will be quite important in the emerging economies of countries such as Russia and Vietnam. The contribution of small business can be measured in terms

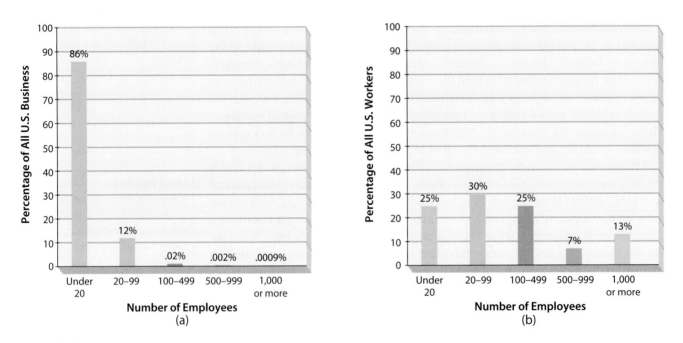

Figure 5.1

THE IMPORTANCE OF SMALL BUSINESS IN THE UNITED STATES

Over 86 percent of all U.S. businesses have no more than 20 employees. The total number of people employed by these small businesses is approximately one-fourth of the entire U.S. workforce. Another 29 percent work for companies with fewer than 100 employees.

Source: U.S. Census Bureau, *Statistical Abstract of the United States,* 2002 (Washington, DC: Government Printing Office, 2003).

of its effects on key aspects of an economic system. In the United States, these aspects include job creation, innovation, and importance to big business.

Job Creation

In the early 1980s, a widely cited study proposed that small businesses create eight of every ten new jobs in the United States. This contention touched off considerable interest in the fostering of small business as a matter of public policy. As we will see, though, relative job growth among businesses of different sizes is not easy to determine. But it is clear that small business—especially in certain industries—is an important source of new (and often well-paid) jobs in the United States. According to the Small Business Administration (SBA), for example, seven of the ten industries that added the most new jobs in 1998 were in sectors dominated by small businesses. Moreover, small businesses currently account for 38 percent of all jobs in high-technology sectors of the economy.[5]

Note that new jobs are also being created by small firms specializing in international business. For example, Bob Knosp operates a small business in Bellevue, Washington, that makes computerized sign-making systems. Knosp gets over half his sales from abroad and has dedicated almost 75 percent of his workforce to handling international sales. Indeed, according to the SBA, small businesses account for 96 percent of all U.S. exporters.[6]

Although small businesses certainly create many new jobs each year, the importance of entrepreneurial big businesses in job creation should also not be overlooked. Although big businesses cut thousands of jobs in the late 1980s and early 1990s, the booming U.S. economy resulted in large-scale job creation in many larger businesses beginning in the mid-1990s. But this trend was reversed in recent years, as many larger companies began to downsize once again. Figure 5.2 details the changes in the number of jobs at 16 large U.S. companies during the ten-year period between 1996 and 2005. As you can see, General Motors eliminated 322,000 jobs while Kmart

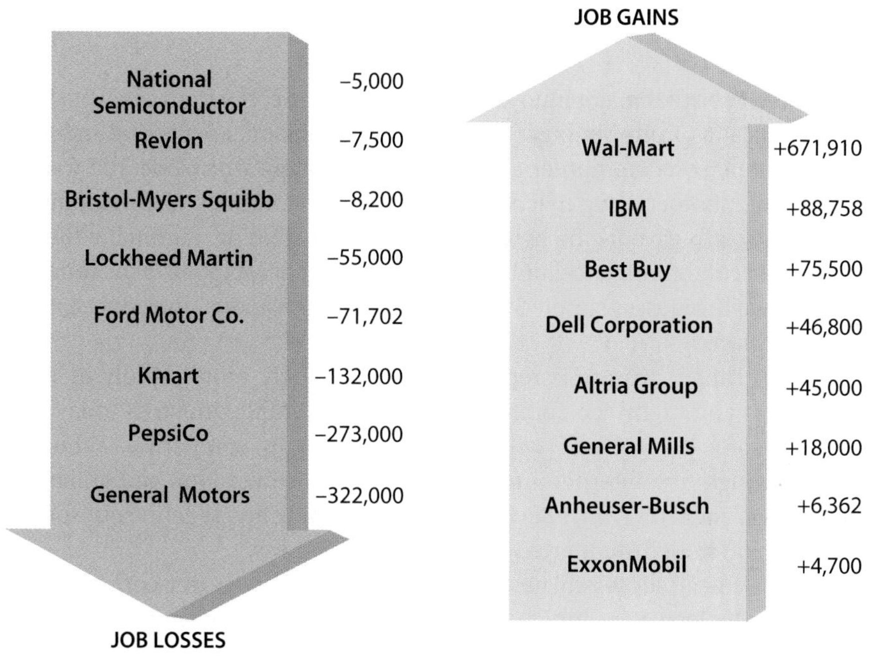

JOB GAINS

JOB LOSSES		JOB GAINS	
National Semiconductor	−5,000	Wal-Mart	+671,910
Revlon	−7,500	IBM	+88,758
Bristol-Myers Squibb	−8,200	Best Buy	+75,500
Lockheed Martin	−55,000	Dell Corporation	+46,800
Ford Motor Co.	−71,702	Altria Group	+45,000
Kmart	−132,000	General Mills	+18,000
PepsiCo	−273,000	Anheuser-Busch	+6,362
General Motors	−322,000	ExxonMobil	+4,700

JOB LOSSES

Figure 5.2

REPRESENTATIVE JOBS CREATED AND LOST BY BIG BUSINESS, 1996–2005

All businesses create and eliminate jobs. Because of their size, the magnitude of job creation and elimination is especially pronounced in bigger businesses. This figure provides several representative examples of job creation and elimination at many big U.S. businesses during the last decade. For example, while General Motors cut 322,000 jobs, Wal-Mart created 671,910 during this period.

eliminated 132,000 jobs. Wal-Mart alone, however, created 671,910 new jobs during the same period, and Best Buy added an additional 75,500.

But even these data have to be interpreted with care. PepsiCo, for example, "officially" eliminated 273,000 jobs. But most of those losses came in 1997, when the firm sold its restaurant chains (KFC, Pizza Hut, and Taco Bell) to Tricon Global Restaurants (since renamed Yum! Brands). In reality, therefore, many of the jobs were not actually eliminated, but simply "transferred" to another employer. Likewise, although most of Wal-Mart's 671,910 new jobs were indeed "new," some came when the company acquired other businesses and thus were not net new jobs.

At least one message is clear: Entrepreneurial business success, more than business size, accounts for most new job creation. Whereas successful retailers like Wal-Mart and Best Buy have been growing and adding thousands of new jobs, struggling chains like Kmart have been eliminating thousands. At the same time, flourishing high-tech giants like Dell, Intel, and Microsoft continue to add jobs at a constant pace. It is also essential to take a long-term view when analyzing job growth. Figure 5.2, for example, shows that IBM has added over 88,000 new jobs. But this ten-year increase follows on the heels of major job cuts at the firm—163,381—between 1990 and 1994. Hence, most firms, especially those in complex and dynamic environments, go through periods of growth when they add new jobs but also have periods when they cut jobs.

The reality, then, is that jobs are created by entrepreneurial companies of all sizes, all of which hire workers and all of which lay them off. Although small firms often hire at a faster rate than large ones, they are also likely to eliminate jobs at a far higher rate. Small firms are also the first to hire in times of economic recovery, whereas large firms are the last. Conversely, however, big companies are also the last to lay off workers during economic downswings. Recent estimates suggest that over one-third of all small businesses in the United States have job openings, and almost 20 percent are planning to hire new employees. On the other hand, the SBA indicates that in 2000 large businesses employed more people than did small businesses for the first time since such statistics has been tracked.[7]

Innovation

History has shown that major innovations are as likely to come from small businesses (or individuals) as from big businesses. For example, small firms and individuals invented the personal computer and the stainless-steel razor blade, the transistor radio and the photocopying machine, the jet engine and the self-developing photograph. They also gave us the helicopter and power steering, automatic transmissions and air conditioning, cellophane, and the 19-cent ballpoint pen. Today, says the SBA, small businesses supply 55 percent of all "innovations" introduced into the U.S. marketplace.[8]

Not surprisingly, history is repeating itself infinitely more rapidly in the age of computers and high-tech communication. For example, much of today's most innovative software is being written at new start-up companies. Yahoo! and Netscape brought the Internet into the average U.S. living room, and online companies such as Amazon.com, eBay, and Google are using it to redefine our shopping habits. Each of these firms started out as a small business.

Of course, not all successful new start-ups are leading-edge dot-com enterprises. Drywall installer Jerry Free, for example, was frustrated by conventional methods of joining angled wallboard. In his spare time, he developed a simple handheld device that makes it easier and faster to perform this common task. He eventually licensed his invention to United States Gypsum, and it is now widely used throughout the construction industry. As for Free, the experience convinced him that "the cliché about invention being 1 percent inspiration and 99 percent perspiration is true."[9] Popular fashion designer Kate Spade has made it big by introducing a line of stylish purses and handbags sold through such exclusive retailers as Neiman Marcus. Rory Stear and Christopher Staines have succeeded with Freeplay Energy Group, a firm making environmentally friendly wind-up radios that need neither batteries nor electricity.[10] Eric Ludewig presides over fast-growing East of Chicago Pizza, a chain he founded when he was 22 years old and just out of college.[11]

Importance to Big Business

Most of the products made by big manufacturers are sold to consumers by small businesses. For example, the majority of dealerships selling Fords, Chevrolets, Toyotas, and Volvos are independently owned and operated. Moreover, small businesses provide big businesses with many of the services, supplies, and raw materials they need. Likewise, Microsoft relies heavily on small businesses in the course of its routine business operations. For example, the software giant outsources much of its routine code-writing functions to hundreds of sole proprietorships and other small firms. It also outsources much of its packaging, delivery, and distribution to smaller companies. Dell Computer uses this same strategy, buying most of the parts and components used in its computers from small suppliers around the world.

Strategy for Entrepreneurial Organizations

One of the most basic challenges facing an entrepreneurial organization is choosing a strategy. The three strategic challenges facing small firms, in turn, are choosing an industry in which to compete, emphasizing distinctive competencies, and writing a business plan.[12]

Choosing an Industry

Not surprisingly, small businesses are more common in some industries than in others. The major industry groups that include successful new ventures and small businesses are services, retailing, construction, finance and insurance, wholesaling, transportation, and manufacturing. Obviously, each group differs in its requirements for employees, money, materials, and machines. In general, the more resources an industry requires, the harder it is to start a business and the less likely that the industry is dominated by small firms. Remember, too, that *small* is a relative term: The criteria (number of employees and total annual sales) differ from industry to industry and are often meaningful only when compared with businesses that are truly large. Figure 5.3 shows the distribution of all U.S. businesses employing fewer than 20 people across industry groups.

Services   Primarily because they require few resources, service businesses are the fastest-growing segment of small-business enterprise. In addition, no other industry group offers a higher return on time invested. Finally, services appeal to the talent for innovation typified by many small enterprises. As Figure 5.3 shows, 37.94 percent of all businesses with fewer than 20 employees are services.

Small-business services range from shoeshine parlors to car rental agencies, from marriage counseling to computer software, from accounting and management consulting to professional dog walking. In Dallas, for example, Jani-King has prospered by selling commercial cleaning services to local companies. In Virginia Beach, Virginia, Jackson Hewitt Tax Services has found a profitable niche in providing computerized tax preparation and electronic tax-filing services. Great Clips, Inc. is a fast-growing family-run chain of hair salons headquartered in Minneapolis.

David Flanary, Richard Sorenson, and Michael Holloway recently established an Internet-based long distance telephone service in Austin, Texas, called PointOne Telecommunications. The basic idea was hatched during a tennis match. Recalls Sorenson, "We started getting excited, volleying at the net, and then finally we put the rackets down and went to the side to talk." The firm is off to a great start. Currently, it acts as a wholesale voice carrier, but as soon as its network is completed, PointOne will start signing up its own commercial customers. Investors agree that the company will soon be a major force in telecommunications.[13]

Retailing A retail business sells products manufactured by other firms directly to consumers. There are hundreds of different kinds of retailers, ranging from wig shops and frozen yogurt stands to automobile dealerships and department stores. Usually, however, people who start small businesses favor specialty shops—for example, big-men's clothing or gourmet coffees—which let them focus limited resources on narrow market segments. Retailing accounts for 12.85 percent of all businesses with fewer than 20 employees.

John Mackey, for example, launched Whole Foods out of his own frustration at being unable to find a full range of natural foods at other stores. He soon found, however, that he had tapped a lucrative market and started an ambitious expansion program. Today, with 90 outlets in 20 states and Washington, D.C., Whole Foods is the largest natural-foods retailer in the United States, three times larger than its biggest competitor.[14] Likewise, when Olga Tereshko found it difficult to locate just the right cloth diapers and breast-feeding supplies for her newborn son, she decided to start selling them herself. Instead of taking the conventional retailing route, however, Tereshko set up shop on the Internet. Her business, called Little Koala, has

Figure 5.3

SMALL BUSINESSES (BUSINESSES WITH FEWER THAN 20 EMPLOYEES) BY INDUSTRY

Small businesses are especially strong in certain industries, such as retailing and services. On the other hand, there are relatively fewer small businesses in industries such as transportation and manufacturing. The differences are affected primarily by factors such as the investment costs necessary to enter markets in these industries. For example, starting a new airline would require the purchase of large passenger aircraft and airport gates, and hiring an expensive set of employees.

Source: U.S. Census Bureau, *Statistical Abstract of the United States: 2005* (125th Edition), Washington, DC, 2005.

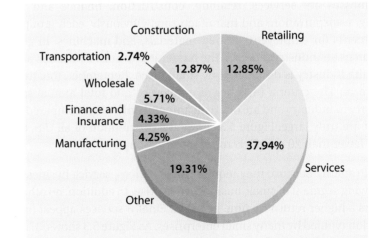

Would-be entrepreneurs can increase their chances of success by identifying a niche or potential market that no other business is serving. Consider, for instance, the success enjoyed by Boston entrepreneur Chris Murphy. He knew that some dog owners felt that they faced the same day-care problems experienced by parents of small children. In response, he started The Common Dog, a service that picks up dogs on a school bus, takes them to a day-kennel while their owners work, and drops them off at the end of the day. The service costs the dog owners $325 a month. At the kennel, the dogs enjoy their own small swimming pool, several lounging couches, and frequent walks. They do, however, have to bring their own lunches!

continued to expand at a rate of about 10 percent a month, and she has established a customer base of 8,000 to 9,000 loyal customers.[15]

Construction   About 13 percent of businesses with fewer than 20 employees are involved in construction. Because many construction jobs are relatively small, local projects, local construction firms are often ideally suited as contractors. Many such firms are begun by skilled craftspeople who start out working for someone else and subsequently decide to work for themselves. Common examples of small construction firms include home builders, wood finishers, roofers, painters, and plumbing, electrical, and roofing contractors.

For example, Marek Brothers Construction in College Station, Texas, was started by two brothers, Pat and Joe Marek. They originally worked for other contractors but started their own partnership in 1980. Their only employee is a receptionist. They manage various construction projects, including new-home construction and remodeling, subcontracting out the actual work to other businesses or to individual craftspeople. Marek Brothers has annual gross income of about $5 million.

Finance and Insurance   Finance and insurance businesses also comprise about 4.3 percent of all firms with fewer than 20 employees. In most cases, these businesses are either affiliates of or sell products provided by larger national firms. Although the deregulation of the banking industry has reduced the number of small local banks, other businesses in this sector are still doing quite well.

Typically, for example, local State Farm Mutual offices are small businesses. State Farm itself is a major insurance company, but its local offices are run by 16,500 independent agents. In turn, agents hire their own staff, run their own offices as independent businesses, and so forth. They sell various State Farm insurance products and earn commissions from the premiums paid by their clients. Some local savings and loan operations, mortgage companies, and pawnshops also fall into this category.

Wholesaling   Small-business owners often do very well in wholesaling, too; about 5.7 percent of businesses with fewer than 20 employees are wholesalers. A wholesale business buys products from manufacturers or other producers and then sells them to retailers. Wholesalers usually buy goods in bulk and store them in quantity at locations that are convenient for retailers. For a given volume of business, therefore, they need fewer employees than manufacturers, retailers, or service providers.

They also serve fewer customers than other providers—usually those who repeatedly order large volumes of goods. Wholesalers in the grocery industry, for instance, buy packaged food in bulk from companies like Del Monte and Campbell and then sell it to both large grocery chains and smaller independent grocers. Luis Espinoza has found a promising niche for Inca Quality Foods, a midwestern wholesaler that imports and distributes Latino foods for consumers from Mexico, the Caribbean, and Central America. Partnered with the large grocery-store chain Kroger, Espinoza's firm continues to grow steadily.[16]

Transportation   Some small firms—about 2.7 percent of all companies with fewer than 20 employees—do well in transportation and transportation-related businesses. Such firms include local taxi and limousine companies, charter airplane services, and tour operators. In addition, in many smaller markets, bus companies and regional airlines subcontract local equipment maintenance to small businesses.

Consider, for example, some of the transportation-related small businesses at a ski resort like Steamboat Springs, Colorado. Most visitors fly to the town of Hayden, about 15 miles from Steamboat Springs. Although some visitors rent vehicles, many others use the services of Alpine Taxi, a small local operation, to transport them to their destinations in Steamboat Springs. While on vacation, they also rely on the local bus service, which is subcontracted by the town to another small business, to get to and from the ski slopes each day. Other small businesses offer van tours of the region, hot-air balloon rides, and helicopter lifts to remote areas for extreme skiers. Still others provide maintenance support at Hayden for Continental, American, and United aircraft that serve the area during ski season.

Manufacturing   More than any other industry, manufacturing lends itself to big business—and for good reason. Because of the investment normally required in equipment, energy, and raw materials, a good deal of money is usually needed to start a manufacturing business. Automobile manufacturing, for example, calls for billions of dollars of investment and thousands of workers before the first automobile rolls off the assembly line. Obviously, such requirements shut out most individuals. Although Henry Ford began with $28,000, it has been a long time since anyone started a new U.S. car company from scratch.

Research has shown that manufacturing costs often fall as the number of units produced by an organization increases. This relationship between cost and production is called an *economy of scale*.[17] Small organizations usually cannot compete effectively on the basis of economies of scale. As depicted in Figure 5.4(a), organizations with higher levels of production have a major cost advantage over those with lower levels of production. Given the cost positions of small and large firms when there are strong economies of scale in manufacturing, it is not surprising that small manufacturing organizations generally do not do as well as large ones.

Interestingly, when technology in an industry changes, it often shifts the economies-of-scale curve, thereby creating opportunities for smaller organizations.

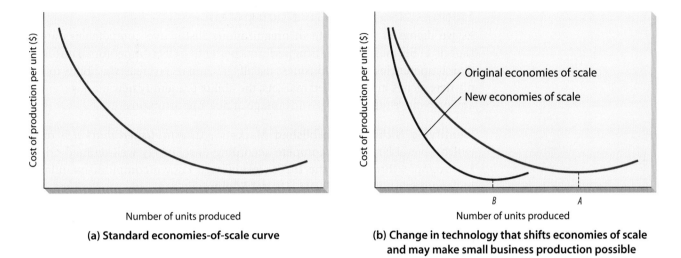

(a) **Standard economies-of-scale curve**

(b) **Change in technology that shifts economies of scale and may make small business production possible**

Figure 5.4
ECONOMIES OF SCALE IN
SMALL-BUSINESS ORGANIZATIONS

Small businesses sometimes find it difficult to compete in manufacturing-related industries because of the economies of scale associated with plant, equipment, and technology. As shown in (a), firms that produce a large number of units (that is, larger businesses) can do so at a lower per-unit cost. At the same time, however, new forms of technology occasionally cause the economies-of-scale curve to shift, as illustrated in (b). In this case, smaller firms may be able to compete more effectively with larger ones because of the drop in per-unit manufacturing cost.

For example, steel manufacturing was historically dominated by a few large companies, which owned several huge facilities. With the development of minimill technology, however, extracting economies of scale at a much smaller level of production became possible. This type of shift is depicted in Figure 5.4(b). Point *A* in this panel is the low-cost point with the original economies of scale. Point *B* is the low-cost point with the economies of scale brought on by the new technology. Notice that the number of units needed for low costs is considerably fewer for the new technology. This has allowed the entry of numerous smaller firms into the steel industry. Such entry would not have been possible with the older technology.

This is not to say that there are no small-business owners who do well in manufacturing—about 4 percent of businesses with fewer than 20 employees are involved in some aspect of manufacturing. Indeed, it is not uncommon for small manufacturers to outperform big business in such innovation-driven industries as chemistry, electronics, toys, and computer software. Some small manufacturers prosper by locating profitable niches. For example, brothers Dave and Dan Hanlon and Dave's wife Jennie recently started a new motorcycle-manufacturing business called Excelsior-Henderson. (Excelsior and Henderson are actually names of classic motorcycles from the early years of the twentieth century; the Hanlons acquired the rights to these brand names because of the images they evoke among motorcycle enthusiasts.) The Hanlons started by building 4,000 bikes in 1999 and will soon have annual production of 20,000 per year. So far, Excelsior-Henderson motorcycles have been well received (the top-end Excelsior-Henderson Super X sells for about $18,000), and many Harley-Davidson dealers have started to sell them as a means of diversifying their product line.[18]

Emphasizing Distinctive Competencies

As we define in Chapter 4, an organization's distinctive competencies are the aspects of business that the firm performs better than its competitors. The distinctive competencies of small business usually fall into three areas: the ability to identify new niches in established markets, the ability to identify new markets, and the ability to move quickly to take advantage of new opportunities.

Identifying Niches in Established Markets An ***established market*** is one in which several large firms compete according to relatively well-defined criteria. For example, throughout the 1970s, several well-known computer-manufacturing companies, including IBM, Digital Equipment, and Hewlett-Packard, competed according to three product criteria: computing power, service, and price. Over the years, the computing power and quality of service delivered by these firms continued to improve, while prices (especially relative to computing power) continued to drop.

Enter Apple and the personal computer. For Apple, user-friendliness, not computing power, service, or price, was to be the basis of competition. Apple targeted every manager, every student, and every home as the owner of a personal computer. Apple's major entrepreneurial act was not to invent a new technology (indeed, the first Apple computers used all standard parts taken from other computers), but to recognize a new kind of computer and a new way to compete in the computer industry.

Apple's approach to competition was to identify a new niche in an established market. A ***niche*** is simply a segment of a market that is not currently being exploited.

established market
A market in which several large firms compete according to relatively well-defined criteria

niche
A segment of a market not currently being exploited

As noted in the text, successful entrepreneurs must choose an industry, emphasize their distinctive competencies, and develop an effective business plan. Unfortunately, entrepreneurs frequently misjudge or do not effectively implement one or more of these activities. As illustrated in this cartoon, for example, providing a product that people do not really want is almost certain to result in failure.

© The New Yorker Collection 1997 J.P. Rini from cartoonbank.com. All Rights Reserved.

In general, small entrepreneurial businesses are better at discovering these niches than are larger organizations. Large organizations usually have so many resources committed to older, established business practices that they may be unaware of new opportunities. Entrepreneurs can see these opportunities and move quickly to take advantage of them.[19]

Identifying New Markets Successful entrepreneurs also excel at discovering whole new markets. Discovery can happen in at least two ways. First, an entrepreneur can transfer a product or service that is well established in one geographic market to a second market. This is what Marcel Bich did with ballpoint pens, which occupied a well-established market in Europe before Bich introduced them to this country. Bich's company, Société Bic, eventually came to dominate the U.S. market.

Second, entrepreneurs can sometimes create entire industries. Entrepreneurial inventions of the dry paper copying process and the semiconductor have created vast new industries. Not only have the first companies into these markets been very successful (Xerox and National Semiconductor, respectively), but their entrepreneurial activity has spawned the development of hundreds of other companies and hundreds of thousands of jobs. Again, because entrepreneurs are not encumbered with a history of doing business in a particular way, they are usually better at discovering new markets than are larger, more mature organizations.

First-Mover Advantages A ***first-mover advantage*** is any advantage that comes to a firm because it exploits an opportunity before any other firm does. Sometimes large firms discover niches within existing markets or new markets at just about the same time small entrepreneurial firms do, but they are not able to move as quickly as small companies to take advantage of these opportunities.

There are numerous reasons for this difference. For example, many large organizations make decisions slowly because each of their many layers of hierarchy has to approve an action before it can be implemented. Also, large organizations may sometimes put a great deal of their assets at risk when they take advantage of new opportunities. Every time Boeing decides to build a new model of a commercial jet, it is making a decision that could literally bankrupt the company if it does not turn out well. The size of the risk may make large organizations cautious. The dollar value of the assets at risk in a small organization, in contrast, is quite small. Managers may be willing to "bet the company" when the value of the company is only $100,000. They might be unwilling to "bet the company" when the value of the company is $1 billion.

first-mover advantage
Any advantage that comes to a firm because it exploits an opportunity before any other firm does

Writing a Business Plan

Once an entrepreneur has chosen an industry to compete in and determined which distinctive competencies to emphasize, these choices are usually included in a document called a business plan. In a ***business plan*** the entrepreneur summarizes the business strategy and how that strategy is to be implemented. The very act of preparing a business plan forces prospective entrepreneurs to crystallize their thinking about what they must do to launch their business successfully and obliges them to develop their business on paper before investing time and money in it. The idea of a business plan is not new. What is new is the growing use of specialized business plans by entrepreneurs, mostly because creditors and investors demand them for use in deciding whether to help finance a small business.

business plan
A document that summarizes the business strategy and structure

The plan should describe the match between the entrepreneur's abilities and the requirements for producing and marketing a particular product or service. It should define strategies for production and marketing, legal aspects and organization, and accounting and finance. In particular, it should answer three questions: (1) What are the entrepreneur's goals and objectives? (2) What strategies will the entrepreneur use to obtain these goals and objectives? (3) How will the entrepreneur implement these strategies?

Business plans should also account for the sequential nature of much strategic decision making in small businesses. For example, entrepreneurs cannot forecast sales revenues without first researching markets. The sales forecast itself is one of the most important elements in the business plan. Without such forecasts, it is all but impossible to estimate intelligently the size of a plant, store, or office, or to determine how much inventory to carry or how many employees to hire.

Another important component of the overall business plan is financial planning, which translates all other activities into dollars. Generally, the financial plan is made up of a cash budget, an income statement, balance sheets, and a breakeven chart. The most important of these statements is the cash budget because it tells entrepreneurs how much money they need before they open for business and how much money they need to keep the business operating.

Entrepreneurship and International Management

Finally, although many people associate international management with big business, many smaller companies are also finding expansion and growth opportunities

---

Eye on Management

Sandwich Chef: A Start Up

This ten-minute video shows an entrepreneur meeting with a banker to discuss borrowing money to fund a new business, a café called Sandwich Chef. The conversation covers many of the important issues in entrepreneurial start-ups, including the entrepreneur's motivation and experience, market research, the business model, and cash flow and finance.

View the video and then answer the following questions individually or as a class.

1. In your opinion, did the entrepreneur do sufficient market research? What else could he have done to be more thorough in this area?

2. The banker repeatedly discusses the business model. For example, he questions the business name, eat-in versus take-out customers, and the product mix. Why are these issues so critical? What would be the likely consequences if the entrepreneur does not do a

satisfactory job of answering those questions before he begins?

3. The banker mentions that banks do not usually fund start-ups. The entrepreneur will contribute $15,000 of his personal money toward the business, but otherwise isn't financially committed. What are some possible sources of funds that this entrepreneur should consider, other than personal savings or bank loans?

4. If you were the banker, would you be inclined to make the loan? If you would, explain what conditions you would require. If you would not, explain why not.

View the two-minute follow-up video. In this video, the banker discusses his reactions to the meeting and his thoughts about the future of this deal.

5. Were you surprised by the issues that the banker felt were important? Did the banker fail to address any issues that you consider important? Discuss.

in foreign countries. For example, Fuci Metals, a small but growing enterprise, buys metal from remote locations in areas such as Siberia and Africa, and then sells it to big auto makers like Ford and Toyota. Similarly, California-based Gold's Gym is expanding into foreign countries and has been especially successful in Russia.[20] And Markel Corporation, a small Philadelphia-based firm that manufactures tubing and insulated wiring, derives 40 percent of its annual revenues (currently around $26 million) from international sales.[21] Although such ventures are accompanied by considerable risks, they also give entrepreneurs new opportunities and can be a real catalyst for success.

Structure of Entrepreneurial Organizations

With a strategy in place and a business plan in hand, the entrepreneur can then proceed to devise a structure that turns the vision of the business plan into a reality. Many of the same concerns in structuring any business, which are described in the next three chapters of this book, are also relevant to small businesses. For example, entrepreneurs need to consider organization design and develop job descriptions, organization charts, and management control systems.

The Internet, of course, is rewriting virtually all of the rules for starting and operating a small business. Getting into business is easier and faster than ever before, there are many more potential opportunities than at any other time in history, and the ability to gather and assimilate information is at an all-time high. Even so, would-be entrepreneurs must still make the right decisions when they start. They must decide, for example, precisely how to get into business. Should they buy an existing business or build from the ground up? In addition, would-be entrepreneurs must find appropriate sources of financing and decide when and how to seek the advice of experts.

Starting a new business can include starting from scratch or buying an existing business—or both. Take Amy Brown, for example. Ms. Brown started Blue Heron Bags to sell purses and related products at kiosks in shopping malls. To fuel growth at her fledgling business, she recently bought a competing enterprise called Bags and Sew On and transformed its outlets into Blue Heron stores. She also plans to buy other small competitors in the next few years and change them to the Blue Heron nameplate as well.

Starting the New Business

The first step in starting a new business is the individual's commitment to becoming a business owner. Next comes choosing the goods or services to be offered—a process that means investigating one's chosen industry and market. Making this choice also requires would-be entrepreneurs to assess not only industry trends but also their own skills. Like the managers of existing businesses, new business owners must also be sure that they understand the true nature of the enterprise in which they are engaged.

Buying an Existing Business   After choosing a product and making sure that the choice fits their own skills and interests, entrepreneurs must decide whether to buy an existing business or to start from scratch. Consultants often recommend the first approach. Quite simply, the odds are better: If successful, an existing business has already proved its ability to draw customers at a profit. It has also established working relationships with lenders, suppliers, and the community. Moreover, the track record of an existing business gives potential buyers a much clearer picture of what to expect than any estimate of a new business's prospects. Around 30 percent of the new businesses started in the past decade were bought from someone else. The McDonald's empire, for example, was started when Ray Kroc bought an existing hamburger business and then turned it into a global phenomenon. Likewise, Starbucks was a struggling mail-order business when Howard Schultz bought it and turned his attention to retail expansion.

Starting from Scratch   Some people, however, prefer the satisfaction that comes from planting an idea, nurturing it, and making it grow into a strong and sturdy business. There are also practical reasons to start a business from scratch. A new business does not suffer the ill effects of a prior owner's errors. The start-up owner is also free to choose lenders, equipment, inventories, locations, suppliers, and workers, unbound by a predecessor's commitments and policies. Of the new businesses begun in the past decade, 64 percent were started from scratch.

Not surprisingly, though, the risks of starting a business from scratch are greater than those of buying an existing firm. Founders of new businesses can make only predictions and projections about their prospects. Success or failure thus depends heavily on identifying a genuine business opportunity—a product for which many customers will pay well but which is currently unavailable to them. To find openings, entrepreneurs must study markets and answer the following questions: (1) Who are my customers? (2) Where are they? (3) At what price will they buy my product? (4) In what quantities will they buy? (5) Who are my competitors? (6) How will my product differ from those of my competitors?

Finding answers to these questions is a difficult task even for large, well-established firms. But where can the new business owner get the necessary information? Other sources of assistance are discussed later in this chapter, but we briefly describe three of the most accessible here. For example, the best way to gain knowledge about a market is to work in it before going into business in it. For example, if you once worked in a bookstore and now plan to open one of your own, you probably already have some idea about the kinds of books people request and buy. Second, a quick scan of the local Yellow Pages or an Internet search will reveal many potential competitors, as will advertisements in trade journals. Personal visits to these establishments and websites can give you insights into their strengths and weaknesses. And, third, studying magazines, books, and websites aimed specifically at small businesses can also be of help, as can hiring professionals to survey the market for you.

Financing the New Business

Although the choice of how to start is obviously important, it is meaningless unless a new business owner can obtain the money to set up shop. Among the more common sources for funding are family and friends, personal savings, banks and similar lending institutions, investors, and government agencies. Lending institutions are more likely to help finance the purchase of an existing business than a new business because the risks are better understood. Individuals starting up new businesses, on the other hand, are more likely to have to rely on their personal resources.

Personal Resources According to a study by the National Federation of Independent Business, an owner's personal resources, not loans, are the most important source of money. Including money borrowed from friends and relatives, personal resources account for over two-thirds of all money invested in new small businesses and one-half of that invested in the purchase of existing businesses. When Michael Dorf and his friends decided to launch a New York nightclub dubbed the Knitting Factory, he started with $30,000 of his own money. Within four months of opening, Dorf asked his father to co-sign the first of four consecutive Milwaukee bank loans (for $70,000, $200,000, $300,000, and to move to a new facility, $500,000, respectively). Dorf and his partners also engaged in creative bartering, such as putting a sound system company's logo on all its advertising in exchange for free equipment. Finally, because the Knitting Factory has become so successful, other investors are now stepping forward to provide funds—$650,000 from one investor and $4.2 million from another.[22]

Strategic Alliances Strategic alliances are also becoming a popular method for financing business growth. When Steven and Andrew Grundy decided to launch an Internet CD-exchange business called Spun.com, they had very little capital and thus made extensive use of alliances with other firms. They partnered, for example, with wholesaler Alliance Entertainment Corporation as a CD supplier. Orders to Spun.com actually go to Alliance, which ships products to customers and bills Spun.com directly. This setup has allowed Spun.com to promote a vast inventory of labels without actually having to buy inventory. All told, the firm created an alliance network that has provided the equivalent of $40 million in capital.[23]

Lenders Although banks, independent investors, and government loans all provide much smaller portions of start-up funds than the personal resources of owners, they are important in many cases. Getting money from these sources, however, requires some extra effort. Banks and private investors usually want to see formal business plans—detailed outlines of proposed businesses and markets, owners' backgrounds, and other sources of funding. Government loans have strict eligibility guidelines.

Venture Capital Companies *Venture capital companies* are groups of small investors seeking to make profits on companies with rapid growth potential. Most of these firms do not lend money: They invest it, supplying capital in return for

venture capital company
A group of small investors seeking to make profits on companies with rapid growth potential.

stock. The venture capital company may also demand a representative on the board of directors. In some cases, managers may even need approval from the venture capital company before making major decisions. Of all venture capital currently committed in the United States, 29 percent comes from true venture capital firms.[24] In 2005, venture capital firms invested $21 billion in new start-ups in the United States.

For example, Dr. Drew Pinsky, cohost of MTV's Loveline, got venture capital funding to extend his program to the Internet from a group of investors collectively known as Garage.com. Garage.com is comprised of several individuals and other investors who specialize in financing Internet start-ups.[25] Similarly, SOFTBANK is a venture capital firm that has provided funds to over 300 web companies, including Yahoo! and E*Trade. As founder Masayoshi Son puts it, "We're a strategic holding company, investing in companies that are very important in the digital information industry—in e-commerce, financial services, and media."

Small-Business Investment Companies Taking a more balanced approach in their choices than venture capital companies, small-business investment companies (SBICs) seek profits by investing in companies with potential for rapid growth. Created by the Small Business Investment Act of 1958, SBICs are federally licensed to borrow money from the SBA and to invest it in or lend it to small businesses. They are themselves investments for their shareholders. Past beneficiaries of SBIC capital include Apple Computer, Intel, and Federal Express. In addition, the government has recently begun to sponsor minority enterprise small-business investment companies (MESBICs). As the name suggests, MESBICs specialize in financing businesses that are owned and operated by minorities.

SBA Financial Programs Since its founding in 1953, the SBA has offered more than 20 financing programs to small businesses that meet standards of size and independence. Eligible firms must also be unable to get private financing at reasonable terms. Because of these and other restrictions, SBA loans have never been a major source of small-business financing. In addition, budget cutbacks at the SBA have reduced the number of firms benefiting from loans. Nevertheless, several SBA programs currently offer funds to qualified applicants.

For example, under the SBA's guaranteed loans program, small businesses can borrow from commercial lenders. The SBA guarantees to repay 75 to 85 percent of the loan amount, not to exceed $750,000. Under a related program, companies engaged in international trade can borrow up to $1.25 million. Such loans may be made for as long as 15 years. Most SBA lending activity flows through this program.

Sometimes, however, both desired bank and SBA-guaranteed loans are unavailable (perhaps because the business cannot meet stringent requirements). In such cases, the SBA may help finance the entrepreneur through its immediate participation loans program. Under this arrangement, the SBA and the bank each puts up a share of the money, with the SBA's share not to exceed $150,000. Under the local development companies (LDCs) program, the SBA works with a corporation (either for-profit or nonprofit) founded by local citizens who want to boost the local economy. The SBA can lend up to $500,000 for each small business to be helped by an LDC.

Spurred in large part by the boom in Internet businesses, both venture capital and loans are becoming easier to get. Most small businesses, for example, report that it has generally become increasingly easier to obtain loans over the last ten years. Indeed, some technology companies are being offered so much venture capital that they are turning down part of it to keep from unnecessarily diluting their ownership.

Sources of Management Advice

Financing is not the only area in which small businesses need help. Until World War II, for example, the business world involved few regulations, few taxes, few records, few big competitors, and no computers. Since then, simplicity has given way to complexity. Today, few entrepreneurs are equipped with all the business skills they need to survive. Small-business owners can no longer be their own troubleshooters, lawyers, bookkeepers, financiers, and tax experts. For these jobs, they rely on professional help. To survive and grow, however, small businesses also need advice regarding management. This advice is usually available from four sources: advisory boards, management consultants, the SBA, and a process called "networking."

Advisory Boards   All companies, even those that do not legally need boards of directors, can benefit from the problem-solving abilities of advisory boards. Thus some small businesses create boards to provide advice and assistance. For example, an advisory board might help an entrepreneur determine the best way to finance a plant expansion or to start exporting products to foreign markets.

Management Consultants   Opinions vary widely about the value of management consultants—experts who charge fees to help managers solve problems. They often specialize in one area, such as international business, small business, or manufacturing. Thus they can bring an objective and trained outlook to problems and provide logical recommendations. They can be quite expensive, however, as some consultants charge $1,000 or more for a day of assistance.

Like other professionals, consultants should be chosen with care. They can be found through major corporations that have used their services and that can provide references and reports on their work. Not surprisingly, they are most effective when the client helps (for instance, by providing schedules and written proposals for work to be done).

The Small Business Administration   Even more important than its financing role is the SBA's role in helping small-business owners improve their management skills. It is easy for entrepreneurs to spend money; SBA programs are designed to show them how to spend it wisely. The SBA offers small businesses four major management-counseling programs at virtually no cost.

A small-business owner who needs help in starting a new business can get it free through the Service Corps of Retired Executives (SCORE). All SCORE members are retired executives, and all are volunteers. Under this program, the SBA tries to match the expert to the need. For example, if a small-business owner needs help putting together a marketing plan, the SBA will send a SCORE counselor with marketing expertise.

Like SCORE, the Active Corps of Executives (ACE) program is designed to help small businesses that cannot afford consultants. The SBA recruits ACE volunteers from virtually every industry. All ACE volunteers are currently involved in successful activities, mostly as small-business owners themselves. Together, SCORE and ACE have more than 12,000 counselors working out of 350 chapters throughout the United States. They provide assistance to some 140,000 small businesses each year.

The talents and skills of students and instructors at colleges and universities are fundamental to the Small Business Institute (SBI). Under the guidance of seasoned professors of business administration, students seeking advanced degrees work closely with small-business owners to help solve specific problems, such as sagging sales or rising costs. Students earn credit toward their degree, with their grades depending on how well they handle a client's problems. Several hundred colleges and universities counsel thousands of small-business owners through this program every year.

Finally, the newest of the SBA's management counseling projects is its Small Business Development Center (SBDC) program. Begun in 1976, SBDCs are designed to consolidate information from various disciplines and institutions, including technical and professional schools. Then they make this knowledge available to new and existing small businesses. In 1995 universities in 45 states took part in the program.

Networking More and more, small-business owners are discovering the value of networking—meeting regularly with one another to discuss common problems and opportunities and, perhaps most important, to pool resources. Businesspeople have long joined organizations such as the local chamber of commerce and the National Federation of Independent Businesses (NFIB) to make such contacts.

Today, organizations are springing up all over the United States to facilitate small-business networking. One such organization, the Council of Smaller Enterprises of Cleveland, boasts a total membership of more than 10,000 small-business owners, the largest number in the country. This organization offers its members not only networking possibilities but also educational programs and services tailored to their needs. In a typical year, its 85 educational programs draw more than 8,500 small-business owners.

In particular, women and minorities have found networking to be an effective problem-solving tool. The National Association of Women Business Owners (NAWBO), for example, provides a variety of networking forums. The NAWBO also has chapters in most major cities, where its members can meet regularly. Increasingly, women are relying more on other women to help locate venture capital, establish relationships with customers, and provide such essential services as accounting and legal advice. According to Patty Abramson of the Women's Growth Capital Fund, all of these tasks have traditionally been harder for women because, until now, they have never had friends in the right places. "I wouldn't say this is about discrimination," adds Abramson. "It's about not having the relationships, and business is about relationships."

Franchising

The next time you drive or walk around town, be on the alert for a McDonald's, Taco Bell, Subway, or KFC restaurant; a Jamba Juice smoothie store; a 7-Eleven or Circle K convenience store; a RE/MAX or Coldwell Banker real estate office; a Super 8 or Ramada Inn motel; a Blockbuster Video store; a Sylvan Learning Center educational center; an Express Oil Change or Precision Auto Wash service center; or a

Supercuts hair salon. What do these businesses have in common? In most cases, they are franchised operations, operating under licenses issued by parent companies to local entrepreneurs who own and manage them.

As many would-be businesspeople have discovered, ***franchising agreements*** are an accessible doorway to entrepreneurship. A franchise is an arrangement that permits the *franchisee* (buyer) to sell the product of the *franchiser* (seller, or parent company). Franchisees can thus benefit from the selling corporation's experience and expertise. They can also consult the franchiser for managerial and financial help.

For example, the franchiser may supply financing. It may pick the store location, negotiate the lease, design the store, and purchase necessary equipment. It may train the first set of employees and managers and provide standardized policies and procedures. Once the business is open, the franchiser may offer franchisees savings by allowing them to purchase from a central location. Marketing strategy (especially advertising) may also be handled by the franchiser. Finally, franchisees may benefit from continued management counseling. In short, franchisees receive—that is, invest in—not only their own ready-made business but also expert help in running it.

Franchises offer many advantages to both sellers and buyers. For example, franchisers benefit from the ability to grow rapidly by using the investment money provided by franchisees. This strategy has enabled giant franchisers such as McDonald's and Baskin-Robbins to mushroom from small start-ups into billion-dollar enterprises..

For the franchisee, the arrangement combines the incentive of owning a business with the advantage of access to big-business management skills. Unlike the person who starts from scratch, the franchisee does not have to build a business step by step. Instead, the business is established virtually overnight. Moreover, because each franchise outlet is probably a carbon copy of every other outlet, the chances of failure are reduced. McDonald's, for example, is a model of consistency—Big Macs taste the same everywhere.

Of course, owning a franchise also involves certain disadvantages. Perhaps the most significant is the start-up cost. Franchise prices vary widely. Fantastic Sams hair salon franchise fees are $30,000, but a Gingiss Formalwear franchise can run as high as $125,000. Extremely profitable or hard-to-get franchises are even more expensive. A McDonald's franchise costs at least $650,000 to $750,000, and a professional sports team can cost several hundred million dollars. Franchisees may also have continued obligations to contribute percentages of sales to the parent corporation.

Buying a franchise also entails less tangible costs. For one thing, the small-business owner sacrifices some independence. A McDonald's franchisee cannot change the way its hamburgers or milkshakes are made. Nor can franchisees create an individual identity in their community; for all practical purposes, the McDonald's owner is anonymous. In addition, many franchise agreements are difficult to terminate.

Finally, although franchises minimize risks, they do not guarantee success. Many franchisees have seen their investments—and their dreams—disappear because of poor location, rising costs, or lack of continued franchiser commitment. Moreover, figures on failure rates are artificially low because they do not include failing franchisees bought out by their franchising parent companies. An additional

franchising agreement
A contract between an entrepreneur (the franchisee) and a parent company (the franchiser); the entrepreneur pays the parent company for the use of its trademarks, products, formulas, and business plans

risk is that the chain itself could collapse. In any given year, dozens—sometimes hundreds—of franchisers close shop or stop selling franchises.

The Performance of Entrepreneurial Organizations

The formulation and implementation of an effective strategy plays a major role in determining the overall performance of an entrepreneurial organization. This section examines how entrepreneurial firms evolve over time and the attributes of these firms that enhance their chances of success. For every Henry Ford, Walt Disney, Mary Kay Ash, or Bill Gates—people who transformed small businesses into major corporations—there are many small-business owners and entrepreneurs who fail.

Figure 5.5 illustrates recent trends in new business start-ups and failures. As you can see, new business start-ups have generally run between around 150,000 and 190,000 per year. Business failures have generally run between 50,000 and 100,000, per year. In this section, we look first at a few key trends in small-business start-ups. Then we examine some of the main reasons for success and failure in small-business undertakings.

Trends in Small-Business Start-Ups

Thousands of new businesses are started in the United States every year. Several factors account for this trend, and in this section we focus on four of them.

Emergence of E-Commerce   Clearly, one of the most significant recent trends in small-business start-ups is the rapid emergence of electronic commerce. Because the Internet has provided fundamentally new ways of doing business, savvy

Figure 5.5
BUSINESS START-UP SUCCESSES
AND FAILURES

Over the most recent ten-year period for which data are available, new business start-ups numbered between 150,000 and 190,000 per year. Business failures during this same period, meanwhile, ranged from about 50,000 to nearly 100,000 per year.

Source: U.S. Census Bureau, *Statistical Abstract of the United States,* 2002 (Washington, DC: Government Printing Office, 2002).

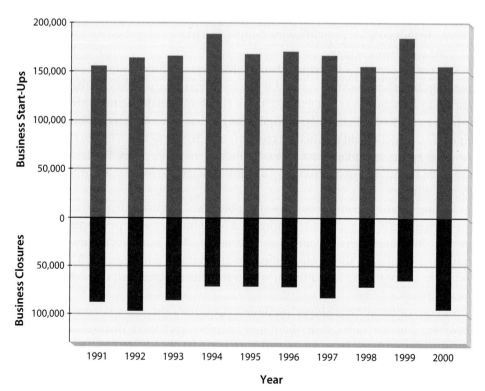

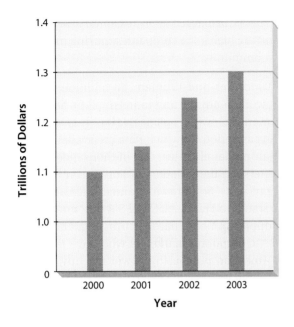

Figure 5.6

THE GROWTH OF ONLINE COMMERCE

Online commerce is becoming an increasingly important part of the U.S. economy. As shown here, for example, online commerce has grown from about $1.1 trillion in 2000 to an estimated $1.3 trillion by 2003. And most indicators suggest that this trend will continue.

Source: U.S. Census Bureau, *Statistical Abstract of the United States*, 2005 (Washington, DC: Government Printing Office, 2005).

entrepreneurs have been able to create and expand new businesses faster and more easily than ever before. Such leading-edge firms as America Online and eBay, for example, owe their very existence to the Internet. At the same time, however, many would-be Internet entrepreneurs have gone under in the last few years, as the so-called dot-com boom quickly faded. Figure 5.6 summarizes trends in online commerce from 2000 through 2003. In addition, one recent study reported that in 1999 the Internet economy grew overall by 62 percent over the previous year and provided jobs for 2.5 million people.[26]

Indeed, it seems as if new ideas emerge virtually every day. Andrew Beebe, for example, is scoring big with Bigstep, a web business that essentially creates, hosts, and maintains websites for other small businesses. So far, Bigstep has signed up 75,000 small-business clients. Beebe actually provides his basic services for free but earns money by charging for such so-called premium services as customer billing. Karl Jacob's Keen.com is a web business that matches people looking for advice with experts who have the answers. Keen got the idea when he and his father were struggling to fix a boat motor and did not know where to turn for help. Keen.com attracted 100,000 subscribers in just three months.[27]

Crossovers from Big Business   It is interesting to note that increasingly more businesses are being started by people who have opted to leave big corporations and put their experience and know-how to work for themselves. In some cases, these individuals see great new ideas they want to develop. Often, they get burned out working for a big corporation. Sometimes they have lost their job, only to discover that working for themselves was a better idea anyway.

Cisco Systems CEO John Chambers is acknowledged as one of the best entrepreneurs around. But he spent several years working first at IBM and then at Wang Laboratories before he set out on his own. Under his leadership, Cisco has become one of the largest and most important technology companies in the world. Indeed, for a few days in March 2000, Cisco had the world's highest market capitalization, and it remains one of the world's most valuable companies.[28] In a more unusual case, Gilman Louie recently left an executive position at Hasbro toy company's online group to head up a CIA-backed venture capital firm called In-Q-It. The firm's mission is to help nurture high-tech companies making products of interest to the nation's intelligence community.[29]

Opportunities for Minorities and Women   In addition to big-business expatriates, minorities and women are starting more small businesses. For example, the number of African American–owned businesses has increased by 46 percent during the most recent five-year period for which data are available and now totals about 620,000. Chicago's Gardner family is just one of thousands of examples illustrating this trend. The Gardners are the founders of Soft Sheen Products, a firm specializing in ethnic hair products. Soft Sheen attained sales of $80 million in the year before the Gardners sold it to France's L'Oréal S.A. for more than $160 million. The emergence of such opportunities is hardly surprising, either to African American entrepreneurs or to the corporate marketers who have taken an interest in their companies. African American purchasing power recently topped $530 billion. Up from just over $300 billion in 1990, that increase of 73 percent far outstrips the 57 percent increase experienced by all Americans.[30]

Latino-owned businesses have grown at an even faster rate of 76 percent and now number about 862,000. Other ethnic groups are also making their presence felt among U.S. business owners. Business ownership among Asians and Pacific Islanders has increased 56 percent, to over 600,000. Although the number of businesses owned by American Indians and Alaska Natives is still somewhat small, at slightly over 100,000, the total nevertheless represents a five-year increase of 93 percent.[31]

The number of women entrepreneurs is also growing rapidly. Celeste Johnson, for example, left a management position at Pitney Bowes to launch Obex, Inc., which makes gardening and landscaping products from mixed recycled plastics. Katrina Garnett gave up a lucrative job at Oracle to start her own software company, Crossworlds Software. Laila Rubenstein closed her management-consulting practice to create Greeting Cards.com, Inc., an Internet-based business selling customizable electronic greetings. "Women-owned business," says Teresa Cavanaugh, director of the Women Entrepreneur's Connection at BankBoston, "is the largest emerging segment of the small-business market. Women-owned businesses are an economic force that no bank can afford to overlook."[32]

There are now 9.1 million businesses owned by women—about 40 percent of all businesses in the United States. Combined, they generate nearly $4 trillion in revenue a year—an increase of 132 percent since 1992. The number of people employed nationwide at women-owned businesses since 1992 has grown to around 27.5 million—an increase of 108 percent.[33] Figure 5.7 summarizes the corporate backgrounds of women entrepreneurs and provides some insight into what they like about running their own businesses. Former corporate positions in general management (25 percent), sales (21 percent), and accounting and finance (18 percent) account for almost two-thirds of the women who start their own businesses. Once in charge of their own business, women also report that they like being their own bosses, setting their own hours, controlling their own destinies, pleasing customers, having independence, making decisions, and achieving goals.

Better Survival Rates   Finally, more people are encouraged to test their skills as entrepreneurs because the failure rate among small businesses has been declin-

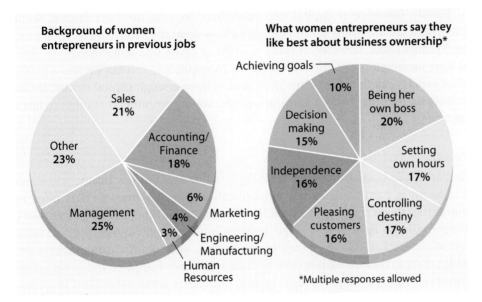

Figure 5.7

WHERE WOMEN ENTREPRENEURS COME FROM AND WHAT THEY LIKE ABOUT THEIR WORK

Women entrepreneurs come from all sectors of large businesses, although management and sales are especially well represented. Women entrepreneurs indicate that they really like being their own bosses, setting their own hours, controlling their own destinies, and being independent.

Source: From "Women Entrepreneurs," *Wall Street Journal*, May 24, 1999. Copyright © 1999 by Dow Jones & Co., Inc. Reproduced with permission of Dow Jones & Co., Inc. via Copyright Clearance Center.

ing in recent years. During the 1960s and 1970s, for example, less than half of all new start-ups survived more than 18 months; only one in five lasted 10 years. Now, however, new businesses have a better chance of surviving. Of new businesses started in the 1980s, for instance, over 77 percent remained in operation for at least 3 years. Today, the SBA estimates that at least 40 percent of all new businesses can expect to survive for 6 years. For the reasons discussed in the next section, small businesses suffer a higher mortality rate than larger concerns. Among those that manage to stay in business for 6 to 10 years, however, the survival rate levels off.

Reasons for Failure

Unfortunately, 63 percent of all new businesses will not celebrate a sixth anniversary. Why do some succeed and others fail? Although no set pattern has been established, four general factors contribute to new business failure. One factor is managerial incompetence or inexperience. Some would-be entrepreneurs assume that they can succeed through common sense, overestimate their own managerial acumen, or think that hard work alone will lead to success. But if managers do not know how to make basic business decisions or understand the basic concepts and principles of management, they are unlikely to be successful in the long run.

Neglect can also contribute to failure. Some entrepreneurs try either to launch their ventures in their spare time or to devote only a limited amount of time to a new business. But starting a new business requires an overwhelming time commitment. Entrepreneurs who are not willing to put in the time and effort that a business requires are unlikely to survive.

Third, weak control systems can lead to serious problems. Effective control systems are needed to keep a business on track and to help alert entrepreneurs to potential trouble. If control systems do not signal impending problems, managers may be in serious trouble before more visible difficulties alert them.

Finally, insufficient capital can contribute to new business failure. Some entrepreneurs are overly optimistic about how soon they will start earning profits. In most cases, however, it takes months or years before a business is likely to start turning a profit. Amazon.com, for example, has still not earned a profit. Most experts say that a new business should have enough capital to operate for at least six months without earning a profit; some recommend enough to last a year.[34]

Reasons for Success

Similarly, four basic factors are typically cited to explain new business success. One factor is hard work, drive, and dedication. New business owners must be committed to succeeding and be willing to put in the time and effort to make it happen. Gladys Edmunds, a single teenage mother in Pittsburgh, washed laundry, made chicken dinners to sell to cab drivers, and sold fire extinguishers and Bibles door to door to earn money to launch her own business. Today, Edmunds Travel Consultants employs eight people and earns about $6 million in annual revenues.[35]

Careful analysis of market conditions can help new business owners assess the probable reception of their products in the marketplace. This will provide insights about market demand for proposed products and services. Whereas attempts to expand local restaurants specializing in baked potatoes, muffins, and gelato have been largely unsuccessful, hamburger and pizza chains continue to have an easier time expanding into new markets.

Managerial competence also contributes to success. Successful new business owners may acquire competence through training or experience or by using the expertise of others. Few successful entrepreneurs succeed alone or straight out of college. Most spend time working in successful companies or partner with others in order to bring more expertise to a new business.

Finally, luck also plays a role in the success of some firms. For example, after Alan McKim started Clean Harbors, an environmental cleanup firm based in New England, he struggled to keep his business afloat. Then the U.S. government committed $1.6 billion to toxic waste cleanup—McKim's specialty. He was able to get several large government contracts and put his business on solid financial footing. Had the government fund not been created at just the right time, McKim may well have failed.

Summary of Key Points

1. Discuss the nature of entrepreneurship.
   - Entrepreneurship is the process of planning, organizing, operating, and assuming the risk of a business venture.
   - An entrepreneur is someone who engages in entrepreneurship. In general, entrepreneurs start small businesses.

2. Describe the role of entrepreneurship in society.
   - Small businesses are an important source of innovation.
   - Small businesses create numerous jobs.
   - Small businesses contribute to the success of large businesses.

3. Understand the major issues involved in choosing strategies for small firms and the role of international management in entrepreneurship.
   - In choosing strategies, entrepreneurs have to consider the characteristics of the industry in which they are going to conduct business.
   - Small businesses generally have several distinctive competencies that they should exploit in choosing their strategy. Small businesses are usually skilled at identifying niches in established markets, identifying new markets, and acting quickly to obtain first-mover advantages.
   - Small businesses are usually not skilled at exploiting economies of scale.
   - Once an entrepreneur has chosen a strategy, the strategy is normally written down in a business plan. Writing a business plan forces an entrepreneur to plan thoroughly and to anticipate problems that might occur.

4. Discuss the structural challenges unique to entrepreneurial firms.
   - With a strategy and business plan in place, entrepreneurs must choose a structure to implement them. All of the structural issues summarized in the next three chapters of this book are relevant to the entrepreneur.
   - In addition, the entrepreneur has structural choices to make. For example, the entrepreneur can buy an existing business or start a new one.
   - In determining financial structure, an entrepreneur has to decide how much personal capital to invest in an organization, how much bank and government support to obtain, and whether to encourage venture capital firms to invest.
   - Entrepreneurs can also rely on various sources of advice.

5. Understand the determinants of the performance of small firms.
   - Several interesting trends characterize new business start-ups today. These include the emergence of electronic commerce, crossovers from big business, increased opportunities for women and minorities, and better survival rates.
   - There are several reasons why some new businesses fail and others succeed. Reasons for failure include incompetence or inexperience, neglect, weak control systems, and insufficient capital. Reasons for success include hard work, drive, and dedication, market awareness, managerial competence, and luck.

Discussion Questions

Questions for Review

1. Describe the similarities and differences between entrepreneurial firms and large firms in terms of their job creation and innovation.

2. What characteristics make an industry attractive to entrepreneurs? Based on these characteristics, which industries are most attractive to entrepreneurs?

3. Describe recent trends in new business start-ups.

Questions for Analysis

6. Entrepreneurs and small businesses play a variety of important roles in society. If these roles are so important, do you think that the government should do more to encourage the development of small business? Why or why not?

4. What are the different sources of advice for entrepreneurs? What type of information would an entrepreneur be likely to get from each source? What are the drawbacks or limitations for each source?

5. What are the basic reasons why small businesses succeed, and what are the basic reasons they fail?

7. Consider the four major reasons for new business failure. What actions can entrepreneurs take to minimize or avoid each cause of failure?

8. The U.S. automotive industry is well established, with several large and many small competitors. Describe

the unexploited niches in the U.S. auto industry and tell how entrepreneurs could offer products that fill those niches.

9. List five entrepreneur-owned businesses in your community. In which industry does each business compete? Based on the industry, how do you rate each business's long-term chances for success? Explain your answers.

10. Using the information about managing a small business presented in this chapter, analyze whether you would like to work in a small business—either as an employee or as a founder. Given your personality, background, and experience, does working in or starting a new business appeal to you? What are the reasons for your opinion?

Building Effective Diagnostic Skills

Exercise Overview

Diagnostic skills are the skills that enable a manager to visualize the most appropriate response to a situation. This exercise develops your diagnostic skills by asking you to consider the factors that may increase the odds of your choosing an entrepreneurial career.

Exercise Background

Scholars of entrepreneurship are concerned with understanding why some individuals choose to start a new business, whereas others do not. Investigators have surveyed thousands of individuals, entrepreneurs and non-entrepreneurs, in an attempt to discover factors that can distinguish between the two groups. Hundreds of studies have been conducted, and some consensus has emerged. Judging on the basis of numerous studies, entrepreneurship is more likely when an individual

- is the parent, child, spouse, or sibling of an entrepreneur.

- is an immigrant to the United States or the child of an immigrant.
- is a parent.
- is a member of the Jewish or Protestant faith.
- holds a professional degree in a field such as medicine, law, or engineering.
- has recently experienced a life-changing event, such as getting married, having a child, moving to a new city, or losing a job.

Exercise Task

With the background information above as context, do the following:

1. Choose one of the categories above and explain why this factor might make an individual more likely to become a business owner.

2. From the categories listed above, choose one that is true of yourself. (Choose a different category from the one you discussed in your answer to Question 1.) In your opinion, does that factor make it more likely that you will become an entrepreneur? Why or why not? If none of the categories above applies to you, tell whether that fact makes it less likely that you will become an entrepreneur, and explain why.

Building Effective Interpersonal Skills

Exercise Overview

Interpersonal skills reflect the manager's ability to understand and motivate individuals and groups. This exercise asks you to assess personality traits associated with entrepreneurship.

Exercise Background

Studies of successful entrepreneurs have found that they share three personality traits. This is not to say that everyone who exhibits a high level of these three traits will become an entrepreneur. Rather, people are more likely to be successful as entrepreneurs if they have these three traits. It follows that people are not likely to be successful as entrepreneurs if they do not have the three traits. Finally, note that the research points out merely what is likely, not what is certain.

After you complete the following questionnaire, your professor will describe the three personality traits and your class will discuss them.

An interesting variation on this activity is to ask someone else to complete the questionnaire. Then you can assess the entrepreneurial aspects of his or her personality.

Exercise Task

With this background information as context, answer the following questions and record your answers. There are no right or wrong choices. Your professor will show you how to score your answers.

	Strongly Disagree	Disagree	Don't Know	Agree	Strongly Agree
1. I believe success depends on ability, not luck.					
2. I am consistent.					
3. I have little influence over things that happen to me.					
4. I have original ideas.					
5. I am stimulating.					
6. I am thorough.					
7. I often risk doing things differently.					
8. I can stand out in disagreement against a group.					
9. I prefer to work on one problem at a time.					
10. I enjoy detailed work.					
11. I prefer friends who do not "rock the boat."					
12. I will always think of something when stuck.					
13. I am methodical.					
14. I need the stimulation of frequent change.					
15. I like to vary my routines at a moment's notice.					
16. I never seek to bend or break the rules.					
17. I am predictable.					
18. When I make plans, I am sure I can achieve them.					
19. I prefer changes to occur gradually.					
20. I am more willing than other people to take risks.					

Reprinted by permission of the author Margaret Hill.

Building Effective Conceptual Skills

Exercise Overview

Conceptual skills reflect the manager's ability to think in the abstract. This exercise will help you relate conceptual skills to entrepreneurship.

Exercise Background

Assume that you have made the decision to open a small business in the local community when you graduate (the community where you are attending college, not your home). Assume that you have funds to start a business without having to worry about finding other investors.

Without regard for market potential, profitability, or similar considerations, list five businesses that you might want to open and operate, solely on the basis of your personal interests. For example, if you enjoy bicycling, you might enjoy opening a shop that caters to cyclists.

Next, without regard for personal attractiveness, list five businesses that you might want to open and operate, solely on the basis of market opportunity. Use the Internet to help you determine which businesses might be profitable in your community, judging on the basis of factors such as population, local economic conditions, local competition, franchising opportunities, and so on.

Evaluate the prospects for success for each of the ten businesses.

Exercise Task

With the background information as context, do the following:

1. Form a small group with three or four classmates and discuss your respective lists. Look for instances where the same type of business appears on multiple lists. Also look for cases where the same business appears with similar or dissimilar prospects for success.

2. How important is personal interest in small-business success?

3. How important is market potential in small-business success?

Skills Self-Assessment Instrument

An Entrepreneurial Quiz

Introduction: Entrepreneurs are starting ventures all the time. These new businesses are vital to the economy. The following assessment is designed to help you understand your readiness to start your own business—to be an entrepreneur.

Instructions: Place a checkmark or an X in the box next to the response that best represents your self-evaluation.

1. Are you a self-starter?
   - ☐ I do things on my own. Nobody has to tell me to get going.
   - ☐ If someone gets me started, I keep going all right.
   - ☐ Easy does it. I don't push myself until I have to.

2. How do you feel about other people?
   - ☐ I like people. I can get along with just about anybody.
   - ☐ I have plenty of friends—I don't need anybody else.
   - ☐ Most people irritate me.

3. Can you lead others?
   - ☐ I can get most people to go along when I start something.
   - ☐ I can give orders if someone tells me what we should do.
   - ☐ I let someone else get things moving. Then I go along if I feel like it.

4. Can you take responsibility?
   - ☐ I like to take charge of things and see them through.
   - ☐ I'll take over if I have to, but I'd rather let someone else be responsible.
   - ☐ There are always eager beavers around wanting to show how smart they are. I let them.

5. How good an organizer are you?
   - ☐ I like to have a plan before I start. I'm usually the one to get things lined up when the group wants to do something.
   - ☐ I do all right unless things get too confused. Then I quit.
   - ☐ You get all set and then something comes along and presents too many problems. So I just take things as they come.

6. How good a worker are you?
   - ☐ I can keep going as long as I need to. I don't mind working hard for something I want.
   - ☐ I'll work hard for a while, but when I've had enough, that's it.
   - ☐ I can't see that hard work gets you anywhere.

7. Can you make decisions?
   - ☐ I can make up my mind in a hurry if I have to. It usually turns out okay, too.
   - ☐ I can if I have plenty of time. If I have to make up my mind fast, I think later I should have decided the other way.
   - ☐ I don't like to be the one who has to decide things.

8. Can people trust what you say?
   - ☐ You bet they can. I don't say things I don't mean.
   - ☐ I try to be on the level most of the time, but sometimes I just say what's easiest.
   - ☐ Why bother if the other person doesn't know the difference?

9. Can you stick with it?
   - ☐ If I make up my mind to do something, I don't let *anything* stop me.
   - ☐ I usually finish what I start—if it goes well.
   - ☐ If it doesn't go well right away, I quit. Why beat your brains out?

10. How good is your health?
    - ☐ I *never* run down!
    - ☐ I have enough energy for most things I want to do.
    - ☐ I run out of energy sooner than most of my friends.

Total the checks or Xs in each column here:
1st col. _____, 2nd col. _____, 3rd col. _____.

From *Business Startup Basics* by Donald Dible, pp. 9–10, © 1978. Adapted by permission of Prentice-Hall, Inc., Upper Saddle River, N.J.
For interpretation, see Interpretations of Skills Self-Assessment Instruments in the appendix near the end of this text.

Experiential Exercise

Negotiating a Franchise Agreement

Step 1: Assume that you are the owner of a rapidly growing restaurant chain. In order to continue your current level of growth, you are considering the option of selling franchises for new restaurants. Working alone, outline the major points of most concern to you that you would want to have in a franchising agreement. Also note the characteristics you would look for in potential franchisees.

Step 2: Assume that you are an individual investor looking to buy a franchise in a rapidly growing restaurant chain. Again working alone, outline the major factors that might determine which franchise you elect to buy. Also note the characteristics you would look for in a potential franchiser.

Step 3: Now form small groups of four. Randomly select one member of the group to play the role of the franchiser; the other three members will play the roles of potential franchisees. Role-play a negotiation meeting. The franchiser should stick as closely as possible to the major points developed in Step 1. Similarly, the potential franchisees should try to adhere to the points they developed in Step 2.

Follow-up Questions

1. Did doing both Step 1 and Step 2 in advance help or hinder your negotiations?
2. Can a franchising agreement be so one-sided as to damage the interests of both parties? How so?

CHAPTER CLOSING CASE

ENTREPRENEURIAL SPIRIT FLIES HIGH AT JETBLUE

JetBlue was founded by David Neeleman, an airline industry veteran, in 1999. By the end of 2000, the company serviced cities around the country and more destinations were added each year. Today, JetBlue flies to 53 cities. In the challenging environment of the modern airline industry, JetBlue is an entrepreneurial success story. While rival airline start-ups struggle and fail, JetBlue prospers. How does JetBlue succeed?

JetBlue draws upon a number of distinctive competencies. One strength springs from the talent and experience of Neeleman and his team of top managers. Neeleman started Morris Air in 1984, when he was just 24 years old. Morris Air was sold to Southwest Airlines in 1994. Then Neeleman helped to found WestJet Airlines before developing the JetBlue concept. Neeleman recruited industry veterans such as COO Dave Barger and CFO John Owen, previously vice presidents at Continental and Southwest.

The airline's second-mover strategy, which imitates competitor Southwest, also provides advantages. The airline industry traditionally offered differentiated service at relatively high prices. Southwest was the first to offer discount air travel. Neeleman, thanks to his experiences, helped JetBlue to duplicate every piece of Southwest's strategy, including low labor costs, reliance on a single type of aircraft and class of service, and use of lower-cost airports.

However, JetBlue adds its own unique take on Southwest's strategy.

Neeleman improved on Southwest's formula by offering differentiation in addition to low costs. All of JetBlue's aircraft have luxurious leather seats and individual seat-back televisions, setting it apart from other low-fare carriers. DirecTV, movies, XM satellite radio, fine wines, and even a Bliss Spa kit, pamper passengers. Together, the strategies allow JetBlue to reduce expenses while charging prices greater than other discount carriers, increasing profits. Neeleman identifies three important factors in JetBlue's business model, "low costs, a great product, and capitalization."

Much of JetBlue's capital comes from Neeleman's personal fortune, which was considerable following the lucrative sale of Morris Air. Neeleman's industry contacts gave $160 million of financial support to the start-up. In 2002, JetBlue held an initial public offering that raised $158 million and gave the company another source for future funding needs.

Today, Neeleman must help JetBlue make the transition from a small, entrepreneurial start-up into the big leagues of major airlines. JetBlue's situation is reminiscent of People Express, a new airline that had $1 billion in sales within five years of start-up, and then went bankrupt just one year later. The company didn't have the funds or other resources to sustain rapid growth. Chris Collins, a former People Express manager, is now part of JetBlue's executive team. "[At People Express], we were the best thing going. A year later, we're gone because we couldn't sustain

growth," Collins says. "You know what keeps me up at night [now]? Figuring out what we're going to need, not next year but five years from now."

Neeleman needs to figure out a way to grow, while maintaining the cohesive culture and small-company feel of JetBlue. One way is through what he calls "visible leadership." Senior managers spend a day with crew members in different cities, working alongside them and talking about their concerns. Training managers in the JetBlue culture is important too.

In spite of its success, there is some indication that the company may have grown too fast and become more focused on efficiency than on effectiveness. JetBlue typically has a high proportion of flights that depart on time, one important measure of airline performance. Yet in February 2007, a severe ice storm in the eastern United States delayed air travel. Other airlines canceled flights and sent passengers home for a day or two, then resumed operations. JetBlue managers believed the weather would clear up soon and tried to stay on schedule. Some customers spent ten or more hours sitting in a plane on a runway in New York City. Others slept in airports for up to a week. Fliers were so angry that some flights had to be canceled due to concerns about the safety of the crews. The company admits that its scheduling and reservations systems were understaffed and inadequate. Losses will likely top $40 million. The lost goodwill cost may be much greater.

Whether JetBlue can recover from this incident and become a major national airline is still to be seen. Neeleman's focus on people, culture, strategy, and operations is a good start, but more will be required to keep the company flying in the right direction.

CASE QUESTIONS

1. How does being a second mover contribute to JetBlue's success? How does its second-mover strategy present potential difficulties for the firm? Would a first-mover strategy have been better? Why or why not?

2. Consider the factors that lead to success for entrepreneurial firms. In your opinion, does JetBlue have what it takes to be a success? Explain.

3. Consider the factors that lead to failure for entrepreneurial firms. In your opinion, is JetBlue likely to experience failure? Explain.

REFERENCES

"2005 Annual Report," "Fact Sheet," JetBlue website, www.jetblue.com on April 10, 2006; Jeff Bailey, "JetBlue's C.E.O. Is 'Mortified' After Fliers Are Stranded," *New York Times*, February 19, 2007, www.nytimes.com on February 23, 2007; Stacy Perman, "How JetBlue Can Regain Its Golden Image," *BusinessWeek*, September 23, 2005, www.businessweek.com on April 10, 2006; Chuck Salter, "And Now the Hard Part," *Fast Company*, May 2004, www.fastcompany.com on April 10, 2006; Wendy Zellner, "Is JetBlue's Flight Plan Flawed?" *BusinessWeek*, February 16, 2004, www.businessweek.com on April 10, 2006.

YOU MAKE THE CALL

Founding Facebook

1. If you use Facebook, what are the properties of the site that cause you to use it?

2. If you do not use Facebook, what might cause you to become a user?

3. Identify the primary factors that led to Facebook's success.

4. What factors should Mark Zuckerberg keep in mind as possible threats to his firm?

5. Try to identify other potential networking concepts that might be extended from Facebook.

6. Would you be willing to invest in Facebook? Why or why not?

Test Prepper

college.hmco.com/pic/griffinfund5e

You've read the chapter, studied the key terms, and the exam is any day now. Think you're ready to ace it? Take this sample test to gauge your comprehension of chapter material. You can check your answers at the back of the book. Want more test questions? Visit the student website at http://college.hmco.com/pic/griffinfund5e/ and take the ACE quizzes for more practice.

1. T F Samuel Palmisano, CEO of IBM, is an entrepreneur.

2. T F Small businesses are generally the first to hire during economic growth and the first to fire during economic slowdowns.

3. T F The service industry appeals to entrepreneurs because it has relatively low start-up cost, it offers a high return on time invested, and it appeals to those with a talent for innovation.

4. T F Eduardo wants to go into business for himself. He is more likely to have success starting from scratch than buying an existing business.

5. T F Mark Zuckerberg, founder of Facebook, is an entrepreneur.

6. The majority of workers in the United States are employed by companies with _____ employees.

   a. fewer than 20

   b. fewer than 100

   c. fewer than 1,000

   d. fewer than 10,000

   e. more than 10,000

7. During the 1990s Wal-Mart added 639,000 jobs, whereas Kmart eliminated 86,475 jobs. Which of the following statements is true about job creation?

   a. Large firms are the first to hire during economic recovery.

   b. Large firms are the first to fire during economic downswings.

   c. Large firms create most of the new jobs.

   d. Business success creates jobs.

   e. All of the above

8. Opportunities to take advantage of economies of scale are MOST obvious in which industry?

   a. Transportation

   b. Retail

   c. Construction

   d. Wholesale

   e. Manufacturing

9. A business plan should include all EXCEPT which of the following?

   a. Goals and objectives

   b. Strategies and structure

   c. Implementation

   d. Salary expectations

   e. Distinctive competencies

10. Maria joined the National Association of Women Business Owners. She went to a conference and met someone who helped her get venture capital for her business. Maria used _____ as a source of management advice.

   a. management consultants

   b. an advisory board

   c. the SBA

   d. networking

   e. All of the above

! Meeting of the Minds

Parts One and Two: Managing in the Soft-Drink Industry

There are four running case segments, each related to major sections of the text. All segments of the running case focus on Coca-Cola and PepsiCo. Your small group will be assigned to one of these companies.

For each case, read the information and do research as a group to learn more about your firm. You may use any source, including library materials and conversations with employees. After your group answers the discussion questions, share your answers.

As a result of working on this case, you will increase your knowledge of these companies and the industry. You will practice your research and analytical skills. And your knowledge of management will grow and deepen as you apply the concepts from the textbook to understanding real organizations.

This part of the running case addresses issues raised in Parts One and Two of the text, covering Chapters 1 through 5.

History of The Coca-Cola Company

Coca-Cola was invented in Atlanta in 1886. The drink contained cocaine (removed in 1903) and was prescribed for nervous complaints. National sales began in 1892, and the company went public in 1919. Coke spread worldwide, especially during World War II. In the 1960s, Coca-Cola purchased the Minute Maid juice company. Coke quadrupled sales between 1975 and 1995. The company experimented with diversification, buying Columbia Pictures in 1982 before divesting in 1989. New products were big hits, but Coke stumbled with New Coke in 1985. During the 1990s, Coca-Cola was more profitable and grew faster than rival Pepsi, which began to catch up after 2000. Today, Coke has achieved total sales of over 6 trillion servings and has experienced 52 years of growth.

History of PepsiCo

Pepsi was invented in North Carolina in the 1890s. It was intended to treat stomach pain, or dyspepsia. After a bankruptcy in the 1920s, the firm regained its popularity during the Depression, as the result of a price war with Coke. In the 1960s, Pepsi acquired Mountain Dew and then purchased snack maker Frito-Lay,

forming PepsiCo. Pepsi entered the USSR, where it was the first American consumer product sold in that country. During the 1970s and 1980s, Pepsi acquired several companies, including North American Van Lines and Wilson Sporting Goods. They were later sold.

Pepsi also acquired Pizza Hut, Taco Bell, and Kentucky Fried Chicken. In 1997, the restaurant units were spun off, creating Yum! Brands. Pepsi purchased juice bottler Tropicana-Dole and also acquired many foreign competitors. Pepsi bought Quaker Oats, which owns Gatorade, in 2001. Today, Pepsi is growing at 8 percent annually, and its products control more grocery-store shelf space than any other company's.

The Soft-Drink Industry

Coca-Cola and PepsiCo are the two largest global firms competing in the soft-drink manufacturing industry, NAICS code 31211. The companies' most important functions are marketing, distribution, and new-product development. In addition, corporate finance is important to support acquisitions.

The ultimate soft-drink consumers are individuals. The manufacturing firms sell to two customer groups. They sell syrups to independent bottling companies, who add water and then bottle and distribute the final product. Second, the manufacturers own some bottling facilities. Coca-Cola owns approximately 45 percent of its bottling capacity and PepsiCo owns about 10 percent. Both independent and company-owned bottlers sell to grocery, convenience, and discount stores; vending operators; and restaurants.

Rivalry in the industry is fierce, with aggressive competition. However, the intensity increased in 1976 when Pepsi conducted the first blind taste test. (See more about this in Part Five.) The companies mimic each other's products and methods closely. However, the rivalry is honest. In July 2006, when Coke employees tried to sell trade secrets to Pepsi, the company informed Coke and then cooperated with the FBI.

Since 2000, domestic soft-drink sales have declined after decades of growth. Explanations include consumers' increasing interest in health, a backlash against large multinationals, a trend toward nonsoda beverages, and the popularity of smaller soft-drink brands.

Online Resources for Further Research

In addition to the sites listed below, a search through Google or other portals using company names or "soft drink industry" will yield good results. Use an index to locate reputable print media such as *BusinessWeek*, *Fortune*, and the *Wall Street Journal*. All of the information you need can be gathered for free—there is no need to pay for it.

1. Coca-Cola's home page at www.thecoca-colacompany.com. Especially useful is the "Our Company" section and "Investors" for the most recent Annual Review and Message from the CEO.
2. PepsiCo's home page at www.pepsico.com. Especially useful is the "Company" section and "Investors" for the most recent Annual Report and Message from the CEO.
3. Industry news and data at Beverage World, www.beverageworld.com. Look at their "State of the Industry" report.
4. More industry news at BevNet, accessed at www.bevnet.com. Look at their "Industry News" section.
5. Industry news at www.beveragedaily.com.
6. London-based newsletter for international news at www.drinks-business-review.com. Click on "Soft Drinks."
7. The beverage industry trade association at www.ameribev.org. Be wary of potential favorable bias.

Case Discussion Questions

Each of the issues raised below should be answered briefly, that is, in no more than a paragraph or two.

1. Briefly describe your company (Coca-Cola or PepsiCo) today. What are its most important products or services? Where are its most important markets? Who are its most important customers? Tell a little about your company's financial performance.
2. Briefly describe the three factors in the general environment facing your company today. Tell whether each factor presents any significant threats or opportunities for your firm.
3. Briefly describe the five dimensions of the task environment facing your company today. Tell whether each dimension presents any significant threats or opportunities for your firm.
4. Which of Porter's generic strategies is your company pursuing? Explain how you arrived at your answer.
5. Which corporate-level strategy is your company pursuing? Explain how you arrived at your answer.
6. What are the opportunities you see in the soft-drink industry today for market entry by smaller, local manufacturers? Examples of smaller, successful firms include new firms Jones Soda and Red Bull, as well as existing companies such as Cheerwine, Bubble Up, and Big Red.

Organization Structure and Design

chapter 6

FIRST THINGS FIRST

Did You Hear the One About . . . Delegation?

"You have to delegate when you're doing 22 episodes a season."

—ROB BURNETT, EXECUTIVE PRODUCER, WORLDWIDE PANTS, MAKER
OF *EVERYBODY LOVES RAYMOND*

"People say New Yorkers can't get along. Not true. I saw two New Yorkers, complete strangers, sharing a cab. One guy took the tires and the radio; the other guy took the engine."

—DAVID LETTERMAN

Everybody who's anybody delegates. CEOs, the president, military commanders all delegate. Delegation can help leaders manage time better, bring more resources to bear, and develop subordinates' confidence and abilities. It is also risky. Some subordinates may not have the capability to make effective decisions. When that happens, managers are responsible for the results.

Imagine this: You are a television show host, known for your unique brand of humor. However, the reality is that you could never write enough material to fill an hour-long show every day. So you must delegate. From producers to direc-

The creative team behind David Letterman's Late Show *practices several forms of delegation. Their creative talents are recognized here by being named as Emmy Award winners.*

LEARNING OBJECTIVES

After studying this chapter, you should be able to:

- Identify the basic elements of organizations.
- Describe the bureaucratic perspective on organization design.
- Identify and explain several situational influences on organization design.
- Describe the basic forms of organization design that characterize many organizations.
- Describe emerging issues in organization design.

tors to joke writers, your team makes most of the decisions that will have a high impact on your career. This is the situation facing late-night TV personalities such as David Letterman, Jon Stewart, and Jay Leno. They rely on a host of coworkers to make them appear funny, night after night.

The executive producer of a talk show is the equivalent of a corporate CEO. They supervise lower-level employees, including producers, directors, and the host. They delegate most of the decisions about the day-to-day running of the show. The producer is the liaison between the director and the studio, while the director is head of the production team. Good producers and directors guarantee high-quality guests and a focused and effective staff.

"Don't forget Mother's Day. Or as they call it in Beverly Hills, Dad's Third Wife Day."
—JAY LENO

Letterman's *Late Show* is produced by Worldwide Pants, a company he founded. The executive producer is Rob Burnett, who also produces *Everybody Loves Raymond* and *Ed,* also Worldwide Pants shows. Burnett claims that being responsible for enacting Letterman's vision and voice is "a gigantic responsibility fraught with an enormous amount of pressure."

Late Show employs teams of joke writers in addition to the host's material and ideas submitted by freelance writers. At the bottom of this hierarchy, freelance joke writers make $100 for each joke used on the air. Jokes are the comic's bottom line. Comedians use physical humor, voice control, and comic timing, but in the end, they are only as funny as their joke writers make them.

"After going to war against the U.N.'s expressed wishes, the U.S. is now admitting it needs the U.N.'s help. It's the geopolitical equivalent of the 2 A.M. phone call every parent dreads: 'Mom, I'm not saying I wrecked the car, but I need a ride home.'"
—JON STEWART

On *Late Show*, writers begin work in the late morning, with a brainstorming meeting that leaves everyone laughing and productive. Some are working on that night's show, some on later ones. Writers are given "setups," the serious straight line that begins the comic routine. The setups provide topics and shape the show. After a period of intense writing, there is a rehearsal and the host gives feedback. Letterman trusts his writers to plan a show that is varied, funny, and topical.

Burnett has learned what he can safely delegate and what he cannot. *Late Show* joke writers can write funny material that fits with Letterman's on-screen persona. On the other hand, *Everybody Loves Raymond* is Burnett's "baby," a concept developed by him. *Raymond* contributors typically leave after one season. "Writers are afraid to come to this show because they know how involved the creators are," one crew member relates. "You have to [delegate] when you're doing 22 episodes a season," Burnett adds. "But when we do, it's not the same. It's like a signature. We sign our names a certain way."

Letterman delegates to Burnett, who delegates back to Letterman. When the *Raymond* character Phil Stubbs needed to utter a ridiculous catchphrase, Letterman supplied, "Shave my poodle."

"I cannot sing, dance or act; what else would I be but a talk show host?"

—DAVID LETTERMAN[1]

One of the major ingredients in managing any business is deciding what tasks can be delegated to others and what tasks must be retained by the manager. Decisions about delegation, in turn, play an important role in the creation of an organization design that links the various elements that comprise the organization. This chapter, the first of three devoted to organizing, discusses many of the critical elements of organization structure and design that managers can control. We first identify and describe the various elements of organization. We then summarize the first common approach to organization, bureaucracy. Next we introduce situational influences on organization design and then discuss the basic forms of design used today. We conclude with a look at emerging issues in organization design.

The Basic Elements of Organizing

The phrase **organization structure and design** refers to the overall set of elements that can be used to configure an organization. This section introduces and describes these elements: job specialization, departmentalization, reporting relationships, distribution of authority, and coordination.[2]

> **organization structure and design**
> The set of elements that can be used to configure an organization

Job Specialization

The first element of organization structure is job specialization. **Job specialization** is the degree to which the overall task of the organization is broken down and divided into smaller component parts. Job specialization is a normal extension of organizational growth. For example, when Walt Disney started his company, he did everything himself—wrote cartoons, drew them, and then marketed them to theaters. As the business grew, he eventually hired others to perform many of these same functions. As growth continued, so, too, did specialization. For example, as animation artists work on Disney/Pixar movies today, they may specialize in generating computer images of a single character or doing only background scenery. And today, the Walt Disney Company has thousands of different specialized jobs. Clearly, no one person could perform them all.

> **job specialization**
> The degree to which the overall task of the organization is broken down and divided into smaller component parts

Benefits and Limitations of Specialization   Job specialization provides four benefits to organizations.[3] First, workers performing small, simple tasks will become very proficient at each task. Second, transfer time between tasks decreases. If employees perform several different tasks, some time is lost as they stop doing the first task and start doing the next. Third, the more narrowly defined a job is, the easier it is to develop specialized equipment to assist with that job. Fourth, when an employee who performs a highly specialized job is absent or resigns, the manager is able to train someone new at relatively low cost. Although specialization is generally thought of in terms of operating jobs, many organizations have

Job specialization is a key element underlying most mass production facilities. Assembly lines have long been used to manufacture such products as automobiles, appliances, and home computers. But job specialization and assembly lines are also commonly found in newer forms of production as well. These workers, for example, work for Earthbound Farms in Yuma, Arizona. They are stationed along an assembly line that is mixing and packaging organic salads. Each individual has a specific job to be performed to insure that the spinach and lettuce get to consumers in perfect condition.

extended the basic elements of specialization to managerial and professional levels as well.[4]

On the other hand, job specialization can have negative consequences. The foremost criticism is that workers who perform highly specialized jobs may become bored and dissatisfied. The job may be so specialized that it offers no challenge or stimulation. Boredom and monotony set in, absenteeism rises, and the quality of the work may suffer. Furthermore, the anticipated benefits of specialization do not always occur. For example, a classic study conducted at Maytag found that the time spent moving work in process from one worker to another was greater than the time needed for the same individual to change from job to job.[5] Thus, although some degree of specialization is necessary, it should not be carried to extremes because of the possible negative consequences. Managers must be sensitive to situations in which extreme specialization should be avoided. And indeed, several alternative approaches to designing jobs have been developed.

Alternatives to Specialization

To counter the problems associated with specialization, managers have sought other approaches to job design that achieve a better balance between organizational demands for efficiency and productivity and individual needs for creativity and autonomy. Five alternative approaches are job rotation, job enlargement, job enrichment, the job characteristics approach, and work teams.[6]

Job rotation involves systematically moving employees from one job to another. A worker in a warehouse might unload trucks on Monday, carry incoming inventory to storage on Tuesday, verify invoices on Wednesday, pull outgoing inventory from storage on Thursday, and load trucks on Friday. Thus the jobs do not change, but instead, workers move from job to job. Unfortunately, for this very reason,

job rotation
An alternative to job specialization that involves systematically moving employees from one job to another

job rotation has not been very successful in enhancing employee motivation or satisfaction. Jobs that are amenable to rotation tend to be relatively standard and routine. Workers who are rotated to a "new" job may be more satisfied at first, but satisfaction soon wanes. Although many companies (among them American Cyanamid, Bethlehem Steel, Ford, Prudential Insurance, TRW, and Western Electric) have tried job rotation, it is most often used today as a training device to improve worker skills and flexibility.

Job enlargement was developed to increase the total number of tasks workers perform. As a result, all workers perform a wide variety of tasks, which presumably reduces the level of job dissatisfaction. Many organizations have used job enlargement, including IBM, Detroit Edison, AT&T, the U.S. Civil Service, and Maytag. At Maytag, for example, the assembly line for producing washing-machine water pumps was systematically changed so that work that had originally been performed by six workers, who passed the work sequentially from one person to another, was performed by four workers, each of whom assembled a complete pump.[7] Unfortunately, although job enlargement does have some positive consequences, they are often offset by some disadvantages: (1) training costs usually increase, (2) unions have argued that pay should increase because the worker is doing more tasks, and (3) in many cases the work remains boring and routine even after job enlargement.

> **job enlargement**
> An alternative to job specialization that involves giving the employee more tasks to perform

A more comprehensive approach, ***job enrichment***, assumes that increasing the range and variety of tasks is not sufficient by itself to improve employee motivation.[8] Thus job enrichment attempts to increase both the number of tasks a worker does and the control the worker has over the job. To implement job enrichment, managers remove some controls from the job, delegate more authority to employees, and structure the work in complete, natural units. These changes increase subordinates' sense of responsibility. Another part of job enrichment is to continually assign new and challenging tasks, thereby increasing employees' opportunity for growth and advancement. AT&T, Texas Instruments, IBM, and General Foods are among the firms that have used job enrichment. This approach, however, also has disadvantages. For example, work systems need to be analyzed before enrichment, but this seldom happens, and managers rarely ask for employee preferences when enriching jobs.

> **job enrichment**
> An alternative to job specialization that involves increasing both the number of tasks the worker does and the control the worker has over the job

The ***job characteristics approach*** is an alternative to job specialization that does take into account the work system and employee preferences.[9] As illustrated in Figure 6.1, the job characteristics approach suggests that jobs should be diagnosed and improved along five core dimensions:

> **job characteristics approach**
> An alternative to job specialization that suggests that jobs should be diagnosed and improved along five core dimensions, taking into account both the work system and employee preferences

1. *Skill variety,* the number of things a person does in a job

2. *Task identity,* the extent to which the worker does a complete or identifiable portion of the total job

3. *Task significance,* the perceived importance of the task

4. *Autonomy,* the degree of control the worker has over how the work is performed

5. *Feedback,* the extent to which the worker knows how well the job is being performed

Increasing the presence of these dimensions in a job presumably leads to higher motivation, high-quality work performance, high satisfaction, and low absenteeism and turnover. Numerous studies have been conducted to test the usefulness

Figure 6.1

THE JOB CHARACTERISTICS APPROACH

The job characteristics approach to job design provides a viable alternative to job specialization. Five core job dimensions may lead to critical psychological states that, in turn, may enhance motivation, performance, and satisfaction while also reducing absenteeism and turnover.

Source: J. R. Hackman and G. R. Oldham, "Motivation Through the Design of Work: Test of a Theory," *Organizational Behavior and Human Performance*, Vol. 16 (1976), pp. 250–279. Copyright © Academic Press, Inc. Reprinted by permission of Academic Press and the authors.

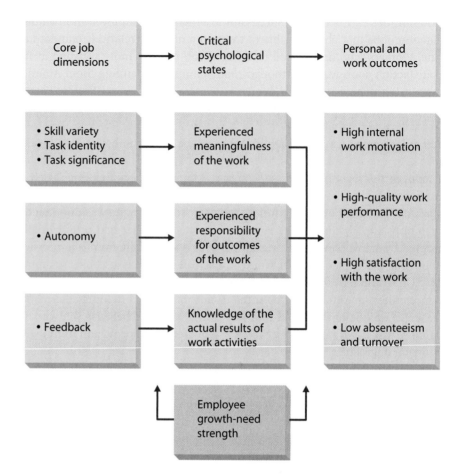

of the job characteristics approach. The Southwestern Division of Prudential Insurance, for example, used this approach in its claims division. Results included moderate declines in turnover and a small but measurable improvement in work quality. Other research findings have not supported this approach as strongly. Thus, although the job characteristics approach is one of the most promising alternatives to job specialization, it is probably not the final answer.

Another alternative to job specialization is **work teams**. Under this arrangement, a group is given responsibility for designing the work system to be used in performing an interrelated set of tasks. In the typical assembly-line system, the work flows from one worker to the next, and each worker has a specified job to perform. In a work team, however, the group itself decides how jobs will be allocated. For example, the work team assigns specific tasks to members, monitors and controls its own performance, and has autonomy over work scheduling.[10]

---

work team
An alternative to job specialization that allows an entire group to design the work system it will use to perform an interrelated set of tasks

---

Grouping Jobs: Departmentalization

The second element of organization structure is the grouping of jobs according to some logical arrangement. The process of grouping jobs is called *departmentalization.* When organizations are small, the owner-manager can personally oversee everyone who works there. As an organization grows, however, personally supervising all the employees becomes more and more difficult for the owner-manager. Consequently, new managerial positions are created to supervise the work of

---

departmentalization
The process of grouping jobs according to some logical arrangement

---

others. Employees are not assigned to particular managers randomly. Rather, jobs are grouped according to some plan. The logic embodied in such a plan is the basis for all departmentalization.[11]

Functional Departmentalization   The most common base for departmentalization, especially among smaller organizations, is by function. ***Functional departmentalization*** groups together those jobs involving the same or similar activities. (The word *function* is used here to mean organizational functions such as finance and production, rather than the basic managerial functions, such as planning or controlling.) This approach, which is most common in smaller organizations, has three primary advantages. First, each department can be staffed by experts in that functional area. Marketing experts can be hired to run the marketing function, for example. Second, supervision is facilitated because an individual manager needs to be familiar with only a relatively narrow set of skills. And, third, coordinating activities inside each department is easier.

> *functional departmentalization*
> Grouping jobs involving the same or similar activities

On the other hand, as an organization begins to grow in size, several disadvantages of this approach may emerge. For one, decision making tends to become slower and more bureaucratic. Employees may also begin to concentrate too narrowly on their own unit and lose sight of the total organizational system. Finally, accountability and performance become increasingly difficult to monitor. For example, determining whether a new product fails because of production deficiencies or a poor marketing campaign may not be possible.

Product Departmentalization   ***Product departmentalization***, a second common approach, involves grouping and arranging activities around products or product groups. Most larger businesses adopt this form of departmentalization for grouping activities at the business or corporate level. Product departmentalization has three major advantages. First, all activities associated with one product or product group can be easily integrated and coordinated. Second, the speed and effectiveness of decision making are enhanced. Third, the performance of individual products or product groups can be assessed more easily and objectively, thereby improving the accountability of departments for the results of their activities.

> *product departmentalization*
> Grouping activities around products or product groups

Product departmentalization also has two major disadvantages. For one, managers in each department may focus on their own product or product group to the exclusion of the rest of the organization. For example, a marketing manager may see her or his primary duty as helping the group rather than helping the overall organization. For another, administrative costs rise because each department must have its own functional specialists for areas such as market research and financial analysis.

Customer Departmentalization   Under ***customer departmentalization***, the organization structures its activities to respond to and interact with specific customers or customer groups. The lending activities in most banks, for example, are usually tailored to meet the needs of different kinds of customers (business, consumer, mortgage, and agricultural loans). The basic advantage of this approach is that the organization is able to use skilled specialists to deal with unique customers or customer groups. It takes one set of skills to evaluate a balance sheet and lend a business $500,000 for operating capital, and a different set of skills to evaluate an individual's creditworthiness and lend $20,000 for a new car. However, a fairly large administrative staff is required to integrate the activities of the various departments.

> *customer departmentalization*
> Grouping activities to respond to and interact with specific customers or customer groups

In banks, for example, coordination is necessary to make sure that the organization does not overcommit itself in any one area and to handle collections on delinquent accounts from a diverse set of customers.

Location Departmentalization   *Location departmentalization* groups jobs on the basis of defined geographic sites or areas. The defined sites or areas may range in size from a hemisphere to only a few blocks of a large city. Transportation companies, police departments (precincts represent geographic areas of a city), and the Federal Reserve Bank all use location departmentalization. The primary advantage of location departmentalization is that it enables the organization to respond easily to unique customer and environmental characteristics in the various regions. On the negative side, a larger administrative staff may be required if the organization must keep track of units in scattered locations.

Establishing Reporting Relationships

The third basic element of organizing is the establishment of reporting relationships among positions. The purpose of this activity is to clarify the chain of command and the span of management.

Chain of Command   Chain of command is an old concept, first popularized in the early years of the twentieth century. For example, early writers about the *chain of command* argued that clear and distinct lines of authority need to be established among all positions in an organization. The chain of command actually has two components. The first, called *unity of command*, suggests that each person within an organization must have a clear reporting relationship to one and only one boss (as we see later in this chapter, newer models of organization design routinely—and successfully—violate this premise). The second, called the *scalar principle*, suggests that there must be a clear and unbroken line of authority that extends from the lowest to the highest position in the organization. The popular saying "The buck stops here" is derived from this idea—someone in the organization must ultimately be responsible for every decision.

Span of Management   Another part of establishing reporting relationships is determining how many people will report to each manager. This defines the *span of management* (sometimes called the *span of control*). For years, managers and researchers sought to determine the optimal span of management. Today we recognize that the span of management is a crucial factor in structuring organizations but that there are no universal, cut-and-dried prescriptions for an ideal or optimal span.[12]

Tall Versus Flat Organizations   In recent years, managers have begun to focus attention on the optimal number of layers in their organizational hierarchy. Having more layers results in a taller organization, whereas having fewer layers leads to a flatter organization. What difference does it make whether the organization is tall or flat? One early study at Sears found that a flat structure led to higher levels of employee morale and productivity.[13] Researchers have also argued that a tall structure is more expensive (because of the larger number of managers involved) and that it fosters more communication problems (because of the increased number of people through whom information must pass). On the other hand, a wide span of management in a flat organization may result in a manager's

---

location departmentalization
Grouping jobs on the basis of defined geographic sites or areas

chain of command
A clear and distinct line of authority among the positions in an organization

span of management
The number of people who report to a particular manager

DILBERT: © Scott Adams/Dist. by United Feature Syndicate, Inc.

Distributing authority is a key building block in creating an effective organization. Unfortunately, some managers prefer to avoid accountability for decisions and work to ensure that someone else can always be held responsible for mistakes and errors. This Dilbert cartoon offers a whimsical view of a manager teaching others to avoid accountability and pass the buck.

having more administrative responsibility (because there are fewer managers) and more supervisory responsibility (because there are more subordinates reporting to each manager). If these additional responsibilities become excessive, the flat organization may suffer.[14]

Many experts agree that businesses can function effectively with fewer layers of organization than they currently have. The Franklin Mint, for example, reduced its number of management layers from 6 to 4. At the same time, the CEO increased his span of management from 6 to 12. In similar fashion, IBM has eliminated several layers of management. One additional reason for this trend is that improved organizational communication networks allow managers to stay in touch with a larger number of subordinates than was possible even just a few years ago.[15]

Distributing Authority

Another important building block in structuring organizations is the determination of how authority is to be distributed among positions. **Authority** is power that has been legitimized by the organization.[16] Two specific issues that managers must address when distributing authority are delegation and decentralization.[17]

The Delegation Process   Delegation is the establishment of a pattern of authority between a superior and one or more subordinates. Specifically, **delegation** is the process by which managers assign a portion of their total workload to others.[18] In theory, the delegation process involves three steps. First, the manager assigns responsibility or gives the subordinate a job to do. The assignment of responsibility might range from telling a subordinate to prepare a report to placing the person in charge of a task force. Along with the assignment, the individual is also given the authority to do the job. The manager may give the subordinate the power to requisition needed information from confidential files or to direct a group of other workers. Finally, the manager establishes the subordinate's accountability—that is, the subordinate accepts an obligation to carry out the task assigned by the manager. For instance, the CEO of AutoZone will sign off for the company on

authority
Power that has been legitimized by the organization

delegation
The process by which a manager assigns a portion of his or her total workload to others

financial performance only when the individual manager responsible for each unit has certified his or her own results as being accurate. The firm believes that this high level of accountability will help it avoid the kind of accounting scandal that has hit many businesses in recent times.[19]

Decentralization and Centralization Just as authority can be delegated from one individual to another, organizations also develop patterns of authority across a wide variety of positions and departments. *Decentralization* is the process of systematically delegating power and authority throughout the organization to middle and lower-level managers. It is important to remember that decentralization is actually one end of a continuum anchored at the other end by *centralization*, the process of systematically retaining power and authority in the hands of higher-level managers. Hence, a decentralized organization is one in which decision-making power and authority are delegated as far down the chain of command as possible. Conversely, in a centralized organization, decision-making power and authority are retained at the higher levels of management.

What factors determine an organization's position on the decentralization-centralization continuum? One common determinant is the organization's external environment. Usually, the greater the complexity and uncertainty of the environment, the greater is the tendency to decentralize. Another crucial factor is the history of the organization. Firms have a tendency to do what they have done in the past, so there is likely to be some relationship between what an organization did in its early history and what it chooses to do today in terms of centralization or decentralization. The nature of the decisions being made is also considered. The costlier and riskier the decisions, the more pressure there is to centralize. In short, managers have no clear-cut guidelines for determining whether to centralize or decentralize. Many successful organizations, such as Sears and General Electric, are quite decentralized. Equally successful firms, such as McDonald's and Wal-Mart, have remained centralized.

Coordinating Activities

A fifth major element of organizing is coordination. As we discuss earlier, job specialization and departmentalization involve breaking jobs down into small units and then combining those jobs into departments. Once this has been accomplished, the activities of the departments must be linked—systems must be put into place to keep the activities of each department focused on the attainment of organizational goals. This is accomplished by *coordination*—the process of linking the activities of the various departments of the organization.[20]

The Need for Coordination The primary reason for coordination is that departments and work groups are interdependent—they depend on one another for information and resources to perform their respective activities. The greater the interdependence between departments, the more coordination the organization requires if departments are to be able to perform effectively. There are three major forms of interdependence: pooled, sequential, and reciprocal.[21]

Pooled interdependence represents the lowest level of interdependence. Units with pooled interdependence operate with little interaction—the output of the units is pooled at the organizational level. Gap clothing stores operate with pooled interdependence. Each store is considered a "department" by the parent

---

decentralization
The process of systematically delegating power and authority throughout the organization to middle and lower-level managers

centralization
The process of systematically retaining power and authority in the hands of higher-level managers

coordination
The process of linking the activities of the various departments of the organization

pooled interdependence
When units operate with little interaction, their output is simply pooled

corporation. Each has its own operating budget, staff, and so forth. The profits or losses from each store are "added together" at the organizational level. The stores are interdependent to the extent that the final success or failure of one store affects the others, but they do not generally interact on a day-to-day basis.

In *sequential interdependence*, the output of one unit becomes the input for another in a sequential fashion. This creates a moderate level of interdependence. At Nissan, for example, one plant assembles engines and then ships them to a final assembly site at another plant, where the cars are completed. The plants are interdependent in that the final assembly plant must have the engines from engine assembly before it can perform its primary function of producing finished automobiles. But the level of interdependence is generally one way—the engine plant is not necessarily dependent on the final assembly plant.

Reciprocal interdependence exists when activities flow both ways between units. This form is clearly the most complex. Within a Marriott hotel, for example, the reservations department, front-desk check-in, and housekeeping are all reciprocally interdependent. Reservations has to provide front-desk employees with information about how many guests to expect each day, and housekeeping needs to know which rooms require priority cleaning. If any of the three units does not do its job properly, all the others will be affected.

> *sequential interdependence*
> When the output of one unit becomes the input for another in sequential fashion

> *reciprocal interdependence*
> When activities flow both ways between units

Structural Coordination Techniques   Because of the obvious coordination requirements that characterize most organizations, many techniques for achieving coordination have been developed. Some of the most useful devices for maintaining coordination among interdependent units are the managerial hierarchy, rules and procedures, liaison roles, task forces, and integrating departments.[22]

Eye on Management

Managing Reporting Relationships in Teams

This five-minute video shows an IT worker for a video game company that employs a project-based team organization. This worker has two individuals who supervise his work. The worker and one of the supervisors apparently just went to lunch today and made the decision that they would start a blog for the company's newest product. The second supervisor has concerns not only about the blog, but also about why she was not included in the lunch/decision and what the process should be in the future. One key issue is communication in general and another is establishment of appropriate reporting relationships.

View the video and then answer the following questions individually or as a class.

1. Why do you think this worker has two supervisors? One is described as "on-site" while the other is "off-site." Which functions or departments do you think these managers might represent?

2. What will be the potential problems for the worker who has two supervisors? Do you think the conversation you just heard clarifies the reporting relationships, or will further attention be needed on this issue?

3. How do you think each of the two supervisors feels about this conversation? How do you think the worker feels? What could the others do to alleviate any uncomfortable or negative feelings?

4. In your opinion, what types of coordinating activities would be most effective for these three employees? Why?

5. How will the use of teams contribute to the organization's effectiveness for this project? What steps can managers take to minimize any negative impact of the use of teams?

Organizations that use the hierarchy to achieve coordination place one manager in charge of interdependent departments or units. In Wal-Mart distribution centers, major activities include receiving and unloading bulk shipments from railroad cars and loading other shipments onto trucks for distribution to retail outlets. The two groups (receiving and shipping) are interdependent in that they share the loading docks and some equipment. To ensure coordination and minimize conflict, one manager is in charge of the whole operation.

Routine coordination activities can be handled via rules and standard procedures. In the Wal-Mart distribution center, an outgoing truck shipment has priority over an incoming rail shipment. Thus, when trucks are to be loaded, the shipping unit is given access to all of the center's auxiliary forklifts. This priority is specifically stated in a rule. But, as useful as rules and procedures often are in routine situations, they are not particularly effective when coordination problems are complex or unusual.

As a device for coordination, a manager in a liaison role coordinates interdependent units by acting as a common point of contact. This individual may not have any formal authority over the groups but instead simply facilitates the flow of information between units. Two engineering groups working on component systems for a large project might interact through a liaison. The liaison maintains familiarity with each group as well as with the overall project. She can answer questions and otherwise serve to integrate the activities of all the groups.

A task force may be created when the need for coordination is acute. When interdependence is complex and several units are involved, a single liaison person may not be sufficient. Instead, a task force might be assembled by drawing one representative from each group. The coordination function is thus spread across several individuals, each of whom has special information about one of the groups involved. When the project is completed, task force members return to their original positions. For example, a college overhauling its degree requirements might establish a task force made up of representatives from each department affected by the change. Each person retains her or his regular departmental affiliation and duties but also serves on the special task force. After the new requirements are agreed on, the task force is dissolved.

Integrating departments are occasionally used for coordination. These are somewhat similar to task forces but are more permanent. An integrating department generally has some permanent members as well as members who are assigned temporarily from units that are particularly in need of coordination. One study found that successful firms in the plastics industry, which is characterized by complex and dynamic environments, used integrating departments to maintain internal integration and coordination.[23] An integrating department usually has more authority than a task force and may even be given some budgetary control by the organization.

Electronic Coordination Recent advances of electronic information technology are also providing useful mechanisms for coordination. Email, for example, makes it easier for people to communicate with one another. This communication, in turn, enhances coordination. Similarly, many people in organizations today use electronic scheduling, at least some of which is accessible to others. Hence, if someone needs to set up a meeting with two colleagues, he can often check their electronic schedules to determine their availability, making it easier to coordinate their activities.

Local networks, increasingly managed by handheld electronic devices, are also making it easier to coordinate activities. Bechtel, for example, now requires its contractors, subcontractors, and suppliers to use a common web-based communication system to improve coordination among their myriad activities. The firm estimates that this improved coordination technology routinely saves it thousands of dollars on every big construction project it undertakes.

The Bureaucratic Model of Organization Design

Max Weber, an influential German sociologist, was a pioneer of classical organization theory. At the core of Weber's writings was the bureaucratic model of organizations.[24] The Weberian perspective suggests that a ***bureaucracy*** is a model of organization design based on a legitimate and formal system of authority. Many people associate bureaucracy with "red tape," rigidity, and passing the buck. For example, how many times have you heard people refer disparagingly to "the federal bureaucracy"? And many U.S. managers believe that bureaucracy in the Chinese government is a major impediment to U.S. firms' ability to do business there.

bureaucracy
A model of organization design based on a legitimate and formal system of authority

Weber viewed the bureaucratic form of organization as logical, rational, and efficient. He offered the model as a framework to which all organizations should aspire—the "one best way" of doing things. According to Weber, the ideal bureaucracy exhibits five basic characteristics:

1. The organization should adopt a distinct division of labor, and each position should be filled by an expert.

2. The organization should develop a consistent set of rules to ensure that task performance is uniform.

3. The organization should establish a hierarchy of positions or offices that creates a chain of command from the top of the organization to the bottom.

4. Managers should conduct business in an impersonal way and maintain an appropriate social distance between themselves and their subordinates.

5. Employment and advancement in the organization should be based on technical expertise, and employees should be protected from arbitrary dismissal.

Perhaps the best examples of bureaucracies today are government agencies and universities. Consider, for example, the steps you must go through and the forms you must fill out to apply for admission to college, request housing, register each semester, change majors, submit a degree plan, substitute a course, and file for graduation. Even when paper is replaced with electronic media, the steps are often the same. The reason these procedures are necessary is that universities deal with large numbers of people who must be treated equally and fairly. Hence, rules, regulations, and standard operating procedures are needed. Large labor unions are also usually organized as bureaucracies.[25]

Some bureaucracies, such as the U.S. Postal Service, are trying to portray themselves as less mechanistic and impersonal. The strategy of the Postal Service is to become more service oriented as a way to fight back against competitors like Federal Express and UPS.

A primary strength of the bureaucratic model is that several of its elements (such as reliance on rules and employment based on expertise) do, in fact, often improve efficiency. Bureaucracies also help prevent favoritism (because everyone must follow the rules) and make procedures and practices very clear to everyone. Unfortunately, however, this approach also has several disadvantages. One major disadvantage is that the bureaucratic model results in inflexibility and rigidity. Once rules are created and put in place, making exceptions or changing them is often difficult. In addition, the bureaucracy often results in the neglect of human and social processes within the organization.

Situational Influences on Organization Design

situational view of organization design
Based on the assumption that the optimal design for any given organization depends on a set of relevant situational factors

The ***situational view of organization design*** is based on the assumption that the optimal design for any given organization depends on a set of relevant situational factors. In other words, situational factors play a role in determining the best organization design for any particular circumstance. Four basic situational factors—technology, environment, size, and organizational life cycle—are discussed here.

Core Technology

technology
Conversion processes used to transform inputs into outputs

Technology consists of the conversion processes used to transform inputs (such as materials or information) into outputs (such as products or services). Most organizations use multiple technologies, but an organization's most important one is called its *core technology*. Although most people visualize assembly lines and machinery when they think of technology, the term can also be applied to service organizations. For example, an investment firm like Vanguard uses technology to transform investment dollars into income in much the same way that Union Carbide uses natural resources to manufacture chemical products.

The link between technology and organization design was first recognized by Joan Woodward.[26] Woodward studied 100 manufacturing firms in southern England. She collected information about such aspects as the history of each organization, its manufacturing processes, its forms and procedures, and its financial performance. Woodward expected to find a relationship between the size of an organization and its design, but no such relationship emerged. As a result, she began to seek other explanations for differences. Close scrutiny of the firms in her sample led her to recognize a potential relationship between technology and organization design. This follow-up analysis led Woodward to first classify the organizations according to their technology. Three basic forms of technology were identified by Woodward:

1. *Unit or small-batch technology.* The product is custom-made to customer specifications or produced in small quantities. Organizations using this form of technology include a tailor shop (custom suits), a printing shop like Kinko's (business cards, company stationery), and a photography studio.

2. *Large-batch or mass-production technology.* The product is manufactured in assembly-line fashion by combining component parts into another part or finished product. Examples include automobile manufacturers like Subaru, appliance makers like Whirlpool Corporation, and electronics firms like Philips.

3. *Continuous-process technology.* Raw materials are transformed to a finished product by a series of machine or process transformations. The composition of the materials themselves is changed. Examples include petroleum refineries like ExxonMobil and Shell, and chemical refineries like Dow Chemical and Hoechst AG.

These forms of technology are listed in order of their assumed levels of complexity. In other words, unit or small-batch technology is presumed to be the least complex and continuous-process technology the most complex. Woodward found that different configurations of organization design were associated with each technology.

Specifically, Woodward found that the two extremes (unit or small-batch and continuous-process) tended to have little bureaucracy, whereas the middle-range organizations (large-batch or mass-production) were much more bureaucratic in nature. The large-batch and mass-production organizations also had a higher level of specialization.[27] Finally, she found that organizational success was related to the extent to which organizations followed the typical pattern. For example, successful continuous-process organizations tended to have less bureaucracy, whereas less-successful firms with the same technology tended to be more bureaucratic.

Environment

Environmental elements and organization design are specifically linked in a number of ways.[28] The first widely recognized analysis of environment-organization design linkages was provided by Tom Burns and G. M. Stalker.[29] Like Woodward, Burns and Stalker worked in England. Their first step was identifying two extreme forms of organizational environment: stable (one that remains relatively constant over time) and unstable (subject to uncertainty and rapid change). Next they studied the designs of organizations in each type of environment. Not surprisingly, they found that organizations in stable environments tended to have a different kind of design than did organizations in unstable environments. The two kinds of design that emerged were called mechanistic and organic organization.

A **mechanistic organization**, quite similar to the bureaucratic model, was most frequently found in stable environments. Free from uncertainty, organizations structured their activities in rather predictable ways by means of rules, specialized jobs, and centralized authority. Although no environment is completely stable, Abercrombie & Fitch and Wendy's use mechanistic designs. Each A&F store, for example, has prescribed methods for store design and merchandise-ordering processes. No deviations are allowed from these methods. An **organic organization**, on the other hand, was most often found in unstable and unpredictable environments, in which constant change and uncertainty usually dictate a much higher level of fluidity and flexibility. Motorola (facing rapid technological change) and Limited Brands (facing constant change in consumer tastes) both use organic designs. A manager at Motorola, for example, has considerable discretion over how work is performed and how problems can be solved.

mechanistic organization
Similar to the bureaucratic model, most frequently found in stable environments

organic organization
Very flexible and informal model of organization design, most often found in unstable and unpredictable environments

These ideas were extended in the United States by Paul R. Lawrence and Jay W. Lorsch.[30] They agreed that environmental factors influence organization design but believed that this influence varies between different units of the same organization. In fact, they predicted that each organizational unit has its own unique environment and responds by developing unique attributes. Lawrence and Lorsch suggested that organizations could be characterized along two primary dimensions.

One of these dimensions, **differentiation**, is the extent to which the organization is broken down into subunits. A firm with many subunits is highly differentiated; one with few subunits has a low level of differentiation. The second

differentiation
Extent to which the organization is broken down into subunits

integration
Degree to which the various subunits must work together in a coordinated fashion

organizational size
Total number of full-time or full-time-equivalent employees

organizational life cycle
Progression through which organizations evolve as they grow and mature

dimension, **integration**, is the degree to which the various subunits must work together in a coordinated fashion. For example, if each unit competes in a different market and has its own production facilities, they may need little integration. Lawrence and Lorsch reasoned that the degree of differentiation and integration needed by an organization depends on the stability of the environments that its subunits face.

Organizational Size and Life Cycle

The size and life cycle of an organization may also affect its design.[31] Although several definitions of size exist, we define **organizational size** as the total number of full-time or full-time-equivalent employees. A team of researchers at the University of Aston in Birmingham, England, believed that Woodward had failed to find a size-structure relationship (which was her original expectation) because almost all of the organizations she studied were relatively small (three-fourths had fewer than 500 employees).[32] Thus they decided to undertake a study of a wider array of organizations to determine how size and technology both individually and jointly affect an organization's design.

Their primary finding was that technology did in fact influence structural variables in small firms, probably because all of their activities tend to be centered on their core technologies. In large firms, however, the strong technology-design link broke down, most likely because technology is not as central to ongoing activities in large organizations. The Aston studies yielded a number of basic generalizations: when compared to small organizations, large organizations tend to be characterized by higher levels of job specialization, more standard operating procedures, more rules, more regulations, and a greater degree of decentralization. Wal-Mart is a good case in point. The firm expects to continue its dramatic growth for the foreseeable future, adding as many as 800,000 new jobs in the next few years. But, as it grows, the firm acknowledges that it will have to become more decentralized for its first-line managers to stay in tune with their customers.[33]

Of course, size is not constant. As we note in Chapter 5, for example, some small businesses are formed but soon disappear. Others remain as small, independently operated enterprises as long as their owner-manager lives. A few, like Dell Computer, JetBlue, and Starbucks, skyrocket to become organizational giants. And occasionally large organizations reduce their size through layoffs or divestitures. For example, Navistar is today far smaller than was its previous incarnation as International Harvester Company.

Although no clear pattern explains changes in size, many organizations progress through a four-stage **organizational life cycle**.[34] The first stage is the *birth* of the organization. The second stage, *youth*, is characterized by growth and the expansion of organizational resources. *Midlife* is a period of gradual growth evolving eventually into stability. Finally, *maturity* is a period of stability, perhaps eventually evolving into decline.

Managers must confront a number of organization design issues as the organization progresses through these stages. In general, as an organization passes from one stage to the next, it becomes bigger, more mechanistic, and more decentralized. It also becomes more specialized, devotes more attention to planning, and takes on an increasingly large staff component. Finally, coordination demands increase, formalization increases, organizational units become geographically more dispersed, and control systems become more extensive. Thus an organization's size and design are clearly linked, and this link is dynamic because of the organizational life cycle.[35]

Basic Forms of Organization Design

Because technology, environment, size, and life cycle can all influence organization design, it should come as no surprise that organizations adopt many different kinds of designs. Most designs, however, fall into one of four basic categories. Others are hybrids based on two or more of the basic forms.

Functional (U-Form) Design

The *functional design* is an arrangement based on the functional approach to departmentalization. This design has been termed the *U form* (for unitary).[36] Under the U-form arrangement, the members and units in the organization are grouped into functional departments such as marketing and production.

For the organization to operate efficiently in this design, there must be considerable coordination across departments. This integration and coordination are most commonly the responsibility of the CEO and members of senior management. Figure 6.2 shows the U-form design applied to the corporate level of a small manufacturing company. In a U-form organization, none of the functional areas can survive without the others. Marketing, for example, needs products from operations to sell and funds from finance to pay for advertising. The WD-40 Company, which makes a popular lubricating oil, and the McIlhenny Company, which makes TABASCO sauce, are both examples of firms that use the U-form design.

> **functional (U-form) design**
> An arrangement based on the functional approach to departmentalization

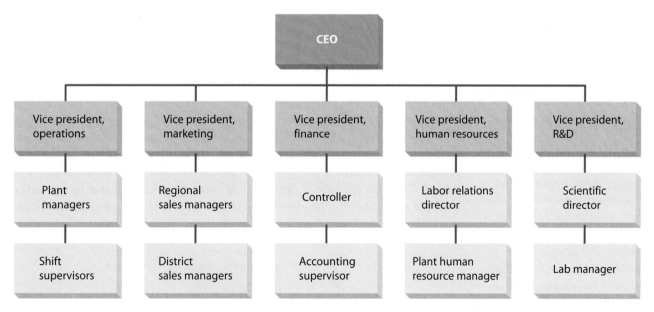

Figure 6.2

FUNCTIONAL OR U-FORM DESIGN FOR A SMALL MANUFACTURING COMPANY

The U-form design is based on functional departmentalization. This small manufacturing firm uses managers at the vice-presidential level to coordinate activities within each functional area of the organization. Note that each functional area is dependent on the others.

In general, this approach shares the basic advantages and disadvantages of functional departmentalization. Thus it allows the organization to staff all important positions with functional experts and facilitates coordination and integration. On the other hand, it also promotes a functional, rather than an organizational focus and tends to promote centralization. Functionally based designs are most commonly used in small organizations because an individual CEO can more readily oversee and coordinate the entire organization. As an organization grows, the CEO finds staying on top of all functional areas increasingly difficult.

Conglomerate (H-Form) Design

> **conglomerate (H-form) design**
> Used by an organization made up of a set of unrelated businesses

Another common form of organization design is the **conglomerate,** or **H-form,** approach.[37] This design is used by an organization made up of a set of unrelated businesses. Thus the H-form design is essentially a holding company that results from unrelated diversification. (The *H* in this term stands for holding.) This approach is based loosely on the product form of departmentalization. Each business or set of businesses is operated by a general manager who is responsible for its profits or losses, and each general manager functions independently of the others. Samsung Group, a South Korean firm, uses the H-form design. As illustrated in Figure 6.3, Samsung consists of four basic business groups. Other firms that use the H-form design include General Electric (aircraft engines, appliances, broadcasting, financial services, lighting products, plastics, and other unrelated businesses) and Tenneco (pipelines, auto parts, financial services, and other unrelated businesses).

In an H-form organization, a corporate staff usually evaluates the performance of each business, allocates corporate resources across companies, and shapes decisions about buying and selling businesses. The basic shortcoming of the H-form design is the complexity associated with holding diverse and unrelated businesses. Managers usually find comparing and integrating activities across a large number of diverse operations difficult. Research by Michael Porter suggests that many organizations following this approach achieve only average-to-weak financial performance.[38] Thus, although some U.S. firms are still using the H-form design, many others have abandoned it for other approaches.

> **divisional (M-form) design**
> An organization design based on multiple businesses in related areas operating within a larger organizational framework

Divisional (M-Form) Design

In this divisional design, which is becoming increasingly popular, a product form of organization is also used; in contrast to the H-form, however, the divisions are related. Thus the **divisional design, or M-form** (for multidivisional), is based on multiple businesses in related areas operating within a larger organizational framework. This design results from a strategy of related diversification.

Figure 6.3

CONGLOMERATE (H-FORM) DESIGN AT SAMSUNG

Samsung Group, a South Korean firm, uses the conglomerate form of organization design. This design, which results from a strategy of unrelated diversification, is a complex one to manage. Managers find that comparing and integrating activities among the dissimilar operations are difficult. Companies may abandon this design for another approach, such as the M-form design.

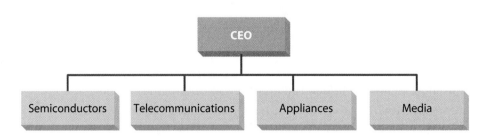

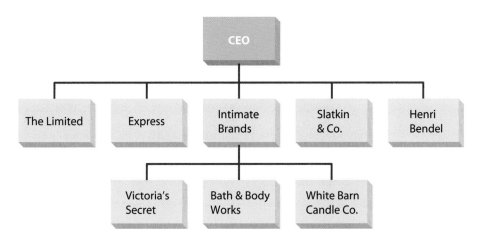

Figure 6.4

MULTIDIVISIONAL (M-FORM) DESIGN AT LIMITED BRANDS

Limited Brands uses the multidivisional approach to organization design. Although each unit operates with relative autonomy, all units function in the same general market. This design resulted from a strategy of related diversification. Other firms that use M-form designs include PepsiCo and the Walt Disney Company.

Some activities are extremely decentralized down to the divisional level; others are centralized at the corporate level.[39] For example, as shown in Figure 6.4, Limited Brands uses this approach. Each of its divisions is headed by a general manager and operates with reasonable autonomy, but the divisions also coordinate their activities as is appropriate. Other firms that use this approach are the Walt Disney Company (theme parks, movies, and merchandising units, all interrelated) and Hewlett-Packard (computers, printers, scanners, electronic medical equipment, and other electronic instrumentation).

The opportunities for coordination and shared resources represent one of the biggest advantages of the M-form design. Limited Brand's market research and purchasing departments are centralized. Thus a buyer can inspect a manufacturer's entire product line, buy some designs for The Limited stores, others for Express, and still others for Henri Bendel. The M-form design's basic objective is to optimize internal competition and cooperation. Healthy competition for resources among divisions can enhance effectiveness, but cooperation should also be promoted. Research suggests that the M-form organization that can achieve and maintain this balance will outperform large U-form and all H-form organizations.[40]

Matrix Design

The **matrix design**, another common approach to organization design, is based on two overlapping bases of departmentalization.[41] The foundation of a matrix is a set of functional departments. A set of product groups, or temporary departments, is then superimposed across the functional departments. Employees in a matrix are simultaneously members of a functional department (such as engineering) and of a project team.

matrix design
Based on two overlapping bases of departmentalization

Figure 6.5 shows a basic matrix design. At the top of the organization are functional units headed by vice presidents of engineering, production, finance, and marketing. Each of these managers has several subordinates. Along the side of the organization are a number of positions called *project manager*. Each project manager heads a project group composed of representatives or workers from the functional departments. Note from the figure that a matrix reflects a *multiple-command structure*—any given individual reports to both a functional superior and one or more project managers.

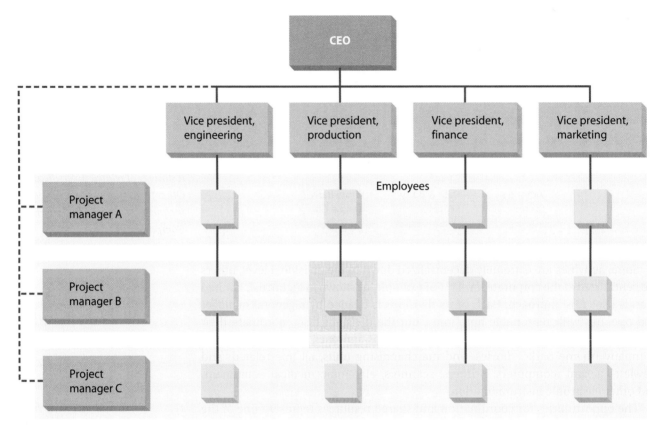

Figure 6.5
A MATRIX ORGANIZATION

A matrix organization design is created by superimposing a product form of departmentalization on an existing functional organization. Project managers coordinate teams of employees drawn from different functional departments. Thus a matrix relies on a multiple-command structure.

The project groups, or teams, are assigned to designated projects or programs. For example, the company might be developing a new product. Representatives are chosen from each functional area to work as a team on the new product. They also retain membership in the original functional group. At any given time, a person may be a member of several teams as well as a member of a functional group. Martha Stewart uses a matrix organization for her lifestyle business. The company was first organized broadly into media and merchandising groups, each of which has a specific product or group of related products. Layered on top of this structure are teams of lifestyle experts organized into groups such as cooking, crafts, weddings, and so forth. Each of these groups is targeted toward specific customer needs, but they work as necessary across all of the product groups. For example, a wedding expert might contribute to an article on wedding planning for a *Martha Stewart Living* magazine, contribute a story idea for a cable television program, and supply content for a Martha Stewart website. This same individual might also help select fabrics suitable for wedding gowns for retailing.[42]

The matrix form of organization design is most often used in one of three situations.[43] First, a matrix may work when there is strong pressure from the environment. For example, intense external competition may dictate the sort of strong marketing thrust that is best spearheaded by a functional department, but the diversity of a company's products may argue for product departments. Second, a matrix may be appropriate when large amounts of information need to be processed. For example, creating lateral relationships by means of a matrix is one effective way to increase the organization's capacity for processing information. Third, the matrix design may work when there is pressure for shared resources. For example, a company with ten product departments may have resources for only three marketing specialists. A matrix design would allow all the departments to share the company's scarce marketing resources.

Both advantages and disadvantages are associated with the matrix design. Researchers have observed six primary advantages of matrix designs. First, they enhance flexibility because teams can be created, redefined, and dissolved as needed. Second, because they assume a major role in decision making, team members are likely to be highly motivated and committed to the organization. Third, employees in a matrix organization have considerable opportunity to learn new skills. A fourth advantage of a matrix design is that it provides an efficient way for the organization to take full advantage of its human resources. Fifth, team members retain membership in their functional unit so that they can serve as a bridge between the functional unit and the team, enhancing cooperation. Sixth, the matrix design gives top management a useful vehicle for decentralization. Once the day-to-day operations have been delegated, top management can devote more attention to areas such as long-range planning.

On the other hand, the matrix design also has some major disadvantages. Employees may be uncertain about reporting relationships, especially if they are simultaneously assigned to a functional manager and to several project managers. To complicate matters, some managers see the matrix as a form of anarchy in which they have unlimited freedom. Another set of problems is associated with the dynamics of group behavior. Groups take longer than individuals to make decisions, may be dominated by one individual, and may compromise too much. They may also get bogged down in discussion and not focus on their primary objectives. Finally, in a matrix, more time may also be required for coordinating task-related activities.[44]

Hybrid Designs

Some organizations use a design that represents a hybrid of two or more of the common forms of organization design.[45] For example, an organization may have five related divisions and one unrelated division, making its design a cross between an M-form and an H-form. Indeed, few companies use a design in its pure form; most firms have one basic organization design as a foundation for managing the business but maintain sufficient flexibility so that temporary or permanent modifications can be made for strategic purposes. Ford, for example, used the matrix approach to design the Focus and the newest Mustang, but the company is basically a U-form organization showing signs of moving to an M-form design. As we note earlier, any combination of factors may dictate the appropriate form of design for any particular company.

Emerging Issues in Organization Design

Finally, in today's complex and ever-changing environment, it should come as no surprise that managers continue to explore and experiment with new forms of

New approaches to organization design are emerging all the time. Take these two men, for instance. They work for a San Francisco company called Tailrank, a news collection and dissemination business. But Tailrank has no address and no physical location. Its owner and employees work online from wherever they happen to be. When it's necessary for them to meet in person, they get together at a convenient coffee house such as Ritual Roasters in San Francisco's Mission district. Kevin Burton, on the left, is the owner of Tailrank; he is shown here with an employee named Jonathan Moore.

organization design. Many organizations today are creating designs for themselves that maximize their ability to adapt to changing circumstances and to a changing environment. They try to accomplish this by not becoming too compartmentalized or too rigid. As we note earlier, bureaucratic organizations are hard to change, slow, and inflexible. To avoid these problems, then, organizations can try to be as different from bureaucracies as possible—relatively few rules, general job descriptions, and so forth. This final section highlights some of the more important emerging issues.[46]

The Team Organization

team organization An approach to organization design that relies almost exclusively on project-type teams, with little or no underlying functional hierarchy	Some organizations today are using the ***team organization***, an approach to organization design that relies almost exclusively on project-type teams, with little or no underlying functional hierarchy. Within such an organization, people float from project to project as necessitated by their skills and the demands of those projects. At Cypress Semiconductor, T. J. Rodgers refuses to allow the organization to grow so large that it cannot function this way. Whenever a unit or group starts getting too large, he simply splits it into smaller units. Consequently, all units within the organization are small. This allows them to change direction, explore new ideas, and try new methods without dealing with a rigid bureaucratic organizational context. Although few organizations have actually reached this level of adaptability, Apple Computer and Xerox are among those moving toward it.[47]

The Virtual Organization

virtual organization One that has little or no formal structure	Closely related to the team organization is the virtual organization. A ***virtual organization*** is one that has little or no formal structure. Such an organization typically has only a handful of permanent employees and a very small staff and administrative headquarters facility. As the needs of the organization change,

its managers bring in temporary workers, lease facilities, and outsource basic support services to meet the demands of each unique situation. As the situation changes, the temporary workforce changes in parallel, with some people leaving the organization and others entering. Facilities and the services subcontracted to others change as well. Thus the organization exists only in response to its needs. And, increasingly, virtual organizations are conducting most—if not all—of their businesses online.[48]

For example, Global Research Consortium is a virtual organization. GRC offers research and consulting services to firms doing business in Asia. As clients request various services, GRC's staff of three permanent employees subcontracts the work to an appropriate set of several dozen independent consultants and researchers with whom it has relationships. At any given time, therefore, GRC may have several projects under way and 20 or 30 people working on projects. As the projects change, so, too, does the composition of the organization.

The Learning Organization

Another recent approach to organization design is the so-called learning organization. Organizations that adopt this approach work to integrate continuous improvement with continuous employee learning and development. Specifically, a *learning organization* is one that works to facilitate the lifelong learning and personal development of all of its employees while continually transforming itself to respond to changing demands and needs.[49]

> *learning organization*
> One that works to facilitate the lifelong learning and personal development of all of its employees while continually transforming itself to respond to changing demands and needs

Although managers might approach the concept of a learning organization from a variety of perspectives, improved quality, continuous improvement, and performance measurement are frequent goals. The idea is that the most consistent and logical strategy for achieving continuous improvement is by constantly upgrading employee talent, skill, and knowledge. For example, if each employee in an organization learns one new thing each day and can translate that knowledge into work-related practice, continuous improvement will logically follow. Indeed, organizations that wholeheartedly embrace this approach believe that only through constant learning by employees can continuous improvement really occur.

In recent years, many different organizations have implemented this approach. For example, Shell Oil recently purchased an executive conference center north of its headquarters in Houston. The center boasts state-of-the-art classrooms and instructional technology, lodging facilities, a restaurant, and recreational amenities such as a golf course, swimming pool, and tennis courts. Line managers at the firm rotate through the Shell Learning Center, as the facility has been renamed, and serve as teaching faculty. Such teaching assignments last anywhere from a few days to several months. At the same time, all Shell employees routinely attend training programs, seminars, and related activities, all the while learning the latest information that they need to contribute more effectively to the firm. Recent seminar topics have ranged from time management, to implications of the Americans with Disabilities Act, to balancing work and family demands, to international trade theory.

Summary of Key Points

1. Identify the basic elements of organizations.
   - Organizations are made up of five basic elements:
     - job specialization
     - departmentalization
     - reporting relationships
     - distribution of authority
     - coordination

2. Describe the bureaucratic perspective on organization design.
   - The bureaucratic model attempts to prescribe how all organizations should be designed.
   - It is based on the presumed need for legitimate, logical, and formal rules, regulations, and procedures.

3. Identify and explain several situational influences on organization design.
   - The situational view of organization design is based on the assumption that the optimal organization design is a function of situational factors.

   - Four important situational factors are:
     - technology
     - environment
     - size
     - organizational life cycle

4. Describe the basic forms of organization design that characterize many organizations.
   - Many organizations today adopt one of four basic organization designs:
     - functional (U-form)
     - conglomerate (H-form)
     - divisional (M-form)
     - matrix
   - Other organizations use a hybrid design derived from two or more of these basic designs.

5. Describe emerging issues in organization design.
   - Emerging issues in organization design are
     - team organization
     - virtual organization
     - learning organization

Discussion Questions

Questions for Review

1. What is job specialization? What are its advantages and its disadvantages?

2. What is departmentalization? What are its most common forms?

3. Distinguish between centralization and decentralization, and comment on their relative advantages and disadvantages.

4. Describe the basic forms of organization design. What are the advantages and disadvantages of each?

5. Compare and contrast the matrix organization and the team organization, citing their similarities and differences.

Questions for Analysis

6. How is specialization applied in such settings as a hospital, restaurant, school, and church?

7. Learn how your school is organized. Analyze the advantages and disadvantages of this form of departmentalization, and then comment on how well or how poorly other forms of departmentalization might work.

8. Identify at least five ways in which electronic coordination affects your daily life.

9. Each of the organization designs is appropriate for some firms but not for others. Describe the characteristics that a firm using the U-form design should

have. Then do the same for the H-form, the M-form, and the matrix design. For each item, explain the relationship between that set of characteristics and the choice of organization design.

10. What are the benefits of using the learning organization approach to design? Now consider that in order to learn, organizations must be willing to tolerate many mistakes, because it is only through the effort to understand mistakes that learning can occur. With this statement in mind, what are some of the potential problems with the use of the learning organization approach?

Building Effective Conceptual Skills

Exercise Overview

Conceptual skills reflect a person's abilities to think in the abstract. Conceptual skills are developed in this exercise as you practice analyzing organization structure.

Exercise Background

Looking at an organization chart enables one to understand a company's structure, such as its distribution of authority, its divisions, its levels of hierarchy, its reporting relationships, and more. The reverse is also true; that is, when one understands the elements of a company's structure, one can draw an organization chart that reflects that structure. In this exercise, you will use the Internet to research a firm's structure and will then draw the appropriate organization chart.

Exercise Task

1. Alone or with a partner, use the Internet to research a publicly traded U.S. firm in which you are interested. Gather information about the firm that will help you understand its structure. For example, if you researched Ford Motor Company, you would find information about different types of vehicles, different regions where Ford products are sold, different functions that are performed at Ford, and so on. (*Hint:* The firm's annual report is usually available online and usually contains a great deal of helpful information, particularly in the section that includes an editorial message from the chair or CEO. The section that summarizes financial information is very helpful. "Segment" data also point to divisional structure in many cases.)

2. On the basis of what you have discovered in your research, draw an appropriate organization structure.

3. Share your results with another group or with the class, justifying your decisions.

Building Effective Technical Skills

Exercise Overview

Technical skills are the skills necessary to accomplish or understand the specific work being done in an organization. This exercise asks you to develop technical skills related to understanding the impact of an organization's strategy on its structure.

Exercise Background

Assume that you are a manager of a firm that has developed a new, innovative line of athletic performance clothing, such as the Under Armour®. (If you are not familiar with Under Armour, visit the website at www.uabiz.com and learn about the product.)

Exercise Task

Using the information about strategy given in each question below and your knowledge of the Under Armour product, choose the appropriate form of organization structure.

1. What would be the most appropriate organization structure if Under Armour's corporate-level strategy were to continue to produce a limited line of very similar products for sale in the United States?

2. What would be the most appropriate organization structure if Under Armour's corporate-level strategy were to continue to produce only its original product but to sell it in Asia and Europe as well as in North America?

3. What would be the most appropriate organization structure if Under Armour's corporate-level strategy were to move into related areas, using the innovations

developed in the design of its heat-handling fabrics to help design other innovative products, such as heat-blocking curtains or safety suits for firefighters?

4. What would be the most appropriate organization structure if Under Armour's corporate-level strategy were to use its expertise in fabric innovations to move into other areas, such as clothing design?

5. What would be the most appropriate organization structure if Under Armour's corporate-level strategy were to use the funds generated by Under Armour sales to finance moves into several unrelated industries?

6. For each of the five strategies listed above, tell how that strategy influenced your choice of organization design.

Building Effective Decision-Making Skills

Exercise Overview

Decision-making skills reflect the manager's ability to recognize and define problems and opportunities correctly and then to select an appropriate course of action to solve problems and capitalize on opportunities. The purpose of this exercise is to give you insights into how managers must make decisions within the context of creating an organization design.

Exercise Background

Assume that you have decided to open a handmade chocolates business in your local community. Your products will be traditional bars and novelty shaped chocolates, truffles, other chocolate products such as ice cream, and gift baskets and boxes featuring chocolates. You have hired a talented chef and believe that her expertise, coupled with your unique designs and high-quality ingredients, will make your products very popular. You have also inherited enough money to get your business up and running and to cover about one year of living expenses (in other words, you do not need to pay yourself a salary).

You intend to buy food items including chocolate, cocoa, white chocolate, nuts, and fruit from suppliers who deliver to your area. Your chef will then turn those ingredients into luscious products that will then be attractively packaged. Local grocery store owners and restaurant chefs have seen samples of your products and indicated a keen interest in selling them. You know, however, that you will still need to service accounts and keep your customers happy.

At the present time, you are trying to determine how many people you need to get your business going and how to group them most effectively into an organization. You realize that you can start out quite small and then expand as sales warrant. However, you also worry that if you are continually adding people and rearranging your organization, confusion and inefficiency may result.

Exercise Task

Under each of the scenarios below, decide how best to design your organization. Sketch a basic organization chart to show your thoughts.

• *Scenario 1*—You will design and sell the products yourself, as well as oversee production. You will start with a workforce of five people.

• *Scenario 2*—You intend to devote all of your time to sales in order to increase revenues, leaving all other functions to others. You will start with a workforce of nine people.

• *Scenario 3*—You do not intend to handle any one function yourself but will instead oversee the entire operation and will start with a workforce of fifteen people.

1. After you have created your organization chart, form small groups of four to five people each. Compare your various organization charts, focusing on similarities and differences.

2. Working in the same group, assume that five years have passed and that your business has been a big success. You have a large factory for making your chocolates and are shipping them to fifteen states. You employ almost 500 people. Create the organization design that you think best fits this organization.

Follow-up Questions

1. How clear (or how ambiguous) were the decisions about organization design?

2. What are your thoughts about starting out too large to maintain stability, as opposed to starting small and then growing?

3. What basic factors did you consider in choosing a design?

Skills Self-Assessment Instrument

Delegation Aptitude Survey

Purpose: To help students gain insight into the process of and the attitudes important to delegation.

Introduction: Delegation has a number of advantages for managers, workers, and organizations, but it also presents challenges. Managers who understand the benefits of delegation, who trust their subordinates, and who have the emotional maturity to allow others to succeed, are more likely to be effective delegators.

Instructions:

1. Complete the Delegation Aptitude Survey on page 184. You should think of work-related or group situations in which you have had the opportunity to delegate responsibility to others. If you have not had such experiences, try to imagine how you would respond in such a situation. Circle the response that best typifies your attitude or behavior.

2. Score the survey according to the directions that follow. Calculate your overall score.

3. Working with a small group, compare individual scores and prepare group responses to the discussion questions.

4. Calculate a class-average score. Have one member of the group present the group's responses to the discussion questions.

Delegation Aptitude Survey

Statement	Strongly Agree	Slightly Agree	Not Sure	Slightly Disagree	Strongly Disagree
1. I don't think others can do the work as well as I can.	1	2	3	4	5
2. I often take work home with me.	1	2	3	4	5
3. Employees who can make their own decisions tend to be more efficient.	5	4	3	2	1
4. I often have to rush to meet deadlines.	1	2	3	4	5
5. Employees with more responsibility tend to have more commitment to group goals.	5	4	3	2	1
6. When I delegate, I always explain precisely how the task is to be done.	1	2	3	4	5
7. I always seem to have too much to do and too little time to do it in.	1	2	3	4	5
8. When employees have the responsibility to do a job, they usually do it well.	5	4	3	2	1
9. When I delegate, I make clear the end results I expect.	5	4	3	2	1
10. I usually only delegate simple, routine tasks.	1	2	3	4	5
11. When I delegate, I always make sure everyone concerned is so informed.	5	4	3	2	1
12. If I delegate, I usually wind up doing the job over again to get it right.	1	2	3	4	5
13. I become irritated watching others doing a job I can do better.	1	2	3	4	5
14. When I delegate, I feel I am losing the control I need.	1	2	3	4	5
15. When I delegate, I always set specific dates for progress reports.	5	4	3	2	1
16. When I do a job, I do it to perfection.	1	2	3	4	5
17. I honestly feel that I can do most jobs better than my subordinates can.	1	2	3	4	5
18. When employees make their own decisions, it tends to cause confusion.	1	2	3	4	5
19. It's difficult for subordinates to make decisions because they don't know the organization's goals.	1	2	3	4	5
20. When employees are given responsibility, they usually do what is asked of them.	5	4	3	2	1

Discussion Questions

1. In what respects do the survey responses agree or disagree?

2. What might account for some of the differences in individual scores?

3. How can you make constructive use of the survey results?

Linda Morable, *Exercises in Management*, 8th edition. © 2005. pp. 82–84. For interpretation, see Interpretations of Skills Self-Assessment Instruments in the appendix near the end of this text.

CHAPTER CLOSING CASE

MANUFACTURING JOBS, JAPANESE-STYLE

Japanese auto manufacturers are winning the battle for U.S. buyers, dominating their American competitors in sales, profits, and innovation. In 2006, Toyota's market share grew by 2 percent, or over 330,000 vehicles, while GM's dropped by 6 percent. Toyota's global profits for 2005 were $11 billion, as compared to a loss of $10.5 billion at GM. Toyota sells innovative, award-winning products including the popular Prius hybrid whereas GM's styles and technology are not cutting edge. There are many, complex reasons for the disparity. Those reasons extend down to the lowest-level line employees, where Japanese firms utilize superior job designs and better reporting relationships.

Consider the Dundee, Michigan, engine making plant of the Global Engine Manufacturing Alliance (GEMA), a partnership spearheaded by Japan-based Mitsubishi, along with DaimlerChrysler and Hyundai of South Korea. The Dundee plant is new, clean, and bright, contrasting sharply with traditional auto factories, which can be dark, greasy, and smelly. The plant makes extensive use of automation and robotics, reducing labor usage. Older Detroit factories average nearly five hours to produce one engine, the second-slowest in the industry. Toyota, the current industry leader, can produce one engine in just three hours. The GEMA plant, which makes extensive use of automation and robots, has the goal of one engine every two hours. The first GEMA plant has been so successful that a second plant became operative in 2006, doubling capacity.

Yet the most important innovation isn't the number of workers, but the way the work itself is designed. Instead of the phone-book-sized union contract used at traditional factories, the GEMA plant's contract with the United Auto Workers (UAW) is a slim booklet. Instead of the dozens of highly specialized jobs called for in most contracts, the GEMA contract uses just one category, "team member," for all hourly workers. Every worker learns every job on the assembly line, in keeping with the plant's philosophy of "anyone, anywhere, anything, anytime." Over the course of a typical 10-hour shift, one employee might be responsible for 15 to 20 different tasks.

Another Toyota joint venture, this time with GM, is organized around self-regulating teams. The plant was started in Fremont, California in 1984, by renovating a troubled GM plant and renaming it NUMMI, or New United Motor Manufacturing Inc. NUMMI's workforce makes decisions and assigns tasks without intervention from supervisors. Reporting relationships are not very hierarchical and the most important communications take place with other team members, not superiors. Every worker's opinion is valued. For example, workers have the power to stop the assembly line when quality problems are occurring. Workers who stop the line are congratulated for taking responsibility for fixing the problems.

To coordinate the work, NUMMI relies on building strong personal relationships across workers. Supervisors have friendly interactions with employees and spend time socializing with them outside of work. These close relationships facilitate sharing information up, down, and across the management hierarchy. Toyota's approach builds strong bonds between managers and workers, so that the manager functions almost like a father to his employees.

In contrast, Honda uses teams extensively at its plant in Marysville, Ohio, but with an entirely different culture. Honda emphasizes innovation and encourages employees to challenge and question managers in order to make the company stronger. Honda's teams group quickly when a problem occurs and then are disbanded when the problem is solved. They are led by whichever team member has the most expertise relevant to the problem at hand. This approach works just as well as Toyota's in motivating workers.

The cooperation of American labor unions is key to the success of the Japanese-style factories. The UAW is aware that automakers are struggling in today's economy. It is showing support by being flexible about job design, allowing the same conditions that have been common in Japanese factories for years. American workers are being flexible too, and demonstrating that they prefer more autonomy and variety in their tasks.

Even Ford and GM, which are struggling to update their facilities and management practices, have taken notice of the Japanese auto makers' success. Both companies have announced plans to build a Japanese-style facility in the United States. Let's hope they don't miss the critical issue. The factory facility is important, the union contract is important, but most important is remaking the organization structure, starting with job design and coordination techniques.

CASE QUESTIONS

1. What benefits and potential disadvantages do American firms gain from use of specialized job designs? What benefits and potential disadvantages do Japanese firms gain from use of broadly defined jobs?
2. Would you expect a traditional American firm to have a relatively tall or flat organization structure? What about a traditional Japanese firm? Explain.
3. The Japanese firms described in the case use culture and relationships as coordination mechanisms. Do you think these are more or less effective than the more traditional coordination techniques mentioned in your text? Why or why not?

REFERENCES

Gina Chon, "GM and Ford Lose More Market Share," *Wall Street Journal*, January 5, 2006, www.wsj.com on April 12, 2006; Roland Jones, "Road Ahead for Automotive Industry Still Bumpy," MSNBC websites, www.msnbc.com on April 12, 2006; Micheline Maynard, "Carmakers' Big Idea: Think Small," *New York Times*, February 5, 2006, pp. BU1, 7.

YOU MAKE THE CALL

Did You Hear the One About . . . Delegation?

1. What do you see as the potential major problems with the delegation relationship between talk show hosts and their writers?
2. Can you identify more traditional job settings that might have similar working relationships between managers and their subordinates?
3. In addition to delegation, how do other elements of organizing relate to the setting of talk show hosts?
4. How might new and emerging technologies change the working relationships between talk show hosts and their writers?
5. There are actually several different kinds of talk shows on television in addition to the late-night variety—afternoon shows, weekly shows, music talk shows, sports talk shows, and serious news shows, for example. Identify three such kinds of talk shows and comment on how delegation in those shows might be similar to and different from that used by the late-night shows.

Test Prepper

college.hmco.com/pic/griffinfund5e

You've read the chapter, studied the key terms, and the exam is any day now. Think you're ready to ace it? Take this sample test to gauge your comprehension of chapter material. You can check your answers at the back of the book. Want more test questions? Visit the student website at http://college.hmco.com/pic/griffinfund5e/ and take the ACE quizzes for more practice.

1. T F Yu Soon works in the public relations office of a university. Her boss initially gave her assignments maintaining alumni records and then added arranging some interviews. Eventually, she was given the authority to accept or reject interview requests. Her boss uses job rotation.

2. T F The U.S. Armed Forces has four-star commanders responsible for Central Command, European Command, Pacific Command, and Southern Command. The military uses location departmentalization.

3. T F A flat organization has more layers of management than a tall organization.

4. T F A small medical practice employing two physicians is likely to choose the functional design.

5. T F A management consulting company in which consultants come together for projects and then disband is designed as a virtual organization.

6. Which of the following is a disadvantage of job specialization?
   a. Boredom
   b. Training costs
   c. Need for specialized equipment
   d. Proficiency
   e. Increased transfer time

7. At Harley-Davidson, a production-line worker has the authority to shut down assembly when he sees a minor defect in a part. According to the job characteristics approach, he has
   a. skill variety.
   b. task identity.
   c. autonomy.
   d. decentralization.
   e. task significance.

8. Max Weber, the sociologist, viewed the bureaucratic model as
   a. the "one best way" of doing things.
   b. corrupt.
   c. motivational.
   d. inefficient.
   e. flexible.

9. Siemens AG, a large German conglomerate, manufactures many products. One of these is telecommunication equipment, which it produces in high volume. What production technology would you expect Siemens to use for that product?
   a. Unit
   b. Small-batch
   c. Medium-batch
   d. Large-batch
   e. Continuous-process

10. An organization with little or no formal structure is a(n) _____ organization.
    a. team
    b. virtual
    c. international
    d. hybrid
    e. learning

chapter 7

Organization Change and Innovation

FIRST THINGS FIRST

Innovative Ikea

"Designing beautiful-but-expensive products is easy. Designing products that are inexpensive and functional is a huge challenge."

—JOSEPHINE RYDBERG-DUMONT, PRESIDENT, IKEA SWEDEN

Ever craved a couch? Enough to camp outside a furniture store for a week? That's what customers did when modern design retailer Ikea opened a store in Atlanta. The brand is so popular that thousands lined up on grand opening day. In April 2006, Ikea's new Tokyo store, the first in Japan, attracted 35,000 customers on its first day. A store opening in Hong Kong created a day-long traffic jam.

Ikea is a cult. Customers are fiercely loyal to the company's unique products that combine high style and low cost. Founder Ingvar Kamprad, who grew up on a small Swedish farm, started Ikea in 1943. He was just 17 when he began selling inexpensive small goods. Over time, his product line evolved to include furniture made by local carpenters. It took 16 years for Kamprad to open his first store, in 1957. After that slow start, Ikea's growth increased gradually at first but then more rapidly. The company now encompasses 237 stores in 35 countries with over 20 new locations annually.

Ikea's vision statement is "Good design and function at low prices," so one important element of their business model is style. Scandinavian designers produce clean-lined, contemporary pieces. Ikea's style emphasizes light, natural wood tones and bright, clear colors. Curvy shapes, unusual materials, and whimsical designs predominate. Furniture is designed to fit in a variety of spaces and adapt to any decorating scheme. For example, one of Ikea's most popular products worldwide is the Klippan sofa, a simple two-seat couch covered in white cotton with silvery steel legs. Bright slipcovers customize the look.

The other important element of Ikea's business model is affordability. Kamprad is a frugal man who buses to work, despite the fact that he is a multibillionaire and the fourth-richest person alive. His passion for reducing costs has led Ikea on a relentless quest for the best bargain. By looking for the lowest-cost deal, whether made in-house or from a global supplier, Ikea drives prices down, sometimes by as much as 50 percent. The Klippan sofa, for example, cost $395 in 1985 but retails for $249 today.

Ikea's emphasis on design and low cost is innovative. "Designing beautiful-but-expensive products is easy," says Ikea Sweden president Josephine

Rydberg-Dumont. "Designing products that are inexpensive and functional is a huge challenge."

Ikea is innovative in shaping buyer preferences. It encourages consumers to stop thinking of furniture as a durable good. Ikea manager Christian Mathieu claims that holding on to older furniture is a habit that makes no sense. "Americans change their spouse as often as their dining-room tables, about 1.5 times in a lifetime," he says. Of course, this risk-taking approach increases furniture sales for Ikea.

Product innovations go beyond the merely stylistic. Ikea supports the natural environment by using renewable soft woods like pine in most of its goods and publishing recycling instructions for every item. To save energy in transportation, most of the items are "knocked down," or shipped as parts that buyers assemble at home. Cheaper woods and knock-down design also save Ikea money, enabling lower prices and higher profit margins. Ikea's operating margin is 10 percent, above industry average and far surpassing rival Pier 1 whose margin was a negative 2 percent in 2006.

Even Ikea's store design is innovative. Displays are unique and fun. Customers walk through the store, writing down the items they want on a company-supplied notepad. Then they find items themselves in a warehouse section of the store. Stores include extras that both pamper shoppers and keep them in the store longer, including in-store restaurants with Swedish treats and a supervised play area for children. After purchase, buyers may rent Ikea-owned vans to cart home large items.

Ikea's popularity has led to imitation by low-cost competitors Target and Kmart, who created their own lines of trendy but affordable furniture.

LEARNING OBJECTIVES

After studying this chapter, you should be able to:

- Describe the nature of organization change, including forces for change and planned versus reactive change.
- Discuss the steps in organization change and how to manage resistance to change.
- Identify and describe major areas of organization change and discuss the assumptions, techniques, and effectiveness of organization development.
- Describe the innovation process, forms of innovation, the failure to innovate, and how organizations can promote innovation.

Ikea has used planned change and innovation to become an international furniture retailing powerhouse.

> The company's continued success will rely on its ability to stay innovative and keep one step ahead of the rest of the industry. With a staff personally trained by Kamprad and corporate assets valued at more than $50 billion, Ikea is poised to do just that.[1]

Managers at Ikea are keeping the firm at the forefront of its industry through the astute management of innovation. The firm uses innovative product designs, innovative cost structures, innovative marketing practices, and innovative store layouts to grow and prosper. At a broader level, Ikea also embraces change. As we will see, understanding when and how to implement change is a vital part of management. This chapter describes how organizations manage change. We first examine the nature of organization change and identify the basic issues of managing change. We then identify and describe major areas of change, including business process change, a major type of change undertaken by many firms recently. We then examine organization development and conclude by discussing organizational innovation as a vital form of change dramatically illustrated by Ikea.

The Nature of Organization Change

organization change
Any substantive modification to some part of the organization

Organization change is any substantive modification to some part of the organization.[2] Thus change can involve virtually any aspect of an organization: work schedules, bases for departmentalization, span of management, machinery, organization design, people themselves, and so on. It is important to keep in mind that any change in an organization may have effects extending beyond the actual area where the change is implemented. For example, when Northrop Grumman recently installed a new automated production system at one of its plants, employees were trained to operate new equipment, the compensation system was adjusted to reflect new skill levels, the span of management for supervisors was altered, and several related jobs were redesigned. Selection criteria for new employees were also changed, and a new quality control system was installed.[3] In addition, it is quite common for multiple organization change activities to be going on simultaneously.[4]

Forces for Change

Why do organizations find change necessary? The basic reason is that something relevant to the organization either has changed or is likely to change in the foreseeable future. The organization therefore may have little choice but to change as well. Indeed, a primary reason for the problems that organizations often face is failure to anticipate or respond properly to changing circumstances. The forces that compel change may be external or internal to the organization.[5]

External Forces   External forces for change derive from the organization's general and task environments. For example, two energy crises, an aggressive Japanese automobile industry, floating currency exchange rates, and floating international interest rates—all manifestations of the international dimension of the general environment—profoundly influenced U.S. automobile companies. New rules of production and competition forced them to dramatically alter the way they do

There are a variety of forces that can create a need for change, some external and some internal. This shopper is checking out her own purchases at a Kroger supermarket. Several factors—new technology (that facilitates cashless transactions), customer preferences for convenience (that causes them to want to get in and out of the store quickly), and the firm's interests in lowering costs (by hiring fewer check-out operators)—have together led to this increasingly popular change.

business. In the political area, new laws, court decisions, and regulations affect organizations. The technological dimension may yield new production techniques that the organization needs to explore. The economic dimension is affected by inflation, the cost of living, and money supplies. The sociocultural dimension, reflecting societal values, determines what kinds of products or services will be accepted in the market.

Because of its proximity to the organization, the task environment is an even more powerful force for change. Competitors influence an organization through their price structures and product lines. When Dell lowers the prices it charges for computers, Gateway may have little choice but to follow suit. Because customers determine what products can be sold at what prices, organizations must be concerned with consumer tastes and preferences. Suppliers affect organizations by raising or lowering prices or changing product lines. Regulators can have dramatic effects on an organization. For example, if OSHA rules that a particular production process is dangerous to workers, it can force a firm to close a plant until it meets higher safety standards. Unions can force change when they negotiate for higher wages or go on strike.[6]

Internal Forces   A variety of forces inside the organization may cause change. If top management revises the organization's strategy, organization change is likely to result. A decision by a consumer electronics company to enter the video game market or a decision to increase a ten-year product sales goal by 3 percent would occasion many organizational changes. Other internal forces for change may be reflections of external forces. As sociocultural values shift, for example, workers' attitudes toward their job may also shift—and workers may demand a change in working hours or working conditions. In such a case, even though the force is rooted in the external environment, the organization must respond directly to the internal pressure it generates.[7]

Planned Versus Reactive Change

Some change is planned well in advance; other change comes about as a reaction to unexpected events. ***Planned change*** is change that is designed and implemented in an orderly and timely fashion in anticipation of future events. ***Reactive change*** is a piecemeal response to circumstances as they develop. Because reactive change may be hurried, the potential for poorly conceived and executed change is increased. Planned change is almost always preferable to reactive change.[8]

Georgia-Pacific, a large forest products business, is an excellent example of a firm that went through a planned and well-managed change process. When A. D. Correll became CEO, he quickly became alarmed at the firm's high accident rate—9 serious injuries per 100 employees each year, and 26 deaths during the previous five-year period. Although the forest products business is inherently dangerous, Correll believed that the accident rate was far too high and set out on a major change effort to improve things. He and other top managers developed a multistage change program intended to educate workers about safety, improve safety equipment in the plant, and eliminate a long-standing part of the firm's culture that made injuries almost a badge of courage. As a result, Georgia-Pacific has achieved the best safety record in the industry and has relatively few injuries.[9]

On the other hand, Caterpillar was caught flat-footed by a worldwide recession in the construction industry, suffered enormous losses, and took several years to recover. Had managers at Caterpillar anticipated the need for change earlier, they might have been able to respond more quickly. Similarly, Kodak had to cut 12,000 jobs in reaction to sluggish sales and profits.[10] Again, better anticipation might have forestalled those job cuts. The importance of approaching change from a planned perspective is reinforced by the frequency of organization change. Most companies or divisions of large companies implement some form of moderate change at least every year and one or more major changes every four to five years.[11] Managers who sit back and respond only when they have to are likely to spend a lot of time hastily changing and rechanging things. A more effective approach is to anticipate forces compelling change and plan ahead to deal with them.[12]

planned change
Change that is designed and implemented in an orderly and timely fashion in anticipation of future events

reactive change
A piecemeal response to circumstances as they develop

Managing Change in Organizations

Organization change is a complex phenomenon. A manager cannot simply wave a wand and implement a planned change like magic. Instead, any change must be systematic and logical to have a realistic opportunity to succeed.[13] To carry this off, the manager needs to understand the steps of effective change and how to counter employee resistance to change.[14]

Steps in the Change Process

Researchers have over the years developed a number of models or frameworks outlining steps for change.[15] The Lewin model was one of the first, although a more comprehensive approach is usually more useful in today's complex business environment.

The Lewin Model   Kurt Lewin, a noted organizational theorist, suggested that every change requires three steps.[16] The first step is *unfreezing*—individuals who will be affected by the impending change must be led to recognize why the change is necessary. Next, the *change itself* is implemented. Finally, *refreezing* involves reinforcing and supporting the change so that it becomes a part of the system.[17] For example, one of the changes Caterpillar faced in response to the recession noted earlier involved a massive workforce reduction. The first step (unfreezing) was convincing the United Auto Workers to support the reduction because of its importance to long-term effectiveness. After this unfreezing was accomplished, 30,000 jobs were eliminated (implementation). Then Caterpillar worked to improve its damaged relationship with its workers (refreezing) by guaranteeing future pay hikes and promising no

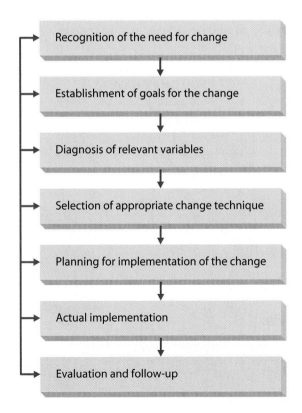

Recognition of the need for change

Establishment of goals for the change

Diagnosis of relevant variables

Selection of appropriate change technique

Planning for implementation of the change

Actual implementation

Evaluation and follow-up

Figure 7.1
STEPS IN THE CHANGE PROCESS

Managers must understand how and why to implement change. A manager who, when implementing change, follows a logical and orderly sequence like the one shown here is more likely to succeed than a manager whose change process is haphazard and poorly conceived.

more cutbacks. As interesting as Lewin's model is, it unfortunately lacks operational specificity. Thus a more comprehensive perspective is often needed.

A Comprehensive Approach to Change   The comprehensive approach to change takes a systems view and delineates a series of specific steps that often leads to successful change. This expanded model is illustrated in Figure 7.1. The first step is recognizing the need for change. Reactive change might be triggered by employee complaints, declines in productivity or turnover, court injunctions, sales slumps, or labor strikes. Recognition may simply be managers' awareness that change in a certain area is inevitable. For example, managers may be aware of the general frequency of organizational change undertaken by most organizations and recognize that their organization should probably follow the same pattern. The immediate stimulus might be the result of a forecast indicating new market potential, the accumulation of a cash surplus for possible investment, or an opportunity to achieve and capitalize on a major technological breakthrough. Managers might also initiate change today because indicators suggest that it will be necessary in the near future and they want to get a head start.[18]

Managers must next set goals for the change. To increase market share, to enter new markets, to restore employee morale, to settle a strike, and to identify investment opportunities all might be goals for change. Third, managers must diagnose what brought on the need for change. Turnover, for example, might be caused by low pay, poor working conditions, poor supervisors, or employee dissatisfaction. Thus, although turnover may be the immediate stimulus for change, managers must understand its causes to make the right changes.

The next step is to select a change technique that will accomplish the intended goals. If turnover is caused by low pay, a new reward system may be needed. If the cause is poor supervision, interpersonal skills training may be called for. (Various change techniques are summarized later in this chapter.) After the appropriate

People in organizations may resist change for a variety of reasons, including uncertainty, threats to self-interests, different perceptions, and feelings of loss. Unless managers understand and appreciate these factors and systematically work to overcome resistance to change, people like Morris here may find it very difficult to accept new ways of doing things.

MORRIS WAS FINDING IT MORE DIFFICULT THAN MOST TO ADJUST TO THE CONCEPT OF A 'PAPERLESS' OFFICE

www.CartoonStock.com

technique has been chosen, its implementation must be planned. Issues to consider include the costs of the change, its effects on other areas of the organization, and the degree of employee participation appropriate for the situation. If the change is implemented as planned, the results should then be evaluated. If the change was intended to reduce turnover, managers must check turnover after the change has been in effect for a while. If turnover is still too high, additional changes may be necessary.[19]

Understanding Resistance to Change

Another element in the effective management of change is understanding the resistance that often accompanies change.[20] Managers need to know why people resist change and what can be done about their resistance. When Westinghouse first provided all of its managers with personal computers, most people responded favorably. One manager, however, resisted the change to the point where he began leaving work every day at noon! It was some time before he began staying in the office all day again. Such resistance is common for a variety of reasons.[21]

Uncertainty Perhaps the biggest cause of employee resistance to change is uncertainty. In the face of impending change, employees may become anxious and nervous. They may worry about their ability to meet new job demands, they may think that their job security is threatened, or they may simply dislike ambiguity. Nabisco was once the target of an extended and confusing takeover battle, and during the entire time, employees were nervous about the impending change. The *Wall Street Journal* described them this way: "Many are angry at their leaders and fearful for their jobs. They are swapping rumors and spinning scenarios for the ultimate outcome of the battle for the tobacco and food giant. Headquarters staffers in Atlanta know so little about what's happening in New York that some call their office 'the mushroom complex,' where they are kept in the dark."[22]

Threatened Self-Interests Many impending changes threaten the self-interests of some managers within the organization. A change might diminish their power or influence within the company, so they fight it. Managers at Sears once developed a plan calling for a new type of store. The new stores would be somewhat smaller than a typical Sears store and would not be located in large shopping malls. Instead, they would be located in smaller strip centers. They would carry clothes and other "soft goods," but not hardware, appliances, furniture, or automotive products. When executives in charge of the excluded product lines heard about the plan, they raised such strong objections that the plan was canceled.

Different Perceptions A third reason that people resist change is due to different perceptions. A manager may make a decision and recommend a plan for change on the basis of her own assessment of a situation. Others in the organization may resist the change because they do not agree with the manager's assessment or perceive the situation differently.[23] Executives at 7-Eleven battled this problem as they attempted to initiate a major organizational change. The corporation wanted to take its convenience stores a bit "upscale" and begin selling fancy fresh foods to go, the newest hardcover novels, some gourmet products, and higher-quality coffee. But many franchisees balked because they saw this move as taking the firm away from its core blue-collar customers.

Feelings of Loss   Many changes involve altering work arrangements in ways that disrupt existing social networks. Because social relationships are important, most people resist any change that might adversely affect those relationships. Other intangibles threatened by change include power, status, security, familiarity with existing procedures, and self-confidence.

Overcoming Resistance to Change

Of course, a manager should not give up in the face of resistance to change. Although there are no sure-fire cures, there are several techniques that at least have the potential to overcome resistance.[24]

Participation   Participation is often the most effective technique for overcoming resistance to change. Employees who participate in planning and implementing a change are better able to understand the reasons for the change. Uncertainty is reduced, and self-interests and social relationships are less threatened. Having had an opportunity to express their ideas and assume the perspectives of others, employees are more likely to accept the change gracefully. A classic study of participation monitored the introduction of a change in production methods among four groups in a Virginia pajama factory.[25] The two groups that were allowed to fully participate in planning and implementing the change improved significantly in their productivity and satisfaction, relative to the two groups that did not participate. 3M Company recently attributed $10 million in cost savings to employee participation in several organization change activities.[26]

Education and Communication   Educating employees about the need for and the expected results of an impending change should reduce their resistance. If open communication is established and maintained during the change process, uncertainty can be minimized. Caterpillar used these methods during many of its cutbacks to reduce resistance. First, it educated UAW representatives about the need for and potential value of the planned changes. Then management told all employees what was happening, when it would happen, and how it would affect them individually.

Facilitation   Several facilitation procedures are also advisable. For instance, making only necessary changes, announcing those changes well in advance, and allowing time for people to adjust to new ways of doing things can help reduce resistance to change.[27] One manager at a Prudential regional office spent several months systematically planning a change in work procedures and job design. He then became too hurried, coming in over the weekend with a work crew and rearranging the office layout. When employees walked in on Monday morning, they were hostile, anxious, and resentful. What was a promising change became a disaster, and the manager had to scrap the entire plan.

Force-Field Analysis   Although force-field analysis may sound like something out of a *Star Trek* movie, it can help overcome resistance to change. In almost any change situation, forces are acting for and against the change. To facilitate the change, managers start by listing each set of forces and then trying to tip the balance so that the forces facilitating the change outweigh those hindering the change. It is especially important to try to remove or at least minimize some of the forces acting against the change. Suppose, for example, that General Motors

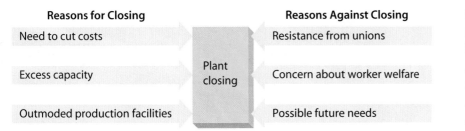

Reasons for Closing

Need to cut costs

Excess capacity

Outmoded production facilities

Plant closing

Reasons Against Closing

Resistance from unions

Concern about worker welfare

Possible future needs

Figure 7.2

FORCE-FIELD ANALYSIS FOR PLANT CLOSING AT GENERAL MOTORS

A force-field analysis can help a manager facilitate change. A manager able to identify forces acting both for and against a change can see where to focus efforts to remove barriers to change (such as offering training and relocation to displaced workers). Removing the forces against the change can at least partially overcome resistance.

is considering a plant closing as part of a change. As shown in Figure 7.2, three factors are reinforcing the change: GM needs to cut costs, it has excess capacity, and the plant has outmoded production facilities. At the same time, there is resistance from the UAW, concern for workers being put out of their jobs, and a feeling that the plant might be needed again in the future. GM might start by convincing the UAW that the closing is necessary by presenting profit and loss figures. It could then offer relocation and retraining to displaced workers. And it might shut down the plant and put it in "mothballs" so that it can be renovated later. The three major factors hindering the change are thus eliminated or reduced in importance.[28]

Areas of Organization Change

We note earlier that change can involve virtually any part of an organization. In general, however, most change interventions involve organization structure and design, technology and operations, or people. In addition, many organizations have gone through massive and comprehensive business process change programs.

Changing Organization Structure and Design

Organization change might be focused on any of the basic components of organization structure or on the organization's overall design. Thus the organization might change the way it designs its jobs or its bases of departmentalization. Likewise, it might change reporting relationships or the distribution of authority. For example, we note in Chapter 6 the trend toward flatter organizations. Coordination mechanisms and line-and-staff configurations are also subject to change. On a larger scale, the organization might change its overall design. For example, a growing business could decide to drop its functional design and adopt a divisional design. Or it might transform itself into a matrix. Changes in culture usually involve the structure and design of the organization as well (recall that we discussed changing culture back in Chapter 2). Finally, the organization might change any part of its human resource management system, such as its selection criteria, its performance appraisal methods, or its compensation package.[29]

Changing Technology and Operations

Technology is the conversion process used by an organization to transform inputs into outputs. Because of the rapid rate of all technological innovation, technological changes are becoming increasingly important to many organizations. One important area of change today revolves around information technology. The adoption and institutionalization of information technology innovations is almost constant

New forms of technology can improve efficiency, boost productivity, and lower costs. They can also help protect the safety and health of employees. For decades automobile assembly line workers had to bend, stoop, and stretch to work on cars as they passed along a moving assembly line. But now, workers in some factories, such as this one, can sit in ergonomically designed seats that move the worker up, down, forward, and backward as the job requires. This approach helps reduce injuries and other associated medical problems that have sometimes plagued automobile workers.

Enterprise resource planning (ERP)
A large-scale information system for integrating and synchronizing the many activities in an extended enterprise

in most firms today. Sun Microsystems, for example, adopted a very short-range planning cycle to be best prepared for environmental changes.[30] Another important form of technological change involves equipment. To keep pace with competitors, firms periodically find that replacing existing machinery and equipment with newer models is necessary.

And changes in work processes or work activities may be necessary if new equipment is introduced or new products are manufactured. Organizational control systems may also be targets of change.

Many businesses have also been working to implement technological and operations change by installing and using complex and integrated software systems that link virtually all facets of the business into an integrated system, making it easier for managers to keep abreast of related developments. Known as ***enterprise resource planning, or ERP,*** such a large-scale information system integrates and synchronizes the many activities in the extended enterprise. In most cases these systems are purchased from external vendors who then tailor their products to the client's unique needs and requirements. Companywide processes—such as materials management, production planning, order management, and financial reporting—can all be managed via ERP. In effect, these are the processes that cut across product lines, departments, and geographic locations.

The ERP integrates all activities and information flows that relate to the firm's critical processes. It also keeps updated real-time information on their current status, reports recent past transactions and upcoming planned transactions, and provides electronic notices that action is required on some items if planned schedules are to be met. It coordinates internal operations with activities by outside suppliers and notifies business partners and customers of current status and upcoming deliveries and billings. It can integrate financial flows among the firm, its suppliers, its customers, and commercial bank deposits for up-to-the-minute status reports that can be used to create real-time financial reports at a moment's notice, rather than in the traditional one-month (or longer) time span for producing a financial statement. ERP's multilanguage capabilities also allow real-time correspondence in various languages to facilitate international transactions.

Changing People, Attitudes, and Behaviors

A third area of organization change has to do with human resources. For example, an organization might decide to change the skill level of its workforce. This change might be prompted by changes in technology or by a general desire to upgrade the quality of the workforce. Thus training programs and new selection criteria might be needed. The organization might also decide to improve its workers' performance level. In this instance, a new incentive system or performance-based training might be in order. *Reader's Digest* has attempted to implement significant changes in its workforce. For example, the firm eliminated 17 percent of its employees, reduced retirement benefits, and took away many of the "perks" (perquisites, or job benefits) that employees once enjoyed. Part of the reason for the changes was to instill in the remaining employees a sense of urgency and the need to adopt a new perspective on how they do their job.[31] Similarly, Saks Fifth Avenue recently changed its entire top management team as a way to breathe new life into the luxury retailer.[32]

Perceptions and expectations are also a common focus of organization change. Workers in an organization might believe that their wages and benefits are not as high as they should be. Management, however, might have evidence that shows the firm is paying a competitive wage and providing a superior benefit package. The change, then, would be centered on informing and educating the workforce about the comparative value of its compensation package. A common way to do this is to publish a statement that places an actual dollar value on each benefit provided and compares that amount to what other local organizations are providing their workers. Change might also be directed at employee attitudes and values. In many organizations today, managers are trying to eliminate adversarial relationships with workers and to adopt a more collaborative relationship. In many ways, changing attitudes and values is perhaps the hardest thing to do.

Changing Business Processes

Many organizations today have gone through massive and comprehensive change programs involving all aspects of organization design, technology, and people. Although various descriptions are used, the terms currently in vogue for these changes are *business process change,* or *reengineering.* Specifically, **business process change, or reengineering,** is the radical redesign of all aspects of a business to achieve major improvements in cost, service, or time.[33] ERP, as described above, is a common platform for changing business processes. However, business process change is a more comprehensive set of changes that goes beyond software and information systems.

business process change (reengineering)
The radical redesign of all aspects of a business to achieve major improvements in cost, service, or time

Corning, for example, has undergone major reengineering over the last few years. Whereas the 150-year-old business once manufactured cookware and other durable consumer goods, it has transformed itself into a high-tech powerhouse making such products as the ultrathin screens used in products like Palm Pilots and laptop computers.[34] Similarly, the dramatic overhauls of Kodak away from print film to other forms of optical imaging, of Yellow into a sophisticated freight delivery firm, and of UPS into a major international delivery giant all required business process changes throughout these organizations.

The Need for Business Process Change Why are so many organizations finding it necessary to undergo business process change? We note in Chapter 1 that all systems, including organizations, are subject to entropy—a normal process leading to system decline. An organization is behaving most typically when it maintains the status quo, does not change in synch with its environment, and starts consuming its own resources to survive. In a sense, that is what happened to Kmart. In the early and mid-1970s, Kmart was in such a high-flying growth mode that it passed first JCPenney and then Sears to become the world's largest retailer. But then the firm's managers grew complacent and assumed that the discount retailer's prosperity would continue and that they need not worry about environmental shifts, the growth of Wal-Mart, and so forth—and entropy set in. The key is to recognize the beginning of the decline and immediately move toward changing relevant business processes. Major problems occur when managers either do not recognize the onset of entropy until it is well advanced or are complacent in taking steps to correct it.

Approaches to Business Process Change Figure 7.3 shows general steps in changing business processes, or reengineering. The first step is setting goals and developing a strategy for the changes. The organization must know in advance what new business processes are supposed to accomplish and how those accomplishments will be achieved. Next, top managers must begin and direct the reengineering effort. If a CEO simply announces that business process change is to occur but does nothing else, the program is unlikely to be successful. But, if the CEO is constantly involved in the process, underscoring its importance and taking the lead, business process change stands a much better chance of success.

Most experts also agree that successful business process change is usually accompanied by a sense of urgency. People in the organization must see the clear and present need for the changes being implemented and appreciate their importance. In addition, most successful reengineering efforts start with a new, clean slate. In other words, rather than assuming that the existing organization is a starting point and then trying to modify it, business process change usually starts

Figure 7.3
THE REENGINEERING PROCESS

Reengineering is a major redesign of all areas of an organization. To be successful, reengineering requires a systematic and comprehensive assessment of the entire organization. Goals, top management support, and a sense of urgency help the organization re-create itself and blend both top-level and bottom-up perspectives.

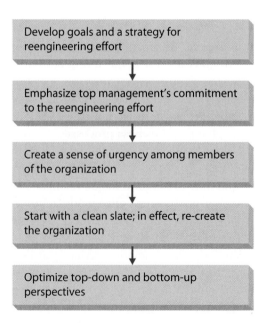

by asking questions such as how customers are best served and competitors best neutralized. New approaches and systems are then created and imposed in place of existing ones.

Finally, business process change requires a careful blend of top-down and bottom-up involvement. On the one hand, strong leadership is necessary, but too much involvement by top management can make the changes seem autocratic. Similarly, employee participation is also important, but too little involvement by leaders can undermine the program's importance and create a sense that top managers do not care. Thus care must be taken to carefully balance these two countervailing forces. Our next section explores more fully one related but distinct approach called *organization development.*

Organization Development

We note in several places the importance of people and change. Beyond those change interests discussed above, a special area of interest that focuses almost exclusively on people is organization development (OD).

OD Assumptions   Organization development is concerned with changing attitudes, perceptions, behaviors, and expectations. More precisely, **organization development (OD)** is a planned effort that is organization-wide and managed from the top, intended to increase organizational effectiveness and health through planned interventions in the organization's process, using behavioral science knowledge.[35] The theory and practice of OD are based on several very important assumptions. The first is that employees have a desire to grow and develop. Another is that employees have a strong need to be accepted by others within the organization. Still another critical assumption of OD is that the total organization and the way it is designed will influence the way individuals and groups within the organization behave. Thus some form of collaboration between managers and their employees is necessary to (1) take advantage of the skills and abilities of the employees and (2) eliminate aspects of the organization that retard employee growth, development, and group acceptance. Because of the intense personal nature of many OD activities, many large organizations rely on one or more OD consultants (either full-time employees assigned to this function or outside experts hired specifically for OD purposes) to implement and manage their OD program.[36]

> *organization development (OD)*
> An effort that is planned, organization-wide, and managed from the top, intended to increase organizational effectiveness and health through planned interventions in the organization's process, using behavioral science knowledge

OD Techniques   Several kinds of interventions or activities are generally considered part of organization development.[37] Some OD programs may use only one or a few of these; other programs use several of them at once.

- *Diagnostic activities.* Just as a physician examines patients to diagnose their current condition, an OD diagnosis analyzes the current condition of an organization. To carry out this diagnosis, managers use questionnaires, opinion or attitude surveys, interviews, archival data, and meetings to assess various characteristics of the organization. The results of this diagnosis may generate profiles of the organization's activities, which can then be used to identify problem areas in need of correction.

- *Team building.* Team-building activities are intended to enhance the effectiveness and satisfaction of individuals who work in groups or teams and to promote overall group effectiveness. Given the widespread use of teams today, these activities have taken on increased importance. An OD consultant might interview team members to determine how they feel about the group; then an off-site meeting could be held to discuss the issues that surfaced and iron out any problem areas or member concerns. Caterpillar used team building as one method for changing the working relationships between workers and supervisors from confrontational to cooperative. An interesting new approach to team building involves having executive teams participate in group cooking classes to teach them the importance of interdependence and coordination.[38]

- *Survey feedback.* In survey feedback, each employee responds to a questionnaire intended to measure perceptions and attitudes (for example, satisfaction and supervisory style). Everyone involved, including the supervisor, receives the results of the survey. The aim of this approach is usually to change the behavior of supervisors by showing them how their subordinates view them. After the feedback has been provided, workshops may be conducted to evaluate results and suggest constructive changes.

- *Third-party peacemaking.* Another approach to OD is through third-party peacemaking, which is most often used when substantial conflict exists within the organization. Third-party peacemaking can be appropriate on the individual, group, or organizational level. The third party, usually an OD consultant, uses a variety of mediation or negotiation techniques to resolve any problems or conflicts among individuals or groups.

- *Process consultation.* In process consultation, an OD consultant observes groups in the organization to develop an understanding of their communication patterns, decision-making and leadership processes, and methods of cooperation and conflict resolution. The consultant then provides feedback to the involved parties about the processes he or she has observed. The goal of this form of intervention is to improve the observed processes. A leader who is presented with feedback outlining deficiencies in his or her leadership style, for example, might be expected to change to overcome them.

- *Life and career planning.* Life and career planning helps employees formulate their personal goals and evaluate strategies for integrating their goals with the goals of the organization. Such activities might include specification of training needs and plotting a career map. General Electric has a reputation for doing an outstanding job in this area.

- *Coaching and counseling.* Coaching and counseling provide nonevaluative feedback to individuals. The purpose is to help people develop a better sense of how others see them and learn behaviors that will assist others in achieving their work-related goals. The focus is not on how the individual is performing today; instead, it is on how the person can perform better in the future.

The Effectiveness of OD   Given the diversity of activities encompassed by OD, it is not surprising that managers report mixed results from various OD interventions. Organizations that actively practice some form of OD include American Airlines, Texas Instruments, Procter & Gamble, and Goodrich Corporation. Goodrich, for example, has trained 60 persons in OD processes and techniques. These trained experts have subsequently become internal OD consultants to assist other managers in applying the techniques.[39] Many other managers, in contrast, report that they have tried OD but discarded it.[40]

OD will probably remain an important part of management theory and practice. Of course, there are no sure things when dealing with social systems such as organizations, and the effectiveness of many OD techniques is difficult to evaluate. Because all organizations are open systems interacting with their environments, an improvement in an organization after an OD intervention may be attributable to the intervention, but it may also be attributable to changes in economic conditions, luck, or other factors.[41]

Organizational Innovation

A final element of organization change that we address is innovation. **Innovation** is the managed effort of an organization to develop new products or services or new uses for existing products or services. Innovation is clearly important because, without new products or services, any organization will fall behind its competition.[42]

innovation
The managed effort of an organization to develop new products or services or new uses for existing products or services

The Innovation Process

The organizational innovation process consists of developing, applying, launching, growing, and managing the maturity and decline of creative ideas.[43] This process is depicted in Figure 7.4.

Innovation Development Innovation development involves the evaluation, modification, and improvement of creative ideas. Innovation development can transform a product or service with only modest potential into a product or service with significant potential. Parker Brothers, for example, decided during innovation development not to market an indoor volleyball game but instead to sell separately the appealing little foam ball designed for the game. The firm will never know how well the volleyball game would have sold, but the Nerf ball and numerous related products generated millions of dollars in revenues for Parker Brothers.

Innovation Application Innovation application is the stage in which an organization takes a developed idea and uses it in the design, manufacturing, or delivery of new products, services, or processes. At this point the innovation emerges from

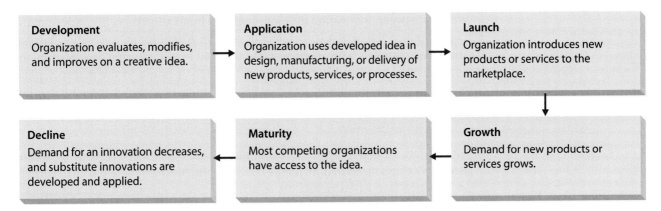

Figure 7.4
THE INNOVATION PROCESS

Organizations actively seek to manage the innovation process. These steps illustrate the general life cycle that characterizes most innovations. Of course, as with creativity, the innovation process will suffer if it is approached too mechanically and rigidly.

the laboratory and is transformed into tangible goods or services. One example of innovation application is the use of radar-based focusing systems in Polaroid's instant cameras. The idea of using radio waves to discover the location, speed, and direction of moving objects was first applied extensively by Allied forces during World War II. As radar technology developed during the following years, the electrical components needed became smaller and more streamlined. Researchers at Polaroid applied this well-developed technology in a new way.[44]

Application Launch Application launch is the stage at which an organization introduces new products or services to the marketplace. The important question is not "Does the innovation work?" but "Will customers want to purchase the innovative product and service?" History is full of creative ideas that did not generate enough interest among customers to be successful. Some notable innovation failures include Sony's seat warmer, the Edsel automobile, and Polaroid's SX-70 instant camera (which cost $3 billion to develop, but never sold more than 100,000 units in a year).[45] Thus, despite development and application, new products and services can still fail at the launch phase.

Application Growth Once an innovation has been successfully launched, it then enters the stage of application growth. This is a period of high economic performance for an organization because demand for the product or service is often greater than supply. Organizations that fail to anticipate this stage may unintentionally limit their growth, as Apple did by not anticipating demand for its iMac computer.[46] At the same time, overestimating demand for a new product can be just as detrimental to performance. Unsold products can sit in warehouses for years.

Innovation Maturity After a period of growing demand, an innovative product or service often enters a period of maturity. Innovation maturity is the stage at which most organizations in an industry have access to an innovation and are applying it in approximately the same way. The technological application of an innovation during this stage of the innovation process can be very sophisticated. Because most firms have access to the innovation, however, either as a result of their developing the innovation on their own or copying the innovation of others, it does not provide competitive advantage to any one of them. The time that elapses between innovation development and innovation maturity varies notably depending on the particular product or service. Whenever an innovation involves the use of complex skills (such as a complicated manufacturing process or highly sophisticated teamwork), moving from the growth phase to the maturity phase will take longer. In addition, if the skills needed to implement these innovations are rare and difficult to imitate, then strategic imitation may be delayed, and the organization may enjoy a period of sustained competitive advantage.

Innovation Decline Every successful innovation bears its own seeds of decline. Because an organization does not gain a competitive advantage from an innovation at maturity, it must encourage its creative scientists, engineers, and managers to begin looking for new innovations. This continued search for competitive advantage usually leads new products and services to move from the creative process through innovation maturity, and finally to innovation decline. Innovation decline is the stage during which demand for an innovation decreases and substitute innovations are developed and applied.

Managing in Times of Change

Out With the Old, In With the New

Good-bye, Knowledge Economy. Hello, Creativity Economy. As knowledge work becomes globalized, outsourced, and imitated, firms in developed nations must reinvent themselves and innovate with new products and customer experiences. Here's a sample of radically innovative companies and their methods.

Incremental innovations are the norm for the household products industry, but while researching cleaning techniques, Procter & Gamble (P&G) found that an electrostatic cloth picks up more dirt than a wet cloth. Thus, the Swiffer mop was born. The Swiffer brand is so popular that it may reach $1 billion in sales in 2007.

Founded in Montreal in 1984, Cirque du Soleil is a complete re-imagination of a traditional circus. Although Cirque uses traditional circus elements, the experience is quite new. The company founders, formerly street performers, keep creativity high by providing financial support for their artists to attend and to stage cultural events. They also run and recruit from circus schools in Europe, Africa, and Latin America, increasing the diversity of ideas and experiences of their employees.

Customercentric design is critical in the Creativity Economy. Consider how JetBlue improved on a traditional airline by offering seat-back entertainment and more leg room. eBay's success comes from its ability to empower customers. NetFlix is much more convenient than standard video stores. Target created a prescription bottle with large type, color coding, and an easy-open top after observing patients struggle to manage their medications. P&G developed a bathroom scrubber on a long pole after surveying consumers who hated stepping into the tub to clean it.

Companies that innovate continuously start with customer observation and then do extensive testing of prototype products. Storytelling is important, too, to connect emotionally with users. The final challenge is to build an organizational process that does these things repeatedly and routinely. To do this, General Electric trains managers in five design leadership traits: external focus, decisiveness, imagination and courage, inclusiveness, and (product-market) expertise.

Today, experts estimate that 96 percent of all corporate innovations fail to meet their performance targets. Clearly, if the United States and other developed nations want to dominate the Creativity Economy, they will have to learn how to continually reinvent themselves.

References: Bruce Nussbaum, "How to Build Innovative Companies," *BusinessWeek*, August 1, 2005, pp. 60–68; "The Company—Cultural Action," Cirque du Soleil website, www.cirquedusoleil.com on January 22, 2007; "Who We Are," Procter & Gamble website, www.pg.com on January 22, 2007.

Forms of Innovation

Each creative idea that an organization develops poses a different challenge for the innovation process. Innovations can be radical or incremental, technical or managerial, and product or process.

Radical Versus Incremental Innovations   ***Radical innovations*** are new products, services, or technologies developed by an organization that completely replace the existing products, services, or technologies in an industry.[47] ***Incremental innovations*** are new products or processes that modify existing ones. Firms that implement radical innovations fundamentally shift the nature of competition and the interaction of firms within their environments. Firms that implement incremental innovations alter, but do not fundamentally change, competitive interaction in an industry.

Over the last several years, organizations have introduced many radical innovations. For example, compact disk technology has virtually replaced long-playing vinyl records in the recording industry, DVDs are replacing videocassettes, and high-definition television seems likely to replace regular television technology in the near future. Whereas radical innovations like these tend to be very visible and public, incremental innovations actually are more numerous. One example is Ford's

radical innovation
A new product, service, or technology that completely replaces an existing one

incremental innovation
A new product, service, or technology that modifies an existing one

sport-utility vehicle, Explorer. Although other companies had similar products, Ford more effectively combined the styling and engineering that resulted in increased demand for all sport-utility vehicles.

Technical Versus Managerial Innovations   *Technical innovations* are changes in the physical appearance or performance of a product or service, or of the physical processes through which a product or service passes. Many of the most important innovations over the last 50 years have been technical. For example, the serial replacement of the vacuum tube with the transistor, the transistor with the integrated circuit, and the integrated circuit with the microchip has greatly enhanced the power, ease of use, and speed of operation of a wide variety of electronic products. Not all innovations developed by organizations are technical, however. *Managerial innovations* are changes in the management process by which products and services are conceived, built, and delivered to customers. Managerial innovations do not necessarily affect the physical appearance or performance of products or services directly. In effect, business process change or reengineering, as we discuss earlier, represents a managerial innovation.

Product Versus Process Innovations   Perhaps the two most important types of technical innovations are product innovations and process innovations. *Product innovations* are changes in the physical characteristics or performance of existing products or services or the creation of brand-new products or services. *Process innovations* are changes in the way products or services are manufactured, created, or distributed. Whereas managerial innovations generally affect the broader context of development, process innovations directly affect manufacturing.

Japanese organizations have often excelled at process innovation. The market for 35mm cameras was dominated by German and other European manufacturers when, in the early 1960s, Japanese organizations such as Canon and Nikon began making cameras. Some of these early Japanese products were not very successful, but these companies continued to invest in their process technology and eventually were able to increase quality and decrease manufacturing costs.[48] The Japanese organizations came to dominate the worldwide market for 35mm cameras, and the German companies, because they were not able to maintain the same pace of process innovation, struggled to maintain market share and profitability. And as film technology gives way to digital photography, the same Japanese firms are effectively transitioning to leadership in this market as well.

The Failure to Innovate

To remain competitive in today's economy, organizations must be innovative. And yet many organizations that should be innovative are not successful at bringing out new products or services or do so only after innovations created by others are very mature. Organizations may fail to innovate for at least three reasons.

Lack of Resources   Innovation is expensive in terms of dollars, time, and energy. If a firm does not have sufficient money to fund a program of innovation or does not currently employ the kinds of workers it needs to be innovative, it may lag behind in innovation. Even highly innovative organizations cannot become involved in every new product or service its employees think up. For example, numerous other commitments in the electronic instruments and computer industry forestalled

---

technical innovation
A change in the appearance or performance of products or services, or of the physical processes through which a product or service passes

managerial innovation
A change in the management process in an organization

product innovation
A change in the physical characteristics or performance of an existing product or service or the creation of new ones

process innovation
A change in the way a product or service is manufactured, created, or distributed

Hewlett-Packard from investing in Steve Jobs and Steve Wozniak's original idea for a personal computer. With infinite resources of money, time, and technical and managerial expertise, HP might have entered this market early. Because the firm did not have this flexibility, however, it had to make some difficult choices about which innovations to invest in.

Failure to Recognize Opportunities   Because firms cannot pursue all innovations, they need to develop the capability to carefully evaluate innovations and to select the ones that hold the greatest potential. To obtain a competitive advantage, an organization usually must make investment decisions before the innovation process reaches the mature stage. The earlier the investment, however, the greater the risk. If organizations are not skilled at recognizing and evaluating opportunities, they may be overly cautious and fail to invest in innovations that later turn out to be successful for other firms.

Resistance to Change   As we discuss earlier, many organizations tend to resist change. Innovation means giving up old products and old ways of doing things in favor of new products and new ways of doing things. These kinds of changes can be personally difficult for managers and other members of an organization. Thus resistance to change can slow the innovation process.

Promoting Innovation in Organizations

A wide variety of ideas for promoting innovation in organizations has been developed over the years. Three specific ways for promoting innovation are through the reward system, through the organizational culture, and through a process called *intrapreneurship.*[49]

The Reward System   A firm's reward system is the means by which it encourages and discourages certain behaviors by employees. Major components of the reward system include salaries, bonuses, and perquisites. Using the reward system to promote innovation is a fairly mechanical but nevertheless effective management technique. The idea is to provide financial and nonfinancial rewards to people and groups who develop innovative ideas. Once the members of an organization understand that they will be rewarded for such activities, they are more likely to work creatively. With this end in mind, Monsanto gives a $50,000 award each year to the scientist or group of scientists who develop the biggest commercial breakthrough.

It is important for organizations to reward creative behavior, but it is vital to avoid punishing creativity when it does not result in highly successful innovations. It is the nature of the creative and innovative processes that many new product ideas will simply not work out in the marketplace. Each process is fraught with too many uncertainties to generate positive results every time. An individual may have prepared herself to be creative, but an insight may not be forthcoming. Or managers may attempt to apply a developed innovation, only to recognize that it does not work. Indeed, some organizations operate according to the assumption that, if all their innovative efforts succeed, then they are probably not taking enough risks in research and development. At 3M, nearly 60 percent of the creative ideas suggested each year do not succeed in the marketplace.

Managers need to be very careful in responding to innovative failure. If innovative failure is due to incompetence, systematic errors, or managerial sloppiness, then a firm should respond appropriately, for example, by withholding raises or reducing promotion opportunities. People who act in good faith to develop an innovation that simply does not work out, however, should not be punished for failure. If they are, they will probably not be creative in the future. A punitive reward system will discourage people from taking risks and therefore reduce the organization's ability to obtain competitive advantages.

Organization Culture   As we discussed in Chapter 2, an organization's culture is the set of values, beliefs, and symbols that help guide behavior. A strong, appropriately focused organizational culture can be used to support innovative activity. A well-managed culture can communicate a sense that innovation is valued and will be rewarded and that occasional failure in the pursuit of new ideas is not only acceptable but even expected. In addition to reward systems and intrapreneurial activities, firms such as 3M, Corning, Monsanto, Procter & Gamble, Texas Instruments, Johnson & Johnson, and Merck are all known to have strong, innovation-oriented cultures that value individual creativity, risk taking, and inventiveness.[50]

Intrapreneurship in Larger Organizations   In recent years, many large businesses have realized that the entrepreneurial spirit that propelled their growth becomes stagnant after they transform themselves from a small but growing concern into a larger one.[51] To help revitalize this spirit, some firms today encourage what they call "intrapreneurship." **Intrapreneurs** are similar to entrepreneurs except that they develop a new business in the context of a large organization. There are three intrapreneurial roles in large organizations.[52] To successfully use intrapreneurship to encourage creativity and innovation, the organization must find one or more individuals to perform these roles.

The *inventor* is the person who actually conceives of and develops the new idea, product, or service by means of the creative process. Because the inventor may lack the expertise or motivation to oversee the transformation of the product or service from an idea into a marketable entity, however, a second role comes into play. A *product champion* is usually a middle manager who learns about the project and becomes committed to it. He or she helps overcome organizational resistance and convinces others to take the innovation seriously. The product champion may have only limited understanding of the technological aspects of the innovation. Nevertheless, product champions are skilled at knowing how the organization works, whose support is needed to push the project forward, and where to go to secure the resources necessary for successful development. A *sponsor* is a top-level manager who approves of and supports a project. This person may fight for the budget needed to develop an idea, overcome arguments against a project, and use organizational politics to ensure the project's survival. With a sponsor in place, the inventor's idea has a much better chance of being successfully developed.

Several firms have embraced intrapreneurship as a way to encourage creativity and innovation. Colgate-Palmolive has created a separate unit, Colgate Venture Company, staffed with intrapreneurs who develop new products. General Foods developed Culinova as a unit to which employees can take their ideas for possible development. S.C. Johnson & Son established a $250,000 fund to support new product ideas, and Texas Instruments refuses to approve a new innovative project unless it has an acknowledged inventor, champion, and sponsor.

intrapreneurs
Similar to entrepreneurs except that they develop new businesses in the context of a large organization

Summary of Key Points

1. Describe the nature of organization change, including forces for change and planned versus reactive change.
   - Organization change is any substantive modification to some part of the organization.
   - Change may be prompted by forces internal or external to the organization.
   - In general, planned change is preferable to reactive change.

2. Discuss the steps in organization change and how to manage resistance to change.
   - The Lewin model provides a general perspective on the steps involved in change.
   - A comprehensive model is usually more effective.
   - People tend to resist change because of uncertainty, threatened self-interests, different perceptions, and feelings of loss.
   - Participation, education and communication, facilitation, and force-field analysis are methods for overcoming this resistance.

3. Identify and describe major areas of organization change and discuss the assumptions, techniques, and effectiveness of organization development.
   - The most common areas of change involve changing organizational structure and design, technology and operations, and people.

   - Business process change is a more massive and comprehensive change.
   - Organization development is concerned with changing attitudes, perceptions, behaviors, and expectations. Its effective use relies on an important set of assumptions.
   - There are conflicting opinions about the effectiveness of several OD techniques.

4. Describe the innovation process, forms of innovation, the failure to innovate, and how organizations can promote innovation.
   - The innovation process has six steps: development, application, launch, growth, maturity, and decline.
   - Basic categories of innovation include radical, incremental, technical, managerial, product, and process innovations.
   - Despite the importance of innovation, many organizations fail to innovate because they lack the required creative individuals or are committed to too many other creative activities, fail to recognize opportunities, or resist the change that innovation requires.
   - Organizations can use a variety of tools to overcome these problems, including the reward system, organization culture, and intrapreneurship.

Discussion Questions

Questions for Review

1. What forces or kinds of events lead to organization change? Identify each force or event as a planned or a reactive change.

2. Compare planned and reactive change. What are the advantages of planned change, as compared to reactive change?

3. Identify the primary reasons people resist change, and then summarize the primary methods managers can use to overcome such resistance.

4. In a brief sentence or just a phrase, describe each of the organizational development (OD) techniques.

5. Consider the following list of products. Categorize each along all three dimensions of innovation, if

possible (radical versus incremental, technical versus managerial, and product versus process). Explain your answers.
   - Teaching college courses by videotaping the instructor and sending the image over the Internet
   - The rise in popularity of virtual organizations (discussed in Chapter 6)
   - Checking the security of packages on airlines with the type of MRI scanning devices that are common in health care
   - A device combining features of a cell phone and a handheld computer with Internet capability

- Robotic arms that can perform surgery that is too precise for a human surgeon's hands
- Hybrid automobiles, which run on both batteries and gasoline

- Using video games to teach soldiers how to plan and execute battles

Questions for Analysis

1. What are the symptoms that a manager should look for in determining whether an organization needs to change? What are the symptoms that indicate that an organization has been through too much change?

2. Assume that you are the manager of an organization that has a routine way of performing a task and now faces a major change in how it performs that task. Using Lewin's model, tell what steps you would take to implement the change. Using the comprehensive approach, tell what steps you would take. For each step, give specific examples of actions you would take at that step.

3. Think back to a time when a professor announced a change that you, the student, did not want to adopt. What were the reasons for your resistance to change? Was the professor able to overcome your resistance?

If so, tell what he or she did. If not, tell what he or she could have done that might have been successful.

4. Some people resist change, whereas others welcome it enthusiastically. To deal with the first group, one needs to overcome resistance to change; to deal with the second, one needs to overcome resistance to stability. What advice can you give a manager facing the latter situation?

5. Do you think it is possible for a change made in one area of an organization—in technology, for instance—not to lead to change in other areas? If you think that change in one area must lead to change in other areas, describe an example of an organization change to illustrate your point. If you think that change can occur in just one area without causing change in other areas, describe an example of an organization change that illustrates your point.

Building Effective Time-Management Skills

Exercise Overview

Time-management skills reflect the manager's ability to prioritize work, to work efficiently, and to delegate appropriately. This exercise demonstrates both the importance and the difficulty of change by seeking to change your use of time.

Exercise Background

Conduct the following thought experiment. What if you found out, with absolute certainty, that the world would end in one month? Some unstoppable force—say, a giant meteor—is hurtling directly toward the earth, and there is no chance of destroying or diverting it. Everyone on the planet knows the exact time of impact, which is precisely one month from today. No one will be able to survive or escape. Death will occur for everyone, instantly. (Of course, this grim scenario is totally fictitious and unrealistic.)

What would you do with the next month? How would you spend your time? Whom would you see? Which activities are essential? And, just as important, what would you cease doing? Whom would you stop spending time with? Which activities are just not essential? The experiment is a bit far-fetched, but attempting to answer seriously works best.

Exercise Task

With the background material above serving as context, do the following:

1. List activities, people, priorities, places, and so on that would be important to you.

2. Compare your list to your current allocation of time. Are there activities that are important to you that receive little or no time today? Are there activities that you do today that are not very important, based on your list?

3. What does the comparison suggest to you about better uses of your time? What should you do more or less of?

4. Share your answers, in general terms, with a small group of classmates. Are there common themes? Do their answers suggest any new ideas to you?

Follow-up Questions

Clearly, taking this exercise too far can lead to absurd results. For example, if we only had thirty days to live, few of us would visit the dentist or go on a diet. Yet those activities can have important consequences if our lives are longer, as they surely will be. Thus this exercise does not provide a prescription of how to spend every day for the rest of your life, but it can highlight those things that are truly important to us, things that tend to get overlooked in the hustle and bustle of daily tasks.

For a variation on this exercise, consider what you would do if the time remaining were one year, one week, or just one day.

For an extension of this exercise, share your list with the people in your life, especially people who appear on the list. Some interesting conversations are sure to result!

Reprinted by permission of the author Margaret Hill.

Building Effective Diagnostic Skills

Exercise Overview

Diagnostic skills help a manager visualize the most appropriate response to a situation. These skills are especially important during a period of organization change.

Exercise Background

Assume that you are the general manager of a hotel located on a tropical island. The hotel is situated along a beautiful stretch of beach and is one of six large resorts in the immediate area. The hotel is owned by a group of foreign investors and is one of the oldest on the island. For several years, the hotel has been operated as a franchise unit of a large international hotel chain, as are all of the others on the island.

For the last few years, the hotel's owners have been taking most of the profits for themselves and putting relatively little back into the hotel. They have also let you know that their business is not in good financial health; the money earned from your hotel is being used to offset losses they are incurring elsewhere. In contrast, most of the other hotels around have recently been refurbished, and plans have just been announced to build two new ones in the near future.

A team of executives from franchise headquarters has just visited your hotel. They expressed considerable disappointment in the property. They felt that it has not kept pace with the other resorts on the island. They also informed you that if the property is not brought up to their standards, the franchise agreement, which comes up for review in a year, will be revoked. You see this move as potentially disastrous because you would lose the franchisor's brand name, access to their reservation system, and so forth.

Sitting alone in your office, you have identified several alternatives that seem viable:

1. Try to convince the owners to remodel the hotel. You estimate that it will take $10 million to meet the franchisor's minimum standards and another $10 million to bring the hotel up to the standards of the top resort on the island.

2. Try to convince the franchisor to give you more time and more options for upgrading the facility.

3. Allow the franchise agreement to terminate and try to succeed as an independent hotel.

4. Assume that the hotel will fail and start looking for another job. You have a good reputation, although you might have to start at a lower level (perhaps as an assistant manager) with another firm.

Exercise Task

With the background information presented above, do the following:

1. Rank-order the four alternatives in terms of their potential success. Make assumptions as appropriate.

2. Identify other alternatives not noted above.

3. Can any alternatives be pursued simultaneously?

4. Develop an overall strategy for trying to save the hotel while also protecting your own interests.

Building Effective Technical Skills

Exercise Overview

Technical skills are the skills necessary to accomplish or understand the specific work being done in an organization. This exercise helps you to develop technical skills as they present a framework for dealing with the forces of change and how that framework can be used in strategy formulation.

Exercise Background

Force-field analysis is a technique for identifying driving forces, the forces that act to encourage change, and restraining forces, the forces that act to discourage change. (See Figure 7.2 in this chapter for an illustration.) Thus, change is generally seen as a slow process in which the driving forces overcome the restraining forces. At any point in time, the situation may seem to be somewhat stable with the two types of forces opposing each other in an unsteady balance, as follows:

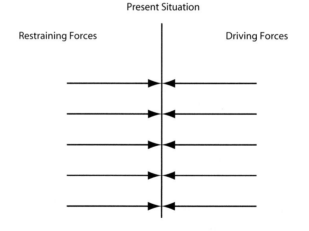

Present Situation

Restraining Forces   Driving Forces

The results of a force-field analysis can be used to formulate strategies that help to manage the change process effectively. Organizations may choose to encourage the change, discourage the change, or redirect the change in some way, depending on the nature of the change. Efforts to manage the change process can be summarized in the following actions:

1. promoting the change by facilitating the driving forces,

2. promoting the change by weakening or eliminating the restraining forces,

3. resisting the change by weakening or eliminating the driving forces,

4. resisting the change by facilitating the restraining forces, or

5. redirecting the change by manipulating the driving and restraining forces.

Exercise Task

1. Your instructor will divide the class into small groups and assign each group one of the following changes taking place in business today.
   - Increased use of wireless communications such as cell phones, Wi-Fi, PDAs
   - Concerns for the balance of work and family life
   - An increase in workplace rage, hostility, and violence
   - More diversity in the workplace
   - Increased threats of possible terrorist attacks
   - Decline in workplace ethics
   - Poor product and customer service quality
   - Loss of American jobs to other countries
   - Decline of employee and customer privacy in the workplace

2. In small groups, discuss the issues. Then complete the Change Analysis Sheet on the following pages.

3. Present the group's findings to the class and discuss.

Change Analysis Sheet

Assigned Change for Analysis: _____

Driving Forces: _____

_____

_____

_____

_____

_____

_____

_____

_____

_____

_____

_____

Restraining Forces: _____

_____

_____

_____

_____

_____

_____

_____

_____

_____

_____

Linda Morable, *Exercises in Management*, 8th edition. © 2005. pp. 95–98.

Identify the management efforts that might be used to manage the change.

1.   Promote change by facilitating the Driving Forces: _____

_____

_____

_____

_____

_____

2.   Promote change by weakening or eliminating the Restraining Forces: _____

_____

_____

_____

_____

_____

3.   Resist the change by weakening or eliminating the Driving Forces: _____

_____

_____

_____

_____

_____

4.   Resist the change by facilitating the Restraining Forces: _____

_____

_____

_____

_____

_____

5.   Redirect the change by manipulating the forces: _____

_____

_____

_____

_____

_____

Skills Self-Assessment Instrument

Innovation and Learning Styles

Introduction: David Kolb, a professor at Case Western University, has described a learning model that tells about different learning styles. While individuals move through all four activities, most express a preference for either hands-on learning or learning by indirect observation; and most express a preference for either learning about abstract concepts or learning about concrete experience. When these two dimensions are combined, the following learning styles are created.

	Active Experimentation	*Reflective Observation*
Concrete Experience	*Accommodator*	*Diverger*
Abstract Conceptualization	*Converger*	*Assimilator*

Individuals with any of these styles can be creative and innovative, although the way they will approach creativity and the contribution they can make to the innovation process differs. If you understand your learning style, you'll be better equipped to participate in innovation.

Instructions: Fill out the following tables.

	Rank from 1 to 4 *1 = Least like you,* *4 = Most Like you*
1. *a.* I want to try something out first.	
b. *I need to feel personally involved with things.*	
c. *I focus on useful practical applications.*	
d. *I look for differences and distinctions.*	

	Rank from 1 to 4 *1 = Least like you,* *4 = Most Like you*
2. *a.* I work mainly by intuition.	
b. I tend to ask myself questions.	
c. I always try to think logically.	
d. I am very results-oriented.	

	Rank from 1 to 4 *1 = Least like you,* *4 = Most Like you*
3. *a.* I let everything filter through my head and think about it.	
b. I am interested in the here and now.	
c. I have a mainly practical nature.	
d. I am mostly interested in the future.	

	Rank from 1 to 4 *1 = Least like you,* *4 = Most Like you*

4.   *a.*   I consider the facts, and then I act.

      b.   I act.

      c.   I ponder until I have evaluated every option, and then I act.

      d.   I would rather dream or imagine than think about the facts.

Interpretation: Add scores for 1a, 2d, 3b, and 4b. This is your Accommodator Score.

Add scores for 1b, 2a, 3d, and 4d. This is your Diverger Score.

Add scores for 1c, 2c, 3c, and 4a. This is your Converger Score.

Add scores for 1d, 2b, 3a, and 4c. This is your Assimilator Score.

While everyone uses each of the four styles at times, whichever score is higher is your preferred mode.

For interpretation, see Interpretations of Skills Self-Assessment Instruments in the appendix near the end of this text.

Experiential Exercise

Team Innovation

Purpose: The purpose of this exercise is to give you practice related to innovation as a team activity.

Introduction: Assume that your group is a team of professionals who are in charge of new-product design at your company.

Instructions:

Step 1: Using *only* the materials your professor will give to you, design and construct a new product. This product can be something wholly new or an improvement on an existing product.

Step 2: Present your product to the class. Explain its use, features, and appeal to consumers.

Follow-up Questions

1. How much influence did the selection of materials have on your design? What, if anything, does this suggest to you about organization resources and their effect on innovation?

2. Explain the process your group used to come up with the design. Describe the number of people who participated, how they participated, how any disagreements were resolved, and so on. What, if anything, does this suggest to you about some of the potential advantages as well as the challenges of team-based innovation in organizations?

3. Describe the various roles played by members of your group. For example, did anyone function primarily as a "voice of caution"? Did anyone serve as a devil's advocate? Did anyone work as a facilitator, smoothing over feelings and resolving conflicts? Were some members better at design, or at implementation? What, if anything, does this tell you regarding the various roles that individuals take in the innovation process in organizations?

CHAPTER CLOSING CASE

WHOLE FOODS CHANGES THE GROCERY INDUSTRY

Austin, Texas, in 1979 was a counterculture haven. A twenty-five-year-old student named John Mackey began a natural foods store called SaferWay. He and his friends sold groceries from a storefront, lived above the store, and showered in the commercial dishwasher. A quarter of a century later, Mackey looks back at that time and says, "When you're young, you don't know what you can't do." Today, it seems there is nothing Mackey can't do. He is the CEO of Whole Foods Market, the nation's largest natural and organic food store, with 192 locations, 39,000 employees, and $5.6 billion of sales in 2006. From its unusual beginning, Whole Foods developed into the supermarket industry leader, at the forefront of new ideas and change.

Traditional grocers are mimicking Wal-Mart, driving down prices and optimizing the supply chain, but at Whole Foods, it's all about innovative food. "Selling the highest quality natural and organic products available" is the first of the firm's core values. Its website claims, "We feature foods that are free of artificial preservatives, colors, flavors, sweeteners, and hydrogenated oils." Instead of standard grocery items, offerings are more numerous and varied, with a focus on handmade, local products. In the Austin store, for example, shoppers can choose from 600 cheeses, 400 beers, and a wide variety of ready-to-eat food.

Whole Foods is moving beyond the traditional grocery chain in other ways, too. In 2006, the company opened an 80,000-square-foot store in the UK, making it the largest food retailer in London and the first multinational organic foods operation. In Los Angeles, Whole Foods is experimenting with a Lifestyle store to sell home and personal items such as bamboo furniture, hemp purses, and organic cotton baby clothes. Whole Foods subsidiaries process natural seafood, inspect organic produce, and purchase fair-trade coffee.

Workers at Whole Foods enjoy an organization culture, benefits plan, and human resources policies that surpass that of any other foods company. For example, the CEO makes a salary just fourteen times that of the average pay of hourly workers. Employees vote on their choices of benefits, resulting in no-cost health insurance. A new employee must be "voted in" by two-thirds of his or her work team to become a permanent employee. Walter Robb, former Whole Foods president, says, "Happy team members make happy customers. Our job as management is simply to make that a reality."

To foster innovation, store managers may spend up to $100,000 each year without seeking approval from their superiors. According to Mackey, his policy is that "it's better to ask forgiveness than permission." These funds are used for experimentation, and successes are adopted throughout the organization. "Most businesses have . . . a mass market football model of executing the game plan—don't fumble the ball," says Mackey. "Whole Foods is more like a fast-breaking basketball team. We're driving down the court, but we don't exactly know how the play is going

to evolve." He adds, "We're creating an organization based on love instead of fear."

Most grocery chains today offer more organic and natural foods, thanks in part to the success of Whole Foods. When Whole Foods asked Dole to provide organic pineapples, Dole complied but was surprised to find that half of the demand now comes from traditional grocers. Even Wal-Mart announced in October 2005 that it would increase its healthy offerings. Whole Foods, called "Whole Paycheck" by some critics, seems vulnerable to Wal-Mart–style price competition. So far, though, no competitors have matched the leader, where annual same-store sales growth is 11 percent, higher than the industry average of 1 to 2 percent. "I keep waiting for the competition I've been hearing about, but nobody else is doing quite what we're doing," claims Mackey.

Yet Whole Foods is not content with revolutionizing the grocery industry; it wants to change the world. From improving health to saving the planet, managers at the firm have always had big agendas, as shown in this excerpt from the mission statement: "Our mission is to promote the vitality and well-being of all individuals by supplying the highest quality, most wholesome foods available. . . . [We are] devoted to the promotion of organically grown foods, food safety concern, and sustainability of our entire eco-system." The biggest goal, however, may be changing the way that corporate managers view their companies. CEO Mackey feels that profitability will follow when companies have a strong vision and purpose. "To be sustainable, business has to be profitable," says Mackey. "[Yet] neither does business exist primarily to make a profit. It exists to fulfill its purpose, whatever that might be." He goes on to add, "[Business] can make money and do good."

CASE QUESTIONS

1. What internal and external forces for change have supported the innovations made at Whole Foods?
2. Traditional grocers try unsuccessfully to compete with Wal-Mart on price, when instead they could be developing a new model of competition, as Whole Foods has. What types of resistance to change contribute to this situation? What could managers do to overcome this resistance?
3. What specific actions does Whole Foods take to encourage and promote continuous innovation throughout the company? In your opinion, will these actions continue to be successful in promoting further innovation in the future?

REFERENCES

"2006 Annual Report," Whole Foods website, www.wholefoodsmarket.com on February 21, 2007; Parija Bhatnagar, "Eat Tofu, Drink Aloe, Wear Soy?" *CNN Money*, November 1, 2004, www.cnnmoney.com on January 22, 2006; Parija Bhatnagar, "What's for Dinner in 2006," *CNN Money*, January 11, 2006, www.cnnmoney.com on January 22, 2006; Diane Brady, "Eating Too Fast at Whole Foods," *BusinessWeek*, October 24, 2005, www.businessweek.com on January 22, 2006; Michael V. Copeland, "The Whole Lifestyle," *Business 2.0*, November 1, 2005, www.cnnmoney.com on January 22, 2006; Charles Fishman, "The Anarchist's Cookbook," *Fast Company*, July 2004, www.fastcompany.com on January 22, 2006; Evan Smith, "John Mackey," *Texas Monthly*, March 2005, pp. 122–132; Ryan Underwood, "Employee Innovator Runner-Up," *Fast Company*, October 2005, www.fastcompany.com on January 22, 2006.

YOU MAKE THE CALL

Innovative Ikea

1. Identify key external and internal forces for change that affect Ikea.
2. Assume that you are the manager of an Ikea store. Corporate headquarters has instructed you to change the layout of your store in a dramatic new way but has left the details of the new design to your discretion. You want to manage this as a planned change. What actions would you take?
3. Using the change process created in response to Question 2, identify the major reasons that your employees might resist the change and how you might best overcome that resistance.
4. What forces might cause Ikea to be forced to engage in reactive as opposed to planned change?
5. Using the various forms of innovation discussed in the chapter, identify a real or likely example of each as practiced at Ikea.
6. Would you want to manage an Ikea store? Why or why not?

Test Prepper

You've read the chapter, studied the key terms, and the exam is any day now. Think you're ready to ace it? Take this sample test to gauge your comprehension of chapter material. You can check your answers at the back of the book. Want more test questions? Visit the student website at http://college.hmco.com/pic/griffinfund5e/ and take the ACE quizzes for more practice.

1. T F Making change announcements well in advance of implementation is called facilitation.

2. T F Organization development (OD) is planned change that bubbles up from line managers intending to increase effectiveness using behavioral science knowledge.

3. T F Xavier is looking for a mentor who will help guide him to work-related goals and give him a better idea of how people see him in the organization. He is interested in the organization development (OD) technique known as coaching.

4. T F The stage where innovation decreases and substitute innovations are developed and applied is called innovation maturity.

5. T F The reward system is a fairly mechanical yet effective management technique for promoting innovation.

6. Which of the following is an example of an internal force that affects the performance of an organization?
   a. A change in the organization's strategy
   b. Identification of a new set of customers
   c. An increase in the intensity of industry competition
   d. A reduction in regulatory enforcement
   e. A sociocultural values shift

7. Which of the following techniques has NOT been identified as being effective in battling resistance to change?
   a. Participation
   b. Education

   c. Force-field analysis
   d. Cost analysis
   e. Communication

8. When an organization creates a radical redesign of all aspects of its business in order to achieve major cost savings, this is an example of
   a. refreezing.
   b. sponsorship.
   c. a product champion.
   d. intrapreneurship.
   e. reengineering.

9. The creation of one-handed foods that can be consumed while driving a car is an example of what kind of innovation?
   a. Ineffective
   b. Radical
   c. Incremental
   d. Process
   e. Managerial

10. A top manager will be responsible for bringing a lower-level employee's invention to market. The top manager is called the
   a. inventor.
   b. intrapreneur.
   c. champion.
   d. entrepreneur.
   e. sponsor.

Managing Human Resources in Organizations

FIRST THINGS FIRST

Results-Only Work Environment at Best Buy

"[At Best Buy,] work is no longer a place you go, but something you do."
—MICHELLE CONLIN, WRITER, *BUSINESSWEEK*

Best Buy, a successful big box retailer, is facing tough competitors, notably Dell and Wal-Mart. So CEO Brad Anderson is trying some new strategies. One new approach is to differentiate Best Buy from low-cost competitors by offering excellent customer service. The company's Geek Squad, which provides training, installation, and repairs, is one tactic to improve service. Another strategy is development of "customer-centricity." Through careful analysis of sales, Best Buy can divide its customers into "angel" and "demon" groups, based on the profitability of those sales. Catering to the angels while ignoring the demons has increased profitability.

Yet the most startling new approach is the radical rethinking of human resources. Best Buy is at the forefront of a movement to change the fundamental structure of work. Avram Miller, a former Intel vice president and now a management consultant, explains, "Most organizations today are run the same way as early-twentieth-century businesses. Everyone goes to his car, drives to work, has certain hours, has a certain job. It's all built on the factory model. Moving forward . . . ideas are being worked on 24 hours a day. Nobody seems surprised anymore if I wake up in the middle of the night and start [working], because the fact is, they don't even know where I am. And it doesn't matter." Michelle Conlin, a *BusinessWeek* writer, says it this way, "Work is no longer a place you go, but something you do."

Miller is describing a profound change in our notion of work, moving away from tasks that must be performed at a specific place and during specific hours, and toward a model that is flexible in both time and place. At its Minneapolis corporate headquarters, Best Buy has implemented a system they call ROWE, for "results-only work environment." ROWE allows workers to set their own schedules, to work from any location, and to change both spontaneously. Workers are judged solely on performance, not on hours.

One employee relations worker took his PDA with him on weekday hunting trips. Another spent months creating training programs, while on a national road tour of his favorite band. A single mother designed in-store promotion campaigns until the midafternoon, leaving to pick up her school-age children, then finished after they were asleep. Other workers leave midday to attend college classes or the movies. It's unorthodox, but it works. Productivity is up an average of 35 percent in the divisions that have switched to ROWE. Morale has soared; turnover is plummeting.

The ROWE program has worked so well that Best Buy will be testing it in stores by late 2007. And Best Buy isn't the only "post-geographic" firm. Forty percent of IBM employees have no office; at AT&T, it's one-third of all managers. Sun Microsystems reports saving $300 million a year in real estate costs because one-half of the workforce works elsewhere. IBM cut real estate costs 40 percent. More companies will be adopting this change in the future. Eighty-five percent of corporate executives think the trend will accelerate over the next five years.

Globalization is one underlying factor supporting the use of off-site workers. When a team consists of members from around the world, time zones become meaningless. Employees must be able to communicate at any time. Technology also drives this trend. PDAs, cell phones, and wireless networked laptops mean that workers can do their work at any location. Changing demographics and social values are also a factor. As baby boomers retire, the labor supply isn't keeping up with demand. Younger employees are demanding and receiving employment concessions including telecommuting and flexible schedules. Finally, putting the structure of work under the control of workers goes a long way toward creating

LEARNING OBJECTIVES

After studying this chapter, you should be able to:

- Describe the environmental context of human resource management, including its strategic importance and its relationship with legal and social factors.

- Discuss how organizations attract human resources, including human resource planning, recruiting, and selecting.

- Describe how organizations develop human resources, including training and development, performance appraisal, and performance feedback.

- Discuss how organizations maintain human resources, including the determination of compensation and benefits and career planning.

- Discuss the nature of diversity, including its meaning, associated trends, impact, and management.

- Discuss labor relations, including how employees form unions and the mechanics of collective bargaining.

- Describe the issues associated with managing knowledge and contingent and temporary workers.

Best Buy is allowing many of its employees to work when and where they want.

work/life balance, one of the features most desired by today's workforce. Work/life balance isn't just for parents—it's for the 90-plus percent of workers who believe work interferes with their nonwork life.

Thus far, Brad Anderson's strategies are paying off. Earnings per share rose 16 percent in 2006. In a corporate world where "80 percent of success is showing up," as comedian Woody Allen says, long hours and longer workweeks may be the most measurable indicator of performance. They are no longer the best indicator.[1]

Most successful businesses recognize that their employees are critical to their firm's success. Indeed, firms like Best Buy have found that they can achieve even greater success by treating their employees like mature and responsible adults. And as in the case of Best Buy, taking such an enlightened view often pays off in numerous ways—higher productivity, lower turnover, and improved morale.

This chapter is about how organizations manage the people that comprise them. This set of processes is called "human resource management," or HRM. We start by describing the environmental context of HRM. We then discuss how organizations attract human resources. Next we describe how organizations seek to further develop the capacities of their human resources. We also look at workforce diversity and examine how high-quality human resources are maintained by organizations. We conclude by discussing labor relations and new challenges in the workplace.

The Environmental Context of Human Resource Management

human resource management (HRM)
The set of organizational activities directed at attracting, developing, and maintaining an effective workforce

Human resource management (HRM) is the set of organizational activities directed at attracting, developing, and maintaining an effective workforce.[2] Human resource management takes place within a complex and ever-changing environmental context. Three particularly vital components of this context are HRM's strategic importance and the legal and social environments of HRM.

The Strategic Importance of HRM

Human resources are critical for effective organizational functioning. HRM (or "personnel," as it is sometimes called) was once relegated to second-class status in many organizations, but its importance has grown dramatically in the last two decades. Its new importance stems from increased legal complexities, the recognition that human resources are a valuable means for improving productivity, and the awareness today of the costs associated with poor human resource management.[3]

Indeed, managers now realize that the effectiveness of their HR function has a substantial impact on the bottom-line performance of the firm. Poor human resource planning can result in spurts of hiring followed by layoffs—costly in terms of unemployment compensation payments, training expenses, and morale. Haphazard compensation systems do not attract, keep, and motivate good employees, and outmoded recruitment practices can expose the firm to expensive and embarrassing discrimination lawsuits. Consequently, the chief human resource executive of most large businesses is a vice president directly accountable to the CEO, and many firms are developing strategic HR plans and integrating those plans with other strategic planning activities.[4]

Even organizations with as few as 200 employees usually have a human resource manager and a human resource department charged with overseeing these activities. Responsibility for HR activities, however, is shared between the HR department and line managers. The HR department may recruit and initially screen candidates, but the final selection is usually made by managers in the department where the new employee will work. Similarly, although the HR department may establish performance appraisal policies and procedures, the actual evaluation and coaching of employees is done by their immediate superiors.

The growing awareness of the strategic significance of human resource management has even led to new terminology to reflect a firm's commitment to people. **Human capital** reflects the organization's investment in attracting, retaining, and motivating an effective workforce. Hence, just as the phrase *financial capital* is an indicator of a firm's financial resources and reserves, so, too, does *human capital* serve as a tangible indicator of the value of the people who comprise an organization.[5]

> **human capital**
> Reflects the organization's investment in attracting, retaining, and motivating an effective workforce

The Legal Environment of HRM

A number of laws regulate various aspects of employee-employer relations, especially in the areas of equal employment opportunity, compensation and benefits, labor relations, and occupational safety and health. Several major ones are summarized in Table 8.1.

Equal Employment Opportunity *Title VII of the Civil Rights Act of 1964* forbids discrimination in all areas of the employment relationship. The intent of Title VII is to ensure that employment decisions are made on the basis of an individual's qualifications rather than on the basis of personal biases. The law has reduced direct forms of discrimination (refusing to promote African Americans into management, failing to hire men as flight attendants, refusing to hire women as construction workers) as well as indirect forms of discrimination (using employment tests that whites pass at a higher rate than African Americans).

Employment requirements such as test scores and other qualifications are legally defined as having an **adverse impact** on minorities and women when such individuals meet or pass the requirement at a rate less than 80 percent of the rate of majority group members. Criteria that have an adverse impact on protected groups can be used only when there is solid evidence that they effectively identify individuals who are better able than others to do the job. The **Equal Employment Opportunity Commission** is charged with enforcing Title VII as well as several other employment-related laws.

The **Age Discrimination in Employment Act,** passed in 1967, amended in 1978, and amended again in 1986, is an attempt to prevent organizations from discriminating against older workers. In its current form, it outlaws discrimination against people older than 40 years. Both the Age Discrimination in Employment Act and Title VII require passive nondiscrimination, or equal employment opportunity. Employers are not required to seek out and hire minorities, but they must treat all who apply fairly.

Several executive orders, however, require that employers holding government contracts engage in **affirmative action**—intentionally seeking and hiring employees from groups that are underrepresented in the organization. These organizations must have a written affirmative action plan that spells out employment goals for underutilized groups and how those goals will be met. These employers are

> **Title VII of the Civil Rights Act of 1964**
> Forbids discrimination on the basis of sex, race, color, religion, or national origin in all areas of the employment relationship

> **adverse impact**
> When minority group members pass a selection standard at a rate less than 80 percent of the pass rate of majority group members

> **Equal Employment Opportunity Commission**
> Charged with enforcing Title VII of the Civil Rights Act of 1964

> **Age Discrimination in Employment Act**
> Outlaws discrimination against people older than forty years; passed in 1967, amended in 1978 and 1986

Table 8.1

THE LEGAL ENVIRONMENT OF HUMAN RESOURCE MANAGEMENT

As much as any area of management, HRM is subject to wide-ranging laws and court decisions. These laws and decisions affect the human resource function in many areas. For example, AT&T was once fined several million dollars for violating Title VII of the Civil Rights Act of 1964.

Equal Employment Opportunity

Title VII of the Civil Rights Act of 1964 (as amended by the Equal Employment Opportunity Act of 1972). Forbids discrimination in all areas of the employment relationship.

Age Discrimination in Employment Act. Outlaws discrimination against people older than 40 years.

Various executive orders, especially Executive Order 11246 in 1965. Requires employers with government contracts to engage in affirmative action.

Pregnancy Discrimination Act. Specifically outlaws discrimination on the basis of pregnancy.

Vietnam Era Veterans Readjustment Assistance Act. Extends affirmative action mandate to military veterans who served during the Vietnam War.

Americans with Disabilities Act. Specifically outlaws discrimination against disabled persons.

Civil Rights Act of 1991. Makes it easier for employees to sue an organization for discrimination but limits punitive damage awards if they win.

Compensation and Benefits

Fair Labor Standards Act. Establishes minimum wage and mandated overtime pay for work in excess of 40 hours per week.

Equal Pay Act of 1963. Requires that men and women be paid the same amount for doing the same job.

Employee Retirement Income Security Act of 1974 (ERISA). Regulates how organizations manage their pension funds.

Family and Medical Leave Act of 1993. Requires employers to provide up to 12 weeks of unpaid leave for family and medical emergencies.

Labor Relations

National Labor Relations Act. Spells out procedures by which employees can establish labor unions and requires organizations to bargain collectively with legally formed unions; also known as the *Wagner Act.*

Labor-Management Relations Act. Limits union power and specifies management rights during a union-organizing campaign; also known as the *Taft-Hartley Act.*

Health and Safety

Occupational Safety and Health Act of 1970 (OSHA). Mandates the provision of safe working conditions.

---

affirmative action
Intentionally seeking and hiring qualified or qualifiable employees from racial, sexual, and ethnic groups that are underrepresented in the organization

Americans with Disabilities Act
Prohibits discrimination against people with disabilities

Civil Rights Act of 1991
Amends the original Civil Rights Act, making it easier to bring discrimination lawsuits while also limiting punitive damages

also required to act affirmatively in hiring Vietnam-era veterans (as a result of the Vietnam Era Veterans Readjustment Assistance Act) and qualified handicapped individuals. Finally, the Pregnancy Discrimination Act forbids discrimination against women who are pregnant.

In 1990 Congress passed the ***Americans with Disabilities Act,*** which forbids discrimination on the basis of disabilities and requires employers to provide reasonable accommodations for disabled employees. More recently, the ***Civil Rights Act of 1991*** amended the original Civil Rights Act as well as other related laws by making it easier to bring discrimination lawsuits while simultaneously limiting the amount of punitive damages that can be awarded in those lawsuits.

Compensation and Benefits   Laws also regulate compensation and benefits. The ***Fair Labor Standards Act,*** passed in 1938 and amended frequently since then, sets a minimum wage and requires the payment of overtime rates for work in excess of 40 hours per week. Salaried professional, executive, and administrative employees are exempt from the minimum hourly wage and overtime provisions. The ***Equal Pay Act of 1963*** requires that men and women be paid the same amount for doing the same job. Attempts to circumvent the law by having different job titles and pay rates for men and women who perform the same work are also illegal. Basing an employee's pay on seniority or performance is legal, however, even if it means that a man and woman are paid different amounts for doing the same job.

The provision of benefits is also regulated in some ways by state and federal laws. Certain benefits are mandatory—for example, worker's compensation insurance for employees who are injured on the job. Employers who provide a pension plan for their employees are regulated by the ***Employee Retirement Income Security Act of 1974 (ERISA).*** The purpose of this act is to help ensure the financial security of pension funds by regulating how they can be invested. The ***Family and Medical Leave Act of 1993*** requires employers to provide up to 12 weeks of unpaid leave for family and medical emergencies.

In the last few years some large employers, most notably Wal-Mart, have come under fire because they do not provide health care for all of their employees. In response to this, the state of Maryland recently passed a law, informally called the "Wal-Mart bill," that requires employers with more than 10,000 workers to spend at least 8 percent of their payrolls on health care or else pay a comparable amount into a general fund for uninsured workers. Wal-Mart is considering appealing this ruling; meanwhile, several other states are considering the passage of similar laws.[6]

Labor Relations   Union activities and management's behavior toward unions constitute another heavily regulated area. The ***National Labor Relations Act*** (also known as the Wagner Act), passed in 1935, sets up a procedure for employees to vote on whether to have a union. If they vote for a union, management is required to bargain collectively with the union. The ***National Labor Relations Board (NLRB)*** was established by the Wagner Act to enforce its provisions. Following a series of severe strikes in 1946, the ***Labor-Management Relations Act*** (also known as the Taft-Hartley Act) was passed in 1947 to limit union power. The law increases management's rights during an organizing campaign. The Taft-Hartley Act also contains the National Emergency Strike provision, which allows the president of the United States to prevent or end a strike that endangers national security. Taken together, these laws balance union and management power. Employees can be represented by a legally created and managed union, but the business can make non-employee-related business decisions without interference.

Health and Safety   The ***Occupational Safety and Health Act of 1970 (OSHA)*** directly mandates the provision of safe working conditions. It requires that employers (1) provide a place of employment that is free from hazards that may cause death or serious physical harm and (2) obey the safety and health standards established by the Department of Labor. Safety standards are intended to prevent accidents, whereas occupational health standards are concerned with preventing occupational disease. For example, standards limit the concentration of cotton dust in the air because this contaminant has been associated with lung disease in textile workers. The standards are enforced by OSHA inspections, which are conducted when an employee files a complaint of unsafe conditions or when a serious accident occurs. Spot inspections of plants in especially hazardous industries such as mining and chemicals are also made. Employers who fail to meet OSHA standards may be fined.

Fair Labor Standards Act
Sets a minimum wage and requires overtime pay for work in excess of 40 hours per week; passed in 1938 and amended frequently since then

Equal Pay Act of 1963
Requires that men and women be paid the same amount for doing the same job

Employee Retirement Income Security Act of 1974 (ERISA)
A law that sets standards for pension plan management and provides federal insurance if pension funds go bankrupt

Family and Medical Leave Act of 1993
Requires employers to provide up to 12 weeks of unpaid leave for family and medical emergencies

National Labor Relations Act
Passed in 1935 to set up procedures for employees to vote on whether to have a union; also known as the Wagner Act

National Labor Relations Board (NLRB)
Established by the Wagner Act to enforce its provisions

Labor-Management Relations Act
Passed in 1947 to limit union power; also known as the Taft-Hartley Act

Occupational Safety and Health Act of 1970 (OSHA)
Directly mandates the provision of safe working conditions

Investigators are looking into claims that chemical agents in the butter flavoring used in microwave popcorn are harmful to workers where such products are made. At least 30 workers at one plant in Jasper, Missouri, have contracted a rare lung disease, and some doctors believe that it resulted from conditions on their job site. Although federal health officials point out that there is no danger to those cooking or eating microwave popcorn, research is ongoing into potential hazards to those who work in the industry.[7]

Emerging Legal Issues Several other areas of legal concern have emerged during the past few years. One is sexual harassment. Although sexual harassment is forbidden under Title VII, it has received additional attention in the courts recently, as more and more victims have decided to publicly confront the problem. Another emerging human resource management issue is alcohol and drug abuse. Both alcoholism and drug dependence are major problems today. Recent court rulings have tended to define alcoholics and drug addicts as disabled, protecting them under the same laws that protect other handicapped people. Finally, AIDS has emerged as an important legal issue as well. AIDS victims, too, are most often protected under various laws protecting the disabled.

Attracting Human Resources

With an understanding of the environmental context of human resource management as a foundation, we are now ready to address its first substantive concern—attracting qualified people who are interested in employment with the organization.

Human Resource Planning

The starting point in attracting qualified human resources is planning. HR planning, in turn, involves job analysis and forecasting the demand and supply of labor.

job analysis
A systematized procedure for collecting and recording information about jobs within an organization

Job Analysis *Job analysis* is a systematic analysis of jobs within an organization. A job analysis is made up of two parts. The job description lists the duties of a job, the job's working conditions, and the tools, materials, and equipment used to perform it. The job specification lists the skills, abilities, and other credentials needed to do the job. Job analysis information is used in many human resource activities. For instance, knowing about job content and job requirements is necessary to develop appropriate selection methods and job-relevant performance appraisal systems and to set equitable compensation rates.

Forecasting Human Resource Demand and Supply After managers fully understand the jobs to be performed within the organization, they can start planning for the organization's future human resource needs. Figure 8.1 summarizes the steps most often followed. The manager starts by assessing trends in past human resources usage, future organizational plans, and general economic trends. A good sales forecast is often the foundation, especially for smaller organizations. Historical ratios can then be used to predict demand for such employees as operating employees and sales representatives. Of course, large organizations use much more complicated models to predict their future human resource needs. Wal-Mart completed an exhaustive planning process that projects that the firm will need to hire 1 million people by 2010. Of this total, 800,000 are for new positions created

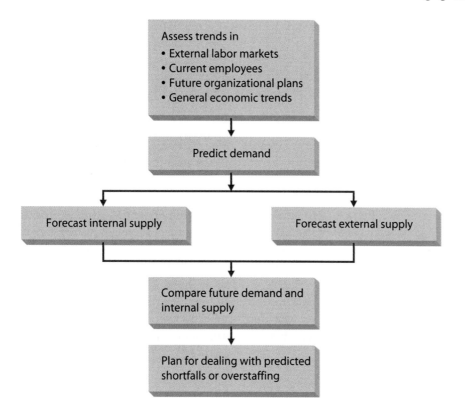

Figure 8.1
HUMAN RESOURCE PLANNING

Attracting human resources cannot be left to chance if an organization expects to function at peak efficiency. Human resource planning involves assessing trends, forecasting supply of and demand for labor, and then developing appropriate strategies for addressing any differences.

as the firm grows, and the other 200,000 will replace current workers who leave for various reasons.[8]

Forecasting the supply of labor is really two tasks: forecasting the internal supply (the number and type of employees who will be in the firm at some future date) and forecasting the external supply (the number and type of people who will be available for hiring in the labor market at large). The simplest approach merely adjusts present staffing levels for anticipated turnover and promotions. Again, though, large organizations use extremely sophisticated models to make these forecasts. At higher levels of the organization, managers plan for specific people and positions. The technique most commonly used is the ***replacement chart***, which lists each important managerial position, who occupies it, how long he or she will probably stay in it before moving on, and who (by name) is now qualified or soon will be qualified to move into the position. This technique allows ample time to plan developmental experiences for persons identified as potential successors to critical managerial jobs.[9]

To facilitate both planning and identifying persons for current transfer or promotion, some organizations also have an ***employee information system***, or ***skills inventory***. Such systems are usually computerized and contain information on each employee's education, skills, work experience, and career aspirations. Such a system can quickly locate all the employees in the organization who are qualified to fill a position requiring, for instance, a degree in chemical engineering, three years of experience in an oil refinery, and fluency in Spanish. Enterprise resource planning (ERP) systems, as described in Chapter 7, generally include capabilities for measuring and managing the internal supply of labor in ways that best fit the needs of the organization.

replacement chart
Lists each important managerial position in the organization, who occupies it, how long he or she will probably remain in the position, and who is or will be a qualified replacement

employee information system (skills inventory)
Contains information on each employee's education, skills, experience, and career aspirations; usually computerized

Forecasting the external supply of labor is a different problem altogether. How does a manager, for example, predict how many electrical engineers will be seeking work in Georgia three years from now? To get an idea of the future availability of labor, planners must rely on information from such outside sources as state employment commissions, government reports, and figures supplied by colleges on the number of students in major fields.

Matching Human Resource Supply and Demand After comparing future demand and internal supply, managers can make plans to manage predicted shortfalls or overstaffing. If a shortfall is predicted, new employees can be hired, present employees can be retrained and transferred into the understaffed area, individuals approaching retirement can be convinced to stay on, or labor-saving or productivity-enhancing systems can be installed. If the organization needs to hire, the external labor supply forecast helps managers plan how to recruit, based on whether the type of person needed is readily available or scarce in the labor market. As we note later in the chapter, the trend toward using temporary workers also helps managers by affording them extra flexibility in staffing. If overstaffing is expected to be a problem, the main options are transferring the extra employees, not replacing individuals who quit, encouraging early retirement, and laying people off.

Recruiting Human Resources

Once an organization has an idea of its future human resource needs, the next phase is usually recruiting new employees.[10] *Recruiting* is the process of attracting qualified persons to apply for jobs that are open. Where do recruits come from? Some recruits are found internally; others come from outside the organization.

recruiting
The process of attracting individuals to apply for jobs that are open

internal recruiting
Considering current employees as applicants for higher-level jobs in the organization

Internal recruiting means considering present employees as candidates for openings. Promotion from within can help build morale and keep high-quality employees from leaving the firm. In unionized firms, the procedures for notifying employees of internal job change opportunities are usually spelled out in the union contract. For higher-level positions, a skills inventory system may be used to identify internal candidates, or managers may be asked to recommend individuals who should be considered. Most businesses today routinely post job openings on their internal communication network, or intranet. One disadvantage of internal recruiting is its ripple effect. When an employee moves to a different job, someone else must be found to take his or her old job. In one organization, 454 job movements were necessary as a result of filling 195 initial openings!

external recruiting
Getting people from outside the organization to apply for jobs

External recruiting involves attracting persons outside the organization to apply for jobs. External recruiting methods include advertising, campus interviews, employment agencies or executive search firms, union hiring halls, referrals by present employees, and hiring "walk-ins" or "gate-hires" (people who show up without being solicited). Increasingly, firms are using the Internet to post job openings and to solicit applicants. Of course, a manager must select the most appropriate methods, using the state employment service to find maintenance workers but not a nuclear physicist, for example. Private employment agencies can be a good source of clerical and technical employees, and executive search firms specialize in locating top-management talent. Newspaper ads are often used because they reach a wide audience and thus allow minorities equal opportunity to find out about and apply for job openings.

Recruiting is the process of attracting individuals to apply for jobs that are open. Recruiting is usually done though a variety of channels, including the Internet, print advertising, and employment agencies. Job or career fairs are also commonly used. This Army recruiter is participating in a recent career fair on a college campus. He is providing this student with information about career opportunities in the military.

One generally successful method for facilitating a good person-job fit is the so-called ***realistic job preview (RJP)***. As the term suggests, the RJP involves providing the applicant with a real picture of what it would be like to perform the job that the organization is trying to fill.[11] For example, it would not make sense for a firm to tell an applicant that the job is exciting and challenging when in fact it is routine and straightforward, yet some managers do this to hire the best people. The likely outcome will be a dissatisfied employee who will quickly be looking for a better job. If the company is more realistic about a job, though, the person hired will be more likely to remain in the job for a longer period of time.

> *realistic job preview (RJP)*
> Provides the applicant with a real picture of what it would be like to perform the job that the organization is trying to fill

Selecting Human Resources

Once the recruiting process has attracted a pool of applicants, the next step is to select whom to hire. The intent of the selection process is to gather from applicants information that will predict their job success and then to hire the candidates likely to be most successful. Of course, the organization can gather information only about factors that are predictive of future performance. The process of determining the predictive value of information is called ***validation***.

> *validation*
> Determining the extent to which a selection device is really predictive of future job performance

Application Blanks The first step in selection is usually asking the candidate to fill out an application blank. While application blanks were historically paper documents, they are increasingly completed online. Application blanks are an efficient method of gathering information about the applicant's previous work history, educational background, and other job-related demographic data. They should not contain questions about areas not related to the job, such as gender, religion, or national origin. Application blank data are generally used informally to decide whether a candidate merits further evaluation, and interviewers use application blanks to familiarize themselves with candidates before interviewing them. Unfortunately, in recent years there has been a trend toward job applicants' either falsifying or inflating their credentials to stand a better chance of getting a job. Indeed, one recent survey of 2.6 million job applications found that an astounding 44 percent of them contained some false information.[12]

Tests Tests of ability, skill, aptitude, or knowledge that is relevant to the particular job are usually the best predictors of job success, although tests of general intelligence or personality are occasionally useful as well. In addition to being validated, tests should be administered and scored consistently. All candidates should be given the same directions, should be allowed the same amount of time, and should experience the same testing environment (temperature, lighting, distractions).[13]

Interviews Although a popular selection device, interviews are sometimes poor predictors of job success. For example, biases inherent in the way people perceive and judge others at a first meeting affect subsequent evaluations by the interviewer. Interview validity can be improved by training interviewers to be aware of potential biases and by increasing the structure of the interview. In a structured interview, questions are written in advance, and all interviewers follow the same question list with each candidate they interview. This procedure introduces consistency into the interview procedure and allows the organization to validate the content of the questions to be asked.[14]

Assessment Centers Assessment centers are a popular method used to select managers and are particularly good for selecting current employees for promotion. The assessment center is a content-valid simulation of major parts of the managerial job. A typical center lasts two to three days, with groups of 6 to 12 persons participating in a variety of managerial exercises. Centers may also include interviews, public speaking, and standardized ability tests. Candidates are assessed by several trained observers, usually managers several levels above the job for which the candidates are being considered. Assessment centers are quite valid if properly designed and if they are fair to members of minority groups and women.[15] For some firms, the assessment center is a permanent facility created for these activities. For other firms, the assessment activities are performed in a multipurpose location such as a conference room. AT&T pioneered the assessment center concept. For years the firm has used assessment centers to make virtually all of its selection decisions for management positions.

Other Techniques Organizations also use other selection techniques depending on the circumstances. Polygraph tests, once popular, are declining in popularity. On the other hand, more and more organizations are requiring that applicants in whom they are interested take physical exams. Organizations are also increasingly using drug tests, especially in situations in which drug-related performance problems could create serious safety hazards. For example, applicants for jobs in a nuclear power plant would likely be tested for drug use. And some organizations today even run credit checks on prospective employees.

Developing Human Resources

Regardless of how effective a selection system is, however, most employees need additional training if they are to grow and develop in their jobs. Evaluating their performance and providing feedback are also necessary.

Training and Development

In HRM, **training** usually refers to teaching operational or technical employees how to do the job for which they were hired. **Development** refers to teaching managers and professionals the skills needed for both present and future jobs. Most organizations provide regular training and development programs for managers and employees. For example, IBM spends more than $700 million annually on programs and has a vice president in charge of employee education. U.S. businesses spend more than $30 billion annually on training and development programs away from the workplace. And this figure does not include wages and benefits paid to employees while they are participating in such programs.

> *training*
> Teaching operational or technical employees how to do the job for which they were hired

> *development*
> Teaching managers and professionals the skills needed for both present and future jobs

Assessing Training Needs   The first step in developing a training plan is to determine what needs exist. For example, if employees do not know how to operate the machinery necessary to do their job, a training program on how to operate the machinery is clearly needed. On the other hand, when a group of office workers is performing poorly, training may not be the answer. The problem could be motivation, aging equipment, poor supervision, inefficient work design, or a deficiency of skills and knowledge. Only the last could be remedied by training. As training programs are being developed, the manager should set specific and measurable goals specifying what participants are to learn. Managers should also plan to evaluate the training program after employees complete it.

Common Training Methods   Many different training and development methods are available. Selection of methods depends on many considerations, but perhaps the most important is training content. When the training content is factual material (such as company rules or explanations for how to fill out forms), assigned reading, programmed learning, and lecture methods work well. When the content is interpersonal relations or group decision making, however, firms must use a method that allows interpersonal contact, such as role-playing or case discussion groups. When employees must learn a physical skill, methods allowing practice and the actual use of tools and materials are needed, as in on-the-job training or vestibule training. (Vestibule training enables participants to focus on safety, learning, and feedback rather than on productivity.)

Web-based and other electronic media-based training are becoming very popular. Such methods allow a mix of training content, are relatively easy to update and revise, let participants use a variable schedule, and lower travel costs.[16] On the other hand, they are limited in their capacity to simulate real activities and facilitate face-to-face interaction. Xerox, Massachusetts Mutual Life Insurance, and Ford have all reported tremendous success with these methods. In addition, most training programs actually rely on a mix of methods. Boeing, for example, sends managers to an intensive two-week training seminar involving tests, simulations, role-playing exercises, and CD-ROM flight simulation exercises.[17]

Finally, some larger businesses have started creating their own self-contained training facility, often called a *corporate university*. McDonald's was among the first to start this practice with its so-called Hamburger University in Illinois. All management trainees for the firm attend training programs there to learn exactly how long to grill a burger, how to maintain good customer service, and so on. Other firms that use this approach include Shell Oil and General Electric.

Evaluation of Training   Training and development programs should always be evaluated. Typical evaluation approaches include measuring one or more relevant criteria (such as attitudes or performance) before and after the training, and determining whether the criteria changed. Evaluation measures collected at the end of training are easy to get, but actual performance measures collected when the trainee is on the job are more important. Trainees may say that they enjoyed the training and learned a lot, but the true test is whether their job performance improves after their training.

Performance Appraisal

performance appraisal
A formal assessment of how well an employee is doing his or her job

Once employees are trained and settled into their jobs, one of management's next concerns is performance appraisal. **Performance appraisal** is a formal assessment of how well employees are doing their jobs. Employees' performance should be evaluated regularly for many reasons. One reason is that performance appraisal may be necessary for validating selection devices or assessing the impact of training programs. A second reason is administrative—to aid in making decisions about pay raises, promotions, and training. Still another reason is to provide feedback to employees to help them improve their present performance and plan future careers.[18] Because performance evaluations often help determine wages and promotions, they must be fair and nondiscriminatory.

Common Appraisal Methods   Two basic categories of appraisal methods commonly used in organizations are objective methods and judgmental methods. Objective measures of performance include actual output (that is, number of units produced), scrap rate, dollar volume of sales, and number of claims processed. Objective performance measures may be contaminated by "opportunity bias" if some persons have a better chance to perform than others. For example, a sales representative selling snow blowers in Michigan has a greater opportunity than does a colleague selling the same product in Arkansas. Fortunately, adjusting raw performance figures for the effect of opportunity bias and thereby arriving at figures that accurately represent each individual's performance is often possible.

Another type of objective measure, the special performance test, is a method in which each employee is assessed under standardized conditions. This kind of appraisal also eliminates opportunity bias. For example, Verizon Southwest has a series of prerecorded calls that operators in a test booth answer. The operators are graded on speed, accuracy, and courtesy in handling the calls. Performance tests measure ability but do not measure the extent to which one is motivated to use that ability on a daily basis. (A high-ability person may be a lazy performer except when being tested.) Special performance tests must therefore be supplemented by other appraisal methods to provide a complete picture of performance.

Judgmental methods, including ranking and rating techniques, are the most common way to measure performance. Ranking compares employees directly with one another and orders them from best to worst. Ranking has a number of drawbacks. Ranking is difficult for large groups, because the persons in the middle of the distribution may be hard to distinguish from one another accurately. Comparisons of people in different work groups are also difficult. For example, an employee ranked third in a strong group may be more valuable than an employee ranked first in a weak group. Another criticism of ranking is that the manager must rank people on the basis of overall performance, although each person likely has both strengths and weaknesses. Furthermore, rankings do not provide useful information for feedback. To be told that one is ranked third is not nearly as helpful as to be told that the quality of one's work is outstanding, its quantity is satisfactory, one's punctuality could use improvement, or one's paperwork is seriously deficient.

Rating differs from ranking in that it compares each employee with a fixed standard rather than comparison with other employees. A rating scale provides the standard. Figure 8.2 gives examples of three graphic rating scales for a bank teller. Each consists of a performance dimension to be rated (punctuality, congeniality, and accuracy) followed by a scale on which to make the rating. In constructing graphic rating scales, performance dimensions that are relevant to job performance must be selected. In particular, they should focus on job behaviors and results rather than on personality traits or attitudes.

The ***Behaviorally Anchored Rating Scale (BARS)*** is a sophisticated and useful rating method. Supervisors construct rating scales with associated behavioral anchors. They first identify relevant performance dimensions and then generate anchors—specific, observable behaviors typical of each performance level.

Behaviorally Anchored Rating Scale (BARS)
A sophisticated rating method in which supervisors construct a rating scale associated with behavioral anchors

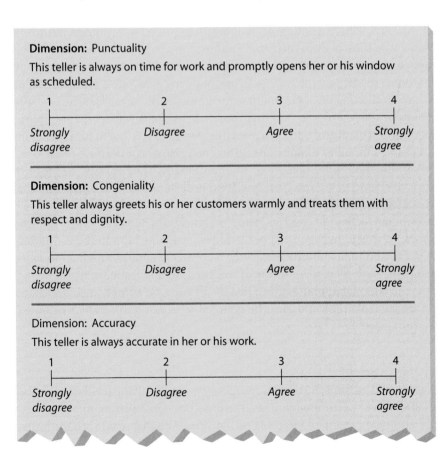

Figure 8.2
GRAPHIC RATING SCALES FOR A BANK TELLER

Graphic rating scales are very common methods for evaluating employee performance. The manager who is doing the rating circles the point on each scale that best reflects her or his assessment of the employee on that scale. Graphic rating scales are widely used for many different kinds of jobs.

Figure 8.3

BEHAVIORALLY ANCHORED RATING SCALE

Behaviorally anchored rating scales help overcome some of the limitations of standard rating scales. Each point on the scale is accompanied by a behavioral anchor—a summary of an employee behavior that fits that spot on the scale.

Job: Specialty store manager
Dimension: Inventory control

7 — Always orders in the right quantities and at the right time

6 — Almost always orders at the right time but occasionally orders too much or too little of a particular item

5 — Usually orders at the right time and almost always in the right quantities

4 — Often orders in the right quantities and at the right time

3 — Occasionally orders at the right time but usually not in the right quantities

2 — Occasionally orders in the right quantities but usually not at the right time

1 — Never orders in the right quantities or at the right time

Figure 8.3 shows an example of a behaviorally anchored rating scale for the dimension "Inventory control."

Errors in Performance Appraisal Errors or biases can occur in any kind of rating or ranking system. One common problem is *recency error*—the tendency to base judgments on the subordinate's most recent performance because it is most easily recalled. Often a rating or ranking is intended to evaluate performance over an entire time period, such as six months or a year, so the recency error does introduce error into the judgment. Other errors include overuse of one part of the scale—being too lenient, being too severe, or giving everyone a rating of "average." *Halo error* is allowing the assessment of an employee on one dimension to "spread" to ratings of that employee on other dimensions. For instance, if an employee is outstanding on quality of output, a rater might tend to give her or him higher marks than deserved on other dimensions. Errors can also occur because of race, sex, or age discrimination, intentionally or unintentionally. The best way to offset these errors is to ensure that a valid rating system is developed at the outset and then to train managers carefully in its use.

360-degree feedback
A performance appraisal system in which managers are evaluated by everyone around them—their boss, their peers, and their subordinates

A popular technique used in many organizations today is called **360-degree feedback**, in which managers are evaluated by everyone around them—their boss, their peers, and their subordinates. Such a complete and thorough approach provides people with a far richer array of information about their performance than does a conventional appraisal given just by the boss. Of course, such a system also takes considerable time and must be handled so as not to breed fear and mistrust in the workplace.[19]

Performance Feedback

The last step in most performance appraisal systems is giving feedback to subordinates about their performance. This is usually done in a private meeting between the person being evaluated and his or her boss. The discussion should generally be focused on the facts—the assessed level of performance, how and why that

"I'm razzled, but not dazzled."

www.CartoonStock.com

The last—and sometimes the hardest—part of performance appraisal is providing constructive feedback to employees about how they can improve their work. It is generally most helpful if perform-ance feedback is objective and con-structive. But sometimes, ill-chosen words such as this manager is using provide little insight into what exactly needs to be done to improve performance.

assessment was made, and how it can be improved in the future. Feedback inter-views are not easy to conduct. Many managers are uncomfortable with the task, especially if feedback is negative and subordinates are disappointed by what they hear. Properly training managers, however, can help them conduct more effective feedback interviews.[20]

Some firms use a very aggressive approach to terminating people who do not meet expectations. General Electric uses a system whereby each year the bottom 10 percent of its workforce is terminated and replaced with new employees. Company executives claim that this approach, although stressful for all employees, helps it to continuously upgrade its workforce. While other firms continue to experiment with this and similar methods, both Ford and Goodyear agreed to abandon an approach similar to that used by GE in response to age discrimination lawsuits.[21]

Maintaining Human Resources

After organizations have attracted and developed an effective workforce, they must also make every effort to maintain that workforce. To do so requires effective com-pensation and benefits as well as career planning.

Determining Compensation

Compensation is the financial remuneration given by the organization to its employees in exchange for their work. There are three basic forms of compen-sation. *Wages* are the hourly compensation paid to operating employees. The minimum hourly wage paid in the United States was $5.15 for the last several years but was recently increased to $7.25. (Several states, however, have laws that set minimum wages that are higher than the national minimum wage.) *Salary* refers to compensation paid for total contributions, as opposed to pay based on hours

> **compensation**
> The financial remuneration given by the organization to its employees in exchange for their work

worked. For example, managers earn an annual salary, usually paid monthly. They receive the salary regardless of the number of hours they work. Some firms have started paying all their employees a salary instead of hourly wages. For example, all employees at Chaparral Steel earn a salary, starting at $30,000 a year for entry-level operating employees. Finally, *incentives* represent special compensation opportunities that are usually tied to performance. Sales commissions and bonuses are among the most common incentives. A good compensation system can help attract qualified applicants, retain present employees, and stimulate high performance at a cost reasonable for one's industry and geographic area. To set up a successful system, management must make decisions about wage levels, the wage structure, and the individual wage determination system.

Wage-Level Decision   The wage-level decision is a management policy decision about whether the firm wants to pay above, at, or below the going rate for labor in the industry or the geographic area. Most firms choose to pay near the average, although those that cannot afford more pay below average. Large, successful firms may like to cultivate the image of being "wage leaders" by intentionally paying more than average and thus attracting and keeping high-quality employees. IBM, for example, pays top dollar to get the new employees it wants. McDonald's, on the other hand, often pays close to the minimum wage. The level of unemployment in the labor force also affects wage levels. Pay declines when labor is plentiful and increases when labor is scarce. Once managers make the wage-level decision, they need information to help set actual wage rates. Managers need to know what the maximum, minimum, and average wages are for particular jobs in the appropriate labor market. This information is collected by means of a wage survey. Area wage surveys can be conducted by individual firms or by local HR or business associations. Professional and industry associations often conduct surveys and make the results available to employers.

Wage Structure Decision   Wage structures are usually set up through a procedure called ***job evaluation***—an attempt to assess the worth of each job relative to other jobs. The simplest method for creating a wage structure is to rank jobs from those that should be paid the most (for example, the president) to those that should be paid the least (for example, a mail clerk or a janitor). In a smaller firm with few jobs this method is quick and practical, but larger firms with many job titles require more sophisticated methods. The next step is setting actual wage rates on the basis of a combination of survey data and the wage structure that results from job evaluation. Jobs of equal value are often grouped into wage grades for ease of administration.

job evaluation
An attempt to assess the worth of each job relative to other jobs

Individual Wage Decisions   After wage-level and wage structure decisions are made, the individual wage decision must be addressed. This decision concerns how much to pay each employee in a particular job. Although the easiest decision is to pay a single rate for each job, more typically a range of pay rates is associated with each job. For example, the pay range for an individual job might be $8.00 to $9.50 per hour, with different employees earning different rates within the range.

A system is then needed for setting individual rates. This may be done on the basis of seniority (enter the job at $8.00, for example, and increase 10 cents per hour every six months on the job until the employee hits $9.50), initial qualifications (inexperienced people start at $8.00; more experienced people start at a higher rate), or merit (raises above the entering rate are given for good performance). Combinations of these bases may also be used.

The Internet is also playing a key role in compensation patterns today because both job seekers and current employees can more easily get a sense of what their true market value is. If they can document the claim that their value is higher than what their current employer now pays or is offering, they are in a position to demand a higher salary. Consider the case of one compensation executive who met recently with a subordinate to discuss her raise. He was surprised when she produced data from five different websites backing up her claim for a bigger raise than he had intended to offer.[22]

Determining Benefits

Benefits are things of value other than compensation that the organization provides to its workers. (Benefits are sometimes called *indirect compensation.*) The average company spends an amount equal to more than one-third of its cash payroll on employee benefits. Thus an average employee who is paid $18,000 per year averages about $6,588 more per year in benefits. Benefits come in several forms. Pay for time not worked includes sick leave, vacation, holidays, and unemployment compensation. Insurance benefits often include life and health insurance for employees and their dependents. Workers' compensation is a legally required insurance benefit that provides medical care and disability income for employees injured on the job. Social security is a government pension plan to which both employers and employees contribute. Many employers also provide a private pension plan to which they and their employees contribute. Employee service benefits include such extras as tuition reimbursement and recreational opportunities.

> **benefits**
> Things of value other than compensation that an organization provides to its workers

Some organizations use "cafeteria benefit plans," whereby basic coverage is provided for all employees but employees are then allowed to choose which additional benefits they want (up to a cost limit based on salary). An employee with five children might choose medical and dental coverage for dependents, a single employee might prefer more vacation time, and an older employee might elect increased pension benefits. Flexible systems are expected to encourage people to stay in the organization and even help the company attract new employees.[23]

Managing Workforce Diversity

Workforce diversity has become a very important issue in many organizations. The management of diversity is often seen as a key human resource function.

The Meaning of Diversity

Diversity exists in a community of people when its members differ from one another along one or more important dimensions. In the business world, the term *diversity* is generally used to refer to demographic differences among people—differences in gender, age, ethnicity, and so forth. For instance, the average age of the U.S. workforce is gradually increasing, and so is the number of women in the labor force. Likewise, the labor force reflects growing numbers of African Americans, Latinos, and Asians, as well as more dual-career couples, same-gender couples, single parents, and physically challenged employees.

> **diversity**
> A characteristic of a group or organization whose members differ from one another along one or more important dimensions, such as age, gender, or ethnicity

The Impact of Diversity

There is no question that organizations are becoming ever more diverse. But how does this affect organizations? Diversity provides both opportunities and challenges for organizations.

Diversity as a Competitive Advantage   Many organizations are finding that diversity can be a source of competitive advantage in the marketplace (in addition to the fact that hiring and promoting in such as way as to enhance diversity is simply the right thing to do). For instance, organizations that manage diversity effectively often have higher levels of productivity and lower levels of turnover and absenteeism. Likewise, organizations that manage diversity effectively become known among women and minorities as good places to work. These organizations are thus better able to attract qualified employees from among these groups. Organizations with a diverse workforce are also better able to understand different market segments than are less diverse organizations. For example, a cosmetics firm such as Avon, which wants to sell its products to women and African Americans, can better understand how to create such products and effectively market them if women and African American managers are available to provide and solicit inputs into product development, design, packaging, advertising, and so forth.[24] Finally, organizations with diverse workforces are generally more creative and innovative than other organizations.

Diversity as a Source of Conflict   Unfortunately, diversity in an organization can also create conflict. This conflict can arise for a variety of reasons.[25] One potential source of conflict exists when an individual thinks that someone else has been hired, promoted, or fired because of her or his diversity status. Another source of conflict is when diversity is misunderstood, misinterpreted, or leads to inappropriate interactions among people of different groups.[26] Conflict may also arise if there is an environment of fear, distrust, or individual prejudice. Members of the dominant group in an organization may worry that newcomers from other groups pose a personal threat to their own position in the organization. For example, when U.S. firms have been taken over by Japanese firms, U.S. managers have sometimes been resentful of or hostile toward Japanese managers assigned to work with them. A final source of conflict exists when people are unwilling to accept people different from themselves. Personal bias and prejudices are still very real among some people today and can lead to potentially harmful conflict.

Managing Diversity in Organizations

Because of the tremendous potential that diversity holds for competitive advantage, as well as the importance of trying to avoid the negative consequences of associated conflict, much attention has been focused in recent years on how individuals and organizations can function more effectively in diverse contexts.

Individual Strategies   One important element of managing diversity and multiculturalism in an organization consists of things that individuals themselves can do. Understanding, of course, is the starting point. For instance, although people need to be treated fairly and equitably, managers must understand that differences among people do, in fact, exist. Thus any effort to treat everyone the same, without regard for their fundamental human differences, will lead only to

Eye on Management

Equality

This seven-minute video shows Doug, a professional worker, bringing a concern to his superior, Elaine. Doug is single and does not have children. He perceives that employees without families are more frequently called upon to work extra hours to meet client deadlines. On the other hand, employees with children are often excused from this work and in fact, receive extra time off. Doug states that he is not the only worker concerned about this issue. Elaine is surprised and asks Doug several questions to explore the issues further.

View the video and then answer the following questions individually or as a class.

1. Is the company in violation of any of the major work-related laws or court decisions? Explain.

2. What assumptions are company managers apparently making in regard to age, gender, sexual orientation, and other demographic variables?

3. In your opinion, what actions can employers take to remain family-friendly while still being fair to all workers, both those with and those without families?

View the two-minute follow-up video. In this video, Elaine tells about the surprise she experienced when hearing Doug's concern.

4. Elaine says that company managers thought, "Family comes first and if you don't have family, what could possibly be more important than that?" She also says that managers assumed that the burden of extra work would "even out" over time because senior employees would eventually have families of their own. Do these and other similar comments reflect the realities of today's workforce? Tell why or why not.

5. Should Elaine or another manager have anticipated these concerns? What are the consequences that could result due to their failure to anticipate?

---

problems. People in an organization should also try to understand the perspectives of others. Further, even though people may learn to understand others, and even though they may try to empathize with others, the fact remains that they still may not accept or enjoy some aspect of their behavior. So, tolerance is also required. Finally, communication is also required. For example, suppose that a young employee has a habit of making jokes about the age of an older colleague. Perhaps the young colleague means no harm and is just engaging in what she sees as good-natured kidding. But the older employee may find the jokes offensive. If the two do not communicate, the jokes will continue, and the resentment will grow. Eventually, what started as a minor problem may erupt into a much bigger one.

Organizational Approaches to Managing Diversity Whereas individuals are important in managing diversity and multiculturalism, the organization itself must play a fundamental role.[27] The starting point in managing diversity and multiculturalism is the policies an organization adopts that directly or indirectly affect how people are treated. Another aspect of organizational policies that affects diversity and multiculturalism is how the organization addresses and responds to problems that arise from differences among people. For example, consider the example of a manager charged with sexual harassment. If the organization's policies put an excessive burden of proof on the individual being harassed and invoke only minor sanctions against the guilty party, it is sending a clear signal about the importance of such matters. But the organization that has a balanced set of policies for addressing questions like sexual harassment sends its employees a message that diversity and individual rights and privileges are important.

Organizations can also help manage diversity and multiculturalism through a variety of ongoing practices and procedures. Avon's creation of networks for various groups represents one example of an organizational practice that fosters diversity. In general, the idea is that, because diversity and multiculturalism are characterized by differences among people, organizations can more effectively manage that diversity by following practices and procedures that are based on flexibility rather than on rigidity. Many organizations are finding that diversity and multicultural training is an effective means for managing diversity and minimizing its associated conflict. More specifically, ***diversity and multicultural training*** is designed to better enable members of an organization to function in a diverse and multicultural workplace.[28] Some organizations even go so far as to provide language training for their employees as a vehicle for managing diversity and multiculturalism. Motorola, for example, provides English-language training for its foreign employees on assignment in the United States. At Pace Foods in San Antonio, with a total payroll of over 450 employees, staff meetings and employee handbooks are translated into Spanish for the benefit of the company's 200 or so Latino employees.

diversity and multicultural training
Training that is specifically designed to better enable members of an organization to function in a diverse and multicultural workforce

Managing Labor Relations

labor relations
The process of dealing with employees who are represented by a union

Labor relations is the process of dealing with employees who are represented by a union.[29] Managing labor relations is an important part of HRM. However, most large firms have separate labor relations specialists to handle these activities apart from other human resources functions.

How Employees Form Unions

For employees to form a new local union, several things must occur. First, employees must become interested in having a union. Nonemployees who are professional organizers employed by a national union (such as the Teamsters or United Auto Workers) may generate interest by making speeches and distributing literature outside the workplace. Inside, employees who want a union try to convince other workers of the benefits of a union.

The second step is to collect employees' signatures on authorization cards. These cards state that the signer wishes to vote to determine whether the union will represent him or her. To show the National Labor Relations Board (NLRB) that interest is sufficient to justify holding an election, 30 percent of the employees in the potential bargaining unit must sign these cards. Before an election can be held, however, the bargaining unit must be defined. The bargaining unit consists of all employees who will be eligible to vote in the election and to join and be represented by the union if one is formed.

The election is supervised by an NLRB representative (or, if both parties agree, the American Arbitration Association—a professional association of arbitrators) and is conducted by secret ballot. If a simple majority of those voting (not of all those eligible to vote) votes for the union, then the union becomes certified as the official representative of the bargaining unit.[30] The new union then organizes itself by officially signing up members and electing officers; it will soon be ready to negotiate the first contract. The union-organizing process is diagrammed in Figure 8.4. If workers become disgruntled with their union or if management presents strong

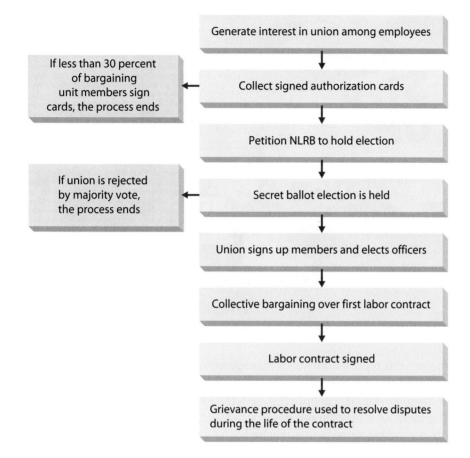

Figure 8.4
THE UNION-ORGANIZING PROCESS

If employees of an organization want to form a union, the law prescribes a specific set of procedures that both employees and the organization must follow. Assuming that these procedures are followed and the union is approved, the organization must engage in collective bargaining with the new union.

evidence that the union is not representing workers appropriately, the NLRB can arrange a decertification election. The results of such an election determine whether the union remains certified.

Organizations usually prefer that employees not be unionized because unions limit management's freedom in many areas. Management may thus wage its own campaign to convince employees to vote against the union. "Unfair labor practices" are often committed at this point. For instance, it is an unfair labor practice for management to promise to give employees a raise (or any other benefit) if the union is defeated. Experts agree that the best way to avoid unionization is to practice good employee relations all the time—not just when threatened by a union election. Providing absolutely fair treatment with clear standards in the areas of pay, promotion, layoffs, and discipline; having a complaint or appeal system for persons who feel unfairly treated; and avoiding any kind of favoritism will help make employees feel that a union is unnecessary. Wal-Mart strives to avoid unionization through these practices.[31]

Collective Bargaining

The intent of ***collective bargaining*** is to agree on a labor contract between management and the union that is satisfactory to both parties. The contract contains agreements about such issues as wages, work hours, job security, promotion, layoffs, discipline, benefits, methods of allocating overtime, vacations, rest periods, and the grievance procedure. The process of bargaining may go on for weeks, months,

collective bargaining
The process of agreeing on a satisfactory labor contract between management and a union

Labor relations is the process of dealing with employees who are represented by a union. As health care costs have skyrocketed in recent years, a major point of negotiation between businesses and unions has focused on health care coverage and payments. These members of the Service Employees International Union in Los Angeles are protesting both their low wages and their employer's efforts to pass along more of the employee insurance premiums to the employees themselves.

grievance procedure
The means by which a labor contract is enforced

or longer, with representatives of management and the union meeting to make proposals and counterproposals. The resulting agreement must be ratified by the union membership. If it is not approved, the union may strike to put pressure on management, or it may choose not to strike and simply continue negotiating until a more acceptable agreement is reached.

The ***grievance procedure*** is the means by which the contract is enforced. Most of what is in a contract concerns how management will treat employees. When employees feel that they have not been treated fairly under the contract, they file a grievance to correct the problem. The first step in a grievance procedure is for the aggrieved employee to discuss the alleged contract violation with her immediate superior. Often the grievance is resolved at this stage. If the employee still believes that she is being mistreated, however, the grievance can be appealed to the next level. A union official can help an aggrieved employee present her case. If the manager's decision is also unsatisfactory to the employee, additional appeals to successively higher levels are made until, finally, all in-company steps are exhausted. The final step is to submit the grievance to binding arbitration. An arbitrator is a labor law expert who is paid jointly by the union and management. The arbitrator studies the contract, hears both sides of the case, and renders a decision that both parties must obey. The grievance system for resolving disputes about contract enforcement prevents any need to strike during the term of the contract.

New Challenges in the Changing Workplace

As we have seen throughout this chapter, human resources managers face several ongoing challenges in their efforts to keep their organizations staffed with effective workforces. To complicate matters, new challenges arise as the economic and social environments of business change. We conclude this chapter with a look at two of the most important human resources management issues facing business today.

Managing Knowledge Workers

Employees traditionally added value to organizations because of what they did or because of their experience. In the "information age," however, many employees add value because of what they know.[32]

The Nature of Knowledge Work These employees are usually called *knowledge workers*, and the skill with which they are managed is a major factor in determining which firms will be successful in the future. Knowledge workers, including computer scientists, engineers, and physical scientists, provide special challenges for the HR manager. They tend to work in high-technology firms and are usually experts in some abstract knowledge base. They often like to work independently and tend to identify more strongly with their profession than with any organization—even to the extent of defining performance in terms recognized by other members of their profession.

> **knowledge workers**
> Workers whose contributions to an organization are based on what they know

As the importance of information-driven jobs grows, the need for knowledge workers continues to grow as well. But these employees require extensive and highly specialized training, and not every organization is willing to make the human capital investments necessary to take advantage of these jobs. In fact, even after knowledge workers are on the job, retraining and training updates are critical to prevent their skills from becoming obsolete. It has been suggested, for example, that the "half-life" of a technical education in engineering is about three years. The failure to update such skills will not only result in the loss of competitive advantage but also increase the likelihood that the knowledge worker will go to another firm that is more committed to updating them.

Knowledge Worker Management and Labor Markets Even though overall demand for labor has slowed in recent years due to the economic downturn, the demand for knowledge workers remains strong. As a result, organizations that need these workers must introduce regular market adjustments (upward) in order to pay them enough to keep them. This is especially critical in areas in which demand is growing, as even entry-level salaries for these employees are high. Once an employee accepts a job with a firm, the employer faces yet another dilemma. Once hired, workers are more subject to the company's internal labor market, which is not likely to be growing as quickly as the external market for knowledge workers as a whole. Consequently, the longer an employee remains with a firm, the further behind the market his or her pay falls—unless, of course, it is regularly adjusted (upward).

Not surprisingly, the growing demand for these workers has inspired some fairly extreme measures for attracting them in the first place.[33] High starting salaries and sign-on bonuses are common. BP Exploration was recently paying starting petroleum engineers with undersea platform-drilling knowledge—not experience, just knowledge—salaries in the six figures, plus sign-on bonuses of over $50,000 and immediate profit sharing. Even with these incentives, HR managers complain that in some areas they cannot retain specialists because young engineers soon leave to accept sign-on bonuses with competitors.

Contingent and Temporary Workers

A final contemporary HR issue of note involves the use of contingent or temporary workers. Indeed, recent years have seen an explosion in the use of such workers by organizations. The FBI, for example, routinely employs a cadre of retired agents in various temporary jobs.[34]

Trends in Contingent and Temporary Employment   In recent years, the number of contingent workers in the workforce has increased dramatically. A contingent worker is a person who works for an organization on something other than a permanent or full-time basis. Categories of contingent workers include independent contractors, on-call workers, temporary employees (usually hired through outside agencies), and contract and leased employees. Another category is part-time workers. The financial services giant Citigroup, for example, makes extensive use of part-time sales agents to pursue new clients. About 10 percent of the U.S. workforce currently uses one of these alternative forms of employment relationships. Experts suggest, however, that this percentage is increasing at a consistent pace.

Managing Contingent and Temporary Workers   Given the widespread use of contingent and temporary workers, HR managers must understand how to use such employees most effectively. In other words, they need to understand how to manage contingent and temporary workers. One key is careful planning. Even though one of the presumed benefits of using contingent workers is flexibility, it is still important to integrate such workers in a coordinated fashion. Rather than having to call in workers sporadically and with no prior notice, organizations try to bring in specified numbers of workers for well-defined periods of time. The ability to do so comes from careful planning.

A second key is understanding contingent workers and acknowledging both their advantages and their disadvantages. In other words, the organization must recognize what it can and cannot achieve from the use of contingent and temporary workers. Expecting too much from such workers, for example, is a mistake that managers should avoid. Third, managers must carefully assess the real cost of using contingent workers. We noted above, for example, that many firms adopt this course of action to save labor costs. The organization should be able to document precisely its labor-cost savings. How much would it be paying people in wages and benefits if they were on permanent staff? How does this cost compare with the amount spent on contingent workers? This difference, however, could be misleading. We also noted, for instance, that contingent workers might be less effective performers than permanent and full-time employees. Comparing employee for employee on a direct-cost basis, therefore, is not necessarily valid. Organizations must learn to adjust the direct differences in labor costs to account for differences in productivity and performance.

Finally, managers must fully understand their own strategies and decide in advance how they intend to manage temporary workers, specifically focusing on how to integrate them into the organization. On a very simplistic level, for example, an organization with a large contingent workforce must make some decisions about the treatment of contingent workers relative to the treatment of permanent, full-time workers. Should contingent workers be invited to the company holiday party? Should they have the same access to such employee benefits as counseling services and child care? There are no right or wrong answers to such questions. Managers must understand that they need to develop a strategy for integrating contingent workers according to some sound logic and then follow that strategy consistently over time.[35]

Summary of Key Points

1. Describe the environmental context of human resource management, including its strategic importance and its relationship with legal and social factors.
   - Human resource management is concerned with attracting, developing, and maintaining the human resources an organization needs.
   - Its environmental context consists of its strategic importance and the legal and social environments that affect human resource management.

2. Discuss how organizations attract human resources, including human resource planning, recruiting, and selecting.
   - Attracting human resources is an important part of the HRM function.
   - Human resource planning starts with job analysis and then focuses on forecasting the organization's future need for employees, forecasting the availability of employees both within and outside the organization, and planning programs to ensure that the proper number and type of employees will be available when needed.
   - Recruitment and selection are the processes by which job applicants are attracted, assessed, and hired.
   - Methods for selecting applicants include application blanks, tests, interviews, and assessment centers.
   - Any method used for selection should be properly validated.

3. Describe how organizations develop human resources, including training and development, performance appraisal, and performance feedback.
   - Organizations must also work to develop their human resources.
   - Training and development enable employees to perform their present job effectively and to prepare for future jobs.
   - Performance appraisals are important for validating selection devices, assessing the impact of training programs, deciding pay raises and promotions, and determining training needs.
   - Both objective and judgmental methods of appraisal can be applied, and a good system usually includes several methods.

   - The validity of appraisal information is always a concern, because it is difficult to accurately evaluate the many aspects of a person's job performance.

4. Discuss how organizations maintain human resources, including the determination of compensation and benefits and career planning.
   - Maintaining human resources is also important.
   - Compensation rates must be fair compared with rates for other jobs within the organization and with rates for the same or similar jobs in other organizations in the labor market.
   - Properly designed incentive or merit pay systems can encourage high performance, and a good benefits program can help attract and retain employees.

5. Discuss the nature of diversity, including its meaning, associated trends, impact, and management.
   - Diversity exists in an organization when its members differ from one another along one or more important dimensions, including gender, age, and ethnicity.
   - Individual strategies for managing diversity include being understanding, tolerant, and communicative with those who are different.
   - Organizational strategies include having fair policies, practices, and procedures; providing diversity training; and maintaining a tolerant culture.

6. Discuss labor relations, including how employees form unions and the mechanics of collective bargaining.
   - If a majority of a company's nonmanagement employees so desire, they have the right to be represented by a union.
   - Management must engage in collective bargaining with the union in an effort to agree on a contract.
   - While a union contract is in effect, the grievance system is used to settle disputes with management.

7. Describe the issues associated with managing knowledge and contingent and temporary workers.
   - Two important new challenges in the workplace include
     - the management of knowledge workers
     - issues associated with the use of contingent and temporary workers

Discussion Questions

Questions for Review

1. Describe the steps in the process of human resource planning. Explain the relationships between the steps.

2. Describe the common selection methods. Which method or methods are the best predictors of future job performance? Which are the worst? Why?

3. Compare training and development, noting any similarities and differences. What are some commonly used training methods?

4. Define wages and benefits. List different benefits that organizations can offer. What are the three decisions that managers must make to determine compensation and benefits? Explain each decision.

5. What are the potential benefits of diversity? How can individuals and organizations more effectively manage diversity?

Questions for Analysis

1. The Family and Medical Leave Act of 1993 is seen as providing much-needed flexibility and security for families and workers. Others think that it places an unnecessary burden on business. Yet another opinion is that the act hurts women, who are more likely to ask for leave, and shuffles them off to a low-paid "mommy track" career path. In your opinion, what are the likely consequences of the act? You can adopt one of the viewpoints expressed above or develop another. Explain your answer.

2. How do you know a selection device is valid? What are the possible consequences of using invalid selection methods? How can an organization ensure that its selection methods are valid?

3. Consider a job that you have held or with which you are familiar. Describe how you think an organization could best provide a realistic job preview for that position. What types of information and experiences should be conveyed to applicants? What techniques should be used to convey the information and experiences?

4. How would managing nonunionized workers differ from managing workers who elected to be in a union? Which would be easier? Why?

5. In what ways would managing temporary workers be easier than managing traditional permanent employees? In what ways would it be more difficult? What differences would likely exist in your own behavior if you were in a contingent or temporary job versus a traditional permanent job?

Building Effective Decision-Making Skills

Exercise Overview

Decision-making skills include the manager's ability to recognize and define problems and opportunities correctly and then to select an appropriate course of action to solve problems and capitalize on opportunities. This exercise gives you practice in making career choices.

Exercise Background

Job seekers must thoroughly understand their own abilities, preferences, and goals in order to make appropriate career choices. This issue is particularly acute for recent college graduates, who are often preparing to enter a career field that is largely unknown to them. Fortunately, a variety of sources of information can help. The Bureau of Labor Statistics maintains data about occupations, employment prospects, compensation, working conditions, and many other issues of interest to job seekers. The information is available by industry, occupation, employer type, and region.

Exercise Task

1. Conduct an online search of the Department of Labor's *National Compensation Survey*, beginning at http://data.bls.gov/oes/search.jsp. (Or search for the survey's title if the page has moved.) Select "Multiple occupations for one geographic area." Then choose "National" or select a state or metropolitan area, if your career plans are focused on a single state or city. Find the detailed data related to the occupation that you think is your most likely career choice upon graduation. Record the "Annual mean wage."

2. Then locate detailed data about two other occupations that you might consider and record the annual mean wage.

3. Judging purely on the basis of salary information, which occupation would be the "best" for you?

4. Now access job descriptions for various occupations at www.bls.gov/oco. Click on the link for the "A-Z Index" and read the descriptions for each of your three choices.

5. Judging purely on the basis of job characteristics, which occupation would be the "best" for you?

6. Is there a conflict between your answers to questions 3 and 5? If so, how do you plan to resolve it?

7. Are there any job characteristics that you desire strongly enough to sacrifice pay in order to have them? What are they? What are the limits, if any, on your willingness to sacrifice pay?

Building Effective Communication Skills

Exercise Overview

Communication skills reflect the manager's ability both to convey ideas and information effectively to others and to receive ideas and information effectively from others.

This exercise gives you practice in presenting yourself in the best possible light to others.

Exercise Background

One of the first tasks that you will be called upon to do in your job search is to introduce yourself to company recruiters at a job fair, career day, informational meeting, or interview. This exercise gives you a two-minute self-introduction tool for making a quick but memorable impression on anyone who might help you in your career advancement. It can be used to make a professional impression on anyone, not just potential employers.

The hour or so that you take to write this introduction and practice using it can be the difference between getting and not getting the job or interview you want. The most common request is "Tell me about yourself." If you can respond to this briefly, by saying something distinctive and memorable, you rise above the crowd.

The two-minute self-introduction should

- Be brief, so the listener will not get bored.
- Highlight what makes you unique.

- Reveal information not necessarily found in your résumé.
- Explain your interest in the firm.
- Show how your goals and background can benefit the firm.
- Encourage the listener to want to know more.
- Highlight aspects that the listener is interested in.
- Sell you—especially your skills, knowledge, and ability.
- Be truthful but positive.
- Be adapted to the particular listener and to his or her firm.
- Tell an interesting story in a conversational way.
- Not mention dates or years, because they are too hard to remember.
- Not include anything that is potentially biasing.

Exercise Task

1. Write a two-minute self-introduction following the format below. Make minor adjustments, if necessary, to accommodate your unique history.

- *Early Life—15 seconds.* Who are you? Where do you come from? What are your roots? "How" did you grow up? Include any unique or memorable fact or early experience or interest that connects to the desired job, even by inference.

- *Education—15 seconds.* Degrees, honors, awards? Major? Significant leadership, interests, or community activity while in school?
- *Work Life—45 seconds.* What are your work habits? Accomplishments (not duties)? How did your interests lead you in this direction? Projects you were enthusiastic about or your proudest moment? What have you learned that is relevant to the listener? If you do not have enough work experience, spend more time talking about your education
- *Sales Pitch—45 seconds.* What do you have to offer? Key skills you have gained, from school, work, leadership, or relationships? How do you want to use your key skills? How do your key skills fit the job or

firm? End with "I want to work for [or I am considering] your company because. . . ." Do not forget to thank them for the opportunity to talk with them!

2. Practice speaking your introduction aloud, with a firm handshake and a smile, until you can say everything in two minutes. One approach is to start alone or in front of a mirror and then work up to saying it to friends.

3. Practice your two-minute self-introduction in class, using classmates as stand-ins for interviewers. Or take turns presenting it in front of the class, with the professor or another student as a partner. Share constructive comments with one another.

Reprinted by permission of the author Margaret Hill.

Building Effective Technical Skills

Exercise Overview

Technical skills reflect the manager's abilities to accomplish or understand work done in an organization. Many managers must have technical skills to be able to hire appropriate people to work in the organization. This exercise will help you, as an individual working in human resource procurement, use technical skills as part of the selection process.

Exercise Background

Variation One. If you currently work or have worked in the past, select two jobs with which you have some familiarity. Select one job that is relatively low in skill level, responsibility, required education, and pay, and select another job that is relatively high in the same categories. It will make the exercise more useful to you if you use real jobs that you can relate to on a personal level.

Variation Two. If you have never worked or are not personally familiar with an array of jobs, assume that you are a manager of a small manufacturing facility. You need to hire individuals to fill two jobs. One job is that of plant custodian. This individual will sweep floors, clean bathrooms, empty trash cans, and so forth. The other person will be an office manager. This individual will supervise a staff of three clerks and secretaries, administer the plant payroll, and coordinate the administrative operations of the plant.

Exercise Task

With the information above as background, do the following:

1. Identify the most basic skills that you think are necessary for the effective performance of each job.

2. Identify the general indicators or predictors of whether or not a given individual can perform each job.

3. Develop a brief set of interview questions that you might use to determine whether an applicant has the qualifications to perform each job.

4. How important is it that a manager hiring employees to perform a job have the technical skills to do that job himself or herself?

Linda Morable, *Exercises in Management*, 8th edition. © 2005. pp. 119–120.

Skills Self-Assessment Instrument

What Do Students Want from Their Jobs?

Purpose: This exercise investigates the job values held by college students at your institution. Then it asks the students to speculate about employers' perceptions of college students' job values. This will help you to understand how college students can be recruited effectively. It also gives you insight into the difficulties of managing and motivating individuals with different values and perceptions.

Introduction: Employees choose careers that match their job values. Employers try to understand employee values in order to better recruit, manage, and motivate them. Job values are important therefore, in every HR process, from job advertisements and interviews, to performance appraisal, to compensation planning.

Instructions:

1. Complete the Job Values Survey below. Consider what you want from your future career. Using Column 1, rank the 14 job values from 1 to 14, with 1 being the most important to you and 14 being the least important.

2. In your opinion, when potential employers try to attract students, how much important do they think students give to each of the values? For Column 2, respond with a + (plus) if you think employers would rank it higher than students or with a – (minus) if you think employers would rate it lower. This is the employers' perception of students' values, not of their own values.

3. In small groups or a class, compute an average ranking for each value. Then discuss the results.

Job Values Survey		
	Column 1 **Your Ranking**	**Column 2** **Employer Ranking**
Working conditions		
Working with people		
Employee benefits		
Challenge		
Location of job		
Self-development		
Type of work		
Job title		
Training program		
Advancement		
Salary		
Company reputation		
Job security		
Autonomy on the job		

Discussion Questions

1. How much variation do you see in the job value rankings in Column 1? That is, are students' values quite different, moderately different, or very similar overall?

2. If there are significant differences between individuals, what impact might these differences have on the recruiting process? On the training process? On the performance evaluation and compensation process?

3. How much variation do you see in the responses for Column 2? That is, does your group or class agree on how employers perceive college students?

4. Is there a large difference between how you think employers perceive college students and your group's

or class's reported job values? If there is a large difference, what difficulties might this create for job seekers and potential employers? How might these difficulties be reduced or eliminated?

For interpretation, see Interpretations of Skills Self-Assessment Instruments in the appendix near the end of this text.

Experiential Exercise

Choosing a Compensation Strategy

Purpose: This exercise helps you better understand how internal and external market forces affect compensation strategies.

Introduction: Assume that you are the head of a large academic department in a major research university. Your salaries are a bit below external market averages. For example, your assistant professors make between $45,000 and $55,000 a year; your associate professors make between $57,000 and $65,000 a year; and your full professors make between $80,000 and $90,000 a year.

Faculty who have been in your department for a long time enjoy the work environment and appreciate the low cost of living in the area. They know that they are somewhat underpaid but have tended to regard the advantages of being in your department as offsetting this disadvantage. Recently, however, external market forces have caused salaries for people in your field to escalate rapidly. Unfortunately, although your university acknowledges this problem, you have been told that no additional funds will be provided to your department.

You currently have four vacant positions that need to be filled. One of these is at the rank of associate professor and the other three are at the rank of assistant professor. You have surveyed other departments in similar universities and you realize that to hire the best new assistant professors, you will need to offer at least $60,000 a year and that to get a qualified associate professor, you will need to pay at least $70,000. You have been given the budget to hire new employees at more competitive salaries but cannot do anything to raise the salaries of faculty currently in your department. You have identified the following options:

1. You can hire new faculty from lower-quality schools. They will likely accept salaries below market rate.

2. You can hire the best people available, pay market salaries, and deal with internal inequities later.

3. You can hire fewer new faculty, use the extra money to boost the salaries of your current faculty, and cut class offerings in the future.

Instructions

Step 1: Working alone, decide how you will proceed.

Step 2: Form small groups with your classmates and compare solutions.

Step 3: Identify the strengths and weaknesses of each option.

Follow-up Questions

1. Are there other options that might be pursued?

2. Assume that you chose Option 2. How would you go about dealing with the internal inequity problems?

3. Discuss with your instructor the extent to which this problem exists at your school.

CHAPTER CLOSING CASE

REI: A PLACE FOR SERIOUS FUN

Imagine you're looking for the perfect kayak for your local lake and the salesclerk is a kayaker who shares her expertise and experiences with you. Imagine shopping for hiking boots and being able to try them out on the store's test "mountain." Imagine a store that sells you exactly the right tent and then helps you practice setting it up. Welcome to REI, an outdoor gear retailer, known for high-quality products as well as excellent customer service. REI's new CEO, Sally Jewell, is beating competitors by providing buyers with experiences, advice, and quality interactions with knowledgeable store staff. "We used to be product-driven . . . relying on customers to trust us to pick the right products," says Jewell. "[Now we are] market-driven, paying attention to who those customers are and how we can adapt to the way they want to recreate."

REI's new strategy is called "experience marketing," and it is powering phenomenal growth for the retailer. The key to the new approach is store personnel. REI needs expert, enthusiastic workers, all the way from top managers to the sales floor. Typically, retail operations have difficulty recruiting enough hourly workers and the annual personnel turnover rate is 30 percent or more. In contrast, REI's turnover is just 12 percent. The firm is ranked twenty-seventh on *Fortune's* 2007 list of "100 Best Companies to Work For." It is also in *Fortune's* "Hall of Fame" as one of just a handful of firms that have appeared on the list every year since it began in 1998. How

does REI attract and keep the kind of employees it needs to provide that exceptional experience for its customers?

To attract the right employees, REI seeks outdoor enthusiasts. The REI website says, "People work for REI because of their passion for outdoor sports." Betty Fujikado, an advertiser for REI, agrees. "Employees are expected to live the brand," she says. REI does a careful job of screening applicants, so it makes sense that they also seek to fill most job vacancies through promotion from within. Former CEO Dennis Madsen worked for REI for 39 years.

Several factors contribute to REI's ability to retain good personnel. The company's culture reflects and supports employees' values. REI is organized as a member cooperative, owned by its approximately 2.8 million customers. This may contribute to its workplace environment, which is characterized by open communication, friendship, and a respect for employees' lives outside of work. Community involvement and social responsibility are also important at REI. Employees are encouraged to volunteer with community organizations that support outdoor recreation. The company makes conservation grants to protect the natural environment and has environmentally friendly policies, such as energy-efficient buildings and recycling programs. Although REI donates millions of dollars in cash and equipment, grant requests are not accepted from outsiders. Instead, REI gives to causes that employees select. REI

uses responsible sourcing, assuring that its products have been made in a way that protects workers and the environment. All of these values have a clear connection to the store's products and mission.

REI's culture has three additional core values that help in employee retention. The first is teamwork. One employee says, "REI is a big team, with a little of the small 'family' shop feel." The company does not pay commissions to sales personnel, who insist that commissions would introduce destructive competition and reduce teamwork. Personal growth is second. Every employee is encouraged to try more activities, acquire training, and learn. Third, REI calls itself "the place for serious fun." The company promotes active lifestyles, adventure, and play through such activities as company-sponsored cycling teams, weekend camping, and lunch-time Frisbee and yoga. "We . . . balance hard work with time off to play," the company's website states.

REI also improves retention through a progressive employee benefit program. Everyone qualifies for life and health insurance, even part-timers and seasonal employees. "This move sends a clear message to its employees that each is highly valued regardless of how many hours they clock," says human resources consultant Thomas Pursley. Additional benefits include generous retirement and profit sharing plans; vacation time, sick pay, and paid holidays for both full- and part-time workers; and subsidy pay for those who commute via public transportation. In addition, employees get discounts that range from 30 percent to 50 percent and free use of any of REI's rental equipment. Thus, salespeople become familiar with REI's products, improving their ability to offer good service.

"REI is a way of life," says one employee. And it seems like a healthy, happy life for both workers and customers.

CASE QUESTIONS

1. Give some specific examples of ways in which REI benefits from its excellent human resources management. As a customer or potential customer of REI, how would you benefit from the company's HRM practices?

2. REI's practices sound expensive. How do you think the company manages to afford these generous policies? For example, how does hiring young, fit workers help REI to manage costs?

3. What could other companies learn from REI's situation? What types of companies would and would not be likely to learn much from REI's situation?

REFERENCES

"100 Best Companies to Work For," "Hall of Fame," *Fortune*, January 20, 2006, www.fortune.com on January 21, 2006; "Benefits," "Culture and Philosophy," "Grants Program," "Join Our Winning Team," "REI Earns Top 10 Ranking," "REI Facts," "Testimonials," REI website, www.rei.com on January 21, 2006; Dale Buss, "REI: Working Out," *BusinessWeek*, November 15, 2005, www.businessweek.com on January 21, 2006; Monica Soto Ouchi, "Sally Jewell: Team Player at Her Peak," *Seattle Times*, March 23, 2005, www.seattletimes.com on January 21, 2006; Alison Overholt, "Smart Strategies: Putting Ideas to Work," *Fast Company*, April 2004, www.fastcompany.com on January 21, 2006.

YOU MAKE THE CALL

Results-Only Work Environment at Best Buy

1. Would you like to work at Best Buy in a department that uses ROWE? Why or why not?

2. Do you think other businesses will adopt an approach similar to Best Buy's? What types of organizations would be most likely to do so? What types of organizations would be unlikely to do so?

3. What are some of the disadvantages of the ROWE system for workers? For managers? For Best Buy?

4. What can Best Buy do to minimize or eliminate potential disadvantages?

Test Prepper

college.hmco.com/pic/griffinfund5e

You've read the chapter, studied the key terms, and the exam is any day now. Think you're ready to ace it? Take this sample test to gauge your comprehension of chapter material. You can check your answers at the back of the book. Want more test questions? Visit the student website at http://college.hmco.com/pic/griffinfund5e/ and take the ACE quizzes for more practice.

1. T F The Fair Labor Standards Act requires that men and women be paid the same amount for doing the same jobs.

2. T F Affirmative action requires all organizations to actively seek and hire employees from underrepresented organization.

3. T F When Phillip wanted to work at Target, he first visited his local store and used a kiosk to answer a series of questions about his education and his work history. In this example, Target is using an assessment center to select human resources.

4. T F Development is teaching managers and professionals the skills needed for both present and future jobs.

5. T F When an employee represented by a union feels that he or she has been treated unfairly, the grievance procedure is used to resolve the issue fairly and legally.

6. A disadvantage of internal recruiting is
   a. the ripple effect.
   b. recruiting expense.
   c. too much information on a recruit.
   d. irrelevance of a replacement chart.
   e. All of the above

7. Providing the applicant with a real picture of job requirements is called
   a. realistic job previews.
   b. reliability.
   c. measurement.
   d. validation.
   e. external recruiting.

8. Verizon Southwest has a series of prerecorded calls that operators in a booth answer. The operators are graded on speed, accuracy, and courtesy in handling the calls. This is an example of which method of performance appraisal?
   a. Interview
   b. Performance appraisal
   c. 360-degree feedback
   d. Performance test
   e. Behaviorally anchored rating scale

9. A worker who is paid $20 per hour is being paid on what type of compensation basis?
   a. Straight commission
   b. Straight salary
   c. Incentives
   d. Wages
   e. Benefits

10. _____ exists in a group or organization when its members differ from one another along one or more important dimensions.
   a. Diversity
   b. Community
   c. Culture
   d. Homogeneity
   e. Affirmative action

Part Three: Managing in the Soft-Drink Industry

This segment of the running case addresses issues raised in Part Three of the text, covering Chapters 6, 7, and 8.

Organization Structure

The Coca-Cola Company and PepsiCo both have complex organization structures, as would be expected for very large, multinational firms. See the organization charts following this segment (pages 256 and 257) for a rough overview of Coke's and Pepsi's global structure. Within regional units, Coke is organized into three sections: "Sparkling Beverages," "Still Beverages," and "Emerging Brands."

You can find more details about the companies' organization structures by looking at the corporate websites. On the Coke website, click "Our Company" and then "Leadership" to see more information. On the Pepsi website, click "Company" and then "Overview." This page summarizes the corporate structure and also contains links to the websites for each of Pepsi's business units.

From executive job titles you should be able to make an educated guess about the company's organization design. By reading the executive biographies, you can draw inferences about the company's policies regarding management of international divisions. Are the divisions run by staff from the company's headquarters country or are they run by staff with extensive local experience?

Another interesting fact you can glean from executive biographies is information about the relative importance of various functions within the corporation. Note the career paths taken by top executives. If most come from marketing backgrounds, for example, then that function is considered highly important and influential throughout the company.

Innovation

In 2006, both the Coca-Cola Company and PepsiCo produced innovations in products, organization structure, operations, and technology. At Coke, for example, for the first time all of the company's bottling investments were brought together into one division reporting to a single president. This allowed for greater coordination between company-owned bottlers and independent bottlers in which the company has partial ownership. Presumably, this change creates improved information flow, better use of shared resources, and other benefits.

Among its innovations, Pepsi purchased the Naked Juice Company, a maker of 100 percent juices that must be refrigerated. This product, along with PepsiCo's Sun Snacks organic chips and Fuelosophy energy drinks, gains the company access to natural food grocers, such as Whole Foods, which do not sell Pepsi's traditional soda products (nor do they sell traditional Coca-Cola products).

See the Coke and Pepsi websites for more detailed data regarding innovations. At Coke, you can find out about innovation by visiting the company's most recent annual review and reading the section titled "Year in Review." For the 2006 annual review, go to www.the-coca-colacompany.com/investors/annualandother-reports/2006/index.html and click "2006 in Review." Pepsi's website has information about innovation in the most recent annual report. From the company's home page, click on "Investors" and "Annual Reports," then select the most recent. In the 2005 annual report, there is a section titled "Innovation" that contains useful data, mostly about product innovation. The 2005 annual report's "Letter to Shareholders" also has useful information about business innovations.

Human Resource Management

In 2000, the Coca-Cola Company settled a discrimination lawsuit brought by a group of 2,200 African American salaried employees. This group of middle managers accused the firm of unequal compensation, having a "glass ceiling" that prevented African Americans from rising to high-ranking positions, and using a "glass wall" that kept members of the group in staff functions such as human resources, while denying them jobs in powerful line functions such as marketing. The settlement cost Coke hundreds of millions of dollars and required their HR practices to be audited by a group of independent outside experts. Visit www.thecoca-colacompany.com/ourcompany/wn20060106_task_force_report.html for a brief overview of the most recent audit report. The page contains a link to the full-scale report if you would like more information. For more information about the company's commitment to diversity, click on "Our Company" and then "Diversity," or visit the "Careers" pages and explore that section.

Pepsi, in contrast to Coca-Cola, has a more visible commitment to diversity. Their corporate CEO is female, as is one of the four business unit CEOs. However, what PepsiCo is most known for in human resources is its ability to nurture excellent HR leaders. For more information, read the *Workforce Management* article titled "PepsiCo—Taste the Success," at www.workforce.com/archive/feature/23/74/10/237412.php.

The Coca-Cola and Pepsi websites can also help you assess the companies' online recruiting efforts. Access the "Careers" section of their websites and visit the various pages related to recruiting.

Online Resources for Further Research

Please look at the list of online resources for Part I for further suggestions.

1. Coca-Cola's home page at www.thecoca-colacompany.com.
2. PepsiCo's home page at www.pepsico.com.

Case Discussion Questions

Each of the questions should be answered briefly, that is, in no more than a paragraph or two for each question.

1. Consider the following situational influences on organization design: core technology, environment, and organizational life cycle. Based on your assessment of your company and the soft-drink industry, what elements of organization design would you expect to find at your company?
2. Describe your company's organization structure in terms of one or more of the basic forms of design.
3. List some recent innovations at your company in as many of the following categories as possible: radical, incremental, technical, managerial, product, and process.
4. Briefly describe some ways that your company encourages innovation. Can you think of anything else the company could do to further innovation? Is there anything your company does that discourages innovation?
5. How would you assess your company's online recruiting efforts? For example, is the website easy to access and navigate? Is the information clear and complete? Does the site seem appealing to job seekers? If you find any areas that are weak or lacking, suggest ways your company might improve their online recruiting.

**Organizational Chart of
The Coca-Cola Company March 2007**

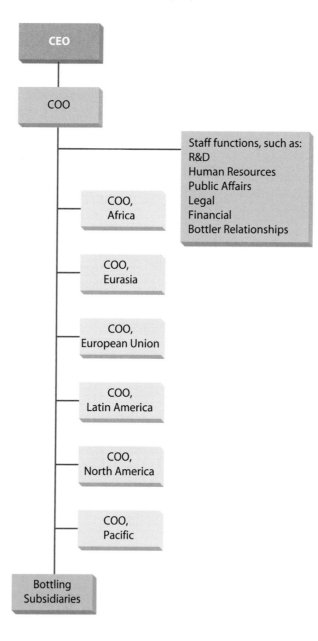

Organizational Chart of PepsiCo
March 2007

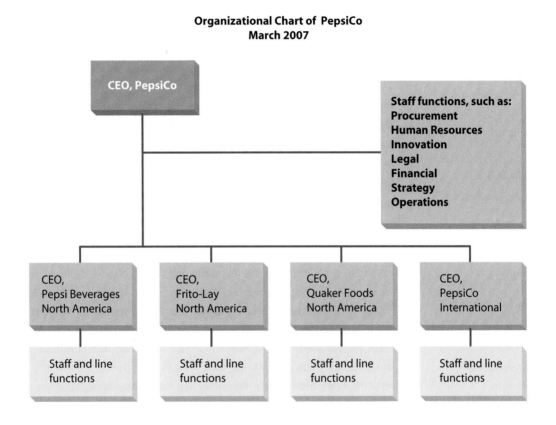

chapter 9

Basic Elements of Individual Behavior in Organizations

FIRST THINGS FIRST

W. L. Gore Nurtures Talent and Creativity

"When I arrived at Gore, I wondered how anything got done here. . . . Who's the boss?"

—DIANE DAVIDSON, ASSOCIATE, W. L. GORE & ASSOCIATES

"Pound for pound, the most innovative company in America is W. L. Gore & Associates," says *Fast Company* writer Alan Deutschman. In searching for the most innovative firm, a few big companies—3M, General Electric—made the cut. Yet midsize, specialized, privately owned Gore tops the list and "proves that brains beat brawn," according to Deutschman.

W. L. Gore founder Bill Gore created the firm's unique organization culture based on two observations. First, he noted "communication really happens in the car pool," at hierarchical companies where workers have few opportunities to speak to colleagues at different levels. Second, Bill Gore noticed that, in times of crisis, companies break through the hierarchy and create cross-functional and cross-level teams. Why wait until there's a crisis? he wondered. Why not do it every day?

Gore's organization culture helps it to effectively manage workers based on their individual differences. While the firm hires self-described "nerdy engineers," these "nerds" aren't sitting alone in a cubicle staring at a computer screen. Each time a worker joins a new team they are asked to spend six months getting to know the team members. That's their entire contribution. "You join a team and you're an idiot. It takes 18 months to build credibility," Gore employee John Mongan says. "[New hires] have trouble believing it—and not contributing when other people are."

All work is teams based, with no hierarchies or job titles outside of the top executive team. Teams are limited in size to a maximum of 200 people in manufacturing. Workspaces are dozens of small buildings located along several miles of rural highway; each houses an autonomous team. Diane Davidson, an outside hire, comparing Gore to her previous employer of 15 years, says, "When I arrived at Gore, I wondered how anything got done here." She kept asking, "Who's the boss?" until her mentor—*not* her boss—told her to quit using the B-word. She eventually figured out the real answer. "Your team is your boss, because you don't want to let them down. Everyone's your boss, and no one's your boss."

No one is designated a leader. If a worker wants to lead, he or she has to have the credibility, passion, ideas, and skills that will attract followers. To encourage creativity, workers are encouraged to spend 10 percent of their time on whatever interests them. Engineer Dave Myers was tinkering with a plastic coating for his mountain bike cables and tried it on guitar strings, among other tests. It seemed to make the strings sound better and resist breakage. He recruited some coworkers who experimented part-time on the idea for three years before they had a viable product. Today Gore is the market leader in acoustic guitar strings, even though their prices are three to five times the cost of other brands.

The W. L. Gore organization does have some designated leaders, including a CEO, four division leaders, and support function leaders in human resources and IT. However, employees are expected to "evolve" their own job descriptions based on their interests and talents. Compensation is determined by a committee, based on assessment of each worker's past, present, and expected future performance. Risk taking is encouraged by this method, as is the sense that everyone in the company is pulling together.

One of these "evolved" jobs is the role of "Sharp Shooter," an individual from outside a development team that volunteers to assess its progress and who may make the decision to stop work. The Sharp Shooters have a fresh perspective and no investment in the project, so halting development is easier. They receive trophies for their decisions. "We're effusive in our thanks," says Gore manager Brad Jones. "We ask them . . . how we could have made the decision [to kill the project] faster." Failed projects are toasted with champagne, just as successes are.

Other job roles include "sponsors" who match workers to project teams and alliance-forming "team leaders" with an idea for a new project team. A "category

LEARNING OBJECTIVES

After studying this chapter, you should be able to:

- Explain the nature of the individual-organization relationship.
- Define personality and describe personality attributes that affect behavior in organizations.
- Discuss individual attitudes in organizations and how they affect behavior.
- Describe basic perceptual processes and the role of attributions in organizations.
- Discuss the causes and consequences of stress and describe how it can be managed.
- Describe creativity and its role in organizations.
- Explain how workplace behaviors can directly or indirectly influence organizational effectiveness.

Gore-Tex has been successful in part because of its ability to acknowledge individual differences among its workers.

champion" is an expert in a set of skills, which may be closely related—sales and advertising—or quite unrelated—metal cable design and music production.

Gore, the maker of Gore-Tex fabrics as well as many medical and industrial products, is a strong competitor, with sales of $2 billion in 2006. The challenge for the fast-growing firm will be keeping that small workgroup feel and encouraging differences, while still growing and remaining effective.[1]

The people who populate today's business world are characterized by a wide variety of personalities and behaviors. Businesses like W. L. Gore that can figure out how best to embrace individuals while not trying to force them into a certain mold or mindset can achieve a significant competitive advantage. Indeed, myriad different and unique characteristics reside in each and every employee. These affect how they feel about the organization, how they will alter their future attitudes about the firm, and how they perform their jobs. These characteristics reflect the basic elements of individual behavior in organizations.

This chapter describes several of these basic elements and is the first of several chapters designed to develop a more complete perspective on the leading function of management. In the next section we investigate the psychological nature of individuals in organizations. The following section introduces the concept of personality and discusses several important personality attributes that can influence behavior in organizations. We then examine individual attitudes and perceptions and their role in organizations. The role of stress in the workplace is then discussed, followed by a discussion of individual creativity. Finally, we describe a number of basic individual behaviors that are important to organizations.

Understanding Individuals in Organizations

As a starting point in understanding human behavior in the workplace, we must consider the basic nature of the relationship between individuals and organizations. We must also gain an appreciation of the nature of individual differences.

The Psychological Contract

Most people have a basic understanding of a contract. Whenever we buy a car or sell a house, for example, both buyer and seller sign a contract that specifies the terms of the agreement. A psychological contract is similar in some ways to a standard legal contract but is less formal and well defined. In particular, a **psychological contract** is the overall set of expectations held by an individual with respect to what he or she will contribute to the organization and what the organization will provide in return.[2] Thus a psychological contract is not written on paper, nor are all of its terms explicitly negotiated.

The essential nature of a psychological contract is illustrated in Figure 9.1. The individual makes a variety of **contributions** to the organization—effort, skills, ability, time, loyalty, and so forth. These contributions presumably satisfy various needs and requirements of the organization. In other words, because the organization may have hired the person because of her skills, it is reasonable for the organization to expect that she will subsequently display those skills in the performance of her job.

psychological contract
The overall set of expectations held by an individual with respect to what he or she will contribute to the organization and what the organization will provide in return

contributions
What the individual provides to the organization

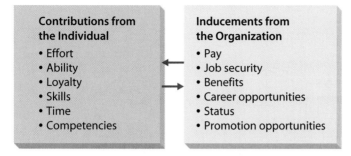

Figure 9.1
THE PSYCHOLOGICAL CONTRACT

Psychological contracts are the basic assumptions that individuals have about their relationships with their organization. Such contracts are defined in terms of contributions by the individual relative to inducements from the organization.

> **inducements**
> What the organization provides to the individual

In return for these contributions, the organization provides **inducements** to the individual. Some inducements, like pay and career opportunities, are tangible rewards. Others, like job security and status, are more intangible. Just as the contributions available from the individual must satisfy the needs of the organization, the inducements offered by the organization must serve the needs of the individual. Thus, if a person accepts employment with an organization because he thinks he will earn an attractive salary and have an opportunity to advance, he will subsequently expect that those rewards will actually be forthcoming.

If both the individual and the organization perceive that the psychological contract is fair and equitable, they will be satisfied with the relationship and will likely continue it. On the other hand, if either party sees an imbalance or inequity in the contract, it may initiate a change. For example, the individual may request a pay raise or promotion, decrease her contributed effort, or look for a better job elsewhere. The organization can also initiate change by requesting that the individual improve his skills through training, transfer the person to another job, or terminate the person's employment altogether.

A basic challenge faced by the organization, then, is to manage psychological contracts. The organization must ensure that it is getting value from its employees. At the same time, it must be sure that it is providing employees with appropriate inducements. If the organization is underpaying its employees for their contributions, for example, they may perform poorly or leave for better jobs elsewhere. On the other hand, if they are being overpaid relative to their contributions, the organization is incurring unnecessary costs.[3]

The Person-Job Fit

One specific aspect of managing psychological contracts is managing the person-job fit. **Person-job fit** is the extent to which the contributions made by the individual match the inducements offered by the organization. In theory, each employee has a specific set of needs that he or she wants fulfilled and a set of job-related behaviors and abilities to contribute. Thus, if the organization can take perfect advantage of those behaviors and abilities and can exactly fulfill his or her needs, it will have achieved a perfect person-job fit.

> **Person-job fit**
> The extent to which the contributions made by the individual match the inducements offered by the organization

Of course, such a precise level of person-job fit is seldom achieved. There are three reasons for this. For one thing, organizational selection procedures are imperfect. Organizations can make approximations of employee skill levels when making hiring decisions and can improve them through training. But even most simple performance dimensions are hard to measure objectively and validly.

Another reason for imprecise person-job fits is that both people and organizations change. An individual who finds a new job stimulating and exciting may find

Person-job fit is a very important construct in organizations. A good person-job fit benefits both the employee and the organization. But a poor person-job fit can result in a dissatisfied and low-performing employee.

"I'M PUTTING YOU ON THE CHINA SHOP ACCOUNT. DO YOU THINK YOU CAN HANDLE IT?"

P.C. Vey

the same job boring and monotonous after performing it for a few years. And when the organization adopts new technology, it has changed the skills it needs from its employees. Still another reason for imprecision in the person-job fit is that each individual is unique. Measuring skills and performance is difficult enough. Assessing needs, attitudes, and personality is far more complex. Each of these individual differences serves to make matching individuals with jobs a difficult and complex process.

The Nature of Individual Differences

individual differences
Personal attributes that vary from one person to another

Individual differences are personal attributes that vary from one person to another. Individual differences may be physical, psychological, or emotional. Taken together, all of the individual differences that characterize any specific person serve to make that individual unique from everyone else. Much of the remainder of this chapter is devoted to individual differences. Before proceeding, however, we must also note the importance of the situation in assessing the behavior of individuals.

Are specific differences that characterize a given individual good or bad? Do they contribute to or detract from performance? The answer, of course, is that it depends on the circumstances. One person may be very dissatisfied, withdrawn, and negative in one job setting, but very satisfied, outgoing, and positive in another. Working conditions, coworkers, and leadership are all important ingredients.

Thus, whenever an organization attempts to assess or account for individual differences among its employees, it must also be sure to consider the situation in which behavior occurs. Individuals who are satisfied or productive workers in one context may prove to be dissatisfied or unproductive workers in another context. Attempting to consider both individual differences and contributions in relation to inducements and contexts, then, is a major challenge for organizations as they attempt to establish effective psychological contracts with their employees and achieve optimal fits between people and jobs.

Personality and Individual Behavior

Personality traits represent some of the most fundamental sets of individual differences in organizations. **Personality** is the relatively stable set of psychological attributes that distinguish one person from another.[4] Managers should strive to understand basic personality attributes and the ways they can affect people's behavior in organizational situations, not to mention their perceptions of and attitudes toward the organization.

> **personality**
> The relatively stable set of psychological and behavioral attributes that distinguish one person from another

The "Big Five" Personality Traits

Psychologists have identified literally thousands of personality traits and dimensions that differentiate one person from another. But, in recent years, researchers have identified five fundamental personality traits that are especially relevant to organizations. Because these five traits are so important and because they are currently the subject of so much attention, they are now commonly referred to as the "**Big Five**" **personality traits**.[5] Figure 9.2 illustrates the Big Five traits.

Agreeableness refers to a person's ability to get along with others. Agreeableness causes some people to be gentle, cooperative, forgiving, understanding, and good-natured in their dealings with others. But it results in others' being irritable, short-tempered, uncooperative, and generally antagonistic toward other people. Although research has not yet fully investigated the effects of agreeableness, it would seem likely that highly agreeable people will be better able to develop good working relationships with coworkers, subordinates, and higher-level managers, whereas less agreeable people will not have particularly good working relationships. This same pattern might also extend to relationships with customers, suppliers, and other key organizational constituents.

Conscientiousness refers to the number of goals on which a person focuses. People who focus on relatively few goals at one time are likely to be organized, systematic, careful, thorough, responsible, and self-disciplined as they work to pursue those

> **"Big Five" personality traits**
> A popular personality framework based on five key traits

> **agreeableness**
> In the "Big Five" model of personality, an individual's ability to get along with others

> **conscientiousness**
> The number of goals on which a person focuses

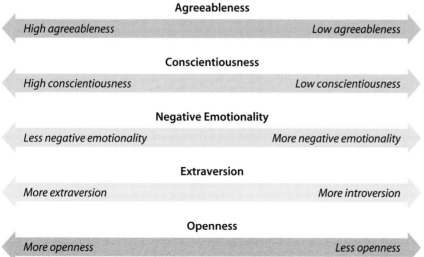

Figure 9.2
THE "BIG FIVE" MODEL OF PERSONALITY

The "Big Five" personality model represents an increasingly accepted framework for understanding personality traits in organizational settings. In general, experts tend to agree that personality traits toward the left end of each dimension, as illustrated in this figure, are more positive in organizational settings, whereas traits closer to the right are less positive.

goals. Others, however, tend to take on a wider array of goals and, as a result, are more disorganized, careless, and irresponsible, as well as less thorough and self-disciplined. Research has found that more conscientious people tend to be higher performers than less conscientious people across a variety of different jobs. This pattern seems logical, of course, because more conscientious people will take their jobs seriously and will approach the performance of their jobs in highly responsible fashions.

The third of the Big Five personality dimensions is **negative emotionality**. People with less negative emotionality will be relatively poised, calm, resilient, and secure. But people with more negative emotionality will be more excitable, insecure, reactive, and subject to extreme mood swings. People with less negative emotionality might be expected to better handle job stress, pressure, and tension. Their stability might also lead them to be seen as more reliable than their less stable counterparts.

Extraversion refers to a person's comfort level with relationships. People who are called "extraverts" are sociable, talkative, assertive, and open to establishing new relationships. But introverts are much less sociable, talkative, and assertive and are less open to establishing new relationships. Research suggests that extraverts tend to be higher overall job performers than introverts and that they are also more likely to be attracted to jobs based on personal relationships, such as sales and marketing positions.

Finally, *openness* refers to a person's rigidity of beliefs and range of interests. People with high levels of openness are willing to listen to new ideas and to change their own ideas, beliefs, and attitudes as a result of new information. They also tend to have broad interests and to be curious, imaginative, and creative. On the other hand, people with low levels of openness tend to be less receptive to new ideas and less willing to change their minds. Further, they tend to have fewer and narrower interests and to be less curious and creative. People with more openness might be expected to be better performers, owing to their flexibility and the likelihood that they will be better accepted by others in the organization. Openness may also encompass an individual's willingness to accept change. For example, people with high levels of openness may be more receptive to change, whereas people with low levels of openness may be more likely to resist change.

The Big Five framework continues to attract the attention of both researchers and managers. The potential value of this framework is that it encompasses an integrated set of traits that appear to be valid predictors of certain behaviors in certain situations. Thus managers who can develop both an understanding of the framework and the ability to assess these traits in their employees will be in a good position to understand how and why employees behave as they do.[6] On the other hand, managers must also be careful not to overestimate their ability to assess the Big Five traits in others. Even assessment using the most rigorous and valid measures, for instance, is still likely to be somewhat imprecise. Another limitation of the Big Five framework is that it is based primarily on research conducted in the United States. Thus there are unanswered questions as to how accurately it applies to workers in other cultures. And, even within the United States, a variety of other factors and traits are also likely to affect behavior in organizations.

negative emotionality
Extent to which a person is poised, calm, resilient, and secure

extraversion
A person's comfort level with relationships

openness
A person's rigidity of beliefs and range of interests

The Myers-Briggs Framework

Another interesting approach to understanding personalities in organizations is the Myers-Briggs framework. This framework, based on the classic work of Carl Jung, differentiates people in terms of four general dimensions. These are defined as follows.

- *Extraversion (E) Versus Introversion (I).* Extraverts get their energy from being around other people, whereas introverts are worn out by others and need solitude to recharge their energy.

- *Sensing (S) Versus Intuition (N).* The sensing type prefers concrete things, whereas intuitives prefer abstract concepts.

- *Thinking (T) Versus Feeling (F).* Thinking individuals base their decisions more on logic and reason, whereas feeling individuals base their decisions more on feelings and emotions.

- *Judging (J) Versus Perceiving (P).* People who are the judging type enjoy completion or being finished, whereas perceiving types enjoy the process and open-ended situations.

To use this framework, people complete a questionnaire designed to measure their personality on each dimension. Higher or lower scores in each of the dimensions are used to classify people into one of 16 different personality categories.

The Myers-Briggs Type Indicator (MBTI) is one popular questionnaire that some organizations use to assess personality types. Indeed, it is among the most popular selection instruments used today, with as many as 2 million people taking it each year. Research suggests that the MBTI is a useful method for determining communication styles and interaction preferences. In terms of personality attributes, however, questions exist about both the validity and the reliability of the MBTI.

Other Personality Traits at Work

Besides the Big Five and the Myers-Briggs framework, there are several other personality traits that influence behavior in organizations. Among the most important

Personality traits such as locus of control and self-efficacy are important determinants of how people behave at work. Many skilled workers in the Caribbean migrate to Europe or the United States in order to find work. But when construction in Jamaica dried up, local architect Mandilee Newton chose a different approach. Because of her confidence in her own capabilities she took a short hop to another Caribbean island, Trinidad, and has been gainfully employed ever since.

are locus of control, self-efficacy, authoritarianism, Machiavellianism, self-esteem, and risk propensity.

Locus of control is the extent to which people believe that their behavior has a real effect on what happens to them.[7]

Some people, for example, believe that, if they work hard, they will succeed. They also may believe that people who fail do so because they lack ability or motivation. People who believe that individuals are in control of their lives are said to have an *internal locus of control.* Other people think that fate, chance, luck, or other people's behavior determines what happens to them. For example, an employee who fails to get a promotion may attribute that failure to a politically motivated boss or just bad luck, rather than to her or his own lack of skills or poor performance record. People who think that forces beyond their control dictate what happens to them are said to have an *external locus of control.*

Self-efficacy is a related but subtly different personality characteristic. Self-efficacy is a person's beliefs about his or her capabilities to perform a task.[8] People with high self-efficacy believe that they can perform well on a specific task, whereas people with low self-efficacy tend to doubt their ability to perform a specific task. Although self-assessments of ability contribute to self-efficacy, so, too, does the individual's personality. Some people simply have more self-confidence than do others. This belief in their ability to perform a task effectively results in their being more self-assured and more able to focus their attention on performance.

Another important personality characteristic is ***authoritarianism***, the extent to which an individual believes that power and status differences are appropriate within hierarchical social systems like organizations.[9] For example, a person who is highly authoritarian may accept directives or orders from someone with more authority purely because the other person is "the boss." On the other hand, although a person who is not highly authoritarian may still carry out appropriate and reasonable directives from the boss, he or she is also more likely to question things, express disagreement with the boss, and even refuse to carry out orders if they are for some reason objectionable. A highly authoritarian manager may be autocratic and demanding, and highly authoritarian subordinates will be more likely to accept this behavior from their leader. On the other hand, a less authoritarian manager may allow subordinates a bigger role in making decisions, and less authoritarian subordinates will respond positively to this behavior.

Machiavellianism is another important personality trait. This concept is named after Niccolo Machiavelli, a sixteenth-century Italian political philosopher. In his book entitled *The Prince*, Machiavelli explained how the nobility could more easily gain and use power. *Machiavellianism* is now used to describe behavior directed at gaining power and controlling the behavior of others. Research suggests that Machiavellianism is a personality trait that varies from person to person. More Machiavellian individuals tend to be rational and nonemotional, may be willing to lie to attain their personal goals, may put little weight on loyalty and friendship, and may enjoy manipulating others' behavior. Less Machiavellian individuals are more emotional, less willing to lie to succeed, value loyalty and friendship highly, and get little personal pleasure from manipulating others. By all accounts, Dennis Kozlowski, the indicted former CEO of Tyco International, had a high degree of Machiavellianism. He apparently came to believe that his position of power in the

---

locus of control
The degree to which an individual believes that his or her behavior has a direct impact on the consequences of that behavior

self-efficacy
An individual's beliefs about her or his capabilities to perform a task

authoritarianism
The extent to which an individual believes that power and status differences are appropriate within hierarchical social systems like organizations

Machiavellianism
Behavior directed at gaining power and controlling the behavior of others

company gave him the right to do just about anything he wanted with company resources.[10]

Self-esteem is the extent to which a person believes that she is a worthwhile and deserving individual.[11] A person with high self-esteem is more likely to seek high-status jobs, be more confident in her ability to achieve higher levels of performance, and derive greater intrinsic satisfaction from her accomplishments. In contrast, a person with less self-esteem may be more content to remain in a lower-level job, be less confident of his ability, and focus more on extrinsic rewards. Among the major personality dimensions, self-esteem is the one that has been most widely studied in other countries. Although more research is clearly needed, the published evidence does suggest that self-esteem as a personality trait does indeed exist in a variety of countries and that its role in organizations is reasonably important across different cultures.[12]

Risk propensity is the degree to which an individual is willing to take chances and make risky decisions. A manager with a high risk propensity, for example, might be expected to experiment with new ideas and gamble on new products. She might also lead the organization in new and different directions. This manager might also be a catalyst for innovation. On the other hand, the same individual might also jeopardize the continued well-being of the organization if the risky decisions prove to be bad ones. A manager with low risk propensity might lead to a stagnant and overly conservative organization or help the organization successfully weather turbulent and unpredictable times by maintaining stability and calm. Thus the potential consequences of risk propensity to an organization are heavily dependent on that organization's environment.

> **self-esteem**
> The extent to which a person believes that he or she is a worthwhile and deserving individual

> **risk propensity**
> The degree to which an individual is willing to take chances and make risky decisions

Emotional Intelligence

The concept of emotional intelligence has been identified in recent years and provides some interesting insights into personality. **Emotional intelligence**, or **EQ**, refers to the extent to which people are self-aware, manage their emotions, motivate themselves, express empathy for others, and possess social skills.[13] These various dimensions can be described as follows:

> **emotional intelligence (EQ)**
> The extent to which people are self-aware, manage their emotions, motivate themselves, express empathy for others, and possess social skills

- *Self-Awareness.* This is the basis for the other components. It refers to a person's capacity for being aware of how they are feeling. In general, more self-awareness allows people to more effectively guide their own lives and behaviors.

- *Managing Emotions.* This refers to a person's capacities to balance anxiety, fear, and anger so that they do not overly interfere with getting things accomplished.

- *Motivating Oneself.* This dimension refers to a person's ability to remain optimistic and to continue striving in the face of setbacks, barriers, and failure.

- *Empathy.* Empathy refers to a person's ability to understand how others are feeling, even without being explicitly told.

- *Social Skill.* This refers to a person's ability to get along with others and to establish positive relationships.

Preliminary research suggests that people with high EQs may perform better than others, especially in jobs that require a high degree of interpersonal interaction and that involve influencing or directing the work of others. Moreover, EQ appears to be something that is not biologically based but can be developed.[14]

Attitudes and Individual Behavior

attitudes
Complexes of beliefs and feelings that people have about specific ideas, situations, or other people

Another important element of individual behavior in organizations is attitudes. **Attitudes** are complexes of beliefs and feelings that people have about specific ideas, situations, or other people. Attitudes are important because they are the mechanism through which most people express their feelings. An employee's statement that he feels underpaid by the organization reflects his feelings about his pay. Similarly, when a manager says that she likes the new advertising campaign, she is expressing her feelings about the organization's marketing efforts.

Attitudes have three components. The *affective component* of an attitude reflects feelings and emotions an individual has toward a situation. The *cognitive component* of an attitude is derived from knowledge an individual has about a situation. It is important to note that cognition is subject to individual perceptions (something we discuss more fully later). Thus one person might "know" that a certain political candidate is better than another, whereas someone else might "know" just the opposite. Finally, the *intentional component* of an attitude reflects how an individual expects to behave toward or in the situation.

To illustrate these three components, consider the case of a manager who places an order for some supplies for his organization from a new office supply firm. Suppose many of the items he orders are out of stock, others are overpriced, and still others arrive damaged. When he calls someone at the supply firm for assistance, he is treated rudely and gets disconnected before his claim is resolved. When asked how he feels about the new office supply firm, he might respond, "I don't like that company [affective component]. They are the worst office supply firm I've ever dealt with [cognitive component]. I'll never do business with them again [intentional component]."

cognitive dissonance
Caused when an individual has conflicting attitudes

People try to maintain consistency among the three components of their attitudes as well as among all their attitudes. However, circumstances sometimes arise that lead to conflicts. The conflict individuals may experience among their own attitudes is called **cognitive dissonance**.[15] Say, for example, that an individual who has vowed never to work for a big, impersonal corporation intends instead to open her own business and be her own boss. Unfortunately, a series of financial setbacks leads her to have no choice but to take a job with a large company and work for someone else. Thus cognitive dissonance occurs: the affective and cognitive components of the individual's attitude conflict with intended behavior. To reduce cognitive dissonance, which is usually an uncomfortable experience for most people, the individual might tell herself that the situation is only temporary and that she can go back out on her own in the near future. Or she might revise her cognitions and decide that working for a large company is more pleasant than she had expected.

Work-Related Attitudes

People in organizations form attitudes about many different things. For example, employees are likely to have attitudes about their salary, promotion possibilities, their boss, employee benefits, the food in the company cafeteria, and the color of the company softball team uniforms. Of course, some of these attitudes are more important than others. Especially important attitudes are job satisfaction or dissatisfaction and organizational commitment.[16]

Job Satisfaction or Dissatisfaction *Job satisfaction or dissatisfaction* is an attitude that reflects the extent to which an individual is gratified by or fulfilled in his or her work. Extensive research conducted on job satisfaction has indicated that personal factors, such as an individual's needs and aspirations, determine this attitude, along with group and organizational factors, such as relationships with coworkers and supervisors, and working conditions, work policies, and compensation.[17]

A satisfied employee also tends to be absent less often, to make positive contributions, and to stay with the organization.[18] In contrast, a dissatisfied employee may be absent more often, may experience stress that disrupts coworkers, and may be continually looking for another job. Contrary to what many managers believe, however, high levels of job satisfaction do not necessarily lead to higher levels of performance. One survey has also indicated that, contrary to popular opinion, Japanese workers are less satisfied with their jobs than their counterparts in the United States.[19]

> **job satisfaction or dissatisfaction**
> An attitude that reflects the extent to which an individual is gratified by or fulfilled in his or her work

Organizational Commitment *Organizational commitment* is an attitude that reflects an individual's identification with and attachment to the organization itself. A person with a high level of commitment is likely to see herself as a true member of the organization (for example, referring to the organization in personal terms like "We make high-quality products"), to overlook minor sources of dissatisfaction with the organization, and to see herself remaining a member of the organization. In contrast, a person with less organizational commitment is more likely to see himself as an outsider (for example, referring to the organization in less personal terms like "They don't pay their employees very well"), to express more dissatisfaction about things, and to not see himself as a long-term member of the organization. Research suggests that Japanese workers may be more committed to their organizations than are American workers.[20]

> **organizational commitment**
> An attitude that reflects an individual's identification with and attachment to the organization itself

Research also suggests that commitment strengthens with an individual's age, years with the organization, sense of job security, and participation in decision making.[21] Employees who feel committed to an organization have highly reliable habits, plan a long tenure with the organization, and muster more effort in performance. Although there are few definitive things that organizations can do to create or promote commitment, there are a few specific guidelines available. For one thing, if the organization treats its employees fairly and provides reasonable rewards and job security, those employees will more likely be satisfied and committed. Allowing employees to have a say in how things are done can also promote all three attitudes.

Affect and Mood in Organizations

Researchers have recently started to focus renewed interest on the affective component of attitudes. Recall from our discussion that the affective component of an attitude reflects our feelings and emotions. Although managers once believed that emotion and feelings varied among people from day to day, research now suggests that, although some short-term fluctuation does indeed occur, there are also underlying stable predispositions toward fairly constant and predictable moods and emotional states.[22]

Some people, for example, tend to have a higher degree of *positive affectivity*. This means that they are relatively upbeat and optimistic, have an overall sense of well-being, and usually see things in a positive light. Thus they always seem to be in a good mood. Other people, those with more *negative affectivity*, are just the

> **positive affectivity**
> A tendency to be relatively upbeat and optimistic, have an overall sense of well-being, see things in a positive light, and seem to be in a good mood

negative affectivity
A tendency to be generally downbeat and pessimistic, see things in a negative way, and seem to be in a bad mood

opposite. They are generally downbeat and pessimistic, and they usually see things in a negative way. They seem to be in a bad mood most of the time.

Of course, as noted above, there can be short-term variations among even the most extreme types. People with a lot of positive affectivity, for example, may still be in a bad mood if they have just received some bad news—being passed over for a promotion, getting extremely negative performance feedback, or being laid off or fired, for instance. Similarly, those with negative affectivity may still be in a good mood—at least for a short time—if they have just been promoted, received very positive performance feedback, or had other good things befall them. After the initial impact of these events wears off, however, those with positive affectivity will generally return to their normal positive mood, whereas those with negative affectivity will gravitate back to their normal bad mood.[23]

Perception and Individual Behavior

As noted earlier, an important element of an attitude is the individual's perception of the object about which the attitude is formed. Because perception plays a role in a variety of other workplace behaviors, managers need to have a general understanding of basic perceptual processes.[24] The role of attributions is also important.

Basic Perceptual Processes

perception
The set of processes by which an individual becomes aware of and interprets information about the environment

Perception is the set of processes by which an individual becomes aware of and interprets information about the environment. As shown in Figure 9.3, basic perceptual processes that are particularly relevant to organizations are selective perception and stereotyping.

selective perception
The process of screening out information that we are uncomfortable with or that contradicts our beliefs

Selective Perception   *Selective perception* is the process of screening out information that we are uncomfortable with or that contradicts our beliefs. For example, suppose a manager is exceptionally fond of a particular worker. The manager has a very positive attitude about the worker and thinks he is a top performer. One day the manager notices that the worker seems to be goofing off. Selective perception may cause the manager to quickly forget what he observed. Similarly, suppose a manager has formed a very negative image of a particular worker. She thinks this worker is a poor performer and never does a good job. When she happens to observe an example of high performance from the worker, she, too, may not remember it for very long. In

Figure 9.3
PERCEPTUAL PROCESSES

Two of the most basic perceptual processes are selective perception and stereotyping. As shown here, selective perception occurs when we screen out information (represented by the – symbols) that causes us discomfort or that contradicts our beliefs. Stereotyping occurs when we categorize or label people on the basis of a single attribute, illustrated here by color.

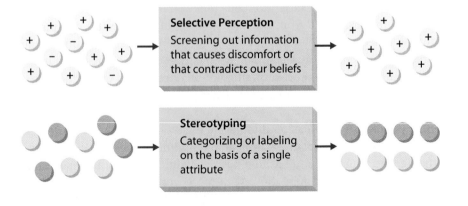

one sense, selective perception is beneficial because it allows us to disregard minor bits of information. Of course, this holds true only if our basic perception is accurate. If selective perception causes us to ignore important information, however, it can become quite detrimental.

Stereotyping *Stereotyping* is the process of categorizing or labeling people on the basis of a single attribute. Common attributes from which people often stereotype are race and sex. Of course, stereotypes along these lines are inaccurate and can be harmful. For example, suppose a manager forms the stereotype that women can perform only certain tasks and that men are best suited for other tasks. To the extent that this affects the manager's hiring practices, the manager is (1) costing the organization valuable talent for both sets of jobs, (2) violating federal law, and (3) behaving unethically. On the other hand, certain forms of stereotyping can be useful and efficient. Suppose, for example, that a manager believes that communication skills are important for a particular job and that speech communication majors tend to have exceptionally good communication skills. As a result, whenever he interviews candidates for jobs, he pays especially close attention to speech communication majors. To the extent that communication skills truly predict job performance and that majoring in speech communication does indeed provide those skills, this form of stereotyping can be beneficial.

stereotyping
The process of categorizing or labeling people on the basis of a single attribute

Perception and Attribution

Perception is also closely linked with another process called attribution. **Attribution** is a mechanism through which we observe behavior and then attribute causes to it.[25] The behavior that is observed may be our own or that of others. For example, suppose someone realizes one day that she is working fewer hours than before, that she talks less about her work, and that she calls in sick more frequently. She might conclude from this that she must have become disenchanted with her job and subsequently decide to quit. Thus she observed her own behavior, attributed a cause to it, and developed what she thought was a consistent response.

attribution
The process of observing behavior and attributing causes to it

More common is attributing cause to the behavior of others. For example, if the manager of the individual described above has observed the same behavior, he might form exactly the same attribution. On the other hand, he might instead decide that she has a serious illness, that he is driving her too hard, that she is experiencing too much stress, that she has a drug problem, or that she is having family problems.

The basic framework around which we form attributions is *consensus* (the extent to which other people in the same situation behave the same way), *consistency* (the extent to which the same person behaves in the same way at different times), and *distinctiveness* (the extent to which the same person behaves in the same way in other situations). For example, suppose a manager observes that an employee is late for a meeting. The manager might further realize that that employee is the only one who is late (low consensus), recall that he is often late for other meetings (high consistency), and subsequently realize that the same employee is sometimes late for work and returning from lunch (low distinctiveness). This pattern of attributions might cause the manager to decide that the individual's behavior is something that should be changed. As a result, the manager might meet with the subordinate and establish some punitive consequences for future tardiness.

Stress and Individual Behavior

stress
An individual's response to a strong stimulus, which is called a stressor

Another important element of behavior in organizations is stress. ***Stress*** is an individual's response to a strong stimulus.[26] This stimulus is called a *stressor*. Stress generally follows a cycle referred to as the ***general adaptation syndrome***, or GAS,[27] shown in Figure 9.4. According to this view, when an individual first encounters a stressor, the GAS is initiated, and the first stage, alarm, is activated. He may feel panic, wonder how to cope, and feel helpless. For example, suppose a manager is told to prepare a detailed evaluation of a plan by his firm to buy one of its competitors. His first reaction may be, "How will I ever get this done by tomorrow?"

general adaptation syndrome (GAS)
General cycle of the stress process

If the stressor is too intense, the individual may feel unable to cope and never really try to respond to its demands. In most cases, however, after a short period of alarm, the individual gathers some strength and starts to resist the negative effects of the stressor. For example, the manager with the evaluation to write may calm down, call home to say he is working late, roll up his sleeves, order out for coffee, and get to work. Thus, at stage 2 of the GAS, the person is resisting the effects of the stressor.

In many cases, the resistance phase may end the GAS. If the manager is able to complete the evaluation earlier than expected, he may drop it in his briefcase, smile to himself, and head home tired but satisfied. On the other hand, prolonged exposure to a stressor without resolution may bring on stage 3 of the GAS—exhaustion. At this stage, the individual literally gives up and can no longer resist the stressor. The manager, for example, might fall asleep at his desk at 3:00 A.M. and never finish the evaluation.

We should note that stress is not all bad. In the absence of stress, we may experience lethargy and stagnation. An optimal level of stress, on the other hand, can result in motivation and excitement. Too much stress, however, can have negative consequences. It is also important to understand that stress can be caused by "good" as well as "bad" things. Excessive pressure, unreasonable demands on our time, and bad news can all cause stress. But even receiving a bonus and then having to decide what to do with the money can be stressful. So, too, can receiving a promotion, gaining recognition, and similar good things.

Type A
Individuals who are extremely competitive, very devoted to work, and have a strong sense of time urgency

One important line of thinking about stress focuses on ***Type A*** and ***Type B*** personalities.[28] Type A individuals are extremely competitive, very devoted to work, and have a strong sense of time urgency. They are likely to be aggressive, impatient, and very work oriented. They have a lot of drive and want to accomplish as much as possible as quickly as possible. Type B individuals are less competitive, less devoted to work, and have a weaker sense of time urgency. Such individuals are less likely to

Figure 9.4
THE GENERAL ADAPTATION SYNDROME

The general adaptation syndrome represents the normal process by which we react to stressful events. At stage 1—alarm—we feel panic and alarm, and our level of resistance to stress drops. Stage 2—resistance—represents our efforts to confront and control the stressful circumstance. If we fail, we may eventually reach stage 3—exhaustion—and just give up or quit.

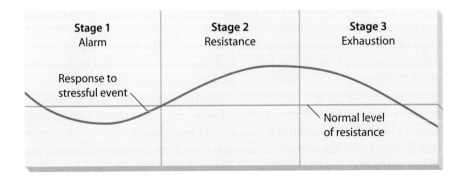

experience conflict with other people and more likely to have a balanced, relaxed approach to life. They are able to work at a constant pace without time urgency. Type B people are not necessarily more or less successful than are Type A people. But they are less likely to experience stress.

> **Type B**
> Individuals who are less competitive, less devoted to work, and have a weaker sense of time urgency

Causes and Consequences of Stress

Stress is obviously not a simple phenomenon. As listed in Figure 9.5, several different things can cause stress. Note that this list includes only work-related conditions. We should keep in mind that stress can also be the result of personal circumstances.[29]

Causes of Stress Work-related stressors fall into one of four categories—task, physical, role, and interpersonal demands. *Task demands* are associated with the task itself. Some occupations are inherently more stressful than others. Having to make fast decisions, decisions with less than complete information, or decisions that have relatively serious consequences are some of the things that can make some jobs stressful. The jobs of surgeon, airline pilot, and stockbroker are relatively more stressful than the jobs of general practitioner, baggage handler, and office receptionist. Although a general practitioner makes important decisions, he is also likely to have time to make a considered diagnosis and fully explore a number of different treatments. But, during surgery, the surgeon must make decisions quickly while realizing that the wrong one may endanger her patient's life.

Physical demands are stressors associated with the job setting. Working outdoors in extremely hot or cold temperatures, or even in an improperly heated or cooled office, can lead to stress. A poorly designed office, which makes it difficult for people to have privacy or promotes too little social interaction, can result in stress, as can poor lighting and inadequate work surfaces. Even more severe are actual threats to health. Examples include jobs like coal mining, poultry processing, and toxic waste handling.

Role demands can also cause stress. (Roles are discussed more fully in Chapter 13.) A role is a set of expected behaviors associated with a position in a group or organization. Stress can result from either role conflict or role ambiguity that

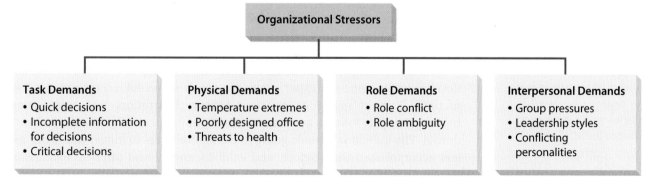

Figure 9.5
CAUSES OF WORK STRESS

There are several causes of work stress in organizations. Four general sets of organizational stressors are task demands, physical demands, role demands, and interpersonal demands.

people can experience in groups. For example, an employee who is feeling pressure from her boss to work longer hours or to travel more, while also being asked by her family for more time at home, will almost certainly experience stress as a result of role conflict.[30] Similarly, a new employee experiencing role ambiguity because of poor orientation and training practices by the organization will also suffer from stress. Excessive meetings are also a potential source of stress.[31]

Interpersonal demands are stressors associated with relationships that confront people in organizations. For example, group pressures regarding restriction of output and norm conformity can lead to stress. Leadership styles may also cause stress. An employee who feels a strong need to participate in decision making may feel stress if his boss refuses to allow participation. And individuals with conflicting personalities may experience stress if required to work too closely together. For example, a person with an internal locus of control might be frustrated when working with someone who prefers to wait and just let things happen.

Consequences of Stress   As noted earlier, the results of stress may be positive or negative. The negative consequences may be behavioral, psychological, or medical. Behaviorally, for example, stress may lead to detrimental or harmful actions, such as smoking, alcohol or drug abuse, and overeating. Other stress-induced behaviors are accident proneness, violence toward self or others, and appetite disorders.

Psychological consequences of stress interfere with an individual's mental health and well-being. These outcomes include sleep disturbances, depression, family problems, and sexual dysfunction. Managers are especially prone to sleep disturbances when they experience stress at work.[32] Medical consequences of stress affect an individual's physiological well-being. Heart disease and stroke have been linked to stress, as have headaches, backaches, ulcers and related disorders, and skin conditions such as acne and hives.

Individual stress also has direct consequences for businesses. For an operating employee, stress may translate into poor-quality work and lower productivity. For a manager, it may mean faulty decision making and disruptions in working relationships. Withdrawal behaviors can also result from stress. People who are having difficulties with stress in their job are more likely to call in sick or to leave the organization. More subtle forms of withdrawal may also occur. A manager may start missing deadlines, for example, or taking longer lunch breaks. Employees may also withdraw by developing feelings of indifference. The irritation displayed by people under great stress can make them difficult to get along with. Job satisfaction, morale, and commitment can all suffer as a result of excessive levels of stress. So, too, can motivation to perform.

Another consequence of stress is **burnout**—a feeling of exhaustion that may develop when someone experiences too much stress for an extended period of time. Burnout results in constant fatigue, frustration, and helplessness. Increased rigidity follows, as do a loss of self-confidence and psychological withdrawal. The individual dreads going to work, often puts in longer hours but gets less accomplished than before, and exhibits mental and physical exhaustion. Because of the damaging effects of burnout, some firms are taking steps to help avoid it. For example, British Airways provides all of its employees with training designed to help them recognize the symptoms of burnout and develop strategies for avoiding it.

burnout
A feeling of exhaustion that may develop when someone experiences too much stress for an extended period of time

Managing Stress

Given the potential consequences of stress, it follows that both people and organizations should be concerned about how to limit its more damaging effects. Numerous ideas and approaches have been developed to help manage stress. Some are strategies for individuals; others are strategies for organizations.[33]

One way people manage stress is through exercise. People who exercise regularly feel less tension and stress, are more self-confident, and feel more optimistic. Their better physical condition also makes them less susceptible to many common illnesses. People who do not exercise regularly, on the other hand, tend to feel more stress and are more likely to be depressed. They are also more likely to have heart attacks. And, because of their physical condition, they are more likely to contract illnesses.

Another method people use to manage stress is relaxation. Relaxation allows individuals to adapt to, and therefore better deal with, their stress. Relaxation comes in many forms, such as taking regular vacations. A recent study found that people's attitudes toward a variety of workplace characteristics improved significantly following a vacation. People can also learn to relax while on the job. For example, some experts recommend that people take regular rest breaks during their normal workday.

People can also use time management to control stress. The idea behind time management is that many daily pressures can be reduced or eliminated if individuals do a better job of managing time. One approach to time management is to make a list every morning of the things to be done that day. The items on the list are then grouped into three categories: critical activities that must be performed, important activities that should be performed, and optional or trivial things that can be delegated or postponed. The individual performs the items on the list in their order of importance.

Finally, people can manage stress through support groups. A support group can be as simple as a group of family members or friends to enjoy leisure time with. Going out after work with a couple of coworkers to a basketball game or a movie, for example, can help relieve stress built up during the day. Family and friends can help people cope with stress on an ongoing basis and during times of crisis. For example, an employee who has just learned that she did not get the promotion she has been working toward for months may find it helpful to have a good friend to lean on, talk to, or yell at. People also may make use of more elaborate and formal support groups. Community centers or churches, for example, may sponsor support groups for people who have recently gone through a divorce, the death of a loved one, or some other tragedy.

Organizations are also beginning to realize that they should be involved in helping employees cope with stress. One argument for this is that because the business is at least partially responsible for stress, it should also help relieve it. Another is that stress-related insurance claims by employees can cost the organization considerable sums of money. Still another is that workers experiencing lower levels of detrimental stress will be able to function more effectively. AT&T has initiated a series of seminars and workshops to help its employees cope with the stress they face in their jobs. The firm was prompted to develop these seminars for all three of the reasons noted above.

A wellness stress program is a special part of the organization specifically created to help deal with stress. Organizations have adopted stress-management programs, health promotion programs, and other kinds of programs for this purpose. The AT&T seminar program noted earlier is similar to this idea, but true wellness programs are ongoing activities that have a number of different components. They commonly include exercise-related activities as well as classroom instruction programs dealing with smoking cessation, weight reduction, and general stress management.

Some companies are developing their own programs or using existing programs of this type. Johns Manville, for example, has a gym at its corporate headquarters. Other firms negotiate discounted health club membership rates with local establishments. For the instructional part of the program, the organization can again either sponsor its own training or perhaps jointly sponsor seminars with a local YMCA, civic organization, or church. Organization-based fitness programs facilitate employee exercise, a very positive consideration, but such programs are also quite costly. Still, more and more companies are developing fitness programs for employees. Similarly, some companies are offering their employees periodic sabbaticals—extended breaks from work that presumably allow people to get revitalized and re-energized. Intel and McDonald's are among the firms offering the benefit.[34]

Creativity in Organizations

Creativity is yet another important component of individual behavior in organizations. *Creativity* is the ability of an individual to generate new ideas or to conceive of new perspectives on existing ideas. What makes a person creative? How do people become creative? How does the creative process work? Although psychologists have not yet discovered complete answers to these questions, examining a few general patterns can help us understand the sources of individual creativity within organizations.[35]

creativity
The ability of an individual to generate new ideas or to conceive of new perspectives on existing ideas

The Creative Individual
Numerous researchers have focused their efforts on attempting to describe the common attributes of creative individuals. These attributes generally fall into three categories: background experiences, personal traits, and cognitive abilities.

Background Experiences and Creativity   Researchers have observed that many creative individuals were raised in environments in which creativity was nurtured. Mozart was raised in a family of musicians and began composing and performing music at age six. Pierre and Marie Curie, great scientists in their own right, also raised a daughter, Irene, who won the Nobel Prize in chemistry. Thomas Edison's creativity was nurtured by his mother. However, people with background experiences very different from theirs have also been creative. Frederick Douglass was born into slavery in Tuckahoe, Maryland, and had very limited opportunities for education. Nonetheless, his powerful oratory and creative thinking helped lead to the Emancipation Proclamation, which outlawed slavery in the United States.

Personal Traits and Creativity   Certain personal traits have also been linked to creativity in individuals. The traits shared by most creative people are openness, an attraction to complexity, high levels of energy, independence and autonomy, strong self-confidence, and a strong belief that one is, in fact, creative. Individuals who possess these traits are more likely to be creative than are those who do not have them.

Some organizations actively seek ways to enhance creativity among their employees. For instance, at Electronic Arts, a videogame developer, creativity is a critical element in the firm's success. Both to counteract the stress inherent in its employees' hectic work lives and to provide a place for calm mental relaxation, Electronic Arts offers a most unusual amenity—a maze. Game developers can walk in the maze whenever they feel that their creative juices need a boost.

Cognitive Abilities and Creativity   Cognitive abilities are an individual's power to think intelligently and to analyze situations and data effectively. Intelligence may be a precondition for individual creativity—although most creative people are highly intelligent, not all intelligent people are necessarily creative. Creativity is also linked with the ability to think divergently and convergently. *Divergent thinking* is a skill that allows people to see differences among situations, phenomena, or events. *Convergent thinking* is a skill that allows people to see similarities among situations, phenomena, or events. Creative people are generally very skilled at both divergent and convergent thinking.

The Creative Process

Although creative people often report that ideas seem to come to them "in a flash," individual creative activity actually tends to progress through a series of stages. Not all creative activity has to follow these four stages, but much of it does.

Preparation   The creative process normally begins with a period of *preparation*. To make a creative contribution to business management or business services, individuals must usually receive formal training and education in business. Formal education and training are usually the most efficient ways of becoming familiar with this vast amount of research and knowledge. This is one reason for the strong

Managing in Times of Change

Managing the Flood of Ideas

Creativity is one of the hottest trends in business today. Universities, whose offerings reflect demand from business employers, have doubled their creativity courses in the past five years. Creativity training focuses on idea generation, encouraging inventiveness and risk taking. Yet some business innovators reject that approach. We don't need more "big ideas," they say. Instead, businesses should focus on effectively managing those ideas.

Margaret Heffernan, a CEO and entrepreneur, says that the problem wasn't too few good ideas, it's too many. "We scarcely had the resources to deliver on *one* good idea," she states. "We were spread way too thin." Resource constraints helped because each new idea was screened carefully. "[Scrutiny] depersonalized the decision-making, making it less stressful and a lot faster. [It] sharpened those creative minds eager to contribute bright ideas." She concludes, "Imagination without discipline wastes everyone's time."

Marissa Ann Mayer agrees, saying, "Creativity loves constraints, but they must be balanced with a healthy disregard for the impossible." As vice president in charge of Google's user experience, she limits the number of items on a toolbar. When that number is exceeded, new functions can only be added by eliminating an existing one. New-product prototyping must last less than one week. "Speed lets you try out more ideas, increasing the odds of success," she says. "Speed also lets you fail faster," so employees don't become overly invested in a poor idea.

Another believer is economics professor Robin Hanson. "To get more innovation we may want less, not more, creativity," she claims. "What society needs is . . . better ways to encourage people to focus on more important issues, identify the most promising ideas, and tell the right people about them," she explains. "We need to better manage the flood of ideas we already have and to reward managers for actually executing them."

The definition of creativity itself is at stake. Is creativity the invention of fashion trends that will last just one season? Or is creativity the invention of a lasting innovation, such as the television or cell phone? If you choose the latter, then creativity is less about the brilliant insight, and more about the hard work, intelligence, and experience to see the insight turned into a real and useful innovation.

References: Jeffrey Gangemi, "Creativity Comes to B-School," *BusinessWeek*, March 26, 2006, www.businessweek.com on February 10, 2007; Robin Hanson, "The Myth of Creativity," *BusinessWeek*, July 3, 2006, www.businessweek.com on February 10, 2007; Margaret Heffernan, "Just Say No," *Fast Company*, March 20, 2006, www.fastcompany.com on February 10, 2007; Marissa Ann Mayer, "Creativity Loves Constraints," *BusinessWeek*, February 13, 2006, www.businessweek.com on February 10, 2007.

demand for undergraduate and master's level business education. Formal business education can be an effective way for an individual to get "up to speed" and begin making creative contributions quickly. Experiences that managers have on the job after their formal training has finished can also contribute to the creative process. In an important sense, the education and training of creative people never really ends. It continues as long as they remain interested in the world and curious about the way things work. Bruce Roth earned a Ph.D. in chemistry and then spent years working in the pharmaceutical industry learning more and more about chemical compounds and how they work in human beings. These forms of learning represent his preparation for creative breakthroughs.

Incubation The second phase of the creative process is *incubation*—a period of less intense conscious concentration during which the knowledge and ideas acquired during preparation mature and develop. A curious aspect of incubation is that it is often helped along by pauses in concentrated rational thought. Some creative people rely on physical activity such as jogging or swimming to provide a break from thinking. Others may read or listen to music. Sometimes sleep may even supply the needed pause. Bruce Roth eventually joined Warner-Lambert, an up-and-coming drug company, to help develop medication to lower cholesterol. In his spare time, Roth read mystery novels and hiked in the mountains. He later acknowledged that this was when he did his best thinking. Similarly, twice a year Bill Gates retreats to a secluded wooded cabin to reflect on trends in technology; it is during these weeks, he says, that he develops his sharpest insights into where Microsoft should be heading.[36]

Insight   Usually occurring after preparation and incubation, *insight* is a spontaneous breakthrough in which the creative person achieves a new understanding of some problem or situation. Insight represents a coming together of all the scattered thoughts and ideas that were maturing during incubation. It may occur suddenly or develop slowly over time. Insight can be triggered by some external event, such as a new experience or an encounter with new data, which forces the individual to think about old issues and problems in new ways, or it can be a completely internal event in which patterns of thought finally coalesce in ways that generate new understanding. One day Bruce Roth was reviewing some data from some earlier studies that had found the new drug under development to be no more effective than other drugs already available. But this time he saw some statistical relationships that had not been identified previously. He knew then that he had a major breakthrough on his hands.

Verification   Once an insight has occurred, *verification* determines the validity or truthfulness of the insight. For many creative ideas, verification includes scientific experiments to determine whether the insight actually leads to the results expected. Verification may also include the development of a product or service prototype. A prototype is one product or a very small number of products built just to see if the ideas behind this new product actually work. Product prototypes are rarely sold to the public but are very valuable in verifying the insights developed in the creative process. Once the new product or service is developed, verification in the marketplace is the ultimate test of the creative idea behind it. Bruce Roth and his colleagues set to work testing the new drug compound and eventually won FDA approval. The drug, named Lipitor, is already the largest-selling pharmaceutical in history. And Pfizer, the firm that bought Warner-Lambert in a hostile takeover, is expected to soon earn more than $10 billion a year on the drug.[37]

Enhancing Creativity in Organizations

Managers who wish to enhance and promote creativity in their organizations can do so in a variety of ways.[38] One important method for enhancing creativity is to make it a part of the organization's culture, often through explicit goals. Firms that truly want to stress creativity, like 3M and Rubbermaid, for example, state goals that some percentage of future revenues are to be gained from new products. This clearly communicates that creativity and innovation are valued.

Another important part of enhancing creativity is to reward creative successes while being careful not to punish creative failures. Many ideas that seem worthwhile on paper fail to pan out in reality. If the first person to come up with an idea that fails is fired or otherwise punished, others in the organization will become more cautious in their own work. And, as a result, fewer creative ideas will emerge.

Types of Workplace Behavior

workplace behavior
A pattern of action by the members of an organization that directly or indirectly influences organizational effectiveness

Now that we have looked closely at how individual differences can influence behavior in organizations, let's turn our attention to what we mean by workplace behavior. *Workplace behavior* is a pattern of action by the members of an organization that directly or indirectly influences organizational effectiveness. Important workplace behaviors include performance and productivity, absenteeism and turnover, and organizational citizenship. Unfortunately, a variety of dysfunctional behaviors can also occur in organizational settings.

Performance Behaviors

performance behaviors
The total set of work-related behaviors that the organization expects the individual to display

Performance behaviors are the total set of work-related behaviors that the organization expects the individual to display. Thus they derive from the psychological contract. For some jobs, performance behaviors can be narrowly defined and easily measured. For example, an assembly-line worker who sits by a moving conveyor and attaches parts to a product as it passes by has relatively few performance behaviors. He or she is expected to remain at the workstation and correctly attach the parts. Performance can often be assessed quantitatively by counting the percentage of parts correctly attached.

For many other jobs, however, performance behaviors are more diverse and much more difficult to assess. For example, consider the case of a research and development scientist at Merck. The scientist works in a lab trying to find new scientific breakthroughs that have commercial potential. The scientist must apply knowledge learned in graduate school with experience gained from previous research. Intuition and creativity are also important elements. And the desired breakthrough may take months or even years to accomplish. As we discussed in Chapter 8, organizations rely on a number of different methods for evaluating performance. The key, of course, is to match the evaluation mechanism with the job being performed.

Withdrawal Behaviors

absenteeism
When an individual does not show up for work

Another important type of work-related behavior is that which results in withdrawal—absenteeism and turnover. *Absenteeism* occurs when an individual does not show up for work. The cause may be legitimate (illness, jury duty, death in the family, and so forth) or feigned (reported as legitimate but actually just an excuse to stay home). When an employee is absent, her or his work does not get done at all, or a substitute must be hired to do it. In either case, the quantity or quality of actual output is likely to suffer. Obviously, some absenteeism is expected. The key concern of organizations is to minimize feigned absenteeism and to reduce legitimate absences as much as possible. High absenteeism may be a symptom of other problems as well, such as job dissatisfaction and low morale.

turnover
When people quit their jobs

Turnover occurs when people quit their jobs. An organization usually incurs costs in replacing individuals who have quit, but if turnover involves especially productive people, it is even more costly. Turnover seems to result from a number of factors, including aspects of the job, the organization, the individual, the labor market, and family influences. In general, a poor person-job fit is also a likely cause of turnover. Moreover, during periods of labor shortages companies may experience higher turnover due to the abundance of attractive alternative jobs that are available to highly qualified individuals.[39]

Efforts to directly manage turnover are frequently fraught with difficulty, even in organizations that concentrate on rewarding good performers. Of course, some turnover is inevitable, and in some cases it may even be desirable. For example, if the organization is trying to cut costs by reducing its staff, having people voluntarily choose to leave is preferable to having to terminate their jobs. And, if the people who choose to leave are low performers or express high levels of job dissatisfaction, the organization may also benefit from turnover.

Organizational Citizenship

Organizational citizenship is the behavior of individuals that makes a positive overall contribution to the organization.[40] Consider, for example, an employee who does work that is acceptable in terms of both quantity and quality. However, she refuses to work overtime, will not help newcomers learn the ropes, and is generally unwilling to make any contribution to the organization beyond the strict performance of her job. Although this person may be seen as a good performer, she is not likely to be seen as a good organizational citizen.

Another employee may exhibit a comparable level of performance. In addition, however, he will always work late when the boss asks him to, take time to help newcomers learn their way around, and is perceived as being helpful and committed to the organization's success. Although his level of performance may be seen as equal to that of the first worker, he is also likely to be seen as a better organizational citizen.

The determinant of organizational citizenship behaviors is likely to be a complex mosaic of individual, social, and organizational variables. For example, the personality, attitudes, and needs of the individual will have to be consistent with citizenship behaviors. Similarly, the social context in which the individual works, or work group, will need to facilitate and promote such behaviors (we discuss group dynamics in Chapter 13). And the organization itself, especially its culture, must be capable of promoting, recognizing, and rewarding these types of behaviors if they are to be maintained. Although the study of organizational citizenship is still in its infancy, preliminary research suggests that it may play a powerful role in organizational effectiveness.[41]

> **organizational citizenship**
> The behavior of individuals that makes a positive overall contribution to the organization

Dysfunctional Behaviors

Some work-related behaviors are dysfunctional in nature. *Dysfunctional behaviors* are those that detract from, rather than contribute to, organizational performance. Two of the more common ones, absenteeism and turnover, are discussed above. But other forms of dysfunctional behavior may be even more costly for an organization. Theft and sabotage, for example, result in direct financial costs for an organization. Sexual and racial harassment also cost an organization, both indirectly (by lowering morale, producing fear, and driving off valuable employees) and directly (through financial liability if the organization responds inappropriately). So, too, can politicized behavior, intentionally misleading others in the organization, spreading malicious rumors, and similar activities. Workplace violence is also a growing concern in many organizations. Violence by disgruntled workers or former workers results in dozens of deaths and injuries each year.[42]

> **dysfunctional behaviors**
> Those that detract from, rather than contribute to, organizational performance

Summary of Key Points

1. Explain the nature of the individual-organization relationship.
   - A basic framework that can be used to facilitate this understanding is the psychological contract—the set of expectations held by people with respect to what they will contribute to the organization and what they expect to get in return.
   - Organizations strive to achieve an optimal person-job fit, but this process is complicated by the existence of individual differences.

2. Define personality and describe personality attributes that affect behavior in organizations.
   - Personality is the relatively stable set of psychological and behavioral attributes that distinguish one person from another.
     - The "Big Five" personality traits are agreeableness, conscientiousness, negative emotionality, extraversion, and openness.
   - The Myers-Briggs framework can also be a useful mechanism for understanding personality.
     - Other important traits are locus of control, self-efficacy, authoritarianism, Machiavellianism, self-esteem, and risk propensity.
   - Emotional intelligence, a fairly new concept, may provide additional insights into personality.

3. Discuss individual attitudes in organizations and how they affect behavior.
   - Attitudes are based on emotion, knowledge, and intended behavior.
   - Whereas personality is relatively stable, some attitudes can be formed and changed easily. Others are more constant.
   - Job satisfaction or dissatisfaction and organizational commitment are important work-related attitudes.

4. Describe basic perceptual processes and the role of attributions in organizations.
   - Perception is the set of processes by which an individual becomes aware of and interprets information about the environment.

   - Basic perceptual processes include selective perception and stereotyping.
   - Perception and attribution are closely related.

5. Discuss the causes and consequences of stress and describe how it can be managed.
   - Stress is an individual's response to a strong stimulus.
   - The general adaptation syndrome outlines the basic stress process.
   - Stress can be caused by task, physical, role, and interpersonal demands.
   - Consequences of stress include organizational and individual outcomes, as well as burnout.
   - Several things can be done to manage stress.

6. Describe creativity and its role in organizations.
   - Creativity is the capacity to generate new ideas.
   - Creative people tend to have certain profiles of background experiences, personal traits, and cognitive abilities.
   - The creative process itself includes preparation, incubation, insight, and verification.

7. Explain how workplace behaviors can directly or indirectly influence organizational effectiveness.
   - Workplace behavior is a pattern of action by the members of an organization that directly or indirectly influences organizational effectiveness.
   - Performance behaviors are the set of work-related behaviors that the organization expects the individual to display to fulfill the psychological contract.
   - Basic withdrawal behaviors are absenteeism and turnover.
   - Organizational citizenship refers to behavior that makes a positive overall contribution to the organization.
   - Dysfunctional behaviors can be very harmful to an organization.

Discussion Questions

Questions for Review

1. What is a psychological contract? List the things that might be included in individual contributions. List the things that might be included in organizational inducements.

2. Describe the three components of attitudes and tell how the components are related. What is cognitive dissonance? How do individuals resolve cognitive dissonance?

3. Identify and discuss the steps in the creative process. What can an organization do to increase employees' creativity?

4. Identify and describe several important workplace behaviors.

Questions for Analysis

1. Organizations are increasing their use of personality tests to screen job applicants. What are the advantages and disadvantages of this approach? What can managers do to avoid some of the potential pitfalls?

2. As a manager, how can you tell that an employee is experiencing job satisfaction? How can you tell that employees are highly committed to the organization? If a worker is not satisfied, what can a manager do to improve satisfaction? What can a manager do to improve organizational commitment?

3. Managers cannot pay equal attention to every piece of information, so selective perception is a fact of life. How does selective perception help managers? How does it create difficulties for them? How can managers increase their "good" selective perception and decrease the "bad"?

4. Write the psychological contract you have in this class. In other words, what do you contribute, and what inducements are available? Ask your professor to tell the class about the psychological contract that he or she intended to establish with the students in your class. How does the professor's intended contract compare with the one you wrote? If there are differences, why do you think the differences exist? Share your ideas with the class.

5. Assume that you are going to hire three new employees for the department store you manage. One will sell shoes, one will manage the toy department, and one will work in the stockroom. Identify the basic characteristics you want in each of the people in order to achieve a good person-job fit.

Building Effective Diagnostic Skills

Exercise Overview

Diagnostic skills help a manager visualize the most appropriate response to a situation. Individual differences in the workplace require that an effective manager have the ability to accurately diagnose situations that vary by individual characteristics.

Exercise Background

Your instructor will divide the class into small groups. Assume that you and your fellow group members are responsible for hiring employees for a sporting goods store. You will need to hire one person for each of the following positions:

- Shoe sales associate
- Designer of in-store displays and advertisements
- Stock clerk
- Manager of human resources
- Outside sales representative to manage sales to local sports teams
- Bookkeeper

Exercise Task

1. As a group, identify a list of characteristics that you would want in each of the new hires in order to achieve a good person-job fit.

2. Note any areas of disagreement and try to understand each member's reasons for their opinion.

3. In what ways should the people's characteristics be similar?

4. In what ways should they be different?

5. Discuss the results as a class. How do individual perceptions and attitudes affect their list of desired characteristics.

Adapted from Jay B. Barney and Ricky W. Griffin, *The Management of Organizations.* Copyright © 1992 by Houghton Mifflin Company. Used with permission.

Building Effective Conceptual Skills

Exercise Overview

Conceptual skills reflect a person's abilities to think in the abstract. Conceptual skills are developed in this exercise as you describe a psychological contract.

Exercise Background

A psychological contract exists between an employee and employer, but it can also exist whenever an understanding between a person and an organization is reached. For example, a psychological contract can exist for volunteers or charitable contributors to organizations, as well as between students and their school or professor. In this exercise, you will analyze a psychological contract by examining the relationship between you and your professor in your Management course.

Exercise Task

1. Study Figure 9.1, The Psychological Contract. Then use the Psychological Contract Sheets in this exercise to list items from the psychological contract you have in this class. What do you contribute to your class, and what inducements are offered by your instructor?

2. Consider the items on the Psychological Contract Sheets. Which inducements are created by your professor and which are offered by your institution? Which contributions are you making to benefit your professor or class, and which are you making for your institution? Is it difficult for you to manage a psychological contract that exists on two levels at once? Why or why not?

3. As a class, compare the information from your Psychological Contract Sheets. In what ways are students' ideas similar and in what ways are they different?

4. This exercise should highlight for you the fact that individuals vary both in the contributions they can or are willing to make and in the inducements they require. In addition, individuals vary in their perceptions of "fairness." What seems fair to one individual may not to another. What lessons does this exercise teach you that might be useful in your future or current career? How can you use your knowledge of psychological contracts in the future?

Adapted from Jay B. Barney and Ricky W. Griffin, *The Management of Organizations.* Copyright © 1992 by Houghton Mifflin Company. Used with permission.

The Psychological Contract Sheets

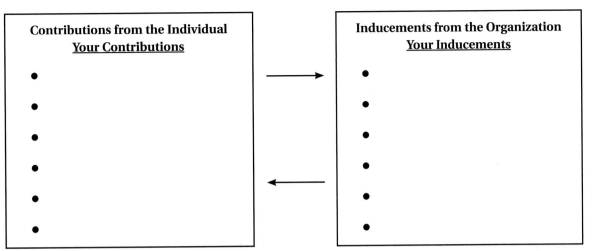

Building Effective Time-Management Skills

Exercise Overview

Time-management skills help people prioritize work, work more efficiently, and delegate appropriately. Poor time-management skills, in turn, may result in stress. This exercise will help you relate time-management skills to stress reduction.

Exercise Background

List several of the major events or expectations that cause stress for you. Stressors might involve school (hard classes, too many exams), work (financial pressures, demanding work schedule), or personal circumstances (friends, romance, family). Be as specific as possible. Also try to identify at least ten different stressors.

Exercise Task

Using the list that you developed, do each of the following:

1. Evaluate the extent to which poor time-management skills on your part play a role in how each stressor affects you. For example, do exams cause stress because you delay studying?

2. Develop a strategy for using time more efficiently in relation to each stressor that is related to time.

3. Note interrelationships among different kinds of stressors and time. For example, financial pressures may cause you to work, but work may interfere with school. Can any of these interrelationships be managed more effectively vis-à-vis time?

4. How do you manage the stress in your life? Is it possible to manage stress in a more time-effective manner?

Skills Self-Assessment Instrument

Personality Types at Work

Interpersonal skills reflect the ability to communicate with, understand, and motivate individuals and groups. This exercise introduces a widely used tool for personality assessment. It shows how an understanding of personality can aid in developing effective interpersonal relationships within organizations.

Introduction: There are many different ways of viewing personality, and one that is widely used is called the Myers-Briggs Type Indicator. According to Isabel Myers, each individual's personality type varies in four dimensions:

1. *Extroversion (E) versus Introversion (I).* Extroverts get their energy from being around other people, whereas

introverts are worn out by others and need solitude to recharge their energy.

2. *Sensing (S) versus Intuition (N).* The sensing type prefers concrete things and physical experiences, whereas intuitives prefer abstract concepts and imagination.

3. *Thinking (T) versus Feeling (F).* Thinking individuals base their decisions more on logic and reason, whereas feeling individuals base their decisions more on feelings and emotions.

4. *Judging (J) versus Perceiving (P).* People who are the judging type enjoy completion or being finished, whereas perceiving types enjoy the process and open-ended situations.

On the basis of their answers to a survey, individuals are classified into sixteen personality types—all the possible combinations of the four dimensions above. The resulting personality type is then expressed as a four-character code, such as ESTP or INFJ. These four-character codes can then be used to describe an individual's preferred way of interacting with others.

Instructions:

1. Use an online Myers-Briggs assessment form to assess your personality type. One place to find the form online is www.keirsey.com/scripts/newkts.cgi. This website also contains additional information about personality type. (Note: This site requires free registration, but you do not need to pay fees or agree to receive emails in order to take the Temperament Sorter.) Alternatively, your institution's Career Center or other organizations may offer a Myers-Briggs assessment service.

2. When you have determined the four-letter code for your personality type, obtain a handout from your professor. The handout will show how your personality type affects your preferred style of working and your leadership style.

Reprinted by permission of the author Margaret Hill.
For interpretation, see Interpretations of Skills Self-Assessment Instruments in the appendix near the end of this text.

Experiential Exercise

Stress Test

Job-related stress is very common in organizations—almost everyone experiences stress some of the time. Stress can also occur in nonwork settings, such as school or family life. While a moderate level of stress can have positive effects, too much stress can lead to physical and mental health problems, absenteeism and turnover, low productivity and morale, and eventually, burnout.

Investigate the demands of your Management class to assess the extent of factors that increase stress, writing down your answers individually. Discuss your perceptions with a small group of classmates. Then as a group, suggest changes that would make your class less stressful.

Step 1: Working alone, assess the task demands associated with your Management class. In this category, include items such as the extent to which you are fully informed and can therefore make informed decisions. Also consider the time pressure and the possible consequences of your actions.

Assess the physical demands associated with your Management class. In this category, include items such

as the location and facilities available in the classroom. Also include lighting, heating, ventilation, seating, amount of space, flexibility of the space, and so on.

Assess the role demands associated with your Management class. In this category, consider the role you play as a student. Do you understand what is expected of you in this role? Are you comfortable in this role? Does your role as a student conflict with any of the other important roles that you play?

Assess the interpersonal demands associated with your Management class. In this category, consider your relationships with the instructor and your fellow students. Any personality conflicts or pressure to conform to group norms would tend to increase stress.

Step 2: In a small group, discuss your answers. Try to recognize patterns of similarities and differences. Then discuss changes that could be made that would reduce stress. Be sure to consider changes that could be made by your institution or department, by your instructor, and by the students.

Step 3: Discuss your conclusions with the class and your instructor.

CHAPTER CLOSING CASE

STEVE JOBS: "THE LEADING-EDGE GUY IN THE WORLD"

Personality can refer to a person of prominence or notoriety. Sometimes the word is used more correctly to refer a set of enduring character traits. Steve Jobs, the charismatic, colorful, and controversial co-founder and head of Apple Computer, fits both definitions. He's a personality who has an interesting personality. Jobs is seen as an inspiring visionary on the one hand, and on the other hand, as difficult and abrasive. His complex personality encompasses many contradictions and yet is a source of his professional success, as well as the success of his several business ventures.

After one semester at Reed College, Jobs worked briefly at Hewlett-Packard, where he met fellow computer geek Steve Wozniak. Jobs had a short stint at Atari, an early video game maker, and backpacked around India. In 1976, when Jobs was 21, he convinced Wozniak to sell a personal computer Wozniak designed and built for himself. This was the first commercially available personal computer. Apple Computer's initial public offering in 1980 created many millionaires, including Jobs.

As CEO of Apple, Jobs oversaw the development of the enormously successful Macintosh. Apple Computer grew tremendously, but Jobs's tenure was marred by controversy and difficulties. His idealistic vision and impossibly high standards drove the firm to ever-greater achievements. Yet after several failed designs and cost overruns, Apple hired John Sculley, former CEO of Pepsi, to run Apple. Jobs and Sculley clashed continually and in 1985, Apple's board of directors forced Jobs to resign. Larry Tesler, then Apple's chief scientist, describes the mood at Apple. "People in the company had very mixed feelings about it. Everyone had been terrorized by Steve Jobs at some point or another, and so there was a certain relief that the terrorist would be gone," says Tesler. "And on the other hand I think there was incredible respect for Steve Jobs by the very same people, and we were all very worried what would happen to this company without the visionary, without the founder, without the charisma."

Jobs protested by selling his Apple stock and starting NeXT, a high-end computer company. NeXT made the PC used by Tim Berners-Lee to write the software code called "WorldWideWeb 1.0," the basis for today's Internet. In 1986, Jobs purchased George Lucas's computer animation studio, Pixar Animation. Jobs's management at Pixar was very hands-off, but he pushed NeXT constantly, resulting in many innovative products.

In 1996, Apple purchased NeXT for $400 million and Jobs returned to his now-ailing and almost bankrupt company. Within a year, he was named CEO of Apple. His leadership produced the iPod and launched the iTunes online music store. Meanwhile, Pixar released hit after hit, including *Toy Story*, *Finding Nemo*, *The Incredibles*, and *Cars*, in partnership with Disney. Disney's then-CEO Michael Eisner and Jobs fought bitterly and publicly, but in 2005, Bob Iger became CEO at Disney. Iger quickly established better relations with Jobs. In 2006, Disney purchased Pixar for $7.4 billion, making Jobs a board member and Disney's largest shareholder, controlling 7 percent of stock.

Today, Jobs is a successful businessman—the forty-ninth richest person in the world, with a net worth estimated at $4.9 billion. His personality has been instrumental in his achievements. "If Steve has a good relationship with you, there's nobody better in the world to work with. He trusts you, and he listens, and he bounces his ideas off you," says Edgar Woolard, Jr., a former Apple board member. Woolard says Jobs is "an absolute perfectionist" who is "incredibly creative with great vision." Colleagues portray Jobs as persuasive, charismatic, energetic, confident, and powerful.

These traits point to success, yet the darker side of these same traits can be problematic. Jobs is seen as both an evangelist and an *enfant terrible*. He can be erratic, tempestuous, mercurial, obsessive, aggressive, demanding, and grandiose. According to some, he's a control freak and a micromanager. He is often outspokenly critical and sarcastic, with unrealistically high standards and a bad temper.

Apple has been transformed into a powerhouse. Its new products are blockbusters. The firm's stock has doubled in the last year and Apple ranks eleventh in *Fortune*'s list of "Most Admired Companies." Pixar and Disney will continue to create award-winning films, and Apple has diversified into Web videos and cell phones. These accomplishments spring from Jobs's drive to improve and innovate. *Fortune* writer Fred Vogelstein admires Jobs, saying, "[He] throws the status quo into disorder and rides that chaos to the front of the pack." "He wants to be the leading-edge guy—which he is," states Woolard, who is also a fan. "He's the leading-edge guy in the world."

CASE QUESTIONS

1. Describe Steve Jobs's personality using the Big Five traits and other personality traits discussed in your text.

2. How does Jobs's personality help him to be a better leader? How does his personality detract from his ability to lead?

3. How do personality traits support creativity? What personality traits allow Jobs to be creative?

REFERENCES

Peter Burrows, "An Insider's Take on Steve Jobs," *BusinessWeek*, January 30, 2006, www.businessweek.com on April 30, 2006; Peter Burrows, "iPods, Sure. But Don't Go Dissing Macs," *BusinessWeek*, April 3, 2006, pp. 68–69; Peter Burrows and Ronald Grover, "Steve Jobs' Magic Kingdom," *BusinessWeek*, February 6, 2006, pp. 63–69; Peter Burrows and Roger O. Crockett, "Turning Cell Phones on Their Ear," *BusinessWeek*, January 22, 2007, pp. 40–41; *Triumph of the Nerds: The Rise of Accidental Empires*, Dir. Robert X. Cringely, PBS, 1996; Richard Siklos, "A Video Business Model Ready to Move Beyond Beta," *New York Times*, September 17, 2006, p. BU3; William C. Taylor and Polly LaBarre, "How Pixar Adds a New School of Thought to Disney," *New York Times*, January 29, 2006, p. BU3; Fred Vogelstein, "Mastering the Art of Disruption," *Fortune*, February 6, 2006, pp. 23–24.

YOU MAKE THE CALL

W. L. Gore Nurtures Talent and Creativity

1. Which personality traits would create a good person-job fit for a prospective employee at W. L. Gore? Which would create a bad fit?

2. Would you like to work at W. L. Gore? Why or why not?

3. Should other organizations attempt to implement some of Gore's practices? What benefits would they receive from doing so? What risks would they take by doing so?

4. In your opinion, will it be possible for Gore's culture to survive intact as the company grows? If yes, tell what actions Gore employees must take to ensure the culture's survival. If no, explain the forces that will make it impossible for the culture to survive.

Test Prepper

college.hmco.com/pic/griffinfund5e

You've read the chapter, studied the key terms, and the exam is any day now. Think you're ready to ace it? Take this sample test to gauge your comprehension of chapter material. You can check your answers at the back of the book. Want more test questions? Visit the student website at http://college.hmco.com/pic/griffinfund5e/ and take the ACE quizzes for more practice.

1. T F The extent to which individual contributions match organizational inducements is called attitude.

2. T F Conscientiousness refers to the number of goals on which a person focuses.

3. T F Type A people are more likely to experience stress than Type B people.

4. T F A feeling of exhaustion that may develop when someone experiences too much stress for an extended period of time is called burnout.

5. T F Sung is good at assimilating information from different sources and recognizing similarities between situations. This is known as contra-dictory thinking.

6. Managers who believe that they are NOT in control of their own destiny and success in the organization are said to have a(n)

    a. external locus of control.

    b. internal locus of control.

    c. negative emotionality.

    d. psychological contract.

    e. positive emotionality.

7. A manager who says, "I'll never work with that person again," is focusing on which component of an attitude?

    a. Cognitive

    b. Affective

    c. Intentional

    d. Risk propensity

    e. Dissonant

8. _____ is an attitude that reflects the extent to which an individual is gratified by or fulfilled in his or her work.

    a. Organizational commitment

    b. Cognitive dissonance

    c. Perception

    d. Machiavellianism

    e. Job satisfaction

9. The process of screening out information that causes us discomfort is known as

    a. positive emotionality.

    b. negative affectivity.

    c. authoritarianism.

    d. selective perception.

    e. stereotyping.

10. For many creative ideas, _____ includes scientific experiments to determine whether or not the insight actually leads to the results expected.

    a. convergent thinking

    b. preparation

    c. incubation

    d. insight

    e. verification

chapter 10

Managing Employee Motivation and Performance

FIRST THINGS FIRST

Motivation Without Borders

"There is nothing like seeing a child deathly skinny and watching that child become healthy. It's amazing."

—LISABETH LIST, RN, MSF VOLUNTEER

It's not just your imagination. The world is becoming a more disastrous place. There were 2.6 times more natural disasters from 1993 to 2002 than there were in the 1960s. When an Indian Ocean tsunami strikes, volunteers from Doctors Without Borders are the first responders. When civil wars break out in Sudan and Congo, Doctors Without Borders go. They also show up for an earthquake in Pakistan, election violence in Haiti, and flooding in Guatemala, wherever a population is in danger. The nonprofit, nongovernmental organization (NGO) treats medical crises, provides aid to victims of war and famine, builds healthcare facilities, fights epidemics, and gives care to excluded groups and refugees.

Doctors Without Borders, another name for Médecins Sans Frontières (MSF), originated in France in 1971. From national headquarters in nineteen countries, MSF served seventy countries in 2005. African nations received the most aid, $260 million in all, while millions more were spent in Afghanistan, Chechnya, Iraq, and Cambodia.

Aid ranges from vaccinations and food to mental health counseling and antiviral medicines. In addition, MSF offers public health education and training for local caregivers. The nonprofit's list of the "Top 10 Most Underreported Humanitarian Stories" raises public awareness about the lack of attention given to worldwide medical crises. One concern MSF highlights: In 2006, of the 14,512 minutes of major evening newscasts in the United States, just 7 minutes focused on humanitarian stories. MSF also participates in a new-drug research consortium. For its efforts, MSF was awarded the Nobel Peace Prize in 1999.

Volunteers are physicians and other health professionals; in addition there are experts in communications, information technology, water and sanitation engineering, and distribution. MSF recruits workers through word of mouth and public relations. Applicants must have specialized and professional qualifications as well as personal characteristics such as adaptability, teamwork, commitment, and ability to function under stress. Volunteers are expected to work continuously, in primitive and stressful conditions, with risky, infectious diseases. MSF volunteers often work in hostile areas and under armed guards, and employees are sometimes the target of violence, as were the five workers killed in a 2004 ambush in Afghanistan. Experienced MSF member and nurse Pierre LePlante tells of working in Rwanda and Somalia for seven days a week, 10 to 16 hours daily, while being threatened with automatic weapons.

Why are highly qualified people, who could be earning top salaries in more conventional and comfortable jobs, volunteering to work under brutal conditions for so little compensation? And why do 70 percent of the members return after their first year's experience? Although experienced volunteers qualify for a small salary and benefits, the pay is low, even compared to that of other nonprofits and NGOs.

Nayana Somaiah, an Indian-trained physician who practiced in Canada, explains her initial motivation: "I was drawn to going back to the developing world. . . . I was going to . . . join an organization that could put my skills and sense of adventure to use." After beginning work in Nigeria, her feelings changed. "Slowly the poverty that surrounded me took away my naïve sense of adventure . . . it hit me really hard." Somaiah's realization of the true nature of her work is echoed in the words of Lisabeth List, a nurse and MSF volunteer. "MSF is not a working holiday," List says, "nor a way to see the world."

What most MSF volunteers cherish most is the chance to make a difference in someone's life. "There is nothing like seeing a child deathly skinny and watching that child become healthy," states List. "It's amazing. I think working with starving people is the best thing I've done." Other members mention the career opportunities and valuable experience they gained as MSF volunteers, including everything from patient care to training to advising local governments.

LEARNING OBJECTIVES
After studying this chapter, you should be able to:
- Characterize the nature of motivation.
- Identify and describe the major content perspectives on motivation.
- Identify and describe the major process perspectives on motivation.
- Describe reinforcement perspectives on motivation.
- Identify and describe popular motivational strategies.
- Describe the role of organizational reward systems in motivation.

These Doctors Without Borders volunteers are transferring medical supplies across a river in southern Lebanon after the only bridge over the river was bombed during a dispute with Israel.

Surgeon Wei Cheng and his wife Karin Moorhouse wrote *No One Can Stop the Rain*, a book about their MSF volunteer experience in Angola. By writing, they fulfill MSF's commitment to *temoinage*, or "bearing witness." They discuss their motives: "[T]he rewards are tremendous. The [Angolans'] ability to endure in terrible circumstances touched us to the core. Our experience was both inspiring and humbling."[1]

Several different factors may cause managers to put in long hours—employer expectations, demanding workloads, or the sheer enjoyment of the work are all things that motivate some people to work nights and weekends. Likewise, a number of factors are also suggesting that change may be in the wind, factors such as a growing desire among younger people to lead more balanced lives and the recognition that long hours may not equate to higher performance. The trick is figuring out how to create a system in which employees can receive rewards that they genuinely want yet lead a balanced life while performing in ways that fit the organization's goals and objectives.

In most settings, people can actually choose how hard they work and how much effort they expend. Thus managers need to understand how and why employees make different choices regarding their own performance. The key ingredient behind this choice is motivation, the subject of this chapter. We first examine the nature of employee motivation and then explore the major perspectives on motivation. Newly emerging approaches are then discussed. We conclude with a description of rewards and their role in motivation.

The Nature of Motivation

motivation
The set of forces that cause people to behave in certain ways

Motivation is the set of forces that cause people to behave in certain ways.[2] On any given day, an employee may choose to work as hard as possible at a job, work just hard enough to avoid a reprimand, or do as little as possible. The goal for the manager is to maximize the likelihood of the first behavior and minimize the likelihood of the last. This goal becomes all the more important when we understand how important motivation is in the workplace.

Individual performance is generally determined by three things: motivation (the desire to do the job), ability (the capability to do the job), and the work environment (the resources needed to do the job). If an employee lacks ability, the manager can provide training or replace the worker. If there is a resource problem, the manager can correct it. But, if motivation is the problem, the task for the manager is more challenging.[3] Individual behavior is a complex phenomenon, and the manager may be hard pressed to figure out the precise nature of the problem and how to solve it. Thus motivation is important because of its significance as a determinant of performance and because of its intangible character.[4]

The motivation framework in Figure 10.1 is a good starting point for understanding how motivated behavior occurs. The motivation process begins with a need or deficiency. For example, when a worker feels that she is underpaid, she experiences a need for more income. In response, the worker searches for ways to satisfy the need, such as working harder to try to earn a raise or seeking a new job. Next she chooses an option to pursue. After carrying out the chosen option—working harder

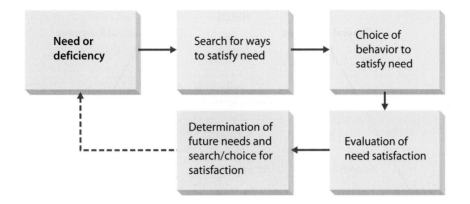

Figure 10.1
THE MOTIVATION FRAMEWORK

The motivation process progresses through a series of discrete steps. Content, process, and reinforcement perspectives on motivation address different parts of this process.

and putting in more hours for a reasonable period of time, for example—she then evaluates her success. If her hard work resulted in a pay raise, she probably feels good about things and will continue to work hard. But, if no raise has been provided, she is likely to try another option.

Content Perspectives on Motivation

Content perspectives on motivation deal with the first part of the motivation process—needs and need deficiencies. More specially, ***content perspectives*** address the question: What factors in the workplace motivate people? Labor leaders often argue that workers can be motivated by more pay, shorter working hours, and improved working conditions. Meanwhile, some experts suggest that motivation can be more effectively enhanced by providing employees with more autonomy and greater responsibility.[5] Both of these views represent content views of motivation. The former asserts that motivation is a function of pay, working hours, and working conditions; the latter suggests that autonomy and responsibility are the causes of motivation. Two widely known content perspectives on motivation are the needs hierarchy and the two-factor theory.

> *content perspectives*
> Approach to motivation that tries to answer the question: What factor or factors motivate people?

The Needs Hierarchy Approach

Needs hierarchies assume that people have different needs that can be arranged in a hierarchy of importance. The best known needs hierarchy was advanced by Abraham Maslow, a human relationist, who argued that people are motivated to satisfy five need levels.[6] ***Maslow's hierarchy of needs*** is shown in Figure 10.2. At the bottom of the hierarchy are the *physiological needs*—things like food, sex, and air, which represent basic issues of survival and biological function. In organizations, these needs are generally satisfied by adequate wages and the work environment itself, which provides restrooms, adequate lighting, comfortable temperatures, and ventilation.

Next are the *security needs* for a secure physical and emotional environment. Examples include the desire for housing and clothing and the need to be free from worry about money and job security. These needs can be satisfied in the workplace by job continuity (no layoffs), a grievance system (to protect against arbitrary supervisory actions), and an adequate insurance and retirement benefit package (for security against illness and provision of income in later life). Even today,

> *Maslow's hierarchy of needs*
> Suggests that people must satisfy five groups of needs in order—physiological, security, belongingness, esteem, and self-actualization

Figure 10.2

MASLOW'S HIERARCHY OF NEEDS

Maslow's hierarchy suggests that human needs can be classified into five categories and that these categories can be arranged in a hierarchy of importance. A manager should understand that an employee may not be satisfied with only a salary and benefits; he or she may also need challenging job opportunities to experience self-growth and satisfaction.

Adapted from Abraham H. Maslow, "A Theory of Human Motivation," *Psychology Review*, 1943, vol. 50, pp. 370–396.

however, depressed industries and economic decline can put people out of work and restore the primacy of security needs.

Belongingness needs relate to social processes. They include the need for love and affection and the need to be accepted by one's peers. These needs are satisfied for most people by family and community relationships outside of work and by friendships on the job. A manager can help satisfy these needs by allowing social interaction and by making employees feel like part of a team or work group.

Esteem needs actually comprise two different sets of needs: the need for a positive self-image and self-respect, and the need for recognition and respect from others. A manager can help address these needs by providing a variety of extrinsic symbols of accomplishment, such as job titles, nice offices, and similar rewards as appropriate. At a more intrinsic level, the manager can provide challenging job assignments and opportunities for the employee to feel a sense of accomplishment.

At the top of the hierarchy are the *self-actualization needs*. These involve realizing one's potential for continued growth and individual development. The self-actualization needs are perhaps the most difficult for a manager to address. In fact, it can be argued that these needs must be met entirely from within the individual. But a manager can help by promoting a culture wherein self-actualization is possible. For instance, a manager could give employees a chance to participate in making decisions about their work and the opportunity to learn new things.

Maslow suggests that the five need categories constitute a hierarchy. An individual is motivated first and foremost to satisfy physiological needs. As long as they remain unsatisfied, the individual is motivated to fulfill only them. When satisfaction of physiological needs is achieved, they cease to act as primary motivational factors, and the individual moves "up" the hierarchy and becomes concerned with security needs. This process continues until the individual reaches the self-actualization level. Maslow's concept of the needs hierarchy has a certain intuitive logic and has been accepted by many managers. But research has revealed certain shortcomings and defects in the theory. Some research has found that five levels of need are not always present and that the order of the levels is not always the same, as postulated by Maslow.[7] In addition, people from different cultures are likely to have different need categories and hierarchies.

The Two-Factor Theory

Another popular content perspective is the ***two-factor theory of motivation.***[8] Frederick Herzberg developed his theory by interviewing 200 accountants and engineers. He asked them to recall occasions when they had been satisfied and motivated and occasions when they had been dissatisfied and unmotivated. Surprisingly, he found that different sets of factors were associated with satisfaction and with dissatisfaction—that is, a person might identify "low pay" as causing dissatisfaction but would not necessarily mention "high pay" as a cause of satisfaction. Instead, different factors—such as recognition or accomplishment—were cited as causing satisfaction and motivation.

This finding led Herzberg to conclude that the traditional view of job satisfaction was incomplete. That view assumed that satisfaction and dissatisfaction are at opposite ends of a single continuum. People might be satisfied, dissatisfied, or somewhere in between. But Herzberg's interviews had identified two different dimensions altogether: one ranging from satisfaction to no satisfaction and the other ranging from dissatisfaction to no dissatisfaction. This perspective, along with several examples of factors that affect each continuum, is shown in Figure 10.3. Note that the factors influencing the satisfaction continuum—called *motivation factors*—are related specifically to the work content. The factors presumed to cause dissatisfaction—called *hygiene factors*—are related to the work environment.

Based on these findings, Herzberg argued that there are two stages in the process of motivating employees. First, managers must ensure that the hygiene factors are not deficient. Pay and security must be appropriate, working conditions must be safe, technical supervision must be acceptable, and so on. By providing hygiene factors at an appropriate level, managers do not stimulate motivation but merely ensure that employees are "not dissatisfied." Employees whom managers attempt to "satisfy" through hygiene factors alone will usually do just enough to get by. Thus managers should proceed to stage two—giving employees the opportunity to experience motivation factors such as achievement and recognition. The result is predicted to be a high level of satisfaction and motivation. Herzberg also went a step further than most other theorists and described exactly how to use the two-factor theory in the workplace. Specifically, he recommended job enrichment, as

> **two-factor theory of motivation**
> Suggests that people's satisfaction and dissatisfaction are influenced by two independent sets of factors—motivation factors and hygiene factors

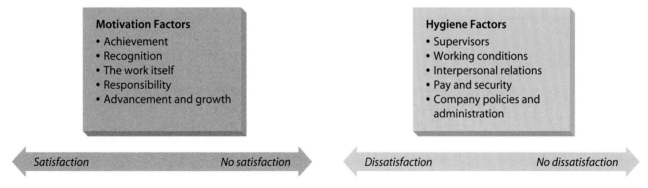

Figure 10.3

THE TWO-FACTOR THEORY OF MOTIVATION

The two-factor theory suggests that job satisfaction has two dimensions. A manager who tries to motivate an employee using only hygiene factors, such as pay and good working conditions, will likely not succeed. To motivate employees and produce a high level of satisfaction, managers must also offer factors such as responsibility and the opportunity for advancement (motivation factors).

discussed in Chapter 6. He argued that jobs should be redesigned to provide higher levels of the motivation factors.

Although widely accepted by many managers, Herzberg's two-factor theory is not without its critics. One criticism is that the findings in Herzberg's initial interviews are subject to different explanations. Another charge is that his sample was not representative of the general population and that subsequent research often failed to uphold the theory.[9] At the present time, Herzberg's theory is not held in high esteem by researchers in the field. The theory has had a major impact on managers, however, and has played a key role in increasing their awareness of motivation and its importance in the workplace.

Individual Human Needs

In addition to these theories, research has focused on specific individual human needs that are important in organizations. The three most important individual needs are achievement, affiliation, and power.[10]

The ***need for achievement***, the best known of the three, is the desire to accomplish a goal or task more effectively than in the past. People with a high need for achievement have a desire to assume personal responsibility, a tendency to set moderately difficult goals, a desire for specific and immediate feedback, and a preoccupation with their task. David C. McClelland, the psychologist who first identified this need, argues that only about 10 percent of the U.S. population has a high need for achievement. In contrast, almost one-quarter of the workers in Japan have a high need for achievement.

The ***need for affiliation*** is less well understood. Like Maslow's belongingness need, the need for affiliation is a desire for human companionship and acceptance. People with a strong need for affiliation are likely to prefer (and perform better in) a job that entails a lot of social interaction and offers opportunities to make friends. One recent survey found that workers with one or more good friends at work are much more likely to be committed to their work. Continental Airlines, for instance, allows flight attendants to form their own teams; those who participate tend to form teams with their friends.[11]

The need for power has also received considerable attention as an important ingredient in managerial success. The ***need for power*** is the desire to be influential in a group and to control one's environment. Research has shown that people with a strong need for power are likely to be superior performers, have good attendance records, and occupy supervisory positions. One study found that managers as a group tend to have a stronger power motive than the general population and that successful managers tend to have stronger power motives than less successful managers.[12] Dennis Kozlowski, disgraced former CEO of Tyco International, clearly had a strong need for power. This was reflected in the way he routinely took control over resources and used them for his own personal gain. Indeed, the things he bought with company money were probably intended to convey to the world the extent of his power.[13]

Process Perspectives on Motivation

Process perspectives are concerned with how motivation occurs. Rather than attempting to identify motivational stimuli, ***process perspectives*** focus on why people

---

need for achievement
The desire to accomplish a goal or task more effectively than in the past

need for affiliation
The desire for human companionship and acceptance

need for power
The desire to be influential in a group and to control one's environment

process perspectives
Approaches to motivation that focus on why people choose certain behavioral options to fulfill their needs and how they evaluate their satisfaction after they have attained these goals

choose certain behavioral options to satisfy their needs and how they evaluate their satisfaction after they have attained these goals. Three useful process perspectives on motivation are the expectancy, equity, and goal-setting theories.

Expectancy Theory

Expectancy theory suggests that motivation depends on two things—how much we want something and how likely we think we are to get it.[14] Assume that you are approaching graduation and looking for a job. You see in the want ads that General Motors is seeking a new vice president with a starting salary of $500,000 per year. Even though you might want the job, you will not apply because you realize that you have little chance of getting it. The next ad you see is for someone to scrape bubble gum from underneath theater seats for a starting salary of $6 an hour. Even though you could probably get this job, you do not apply because you do not want it. Then you see an ad for a management trainee at a big company, with a starting salary of $40,000. You will probably apply for this job because you want it and because you think you have a reasonable chance of getting it.

Expectancy theory rests on four basic assumptions. First, it assumes that behavior is determined by a combination of forces in the individual and in the environment. Second, it assumes that people make decisions about their own behavior in organizations. Third, it assumes that different people have different types of needs, desires, and goals. Fourth, it assumes that people make choices from among alternative plans of behavior, based on their perceptions of the extent to which a given behavior will lead to desired outcomes.

Figure 10.4 summarizes the basic expectancy model. The model suggests that motivation leads to effort and that effort, combined with employee ability and environmental factors, results in performance. Performance, in turn, leads to various outcomes, each of which has an associated value, called its *valence*. The most important parts of the expectancy model cannot be shown in the figure, however. These are the individual's expectation that effort will lead to high performance,

> **expectancy theory**
> Suggests that motivation depends on two things—how much we want something and how likely we think we are to get it

Expectancy theory suggests that motivation depends on how much we want something and how likely we think we are to get it. Daisuke Matsuzaka was a very successful pitcher in the Japanese major leagues. However, he knew that he could earn more money and play on a bigger stage if he moved to the United States. He also was fully confident in his abilities to perform at the highest level. Hence, because he knew what he wanted (more money and greater recognition) and believed he could achieve these things (as a result of self-confidence), he left the security of his Japanese team and signed with the American League's Boston Red Sox.

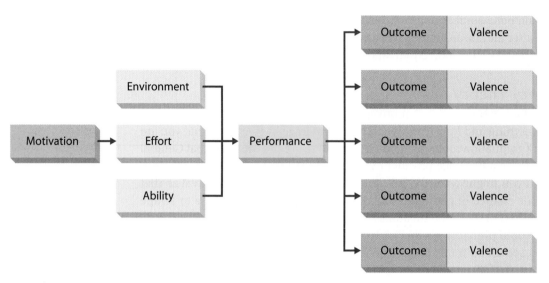

Figure 10.4
THE EXPECTANCY MODEL OF MOTIVATION

The expectancy model of motivation is a complex but relatively accurate portrayal of how motivation occurs. According to this model, a manager must understand what employees want (such as pay, promotions, or status) to begin to motivate them.

that performance will lead to outcomes, and that each outcome will have some kind of value.

Effort-to-Performance Expectancy   The ***effort-to-performance expectancy*** is the individual's perception of the probability that effort will lead to high performance. When the individual believes that effort will lead directly to high performance, expectancy will be quite strong (close to 1.00). When the individual believes that effort and performance are unrelated, the effort-to-performance expectancy is very weak (close to 0). The belief that effort is somewhat but not strongly related to performance carries with it a moderate expectancy (somewhere between 0 and 1.00).

Performance-to-Outcome Expectancy   The ***performance-to-outcome expectancy*** is the individual's perception that performance will lead to a specific outcome. For example, if the individual believes that high performance *will* result in a pay raise, the performance-to-outcome expectancy is high (approaching 1.00). The individual who believes that high performance *may* lead to a pay raise has a moderate expectancy (between 1.00 and 0). The individual who believes that performance has no relationship to rewards has a low performance-to-outcome expectancy (close to 0).

Outcomes and Valences   Expectancy theory recognizes that an individual's behavior results in a variety of ***outcomes***, or consequences, in an organizational setting. A high performer, for example, may get bigger pay raises, faster promotions, and more praise from the boss. On the other hand, she may also be subject to more stress and incur resentment from coworkers. Each of these outcomes also has an associated value, or ***valence***—an index of how much an individual values a particular outcome. If the individual wants the outcome, its valence is positive; if the individual does not want the outcome, its valence is negative; and if the individual is indifferent to the outcome, its valence is zero.

effort-to-performance expectancy
The individual's perception of the probability that effort will lead to high performance

performance-to-outcome expectancy
The individual's perception that performance will lead to a specific outcome

outcomes
Consequences of behaviors in an organizational setting, usually rewards

It is this part of expectancy theory that goes beyond the content perspectives on motivation. Different people have different needs, and they will try to satisfy these needs in different ways. For an employee who has a high need for achievement and a low need for affiliation, the pay raise and promotions cited above as outcomes of high performance might have positive valences, the praise and resentment zero valences, and the stress a negative valence. For a different employee, with a low need for achievement and a high need for affiliation, the pay raise, promotions, and praise might all have positive valences, whereas both resentment and stress could have negative valences.

> **valence**
> An index of how much an individual desires a particular outcome; the attractiveness of the outcome to the individual

For motivated behavior to occur, three conditions must be met. First, the effort-to-performance must be greater than 0 (the individual must believe that if effort is expended, high performance will result). The performance-to-outcome expectancy must also be greater than 0 (the individual must believe that if high performance is achieved, certain outcomes will follow). And the sum of the valences for the outcomes must be greater than 0. (One or more outcomes may have negative valences if they are more than offset by the positive valences of other outcomes. For example, the attractiveness of a pay raise, a promotion, and praise from the boss may outweigh the unattractiveness of more stress and resentment from coworkers.) Expectancy theory suggests that when these conditions are met, the individual is motivated to expend effort.

Starbucks credits its unique stock ownership program with maintaining a dedicated and motivated workforce. Based on the fundamental concepts of expectancy theory, Starbucks employees earn stock as a function of their seniority and performance. Thus their hard work helps them earn shares of ownership in the company.[15]

The Porter-Lawler Extension An interesting extension of expectancy theory has been proposed by Porter and Lawler.[16] Recall from Chapter 1 that the human relationists assumed that employee satisfaction causes good performance. We also noted that research has not supported such a relationship. Porter and Lawler suggested that there may indeed be a relationship between satisfaction and performance but that it goes in the opposite direction—that is, high performance may lead to high satisfaction. Figure 10.5 summarizes Porter and Lawler's logic. Performance results in rewards for an individual. Some of these are extrinsic (such as pay and promotions); others are intrinsic (such as self-esteem and accomplishment). The individual evaluates the equity, or fairness, of the rewards relative to the effort expended and the level of performance attained. If the rewards are perceived to be equitable, the individual is satisfied.

Figure 10.5

THE PORTER-LAWLER EXTENSION OF EXPECTANCY THEORY

The Porter-Lawler extension of expectancy theory suggests that if performance results in equitable rewards, people will be more satisfied. Thus performance can lead to satisfaction. Managers must therefore be sure that any system of motivation includes rewards that are fair, or equitable, for all.

Source: Edward E. Lawler III and Lyman W. Porter, "The Effect of Performance on Job Satisfaction," *Industrial Relations,* October 1967, p. 23. Used with permission of the University of California.

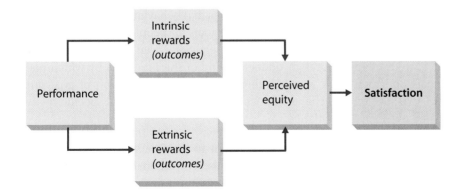

Equity Theory

equity theory
Suggests that people are motivated to seek social equity in the rewards they receive for performance

After needs have stimulated the motivation process and the individual has chosen an action that is expected to satisfy those needs, the individual assesses the fairness, or equity, of the resultant outcome. **Equity theory** contends that people are motivated to seek social equity in the rewards they receive for performance.[17] Equity is an individual's belief that the treatment he or she is receiving is fair relative to the treatment received by others. According to equity theory, outcomes from a job include pay, recognition, promotions, social relationships, and intrinsic rewards. To get these rewards, the individual makes inputs to the job, such as time, experience, effort, education, and loyalty. The theory suggests that people view their outcomes and inputs as a ratio and then compare it to someone else's ratio. This other "person" may be someone in the work group or some sort of group average or composite. The process of comparison looks like this:

$$\frac{\text{Outcomes (self)}}{\text{Inputs (self)}} = \frac{\text{Outcomes (other)}}{\text{Inputs (other)}}$$

Both the formulation of the ratios and comparisons between them are very subjective and based on individual perceptions. As a result of comparisons, three conditions may result: the individual may feel equitably rewarded, underrewarded, or overrewarded. A feeling of equity will result when the two ratios are equal. This may occur even though the other person's outcomes are greater than the individual's own outcomes—provided that the other's inputs are also proportionately greater. Suppose that Mark has a high school education and earns $30,000. He may still feel equitably treated relative to Susan, who earns $35,000, because she has a college degree.

People who feel underrewarded try to reduce the inequity. Such an individual might decrease her inputs by exerting less effort, increase her outcomes by asking for a raise, distort the original ratios by rationalizing, try to get the other person to change her or his outcomes or inputs, leave the situation, or change the object of comparison. An individual may also feel overrewarded relative to another person. This is not likely to be terribly disturbing to most people, but research suggests that some people who experience inequity under these conditions are somewhat motivated to reduce it. Under such a circumstance, the person might increase his inputs by exerting more effort, reduce his outcomes by producing fewer units (if paid on a per-unit basis), distort the original ratios by rationalizing, or try to reduce the inputs or increase the outcomes of the other person.

Goal-Setting Theory

The goal-setting theory of motivation assumes that behavior is a result of conscious goals and intentions.[18] Therefore, by setting goals for people in the organization, a manager should be able to influence their behavior. Given this premise, the challenge is to develop a thorough understanding of the processes by which people set goals and then work to reach them. In the original version of goal-setting theory, two specific goal characteristics—goal difficulty and goal specificity—were expected to shape performance.

Goal Difficulty *Goal difficulty* is the extent to which a goal is challenging and requires effort. If people work to achieve goals, it is reasonable to assume that they will work harder to achieve more difficult goals. But a goal must not be so difficult that it is unattainable. If a new manager asks her sales force to increase sales by 300 percent, the group may become disillusioned. A more realistic but still difficult goal—perhaps a 30 percent increase—would be a better incentive. A substantial body of research supports the importance of goal difficulty. In one study, for example, managers at Weyerhauser set difficult goals for truck drivers hauling loads of timber from cutting sites to wood yards. Over a nine-month period, the drivers increased the quantity of wood they delivered by an amount that would have required $250,000 worth of new trucks at the previous per-truck average load.[19]

Goal Specificity   *Goal specificity* is the clarity and precision of the goal. A goal of "increasing productivity" is not very specific; a goal of "increasing productivity by 3 percent in the next six months" is quite specific. Some goals, such as those involving costs, output, profitability, and growth, are readily amenable to specificity. Other goals, however, such as improving employee job satisfaction, morale, company image and reputation, ethics, and socially responsible behavior, may be much harder to state in specific terms. Like difficulty, specificity has been shown to be consistently related to performance. The study of timber truck drivers mentioned above, for example, also examined goal specificity. The initial loads the truck drivers were carrying were found to be 60 percent of the maximum weight each truck could haul. The managers set a new goal for drivers of 94 percent, which the drivers were soon able to reach. Thus the goal was both specific and difficult.

Because the theory attracted so much widespread interest and research support from researchers and managers alike, an expanded model of the goal-setting process was eventually proposed. The expanded model, shown in Figure 10.6, attempts to capture more fully the complexities of goal setting in organizations.

The expanded theory argues that goal-directed effort is a function of four goal attributes: difficulty and specificity, as already discussed, and acceptance and commitment. *Goal acceptance* is the extent to which a person accepts a goal as his or her own. *Goal commitment* is the extent to which she or he is personally interested in reaching the goal. The manager who vows to take whatever steps are necessary

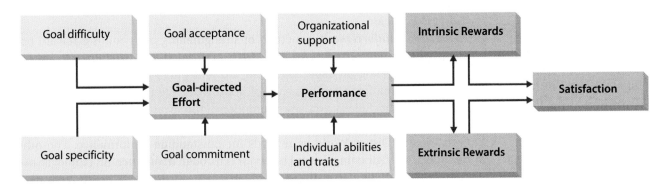

Figure 10.6
THE EXPANDED GOAL-SETTING THEORY OF MOTIVATION

One of the most important emerging theories of motivation is goal-setting theory. This theory suggests that goal difficulty, specificity, acceptance, and commitment combine to determine an individual's goal-directed effort. This effort, when complemented by appropriate organizational support and individual abilities and traits, results in performance. Finally, performance is seen as leading to intrinsic and extrinsic rewards that, in turn, result in employee satisfaction.

Source: Reprinted from *Organizational Dynamics*, Autumn 1979, Gary P. Latham and Edwin A. Locke, "A Motivational Technique That Works," p. 79, copyright © 1979 with permission from Elsevier Science.

to cut costs by 10 percent has made a commitment to achieve the goal. Factors that can foster goal acceptance and commitment include participating in the goal-setting process, making goals challenging but realistic, and believing that goal achievement will lead to valued rewards.

The interaction of goal-directed effort, organizational support, and individual abilities and traits determines actual performance. Organizational support is whatever the organization does to help or hinder performance. Positive support might mean making available adequate personnel and a sufficient supply of raw materials; negative support might mean failing to fix damaged equipment. Individual abilities and traits are the skills and other personal characteristics necessary for doing a job. As a result of performance, a person receives various intrinsic and extrinsic rewards, which in turn influence satisfaction. Note that the latter stages of this model are quite similar to the Porter and Lawler expectancy model discussed earlier.[20]

Reinforcement Perspectives on Motivation

A third element of the motivational process addresses why some behaviors are maintained over time and why other behaviors change. As we have seen, content perspectives deal with needs, whereas process perspectives explain why people choose various behaviors to satisfy needs and how they evaluate the equity of the rewards they get for those behaviors. Reinforcement perspectives explain the role of those rewards as they cause behavior to change or remain the same over time. Specifically, *reinforcement theory* argues that behavior that results in rewarding consequences is likely to be repeated, whereas behavior that results in punishing consequences is less likely to be repeated.[21]

Kinds of Reinforcement in Organizations

There are four basic kinds of reinforcement that can result from behavior—positive reinforcement, avoidance, punishment, and extinction.[22] The first two kinds of reinforcement strengthen or maintain behavior, whereas the other two weaken or decrease behavior.

Positive reinforcement, a method of strengthening behavior, is a reward or a positive outcome after a desired behavior is performed. When a manager observes an employee doing an especially good job and offers praise, the praise serves to positively reinforce the behavior of good work. Other positive reinforcers in organizations include pay raises, promotions, and awards. Employees who work at General Electric's customer service center receive clothing, sporting goods, and even trips to Disney World as rewards for outstanding performance. The other method of strengthening desired behavior is through *avoidance*. An employee may come to work on time to avoid a reprimand. In this instance, the employee is motivated to perform the behavior of punctuality to avoid an unpleasant consequence that is likely to follow tardiness.

Punishment is used by some managers to weaken undesired behaviors. When an employee is loafing, coming to work late, doing poor work, or interfering with the work of others, the manager might resort to reprimands, discipline, or fines. The logic is that the unpleasant consequence will reduce the likelihood that the employee will choose that particular behavior again. Given the counterproductive side effects of punishment (such as resentment and hostility), it is often advisable

---

reinforcement theory
Approach to motivation that argues that behavior that results in rewarding consequences is likely to be repeated, whereas behavior that results in punishing consequences is less likely to be repeated

positive reinforcement
A method of strengthening behavior with rewards or positive outcomes after a desired behavior is performed

avoidance
Used to strengthen behavior by avoiding unpleasant consequences that would result if the behavior were not performed

to use the other kinds of reinforcement if at all possible. **Extinction** can also be used to weaken behavior, especially behavior that has previously been rewarded. When an employee tells an off-color joke and the boss laughs, the laughter reinforces the behavior and the employee may continue to tell off-color jokes. By simply ignoring this behavior and not reinforcing it, the boss can cause the behavior to subside and eventually become "extinct."

Providing Reinforcement in Organizations

Not only is the kind of reinforcement important, but so is when or how often it occurs. Various strategies are possible for providing reinforcement. The **fixed-interval schedule** provides reinforcement at fixed intervals of time, regardless of behavior. A good example of this schedule is the weekly or monthly paycheck. This method provides the least incentive for good work because employees know they will be paid regularly regardless of their efforts. A **variable-interval schedule** also uses time as the basis for reinforcement, but the time interval varies from one reinforcement to the next. This schedule is appropriate for praise or other rewards based on visits or inspections. When employees do not know when the boss is going to drop by, they tend to maintain a reasonably high level of effort all the time.

A **fixed-ratio schedule** gives reinforcement after a fixed number of behaviors, regardless of the time that elapses between behaviors. This results in an even higher level of effort. For example, when Sears is recruiting new credit card customers, salespersons get a small bonus for every fifth application returned from their department. Under this arrangement, motivation will be high because each application gets the person closer to the next bonus. The **variable-ratio schedule**, the most powerful schedule in terms of maintaining desired behaviors, varies the number of behaviors needed for each reinforcement. A supervisor who praises an employee for her second order, the seventh order after that, the ninth after that, then the fifth, and then the third is using a variable-ratio schedule. The employee is motivated to increase the frequency of the desired behavior because each performance increases the probability of receiving a reward. Of course, a variable-ratio schedule is difficult (if not impossible) to use for formal rewards such as pay because it would be too complicated to keep track of who was rewarded when.

Managers wanting to explicitly use reinforcement theory to motivate their employees generally do so with a technique called **behavior modification**, or **OB Mod**.[23] An OB Mod program starts by specifying behaviors that are to be increased (such as producing more units) or decreased (such as coming to work late). These target behaviors are then tied to specific forms or kinds of reinforcement. Although many organizations (such as Procter & Gamble and Ford) have used OB Mod, the best-known application was at Emery Air Freight. Management felt that the containers used to consolidate small shipments into fewer, larger shipments were not being packed efficiently. Through a system of self-monitored feedback and rewards, Emery increased container usage from 45 percent to 95 percent and saved over $3 million during the first three years of the program.[24]

---

punishment
Used to weaken undesired behaviors by using negative outcomes or unpleasant consequences when the behavior is performed

---

extinction
Used to weaken undesired behaviors by simply ignoring or not reinforcing them

---

fixed-interval schedule
Provides reinforcement at fixed intervals of time, such as regular weekly paychecks

---

variable-interval schedule
Provides reinforcement at varying intervals of time, such as occasional visits by the supervisor

---

fixed-ratio schedule
Provides reinforcement after a fixed number of behaviors regardless of the time interval involved, such as a bonus for every fifth sale

---

variable-ratio schedule
Provides reinforcement after varying numbers of behaviors are performed, such as the use of complements by a supervisor on an irregular basis

---

behavior modification (OB Mod)
Method for applying the basic elements of reinforcement theory in an organizational setting

---

Popular Motivational Strategies

Although the various theories discussed thus far provide a solid explanation for motivation, managers must use various techniques and strategies to actually apply them. Among the most popular motivational strategies today are empowerment and participation and alternative forms of work arrangements. Various forms of performance-based reward systems, discussed in the next section, also reflect efforts to boost motivation and performance.

Empowerment and Participation

> **empowerment**
> The process of enabling workers to set their own work goals, make decisions, and solve problems within their sphere of responsibility and authority

Empowerment and participation represent important methods that managers can use to enhance employee motivation. **Empowerment** is the process of enabling workers to set their own work goals, make decisions, and solve problems within their sphere of responsibility and authority. **Participation** is the process of giving employees a voice in making decisions about their own work. Thus empowerment is a somewhat broader concept that promotes participation in a wide variety of areas, including but not limited to work itself, work context, and work environment.[25]

> **participation**
> The process of giving employees a voice in making decisions about their own work

The role of participation and empowerment in motivation can be expressed in terms of both content perspectives and expectancy theory. Employees who participate in decision making may be more committed to executing decisions properly. Furthermore, the successful process of making a decision, executing it, and then seeing the positive consequences can help satisfy one's need for achievement, provide recognition and responsibility, and enhance self-esteem. Simply being asked to participate in organizational decision making also may enhance an employee's self-esteem. In addition, participation should help clarify expectancies; that is, by participating in decision making, employees may better understand the linkage between their performance and the rewards they want most.

Alternative Forms of Work Arrangements

Many organizations today are also experimenting with a variety of alternative work arrangements. These alternative arrangements are generally intended to enhance employee motivation and performance by providing employees with greater flexibility in how and when they work. Among the more popular alternative work

Alternative forms of work arrangements can motivate people in a variety of ways. Take Dr. Orit Wimpfheimer, for example. Many Israeli professionals who train in the United States face a difficult choice: they can remain in the United States away from their homeland, or they can return to Israel but earn much less than their American counterparts. But professionals like Dr. Wimpfheimer are increasingly finding that by relying on new forms of technology they can work in U.S. fields while living in Israel. From her home office near Jerusalem, for instance, Dr. Wimpfheimer maintains a full-time business analyzing medical test results for U.S. hospitals.

arrangements are variable work schedules, flexible work schedules, job sharing, and telecommuting.[26]

Variable Work Schedules Although there are many exceptions, of course, the traditional work schedule starts at 8:00 or 9:00 in the morning and ends at 5:00 in the evening, five days a week (and, of course, many managers work additional hours outside of these times). Unfortunately, this schedule makes it difficult to attend to routine personal business—going to the bank, seeing a doctor or dentist for a routine checkup, having a parent-teacher conference, getting an automobile serviced, and so forth. At a surface level, then, employees locked into this sort of arrangement may find it necessary to take a sick day or a vacation day to handle these activities. At a more unconscious level, some people may also feel so powerless and constrained by their job schedule as to feel increased resentment and frustration.

To help counter these problems, some businesses have adopted a ***compressed work schedule***, working a full 40-hour week in fewer than the traditional five days.[27] One approach involves working 10 hours a day for four days, leaving an extra day off. Another alternative is for employees to work slightly less than 10 hours a day, but to complete the 40 hours by lunchtime on Friday. And a few firms have tried having employees work 12 hours a day for three days, followed by four days off. Organizations that have used these forms of compressed workweeks include John Hancock, BP Amoco, and Philip Morris. One problem with this schedule is that when employees put in too much time in a single day, they tend to get tired and perform at a lower level later in the day.

> **compressed work schedule**
> Working a full 40-hour week in fewer than the traditional five days

A schedule that some organizations today are beginning to use is what they call a "nine-eighty" schedule. Under this arrangement, an employee works a traditional schedule one week and a compressed schedule the next, getting every other Friday off. In other words, they work 80 hours (the equivalent of two weeks of full-time work) in nine days. By alternating the regular and compressed schedules across half of its workforce, the organization can be fully staffed at all times, while still giving employees two full days off each month. Shell Oil and BP Amoco Chemicals are two of the firms that currently use this schedule.

Flexible Work Schedules Another promising alternative work arrangement is ***flexible work schedules***, sometimes called *flextime*. Flextime gives employees more personal control over the times they work. The workday is broken down into two categories: flexible time and core time. All employees must be at their workstation during core time, but they can choose their own schedules during flexible time. Thus one employee may choose to start work early in the morning and leave in midafternoon, another to start in the late morning and work until late afternoon, and still another to start early in the morning, take a long lunch break, and work until late afternoon. Organizations that have used the flexible work schedule method for arranging work include Hewlett-Packard, Microsoft, and Texas Instruments.

> **flexible work schedules**
> Work schedules that allow employees to select, within broad parameters, the hours they work

Job Sharing Yet another potentially useful alternative work arrangement is job sharing. In ***job sharing***, two part-time employees share one full-time job. One person may perform the job from 8:00 A.M. to noon and the other from 1:00 P.M. to 5:00 P.M. Job sharing may be desirable for people who want to work only part time or when job markets are tight. For its part, the organization can accommodate the preferences of a broader range of employees and may benefit from the talents of more people.

> **job sharing**
> When two part-time employees share one full-time job

telecommuting
Allowing employees to spend part of their time working offsite, usually at home

Telecommuting An increasingly popular approach to alternative work arrangements is *telecommuting* —allowing employees to spend part of their time working offsite, usually at home. By using email, the Internet, and other forms of information technology, many employees can maintain close contact with their organization and still get just as much work done at home as if they were in their office. The increased power and sophistication of modern communication technology is making telecommuting easier and easier. About 15 percent of the U.S. workforce does at least some telecommuting, and in some businesses it's much higher. At IBM, for instance, 40 percent of the workforce has no corporate workstation or office; at AT&T, the figure is 35 percent, and at Sun Microsystems, it's 50 percent.[28]

Using Reward Systems to Motivate Performance

reward system
The formal and informal mechanisms by which employee performance is defined, evaluated, and rewarded

Aside from these types of motivational strategies, an organization's reward system is its most basic tool for managing employee motivation. An organizational *reward system* comprises the formal and informal mechanisms by which employee performance is defined, evaluated, and rewarded. Rewards that are tied specifically to performance, of course, have the greatest impact on enhancing both motivation and actual performance.

Performance-based rewards play a number of roles and address a variety of purposes in organizations. The major purposes involve the relationship of rewards to motivation and to performance. Specifically, organizations want employees to perform at relatively high levels and need to make it worth their effort to do so. When rewards are associated with higher levels of performance, employees will presumably be motivated to work harder to achieve those awards. At that point, their own self-interests coincide with the organization's interests. Performance-based rewards are also relevant regarding other employee behaviors, such as retention and citizenship.

Merit Reward Systems

merit pay
Pay awarded to employees on the basis of the relative value of their contributions to the organization

Merit reward systems are one of the most fundamental forms of performance-based rewards. **Merit pay** generally refers to pay awarded to employees on the basis of the relative value of their contributions to the organization. Employees who make greater contributions are given higher pay than those who make lesser contributions. **Merit pay plans**, then, are compensation plans that formally base at least some meaningful portion of compensation on merit.

merit pay plan
Compensation plan that formally bases at least some meaningful portion of compensation on merit

The most general form of merit pay plan is to provide annual salary increases to individuals in the organization based on their relative merit. Merit, in turn, is usually determined or defined based on the individual's performance and overall contributions to the organization. For example, an organization using such a traditional merit pay plan might instruct its supervisors to give all their employees an average pay raise of, say, 4 percent. But the individual supervisor is further instructed to differentiate among high, average, and low performers. Under a simple system, for example, a manager might give the top 25 percent of her employees a 6 percent pay raise, the middle 50 percent a 4 percent or average pay raise, and the bottom 25 percent a 2 percent pay raise.

Incentive Reward Systems

Incentive reward systems are among the oldest forms of performance-based rewards. For example, some companies were using individual piece-rate incentive plans

© Mike Baldwin / Cornered

"Worked all weekend to finish the report, and all I get is a stupid Pat on the back."

www.CartoonStock.com

Incentives and other rewards can play a powerful role in motivating employee performance. But managers must be sure that the incentives they provide are actually seen by the employee as being desirable. For instance, providing dinner with the boss as a reward might backfire if the employee has trouble scheduling a sitter for evenings out or does not really enjoy the boss's companionship. And as shown here even an innocent "pat on the back" can backfire if not handled carefully!

over 100 years ago.[29] Under a ***piece-rate incentive plan***, the organization pays an employee a certain amount of money for every unit she or he produces. For example, an employee might be paid $1 for every dozen units of products that are successfully completed. But such simplistic systems fail to account for such facts as minimum wage levels and rely very heavily on the assumptions that performance is totally under an individual's control and that the individual employee does a single task continuously throughout his or her work time. Thus most organizations today that try to use incentive compensation systems use more sophisticated methodologies.

Incentive Pay Plans   Generally speaking, *individual incentive plans* reward individual performance on a real-time basis. In other words, rather than increasing a person's base salary at the end of the year, an individual instead receives some level of salary increase or financial reward in conjunction with demonstrated outstanding performance in close proximity to when that performance occurred. Individual incentive systems are most likely to be used in cases in which performance can be objectively assessed in terms of number of units of output or similar measures, rather than on a subjective assessment of performance by a superior.

Some variations on a piece-rate system are still fairly popular. Although many of these still resemble the early plans in most ways, a well-known piece-rate system at Lincoln Electric illustrates how an organization can adapt the traditional model to achieve better results. For years, Lincoln's employees were paid individual incentive payments based on their performance. However, the amount of money shared (or the incentive pool) was based on the company's profitability. There was also a well-organized system whereby employees could make suggestions for increasing productivity. There was motivation to do this because the employees received one-third of the profits (another third went to the stockholders, and the last share was retained for improvements and seed money). Thus the pool for incentive payments was determined by profitability, and an employee's share of this pool was a function

piece-rate incentive plan
Reward system wherein the organization pays an employee a certain amount of money for every unit she or he produces

of his or her base pay and rated performance based on the piece-rate system. Lincoln Electric was most famous, however, because of the stories (which were apparently typical) of production workers receiving a year-end bonus payment that equaled their yearly base pay.[30] In recent years, Lincoln has partially abandoned its famous system for business reasons, but it still serves as a benchmark for other companies seeking innovative piece-rate pay systems.

Perhaps the most common form of individual incentive is *sales commissions* that are paid to people engaged in sales work. For example, sales representatives for consumer products firms and retail sales agents may be compensated under this type of commission system. In general, the person might receive a percentage of the total volume of attained sales as her or his commission for a period of time. Some sales jobs are based entirely on commission, whereas others use a combination of base minimum salary with additional commission as an incentive. Notice that these plans put a considerable amount of the salesperson's earnings "at risk." In other words, although organizations often have drawing accounts to allow the salesperson to live during lean periods (the person then "owes" this money back to the organization), if he or she does not perform well, he or she will not be paid much. The portion of salary based on commission is simply not guaranteed and is paid only if sales reach some target level.

Other Forms of Incentive   Occasionally organizations may also use other forms of incentives to motivate people. For example, a nonmonetary incentive, such as additional time off or a special perk, might be a useful incentive. For example, a company might establish a sales contest in which the sales group that attains the highest level of sales increase over a specified period of time will receive an extra week of paid vacation, perhaps even at an arranged place, such as a tropical resort or a ski lodge.[31]

A major advantage of incentives relative to merit systems is that incentives are typically a one-shot reward and do not accumulate by becoming part of the individual's base salary. Stated differently, an individual whose outstanding performance entitles him or her to a financial incentive gets the incentive only one time, based on that level of performance. If the individual's performance begins to erode in the future, then the individual may receive a lesser incentive or perhaps no incentive in the future. As a consequence, his or her base salary remains the same or is perhaps increased at a relatively moderate pace; he or she receives one-time incentive rewards as recognition for exemplary performance. Furthermore, because these plans, by their very nature, focus on one-time events, it is much easier for the organization to change the focus of the incentive plan. At a simple level, for example, an organization can set up an incentive plan for selling one product during one quarter, but then shift the incentive to a different product the next quarter, as the situation requires. Automobile companies like Ford and GM routinely do this by reducing sales incentives for models that are selling very well and increasing sales incentives for models that are selling below expectations or are about to be discontinued.

Team and Group Incentive Reward Systems

The merit compensation and incentive compensation systems described in the preceding sections deal primarily with performance-based reward arrangements for individuals. There also exists a different set of performance-based reward programs that are targeted for teams and groups. These programs are particularly important for managers to understand today, given the widespread trends toward team and group-based methods of work and organizations.[32]

Common Team and Group Reward Systems   There are two commonly used types of team and group reward systems. One type used in many organizations is an approach called gainsharing. ***Gainsharing programs*** are designed to share the cost savings from productivity improvements with employees. The underlying assumption of gainsharing is that employees and the employer have the same goals and thus should appropriately share in incremental economic gains.[33]

In general, organizations that use gainsharing start by measuring team- or group-level productivity. It is important that this measure be valid and reliable and that it truly reflect current levels of performance by the team or group. The team or work group itself is then given the charge of attempting to lower costs and otherwise improve productivity through any measures that its members develop and its manager approves. Resulting cost savings or productivity gains that the team or group is able to achieve are then quantified and translated into dollar values. A predetermined formula is then used to allocate these dollar savings between the employer and the employees themselves. A typical formula for distributing gainsharing savings is to provide 25 percent to the employees and 75 percent to the company.

One specific type of gainsharing plan is an approach called the Scanlon plan. This approach was developed by Joseph Scanlon in 1927. The ***Scanlon plan*** has the same basic strategy as gainsharing plans, in that teams or groups of employees are encouraged to suggest strategies for reducing costs. However, the distribution of these gains is usually tilted much more heavily toward employees, with employees usually receiving between two-thirds and three-fourths of the total cost savings that the plan achieves. Furthermore, the distribution of cost savings resulting from the plan is given not just to the team or group that suggested and developed the ideas, but across the entire organization.

Other Types of Team and Group Rewards   Although gainsharing and Scanlon-type plans are among the most popular group incentive reward systems, there are other systems that are also used by some organizations. Some companies, for example, have begun to use true incentives at the team or group level. Just as with individual incentives, team or group incentives tie rewards directly to performance increases. And, like individual incentives, team or group incentives are paid as they are earned rather than being added to employees' base salary. The incentives are distributed at the team or group level, however, rather than at the individual level. In some cases, the distribution may be based on the existing salary of each employee, with incentive bonuses being given on a proportionate basis. In other settings, each member of the team or group receives the same incentive pay.

Some companies also use nonmonetary rewards at the team or group level—most commonly in the form of prizes and awards. For example, a company might designate the particular team in a plant or subunit of the company that achieves the highest level of productivity increase, the highest level of reported customer satisfaction, or a similar index of performance. The reward itself might take the form of additional time off, as described earlier in this chapter, or a tangible award, such as a trophy or plaque. In any event, the idea is that the reward is at the team level and serves as recognition of exemplary performance by the entire team.

gainsharing programs
Designed to share the cost savings from productivity improvements with employees

Scanlon plan
Similar to gainsharing, but the distribution of gains is tilted much more heavily toward employees

There are also other kinds of team or group level incentives that go beyond the contributions of a specific work group. These are generally organization-wide kinds of incentives. One long-standing method for this approach is *profit sharing*. In a profit-sharing approach, at the end of the year some portion of the company's profits is paid into a profit-sharing pool that is then distributed to all employees. Either this amount is distributed at that time, or it is put into an escrow account and payment is deferred until the employee retires.

Executive Compensation

The top-level executives of most companies have separate compensation programs and plans. These are intended to reward these executives for their performance and for the performance of the organization.

Standard Forms of Executive Compensation   Most senior executives receive their compensation in two forms. One form is a *base salary*. As with the base salary of any staff member or professional member of an organization, the base salary of an executive is a guaranteed amount of money that the individual will be paid. For example, in 2005 Yahoo! paid its CEO, Terry Semel, $600,000 in base salary.

Above and beyond this base salary, however, most executives also receive one or more forms of incentive pay. The traditional method of incentive pay for executives is in the form of bonuses. Bonuses, in turn, are usually determined by the performance of the organization. Thus, at the end of the year, some portion of a corporation's profits may be diverted into a bonus pool. Senior executives then receive a bonus expressed as a percentage of this bonus pool. The chief executive officer and president are obviously likely to get a larger percentage bonus than a vice president. The exact distribution of the bonus pool is usually specified ahead of time in the individual's employment contract. Some organizations intentionally leave the distribution unspecified, so that the board of directors has the flexibility to give larger rewards to those individuals deemed to be most deserving. Yahoo!'s Terry Semel received a cash bonus of about $250,000 in 2005.

Special Forms of Executive Compensation   Beyond base salary and bonuses, many executives receive other kinds of compensation as well. A form of executive compensation that has received a lot of attention in recent years has been various kinds of stock options. A **stock option plan** is established to give senior managers the option to buy company stock in the future at a predetermined fixed price. The basic idea underlying stock option plans is that if the executives contribute to higher levels of organizational performance, then the company stock should increase in value. Then the executive will be able to purchase the stock at the predetermined price, which theoretically should be lower than its future market price. The difference then becomes profit for the individual. Yahoo! awarded Terry Semel stock options with a potential value of $230,000,000.

Stock options continue to grow in popularity as a means of compensating top managers. Options are seen as a means of aligning the interests of the manager with those of the stockholders, and given that they do not cost the organization much (other than some possible dilution of stock values), they will probably be even more popular in the future. In fact, a recent study by KPMG Peat Marwick indicates that for senior management whose salary exceeds $250,000, stock options represent the largest share of the salary mix (relative to salary and other incentives). Furthermore,

stock option plan
Established to give senior managers the option to buy company stock in the future at a predetermined fixed price

when we consider all of top management (annual salary over $750,000), stock options comprise a full 60 percent of their total compensation. And the Peat Marwick report indicates that even among exempt employees at the $35,000-a-year level, stock options represent 13 percent of total compensation.

But events in recent years have raised serious questions about the use of stock options as incentives for executives. For example, several executives at Enron allegedly withheld critical financial information from the markets, cashed in their stock options (while Enron stock was trading at $80 a share), and then watched as the financial information was made public and the stock fell to less than $1 a share. Of course, these actions (if proven) are illegal, but they raise questions in the public's mind about the role of stock options and about the way organizations treat stock options from an accounting perspective. Most organizations have *not* treated stock options as liabilities, even though, when exercised, they are exactly that. There is concern that by not carrying stock options as liabilities, the managers are overstating the value of the company, which, of course, can help raise the stock price. Finally, when stock markets generally fell during the middle of 2002, many executives found that their options were worthless, as the price of the stock fell below the option price. When stock options go "under water" in this way, they have no value to anyone.

Aside from stock option plans, other kinds of executive compensation are also used by some companies. Among the more popular are such perquisites as memberships in private clubs, access to company recreational facilities, and similar considerations. Some organizations also make available to senior executives low- or no-interest loans. These are often given to new executives whom the company is hiring from other companies and serve as an incentive for the individual to leave his or her current job to join a new organization.

Criticisms of Executive Compensation   In recent years, executive compensation has come under fire for a variety of reasons. One major reason is that the levels of executive compensation attained by some managers seem simply too large for the average shareholder to understand. It is not uncommon, for instance, for a senior executive of a major corporation to earn total income from his or her job in a given year of well in excess of $1 million. Sometimes the income of chief executive officers can be substantially more than this. Coca-Cola's Douglas Daft earned a total of $55 million in 2001 from all sources combined. Thus, just as the typical person has difficulty comprehending the astronomical salaries paid to some movie stars and sports stars, so, too, would the average person be aghast at the astronomical salaries paid to some senior executives.

Compounding the problem created by perceptions of executive compensation is the fact that there often seems to be little or no relationship between the performance of the organization and the compensation paid to its senior executives.[34] Certainly, if an organization is performing at an especially high level and its stock price is increasing consistently, then most observers would agree that the senior executives responsible for this growth should be entitled to attractive rewards.[35] However, it is more difficult to understand a case in which executives are paid huge salaries and other forms of rewards when their company is performing at only a marginal level, yet this is fairly common today. For example, in 2002 Oracle's CEO, Lawrence Ellison, pocketed over $700 million from the sale of previously granted stock options, while the value of Oracle stock was dropping by 57 percent.

Finally, we should note that the gap between the earnings of the CEO and the earnings of a typical employee is enormous. First of all, the size of the gap has been increasing in the United States. In 1980 the typical CEO earned 42 times the earnings of an ordinary worker, but by 1990 this ratio had increased to 85 times the earnings of an ordinary worker. In Japan, on the other hand, the relationship in 1990 was that a typical CEO made less than 20 times the earnings of an ordinary worker.[36]

New Approaches to Performance-Based Rewards

Some organizations have started to recognize that they can leverage the value of the incentives that they offer to their employees and to groups in their organization by allowing those individuals and groups to have a say in how rewards are distributed. For example, at the extreme, a company could go so far as to grant salary increase budgets to work groups and then allow the members of those groups themselves to determine how the rewards are going to be allocated among the various members of the group. This strategy would appear to hold considerable promise if everyone understands the performance arrangements that exist in the work group and everyone is committed to being fair and equitable. Unfortunately, it can also create problems if people in a group feel that rewards are not being distributed fairly.[37]

Organizations are also getting increasingly innovative in their incentive programs. For example, some now offer stock options to all their employees, rather than just to top executives. In addition, some firms are looking into ways to purely individualize reward systems. For instance, a firm might offer one employee a paid three-month sabbatical every two years in exchange for a 20 percent reduction in salary. Another employee in the same firm might be offered a 10 percent salary increase in exchange for a 5 percent reduction in company contributions to the person's retirement account. Corning, General Electric, and Microsoft are among the firms closely studying this option.[38]

Regardless of the method used, however, it is also important that managers in an organization effectively communicate what rewards are being distributed and the basis for that distribution. In other words, if incentives are being distributed on the basis of perceived individual contributions to the organization, then members of the organization should be informed of that fact. This will presumably better enable them to understand the basis on which pay increases and other incentives and performance-based rewards have been distributed.

Summary of Key Points

1. Characterize the nature of motivation.
   - Motivation is the set of forces that cause people to behave in certain ways.
   - Motivation is an important consideration for managers because it, along with ability and environmental factors, determines individual performance.

2. Identify and describe the major content perspectives on motivation.
   - Content perspectives on motivation are concerned with what factor or factors cause motivation.

   - Popular content theories include Maslow's needs hierarchy and Herzberg's two-factor theory.
   - Other important needs are the needs for achievement, affiliation, and power.

3. Identify and describe the major process perspectives on motivation.
   - Process perspectives on motivation deal with how motivation occurs.
   - Expectancy theory suggests that people are motivated to perform if they believe that their effort will

result in high performance, that this performance will lead to rewards, and that the positive aspects of the outcomes outweigh the negative aspects.
- Equity theory is based on the premise that people are motivated to achieve and maintain social equity.

4. Describe reinforcement perspectives on motivation.
- The reinforcement perspective focuses on how motivation is maintained.
- Its basic assumption is that behavior that results in rewarding consequences is likely to be repeated, whereas behavior resulting in negative consequences is less likely to be repeated.
- Reinforcement contingencies can be arranged in the form of positive reinforcement, avoidance, punishment, and extinction, and they can be provided on fixed-interval, variable-interval, fixed-ratio, or variable-ratio schedules.

5. Identify and describe popular motivational strategies.
- Managers use a variety of motivational strategies derived from the various theories of motivation.
- Common strategies include empowerment and participation and alternative forms of work arrangements, such as variable work schedules, flexible work schedules, job sharing, and telecommuting.

6. Describe the role of organizational reward systems in motivation.
- Reward systems also play a key role in motivating employee performance.
- Popular methods include merit reward systems, incentive reward systems, and team and group incentive reward systems.
- Executive compensation is intended to serve as motivation for senior managers but has currently come under close scrutiny and criticism.

Discussion Questions

Questions for Review

1. Summarize Maslow's needs hierarchy and the two-factor theory. In what ways are they similar and in what ways are they different?

2. Compare and contrast content, process, and reinforcement perspectives on motivation.

3. Using equity theory as a framework, explain how a person can experience inequity because he or she is paid too much. What are the potential outcomes of this situation?

4. Explain how goal-setting theory works. How is goal setting different from merely asking a worker to "do your best"?

5. Describe some new forms of working arrangements. How do these alternative arrangements increase motivation?

Questions for Analysis

1. Choose one theory from the content perspectives and one from the process perspectives. Describe actions that a manager might take to increase worker motivation under each of the theories. What differences do you see between the theories in terms of their implications for managers?

2. Can factors from both the content and the process perspectives be acting on a worker at the same time? Explain why or why not. Whether you answered yes or no to the previous question, explain the implications for managers.

3. How do rewards increase motivation? What would happen if an organization gave too few rewards? What would happen if it gave too many?

4. Think about the worst job you have held. What approach to motivation was used in that organization? Now think about the best job you have held. What approach to motivation was used there? Can you base any conclusions on this limited information? If so, what are they?

5. Consider a class you have taken. Using just that one class, offer examples of times when the professor used positive reinforcement, avoidance, punishment, and extinction to manage students' behavior.

Building Effective Interpersonal and Communication Skills

Exercise Overview

Interpersonal skills reflect the manager's ability to understand and motivate individuals and groups, and communication skills reflect the ability to send and receive information effectively. This exercise shows, in a very explicit way, how essential understanding and communicating are for motivating workers.

Exercise Background

One implication of reinforcement theory is that both positive reinforcement (reward) and punishment can be effective in altering employee behavior. However, the use of punishment may also cause resentment on the worker's part, which can reduce the effectiveness of punishment over the long term. Therefore, over time, positive reinforcement is more effective.

Exercise Task

Your professor will ask for volunteers to perform a demonstration in front of the class. Consider volunteering or observe the demonstration. Then answer the following questions:

1. On the basis of what you saw, which do you judge to be more effective, positive reinforcement or punishment?

2. How did positive reinforcement and punishment affect the "employee" in the demonstration? How did they affect the "boss"?

3. What do you think are the probable long-term consequences of positive reinforcement and of punishment?

Reprinted by permission of the author Margaret Hill.

Building Effective Decision-Making Skills

Exercise Overview

Decision-making skills include the manager's ability to recognize and define situations correctly and to select courses of action. This exercise offers you an opportunity to build decision-making skills, while using goal-setting theory to help you plan your career.

Exercise Background

Lee Iacocca started his career at Ford in 1946 in an entry-level engineering job. By 1960 he was a vice president and in charge of the group that designed the Mustang. By 1970 he was a president of the firm. After being fired from Ford in 1978, he became a president at Chrysler and rose to the CEO spot, retiring in 1992. What is really remarkable in Iacocca's rise to power is that he had it all planned out, even before he completed college.

As legend has it, Iacocca wrote out a list while he was still an undergraduate of all the positions he would like to hold throughout his career. The first item on his list was "Engineer at an auto maker." He then wrote down all the career steps he planned to make, ending with CEO. He also wrote down a timetable for his promotions. He put the list on a three-by-five-inch card, which he folded and stowed in his wallet. The story tells us that Iacocca took out that card frequently to look at it and that, each time he did so, he gained fresh confidence and drive. Apparently he reached the pinnacle several years earlier than he anticipated and he switched from Ford to Chrysler, but he followed the career path faithfully. Iacocca used goal-setting theory to motivate himself to reach his ultimate career aspirations and you can do the same.

Exercise Task

1. Consider what position you would like to hold at the peak of your career. It may be CEO, or it may be owner of a chain of stores, or partner in a law or accounting firm, or president of a university. It may be something less lofty. Whatever it is, write it down.

2. Choose a career path that will lead you toward that goal. It may help to work "backward"—that is, to start with your final positions and work back in time to an entry-level position. If you do not know the career path that will lead to your ultimate goal, do some research. You can talk to someone in that career field, ask a professor in that subject, or get information online. For example, the AICPA's website has a section titled "Career Development and Workplace Issues," which includes information about career paths and position descriptions for accounting (although it takes a bit of digging down through multiple web pages to find it). Many other occupations have similar information online.

3. Write down each step in your path on a card or a sheet of paper.

4. If you were to carry this paper with you and refer to it often, do you think it would help you achieve your ultimate goal? Why or why not?

Reprinted by permission of the author Margaret Hill.

Building Effective Conceptual and Diagnostic Skills

Exercise Overview

Conceptual skills reflect a manager's ability to think in the abstract, and diagnostic skills focus on responses to situations. These skills must be used together to relate motivation theory to your individual needs and your future career choices.

Exercise Background

First, you will develop a list of things you want from life and categorize them according to one of the theories in the chapter. Then you will find out about motivating factors that tend to be present in a career of your choice. Finally, you will consider how your needs can be met at the career you choose.

Exercise Task

1. Prepare a list of approximately 15 things you want from an entry-level job, the job you will seek following graduation. These can be very specific (such as a new car) or very general (such as a feeling of accomplishment).

2. Choose the content theory that best fits your set of needs. Classify each item on your wish list in terms of the need or needs it might satisfy.

3. Use the Internet to research your entry-level job. (*Hint:* One good source is the *Occupational Outlook Handbook* on the Bureau of Labor Statistics website, at http://www.bls.gov/oco/home.htm.) Investigate any items that are related to the needs you specified in response to Question 1, such as compensation, benefits, working conditions, and so on.

4. Did the theoretical framework help you classify your individual needs? Explain. As a result, do you now place more or less trust in the need theories as viable management tools?

5. In what ways does your chosen entry-level job fulfill your needs? In what ways does it fail to do so? If it does satisfy your needs, will you be motivated? If it does not satisfy your needs, will you be unmotivated, or will you find another way to address any discrepancies (such as working a second job or developing a hobby)? Explain.

Skills Self-Assessment Instrument

Assessing Your Needs

Introduction: Needs are one factor that influences motivation. The following assessment surveys your judgments about some of the personal needs that might be partially shaping your motivation.

Instructions: Judge how descriptively accurate each of the following statements is about you. You may find making a decision difficult in some cases, but you should force yourself to make a choice. Record your answers next to each statement according to the following scale:

Rating Scale

5 Very descriptive of me

4 Fairly descriptive of me

3 Somewhat descriptive of me

2 Not very descriptive of me

1 Not descriptive of me at all

_____ 1. I aspire to accomplish difficult tasks and maintain high standards and am willing to work toward distant goals.

_____ 2. I enjoy being with friends and people in general and accept people readily.

_____ 3. I am easily annoyed and am sometimes willing to hurt people to get my way.

_____ 4. I try to break away from restraints or restrictions of any kind.

_____ 5. I want to be the center of attention and enjoy having an audience.

_____ 6. I speak freely and tend to act on the spur of the moment.

_____ 7. I assist others whenever possible, giving sympathy and comfort to those in need.

_____ 8. I believe in the saying that "there is a place for everything and everything should be in its place." I dislike clutter.

_____ 9. I express my opinions forcefully, enjoy the role of leader, and try to control my environment as much as I can.

_____ 10. I want to understand many areas of knowledge and value synthesizing ideas and generalization.

For interpretation, see Interpretations of Skills Self-Assessment Instruments in the appendix near the end of this text.

Experiential Exercise

Motivation at Bluefield

Bob works at the oldest plant of a fast-growing cosmetics manufacturer in Bluefield, West Virginia. Bob has an MBA from State University and began his career at Bluefield in human resources. He got his first big break when the company, which faced increasing problems with the local minority community, put Bob in charge of a new affirmative action program. Bob is proud of his success in that position. His supervisors were also impressed and promoted him to manager of machine operations. He manages a workforce of 74 employees through seven supervisors and has held this job for only one year.

With a new program to revitalize operations at Bluefield and because of his earlier success, Bob has been asked to develop a motivation plan for his seven subordinate supervisors. Bob needs to review the personnel files and try to identify the needs or motivators for each supervisor. To provide a working framework for

his analysis, Bob decides to use both Maslow's needs hierarchy and Herzberg's two-factor theory, as shown on the Need/Motivation Worksheet.

Bob divides the worksheet into three sections: (1) Maslow's Needs, (2) Motivation Factors, (3) Hygiene Factors. In each category, he plans to rank the appropriate items for each supervisor, using a 1 for the top ranking, a 2 for the second ranking, etc.

Instructions:

1. Read the personnel files below. In addition to other data, each profile contains a supervisor's Performance Measure. This is a score assigned by a computer-based productivity program developed by the industrial engineering department. The program uses a variety of cost and output figures to calculate a Performance Measure (PM) for each supervisor on a scale ranging from 0 (representing very poor performance) to 100 (nearly perfect performance).

2. In small groups, use the Need/Motivation Worksheet to rank the relative importance of each of the motivators for each supervisor. Rank within groups—1 to 5 for Maslow's needs, then 1 to 5 for motivation factors, then 1 to 6 for hygiene factors.

3. Present your group findings to the class and discuss.

Bluefield Plant Supervisor Profiles

JOHN MILLER is the senior supervisor with 21 years of seniority. He is 60 years old and has only a sixth-grade education. His most recent PM score is 50, which is lower than it used to be. John's past appraisals suggest that he has done an average job historically. Bob, who thinks his performance is still average, is sorry to see John's performance declining. His peers are convinced that John is too old to cut the mustard. Bob thinks that John has the easiest job in the group. John is a widower who spends a lot of time at his cabin by the lake. His current salary is $45,000.

MOHAMMAD NAJEED is 52 and has spent 16 years with the firm. His PM is 70 and his salary is $38,000. Mohammad is a high-school graduate, and his wife is quite wealthy. Bob believes that Mohammad has the best overall experience in the group and is a very capable supervisor, although his peers rank him average, the same as his past evaluations. Mohammad supervises a group that has about average responsibilities.

TANIKA FORESTER is 36 with 10 years of seniority. She has a B.S. in management, a PM of 80, and a salary of $31,000. Bob feels she has one of the easier jobs and is doing only a so-so job. He is surprised to find that her earlier appraisals have been very good, an evaluation shared by her peers. Tanika's husband was killed in a car accident, and she has three dependent children.

TOM WILSON is 44 and has spent 14 years with the company. Tom has a high-school diploma, a PM of 50, and a salary of $28,000. Tom has the hardest group to supervise, but his earlier appraisals have only been average, an opinion shared by Tom's peers. Bob agrees that Tom's performance is average and is concerned that it might get worse, as Tom seems to be having too many personal problems lately.

SIDNEY BENTON is 35 and has 8 years of seniority, a PM of 80, and a salary of $26,000. Sidney has a B.S. in industrial technology and is enrolled in State's night M.B.A. program. Sidney has a difficult job, requiring specialized skills, and he would be very hard to replace. Bob believes Sidney to be a top supervisor, an opinion shared by his peers. But Bob is troubled by past appraisals that vary from outstanding to poor.

LI TRAN is 32 with 5 years at the plant, a PM of only 30, and a salary of $22,000. She is a high-school dropout who quit school to have her first child. She is a single parent with four children and works very hard to support them. Li represents one of the affirmative action promotions that Bob arranged when he was the affirmative action officer, and he is disappointed to find that her past and present appraisals are quite poor. Although her present job is perceived to require average skill, her peers consider her to be an incompetent troublemaker who constantly complains about the need for more affirmative action efforts at the plant.

LUIS FUENTES is 26, has only 2 years with the company, a PM of only 20, and a salary of $19,000. He dropped out of school to take care of his sick mother and two younger sisters. Bob hired Luis as part of the affirmative action program. Luis's first appraisal was low, but Bob believes that was because he was in a job requiring too much experience. So Bob moved him to a job with more average demands. Bob thinks that Luis is doing a bit better in the new job and, in time, will be a good supervisor. Peer evaluations are somewhat mixed but above average.

Need/Motivation Worksheet

(In each category. Rank the appropriate items for each supervisor.

Top rank = 1, Second rank = 2, etc.)

Need/Factor	John Miller	Mohammed Najeed	Tanika Forester	Tom Wilson	Sidney Benton	Li Tran	Luis Fuentes
Maslow's Needs							
Physiological							
Security							
Belongingness							
Esteem							
Self-Actualization							
Motivation Factors							
Achivement							
Recognition							
Work Itself							
Responsibility							
Advancement/ Growth							
Hygiene Factors							
Supervision							
Working conditions							
Interpersonal							
Pay							
Security							
Policy & Administration							

Adapted from Morable, *Exercises in Management*, to accompany Griffin, *Management*, 8th edition.

CHAPTER CLOSING CASE

YOU'VE GOT TO LOVE THIS JOB

For most of us, dream jobs are just that—a dream. Yet some individuals are lucky enough to land the perfect job, one that combines their unique talents and interests in a way that is rewarding and also offers unique benefits to employers. Dana Gioia, a Stanford MBA who ultimately became a marketing vice president at General Foods, is one example. For fun, he wrote poetry and was skilled enough to see many of his poems published. After leaving corporate America and spending a decade as a serious writer, President Bush asked him to be chairman of the National Endowment for the Arts. Gioia says, "This is the only job I've ever had in which I use pretty much everything I know."

Others are wise enough to let their dream job evolve over time. Tim Brosnan turned his childhood interest in baseball into a business position with the New York Yankees and today heads corporate sponsorships for Major League Baseball. Rick Steves, a piano teacher, enjoyed travel to Europe to listen to concerts. Ultimately, he began to make presentations about his travel experiences, then to write travel guidebooks. "I'm real thankful that I found something I love doing that works from a business point of view," says Steves. "The joy and reward in my work have always been about teaching." Today he produces a PBS television travel series and owns a travel company.

Firms find that creating positions based on an employee's interests can be a reward for high performance. Steve Gluckman is a bicycle designer for REI, a supplier of outdoor gear. Gluckman worked his way up from service manager to designer over thirteen years. An avid cyclist, he says, "Some people sing. Some people paint. I ride my bike. Like a ballet dancer, like a gymnast, like a skateboarder, I express myself in my job." Starbucks's coffee education manager, Aileen Carrell, travels around the world educating employees about coffee. "I was hired as temporary Christmas help . . . and I fell madly in love with the fact that coffees came from the most amazing places, like Sulawesi." After working as a store manager for several years, Carrell moved into her exciting and challenging position.

Sometimes individuals are so motivated by an activity that they search for an employer who will allow them to do what they love. Holly Brewster Jones was an independent artist for years but wanted more job security. She says, "I applied for a graphic design job at SAS Institute, which I really wasn't qualified for. They called me about a week later for the artist-in-residence job." She paints about sixty works a year for display in the company's campuslike headquarters. "I'll paint until I retire, probably," asserts Jones. "And even then I'll still be an artist."

When high-performing workers define their dream jobs, they can come up with offbeat ideas that take the company in new and interesting directions. At financial services firm Citigroup, Sandra Feagan Stern has carved out a unique niche: ranching. Stern is a private banker, serving clients who invest $3 million or more.

The combination of her extensive knowledge of ranching and her financial savvy makes Stern the perfect person to recommend and manage investments in thoroughbreds and second homes.

Pat Connors found his dream job—managing Agilent's corporate retreat in the Pennsylvania Poconos. He previously worked on the firm's manufacturing line but wanted a change. "I'm a naturalist at heart," says Connors. "I enjoy what I do. I'm living a dream." Connors finds the work itself rewarding, because it utilizes his talents and skills. "It was a round peg in a round hole," he claims.

As these examples show, if companies want to motivate workers, maybe they should focus less on offering incentives to individuals who are doing tasks they find unexciting and uninspiring. Instead, firms could ask employees to tell them how to make their jobs more motivating. Employees are the experts in what motivates them. Perhaps they are also the most effective job designers.

CASE QUESTIONS

1. For each of the employees mentioned in the case, determine which needs they are working to fulfill, using Maslow's hierarchy. Explain how you arrived at your answers.

2. Tell whether the workers described in the case are high or low on satisfaction and dissatisfaction, according to Herzberg's theory. Do the examples tend to support Herzberg's claim that satisfaction and dissatisfaction

are based on two independent sets of factors?

3. Allowing employees control over their job design is empowering. What are some benefits that firms might expect from empowering their employees? What are some problems that firms might encounter as they empower their employees? In the case, are there any examples of the benefits or problems associated with empowerment? If so, describe them.

REFERENCES

Lee Clifford, "Citigroup Bets (on) the Ranch," *Fortune*, January 8, 2002, www.fortune.com on February 6, 2003; Michael A. Prospero, "Dream Jobs," *Fast Company*, July 2005, www.fastcompany.com on January 20, 2006; Curtis Sittenfeld, "Poet-In-Chief," *Fast Company*, November 7, 2005, www.fastcompany.com on January 20, 2006; Eric Wahlgren, "Online Extra: Goodbye, 'Guru of Fun,'" *BusinessWeek*, August 27, 2001, www.businessweek.com on February 6, 2003; "You Get Paid to Do What?" *Fortune*, January 20, 2003, www.fortune.com on January 13, 2003.

YOU MAKE THE CALL

Motivation Without Borders

1. Would working with Doctors Without Borders satisfy your individual needs? Explain why or why not.

2. This case highlights workers for whom intrinsic rewards seem to be more important than extrinsic ones. Do you know anyone for whom the opposite is true; that is, someone for whom extrinsic rewards are more important than intrinsic? How do these individuals differ from the workers described in the case?

3. Although Doctors Without Borders is effective in helping groups of individuals, it cannot affect the underlying causes, such as natural disaster or war. If you worked with the organization, how might this fact affect your motivation?

4. Are there any lessons that profit-making companies can learn from studying motivation as it relates to Doctors Without Borders? Describe them.

Test Prepper

You've read the chapter, studied the key terms, and the exam is any day now. Think you're ready to ace it? Take this sample test to gauge your comprehension of chapter material. You can check your answers at the back of the book. Want more test questions? Visit the student website at http://college.hmco.com/pic/griffinfund5e/ and take the ACE quizzes for more practice.

1. T F Approaches to motivation that try to answer the question "What factor or factors motivate people?" are called needs perspectives.

2. T F Herzberg's two-factor theory of motivation suggests that people's satisfaction and dissatisfaction are influenced by two independent sets of factors: need for achievement and need for affiliation.

3. T F Your supervisor tells you to increase productivity by 10 percent. This manager has created goal commitment.

4. T F Yolanda is paid the last day of each month. This is a fixed-ratio schedule.

5. T F Incentive pay plans usually increase base pay.

6. Which of the following determines performance?

    a. Motivation

    b. Ability

    c. Work environment

    d. The capability to do the job

    e. All of the above

7. An organization contributes to fulfillment of the lowest level of Maslow's need hierarchy through

    a. job challenges.

    b. socialization.

    c. adequate wages.

    d. a pension plan.

    e. job sharing.

8. According to expectancy theory, an index of how much an individual values an outcome is called

    a. the effort-to-performance ratio.

    b. the performance-to-outcome ratio.

    c. a valence.

    d. outcomes.

    e. None of the above

9. Bob works from 6:00 A.M. to 4:00 P.M. four days a week. He uses which alternative work arrangement?

    a. Job sharing

    b. Telecommuting

    c. A compressed workweek

    d. A part-time schedule

    e. All of the above

10. When a factory work team receives 25 percent of the cost savings for a suggestion it made, this is an example of

    a. gainsharing.

    b. a Scanlon plan.

    c. a stock option plan,

    d. a compensation plan.

    e. a benefits plan.

Leadership and Influence Processes

FIRST THINGS FIRST

Watch Out Bud, Miller Is Catching Up

"[Adami's tactics are] a way to build a passion and let people remember once again what we're all about: beer."

—VIRGIS W. COLBERT, BOARD MEMBER, MILLER

When South African Brewing purchased Miller Brewing from Philip Morris (now Altria) in 2003 to create SABMiller PLC, investors were skeptical. After all, SAB was new to the United States and had paid $5.6 billion for Miller, which was losing the competitive battle to arch rival Anheuser-Busch (A-B), maker of Budweiser. When SAB named Norman J. Adami, a South African with no U.S. experience, as CEO of Miller, that seemed to further jeopardize the merged venture. But the skeptics were wrong.

Adami's success arises from his behavior as a leader. According to observers, he is a "charismatic leader [who] has motivated a long-complacent workforce" and the creator of a "seismic cultural shift." Adami's primary skill is vision. When Adami first came on board at Miller, he expected to make only routine changes. Yet he quickly realized that the company was "stuck in a downward cycle, a vicious cycle," he says. "We needed to fundamentally change the direction of the company." Adami embarked on changes throughout the organization, from speeding up decision making to rebuilding relationships with the distributors who are Miller's customers.

Adami's leadership style alternates between personal charm, openness to change, aggressive competitiveness, a sense of humor, and careful attention to operational and financial details. He has been known to send flowers to managers' wives on their birthdays, and he responded to and won a chugging contest with MTV's Jamie Kennedy. Adami encourages advertising that goes head-to-head against A-B. He's pushed the marketing department to respond to new A-B ads in one week, rather than the previous time of 3 to 6 months. "Everything's . . . slightly too slow for Norman," says Denise Smith, Miller Senior Vice President.

Adami has also made some excellent, if controversial, decisions. One was to create Fred's Pub, a 2,700-foot lounge, inside the company's Minneapolis headquarters. Here, coworkers from different departments get a chance to have casual conversations, cross hierarchical boundaries, and enjoy work. Adami visits regularly, getting to know employees and seeking out their honest feedback. "[Beer] makes people brave," jokes Adami. The CEO also began Beer University, a course for all employees to study and sample the company's products. "[Adami's tactics are] a way to build a passion and let people remember once again what we're all about: beer," says Virgis W. Colbert, Miller board member.

Other changes include Miller Chill, modeled after Mexican *chelada* beer, flavored with lime and salt. Adami hope to attract Hispanic customers, who make up the largest, fastest-growing, and youngest ethnic group. A new marketing push will do more to promote imported beers near ethnic communities, for example, to strengthen the Polish brand Tyskie in Chicago. Adami recruited top managers from outside of Miller, including Tom Long from Coca-Cola and Tom Cardella, from rival InBev, a Belgian firm that brews Bass and Beck's, among others.

Adami's leadership got results. Sales of Miller Lite increased by 3.2 percent in 2005, in spite of price cuts. Bud Light sales remained flat and overall industry sales dropped slightly over the same period. A-B's stock price declined 4 percent while SABMiller's soared by 190 percent.

In August 2006, Adami was promoted to CEO of SABMiller Americas, with responsibility for North, Central, and South America. Tom Long moved up to head Miller Brewing of North America. His 17-year career in marketing with Coca-Cola included stints as Coke's head for the Wal-Mart and 7-Eleven accounts.

Miller still faces challenges. "The turnaround phase was tough. There was a lot of fear," says Adami. "The next phase is just as tough." Domestic beer sales are flat. Developing nations offer more opportunities than domestic markets, but an overseas acquisition will be expensive and difficult to integrate. Ad campaigns still need work too. A-B is experimenting with Bud.TV, a website that features YouTube-like videos that they hope will attract the important 20-something demographic.

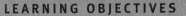

LEARNING OBJECTIVES

After studying this chapter, you should be able to:

- Describe the nature of leadership and relate leadership to management.
- Discuss and evaluate the two generic approaches to leadership.
- Identify and describe the major situational approaches to leadership.
- Identify and describe three related approaches to leadership.
- Describe three emerging approaches to leadership.
- Discuss political behavior in organizations and how it can be managed.

Norman Adami's strong leadership has pumped new life into Miller Brewing since it was purchased by South African Brewing.

In addition, while demand for beer in the United States increased by 3 percent in 2006, Miller sales began to fall. After a strong revival under Adami, the company may be faltering. SAB CEO Graham Mackay sums up the previous situation bluntly, "Anheuser-Busch used to take all the incremental growth, while the rest of the industry got weaker. We've become much stronger, and . . . there's no longer a carcass to feed on." That may be true, but it's going to take more strong leadership to keep Miller Brewing's recovery going strong.[1]

The story of Norman Adami and Miller Brewing provides several vivid examples of the roles and importance of leadership. Different circumstances call for different kinds of leadership. Miller was in a downward spiral and radical changes were needed to reverse things. While Adami did not envision having to make major changes when he took over, he quickly realized that his original assumptions were wrong and that change was indeed necessary. A different leader might have adopted very different kinds of change; likewise, had Adami's original assumptions been correct he would have implemented far less change.

This chapter examines people like Norman Adami more carefully by focusing on leadership and its role in management. We characterize the nature of leadership and trace through the three major approaches to studying leadership—traits, behaviors, and situations. After examining other perspectives on leadership, we conclude by describing another approach to influencing others—political behavior in organizations.

The Nature of Leadership

In Chapter 10, we described various models and perspectives on employee motivation. From the manager's standpoint, trying to motivate people is an attempt to influence their behavior. In many ways, leadership, too, is an attempt to influence the behavior of others. In this section, we first define leadership, then differentiate it from management, and conclude by relating it to power.

The Meaning of Leadership

> **leadership**
>
> As a *process*, the use of noncoercive influence to shape the group's or organization's goals, motivate behavior toward the achievement of those goals, and help define group or organizational culture; as a *property*, the set of characteristics attributed to individuals who are perceived to be leaders

Leadership is both a process and a property.[2] As a process—focusing on what leaders actually do—leadership is the use of noncoercive influence to shape the group or organization's goals, motivate behavior toward the achievement of those goals, and help define group or organizational culture.[3] As a property, leadership is the set of characteristics attributed to individuals who are perceived to be leaders. Thus **leaders** are people who can influence the behaviors of others without having to rely on force or people whom others accept as leaders.

Leadership and Management

From these definitions, it should be clear that leadership and management are related, but they are not the same. A person can be a manager, a leader, both, or neither.[4] Some of the basic distinctions between the two are summarized in Table 11.1. At the left side of the table are four elements that differentiate leadership from management. The two columns show how each element differs when considered from

Activity	Management	Leadership
Creating an agenda	*Planning and Budgeting.* Establishing detailed steps and timetables for achieving needed results; allocating the resources necessary to make those needed results happen	*Establishing Direction.* Developing a vision of the future, often the distant future, and strategies for producing the changes needed to achieve that vision
Developing a human network for achieving the agenda	*Organizing and Staffing.* Establishing some structure for accomplishing plan requirements, staffing that structure with individuals, delegating responsibility and authority for carrying out the plan, providing policies and procedures to help guide people, and creating methods or systems to monitor implementation	*Aligning People.* Communicating the direction by words and deeds to everyone whose cooperation may be needed to influence the creation of teams and coalitions that understand the visions and strategies and accept their validity
Executing plans	*Controlling and Problem Solving.* Monitoring results versus planning in some detail, identifying deviations, and then planning and organizing to solve these problems	*Motivating and Inspiring.* Energizing people to overcome major political, bureaucratic, and resource barriers by satisfying very basic, but often unfulfilled, human needs
Outcomes	Produces a degree of predictability and order and has the potential to produce consistently major results expected by various stakeholders (for example, for customers, always being on time; for stockholders, being on budget)	Produces change, often to a dramatic degree, and has the potential to produce extremely useful change (for example, new products that customers want, new approaches to labor relations that help make a firm more competitive)

Table 11.1

DISTINCTIONS BETWEEN MANAGEMENT AND LEADERSHIP

Management and leadership are related, but distinct, constructs. Managers and leaders differ in how they create an agenda, develop a rationale for achieving the agenda, and execute plans, and in the types of outcomes they achieve.

Source: Reprinted with permission of The Free Press, a division of Simon & Schuster Adult Publishing Group, from *A Force for Change: How Leadership Differs from Management* by John P. Kotter. Copyright © 1990 by John P. Kotter, Inc.

a management and from a leadership point of view. For example, when executing plans, managers focus on monitoring results, comparing them with goals, and correcting deviations. In contrast, the leader focuses on energizing people to overcome bureaucratic hurdles to reach goals.

Organizations need both management and leadership if they are to be effective. Leadership is necessary to create change, and management is necessary to achieve orderly results. Management in conjunction with leadership can produce orderly change, and leadership in conjunction with management can keep the organization properly aligned with its environment. Indeed, perhaps part of the reason why executive compensation has soared in recent years is the belief that management and leadership skills reflect a critical but rare combination that can lead to organizational success.

> *Leaders*
> People who can influence the behaviors of others without having to rely on force; those accepted by others as leaders

Leadership and Power

To fully understand leadership, it is necessary to understand power. **Power** is the ability to affect the behavior of others. One can have power without actually using it. For example, a football coach has the power to bench a player who is not performing up to par. The coach seldom has to use this power because players recognize that the power exists and work hard to keep their starting positions. In organizational settings, there are usually five kinds of power: legitimate, reward, coercive, referent, and expert power.[5]

> *Power*
> The ability to affect the behavior of others

Managing in Times of Change

Measuring Excellent Leadership

What makes a great leader? Is it returns to stockholders, innovation, strengthening core businesses, inspiring workers, wooing customers, or something else entirely? In the 1950s, a "company man" who maintained a stable culture was considered high-performing. In the 1970s, the stock market became the preferred indicator of CEO excellence. Now a new view is emerging.

Today, share price alone isn't enough. During a bull market, even mediocre leaders get rewarded. Focus on share price requires leaders to respond to quarterly earnings targets set by Wall Street analysts, with too much focus on short-term results and the temptation to manipulate financial statements. Share price fluctuates too much. Joshua Fox, a *Fortune* writer, says, "The stock market [is] great at assessing CEOs—if you can wait a decade or two for short-term noise to wash away."

A "balanced scorecard" approach considers stock price but it also takes into account leader behavior outcomes such as customer satisfaction and employee motivation. For example, Best Buy CEO Brad Anderson's performance metrics include customer loyalty, worker turnover, and store revenue. The balanced scorecard is somewhat a return to the 1950s, with its emphasis on maintaining the health of the organization. Yet while CEOs like the balanced scorecard, most investors do not. It has caused leaders such as Anne Mulcahy of

Xerox and Jeff Immelt of GE to receive high compensation even as stock price falls.

Some experts believe that how we measure leadership may not even matter. Research has shown a primarily negative correlation between changing CEOs and corporate performance. "Good leaders can make a small positive difference; bad leaders can make a huge negative difference," says Stanford professor Jeffrey Pfeffer. He believes that it's very difficult for a CEO to cure an ailing company, but very easy to drive a good company into the ground, mainly by scaring away talented personnel.

What's really needed is a way to measure such intangibles as bonding with employees, creating alliances, generating excitement and urgency, and minimizing the impact of political behavior. Another valuable measure could focus on succession planning—choosing and nurturing the next generation of leaders. Until that can be done, we'll have to be satisfied with other, weaker measures.

References: Diane Brady, "Nothing Succeeds Like Succession," *BusinessWeek*, March 25, 2005, www.businessweek.com on February 27, 2007; Justin Fox, "The CEO Stats That Matter," *Fortune*, October 30, 2006, pp. 154–160; Ulrike Malmendier and Geoffrey Tate, "Superstar CEOs," Working paper from Stanford University, May 2005, faculty-gsb.stanford.edu on February 27, 2007; "Succession Screw-Ups," *BusinessWeek*, January 10, 2005, www.businessweek.com on February 27, 2007.

---

legitimate power
Power granted through the organizational hierarchy; the power defined by the organization to be accorded to people occupying particular positions

Legitimate Power *Legitimate power* is power granted through the organizational hierarchy; it is the power defined by the organization to be accorded to people occupying a particular position. A manager can assign tasks to a subordinate, and a subordinate who refuses to do them can be reprimanded or even fired. Such outcomes stem from the manager's legitimate power as defined and vested in her or him by the organization. Legitimate power, then, is authority. All managers have legitimate power over their subordinates. The mere possession of legitimate power, however, does not by itself make someone a leader. Some subordinates follow only orders that are strictly within the letter of organizational rules and policies. If asked to do something not in their job descriptions, they refuse or do a poor job. The manager of such employees is exercising authority but not leadership.

reward power
The power to give or withhold rewards, such as salary increases, bonuses, promotions, praise, recognition, and interesting job assignments

Reward Power *Reward power* is the power to give or withhold rewards. Rewards that a manager may control include salary increases, bonuses, promotion recommendations, praise, recognition, and interesting job assignments. In general, the greater the number of rewards a manager controls and the more important

Referent power is based on identification, imitation, loyalty, or charisma. Professional athletes often have referent power relative to young sports fans. For example, these members of the Orlando Magic professional basketball team are helping build a new playground in Sanford, Florida. The presence of the basketball players attracts involvement from many local kids, and the conduct of those players provides positive role modeling for them as well.

the rewards are to subordinates, the greater is the manager's reward power. If the subordinate sees as valuable only the formal organizational rewards provided by the manager, then he or she is not a leader. If the subordinate also wants and appreciates the manager's informal rewards, such as praise, gratitude, and recognition, however, then the manager is also exercising leadership.

Coercive Power   *Coercive power* is the power to force compliance by means of psychological, emotional, or physical threat. In the past, physical coercion in organizations was relatively common. In most organizations today, however, coercion is limited to verbal reprimands, written reprimands, disciplinary layoffs, fines, demotion, and termination. Some managers occasionally go so far as to use verbal abuse, humiliation, and psychological coercion in an attempt to manipulate subordinates. (Of course, most people would agree that these are not appropriate managerial behaviors.) James Dutt, a legendary former CEO of Beatrice Company, once told a subordinate that if his wife and family got in the way of his working a 24-hour day seven days a week, he should get rid of them.[6] The more punitive the elements under a manager's control and the more important they are to subordinates, the more coercive power the manager possesses. On the other hand, the more a manager uses coercive power, the more likely he is to provoke resentment and hostility and the less likely he is to be seen as a leader.[7]

> **coercive power**
> The power to force compliance by means of psychological, emotional, or physical threat

Referent Power   Compared with legitimate, reward, and coercive power, which are relatively concrete and grounded in objective facets of organizational life, *referent power* is abstract. It is based on identification, imitation, loyalty, or charisma. Followers may react favorably because they identify in some way with a leader, who may be like them in personality, background, or attitudes. In other situations, followers might choose to imitate a leader with referent power by wearing the same kind of clothes, working the same hours, or espousing the same management philosophy. Referent power may also take the form of charisma, an intangible attribute

> **referent power**
> The personal power that accrues to someone based on identification, imitation, loyalty, or charisma

Leaders can exercise a number of different kinds of power. Legitimate, reward, coercive, referent, and expert are common forms of power. The leader shown here seems to be relying on his legitimate power as he attempts to deflect blame on someone else. Of course, this act will also reduce his ability to motivate his employees in the future!

www.CartoonStock.com

of the leader that inspires loyalty and enthusiasm. Thus a manager might have referent power, but it is more likely to be associated with leadership.

Expert Power   ***Expert power*** is derived from information or expertise. A manager who knows how to interact with an eccentric but important customer, a scientist who is capable of achieving an important technical breakthrough that no other company has dreamed of, and a secretary who knows how to unravel bureaucratic red tape all have expert power over anyone who needs that information. The more important the information and the fewer the people who have access to it, the greater is the degree of expert power possessed by any one individual. In general, people who are both leaders and managers tend to have a lot of expert power.

> **expert power**
> The personal power that accrues to someone based on the information or expertise that they possess

Generic Approaches to Leadership

Early approaches to the study of leadership adopted what might be called a "universal" or "generic" perspective. Specifically, they assumed that there was one set of answers to the leadership puzzle. One generic approach focused on leadership traits, and the other looked at leadership behavior.

Leadership Traits

The first organized approach to studying leadership analyzed the personal, psychological, and physical traits of strong leaders. The trait approach assumed that some basic trait or set of traits existed that differentiated leaders from nonleaders. If those traits could be defined, potential leaders could be identified. Researchers thought that leadership traits might include intelligence, assertiveness, above-average height, good vocabulary, attractiveness, self-confidence, and similar attributes.[8]

During the first half of the twentieth century, hundreds of studies were conducted in an attempt to identify important leadership traits. For the most part, the results of the studies were disappointing. For every set of leaders who possessed a common trait, a long list of exceptions was also found, and the list of suggested traits soon grew so long that it had little practical value. Alternative explanations usually existed even for relationships between traits and leadership that initially appeared valid. For example, it was observed that many leaders have good communication skills and are assertive. Rather than those traits being the cause of leadership, however, successful leaders may begin to display those traits after they have achieved a leadership position.

Although most researchers gave up trying to identify traits as predictors of leadership ability, many people still explicitly or implicitly adopt a trait orientation.[9] For example, politicians are all too often elected on the basis of personal appearance, speaking ability, or an aura of self-confidence. In addition, traits like honesty and integrity may very well be fundamental leadership traits that do serve an important purpose. Intelligence also seems to play a meaningful role in leadership.[10]

Leadership Behaviors

Spurred on by their lack of success in identifying useful leadership traits, researchers soon began to investigate other variables, especially the behaviors or actions of leaders. The new hypothesis was that effective leaders somehow behaved differently than less-effective leaders. Thus the goal was to develop a fuller understanding of leadership behaviors.

Michigan Studies   Researchers at the University of Michigan, led by Rensis Likert, began studying leadership in the late 1940s.[11] Based on extensive interviews with both leaders (managers) and followers (subordinates), this research identified two basic forms of leader behavior: job centered and employee centered. Managers using *job-centered leader behavior* pay close attention to subordinates' work, explain work procedures, and are keenly interested in performance. Managers using *employee-centered leader behavior* are interested in developing a cohesive work group and ensuring that employees are satisfied with their jobs. Their primary concern is the welfare of subordinates.

> *job-centered leader behavior*
> The behavior of leaders who pay close attention to the job and work procedures involved with that job

The two styles of leader behavior were presumed to be at the ends of a single continuum. Although this suggests that leaders may be extremely job centered, extremely employee centered, or somewhere in between, Likert studied only the two end styles for contrast. He argued that employee-centered leader behavior generally tends to be more effective.

> *employee-centered leader behavior*
> The behavior of leaders who develop cohesive work groups and ensure employee satisfaction

Ohio State Studies   At about the same time that Likert was beginning his leadership studies at the University of Michigan, a group of researchers at Ohio State University also began studying leadership.[12] The extensive questionnaire surveys conducted during the Ohio State studies also suggested that there are two basic leader behaviors or styles: initiating-structure behavior and consideration behavior. When using *initiating-structure behavior*, the leader clearly defines the leader-subordinate role so that everyone knows what is expected, establishes formal lines of communication, and determines how tasks will be performed. Leaders using *consideration behavior* show concern for subordinates and attempt to establish a warm, friendly, and supportive climate. The behaviors identified at Ohio State are similar to those described at Michigan, but there are important differences. One major difference is that the Ohio State researchers

> *initiating-structure behavior*
> The behavior of leaders who define the leader-subordinate role so that everyone knows what is expected, establish formal lines of communication, and determine how tasks will be performed

consideration behavior
The behavior of leaders who show concern for subordinates and attempt to establish a warm, friendly, and supportive climate

did not interpret leader behavior as being one-dimensional; each behavior was assumed to be independent of the other. Presumably, then, a leader could exhibit varying levels of initiating structure and at the same time varying levels of consideration.

At first, the Ohio State researchers thought that leaders who exhibit high levels of both behaviors would tend to be more effective than other leaders. A study at International Harvester (now Navistar International), however, suggested a more complicated pattern.[13] The researchers found that employees of supervisors who ranked high on initiating structure were high performers but expressed low levels of satisfaction and had a higher absence rate. Conversely, employees of supervisors who ranked high on consideration had low performance ratings but high levels of satisfaction and few absences from work. Later research isolated other variables that make consistent prediction difficult and determined that situational influences also occurred. (This body of research is discussed in the section on situational approaches to leadership.[14])

Leadership Grid   Yet another behavioral approach to leadership is the Leadership Grid.[15] The Leadership Grid provides a means for evaluating leadership styles and then training managers to move toward an ideal style of behavior. The Leadership Grid is shown in Figure 11.1. The horizontal axis represents ***concern for production*** (similar to job-centered and initiating-structure behaviors), and the vertical

concern for production
The part of the Leadership Grid that deals with the job and task aspects of leader behavior

Figure 11.1
THE LEADERSHIP GRID

The Leadership Grid® is a method of evaluating leadership styles. The overall objective of an organization using the Grid® is to train its managers using organization development techniques so that they are simultaneously more concerned for both people and production (9,9 style on the Grid®).

Source: The Leadership Grid Figure for *Leadership Dilemmas—Grid Solutions* by Robert R. Blake and Anne Adams McCanse. (Formerly *The Managerial Grid* by Robert R. Blake and Jane S. Mouton.) Houston: Gulf Publishing Company, p. 29. Copyright © 1997 by Grid International, Inc. Reproduced by permission of the owners.

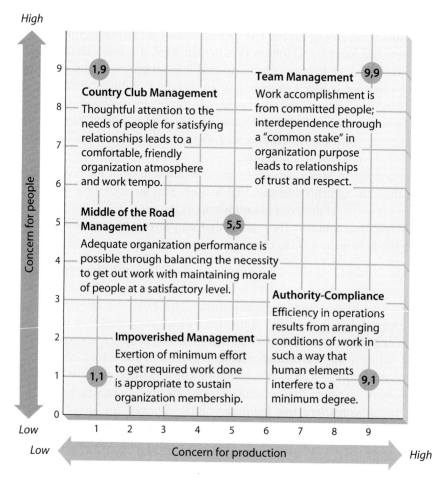

axis represents ***concern for people*** (similar to employee-centered and considera-tion behaviors). Note the five extremes of managerial behavior: the 1,1 manager (impoverished management), who exhibits minimal concern for both production and people; the 9,1 manager (authority-compliance), who is highly concerned about production but exhibits little concern for people; the 1,9 manager (country club management), who has exactly opposite concerns from the 9,1 manager; the 5,5 manager (middle-of-the-road management), who maintains adequate concern for both people and production; and the 9,9 manager (team management), who exhibits maximum concern for both people and production.

According to this approach, the ideal style of managerial behavior is 9,9. There is a six-phase program to assist managers in achieving this style of behavior. A. G. Edwards, Westinghouse, the FAA, Equicor, and other companies have used the Leadership Grid with reasonable success. However, there is little published scientific evidence regarding its true effectiveness.

The leader-behavior theories have played an important role in the develop-ment of contemporary thinking about leadership. In particular, they urge us not to be preoccupied with what leaders are (the trait approach) but to concentrate on what leaders do (their behaviors). Unfortunately, these theories also make univer-sal generic prescriptions about what constitutes effective leadership. When we are dealing with complex social systems composed of complex individuals, however, few, if any, relationships are consistently predictable, and certainly no formulas for success are infallible. Yet the behavior theorists tried to identify consistent relation-ships between leader behaviors and employee responses in the hope of finding a dependable prescription for effective leadership. As we might expect, they often failed. Other approaches to understanding leadership were therefore needed. The catalyst for these new approaches was the realization that although interpersonal and task-oriented dimensions might be useful for describing the behavior of lead-ers, they were not useful for predicting or prescribing it. The next step in the evolu-tion of leadership theory was the creation of situational models.

Situational Approaches to Leadership

Situational models assume that appropriate leader behavior varies from one situa-tion to another. The goal of a situational theory, then, is to identify key situational factors and to specify how they interact to determine appropriate leader behav-ior. In the following sections, we describe four of the most important and widely accepted situational theories of leadership: the LPC theory, the path-goal theory, Vroom's decision tree approach, and the leader-member exchange approach.

LPC Theory

The **LPC theory**, developed by Fred Fiedler, was the first truly situational theory of leadership.[16] As we will discuss later, LPC stands for least-preferred coworker. Beginning with a combined trait and behavioral approach, Fiedler identified two styles of leadership: task oriented (analogous to job-centered and initiating-structure behavior) and relationship oriented (similar to employee-centered and consideration behavior). He went beyond the earlier behavioral approaches by arguing that the style of behavior is a reflection of the leader's personality and that most personalities fall into one of his two categories—task oriented or relationship

---

concern for people
The part of the Leadership Grid that deals with the human aspects of leader behavior

LPC theory
A theory of leadership that suggests that the appropriate style of leadership varies with situational favorableness

least-preferred coworker (LPC) measure
The measuring scale that asks leaders to describe the person with whom he or she is able to work least well

oriented by nature. Fiedler measures leadership style by means of a controversial questionnaire called the ***least-preferred coworker (LPC) measure***. To use the measure, a manager or leader is asked to describe the specific person with whom he or she is able to work least well—the LPC—by filling in a set of 16 scales anchored at each end by a positive or negative adjective. For example, 3 of the 16 scales are:

Helpful	___ ___ ___ ___ ___ ___ ___ ___	Frustrating
	8 7 6 5 4 3 2 1	
Tense	___ ___ ___ ___ ___ ___ ___ ___	Relaxed
	1 2 3 4 5 6 7 8	
Boring	___ ___ ___ ___ ___ ___ ___ ___	Interesting
	1 2 3 4 5 6 7 8	

The leader's LPC score is then calculated by adding up the numbers below the line checked on each scale. Note in these three examples that the higher numbers are associated with positive qualities (helpful, relaxed, and interesting), whereas the negative qualities (frustrating, tense, and boring) have low point values. A high total score is assumed to reflect a relationship orientation and a low score a task orientation on the part of the leader. The LPC measure is controversial because researchers disagree about its validity. Some question exactly what an LPC measure reflects and whether the score is an index of behavior, personality, or some other factor.[17]

Favorableness of the Situation   The underlying assumption of situational models of leadership is that appropriate leader behavior varies from one situation to another. According to Fiedler, the key situational factor is the favorableness of the situation from the leader's point of view. This factor is determined by leader-member relations, task structure, and position power. Leader-member relations refer to the nature of the relationship between the leader and the work group. If the leader and the group have a high degree of mutual trust, respect, and confidence, and if they like one another, relations are assumed to be good. If there is little trust, respect, or confidence, and if they do not like one another, relations are poor. Naturally, good relations are more favorable.

Task structure is the degree to which the group's task is well defined. The task is structured when it is routine, easily understood, and unambiguous, and when the group has standard procedures and precedents to rely on. An unstructured task is nonroutine, ambiguous, and complex, with no standard procedures or precedents. You can see that high structure is more favorable for the leader, whereas low structure is less favorable. For example, if the task is unstructured, the group will not know what to do, and the leader will have to play a major role in guiding and directing its activities. If the task is structured, the leader will not have to get so involved and can devote time to nonsupervisory activities.

Position power is the power vested in the leader's position. If the leader has the power to assign work and to reward and punish employees, position power is assumed to be strong. But, if the leader must get job assignments approved by someone else and does not administer rewards and punishment, position power is weak, and it is more difficult to accomplish goals. From the leader's point of view, strong position power is clearly preferable to weak position power. However, position power is not as important as task structure and leader-member relations.

Favorableness and Leader Style   Fiedler and his associates conducted numerous studies linking the favorableness of various situations to leader style and the effectiveness of the group.[18] The results of these studies—and the overall framework of the theory—are shown in Figure 11.2. To interpret the model, look first at the situational factors at the top of the figure. Good or bad leader-member relations, high or low task structure, and strong or weak leader position power can be combined to yield eight unique situations. For example, good leader-member relations, high task structure, and strong leader position power (at the far left) are presumed to define the most favorable situation; bad leader-member relations, low task structure, and weak leader power (at the far right) are the least favorable. The other combinations reflect intermediate levels of favorableness.

Below each set of situations are shown the degree of favorableness and the form of leader behavior found to be most strongly associated with effective group performance for those situations. When the situation is most and least favorable, Fiedler found that a task-oriented leader is most effective. When the situation is only moderately favorable, however, a relationship-oriented leader is predicted to be most effective.

Flexibility of Leader Style   Fiedler argued that, for any given individual, leader style is essentially fixed and cannot be changed; leaders cannot change their behavior to fit a particular situation because it is linked to their particular personality traits. Thus, when a leader's style and the situation do not match, Fiedler argued that the situation should be changed to fit the leader's style. When leader-member relations are good, task structure low, and position power weak, the leader style that is most likely to be effective is relationship oriented. If the leader is task oriented, a mismatch exists. According to Fiedler, the leader can make the elements of the

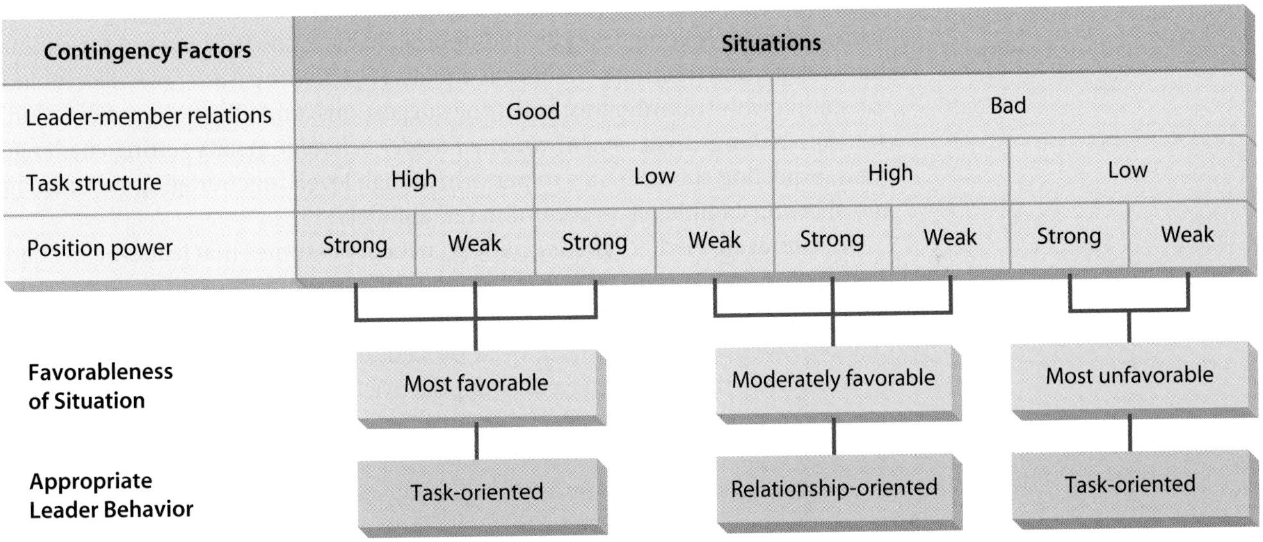

Contingency Factors	Situations							
Leader-member relations	Good				Bad			
Task structure	High		Low		High		Low	
Position power	Strong	Weak	Strong	Weak	Strong	Weak	Strong	Weak

Favorableness of Situation		Most favorable		Moderately favorable		Most unfavorable
Appropriate Leader Behavior		Task-oriented		Relationship-oriented		Task-oriented

Figure 11.2
THE LEAST-PREFERRED COWORKER THEORY OF LEADERSHIP

Fiedler's LPC theory of leadership suggests that appropriate leader behavior varies as a function of the favorableness of the situation. Favorableness, in turn, is defined by task structure, leader-member relations, and the leader's position power. According to the LPC theory, the most and least favorable situations call for task-oriented leadership, whereas moderately favorable situations suggest the need for relationship-oriented leadership.

situation more congruent by structuring the task (by developing guidelines and procedures, for instance) and increasing power (by requesting additional authority or by other means).

Fiedler's LPC theory has been attacked on the grounds that it is not always supported by research, that his findings are subject to other interpretations, that the LPC measure lacks validity, and that his assumptions about the inflexibility of leader behavior are unrealistic.[19] However, Fiedler's theory was one of the first to adopt a situational perspective on leadership. It has helped many managers recognize the important situational factors they must contend with, and it has fostered additional thinking about the situational nature of leadership. Moreover, in recent years Fiedler has attempted to address some of the concerns about his theory by revising it and adding such additional elements as cognitive resources.

Path-Goal Theory

path-goal theory
A theory of leadership suggesting that the primary functions of a leader are to make valued or desired rewards available in the workplace and to clarify for the subordinate the kinds of behavior that will lead to those rewards

The **path-goal theory** of leadership—associated most closely with Martin Evans and Robert House—is a direct extension of the expectancy theory of motivation discussed in Chapter 10.[20] Recall that the primary components of expectancy theory included the likelihood of attaining various outcomes and the value associated with those outcomes. The path-goal theory of leadership suggests that the primary functions of a leader are to make valued or desired rewards available in the workplace and to clarify for the subordinate the kinds of behavior that will lead to goal accomplishment and valued rewards—that is, the leader should clarify the paths to goal attainment.

Leader Behavior   The most fully developed version of path-goal theory identifies four kinds of leader behavior. *Directive leader behavior* lets subordinates know what is expected of them, gives guidance and direction, and schedules work. *Supportive leader behavior* is being friendly and approachable, showing concern for subordinate welfare, and treating members as equals. *Participative leader behavior* includes consulting with subordinates, soliciting suggestions, and allowing participation in decision making. *Achievement-oriented leader behavior* means setting challenging goals, expecting subordinates to perform at high levels, encouraging subordinates, and showing confidence in subordinates' abilities.

In contrast to Fiedler's theory, path-goal theory assumes that leaders can change their style or behavior to meet the demands of a particular situation. For example, when encountering a new group of subordinates and a new project, the leader may be directive in establishing work procedures and in outlining what needs to be done. Next, the leader may adopt supportive behavior to foster group cohesiveness and a positive climate. As the group becomes familiar with the task and as new problems are encountered, the leader may exhibit participative behavior to enhance group members' motivation. Finally, achievement-oriented behavior may be used to encourage continued high performance.

Situational Factors   Like other situational theories of leadership, path-goal theory suggests that appropriate leader style depends on situational factors. Path-goal theory focuses on the situational factors of the personal characteristics of subordinates and environmental characteristics of the workplace.

Important personal characteristics include the subordinates' perception of their own abilities and their locus of control. If people perceive that they are lacking in abilities, they may prefer directive leadership to help them understand path-goal relationships better. If they perceive themselves to have a lot of abilities, however, employees may resent directive leadership. Locus of control is a personality trait. People who have an internal locus of control believe that what happens to them is a function of their own efforts and behavior. Those who have an external locus of control assume that fate, luck, or "the system" determines what happens to them. A person with an internal locus of control may prefer participative leadership, whereas a person with an external locus of control may prefer directive leadership. Managers can do little or nothing to influence the personal characteristics of subordinates, but they can shape the environment to take advantage of these personal characteristics by, for example, providing rewards and structuring tasks.

Environmental characteristics include factors outside the subordinates' control. Task structure is one such factor. When structure is high, directive leadership is less effective than when structure is low. Subordinates do not usually need their boss to continually tell them how to do an extremely routine job. The formal authority system is another important environmental characteristic. Again, the higher the degree of formality, the less directive is the leader behavior that will be accepted by subordinates. The nature of the work group also affects appropriate leader behavior. When the work group provides the employee with social support and satisfaction, supportive leader behavior is less critical. When social support and satisfaction cannot be derived from the group, the worker may look to the leader for this support.

The basic path-goal framework as illustrated in Figure 11.3 shows that different leader behaviors affect subordinates' motivation to perform. Personal and environmental characteristics are seen as defining which behaviors lead to which outcomes. The path-goal theory of leadership is a dynamic and incomplete model. The original intent was to state the theory in general terms so that future research could explore a variety of interrelationships and modify the theory. Research that has been done suggests that the path-goal theory is a reasonably good description of the leadership process and that future investigations along these lines should enable us to discover more about the link between leadership and motivation.[21]

Vroom's decision tree approach
Predicts what kinds of situations call for different degrees of group participation

Vroom's Decision Tree Approach

The third major contemporary approach to leadership is ***Vroom's decision tree approach***. The earliest version of this model was proposed by Victor Vroom and

Figure 11.3
THE PATH-GOAL FRAMEWORK

The path-goal theory of leadership suggests that managers can use four types of leader behavior to clarify subordinates' paths to goal attainment. Personal characteristics of the subordinate and environmental characteristics within the organization both must be taken into account when determining which style of leadership will work best for a particular situation.

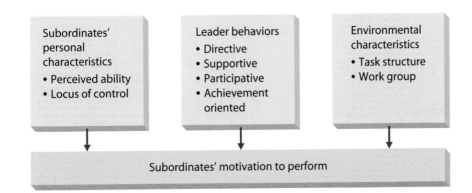

Philip Yetton and later revised and expanded by Vroom and Arthur Jago.[22] Most recently, Vroom has developed yet another refinement of the original model.[23] Like the path-goal theory, this approach attempts to prescribe a leadership style appropriate to a given situation. It also assumes that the same leader may display different leadership styles. But Vroom's approach concerns itself with only a single aspect of leader behavior: subordinate participation in decision making.

Basic Premises Vroom's decision tree approach assumes that the degree to which subordinates should be encouraged to participate in decision making depends on the characteristics of the situation. In other words, no one decision-making process is best for all situations. After evaluating a variety of problem attributes (characteristics of the problem or decision), the leader determines an appropriate decision style that specifies the amount of subordinate participation.

Vroom's current formulation suggests that managers use one of two different decision trees.[24] To do so, the manager first assesses the situation in terms of several factors. This assessment involves determining whether the given factor is high or low for the decision that is to be made. For instance, the first factor is decision significance. If the decision is extremely important and may have a major impact on the organization (such as choosing a location for a new plant), its significance is high. But, if the decision is routine and its consequences are

Figure 11.4
VROOM'S TIME-DRIVEN DECISION TREE

This matrix is recommended for situations where time is of the highest importance in making a decision. The matrix operates like a funnel. You start at the left with a specific decision problem in mind. The column headings denote situational factors that may or may not be present in that problem. You progress by selecting high or low (H or L) for each relevant situational factor. Proceed down the funnel, judging only those situational factors for which a judgment is called, until you reach the recommended process.

Source: Table 2.1, "Decision Methods for Group and Individual Problems" is from *Leadership and Decision Making* by Victor H. Vroom and Philip W. Yetton, © 1973. Adapted and reprinted by permission of University of Pittsburgh Press.

	Decision Significance	Importance of Commitment	Leader Expertise	Likelihood of Commitment	Group Support	Group Expertise	Team Competence	
P R O B L E M S T A T E M E N T	H	H	H	H	—	—	—	Decide
				L	H	H	H	Delegate
							L	Consult (group)
						L	—	
				L	—	—		
			L	H	H	H	Facilitate
						L	Consult (individually)
					L	—	
				L	—	—	
				L	H	H	Facilitate
						L	Consult (group)
				L	—	—	
	L		H	—	—	—	—	Decide
			L	—	H	H	Facilitate
						L	Consult (individually)
				L	—	—	
	L	H		H	—	—	—	Decide
				L	—	—	H	Delegate
							L	Facilitate
		L	—	—	—	—	—	Decide

Decision Significance	Importance of Commitment	Leader Expertise	Likelihood of Commitment	Group Support	Group Expertise	Team Competence	
H	H	—	H	H	H	H	Decide
						L	Facilitate
					L	—	Consult (group)
				L	—	—	Consult (group)
			L	H	H	H	Delegate
						L	Facilitate
					L	—	Facilitate
				L	—	—	Consult (group)
	L	—	—	H	H	H	Delegate
						L	Facilitate
					L	—	Consult (group)
				L	—	—	Consult (group)
L	H	—	H	—	—	—	Decide
			L	—	—	—	Delegate
	L	—	—	—	—	—	Decide

Figure 11.5

VROOM'S DEVELOPMENT-DRIVEN DECISION TREE

This matrix is to be used when the leader is more interested in developing employees than in making the decision as quickly as possible. Just as with the time-driven tree shown in Figure 11.4, the leader assesses up to seven situational factors. These factors, in turn, funnel the leader to a recommended process for making the decision.

Source: Figure 9.3, "Decision-Process Flow Chart for Both Individual and Group Problems" is from *Leadership and Decision Making* by Victor H. Vroom and Philip W. Yetton, © 1973. Adapted and reprinted by permission of the University of Pittsburgh Press.

not terribly important (selecting a color for the firm's softball team uniforms), its significance is low. This assessment guides the manager through the paths of the decision tree to a recommended course of action. One decision tree is to be used when the manager is interested primarily in making the decision as quickly as possible; the other is to be used when time is less critical and the manager is interested in helping subordinates to improve and develop their own decision-making skills.

The two decision trees are shown in Figures 11.4 and 11.5. The problem attributes (situational factors) are arranged along the top of the decision tree. To use the model, the decision maker starts at the left side of the diagram and assesses the first problem attribute (decision significance). The answer determines the path to the second node on the decision tree, where the next attribute (importance of commitment) is assessed. This process continues until a terminal node is reached. In this way, the manager identifies an effective decision-making style for the situation.

Decision-Making Styles The various decision styles reflected at the ends of the tree branches represent different levels of subordinate participation that the manager should attempt to adopt in a given situation. The five styles are defined as follows:

- *Decide.* The manager makes the decision alone and then announces or "sells" it to the group.
- *Consult (individually).* The manager presents the program to group members individually, obtains their suggestions, and then makes the decision.
- *Consult (group).* The manager presents the problem to group members at a meeting, gets their suggestions, and then makes the decision.

- *Facilitate.* The manager presents the problem to the group at a meeting, defines the problem and its boundaries, and then facilitates group member discussion as they make the decision.

- *Delegate.* The manager allows the group to define for itself the exact nature and parameters of the problem and then to develop a solution.

Vroom's decision tree approach represents a very focused but quite complex perspective on leadership. To compensate for this difficulty, Vroom has developed elaborate expert system software to help managers assess a situation accurately and quickly and then to make an appropriate decision regarding employee participation.[25] Many firms, including Halliburton Company, Litton Industries, and Borland International, have provided their managers with training in how to use the various versions of this model.

Evaluation and Implications Because Vroom's current approach is relatively new, it has not been fully scientifically tested. The original model and its subsequent refinement, however, attracted a great deal of attention and were generally supported by research.[26] For example, there is some support for the idea that individuals who make decisions consistent with the predictions of the model are more effective than those who make decisions inconsistent with it. The model therefore appears to be a tool that managers can apply with some confidence in deciding how much subordinates should participate in the decision-making process.

The Leader-Member Exchange Approach

Because leadership is such an important area, managers and researchers continue to study it. As a result, new ideas, theories, and perspectives are continuously being developed. The **leader-member exchange (LMX) model** of leadership, conceived by George Graen and Fred Dansereau, stresses the importance of variable relationships between supervisors and each of their subordinates.[27] Each superior-subordinate pair is referred to as a "vertical dyad." The model differs from earlier approaches in that it focuses on the differential relationship leaders often establish with different subordinates. Figure 11.6 shows the basic concepts of the leader-member exchange theory.

The model suggests that supervisors establish a special relationship with a small number of trusted subordinates, referred to as "the in-group." The in-group usually receives special duties requiring responsibility and autonomy; they may

leader-member exchange (LMX) model
Stresses that leaders have different kinds of relationships with different subordinates

Figure 11.6
THE LEADER-MEMBER EXCHANGE (LMX) MODEL

The LMX model suggests that leaders form unique independent relationships with each of their subordinates. As illustrated here, a key factor in the nature of this relationship is whether the individual subordinate is in the leader's out-group or in-group.

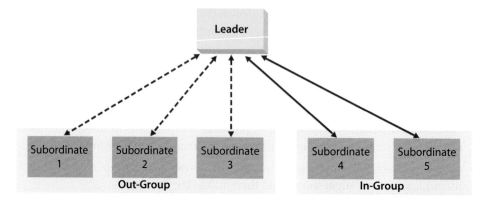

also receive special privileges. Subordinates who are not a part of this group are called "the out-group," and they receive less of the supervisor's time and attention. Note in the figure that the leader has a dyadic, or one-to-one, relationship with each of the five subordinates.

Early in his or her interaction with a given subordinate, the supervisor initiates either an in-group or an out-group relationship. It is not clear how a leader selects members of the in-group, but the decision may be based on personal compatibility and subordinates' competence. Research has confirmed the existence of in-groups and out-groups. In addition, studies generally have found that in-group members have a higher level of performance and satisfaction than do out-group members.[28]

Related Approaches to Leadership

Because of its importance to organizational effectiveness, leadership continues to be the focus of a great deal of research and theory building. New approaches that have attracted much attention are the concepts of substitutes for leadership and transformational leadership.

Substitutes for Leadership

The concept of **substitutes for leadership** was developed because existing leadership models and theories do not account for situations in which leadership is not needed.[29] They simply try to specify what kind of leader behavior is appropriate. The substitutes concept, however, identifies situations in which leader behaviors are neutralized or replaced by characteristics of the subordinate, the task, and the organization. For example, when a patient is delivered to a hospital emergency room, the professionals on duty do not wait to be told what to do by a leader. Nurses, doctors, and attendants all go into action without waiting for directive or supportive leader behavior from the emergency room supervisor.

> **substitutes for leadership**
> A concept that identifies situations in which leader behaviors are neutralized or replaced by characteristics of subordinates, the task, and the organization

Characteristics of the subordinate that may serve to neutralize leader behavior include ability, experience, need for independence, professional orientation, and indifference toward organizational rewards. For example, employees with a high level of ability and experience may not need to be told what to do. Similarly, a subordinate's strong need for independence may render leader behavior ineffective. Task characteristics that may substitute for leadership include routineness, the availability of feedback, and intrinsic satisfaction. When the job is routine and simple, the subordinate may not need direction. When the task is challenging and intrinsically satisfying, the subordinate may not need or want social support from a leader.

Organizational characteristics that may substitute for leadership include formalization, group cohesion, inflexibility, and a rigid reward structure. Leadership may not be necessary when policies and practices are formal and inflexible, for example. Similarly, a rigid reward system may rob the leader of reward power and thereby decrease the importance of the role. Preliminary research has provided support for the concept of substitutes for leadership.[30]

Charismatic Leadership

The concept of **charismatic leadership**, like trait theories, assumes that charisma is an individual characteristic of the leader. **Charisma** is a form of

> **charismatic leadership**
> Assumes that charisma is an individual characteristic of the leader

charisma
A form of interpersonal attraction that inspires support and acceptance

interpersonal attraction that inspires support and acceptance. All else being equal, then, someone with charisma is more likely to be able to influence others than is someone without charisma. For example, a highly charismatic supervisor will be more successful in influencing subordinate behavior than a supervisor who lacks charisma. Thus influence is again a fundamental element of this perspective.

Robert House first proposed a theory of charismatic leadership, based on research findings from a variety of social science disciplines.[31] His theory suggests that charismatic leaders are likely to have a lot of self-confidence, a firm conviction in their beliefs and ideals, and a strong need to influence people. They also tend to communicate high expectations about follower performance and express confidence in followers. Donald Trump is an excellent example of a charismatic leader. Even though he has made his share of mistakes and generally is perceived as only an "average" manager, many people view him as larger than life.[32]

There are three elements of charismatic leadership in organizations that most experts acknowledge today.[33] First, the leader needs to be able to envision the future, set high expectations, and model behaviors consistent with meeting those expectations. Next, the charismatic leader must be able to energize others through a demonstration of personal excitement, personal confidence, and patterns of success. And, finally, the charismatic leader enables others by supporting them, empathizing with them, and expressing confidence in them.[34]

Charismatic leadership ideas are quite popular among managers today and are the subject of numerous books and articles. Unfortunately, few studies have attempted to specifically test the meaning and impact of charismatic leadership. There are also lingering ethical issues about charismatic leadership, however, that trouble some people. For instance, President Bill Clinton was a charismatic leader. But some of his critics argued that this very charisma caused his supporters to overlook his flaws and to minimize some of his indiscretions.

Transformational Leadership

transformational leadership
Leadership that goes beyond ordinary expectations by transmitting a sense of mission, stimulating learning experiences, and inspiring new ways of thinking

Another new perspective on leadership has been called by a number of labels: charismatic leadership, inspirational leadership, symbolic leadership, and transformational leadership. We use the term **transformational leadership** and define it as leadership that goes beyond ordinary expectations by transmitting a sense of mission, stimulating learning experiences, and inspiring new ways of thinking.[35] Because of rapid change and turbulent environments, transformational leaders are increasingly being seen as vital to the success of business.[36]

A recent article in the popular press identified seven keys to successful leadership: trusting one's subordinates, developing a vision, keeping cool, encouraging risk, being an expert, inviting dissent, and simplifying things.[37] Although this list was the result of a simplistic survey of the leadership literature, it is nevertheless consistent with the premises underlying transformational leadership. So, too, are recent examples cited as effective leadership. Take the case of 3M. The firm's new CEO is working to make the firm more efficient and profitable while simultaneously keeping its leadership role in new product innovation. He has also changed the reward system, overhauled procedures, and restructured the entire firm. And so far, at least, analysts have applauded these changes.[38]

Emerging Approaches to Leadership

Recently, three potentially very important new approaches to leadership have emerged. One is called "strategic leadership"; the others deal with cross-cultural leadership and ethical leadership.

Strategic Leadership

Strategic leadership is a new concept that explicitly relates leadership to the role of top management. We define **strategic leadership** as the capability to understand the complexities of both the organization and its environment and to lead change in the organization in order to achieve and maintain a superior alignment between the organization and its environment. This definition reflects an integration of the leadership concepts covered in this chapter with our discussion of strategic management in Chapter 3.

> *strategic leadership*
> The capability to understand the complexities of both the organization and its environment and to lead change in the organization in order to achieve and maintain a superior alignment between the organization and its environment

To be effective in this role, a manager needs to have a thorough and complete understanding of the organization—its history, its culture, its strengths, and its weaknesses. In addition, the leader needs a firm grasp of the organization's environment. This understanding must encompass current conditions and circumstances as well as significant trends and issues on the horizon. The strategic leader also needs to recognize how the firm is currently aligned with its environment—where it relates effectively and where it relates less effectively with that environment. Finally, looking at environmental trends and issues, the strategic leader works to improve both the current alignment and the future alignment.[39]

Jeffrey Immelt (CEO of General Electric), Hector Ruiz (CEO of Advanced Micro Devices), Michael Dell (founder and CEO of Dell Computer), Anne Mulcahy (CEO of Xerox) and A. G. Lafley (CEO of Procter & Gamble) have all been recognized as strong strategic leaders. Reflecting on his dramatic turnaround at Procter & Gamble, for instance, Lafley commented, "I have made a lot of symbolic, very physical changes so people understand we are in the business of leading change." On the other hand, Raymond Gilmartin (CEO of Merck), Scott Livengood (CEO of Krispy Kreme), and Howard Pien (CEO of Chiron) have been cited as less effective strategic leaders. Under Livengood's leadership, for instance, Krispy Kreme's stock has plummeted by 80 percent, and the firm is under investigation by the SEC; moreover, most critics believe that the chain has expanded far too rapidly.[40]

Cross-Cultural Leadership

Another new approach to leadership is based on cross-cultural issues. In this context, culture is used as a broad concept to encompass both international differences and diversity-based differences within one culture. For instance, when a Japanese firm sends an executive to head the firm's operations in the United States, that person will need to become acclimated to the cultural differences that exist between the two countries and to change his or her leadership style accordingly. For example, Japan is generally characterized by collectivism (the group comes before the individual), whereas the United States is based more on individualism (the individual comes before the group). The Japanese executive, then, will find it necessary to recognize the importance of individual contributions and rewards, as well as the differences in individual and group roles, that exist in Japanese and U.S. businesses.

Cross-cultural leadership issues are playing a growing role today as globalization continues to flourish. For instance, these individuals represent three different religious faiths. They are shown here signing an agreement that was negotiated during a recent international conference. Each individual had to learn much about the other two in order to reach an amicable accord.

Similarly, cross-cultural factors play a growing role in organizations as their workforces become more and more diverse. Most leadership research, for instance, has been conducted on samples or case studies involving white male leaders (until several years ago, most business leaders were white males). But, as more females, African Americans, and Latinos achieve leadership positions, it may be necessary to reassess how applicable current theories and models of leadership are when applied to an increasingly diverse pool of leaders.

Ethical Leadership

Most people have long assumed that top managers are ethical people. But in the wake of recent corporate scandals, faith in top managers has been shaken. Perhaps now more than ever, high standards of ethical conduct are being held up as a prerequisite for effective leadership. More specifically, top managers are being called on to maintain high ethical standards for their own conduct, to exhibit ethical behavior unfailingly, and to hold others in their organization to the same standards.

The behaviors of top leaders are being scrutinized more than ever, and those responsible for hiring new leaders for a business are looking more and more closely at the background of those being considered. And the emerging pressures for stronger corporate governance models are likely to further increase commitment to selecting only those individuals with high ethical standards and to hold them more accountable than in the past for both their actions and the consequences of those actions.[41]

Political Behavior in Organizations

political behavior
The activities carried out for the specific purpose of acquiring, developing, and using power and other resources to obtain one's preferred outcomes

Another common influence on behavior is politics and political behavior. ***Political behavior*** describes activities carried out for the specific purpose of acquiring, developing, and using power and other resources to obtain one's preferred outcomes.[42] Political behavior may be undertaken by managers dealing with their subordinates, subordinates dealing with their managers, and managers and subordinates dealing with others at the same level. In other words, it may be directed upward, downward, or laterally. Decisions ranging from where to locate a manufacturing plant to where to put the company coffeemaker are subject to political action. In any situation, individuals may engage in political behavior to further their own ends, to protect themselves from others, to further goals they sincerely believe to be in the organization's best interests, or simply to acquire and exercise power. And power may be sought by individuals, by groups of individuals, or by groups of groups.[43]

Although political behavior is difficult to study because of its sensitive nature, one early survey found that many managers believed that politics influenced salary and hiring decisions in their firm. Many also believed that the incidence of political behavior was greater at the upper levels of their organization and lesser at the lower levels. More than half of the respondents felt that organizational politics was bad, unfair, unhealthy, and irrational, but most suggested that successful executives have to be good politicians and be political to get ahead.[44]

Common Political Behaviors

Research has identified four basic forms of political behavior widely practiced in organizations.[45] One form is *inducement,* which occurs when a manager offers to give something to someone else in return for that individual's support. For example, a product manager might suggest to another product manager that she will put in a good word with his boss if he supports a new marketing plan that she has developed. By most accounts, former WorldCom CEO Bernard Ebbers made frequent use of this tactic to retain his leadership position in the company. For example, he allowed board members to use the corporate jet whenever they wanted and invested heavily in their pet projects.

A second tactic is *persuasion,* which relies on both emotion and logic. An operations manager wanting to construct a new plant on a certain site might persuade others to support his goal on grounds that are objective and logical (is less expensive; taxes are lower) as well as subjective and personal. Ebbers also used this approach. For instance, when one board member attempted to remove him from his position, he worked behind the scenes to persuade the majority of board members to allow him to stay on.

A third political behavior involves the *creation of an obligation.* For example, one manager might support a recommendation made by another manager for a new advertising campaign. Although he might really have no opinion on the new campaign, he might think that by going along, he is incurring a debt from the other manager and will be able to "call in" that debt when he wants to get something done and needs additional support. Ebbers loaned WorldCom board members money, for example, but then forgave the loans in exchange for their continued support.

Coercion is the use of force to get one's way. For example, a manager may threaten to withhold support, rewards, or other resources as a way to influence someone else. This, too, was a common tactic used by Ebbers. He reportedly belittled any board member who dared question him, for example. In the words of one former director, "Ebbers treated you like a prince—as long as you never forgot who was king."[46]

Impression Management

Impression management is a subtle form of political behavior that deserves special mention. **Impression management** is a direct and intentional effort by someone

impression management
A direct and intentional effort by someone to enhance his or her image in the eyes of others

to enhance his or her image in the eyes of others. People engage in impression management for a variety of reasons. For one thing, they may do so to further their own careers. By making themselves look good, they think they are more likely to receive rewards, to be given attractive job assignments, and to receive promotions. They may also engage in impression management to boost their self-esteem. When people have a solid image in an organization, others make them aware of it through compliments, respect, and so forth. Still another reason people use impression management is in an effort to acquire more power and hence more control.

People attempt to manage how others perceive them through a variety of mechanisms. Appearance is one of the first things people think of. Hence, a person motivated by impression management will pay close attention to choice of attire, selection of language, and use of manners and body posture. People interested in impression management are also likely to jockey for association only with successful projects. By being assigned to high-profile projects led by highly successful managers, a person can begin to link his or her own name with such projects in the minds of others.

Sometimes people too strongly motivated by impression management become obsessed with it and may resort to dishonest or unethical means. For example, some people have been known to take credit for others' work in an effort to make themselves look better. People have also been known to exaggerate or even falsify their personal accomplishments in an effort to build an enhanced image.[47]

Managing Political Behavior

By its very nature, political behavior is tricky to approach in a rational and systematic way. But managers can handle political behavior so that it does not do excessive damage.[48] First, managers should be aware that, even if their actions are not politically motivated, others may assume that they are. Second, by providing subordinates with autonomy, responsibility, challenge, and feedback, managers reduce the likelihood of political behavior by subordinates. Third, managers should avoid using power if they want to avoid charges of political motivation. Fourth, managers should get disagreements out in the open so that subordinates will have less opportunity for political behavior through using conflict for their own purposes. Finally, managers should avoid covert activities. Behind-the-scenes activities give the impression of political intent, even if none really exists.[49] Other guidelines include clearly communicating the bases and processes for performance evaluation, tying rewards directly to performance, and minimizing competition among managers for resources.[50]

Of course, these guidelines are much easier to list than they are to implement. The well-informed manager should not assume that political behavior does not exist or, worse yet, attempt to eliminate it by issuing orders or commands. Instead, the manager must recognize that political behavior exists in virtually all organizations and that it cannot be ignored or stamped out. It can, however, be managed in such a way that it will seldom inflict serious damage on the organization. It may even play a useful role in some situations.[51] For example, a manager may be able to use his or her political influence to stimulate a greater sense of social responsibility or to heighten awareness of the ethical implications of a decision.

Summary of Key Points

1. Describe the nature of leadership and relate leadership to management.
   - As a process, leadership is the use of noncoercive influence to shape the group's or organization's goals, motivate behavior toward the achievement of those goals, and help define group or organization culture.
   - As a property, leadership is the set of characteristics attributed to those who are perceived to be leaders.
   - Leadership and management are often related but are also different.
   - Managers and leaders use legitimate, reward, coercive, referent, and expert power.

2. Discuss and evaluate the two generic approaches to leadership.
   - The trait approach to leadership assumed that some basic trait or set of traits differentiated leaders from nonleaders.
   - The leadership behavior approach to leadership assumed that the behavior of effective leaders was somehow different from the behavior of nonleaders.
   - Research at the University of Michigan and Ohio State University identified two basic forms of leadership behavior—one concentrating on work and performance and the other concentrating on employee welfare and support.
   - The Leadership Grid attempts to train managers to exhibit high levels of both forms of behavior.

3. Identify and describe the major situational approaches to leadership.
   - Situational approaches to leadership recognize that appropriate forms of leadership behavior are not universally applicable and attempt to specify situations in which various behaviors are appropriate.
   - The LPC theory suggests that a leader's behaviors should be either task oriented or relationship oriented, depending on the favorableness of the situation.
   - The path-goal theory suggests that directive, supportive, participative, or achievement-oriented leader behaviors may be appropriate, depending on the personal characteristics of subordinates and the environment.
   - Vroom's decision tree approach maintains that leaders should vary the extent to which they allow subordinates to participate in making decisions as a function of problem attributes.
   - The leader-member exchange model focuses on individual relationships between leaders and followers and on in-group versus out-group considerations.

4. Identify and describe three related approaches to leadership.
   - Related leadership perspectives are
     - the concept of substitutes for leadership
     - charismatic leadership
     - the role of transformational leadership in organizations

5. Describe three emerging approaches to leadership.
   - Emerging approaches include
     - strategic leadership
     - cross-cultural leadership
     - ethical leadership

6. Discuss political behavior in organizations and how it can be managed.
   - Political behavior is another influence process frequently used in organizations.
   - Impression management, one especially important form of political behavior, is a direct and intentional effort by someone to enhance his or her image in the eyes of others.
   - Managers can take steps to limit the effects of political behavior.

Discussion Questions

Questions for Review

1. What activities do managers perform? What activities do leaders perform? Do organizations need both managers and leaders? Why or why not?

2. What are the two generic approaches to leadership? What can managers today learn from these approaches?

3. What are the situational approaches to leadership? Briefly describe each and compare and contrast their findings.

4. Describe the subordinates' characteristics, leader behaviors, and environmental characteristics used in path-goal theory. How do these factors combine to influence motivation?

5. In your own words, define political behavior. Describe four political tactics and give an example of each.

Questions for Analysis

1. Even though the trait approach to leadership has no empirical support, it is still widely used. In your opinion, why is this so? In what ways is the use of the trait approach helpful to those who use it? In what ways is it harmful to those who use it?

2. The behavioral theories of leadership claim that an individual's leadership style is fixed. Do you agree or disagree? Give examples to support your position. The behavioral theories also claim that the ideal style is the same in every situation. Do you agree or disagree? Again, give examples.

3. Consider the following list of leadership situations. For each situation, describe in detail the kinds of power the leader has. If the leader were the same but the situation changed—for example, if you thought of the president as the head of his family rather than of the military—would your answers change? Why?
   • The president of the United States is commander-in-chief of the U.S. military.

   • An airline pilot is in charge of a particular flight.
   • Fans look up to a movie star.
   • Your teacher is the head of your class.

4. Think about a decision that would affect you as a student. Use Vroom's decision tree approach to decide whether the administrator making that decision should involve students in the decision. Which parts of the model seem most important in making that decision? Why?

5. Describe a time when you or someone you know was part of an in-group or an out-group. What was the relationship between each of the groups and the leader? What was the relationship between the members of the two different groups? What was the outcome of the situation for the leader? For the members of the two groups? For the organization?

Building Effective Diagnostic Skills

Exercise Overview

Diagnostic skills help a manager visualize appropriate responses to a situation. One situation that leaders often face is deciding how to use different types of power to respond effectively to different situations.

Exercise Background

The president of the United States is one of the most powerful leaders in the world. The president's speeches are usually carefully crafted statements that address specific concerns, but they are also deliberately loaded with language that invokes the power of the office. The annual State of the Union address is often the most detailed and polished public speech given by the president in a year. So it is natural that the State of the Union address would contain many references to the various types of power wielded by the president.

Exercise Task

Read a transcript of the president's most recent State of the Union Address. (One place to look for it is at www.whitehouse.gov. On that page, enter "State of the Union" as a search term and then click on the words "Full Transcript" at the bottom of the page to see the details.) Then answer the following questions:

1. What types of power is the president using in this speech? Give specific examples of each type. As one example, in the 2007 State of the Union speech, George W. Bush says, "I congratulate the Democrat majority." This sentence serves to praise Democrats, a form of reward power.

2. In addition to this speech, list some of the president's other actions or words that, in your opinion, tend to give him or her more power. List some actions or words that tend, in your opinion, to reduce his or her power.

3. Does this speech inspire you to be a follower of the president? Why or why not?

Building Effective Decision-Making Skills

Exercise Overview

Decision-making skills include the manager's ability to recognize and define situations correctly and to select courses of action. Vroom's decision tree approach to leadership is an effective method for determining how much participation a manager might allow his or her subordinates in making a decision. This exercise will enable you to refine your decision-making skills by applying Vroom's approach to a hypothetical situation.

Exercise Background

Assume that you are the branch manager of the West Coast region of the United States for an international manufacturing and sales company. The company is making a major effort to control costs and boost efficiency. As part of this effort, the firm recently installed a networked computer system linking sales representatives, customer service employees, and other sales support staff. The goal of this network was to increase sales while simultaneously cutting sales expenses.

Unfortunately, just the opposite has resulted—sales are down slightly, but expenses are increasing. You have looked into this problem and believe that the computer hardware that people are using is fine. You also believe, however, that the software that is used to run the system is flawed: it is too hard to use and provides less than complete information.

Your employees disagree with your assessment, however. They believe that the entire system is fine. They attribute the problems to poor training in using the system and to a lack of incentives for using it to solve many problems that they already know how to handle using other methods. Some of them also think that their colleagues are merely resistant to change.

Your boss has just called and instructed you to "solve the problem." She indicated that she has complete faith in your ability to do so, that decisions about how to proceed will be left to you, and that she wants a report suggesting a course of action in five days.

Exercise Task

Using the information presented above, do the following:

1. Using your own personal preferences and intuition, describe how you think you would proceed.

2. Now use Vroom's approach to determine a course of action.

3. Compare and contrast your initial approach with the actions suggested by Vroom's approach.

Building Effective Conceptual Skills

Exercise Overview

Conceptual skills reflect the manager's ability to think in the abstract. This exercise gives you an opportunity to analyze the various sources of power and how they manifest themselves in various types of leaders.

Exercise Background

There are five sources of leader power. Different individuals choose to exercise different types of power. However, there are also occupational patterns related to the sources of power.

Exercise Task

1. Individually, complete the Power Base Worksheet, below. For each occupation, place an X for each power base that the person probably possesses in that job.

2. In a small group, achieve consensus on the answers to the Power Base Worksheet. Try to think of specific examples to support your group's answers.

3. Present your group's results to the class and discuss.

4. What conclusions can you draw about how the sources of power are related to various occupations?

Power Base Worksheet					
Occupation	Legitimate Power	Reward Power	Coercive Power	Referent Power	Expert Power
University professor	_____	_____	_____	_____	_____
CEO of a bank	_____	_____	_____	_____	_____
Restaurant chef	_____	_____	_____	_____	_____
A CPA in auditing	_____	_____	_____	_____	_____
Factory manager	_____	_____	_____	_____	_____
Police officer	_____	_____	_____	_____	_____
Small workgroup supervisor	_____	_____	_____	_____	_____

Source: Adapted from Morable, *Exercises in Management*, to accompany Griffin, *Management*, 8th edition.

Skills Self-Assessment Instrument

Managerial Leader Behavior Questionnaire

Introduction: Leadership is now recognized as consisting of a set of characteristics that is important for everyone in an organization to develop. The following assessment surveys the practices or beliefs that you would apply in a management role—that is, your managerial leadership.

Instructions: The following statements refer to different ways in which you might behave in a managerial leadership role. For each statement, indicate how you do behave or how you think you would behave.

Describing yourself may be difficult in some cases, but you should force yourself to make a selection. Record your answers next to each statement according to the following scale:

Rating Scale

5   Very descriptive of me

4   Fairly descriptive of me

3   Somewhat descriptive of me

2   Not very descriptive of me

1   Not descriptive of me at all

_____ 1. I emphasize the importance of performance and encourage everyone to make a maximum effort.

_____ 2. I am friendly, supportive, and considerate toward others.

_____ 3. I offer helpful advice to others on how to advance their careers and encourage them to develop their skills.

_____ 4. I stimulate enthusiasm for the work of the group and say things to build the group's confidence.

_____ 5. I provide appropriate praise and recognition for effective performance and show appreciation for special efforts and contributions.

_____ 6. I reward effective performance with tangible benefits.

_____ 7. I inform people about their duties and responsibilities, clarify rules and policies, and let people know what is expected of them.

_____ 8. Either alone or jointly with others, I set specific and challenging but realistic performance goals.

_____ 9. I provide any necessary training and coaching or arrange for others to do it.

_____ 10. I keep everyone informed about decisions, events, and developments that affect their work.

_____ 11. I consult with others before making work-related decisions.

_____ 12. I delegate responsibility and authority to others and allow them discretion in determining how to do their work.

_____ 13. I plan in advance how to efficiently organize and schedule the work.

_____ 14. I look for new opportunities for the group to exploit, propose new undertakings, and offer innovative ideas.

_____ 15. I take prompt and decisive action to deal with serious work-related problems and disturbances.

_____ 16. I provide subordinates with the supplies, equipment, support services, and other resources necessary to work effectively.

_____ 17. I keep informed about the activities of the group and check on its performance.

_____ 18. I keep informed about outside events that have important implications for the group.

_____ 19. I promote and defend the interests of the group and take appropriate action to obtain necessary resources for the group.

_____ 20. I emphasize teamwork and try to promote cooperation, cohesiveness, and identification with the group.

_____ 21. I discourage unnecessary fighting and bickering within the group and help settle conflicts and disagreements in a constructive manner.

_____ 22. I criticize specific acts that are unacceptable, find positive things to say, and provide an opportunity for people to offer explanations.

_____ 23. I take appropriate disciplinary action to deal with anyone who violates a rule, disobeys an order, or has consistently poor performance.

Source: Reprinted from *Military Leadership: An Organizational Behavior Perspective*, pp. 38–39, David D. Van Fleet and Gary A. Yukl. Copyright © 1986 with permission from Elsevier Science.
For interpretation, see Interpretations of Skills Self-Assessment Instruments in the appendix near the end of this text.

Experiential Exercise

The Leadership/Management Interview Experiment

Purpose: Leadership and management are in some ways the same, but more often they are different. This exercise offers you an opportunity to develop a conceptual framework for leadership and management.

Introduction: Most management behaviors and leadership behaviors are a product of individual work experience, so each leader/manager tends to have a unique leadership/management style. Analyzing leadership/management styles, comparing such styles, and relating them to different organizational contexts are often rewarding experiences in learning.

Instructions: *Fact-finding and Execution of the Experiment*

1. Develop a list of questions related to issues you have studied in this chapter that you want to ask a practicing

manager and leader during a face-to-face interview. Prior to the actual interview, submit your list of questions to your instructor for approval.

2. Arrange to interview a practicing manager and a practicing leader. For purposes of this assignment, a manager or leader is a person whose job priority involves supervising the work of other people. The leader/manager may work in a business or in a public or private agency.

3. Interview at least one manager and at least one leader, using the questions you developed. Take good notes on their comments and on your own observations. Do not take more than one hour of each leader's/manager's time.

Oral Report

Prepare an oral report using the questions here and your interview information. Complete the following report after the interview. (Attach a copy of your interview questions.)

The Leadership/Management Interview Experiment Report

1. How did you locate the leader(s)/manager(s) you interviewed? Describe your initial contacts.

2. Describe the level and responsibilities of your leader(s)/manager(s). Do not supply names—their responses should be anonymous.

3. Describe the interview settings. How long did the interview last?

4. In what ways were the leaders/managers similar or in agreement about issues?

5. What were some of the major differences between the leaders/managers and between the ways in which they approached their jobs?

6. In what ways would the managers agree or disagree with ideas presented in this course?

7. Describe and evaluate your own interviewing style and skills.

8. How did your managers feel about having been interviewed? How do you know that?

CHAPTER CLOSING CASE

STAN O'NEAL LEADS MERRILL LYNCH

Stan O'Neal may seem an unlikely Wall Street CEO. O'Neal, who is African American and was raised in the segregated South, was hired from outside the industry after years at General Motors. His journey to the top of Merrill Lynch is as remarkable as his accomplishments. His controversial leadership is highly profitable and according to reporter David Rynecki, "may have saved [Merrill] from extinction."

Merrill Lynch, founded in 1912 as the first modern investment bank, has long dominated retail investment banking. Yet by the mid-1990s, the firm was inefficient and complacent. Revenues grew by $3 billion between 1996 and 1998, yet profits increased only $100 million. Leadership failed to notice the severity of the problem and continued the firm's indulgent "Mother Merrill" culture. As the new CFO, O'Neal called for cost cuts in a 1999 speech, but his warning went unheeded. Following the stock market crash of 2000, O'Neal was named COO and president in July 2001.

After 12 year at Merrill, O'Neal finally had the chance to exert his leadership and he did so aggressively. To reduce expenses, he cut 24,000 jobs, over one-third of the payroll. Over 300 field offices were closed. The cuts included thousands of brokers and analysts, the front-line workers of Merrill. He also fired dozens of executives, singling out those he felt would not support his strategy. In their places, O'Neal hired younger, hungrier, and more diverse managers.

In another cost-saving tactic, O'Neal segmented Merrill's 9 million retail accounts. He then lavished services on the most profitable customers, while eliminating personal managers for the least profitable. Merrill now serves its small accounts with just 460 agents, as compared to the previous 6,600 brokers. O'Neal looked for cost cuts in every aspect of the business. Divesting low-profit business units, instituting pay freezes, lowering bonuses, even slashing free meals—all became a part of his plan.

The layoffs and cost cutting upset long-time employees and customers. So did O'Neal's management style. However, the CEO was determined to revitalize Merrill Lynch's culture and remake the firm as a meritocracy. *BusinessWeek* writer Emily Thornton says, "[In his first five months as CEO, O'Neal] dragged Merrill though more cultural change than it underwent in the previous five decades." Family connections, Ivy League–school friendships, and seniority used to drive the firm's reward system. Under O'Neal's new regime, managers are encouraged to take risks and given only a few months to demonstrate results. Revenue increases are no longer sufficient; those who do not increase profits are let go.

O'Neal has been described as "ruthless." Other adjectives include "cold," "aloof," and "uninspiring." His hand-picked top team is sometimes referred to as the "Taliban." He is accused of being an ambitious bureaucrat with no concern for his employees. "People say . . . I'm a bean counter," O'Neal says. "I'm not . . . [but] I have a job to do, and it has nothing to do with worrying about what people call me." O'Neal acknowledges that cost cuts and layoffs are painful. He then counters by pointing out that the changes were necessary for Merrill's survival.

In spite of his autocratic decision-making style, O'Neal is a hands-off manager. He holds his subordinates responsible for high performance but allows a lot of latitude in how they achieve it. His communications are blunt rather than tactful. He works through lunch and avoids executive perks such as golf and expense-account lunches. After suffering through disastrous leaks to the press in his early years as CEO, O'Neal rarely grants interviews.

In the last three years, O'Neal has shifted his attention from tearing down the "old" Merrill to rebuilding the "new." Funds saved by cost cutting are being used to make over 30 strategic acquisitions, moving the firm into more profitable segments and regions. The firm is hiring again. O'Neal's growth strategy is cautious, and he is maintaining the pressure for operational efficiency. In spite of a slow worldwide economic recovery, Merrill Lynch has prospered under O'Neal. Revenues increased 33 percent from 2004 to 2006, while earnings improved 69 percent. "This is definitely a period of peak earnings," says analyst Philip Guziec. "[Merrill has] been firing on all cylinders."

O'Neal's background is important in understanding his values today. "No obstacles have been as great in my life . . . as being a young child with no money and on the wrong side of the color line." O'Neal states.

Rynecki, a reporter, writes this article subtitle: "O'Neal may be toughest— some say the most ruthless—CEO in America. Merrill Lynch couldn't be luckier to have him." O'Neal may be tough, but he is effective. And that may make him the kindest CEO of all.

CASE QUESTIONS

1. Which types of power does Stan O'Neal use as CEO of Merrill Lynch? Give examples of each type.
2. Using the framework of the Ohio State studies, analyze O'Neal's leadership behavior. What are the likely outcomes of this type of behavior, according to the Ohio State researchers?
3. Assume that work in the financial services industry is nonroutine and provides few opportunities for social interaction. Assume also that managers and workers in the financial services industry are primarily skilled professionals who have a strong internal locus of control. Use path-goal theory to describe the ideal type of leader behavior for the financial services industry. Then describe O'Neal's behavior, based on information in the case. Is O'Neal using the optimal leader behavior for this industry? Tell why or why not.

REFERENCES

"2006 Financial Highlights," Merrill Lynch website, www.ml.com on February 26, 2007; David Rynecki, "Putting the Muscle Back in the Bull," *Fortune*, April 5, 2004, www.fortune.com on February 26, 2007; Sonja Ryst, "Financial Services: Fattening Up," *BusinessWeek*, July 18, 2006, www.businessweek.com on February 26, 2007; Emily Thornton, "The New Merrill Lynch," *BusinessWeek*, May 5, 2003, www.businessweek.com on February 26, 2007.

YOU MAKE THE CALL

Watch Out Bud, Miller Is Catching Up

1. Would you enjoy working for a leader like Norman Adami? Why or why not?
2. In your opinion, what will new CEO Tom Long have to do to keep Miller on the road to recovery?
3. What can CEO Long do to be as effective a leader as his boss, Norman Adami? Give specific examples.
4. Prior to joining Miller, CEO Long served as Coca-Cola's President of the Northwest Europe Division. Do you think this experience will be a benefit to him as CEO of Miller? Explain why or why not.

Test Prepper

You've read the chapter, studied the key terms, and the exam is any day now. Think you're ready to ace it? Take this sample test to gauge your comprehension of chapter material. You can check your answers at the back of the book. Want more test questions? Visit the student website at http://college.hmco.com/pic/griffinfund5e/ and take the ACE quizzes for more practice.

1. T F Management, as a process, is the use of noncoercive influences to shape the organization's goals, motivate behavior toward the achievement of those goals, and help define organization culture.

2. T F Quarterback of the Indianapolis Colts, Peyton Manning, viewed by some as a role model, can use referent power through personal identification and imitation.

3. T F When a manager "sells" her decision to the group, she uses the consulting style of decision making.

4. T F Leadership that goes beyond ordinary expectations by transmitting a sense of mission, stimulating learning experiences, and inspiring new ways of thinking is called charismatic leadership.

5. T F By providing subordinates with autonomy, responsibility, challenge, and feedback, managers reduce the likelihood of political behavior by subordinates.

6. The power to give salary increases, bonuses, promotions, praise, recognition, and interesting job assignments is called _____ power.

   a. reward
   b. expert
   c. referent
   d. coercive
   e. legitimate

7. Fred is primarily concerned with the efficiency and performance of his subordinates. According to the Michigan studies, he exhibits which leader behavior?

   a. Job-centered
   b. Employee-centered

   c. Initiating-structure
   d. Consideration
   e. Initiating-structure and consideration

8. Which leadership theory is a direct extension of the expectancy theory of motivation?

   a. Vroom's decision tree
   b. Least-preferred coworker (LPC)
   c. Path-goal
   d. Leader-member exchange
   e. Michigan studies

9. A manager presents a problem to the team and then helps team members make the decision. He is exhibiting which decision-making style?

   a. Decide
   b. Facilitate
   c. Delegate
   d. Exchange
   e. Consult

10. Within an organization, political behavior is used for what purpose?

   a. Acquiring power
   b. Developing power
   c. Using power
   d. Using resources to obtain one's preferred outcomes
   e. All of the above

Communication in Organizations

FIRST THINGS FIRST

Talking With Sports Fans

"ESPN listens to its audience very closely."
—SIMON WILLIAMS, CONSULTANT, STEWART BRANDING

Sports fans, regardless of which sports they follow, are passionate about their teams, their players, their games, and their championships. In order to appeal to sports fans, the majority of which are young men between the ages of 18 and 35, the press must meet their demands. First, that their sport be covered. NASCAR fans don't watch Wimbledon and vice versa. Second, that the information be deep and broad within each sport, so that a fan can immerse him- or herself in an infinite sea of data. Third, the use of many media channels to allow access anytime, anywhere. And fourth, that the information be as current as possible. Even an hour's delay is unacceptable for many viewers. ESPN, the first all-sports media company, has dominated the industry on these four measures as surely as the Yankees have dominated the World Series.

ESPN covers 65 sports in all, ranging from the NBA, Major League Baseball, and the NFL, to the Little League World Series and the X Games. A fan can see sports from around the world, for both men's and women's teams, amateurs and professionals, old-school sports and modern ones, current games and past classics. ESPN provides reporting, commentary from more than 50 writers, statistics, and enough in-depth analysis to satisfy any fan. Athletes are accommodated too, through products such as Surfline, which reports surf conditions. ESPN is available in English and Spanish, and in 31 other nations.

ESPN employs a range of media. Broadcast, cable, and pay-per-view television, radio, and magazines are all part of the portfolio, as are new media such as ESPN.com, wireless mobile, and broadband video. The company understands the need for speed. "[ESPN CEO] George Bodenheimer realizes ESPN has to be fast-paced. . . . [If] you stand still you're dead," says Simon Williams, an industry consultant. The company cannibalizes its current offerings when a faster technology comes along. "SportsCenter" was ESPN's first and flagship TV show, yet ESPN.com often reports breaking sports news one to two hours earlier.

ESPN rules the sports media industry through its knowledgeable and extensive content. Yet the most striking feature of ESPN isn't the content but the way that the company engages the fans. Williams says, "ESPN listens to its audience very closely." CEO Bodenheimer listens by walking around. He often leaves his luxury box at a game to walk through the stands. "I want to know what fans are saying—about sports, about ESPN," he says.

Fans are engaged in other ways, too. One is through the dozens of message boards on ESPN.com. ESPN's men's basketball message board, for example, contains over 250,000 messages. Subscribers to ESPN Insider, for $6.95 monthly, can access over 30 blogs hosted by commentators and covering a wide variety of sports. In addition, ESPN offers a dozen fantasy sports leagues, in which individuals compete online using imaginary teams. The message boards, blogs, and fantasy leagues allow two-way communication between the fans and the press.

Better communication—with richer media, more media channels, and two-way transmission—helps build a strong brand. ESPN is the most-watched cable network, averaging 2.5 million households per week. NFL's Monday Night Football alone generates over 20 million views of ESPN.com each Monday. Eighty-eight million viewers watch SportsCenter each month. ESPN and ESPN2 are rated the first- and second-most valuable show on cable by viewers, cable operators, and advertisers. The strong brand leads to greater profits. Revenues flow from subscription services such as ESPN Insider or the $15/month charge for Mobile ESPN from Verizon. ESPN charges cable operators an estimated $2.80 per subscriber per month, versus 40 cents for CNN. In all, ESPN's revenues will likely top $6 billion in 2007. The strong brand also helps ESPN beat its rivals. The firm has topped the market share charts for more than a decade. ESPN also defeats competitors by cross-selling, directing its viewers to its other media and other Disney channels. Finally, ESPN leads in innovation. For example, it is a part-owner of Active.com, an Internet service for organizing and promoting local sports events, such as marathons and soccer leagues.

LEARNING OBJECTIVES

After studying this chapter, you should be able to:

- Describe the role and importance of communication in the manager's job.
- Identify the basic forms of communication in organizations.
- Describe the role of electronic communication in organizations.
- Discuss informal communication, including its various forms and types.
- Describe how the communication process can be managed to recognize and overcome barriers.

Communication plays a vital role in every aspect of business at ESPN.

> Giving fans more options and more choice, and empowering them to respond, is an effective communication strategy and one that rivals will find hard to beat.[1]

Businesses continue to look for effective ways to communicate with their stakeholders. ESPN has done an outstanding job of communicating with its customers. It also does a very effective job of communicating with its employees and the advertisers who purchase commercial time to hawk their wares. Communication has always been a vital part of managerial work. Indeed, managers around the world agree that communication is one of their most important tasks. It is important for them to communicate with others in order to convey their vision and goals for the organization. And it is important for others to communicate with them so that they will better understand what is going on in their environment and how they and their organization can become more effective.

This chapter discusses communication, one of the most basic forms of interaction among people. We begin by examining communication in the context of the manager's job. We then identify and discuss forms of interpersonal, group, and organizational communication. After discussing electronic and informal means of communication, we describe how organizational communication can be effectively managed.

Communication and the Manager's Job

A typical day for a manager includes doing desk work, attending scheduled meetings, placing and receiving telephone calls, reading and answering correspondence (both print and electronic), attending unscheduled meetings, and making tours.[2] Most of these activities involve communication. In fact, managers usually spend over half their time on some form of communication. Communication always involves two or more people, so other behavioral processes, such as motivation, leadership, and group and team interactions, all come into play. Top executives must handle communication effectively if they are to be true leaders.

A Definition of Communication

Imagine three managers working in an office building. The first is all alone but is nevertheless yelling for a subordinate to come help. No one appears, but he continues to yell. The second is talking on the telephone to a subordinate, but static on the line causes the subordinate to misunderstand some important numbers that the manager is providing. As a result, the subordinate sends 1,500 crates of eggs to 150 Fifth Street, when he should have sent 150 crates of eggs to 1500 Fifteenth Street. The third manager is talking in her office with a subordinate who clearly hears and understands what is being said. Each of these managers is attempting to communicate, but with different results.

communication
The process of transmitting information from one person to another

Communication is the process of transmitting information from one person to another. Did any of our three managers communicate? The last did, and the first did not. How about the second? In fact, she did communicate. She transmitted information, and information was received. The problem was that the message transmitted and the message received were not the same. The words spoken by the manager were distorted by static and noise. ***Effective communication***, then, is the process of sending a message in such a way that the message received is as close in meaning as possible to the message intended. Although the second manager engaged in communication, it was not effective.

A key element in effective communication is differentiating between data and information. **Data** are raw figures and facts reflecting a single aspect of reality. The facts that a plant has 35 machines, that each machine is capable of producing 1,000 units of output per day, that current and projected future demand for the units is 30,000 per day, and that workers sufficiently skilled to run the machines make $20 an hour are data. **Information**, meanwhile, is data presented in a way or form that has meaning.[3] Thus combining and summarizing the four pieces of data given above provides information: The plant has excess capacity and is therefore incurring unnecessary costs. Information has meaning to a manager and provides a basis for action. The plant manager might use the information and decide to sell four machines (perhaps keeping one as a backup) and transfer five operators to other jobs.

effective communication
The process of sending a message in such a way that the message received is as close in meaning as possible to the message intended

data
Raw figures and facts reflecting a single aspect of reality

information
Data presented in a way or form that has meaning

Characteristics of Useful Information

What characteristics make the difference between information that is useful and information that is not useful? In general, information is useful if it is accurate, timely, complete, and relevant.

1. *Accurate.* For information to be of real value to a manager, it must be **accurate information**. *Accuracy* means that the information provides a valid and reliable reflection of reality. A Japanese construction company once bought information from a consulting firm about a possible building site in London. The Japanese were told that the land, which would be sold in a sealed-bid auction, would attract bids of close to $250 million. They were also told that the land currently held an old building that could readily be demolished. Thus the Japanese bid $255 million—which ended up being $90 million more than the next-highest bid. And to make matters worse, a few days later the British government declared the building historic, preventing any possibility of demolition. Clearly, the Japanese acted on information that was less than accurate. More recently, President Bush's decision to invade Iraq was apparently based, at least in part, on faulty information regarding that country's possession of weapons of mass destruction.

accurate information
Information that provides a valid and reliable reflection of reality

2. *Timely.* **Information** also needs to be **timely.** *Timeliness* does not necessarily mean speediness; it means only that information needs to be available in time for appropriate managerial action. What constitutes timeliness is a function of the situation facing the manager. When Marriott was gathering information for a new hotel project, managers allowed themselves a six-month period for data collection. They felt this would give them an opportunity to do a good job of getting the information they needed while not delaying things too much. In contrast, Marriott's computerized reservation and accounting system can provide a manager today with last night's occupancy level at any Marriott facility.[4]

timely information
Information that is available in time for appropriate managerial action

3. *Complete.* Information must tell a complete story for it to be useful to a manager. If it is less than **complete information**, the manager is likely to get an inaccurate or distorted picture of reality. For example, managers at Kroger used to think that house-brand products were more profitable than national brands

complete information
Information that provides the manager with all the information he or she needs

because they yielded higher unit profits. On the basis of this information, they gave house brands a great deal of shelf space and organized promotional activities around them. As Kroger's managers became more sophisticated in understanding their information, however, they realized that national brands were actually more profitable over time, because they sold many more units than house brands during any given period of time. Hence, although a store might sell 10 cans of Kroger coffee in a day, with a profit of 50 cents per can (total profit of $5), it would also sell 15 cans of Maxwell House, with a profit of 40 cents per can (total profit of $6), and 10 vacuum bags of Starbucks coffee, with a profit of $1 per bag (total profit of $10). With this more complete picture, managers could do a better job of selecting the right mix of Kroger, Maxwell House, and Starbucks coffee to display and promote.

4. *Relevant.* Finally, information must be relevant if it is to be useful to managers. **Relevant information**, like timely information, is defined according to the needs and circumstances of a particular manager. Operations managers need information on costs and productivity; human resource managers need information on hiring needs and turnover rates; and marketing managers need information on sales projections and advertising rates. As Wal-Mart contemplates various countries as possible expansion opportunities, it gathers information about local regulations, customs, and so forth. But the information about any given country is not really relevant until the decision is made to enter that market.

relevant information
Information that is useful to managers in their particular circumstances for their particular needs

The Communication Process

Figure 12.1 illustrates how communication generally takes place between people. The process of communication begins when one person (the sender) wants to transmit a fact, idea, opinion, or other information to someone else (the receiver).

Figure 12.1
THE COMMUNICATION PROCESS

As the figure shows, noise can disrupt the communication process at any step. Managers must therefore understand that a conversation in the next office, a fax machine out of paper, and the receiver's worries may all thwart the manager's best attempts to communicate.

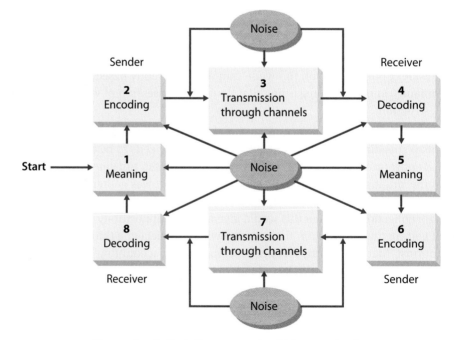

The numbers indicate the sequence in which steps take place.

This fact, idea, or opinion has meaning to the sender, whether it be simple and concrete or complex and abstract.

The next step is to encode the meaning into a form appropriate to the situation. The encoding might take the form of words, facial expressions, gestures, or even artistic expressions and physical actions. After the message has been encoded, it is transmitted through the appropriate channel or medium. The channel by which this encoded message is being transmitted to you is the printed page. Common channels in organizations include meetings, email, memos, letters, reports, and telephone calls. After the message is received, it is decoded back into a form that has meaning for the receiver. As noted earlier, the consistency of this meaning can vary dramatically. In many cases, the meaning prompts a response, and the cycle is continued when a new message is sent by the same steps back to the original sender.

"Noise" may disrupt communication anywhere along the way. Noise can be the sound of someone coughing, a truck driving by, or two people talking close at hand. It can also include disruptions such as a letter lost in the mail, a dead telephone line, an interrupted cell phone call, an email misrouted or infected with a virus, or one of the participants in a conversation being called away before the communication process is completed.

Forms of Communication in Organizations

Managers need to understand several kinds of communication that are common in organizations today.[5] These include interpersonal communication, communication in networks and teams, organizational communication, and electronic communication.

Interpersonal Communication

Interpersonal communication generally takes one of two forms: oral and written. As we will see, each has clear strengths and weaknesses.

Oral Communication *Oral communication* takes place in conversations, group discussions, telephone calls, and other situations in which the spoken word is used to express meaning. One study (conducted before the advent of email) demonstrated the importance of oral communication by finding that most managers spent between 50 and 90 percent of their time talking to people.[6] Oral communication is so prevalent for several reasons. The primary advantage of oral communication is that it promotes prompt feedback and interchange in the form of verbal questions or agreement, facial expressions, and gestures. Oral communication is also easy (all the sender needs to do is talk), and it can be done with little preparation (though careful preparation is advisable in certain situations). The sender does not need pencil and paper, typewriter, or other equipment. In another survey, 55 percent of the executives sampled felt that their own written communication skills were fair or poor, so they chose oral communication to avoid embarrassment![7]

However, oral communication also has drawbacks. It may suffer from problems of inaccuracy if the speaker chooses the wrong words to convey meaning or leaves out pertinent details, if noise disrupts the process, or if the receiver forgets part of the message.[8] In a two-way discussion, there is seldom time for a thoughtful,

> *oral communication*
> Face-to-face conversation, group discussions, telephone calls, and other circumstances in which the spoken word is used to transmit meaning

considered response or for introducing many new facts, and there is no permanent record of what has been said. In addition, although most managers are comfortable talking to people individually or in small groups, fewer enjoy speaking to larger audiences.[9]

Written Communication "Putting it in writing" in a letter, report, memorandum, handwritten note, or email can solve many of the problems inherent in oral communication. Nevertheless, and perhaps surprisingly, ***written communication*** is not as common as one might imagine, nor is it a mode of communication much respected by managers. One sample of managers indicated that only 13 percent of the printed mail they received was of immediate use to them.[10] Over 80 percent of the managers who responded to another survey indicated that the written communication they received was of fair or poor quality.[11]

The biggest single drawback of traditional forms of written communication is that they inhibit feedback and interchange. When one manager sends another manager a letter, it must be written or dictated, typed, mailed, received, routed, opened, and read. If there is a misunderstanding, it may take several days for it to be recognized, let alone rectified. Although the use of email is, of course, much faster, both sender and receiver must still have access to a computer, and the receiver must open and read the message for it to actually be received. A phone call could settle the whole matter in just a few minutes. Thus written communication often inhibits feedback and interchange and is usually more difficult and time consuming than oral communication.

Of course, written communication offers some advantages. It is often quite accurate and provides a permanent record of the exchange. The sender can take the time to collect and assimilate the information and can draft and revise it before it is transmitted. The receiver can take the time to read it carefully and can refer to it repeatedly, as needed. For these reasons, written communication is generally preferable when important details are involved. At times it is important to one or both parties to have a written record available as evidence of exactly what took place. Julie Regan, founder of Toucan-Do, an importing company based in Honolulu, relies heavily on formal business letters in establishing contacts and buying merchandise from vendors in Southeast Asia. She believes that such letters give her an opportunity to carefully think through what she wants to say, tailor her message to each individual, and avoid later misunderstandings.

Choosing the Right Form Which form of interpersonal communication should the manager use? The best medium will be determined by the situation. Oral communication or email may be preferred when the message is personal, nonroutine, and brief. More formal written communication is usually best when the message is more impersonal, routine, and longer. And, given the prominent role that emails have played in several recent court cases, managers should always use discretion when sending messages electronically.[12] For example, private emails made public during legal proceedings have played major roles in litigation involving Enron, Tyco, WorldCom, and Morgan Stanley.[13]

The manager can also combine media to capitalize on the advantages of each. For example, a quick telephone call to set up a meeting is easy and gets an immediate response. Following up the call with a reminder email or handwritten note helps ensure that the recipient will remember the meeting, and it provides a record of

---

written communication
Memos, letters, reports, notes, and other circumstances in which the written word is used to transmit meaning

the meeting's having been called. Electronic communication, discussed more fully later, blurs the differences between oral and written communication and can help each be more effective.

Communication in Networks and Work Teams

Although communication among team members in an organization is clearly interpersonal in nature, substantial research also focuses specifically on how people in networks and work teams communicate with one another. A ***communication network*** is the pattern through which the members of a group or team communicate. Researchers studying group dynamics have discovered several typical networks in groups and teams consisting of three, four, and five members. Representative networks among members of five-member teams are shown in Figure 12.2.[14]

In the wheel pattern, all communication flows through one central person, who is probably the group's leader. In a sense, the wheel is the most centralized network because one person receives and disseminates all information. The Y pattern is slightly less centralized—two people are close to the center. The chain offers a more even flow of information among members, although two people (the ones at each end) interact with only one other person. This path is closed in the circle pattern. Finally, the all-channel network, the most decentralized, allows a free flow of information among all group members. Everyone participates equally, and the group's leader, if there is one, is not likely to have excessive power.

Research conducted on networks suggests some interesting connections between the type of network and group performance. For example, when the group's task is relatively simple and routine, centralized networks tend to perform with greatest efficiency and accuracy. The dominant leader facilitates performance by coordinating the flow of information. When a group of accounting clerks is logging incoming invoices and distributing them for payment, for example, one centralized leader can coordinate things efficiently. When the task is complex and nonroutine, such as making a major decision about organizational strategy, decentralized networks tend to be most effective because open channels of communication permit more interaction and a more efficient sharing of relevant information. Managers should recognize the effects of communication networks on group and organizational performance and should try to structure networks appropriately.

> **communication network**
> The pattern through which the members of a group communicate

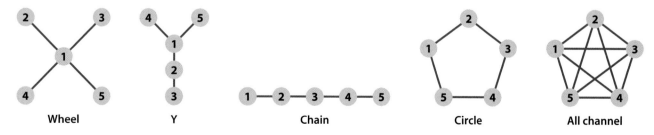

Wheel   Y   Chain   Circle   All channel

Figure 12.2
TYPES OF COMMUNICATION NETWORKS

Research on communication networks has identified five basic networks for five-person groups. These networks vary in terms of information flow, position of the leader, and effectiveness for different types of tasks. Managers might strive to create centralized networks when group tasks are simple and routine. Alternatively, managers can foster decentralized groups when group tasks are complex and nonroutine.

Organizational Communication

Still other forms of communication in organizations are those that flow among and between organizational units or groups. Each of these involves oral or written communication, but each also extends to broad patterns of communication across the organization.[15] As shown in Figure 12.3, two of these forms of communication follow vertical and horizontal linkages in the organization.

Vertical Communication *Vertical communication* is communication that flows up and down the organization, usually along formal reporting lines—that is, it is the communication that takes place between managers and their superiors and subordinates. Vertical communication may involve only two people, or it may flow through several different organizational levels. A common perspective on vertical communication that exists in some organizations is illustrated in the cartoon.

Upward communication consists of messages from subordinates to superiors. This flow is usually from subordinates to their direct superior, then to that person's direct superior, and so on up the hierarchy. Occasionally, a message might bypass a particular superior. The typical content of upward communication is requests, information that the lower-level manager thinks is of importance to the higher-level manager, responses to requests from the higher-level manager, suggestions, complaints, and financial information. Research has shown that upward communication is more subject to distortion than is downward communication. Subordinates are likely to withhold or distort information that makes them look bad. The greater the degree of difference in status between superior and subordinate and the greater the degree of distrust, the more likely the subordinate is to suppress or distort information.[16] For example, subordinates might choose to withhold information about problems from their boss if they think the news will make him angry and if they think they can solve the problem themselves without his ever knowing about it.

Downward communication occurs when information flows down the hierarchy from superiors to subordinates. The typical content of these messages is directives

> **vertical communication**
> Communication that flows up and down the organization, usually along formal reporting lines; takes place between managers and their superiors and subordinates and may involve several different levels of the organization

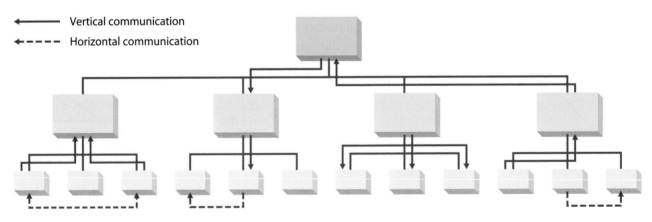

Figure 12.3
FORMAL COMMUNICATION IN ORGANIZATIONS

Formal communication in organizations follows official reporting relationships or prescribed channels. For example, vertical communication, shown here with the solid lines, flows between levels in the organization and involves subordinates and their managers. Horizontal communication, shown with dashed lines, flows between people at the same level and is usually used to facilitate coordination.

on how something is to be done, the assignment of new responsibilities, performance feedback, and general information that the higher-level manager thinks will be of value to the lower-level manager. Vertical communication can and usually should be two-way in nature. In other words, give-and-take communication with active feedback is generally likely to be more effective than one-way communication.[17]

Horizontal Communication   Whereas vertical communication involves a superior and a subordinate, ***horizontal communication*** involves colleagues and peers at the same level of the organization. For example, an operations manager might communicate to a marketing manager that inventory levels are running low and that projected delivery dates should be extended by two weeks. Horizontal communication probably occurs more among managers than among nonmanagers.

horizontal communication
Communication that flows laterally within the organization; involves colleagues and peers at the same level of the organization and may involve individuals from several different organizational units

This type of communication serves a number of purposes.[18] It facilitates coordination among interdependent units. For example, a manager at Motorola was once researching the strategies of Japanese semiconductor firms in Europe. He found a great deal of information that was relevant to his assignment. He also uncovered some additional information that was potentially important to another department, so he passed it along to a colleague in that department, who used it to improve his own operations. Horizontal communication can also be used for joint problem solving, as when two plant managers at Northrop Grumman got together to work out a new method to improve productivity. Finally, horizontal communication plays a major role in work teams with members drawn from several departments.

Electronic Communication

An increasingly important form of organizational communication relies on electronic communication technology. ***Information technology, or IT*** consists of the resources used by an organization to manage information that it needs in order to carry out its mission. IT may consist of computers, computer networks, telephones, fax machines, and other pieces of hardware. In addition, IT involves software that facilitates the system's ability to manage information in a way that is useful for managers. Both formal information systems and personal information technology have reshaped how managers communicate with one another.

information technology (IT)
The resources used by an organization to manage information that it needs in order to carry out its mission

Information Systems

Advances in information technology have made it increasingly easy for managers to use many different kinds of information systems. In this section we discuss the most common kinds of information systems used by businesses today.

Transaction-processing systems (TPS) are applications of information processing for basic day-to-day business transactions. Customer order taking by online retailers, approval of claims at insurance companies, receipt and confirmation of reservations by airlines, payroll processing and bill payment at almost every company—all are routine business processes. Typically, the TPS for first-level (operational) activities is well defined, with predetermined data requirements, and follows the same steps to complete all transactions in the system.

transaction-processing systems (TPS)
An application of information processing for basic day-to-day business transactions

Systems for knowledge workers and office applications support the activities of both knowledge workers and employees in clerical positions. They provide assistance for data processing and other office activities, including the creation

Electronic communication continues to extend its impact throughout the world. Ichimame is a 19-year old maiko, or young geisha. As she progresses through the secretive world of geisha training, Ichimame decided to launch her own blog to provide insights into the geisha world and to recruit other young women to consider a career as a geisha. She is shown here updating her blog at a teahouse in Kyoto, Japan. This convergence of the traditional and the modern would have been unheard of only a few years ago.

of communications documents. Like other departments, the information systems (IS) department includes both knowledge workers and data workers. *Systems for operations and data workers* make sure that the right programs are run in the correct sequence, and they monitor equipment to ensure that it is operating properly. Many organizations also have employees who enter data into the system for processing. *Knowledge-level and office systems* are also increasingly widespread. The explosion of new support systems—word processing, document imaging, desktop publishing, computer-aided design, simulation modeling—has increased the productivity of both knowledge and office workers. Desktop publishing combines graphics and word-processing text to publish professional-quality print and web documents. Document-imaging systems can scan paper documents and images, convert them into digital form for storage on disks, retrieve them, and transmit them electronically to workstations throughout the network.

management information system (MIS)
An information system that supports an organization's managers by providing daily reports, schedules, plans, and budgets

Management information systems (***MIS***) support an organization's managers by providing daily reports, schedules, plans, and budgets. Each manager's information activities vary according to his or her functional area (say, accounting or marketing) and management level. Whereas midlevel managers focus mostly on internal activities and information, higher-level managers are also engaged in external activities. Middle managers, the largest MIS user group, need networked information to plan such upcoming activities as personnel training, materials movements, and cash flows. They also need to know the current status of the jobs and projects being carried out in their department: What stage is it at now? When will it be finished? Is there an opening so we can start the next job? Many of a firm's management information systems—cash flow, sales, production scheduling, shipping—are indispensable in helping managers find answers to such questions.

decision support system (DSS)
An interactive system that locates and presents information needed to support the decision-making process

Decision support systems (***DSS***) are interactive systems that locate and present information needed to support the decision-making process. Whereas some DSSs are devoted to specific problems, others serve more general purposes, allowing managers to analyze different types of problems. Thus a firm that often faces decisions on plant capacity, for example, may have a capacity DSS: The manager inputs data on anticipated levels of sales, working capital, and customer delivery requirements. Then the DSS's built-in transaction processors manipulate the data and make recommendations on the best levels of plant capacity for each future time period. In contrast, a general-purpose system, such as a marketing DSS, might respond to a variety of marketing-related problems. It may be programmed to handle "what if" questions, such as "When is the best time to introduce a new product if my main competitor introduces one in three months, our new product has an eighteen-month expected life, demand is seasonal with a peak in autumn, and my goal is to gain the largest possible market share?" The DSS can help managers make decisions for which predetermined solutions are unknown by using sophisticated modeling tools and data analysis.

An ***executive support system*** (***ESS***) is a quick-reference, easy-access application of information systems specially designed for instant access by upper-level managers. ESSs are designed to assist with executive-level decisions and problems, ranging from "What lines of business should we be in five years from now?" to "Based on forecasted developments in electronic technologies, to what extent should our firm be globalized in five years? in ten years?" The ESS also uses a wide range of both internal information and external sources, such as industry reports, global economic forecasts, and reports on competitors' capabilities. Because senior-level managers do not usually possess advanced computer skills, they prefer systems that are easily accessible and adaptable. Accordingly, ESSs are not designed to address only specific, predetermined problems. Instead, they allow the user some flexibility in attacking a variety of problem situations. They are easily accessible by means of simple keyboard strokes or even voice commands.

> **executive support system (ESS)**
> A quick-reference, easy-access application of information systems specially designed for instant access by upper-level managers

Artificial intelligence (***AI***) can be defined as the construction of computer systems, both hardware and software, to imitate human behavior—in other words, systems that perform physical tasks, use thought processes, and learn. In developing AI systems, knowledge workers (business specialists, modelers, and information technology experts) try to design computer-based systems capable of reasoning, so that computers, instead of people, can perform certain business activities. One simple example is a credit evaluation system that decides which loan applicants are creditworthy and which ones are risky and then composes acceptance and rejection letters accordingly. One special form of AI, the *expert system*, is designed to imitate the thought processes of human experts in a particular field. Expert systems incorporate the rules that an expert applies to specific types of problems, such as the judgments a physician makes in diagnosing illnesses. In effect, expert systems supply everyday users with "instant expertise." A system called MOCA (for Maintenance Operations Center Advisor), by imitating the thought processes of a maintenance manager, schedules routine maintenance for American Airlines' entire fleet.

> **artificial intelligence (AI)**
> The construction of computer systems, both hardware and software, to imitate human behavior—that is, to perform physical tasks, use thought processes, and learn

Intranets, or private Internet networks, are accessible only to employees via entry through electronic firewalls. Firewalls are used to limit access to an intranet. Ford's intranet connects over 100,000 workstations in Asia, Europe, and the United States to thousands of Ford websites containing private information on Ford activities in production, engineering, distribution, and marketing. Sharing such information has helped reduce the lead time for getting models into production from 36 to 24 months. One of Ford's recent projects in improving customer

> **intranet**
> A communications network similar to the Internet but operating within the boundaries of a single organization

service through internal information sharing is called manufacturing on demand. Now, for example, the Mustang that required 50 days' delivery time in 1996 is available in less than two weeks. The savings to Ford, of course, will be billions of dollars in inventory and fixed costs.

Extranets allow outsiders limited access to a firm's intranet. The most common application allows buyers to enter the seller's system to see which products are available for sale and delivery, thus providing product availability information quickly to outside buyers. Industrial suppliers, too, are often linked into their customers' intranets so that they can see planned production schedules and make supplies ready as needed for customers' upcoming operations.

> **extranet**
> A communications network that allows selected outsiders limited access to an organization's internal information system, or intranet

Personal Electronic Technology

In recent years, the nature of organizational communication has changed dramatically, mainly because of breakthroughs in personal electronic communication technology, and the future promises even more change. Electronic typewriters and photocopying machines were early breakthroughs. The photocopier, for example, makes it possible for a manager to have a typed report distributed to large numbers of other people in an extremely short time. Personal computers accelerated the process. Email networks, the Internet, and corporate intranets have carried communication technology even further.

It is also becoming common to have teleconferences in which managers stay at their own location (such as offices in different cities) but are seen on television or computer monitors as they "meet." A manager in New York can keyboard a letter or memorandum at her personal computer, point and click with a mouse, and have it delivered to hundreds or even thousands of colleagues around the world in a matter of seconds. Highly detailed information can be retrieved with ease from large electronic databanks. This has given rise to a new version of an old work arrangement—the cottage industry. In a cottage industry, people work at home (in their "cottage") and periodically bring the products of their labors in to the company. "Telecommuting" is the label given to a new electronic cottage industry. In telecommuting, people work at home on their computer and transmit their work to the company via telephone line or cable modem.

Cellular telephones and facsimile machines have made it even easier for managers to communicate with one another. Many now use cell phones to make calls while commuting to and from work, and some carry them in their briefcases so that they can receive calls while at lunch. Facsimile machines make it easy for people to use written communication media and get rapid feedback. And new personal computing devices, such as Palm Pilots, are revolutionizing how people communicate with one another. Wi-Fi technology is further extending the impact of these devices.

Psychologists, however, are beginning to associate some problems with these communication advances. For one thing, managers who are seldom in their "real" office are likely to fall behind in their field and to be victimized by organizational politics because they are not present to keep in touch with what is going on and to protect themselves. They drop out of the organizational grapevine and miss out on much of the informal communication that takes place. Moreover, the use of electronic communication at the expense of face-to-face meetings and conversations makes it hard to build a strong culture, develop solid working relationships,

Managing in Times of Change

Communicating via Craigslist

Wanted—Director of Business Development. 1999 Harley Davidson for $4500. Ready to build everlasting love? Graduate student seeks housemate. Have you seen my Black Lab? If you read these, you might think you were looking at a newspaper's classified ads, but you'd be wrong. These items are found on craigslist.org, a unique online community bulletin board.

Software developer Craig Newmark founded craigslist in 1995. He began by emailing friends about local parties. The list's popularity grew and information about jobs, housing, and personals was added. Today the website covers 450 cities in the United States and more than 50 other countries. It's the seventh-most-visited English-language website, with 5 billion page views monthly, doubled over the last year.

Is craigslist "reinventing the wheel"? After all, newspapers already provide classifieds. It's surprising that one of the biggest Internet success stories is a company modeled on a low-tech product like the want ads.

Newmark's innovative business model is one source of success. The site has a "dot org" domain name, signifying its nonprofit status. Unlike Google and other Internet companies, the site does not accept advertising. Modest fees of $25 to $75 are charged for help-wanted listings in seven of the largest cities—all other postings are free. Annual revenues are a low $10 million, yet with just four paid employees, expenses are also low.

Another factor in craigslist's success is its direct link with customers. Newmark notes that every new development at craigslist is suggested by users. "In a way, I've only had one idea," Newmark says. "Everything comes from the community." Users also contribute to maintaining the site, by pointing out scammers and illegal messages. More participation leads to greater customer loyalty.

The success of craigslist has inspired some copycats and also scared traditional newspapers. Papers typically receive about 40 percent of their revenues from classifieds, but competition from craigslist is causing ad prices to drop. Internet technology also provides faster and wider distribution than newspapers.

With its grapevine communication style, low prices, and loyal user community, craigslist is the perfect "new economy" company. Craig Newmark refuses to use the term "business model," but by listening to others, he's developed a seemingly unbeatable business.

References: Spencer E. Ante, "Craig Newmark: The Net's Free Force," *BusinessWeek*, August 15, 2005, www.businessweek.com on March 1, 2007; "craigslist factsheet," craigslist website, www.craigslist.org on March 2, 2007; Jeffrey Gangemi, "Small Company, Big Brand," *Small Biz*, August 28, 2006, www.businessweek.com on March 1, 2007; Alex Mindlin, "Searching the Want Ads Moves Online, Too," *New York Times*, September 18, 2006, www.nytimes.com on March 2, 2007.

and create a mutually supportive atmosphere of trust and cooperativeness. Finally, electronic communication is opening up new avenues for dysfunctional employee behavior, such as the passing of lewd or offensive materials to others. For example, in 2000, the *New York Times* fired almost 10 percent of the workers at one of its branch offices for sending inappropriate emails at work.

Informal Communication in Organizations

The forms of organizational communication discussed in the previous section all represent planned and relatively formal communication mechanisms. However, in many cases communication that takes place in an organization transcends these formal channels and instead follows any of several informal methods. Figure 12.4 illustrates numerous examples of informal communication. Common forms of informal communication in organizations include the grapevine, management by wandering around, and nonverbal communication.

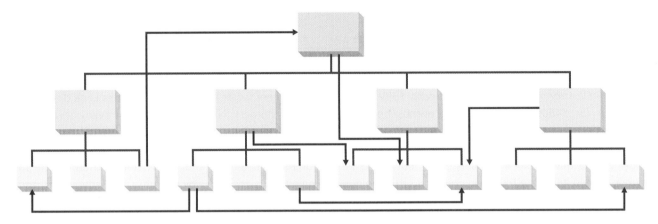

Figure 12.4
INFORMAL COMMUNICATION IN ORGANIZATIONS

Informal communication in organizations may or may not follow official reporting relationships or prescribed channels. It may cross different levels and different departments or work units, and it may or may not have anything to do with official organizational business.

The Grapevine

grapevine
An informal communication network among people in an organization

The **grapevine** is an informal communication network that can permeate an entire organization. Grapevines are found in all organizations except the very smallest, but they do not always follow the same patterns as, nor do they necessarily coincide with, formal channels of authority and communication. Research has identified several kinds of grapevines.[19] The two most common are illustrated in Figure 12.5. The gossip chain occurs when one person spreads the message to many other people. Each one, in turn, may either keep the information confidential or pass it on to others. The gossip chain is likely to carry personal information. The other common grapevine is the cluster chain, in which one person passes the information to a selected few individuals. Some of the receivers pass the information to a few other individuals; the rest keep it to themselves.

There is some disagreement about how accurate the information carried by the grapevine is, but research is increasingly finding it to be fairly accurate, especially when the information is based on fact rather than speculation. One study found that the grapevine may be between 75 percent and 95 percent accurate.[20] That same study also found that informal communication is increasing in many organizations for two basic reasons. One contributing factor is the recent increase in merger, acquisition, and takeover activity. Because such activity can greatly affect the people within an organization, it follows that they may spend more time talking about it.[21] The second contributing factor is that as more and more corporations move facilities from inner cities to suburbs, employees tend to talk less and less to others outside the organization and more and more to one another.

Attempts to eliminate the grapevine are fruitless, but fortunately the manager does have some control over it. By maintaining open channels of communication and responding vigorously to inaccurate information, the manager can minimize the damage the grapevine can do. The grapevine can actually be an asset. By learning who the key people in the grapevine are, for example, the manager can partially control the information they receive and use the grapevine to sound out employee reactions to new ideas, such as a change in human resources policies or benefit

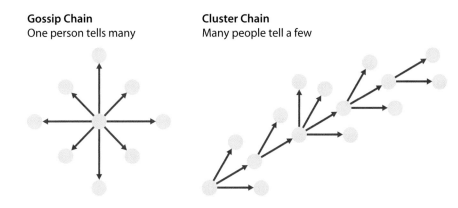

Gossip Chain
One person tells many

Cluster Chain
Many people tell a few

Figure 12.5
COMMON GRAPEVINE CHAINS FOUND IN ORGANIZATIONS

The two most common grapevine chains in organizations are the gossip chain (in which one person communicates messages to many others) and the cluster chain (in which many people pass messages to a few others).

Source: From Keith Davis and John W. Newstrom, *Human Behavior at Work: Organizational Behavior*, Eighth Edition, 1989. Copyright (c) 1989 The McGraw-Hill Companies, Inc. Reprinted with permission.

packages. The manager can also get valuable information from the grapevine and use it to improve decision making.[22]

Management by Wandering Around

Another increasingly popular form of informal communication is called, interestingly enough, ***management by wandering around***.[23] The basic idea is that some managers keep in touch with what is going on by wandering around and talking with people—immediate subordinates, subordinates far down the organizational hierarchy, delivery people, customers, or anyone else who is involved with the company in some way. Bill Marriott, for example, frequently visits the kitchens, loading docks, and custodial work areas whenever he tours a Marriott hotel. He claims that, by talking with employees throughout the hotel, he gets new ideas and has a better feel for the entire company. And, when Continental Airlines CEO Larry Kellner travels, he makes a point of talking to flight attendants and other passengers to gain continuous insights into how the business can be run more effectively.

A related form of organizational communication that really has no specific term is the informal interchange that takes place outside the normal work setting. Employees attending the company picnic, playing on the company softball team, or taking fishing trips together will almost always spend part of their time talking about work. For example, Texas Instruments engineers at TI's Lewisville, Texas, facility often frequent a local bar in town after work. On any given evening, they talk about the Dallas Cowboys, the newest government contract received by the company, the weather, their boss, the company's stock price, local politics, and problems at work. There is no set agenda, and the key topics of discussion vary from group to group and from day to day. Still, the social gatherings serve an important role. They promote a strong culture and enhance understanding of how the organization works.

Nonverbal Communication

Nonverbal communication is a communication exchange that does not use words or uses words to carry more meaning than the literal definition of the words themselves. Nonverbal communication is a powerful but little-understood form of communication in organizations. It often relies on facial expressions, body movements, physical contact, and gestures. One study found that as much as 55 percent of the

management by wandering around
An approach to communication that involves the manager's literally wandering around and having spontaneous conversations with others

nonverbal communication
Any communication exchange that does not use words or uses words to carry more meaning than the strict definition of the words themselves

content of a message is transmitted by facial expressions and body posture and that another 38 percent derives from inflection and tone. Words themselves account for only 7 percent of the content of the message.[24]

Research has identified three kinds of nonverbal communication practiced by managers—images, settings, and body language.[25] In this context, images are the kinds of words people elect to use. "Damn the torpedoes, full speed ahead" and "Even though there are some potential hazards, we should proceed with this course of action" may convey the same meaning. Yet the person who uses the first expression may be perceived as a maverick, a courageous hero, an individualist, or a reckless and foolhardy adventurer. The person who uses the second might be described as aggressive, forceful, diligent, or narrow minded and resistant to change. In short, our choice of words conveys much more than just the strict meaning of the words themselves.

The setting for communication also plays a major role in nonverbal communication. Boundaries, familiarity, the home turf, and other elements of the setting are all important. Much has been written about the symbols of power in organizations. The size and location of an office, the kinds of furniture in the office, and the accessibility of the person in the office all communicate useful information. For example, when H. Ross Perot ran Electronic Data Systems (EDS) he positioned his desk so that it is always between him and a visitor. This signaled that he was in charge. When he wanted a less formal dialogue, he moved around to the front of the desk and sat beside his visitor. Michael Dell of Dell Computer, in contrast, has his desk facing a side window so that, when he turns around to greet a visitor, there is never anything between them.

A third form of nonverbal communication is body language.[26] The distance we stand from someone as we speak has meaning. In the United States, standing very close to someone you are talking to generally signals either familiarity or aggression. The English and Germans stand farther apart than Americans when talking, whereas the Arabs, Japanese, and Mexicans stand closer together.[27] Eye contact is another effective means of nonverbal communication. For example, prolonged eye contact might suggest either hostility or romantic interest. Other kinds of body language include body and hand movement, pauses in speech, and mode of dress.

The manager should be aware of the importance of nonverbal communication and recognize its potential impact. Giving an employee good news about a reward with the wrong nonverbal cues can destroy the reinforcement value of the reward. Likewise, reprimanding an employee but providing inconsistent nonverbal cues can limit the effectiveness of the sanctions. The tone of the message, where and how the message is delivered, facial expressions, and gestures can all amplify or weaken the message or change the message altogether.

Managing Organizational Communication

In view of the importance and pervasiveness of communication in organizations, it is vital for managers to understand how to manage the communication process.[28] Managers should understand how to maximize the potential benefits of communication and minimize the potential problems. We begin our discussion of communication management by considering the factors that might disrupt effective communication and how to deal with them.

Many managers would like to improve communication effectiveness in their organizations. Although there are several basic things that can be done, they sometimes seek out unusual and creative methods as well. Ellen Moore, for instance, is a professional ethnographer—someone who studies cultures and societies through first-hand observation. Moore works as a communications consultant to several businesses. She spends time watching how people interact and communicate with each other and then offers suggestions for making these processes more effective.

Barriers to Communication

Several factors may disrupt the communication process or serve as barriers to effective communication.[29] As shown in Table 12.1, these may be divided into two classes: individual barriers and organizational barriers.

Individual Barriers   Several individual barriers may disrupt effective communication. One common problem is conflicting or inconsistent signals. A manager is sending conflicting signals when she says on Monday that things should be done one way, but then prescribes an entirely different procedure on Wednesday.

Individual Barriers	Organizational Barriers
Conflicting or inconsistent signals	Semantics
Credibility about the subject	Status or power differences
Reluctance to communicate	Different perceptions
Poor listening skills	Noise
Predispositions about the subject	Overload
	Language differences

Table 12.1
BARRIERS TO EFFECTIVE COMMUNICATION
Numerous barriers can disrupt effective communication. Some of these barriers involve individual characteristics and processes. Others are functions of the organizational context in which communication is taking place.

Inconsistent signals are being sent by a manager who says that he has an "open door" policy and wants his subordinates to drop by, but keeps his door closed and becomes irritated whenever someone stops in.

Another barrier is lack of credibility. Credibility problems arise when the sender is not considered a reliable source of information. He may not be trusted or may not be perceived as knowledgeable about the subject at hand. When a politician is caught withholding information or when a manager makes a series of bad decisions, the extent to which he or she will be listened to and believed thereafter diminishes. In extreme cases, people may talk about something they obviously know little or nothing about.

Some people are simply reluctant to initiate a communication exchange. This reluctance may occur for a variety of reasons. A manager may be reluctant to tell subordinates about an impending budget cut because he knows they will be unhappy about it. Likewise, a subordinate may be reluctant to transmit information upward for fear of reprisal or because it is felt that such an effort would be futile.

Poor listening habits can be a major barrier to effective communication. Some people are simply poor listeners. When someone is talking to them, they may be daydreaming, looking around, reading, or listening to another conversation. Because they are not concentrating on what is being said, they may not comprehend part or all of the message. They may even think that they really are paying attention, only to realize later that they cannot remember parts of the conversation.

Receivers may also bring certain predispositions to the communication process. They may already have their minds made up, firmly set in a certain way. For example, a manager may have heard that his new boss is unpleasant and hard to work with. When she calls him in for an introductory meeting, he may go into that meeting predisposed to dislike her and discount what she has to say.

Organizational Barriers   Other barriers to effective communication involve the organizational context in which the communication occurs. Semantics problems arise when words have different meanings for different people. Words and phrases such as *profit, increased output,* and *return on investment* may have positive meanings for managers but less positive meanings for labor.

Communication problems may also arise when people of different power or status try to communicate with each other. The company president may discount a suggestion from an operating employee, thinking, "How can someone at that level help me run my business?" Or, when the president goes out to inspect a new plant, workers may be reluctant to offer suggestions because of their lower status. The marketing vice president may have more power than the human resource vice president and consequently may not pay much attention to a staffing report submitted by the human resources department.

If people perceive a situation differently, they may have difficulty communicating with one another. When two managers observe that a third manager has not spent much time in her office lately, one may believe that she has been to several important meetings, and the other may think she is "hiding out." If they need to talk about her in some official capacity, problems may arise because one has a positive impression and the other a negative impression.

Environmental factors may also disrupt effective communication. As mentioned earlier, noise may affect communication in many ways. Similarly, overload

SALES PER
100,000 WORDS
SPOKEN

SALES PER
100,000 WORDS
LISTENED TO

GoFF

While most managers acknowledge the importance of communication, not as many understand the value of two-way communication. For example, this manager is learning that in his organization the more people talk the less revenue the organization generates. But the more people listen, the more revenue is generated. While no one has studied this phenomenon in exactly this way, common sense suggests that this manager may be on to something!

© 2007 Ted Goff from cartoonbank.com. All Rights Reserved.

may be a problem when the receiver is being sent more information than he or she can effectively handle. As email becomes increasingly common, many managers report getting so many messages each day as to sometimes feel overwhelmed.[30] And, when the manager gives a subordinate many jobs on which to work and at the same time the subordinate is being told by family and friends to do other things, overload may result and communication effectiveness diminishes.

Finally, as businesses become more and more global, different languages can create problems. To counter this problem, some firms are adopting an "official language." For example, when the German chemical firm Hoechst merged with the French firm Rhone-Poulenc, the new company adopted English as its official language. Indeed, English is increasingly becoming the standard business language around the world.[31]

Improving Communication Effectiveness

Considering how many factors can disrupt communication, it is fortunate that managers can resort to several techniques for improving communication effectiveness.[32] As shown in Table 12.2, these techniques include both individual and organizational skills.

Individual Skills The single most important individual skill for improving communication effectiveness is being a good listener.[33] Being a good listener requires that the individual be prepared to listen, not interrupt the speaker, concentrate on both the words and the meaning being conveyed, be patient, and ask questions as appropriate.[34] So important are good listening skills that companies like Delta, IBM, and Boeing conduct programs to train their managers to be better listeners. Figure 12.6 illustrates the characteristics of poor listeners versus good listeners.

Table 12.2

OVERCOMING BARRIERS TO COMMUNICATION

Because communication is so important, managers have developed several methods of overcoming barriers to effective communication. Some of these methods involve individual skills, whereas others are based on organizational skills.

Individual Skills	Organizational Skills
Develop good listening skills	Follow up
Encourage two-way communication	Regulate information flows
Be aware of language and meaning	Understand the richness of media
Maintain credibility	
Be sensitive to receiver's perspective	
Be sensitive to sender's perspective	

In addition to being a good listener, several other individual skills can promote effective communication. Feedback, one of the most important, is facilitated by two-way communication. Two-way communication allows the receiver to ask questions, request clarification, and express opinions that let the sender know whether he or she has been understood. In general, the more complicated the message, the more useful two-way communication is. In addition, the sender should be aware of the meanings that different receivers might attach to various words. For example, when addressing stockholders, a manager might use the word *profits* often. When addressing labor leaders, however, she may choose to use *profits* less often.

Furthermore, the sender should try to maintain credibility. This can be accomplished by not pretending to be an expert when one is not, by "doing one's homework" and checking facts, and by otherwise being as accurate and honest as possible. The sender should also try to be sensitive to the receiver's perspective. A manager who must tell a subordinate that she has not been recommended for a promotion should recognize that the subordinate will be frustrated and unhappy. The content of the message and its method of delivery should be chosen accordingly. The manager should be primed to accept a reasonable degree of hostility and bitterness without getting angry in return.[35]

Finally, the receiver should also try to be sensitive to the sender's point of view. Suppose that a manager has just received some bad news—for example, that his

Figure 12.6

MORE AND LESS EFFECTIVE LISTENING SKILLS

Effective listening skills are a vital part of communication in organizations. There are several barriers that can contribute to poor listening skills by individuals in organizations. Fortunately, there are also several practices for improving listening skills.

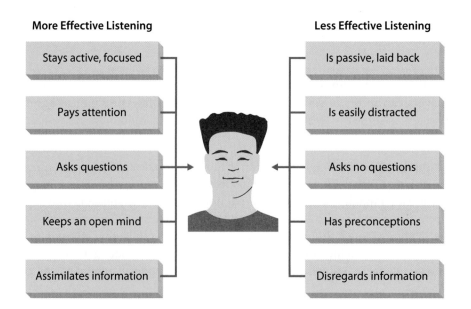

More Effective Listening		Less Effective Listening
Stays active, focused		Is passive, laid back
Pays attention		Is easily distracted
Asks questions		Asks no questions
Keeps an open mind		Has preconceptions
Assimilates information		Disregards information

position is being eliminated next year. Others should understand that he may be disappointed, angry, or even depressed for a while. Thus they might make a special effort not to take too much offense if he snaps at them, and they might look for signals that he needs someone to talk to.[36]

Organizational Skills Three useful organizational skills can also enhance communication effectiveness for both the sender and the receiver—following up, regulating information flow, and understanding the richness of different media. Following up simply involves checking at a later time to be sure that a message has been received and understood. After a manager mails a report to a colleague, she might call a few days later to make sure the report has arrived. If it has, the manager might ask whether the colleague has any questions about it.

Regulating information flow means that the sender or receiver takes steps to ensure that overload does not occur. For the sender, this could mean not passing too much information through the system at one time. For the receiver, it might mean calling attention to the fact that he is being asked to do too many things at once. Many managers limit the influx of information by periodically weeding out the list of journals and routine reports they receive, or they train their assistant to screen phone calls and visitors. Indeed, some executives now get so much email that they have it routed to an assistant. That person reviews the email, discards those that are not useful (such as "spam"), responds to those that are routine, and passes on to the executive only those that require her or his personal attention.

Both parties should also understand the richness associated with different media. When a manager is going to lay off a subordinate temporarily, the message should be delivered in person. A face-to-face channel of communication gives the manager an opportunity to explain the situation and answer questions. When the purpose of the message is to grant a pay increase, written communication may be appropriate because it can be more objective and precise. The manager could then follow up the written notice with personal congratulations.

Summary of Key Points

1. Describe the role and importance of communication in the manager's job.
   - Communication is the process of transmitting information from one person to another.
   - Effective communication is the process of sending a message in such a way that the message received is as close in meaning as possible to the message intended.
   - For information to be useful, it must be accurate, timely, complete, and relevant.
   - The communication process consists of a sender's encoding meaning and transmitting it to one or more receivers, who receive the message and decode it into meaning.
   - In two-way communication, the process continues with the roles reversed.
   - Noise can disrupt any part of the overall process.

2. Identify the basic forms of communication in organizations.
   - Interpersonal communication focuses on communication among a small number of people.
     - Two important forms of interpersonal communication, oral and written, both offer unique advantages and disadvantages.
     - The manager should weigh the pros and cons of each when choosing a medium for communication.

- Communication networks are recurring patterns of communication among members of a group or work team.
- Vertical communication between superiors and subordinates may flow upward or downward.
- Horizontal communication involves peers and colleagues at the same level in the organization.

3. Describe the role of electronic communication in organizations.
   - There are several basic levels of information systems:
     - transaction-processing systems
     - systems for various types of workers
     - basic management information systems
     - decision support systems and executive support systems
     - artificial intelligence, including expert systems
   - Intranets and extranets are also growing in popularity.
   - Electronic communication is having a profound effect on managerial and organizational communication.

4. Discuss informal communication, including its various forms and types.
   - The grapevine is an informal communication network among people in an organization.
   - Management by wandering around is also a popular informal method of communication.
   - Nonverbal communication is expressed through images, settings, and body language.

5. Describe how the communication process can be managed to recognize and overcome barriers.
   - Managing the communication process entails recognizing the barriers to effective communication and understanding how to overcome them.
   - Barriers can be identified at both the individual and the organizational level.
   - Likewise, both individual and organizational skills can be used to overcome these barriers.

Discussion Questions

Questions for Review

1. Describe the difference between communication and effective communication. How can a sender verify that a communication was effective? How can a receiver verify that a communication was effective?

2. Which form of interpersonal communication is best for long-term retention? Why? Which form is best for getting across subtle nuances of meaning? Why?

3. What are the similarities and differences of oral and written communication? What kinds of situations call for the use of oral methods? What situations call for written communication?

4. What forms of electronic communication do you use regularly?

5. Describe the individual and organizational barriers to effective communication. For each barrier, describe one action that a manager could take to reduce the problems caused by that barrier.

Questions for Analysis

1. At what points in the communication process can problems occur? Give examples of how noise can interfere with the communication process. What can managers do to reduce problems and noise?

2. How are electronic communication devices (cell phones, email, and websites) likely to affect the communication process in the future? Describe both the advantages and the disadvantages of these three devices over traditional communication methods, such as face-to-face conversations, written notes, and phone calls.

3. What forms of communication have you experienced today? What form of communication is involved in a face-to-face conversation with a friend? A telephone call from a customer? A traffic light or crossing signal? A picture of a cigarette in a circle with a slash across it? An area around machinery defined by a yellow line painted on the floor?

4. Keep track of your own activities over the course of a few hours of leisure time to determine what forms of communication you encounter.

Which forms were most common? If you had been tracking your communications while at work, how would the list be different? Explain why the differences occur.

5. For each of the following situations, tell which form of communication you would use. Then ask the same question of someone who has been in the workforce for at least ten years. For any differences that occur, ask the worker to explain why his or her choice is better than yours. Do you agree with his or her assessment? Why or why not?

- Describing complex changes in how healthcare benefits are calculated and administered to every employee of a large firm
- Asking your boss a quick question about how she wants something done
- Telling customers that a new two-for-one promotion is available at your store
- Reprimanding an employee for excessive absences on the job
- Reminding workers that no smoking is allowed in your facility

Building Effective Technical Skills

Exercise Overview

Technical skills are the skills necessary to perform the work of the organization. This exercise will help you develop and apply technical skills involving the Internet and its potential for providing raw data that can be turned into information that is relevant to important decisions.

Exercise Background

Assume that you are a manager for a large national retailer. You have been assigned the responsibility for identifying potential locations for the construction of a warehouse and distribution center. The idea behind such a center is that the firm can use its enormous purchasing power to buy many products in bulk quantities at relatively low prices. Individual stores can then order the specific quantities they need from the warehouse.

The location must include a great deal of land. The warehouse itself, for example, will occupy more than four square acres. In addition, it must be close to railroads and major highways, because shipments will be arriving by both rail and truck, although outbound shipments will be exclusively by truck. Other important considerations are that land prices and the cost of living should be relatively low and weather conditions should be mild to minimize disruptions to shipments.

The firm's general experience is that small to mid-size communities work best. Moreover, warehouses are already in place in the western and eastern parts of the United States, so this new one will most likely be in the central or south-central area. Your boss has asked you to identify three or four possible sites.

Exercise Task

With the information above as a framework, do the following:

1. Use the Internet to identify as many as ten possible locations.

2. Using additional information from the Internet, narrow the set of possible locations to three or four.

3. Again using the Internet, find out as much as possible about the potential locations.

Building Effective Communication Skills

Exercise Overview

Communication skills reflect the manager's ability both to convey ideas and information feectively to others and to receive ideas and information effectively from others. This exercise gives you practice in using email to convey and receive ideas and information effectively.

Exercise Background

Email accounts for an increasing percentage of managers' communication time. According to Andy Grove, chairman of the board and former CEO of Intel, email takes time, but, he says, "It also replaces time. I mean, I used to spend probably an hour-and-a-half to two hours a day reading paper mail—and that has almost disappeared."

Grove's email use may be on the low side. One study of high-tech managers showed that, on average, they spent two hours per day reading, sending, or gathering data for email. Given the growing importance and prevalence of email, it is crucial for managers to understand how to use it effectively.

Exercise Task

1. Visit the website of author Virginia Shea's book *Netiquette*, at www.albion.com/netiquette/. The site provides key excerpts from her book. Go to the page "The Core Rules of Netiquette," which gives a useful brief summary of the full text. Read the sections "Introduction" and "Rule 1: Remember the Human."

2. Write an email message to a hypothetical firm describing your dissatisfaction with a product or service they sold to you. Bring the printout of the message to class.

3. Exchange email messages with a classmate. Read each other's messages and prepare useful feedback. Evaluate the clarity and tone of each message. Is the message polite yet firm? Does it clearly indicate the problem? Does it suggest a solution? If you were the employee who received this message, what would be your reaction? Share your feedback with your classmate.

Skills Self-Assessment Instrument

Sex Talk Quiz

Introduction: As more women enter the workforce, communication between men and women will increase. Research shows that men and women often have trouble communicating effectively with one another because they have contrasting values and beliefs about differences between the sexes. The following assessment surveys your beliefs and values about each sex.

Instructions: Mark each statement as either true or false. In some cases, you may find making a decision difficult, but you should force yourself to make a choice.

True/False Questions

_____ 1. Women are more intuitive than men. They have a sixth sense, which is typically called "women's intuition."

_____ 2. At business meetings, coworkers are more likely to listen to men than they are to women.

_____ 3. Women are the "talkers." They talk much more than men in group conversations.

_____ 4. Men are the "fast talkers." They talk much more quickly than women.

_____ 5. Men are more outwardly open than women. They use more eye contact and exhibit more friendliness when first meeting someone than do women.

_____ 6. Women are more complimentary and give more praise than men.

_____ 7. Men interrupt more than women and will answer a question even when it is not addressed to them.

_____ 8. Women give more orders and are more demanding in the way they communicate than are men.

_____ 9. In general, men and women laugh at the same things.

_____ 10. When making love, both men and women want to hear the same things from their partner.

_____ 11. Men ask for assistance less often than do women.

_____ 12. Men are harder on themselves and blame themselves more often than do women.

_____ 13. Through their body language, women make themselves less confrontational than men.

_____ 14. Men tend to explain things in greater detail when discussing an incident than do women.

_____ 15. Women tend to touch others more often than men.

_____ 16. Men appear to be more attentive than women when they are listening.

_____ 17. Women and men are equally emotional when they speak.

_____ 18. Men are more likely than women to discuss personal issues.

_____ 19. Men bring up more topics of conversation than do women.

_____ 20. Today we tend to raise our male children the same way we do our female children.

_____ 21. Women tend to confront problems more directly and are likely to bring up the problem first.

_____ 22. Men are livelier speakers who use more body language and facial animation than do women.

_____ 23. Men ask more questions than women.

_____ 24. In general, men and women enjoy talking about similar things.

_____ 25. When asking whether their partner has had an AIDS test or when discussing safe sex, a woman will likely bring up the topic before a man.

Source: "Sex Talk Quiz," from *He Says, She Says* by Lillian Glass, Ph.D. Copyright 1992 by Lillian Glass, Ph.D. Used by permission of G. P. Putnam's Sons, a division of Penguin Putnam Inc.

For interpretation, see Interpretations of Skills Self-Assessment Instruments in the appendix near the end of this text.

Experiential Exercise

Nonverbal Communication in Groups

Purpose: The role of nonverbal communication in organizations can be just as important as oral or written communication, but is often overlooked. This activity will make you more aware of the power of nonverbal communication and give you some practice in using it.

Instructions:

Step 1: Your instructor will break your class into groups of about 20. Change your seat as needed until the group members are sitting fairly close and facing each other. Count the exact number of members and agree upon the count as a group.

Step 2: Count out loud, one at a time, from 1 up to the total number of group members. The group must do this without discussion or planning about who will say each number. Members may not use any verbal or physical signals, for example, no pointing, nodding, or touching. Each member must say exactly one number and no number may be repeated. No two people may speak simultaneously.

Step 3: If any of the rules are violated, begin the task again from the number 1. Continue until the group successfully completes the task. Then answer the follow-up questions.

Follow-Up Questions

1. What methods of communication did you use to determine who would say each number? How effective was this method?

2. How did the group arrive at this method? For example, did the group try several methods before settling on one?

3. What does this exercise demonstrate to you about the power of nonverbal communication?

4. Can you think of examples of situations that you have experienced in which nonverbal communication played an important role?

5. Can you think of examples of situations that could occur in business organizations in which nonverbal communication might play an important role?

CHAPTER CLOSING CASE

COMMUNICATING THE TRUTH ABOUT SMOKING

A young man stands near a pile of body bags outside the high-rise headquarters of Philip Morris. He shouts up: "We're gonna leave these here, so you can see what 1,200 people actually look like!" The body bags represent the 1,200 daily deaths in the United States attributable to tobacco products. The American Legacy Foundation developed this ad as part of an innovative television campaign to inform and warn teens about the dangers of smoking. So far, the commercials have been remarkably effective.

In 1998 Big Tobacco agreed to pay installments totaling $206 billion as part of a legal settlement against various tobacco makers. Each year, $300 million of that was earmarked for smoking education and prevention, especially among youth. The not-for-profit American Legacy Foundation (ALF) was established to administer those programs.

ALF developed its unique "truth" ads to raise awareness of the dangers of smoking. The commercials feature diverse teens taking direct action against tobacco companies. The style is edgy and confrontational. Market researcher Peter Zollo calls the ads "the 'un-marketing' of high-risk youth behaviors." He explains why the commercials have been so effective with teenagers: "The truth campaign creates a brand with which [teens] want to affiliate. Truth understands teenagers' emotional needs to rebel, defy authority, and assert their independence. So instead of rebelling by smoking, truth encourages teens to rebel by con-

fronting and rejecting the tobacco industry."

The messages appeal to young people's distrust of big business and their desire for nonconformity. Zollo claims, "We've found that humor also goes a long way in gaining teens' acceptance and establishing credibility." High schooler Katie Hardison agrees. "They're not saying 'we're smarter than you; we know what you should do,'" says Hardison. "They never say 'don't smoke.'" In fact, the ads show a teen saying, "If I want to smoke that's my own decision," and another ad claims, "We totally respect people's freedom of choice—different strokes for different folks." Philip Morris's own ad campaign features the tag line "Think. Don't Smoke." ALF contends that the industry's ads present smoking as a behavior that is reserved for adults, which makes smoking appear forbidden and therefore more desirable. Surveys show that teens who view the Philip Morris ads are *more* likely to smoke.

A young woman pushes a baby carriage on a busy city sidewalk. She abruptly runs away, abandoning the carriage near the curb. Bewildered pedestrians approach. Inside, they see a baby doll and a sign proclaims, "Every year, smoking leaves about 13,000 kids motherless." An ALF ad that aired during Super Bowl XXXVIII won an Emmy for the best community service advertisement. ALF not only produces commercials but also creates print ads for publications geared to teens and maintains a website, www.thetruth.com. A truth

tour visits beaches and concerts with vans full of DJs, video monitors, and game consoles. The nonprofit provides money to fund grassroots, youth-led antismoking activities. ALF's research division conducts surveys to evaluate the organization's effectiveness.

Thus far, performance has been high. ALF CEO Cheryl G. Healton claims that after one year of the truth campaign "75 percent of all 12 to 17 year olds . . . could accurately describe at least one of the truth ads." Even more encouraging, truth ads were judged most effective by those at the highest risk—young people who are already smoking or considering smoking. Best of all, in 2005, the *American Journal of Public Health* published research showing that, as a result of the truth campaign, youth smoking declined 22 percent during the first two years, resulting in 300,000 fewer young smokers.

Unfortunately, despite the unprecedented success of the truth campaign, ALF is facing a funding crisis. The payments from tobacco companies ended in 2003, and the company is struggling to find the financing to keep its message in the public view. Focusing on the thousands of expected fatalities if the youth smoking rate climbs to previous levels, the ALF website claims, "If truth dies, it won't die alone." *A teen holds an electronic display, showing the digit 8. The view is grainy, off-center, unsteady. The text reads, "Every 8 seconds, big tobacco loses another customer." Pause. "They die."*

CASE QUESTIONS

1. Describe the steps in the communication process that occur as ALF attempts to educate teens about smoking. Use specific examples from the case.
2. Show how ALF is using oral, written, electronic, and nonverbal communication.
3. In your opinion, why is ALF successful when other organizations sending the same basic message are not? Is there anything ALF could do to increase its effectiveness?

CASE REFERENCES

"American Legacy Foundation," "Applied Research and Evaluation," "Fact Sheet on College Students and Smoking," "First Look Report 9," "Remarks as Prepared for Delivery by Peter Zollo," "Truth Advertising Campaign Takes Home Emmy," American Legacy Foundation website, www.americanlegacy.org on February 1, 2006; Cara B. DiPasquale, "Anti-Tobacco Group Blasts Philip Morris Ads," *Ad Age,* May 29, 2002, www.adage.com on February 16, 2003; Wendy McElroy, "Paying for the Rope That Hangs Them," September 25, 2000, Wendy McElroy's website, www.zetetics.com on February 16, 2003; Alina Tugend, "Cigarette Makers Take Anti-Smoking Ads Personally," *New York Times,* October 27, 2002, p. BU4.

YOU MAKE THE CALL

Talking With Sports Fans

1. Is ESPN managing its communications effectively? Give examples to support your answer.
2. What do you think are the possible disadvantages of ESPN's communication strategies?
3. Do you use ESPN.com? If so, what do you think of the site's interactive features? If you do not use it, tell why. How could ESPN.com gain you as a viewer?
4. In your opinion, is two-way communication between viewers and media companies desirable? Explain.

Test Prepper

college.hmco.com/pic/griffinfund5e

You've read the chapter, studied the key terms, and the exam is any day now. Think you're ready to ace it? Take this sample test to gauge your comprehension of chapter material. You can check your answers at the back of the book. Want more test questions? Visit the student website at http://college.hmco.com/pic/griffinfund5e/ and take the ACE quizzes for more practice.

1. T F Effective communication occurs when the message received is as close as possible to the message sent.

2. T F Studies show that managers generally prefer written communication to verbal communication.

3. T F Wal-Mart reports inventory information to Procter & Gamble daily by email. The two firms are part of an intranet.

4. T F Craig makes a point of leaving his executive office to talk to assembly-line workers about their work. He practices management by wandering around.

5. T F The single most important individual skill for improving communication effectiveness is being a good listener.

6. Which of the following is an example of noise in communication?

   a. A lost memo

   b. Telephone static

   c. An email infected with a virus

   d. A loud helicopter flying overhead

   e. All of the above

7. Which type of network exists when all communication flows through one person?

   a. Chain

   b. Circle

   c. All-channel

   d. Wheel

   e. Y

8. When you make an online hotel reservation on Travelocity, you have just used a(n)

   a. transaction-processing system (TPS).

   b. management information system (MIS).

   c. decision support system (DSS).

   d. executive support system (ESS).

   e. intranet.

9. Which of the following statements is true of the grapevine?

   a. It permeates the entire organization.

   b. The information it contains is usually accurate.

   c. It is impossible to eliminate.

   d. It can be used to improve manager's decision making.

   e. All of the above

10. Organizational barriers to communication include all of the following EXCEPT

    a. language differences.

    b. poor listening skills.

    c. power differences.

    d. overload.

    e. noise.

Managing Work Groups and Teams

chapter 13

FIRST THINGS FIRST

Teamwork for the Tampa Bay Devil Rays

"'What do these kids know? . . . How much baseball will they grasp?' I say, give them a chance."

—DON ZIMMER, SENIOR ADVISOR AND COACH, TAMPA BAY DEVIL RAYS

In 2004, Andrew Friedman spent his days sitting behind a desk at a private equity firm in New Jersey and his nights online, playing fantasy baseball. Today, he is living his fantasy, as executive vice president with the Tampa Bay Devil Rays. Friedman is part of an innovative leadership team at the struggling Devil Rays. The new management team, headed by a former Goldman Sachs executive, recruited its members from the rising-star personnel of investment firms. Team members have a thorough grasp of financial markets and decades' of collective experience applying that knowledge in a practical way. But can Wall Street–style teamwork fix a troubled sports team?

The management team that runs the Tampa Bay Devil Rays includes leaders both on and off of the playing field.

LEARNING OBJECTIVES

After studying this chapter, you should be able to:

- Define and identify types of groups and teams in organizations, discuss reasons why people join groups and teams, and list the stages of group and team development.

- Identify and discuss four essential characteristics of groups and teams.

- Discuss interpersonal and intergroup conflict in organizations.

- Describe how organizations manage conflict.

It began with Stuart Sternberg, a partner who managed options trading for a New York firm. Sternberg, who loved baseball as a child, learned that the Rays were up for sale. At first glance the Rays, who are ranked last in Major League Baseball with a value of $176 million, seemed hopeless. Fans didn't turn out for games, the stadium was unattractive, and management was weak.

Yet Sternberg was intrigued. "I'm a buy-low guy, and if you pay the right price for something, I don't care what it is, you can't go very wrong," he says. Sternberg and five former colleagues paid $48 million for 48 percent of the Devil Rays in 2004. General partner Vince Naimoli, who obtained the MLB franchise in 1995, owns an additional 15 percent. Limited partners, who have no management role, own the rest. In 2006, Naimoli stepped aside, giving management control to Sternberg and his team.

Sternberg's vision is a complete transformation of every aspect of team management. He wants to upgrade Tropicana Park, control costs better, cultivate a deep roster of young talent, and perhaps even change the team's nickname and colors. To do that, he enlisted the help of a protégé, Matthew Silverman. Silverman, also a childhood baseball geek, worked with Sternberg at Goldman Sachs. The 29-year-old was named president of the Tampa Bay team, with responsibility for managing team finances and operations. Rounding out the team is Friedman, also 29, in charge of managing players.

The team is young and inexperienced in baseball management, although clearly intelligent and knowledgeable about finance. Yet Sternberg does not think this poses a problem. He says, "On Wall Street, you want younger, hungry people." The Rays are ready to take risks and everything is under review. "We love where we are right now," says Sternberg, " . . . [but] we'll look at anything that might be more appealing. . . . If somebody knocks our socks off, . . . we're going there."

In Sternberg's view, other teams' managers might be more willing to negotiate with Friedman over player trades, for example, because they are less intimidated by him than by older, more famous team managers. Tampa players, including former catcher Toby Hall, like what the new team has done so far. "Obviously I liked what Sternberg said: They don't fail," says Hall.

The trio is very close, joking around more like fraternity brothers than professional colleagues. A *New York Times* journalist writes, "There is a distinct boys-club feel to the slap-happy camaraderie that binds Mr. Sternberg to his two young executives. It mixes the testosterone of the Wall Street trading floor with the geekiness of those who spend an inordinate amount of time breaking down earned-run averages."

Sternberg, Silverman, and Friedman plan to manage the team like an investments portfolio. Friedman says, "I am purely market driven. I love players I think I can get for less than they are worth. It's positive arbitrage, the valuation asymmetry in the game." Friedman is a believer in "mark-to-market" accounting, in which an asset is valued at its current market price, not the price originally or currently paid for it. For example, Friedman thinks that pitcher Scott Kazmir, who earns just $370,000, is worth $7 million annually to the team. Using mark-to-market,

Friedman values the Devil Rays' payroll at $50 million, about 50 percent more than its actual value of $35 million.

Clearly, Friedman talks and thinks like the Harvard-trained economist that he is. At times, he and the other New Yorkers conflict with the rest of the team's staff, who take a more traditional approach. Don Zimmer, a senior coach with 57 years' experience in baseball doesn't use economic models when evaluating players. He often disagrees with Friedman, but is taking a wait-and-see approach. "People say to me, 'What do these kids know? They look like they are 20 years old. How much baseball will they grasp?'" Zimmer says. "I say, give them a chance."[1]

Andrew Friedman, Stuart Sternberg, and Matthew Silverman are working together as a team. And their goal is to enhance the performance of another team, the Tampa Bay Devil Rays professional baseball franchise. Each member of the management team clearly recognizes the importance of teamwork in organizations. They know, for instance, that if the team is poorly managed it will not succeed. They also recognize that if they do their jobs effectively, then the team will become increasingly competitive.

This chapter is about processes that lead to and follow from activities like those at the Tampa Bay Devil Rays. In our last chapter we established the interpersonal nature of organizations. We extend that discussion here by first introducing basic concepts of group and team dynamics. Subsequent sections explain the characteristics of groups and teams in organizations. We then describe interpersonal and intergroup conflict. Finally, we conclude with a discussion of how conflict can be managed.

Groups and Teams in Organizations

Groups are a ubiquitous part of organizational life. They are the basis for much of the work that gets done, and they evolve both inside and outside the normal structural boundaries of the organization. We will define a ***group*** as two or more people who interact regularly to accomplish a common purpose or goal.[2] The purpose of a group or team may range from preparing a new advertising campaign, to informally sharing information, to making important decisions, to fulfilling social needs.

> **group**
> Two or more people who interact regularly to accomplish a common purpose or goal

Types of Groups and Teams

In general, three basic kinds of groups are found in organizations—functional groups, informal or interest groups, and task groups and teams.[3] These are illustrated in Figure 13.1.

Functional Groups   A ***functional group*** is a permanent group created by the organization to accomplish a number of organizational purposes with an unspecified time horizon. The advertising department at Target, the management department at the University of North Texas, and the nursing staff at the Mayo Clinic are functional groups. The advertising department at Target, for example, seeks to plan effective advertising campaigns, increase sales, run in-store promotions, and develop a unique identity for the company. It is assumed that the functional group will remain in existence after it attains its current objectives—those objectives will be replaced by new ones.

> **functional group**
> A permanent group created by the organization to accomplish a number of organizational purposes with an unspecified time horizon

Figure 13.1

TYPES OF GROUPS IN ORGANIZATIONS

Every organization has many different types of groups. In this hypothetical organization, a functional group is shown within the purple area, a cross-functional team within the yellow area, and an informal group within the green area.

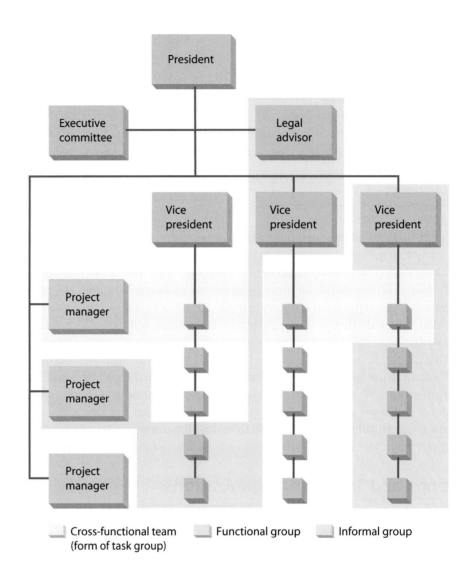

Cross-functional team (form of task group)   Functional group   Informal group

---

informal or interest group
Created by its members for purposes that may or may not be relevant to those of the organization

Informal or Interest Groups   An *informal or interest group* is created by its own members for purposes that may or may not be relevant to organizational goals. It also has an unspecified time horizon. A group of employees who lunch together every day may be discussing productivity, money embezzling, or local politics and sports. As long as the group members enjoy eating together, they will probably continue to do so. When lunches cease to be pleasant, they will seek other company or a different activity.

Informal groups can be a powerful force that managers cannot ignore.[4] One writer described how a group of employees at a furniture factory subverted their boss's efforts to increase production. They tacitly agreed to produce a reasonable amount of work but not to work too hard. One man kept a stockpile of completed work hidden as a backup in case he got too far behind. In another example, auto workers described how they left out gaskets and seals and put soft-drink bottles inside doors.[5] Of course, informal groups can also be a positive force, as demonstrated recently when Continental Airlines employees worked together to buy a new motorcycle for Gordon Bethune, the company's former CEO, to show their support and gratitude for his excellent leadership.

Problem-Solving Team Most popular type of team; comprises knowledge workers who gather to solve a specific problem and then disband

Management Team Consists mainly of managers from various functions like sales and production; coordinates work among other teams

Work Team An increasingly popular type of team; work teams are responsible for the daily work of the organization; when empowered, they are self-managed teams

Virtual Team A new type of work team that interacts by computer; members enter and leave the network as needed and may take turns serving as leader

Quality Circle Declining in popularity, quality circles, comprising workers and supervisors, meet intermittently to discuss workplace problems.

Table 13.1
TYPES OF TEAMS

Source: From *Fortune*, September 5, 1994. Copyright © 1994 Time Inc. All rights reserved.

In recent years the Internet has served as a platform for the emergence of more and different kinds of informal or interest groups. Just as one example, Yahoo! includes a wide array of interest groups that bring together people with common interests. And increasingly workers who lose their jobs as a result of layoffs are banding together electronically to offer moral support to one another and to facilitate networking as they all look for new jobs.[6]

Task Groups   A *task group* is a group created by the organization to accomplish a relatively narrow range of purposes within a stated or implied time horizon. Most committees and task forces are task groups. The organization specifies group membership and assigns a relatively narrow set of goals, such as developing a new product or evaluating a proposed grievance procedure. The time horizon for accomplishing these purposes is either specified (a committee may be asked to make a recommendation within 60 days) or implied (the project team will disband when the new product is developed).

Teams are a special form of task group that have become increasingly popular.[7] In the sense used here, a *team* is a group of workers that functions as a unit, often with little or no supervision, to carry out work-related tasks, functions, and activities. Table 13.1 lists and defines some of the various types of teams that are being used today. Earlier forms of teams included autonomous work groups and quality circles. Today, teams are also sometimes called "self-managed teams," "cross-functional teams," or "high-performance teams." Many firms today are routinely using teams to carry out most of their daily operations.[8]

Organizations create teams for a variety of reasons. For one thing, they give more responsibility for task performance to the workers who are actually performing the tasks. They also empower workers by giving them greater authority and decision-making freedom. In addition, they allow the organization to capitalize on the knowledge and motivation of their workers. Finally, they enable the organization to shed its bureaucracy and to promote flexibility and responsiveness. Ford used teams to design its new Mustang. Similarly, General Motors used a team to develop its newest version of the Chevrolet Blazer. One interesting new trend is the use of virtual teams—teams made up of people from different work locations who interact only through electronic communication media such as the Internet.[9]

When an organization decides to use teams, it is essentially implementing a major form of organization change, as discussed in Chapter 7. Thus it is important to follow a logical and systematic approach to planning and implementing teams

task group
A group created by the organization to accomplish a relatively narrow range of purposes within a stated or implied time horizon

team
A group of workers that functions as a unit, often with little or no supervision, to carry out work-related tasks, functions, and activities

in an existing organization design. It is also important to recognize that resistance may be encountered. This resistance is most likely from first-line managers who will be giving up much of their authority to the team. Many organizations find that they must change the whole management philosophy of such managers away from being a supervisor to being a coach or facilitator.[10]

After teams are in place, managers should continue to monitor their contributions and how effectively they are functioning. In the best circumstances, teams will become very cohesive groups with high performance norms. To achieve this state, the manager can use any or all of the techniques described later in this chapter for enhancing cohesiveness. If implemented properly, and with the support of the workers themselves, performance norms will likely be relatively high. In other words, if the change is properly implemented, the team participants will understand the value and potential of teams and the rewards they may expect to get as a result of their contributions. On the other hand, poorly designed and implemented teams will do a less effective job and may detract from organizational effectiveness.[11]

Why People Join Groups and Teams

People join groups and teams for a variety of reasons. They join functional groups simply by virtue of joining organizations. People accept employment to earn money or to practice their chosen professions. Once inside the organization, they are assigned to jobs and roles and thus become members of functional groups. People in existing functional groups are told, are asked, or volunteer to serve on committees, task forces, and teams. People join informal or interest groups for a variety of reasons, most of them quite complex.[12] Indeed, the need to be a team player has grown so strong today that many organizations will actively resist hiring someone who does not want to work with others.[13]

People join groups and teams for many different reasons. Take Omar Nuñez (center) and Annie Balliro (right), for example. They work for Hard Rock Café in New York. When they recently attended a conference in New Orleans, they took time from their schedule to join these other volunteers at a Habitat for Humanity project. Why did they join this group? Because they wanted to help others.

Interpersonal Attraction One reason why people choose to form informal or interest groups is that they are attracted to one another. Many different factors contribute to interpersonal attraction. When people see a lot of each other, pure proximity increases the likelihood that interpersonal attraction will develop. Attraction is increased when people have similar attitudes, personalities, or economic standings.

Group Activities Individuals may also be motivated to join a group because the activities of the group appeal to them. Jogging, playing bridge, bowling, discussing poetry, playing video games, and flying model airplanes are all activities that some people enjoy. Many of them are more enjoyable to participate in as a member of a group, and most require more than one person. Many large firms like Shell Oil and Apple Computer have a football, softball, or bowling league. A person may join a bowling team, not because of any noticeable attraction to other group members, but simply because being a member of the group allows that person to participate in a pleasant activity. Of course, if the group's level of interpersonal attraction is very low, a person may choose to forgo the activity rather than join the group.

Group Goals The goals of a group may also motivate people to join. The Sierra Club, which is dedicated to environmental conservation, is a good example of this kind of interest group. Various fund-raising groups are another illustration. Members may or may not be personally attracted to the other fundraisers, and they probably do not enjoy the activity of knocking on doors asking for money, but they join the group because they subscribe to its goal. Workers join unions like the United Auto Workers because they support its goals.

Need Satisfaction Still another reason for joining a group is to satisfy the need for affiliation. New residents in a community may join the Newcomers Club partially as a way to meet new people and partially just to be around other people. Likewise, newly divorced people often join support groups as a way to have companionship.

Instrumental Benefits A final reason why people join groups is that membership is sometimes seen as instrumental in providing other benefits to the individual. For example, it is fairly common for college students entering their senior year to join several professional clubs or associations because listing such memberships on a résumé is thought to enhance the chances of getting a good job. Similarly, a manager might join a certain racquet club not because she is attracted to its members (although she might be) and not because of the opportunity to play tennis (although she may enjoy it). The club's goals are not relevant, and her affiliation needs may be satisfied in other ways. However, she may feel that being a member of this club will lead to important and useful business contacts. The racquet club membership is instrumental in establishing those contacts. Membership in civic groups such as the Junior League and Rotary may be solicited for similar reasons.

Stages of Group and Team Development

Imagine the differences between a collection of five people who have just been brought together to form a group or team and a group or team that has functioned like a well-oiled machine for years. Members of a new group or team are unfamiliar with how they will function together and are tentative in their interactions. In a group or team with considerable experience, members are familiar with one another's strengths and weaknesses and are more secure in their roles in the

Figure 13.2
STAGES OF GROUP DEVELOPMENT

As groups mature, they tend to evolve through four distinct stages of development. Managers must understand that group members need time to become acquainted, accept one another, develop a group structure, and become comfortable with their roles in the group before they can begin to work directly to accomplish goals.

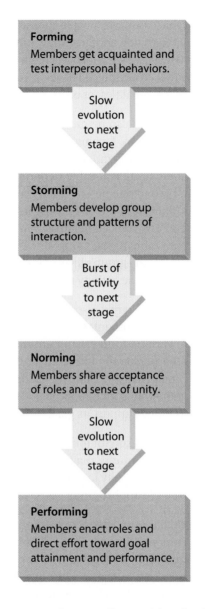

Forming
Members get acquainted and test interpersonal behaviors.

Slow evolution to next stage

Storming
Members develop group structure and patterns of interaction.

Burst of activity to next stage

Norming
Members share acceptance of roles and sense of unity.

Slow evolution to next stage

Performing
Members enact roles and direct effort toward goal attainment and performance.

group. The former group or team is generally considered to be immature; the latter, mature. To progress from the immature phase to the mature phase, a group or team must go through certain stages of development, as shown in Figure 13.2.[14]

The first stage of development is called *forming*. The members of the group or team get acquainted and begin to test which interpersonal behaviors are acceptable and which are unacceptable to the other members. The members are very dependent on others at this point to provide cues about what is acceptable. The basic ground rules for the group or team are established, and a tentative group structure may emerge.[15] At Reebok, for example, a merchandising team was created to handle its sportswear business. The team leader and his members were barely acquainted and had to spend a few weeks getting to know one another.

The second stage of development, often slow to emerge, is *storming*. During this stage, there may be a general lack of unity and uneven interaction patterns. At the same time, some members of the group or team may begin to exert themselves to become recognized as the group leader or at least to play a major role in shaping the group's agenda. In Reebok's team, some members advocated a rapid expansion into the marketplace; others argued for a slower entry. The first faction won, with disastrous results. Because of the rush, product quality was poor and deliveries were late. As a result, the team leader was fired and a new manager placed in charge.

The third stage of development, called *norming*, usually begins with a burst of activity. During this stage, each person begins to recognize and accept her or his role and to understand the roles of others. Members also begin to accept one another and to develop a sense of unity. There may also be temporary regressions to the previous stage. For example, the group or team might begin to accept one particular member as the leader. If this person later violates important norms or otherwise jeopardizes his or her claim to leadership, conflict might reemerge as the group rejects this leader and searches for another. Reebok's new leader transferred several people away from the team and set up a new system and structure for managing things. The remaining employees accepted his new approach and settled into doing their jobs.

Performing, the final stage of group or team development, is also slow to emerge. The team really begins to focus on the problem at hand. The members enact the roles they have accepted, interaction occurs, and the efforts of the group are directed toward goal attainment. The basic structure of the group or team is no longer an issue but has become a mechanism for accomplishing the purpose of the group. Reebok's sportswear business is now growing consistently and has successfully avoided the problems that plagued it at first.

Characteristics of Groups and Teams

As groups and teams mature and pass through the four basic stages of development, they begin to take on four important characteristics—a role structure, norms, cohesiveness, and informal leadership.[16]

Role Structures

Each individual in a team has a part, or *role*, to play in helping the group reach its goals. Some people are leaders, some do the work, some interface with other teams, and so on. Indeed, a person may take on a *task specialist role* (concentrating on getting the group's task accomplished) or a *socioemotional role* (providing social and emotional support to others on the team). A few people, usually the leaders, perform both roles; a few others may do neither. The group's **role structure** is the set of defined roles and interrelationships among those roles that the group or team members define and accept. Each of us belongs to many groups and therefore plays multiple roles—in work groups, classes, families, and social organizations.[17]

Role structures emerge as a result of role episodes, as shown in Figure 13.3. The process begins with the expected role—what other members of the team expect the individual to do. The expected role gets translated into the sent role—the messages and cues that team members use to communicate the expected role to the individual. The perceived role is what the individual perceives the sent role to mean. Finally, the enacted role is what the individual actually does in the role. The enacted role, in turn, influences future expectations of the team. Of course, role episodes seldom unfold this easily. When major disruptions occur, individuals may experience role ambiguity, conflict, or overload.[18]

roles
The parts individuals play in groups in helping the group reach its goals

role structure
The set of defined roles and interrelationships among those roles that the group members define and accept

Figure 13.3
THE DEVELOPMENT OF A ROLE

Roles and role structures within a group generally evolve through a series of role episodes. The first two stages of role development are group processes, as the group members let individuals know what is expected of them. The other two parts are individual processes, as the new group members perceive and enact their roles.

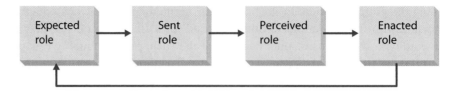

---

role ambiguity
Arises when the sent role is unclear and the individual does not know what is expected of him or her

---

role conflict
Occurs when the messages and cues composing the sent role are clear but contradictory or mutually exclusive

---

Role Ambiguity *Role ambiguity* arises when the sent role is unclear. If your instructor tells you to write a term paper but refuses to provide more information, you will probably experience role ambiguity. You do not know what the topic is, how long the paper should be, what format to use, or when the paper is due. In work settings, role ambiguity can stem from poor job descriptions, vague instructions from a supervisor, or unclear cues from coworkers. The result is likely to be a subordinate who does not know what to do. Role ambiguity can be a significant problem for both the individual who must contend with it and the organization that expects the employee to perform.

Role Conflict *Role conflict* occurs when the messages and cues composing the sent role are clear but contradictory or mutually exclusive.[19] One common form is *interrole conflict*—conflict between roles. For example, if a person's boss says that one must work overtime and on weekends to get ahead, and the same person's spouse says that more time is needed at home with the family, conflict may result. In a matrix organization, interrole conflict often arises between the roles one plays in different teams as well as between team roles and one's permanent role in a functional group.

Intrarole conflict may occur when the person gets conflicting demands from different sources within the context of the same role. A manager's boss may tell her that she needs to put more pressure on subordinates to follow new work rules. At the same time, her subordinates may indicate that they expect her to get the rules changed. Thus the cues are in conflict, and the manager may be unsure about which course to follow. *Intrasender conflict* occurs when a single source sends clear but contradictory messages. This might arise if the boss says one morning that there can be no more overtime for the next month but after lunch tells someone to work late that same evening. *Person-role conflict* results from a discrepancy between the role requirements and the individual's personal values, attitudes, and needs. If a person is told to do something unethical or illegal, or if the work is distasteful (for example, firing a close friend), person-role conflict is likely. Role conflict of all varieties is of particular concern to managers. Research has shown that role conflict may occur in a variety of situations and lead to a variety of adverse consequences, including stress, poor performance, and rapid turnover.

---

role overload
Occurs when expectations for the role exceed the individual's capabilities to perform

---

Role Overload A final consequence of a weak role structure is *role overload*, which occurs when expectations for the role exceed the individual's capabilities. When a manager gives an employee several major assignments at once, while increasing the person's regular workload, the employee will probably experience role overload. Role overload may also result when an individual takes on too many roles at one time. For example, a person trying to work extra hard at work, run for election to the school board, serve on a committee in church, coach Little League baseball, maintain an active exercise program, and be a contributing member to her or his family will probably encounter role overload.

Implications   In a functional group or team, the manager can take steps to avoid role ambiguity, conflict, and overload. Having clear and reasonable expectations and sending clear and straightforward cues go a long way toward eliminating role ambiguity. Consistent expectations that take into account the employee's other roles and personal value system may minimize role conflict. Role overload can be avoided simply by recognizing the individual's capabilities and limits. In friendship and interest groups, role structures are likely to be less formal; hence, the possibility of role ambiguity, conflict, or overload may not be so great. However, if one or more of these problems does occur, they may be difficult to handle. Because roles in friendship and interest groups are less likely to be partially defined by a formal authority structure or written job descriptions, the individual cannot turn to those sources to clarify a role.

Behavioral Norms

Norms are standards of behavior that the group or team accepts for and expects of its members. Most committees, for example, develop norms governing their discussions. A person who talks too much is perceived as doing so to make a good impression or to get his or her own way. Other members may not talk much to this person, may not sit nearby, may glare at the person, and may otherwise "punish" the individual

> *norms*
> Standards of behavior that the group accepts for and expects of its members

Managing in Times of Change

Don't Let a Dream Team Become a Nightmare

Every manager's fantasy is to lead a "dream team." Yet dream teams often fail to produce the anticipated results. Consider the NBA star-studded U.S. Olympic team that placed third in 2004, behind Lithuania. Less well known but just as humiliating, for example, is the bankruptcy of hedge fund Long-Term Capital Management, headed by two Nobel Prize–winning economists. Simply hiring great people and expecting great things is not enough. Team members determine the level of cooperation and performance, but managers can help by providing the right conditions. Here's how.

Don't hire the best people; hire the right people. A top achiever may not work well with others. At Worthington Industries, a steelmaker, team members vote on each new hire. Pay is based on team performance so members choose carefully. "Give us people who are dedicated to making the team work, as opposed to a bunch of talented people with big egos," says CEO John McConnell.

Establish trust and common values. Although team-building exercises can help, trust among team members cannot be rushed. Thus, most corporations, with competitive promotions and frequent job changes, make it difficult to build common vision and trust. Shared values are much easier in small groups. Some of the most effective top management teams consist of just two people, for example, Microsoft's Gates and Ballmer.

Resolve conflicts by getting real. "Put the fish on the table," says professor George Kohlrieser. Out of politeness or self-preservation, managers may not raise difficult issues. Yet honesty is important when addressing fundamental problems and building trust. Stas Preczewski, a crew coach, placed his top performers on the varsity squad and the rest on junior varsity. The JV won two-thirds of the time because the star rowers resented each other. Preczewski arranged a wrestling match, which broke through the tension and fostered teamwork. Former CEO of General Electric Jack Welch implemented open, informal work meetings to "face reality," in his words.

Expect to work hard managing a dream team, but don't worry if you can't attract the top people. A group of intelligent, hard-working team players will likely outperform any dream team. As Michael Jordan notes, "Talent wins games, but teamwork wins championships."

References: Geoffrey Colvin, "Why Dream Teams Fail," *Fortune*, June 1, 2006, www.fortune.com on June 1, 2006; "Remember These Guys?" *BusinessWeek*, June 12, 2006, www.businessweek.com on March 2, 2006; Jerry Useem, How to Build a Great Team," *Fortune*, June 1, 2006, www.fortune.com on March 2, 2006.

Smoothly functioning teams can often be a source of efficiency, innovation, and productivity. However, various obstacles may also limit how well the members of a team work together. For instance, personality conflicts, differences in goals, and similar factors can be problems. Problems can also arise when one or more team members attempt to exert power or control over other team members. The manager in this example is doing just that, and as a result other team members may become resentful or intimidated.

"I don't <u>have</u> to be a team player, Crawford. I'm the team owner."

© The New Yorker Collection 2003 Leo Cullum from cartoonbank.com. All Rights Reserved.

for violating the norm. Norms, then, define the boundaries between acceptable and unacceptable behavior.[20] Some groups develop norms that limit the upper bounds of behavior to "make life easier" for the group—for example, do not make more than two comments in a committee discussion or do not produce any more than you have to. In general, these norms are counterproductive. Other groups may develop norms that limit the lower bounds of behavior—for example, do not come to meetings unless you have read the reports to be discussed or produce as much as you can. These norms tend to reflect motivation, commitment, and high performance. Managers can sometimes use norms for the betterment of the organization. For example, Kodak has successfully used group norms to reduce injuries in some of its plants.[21]

Norm Generalization   The norms of one group cannot always be generalized to another group. Some academic departments, for example, have a norm that suggests that faculty members dress up on teaching days. People who fail to observe this norm are "punished" by sarcastic remarks or even formal reprimands. In other departments, the norm may be casual clothes, and the person unfortunate enough to wear dress clothes may be punished just as vehemently. Even within the same work area, similar groups or teams can develop different norms. One team may strive always to produce above its assigned quota; another may maintain productivity just below its quota. The norm of one team may be to be friendly and cordial to its supervisor; that of another team may be to remain aloof and distant. Some differences are due primarily to the composition of the teams.

Norm Variation   In some cases, there can also be norm variation within a group or team. A common norm is that the least senior member of a group is expected to perform unpleasant or trivial tasks for the rest of the group. These tasks might be to wait on customers who are known to be small tippers (in a restaurant), to deal with complaining customers (in a department store), or to handle the low-commission line of merchandise (in a sales department). Another example is when certain individuals, especially informal leaders, may violate some norms. If the team is going to meet at 8:00 A.M., anyone arriving late will be chastised for holding things up. Occasionally, however, the informal leader may arrive a few minutes late. As long as this does not happen too often, the group probably will not do anything about it.

Norm Conformity   Four sets of factors contribute to norm conformity. First, factors associated with the group are important. For example, some groups or teams may exert more pressure for conformity than others. Second, the initial stimulus that prompts behavior can affect conformity. The more ambiguous the stimulus (for example, news that the team is going to be transferred to a new unit), the more pressure there is to conform. Third, individual traits determine the individual's propensity to conform (for example, more intelligent people are often less susceptible to pressure to conform). Finally, situational factors, such as team size and unanimity, influence conformity. As an individual learns the group's norms, he can do several different things. The most obvious is to adopt the norms. For example, the new male professor who notices that all the other men in the department dress up to teach can also start wearing a suit. A variation is to try to obey the "spirit" of the norm while retaining individuality. The professor may recognize that the norm is actually to wear a tie; thus he might succeed by wearing a tie with his sport shirt, jeans, and sneakers.

The individual may also ignore the norm. When a person does not conform, several things can happen. At first the group may increase its communication with the deviant individual to try to bring her back in line. If this does not work, communication may decline. Over time, the group may begin to exclude the individual from its activities and, in effect, ostracize the person. Finally, we need to briefly consider another aspect of norm conformity—socialization. **Socialization** is generalized norm conformity that occurs as a person makes the transition from being an outsider to being an insider. A newcomer to an organization, for example, gradually begins to learn about such norms as dress, working hours, and interpersonal relations. As the newcomer adopts these norms, she is being socialized into the organizational culture. Some organizations, like Texas Instruments, work to actively manage the socialization process; others leave it to happenstance.

> **socialization**
> Generalized norm conformity that occurs as a person makes the transition from being an outsider to being an insider in the organization

Cohesiveness

A third important team characteristic is cohesiveness. **Cohesiveness** is the extent to which members are loyal and committed to the group. In a highly cohesive team, the members work well together, support and trust one another, and are generally effective at achieving their chosen goals.[22] In contrast, a team that lacks cohesiveness is not very coordinated, its members do not necessarily support one another fully, and it may have a difficult time reaching goals. Of particular interest are the factors that increase and reduce cohesiveness and the consequences of team cohesiveness. These are listed in Table 13.2.

> **cohesiveness**
> The extent to which members are loyal and committed to the group; the degree of mutual attractiveness within the group

Factors That Increase Cohesiveness   Five factors can increase the level of cohesiveness in a group or team. One of the strongest is intergroup competition. When two or more groups are in direct competition (for example, three sales groups competing for top sales honors or two football teams competing for a conference championship),

Table 13.2

FACTORS THAT INFLUENCE GROUP COHESIVENESS

Several different factors can influence the cohesiveness of a group. For example, a manager can establish intergroup competition, assign compatible members to the group, create opportunities for success, establish acceptable goals, and foster interaction to increase cohesiveness. Other factors can be used to decrease cohesiveness.

Factors That Increase Cohesiveness	Factors That Reduce Cohesiveness
Intergroup competition	Group size
Personal attraction	Disagreement on goals
Favorable evaluation	Intragroup competition
Agreement on goals	Domination
Interaction	Unpleasant experiences

each group is likely to become more cohesive. Second, just as personal attraction plays a role in causing a group to form, so, too, does attraction seem to enhance cohesiveness. Third, favorable evaluation of the entire group by outsiders can increase cohesiveness. Thus a group's winning a sales contest or a conference title or receiving recognition and praise from a superior tends to increase cohesiveness.

Similarly, if all the members of the group or team agree on their goals, cohesiveness is likely to increase.[23] And the more frequently members of the group interact with one another, the more likely the group is to become cohesive. A manager who wants to foster a high level of cohesiveness in a team might do well to establish some form of intergroup competition, assign members to the group who are likely to be attracted to one another, provide opportunities for success, establish goals that all members are likely to accept, and allow ample opportunities for interaction.

Factors That Reduce Cohesiveness   There are also five factors that are known to reduce team cohesiveness. First of all, cohesiveness tends to decline as a group increases in size. Second, when members of a team disagree on what the goals of the group should be, cohesiveness may decrease. For example, when some members believe the group should maximize output and others think output should be restricted, cohesiveness declines. Third, intragroup competition reduces cohesiveness. When members are competing among themselves, they focus more on their own actions and behaviors than on those of the group.

Fourth, domination by one or more persons in the group or team may cause overall cohesiveness to decline. Other members may feel that they are not being given an opportunity to interact and contribute, and they may become less attracted to the group as a consequence. Finally, unpleasant experiences that result from group membership may reduce cohesiveness. A sales group that comes in last in a sales contest, an athletic team that sustains a long losing streak, and a work group reprimanded for poor-quality work may all become less cohesive as a result of their unpleasant experiences.

Consequences of Cohesiveness   In general, as teams become more cohesive, their members tend to interact more frequently, conform more to norms, and become more satisfied with the team. Cohesiveness may also influence team performance. However, performance is also influenced by the team's performance norms. Figure 13.4 shows how cohesiveness and performance norms interact to help shape team performance.

When both cohesiveness and performance norms are high, high performance should result because the team wants to perform at a high level (norms) and its members are working together toward that end (cohesiveness). When norms are high and cohesiveness is low, performance will be moderate. Although the team

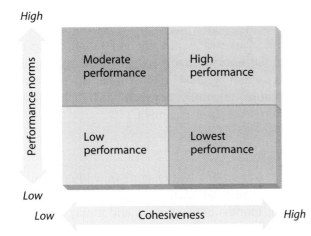

Figure 13.4

THE INTERACTION BETWEEN COHESIVENESS AND PERFORMANCE NORMS

Group cohesiveness and performance norms interact to determine group performance. From the manager's perspective, high cohesiveness combined with high performance norms is the best situation, and high cohesiveness with low performance norms is the worst situation. Managers who can influence the level of cohesiveness and performance norms can greatly improve the effectiveness of a work group.

wants to perform at a high level, its members are not necessarily working well together. When norms are low, performance will be low, regardless of whether group cohesiveness is high or low. The least desirable situation occurs when low performance norms are combined with high cohesiveness. In this case, all team members embrace the standard of restricting performance (owing to the low performance norm), and the group is united in its efforts to maintain that standard (owing to the high cohesiveness). If cohesiveness were low, the manager might be able to raise performance norms by establishing high goals and rewarding goal attainment or by bringing in new group members who are high performers. But a highly cohesive group is likely to resist these interventions.[24]

Formal and Informal Leadership

Most functional groups and teams have a formal leader—that is, one appointed by the organization or chosen or elected by the members of the group. Because friendship and interest groups are formed by the members themselves, however, any formal leader must be elected or designated by the members. Although some groups do designate such a leader (a softball team may elect a captain, for example), many do not. Moreover, even when a formal leader is designated, the group or team may also look to others for leadership. An ***informal leader*** is a person who engages in leadership activities but whose right to do so has not been formally recognized. The formal and the informal leader in any group or team may be the same person, or they may be different people. We noted earlier the distinction between the task specialist and socioemotional roles within groups. An informal leader is likely to be a person capable of carrying out both roles effectively. If the formal leader can fulfill one role but not the other, an informal leader often emerges to supplement the formal leader's functions. If the formal leader can fill neither role, one or more informal leaders may emerge to carry out both sets of functions.

Is informal leadership desirable? In many cases informal leaders are quite powerful because they draw from referent or expert power. When they are working in the best interests of the organization, they can be a tremendous asset. Notable athletes like Brett Favre and Mia Hamm are classic examples of informal leaders. However, when informal leaders work counter to the goals of the organization, they can cause significant difficulties. Such leaders may lower performance norms, instigate walkouts or wildcat strikes, or otherwise disrupt the organization.

informal leader
A person who engages in leadership activities but whose right to do so has not been formally recognized by the organization or group

Interpersonal and Intergroup Conflict

Of course, when people work together in an organization, things do not always go smoothly. Indeed, conflict is an inevitable element of interpersonal relationships in organizations. In this section, we look at how conflict affects overall performance. We also explore the causes of conflict between individuals, between groups, and between an organization and its environment.

The Nature of Conflict

conflict
A disagreement among two or more individuals, groups, or organizations

Conflict is a disagreement among two or more individuals, groups, or organizations. This disagreement may be relatively superficial or very strong. It may be short-lived or exist for months or even years, and it may be work related or personal. Conflict may manifest itself in a variety of ways. People may compete with one another, glare at one another, shout, or withdraw. Groups may band together to protect popular members or oust unpopular members. Organizations may seek legal remedies.

Most people assume that conflict is something to be avoided because it connotes antagonism, hostility, unpleasantness, and dissension. Indeed, managers and management theorists have traditionally viewed conflict as a problem to be avoided.[25] In recent years, however, we have come to recognize that, although conflict can be a major problem, certain kinds of conflict may also be beneficial.[26] For example, when two members of a site selection committee disagree over the best location for a new plant, each may be forced to more thoroughly study and defend his or her preferred alternative. As a result of more systematic analysis and discussion, the committee may make a better decision and be better prepared to justify it to others than if everyone had agreed from the outset and accepted an alternative that was perhaps less well analyzed.

As long as conflict is being handled in a cordial and constructive manner, it is probably serving a useful purpose in the organization. On the other hand, when working relationships are being disrupted and the conflict has reached destructive levels, it has likely become dysfunctional and needs to be addressed.[27] We discuss ways of dealing with such conflict later in this chapter.

Figure 13.5 depicts the general relationship between conflict and performance for a group or organization. If there is absolutely no conflict in the group or

Figure 13.5
THE NATURE OF ORGANIZATIONAL CONFLICT

Either too much or too little conflict can be dysfunctional for an organization. In either case, performance may be low. However, an optimal level of conflict that sparks motivation, creativity, innovation, and initiative can result in higher levels of performance.

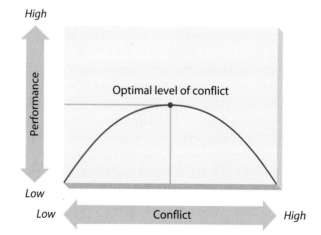

organization, its members may become complacent and apathetic. As a result, group or organizational performance and innovation may begin to suffer. A moderate level of conflict among group or organizational members, on the other hand, can spark motivation, creativity, innovation, and initiative and raise performance. Too much conflict, though, can produce such undesirable results as hostility and lack of cooperation, which lower performance. The key for managers is to find and maintain the optimal amount of conflict that fosters performance. Of course, what constitutes optimal conflict varies with both the situation and the people involved.[28]

Causes of Conflict

Conflict may arise in both interpersonal and intergroup relationships. Occasionally conflict between individuals and groups may be caused by particular organizational strategies and practices. A third arena for conflict is between an organization and its environment.

Interpersonal Conflict   Conflict between two or more individuals is almost certain to occur in any organization, given the great variety in perceptions, goals, attitudes, and so forth among its members. William Gates, founder and CEO of Microsoft, and Kazuhiko Nishi, a former business associate from Japan, ended a long-term business relationship because of interpersonal conflict. Nishi accused Gates of becoming too political, while Gates charged that Nishi became too unpredictable and erratic in his behavior.[29]

A frequent source of interpersonal conflict in organizations is what many people call a "personality clash"—when two people distrust each other's motives, dislike each other, or for some other reason simply cannot get along.[30] Conflict may also arise between people who have different beliefs or perceptions about some aspect of their work or their organization. For example, one manager might want

Conflict can be caused by a number of different factors. J. Mays is Ford's group vice president for design and the firm's chief creative officer. Mays and his group have been charged with developing a large number of cutting edge car and truck designs. But carrying out this charge often comes into conflict with other major efforts at Ford to cut costs and downsize the workforce by 14,000 employees.

the organization to require that all employees use Microsoft Office software in order to promote standardization. Another manager might believe that a variety of software packages should be allowed, in order to recognize individuality. Similarly, a male manager may disagree with his female colleague over whether the organization is guilty of discriminating against women in promotion decisions. Conflict can also result from excess competitiveness among individuals. Two people vying for the same job, for example, may resort to political behavior in an effort to gain an advantage. If either competitor sees the other's behavior as inappropriate, accusations are likely to result. Even after the "winner" of the job is determined, such conflict may continue to undermine interpersonal relationships, especially if the reasons given in selecting one candidate are ambiguous or open to alternative explanations. Robert Allen resigned as CEO of Delta Air Lines a few years ago because he disagreed with other key executives over how best to reduce the carrier's costs. After he began looking for a replacement for one of his rivals without the approval of the firm's board of directors, the resultant conflict and controversy left him no choice but to leave.[31] More recently, similar problems have plagued Boeing as its top executives have publicly disagreed over routine matters and sometimes gone to great lengths to make each other look bad.[32]

Intergroup Conflict   Conflict between two or more organizational groups is also quite common. For example, the members of a firm's marketing group may disagree with the production group over product quality and delivery schedules. Two sales groups may disagree over how to meet sales goals, and two groups of managers may have different ideas about how best to allocate organizational resources.

Many intergroup conflicts arise more from organizational causes than from interpersonal causes. In Chapter 6, we described three forms of group interdependence—pooled, sequential, and reciprocal. Just as increased interdependence makes coordination more difficult, it also increases the potential for conflict. For example, recall that in sequential interdependence, work is passed from one unit to another. Intergroup conflict may arise if the first group turns out too much work (the second group will fall behind), too little work (the second group will not meet its own goals), or poor-quality work.

At one JCPenney department store, conflict arose between stockroom employees and sales associates. The sales associates claimed that the stockroom employees were slow in delivering merchandise to the sales floor so that it could be priced and shelved. The stockroom employees, in turn, claimed that the sales associates were not giving them enough lead time to get the merchandise delivered and failed to understand that they had additional duties besides carrying merchandise to the sales floor.

Just like people, different departments often have different goals. Further, these goals may often be incompatible. A marketing goal of maximizing sales, achieved partially by offering many products in a wide variety of sizes, shapes, colors, and models, probably conflicts with a production goal of minimizing costs, achieved partially by long production runs of a few items. Reebok recently confronted this very situation. One group of managers wanted to introduce a new sportswear line as quickly as possible, but other managers wanted to expand more deliberately and cautiously. Because the two groups were not able to reconcile their differences effectively, conflict between the two factions led to quality problems and delivery delays that plagued the firm for months.

Competition for scarce resources can also lead to intergroup conflict. Most organizations—especially universities, hospitals, government agencies, and businesses in depressed industries—have limited resources. In one New England town, for example, the public works department and the library battled over funds from a federal construction grant. The Buick, Pontiac, and Chevrolet divisions of General Motors have frequently fought over the right to manufacture various new products developed by the company.

Conflict Between Organization and Environment   Conflict that arises between one organization and another is called *interorganizational conflict.* A moderate amount of interorganizational conflict resulting from business competition is expected, of course, but sometimes conflict becomes more extreme. For example, the owners of Jordache Enterprises, Inc., and Guess, Inc., battled in court for years over ownership of the Guess? label, allegations of design theft, and several other issues.[33] Similarly, General Motors and Volkswagen went to court to resolve a bitter conflict that spanned more than four years. It all started when a key GM executive, Jose Ignacio Lopez de Arriortua, left for a position at Volkswagen. GM claimed that he took with him key secrets that could benefit its German competitor. After the messy departure, dozens of charges and countercharges were made by the two firms, and only a court settlement was able to put the conflict to an end.[34]

Conflict can also arise between an organization and other elements of its environment. For example, an organization may conflict with a consumer group over claims it makes about its products. McDonald's faced this problem a few years ago when it published nutritional information about its products that omitted details about fat content. A manufacturer might conflict with a governmental agency such as the federal Occupational Safety and Health Administration (OSHA). For example, the firm's management may believe it is in compliance with OSHA regulations, whereas officials from the agency itself believe that the firm is not in compliance. Or a firm might conflict with a supplier over the quality of raw materials. The firm may think the supplier is providing inferior materials, while the supplier thinks the materials are adequate. Finally, individual managers obviously may have disagreements with groups of workers. For example, a manager may think her workers are doing poor-quality work and that they are unmotivated. The workers, on the other hand, may believe they are doing good jobs and that the manager is doing a poor job of leading them.

Managing Conflict in Organizations

How do managers cope with all this potential conflict? Fortunately, as Table 13.3 shows, there are ways to stimulate conflict for constructive ends, to control conflict before it gets out of hand, and to resolve it if it does. Below we look at ways of managing conflict.[35]

Stimulating Conflict

In some situations, an organization may stimulate conflict by placing individual employees or groups in competitive situations. Managers can establish sales contests, incentive plans, bonuses, or other competitive stimuli to spark competition. As long as the ground rules are equitable and all participants perceive the contest as

Table 13.3

METHODS FOR MANAGING CONFLICT

Conflict is a powerful force in organizations and has both negative and positive consequences. Thus managers can draw on several different techniques to stimulate, control, or resolve and eliminate conflict, depending on their unique circumstances.

Stimulating Conflict	Increase competition among individuals and teams.
	Hire outsiders to shake things up.
	Change established procedures.
Controlling Conflict	Expand resource base.
	Enhance coordination of interdependence.
	Set superordinate goals.
	Match personalities and work habits of employees.
Resolving and Eliminating Conflict	Avoid conflict.
	Convince conflicting parties to compromise.
	Bring conflicting parties together to confront and negotiate conflict.

fair, the conflict created by the competition is likely to be constructive because each participant will work hard to win (thereby enhancing some aspect of organizational performance).

Another useful method for stimulating conflict is to bring in one or more outsiders who will shake things up and present a new perspective on organizational practices. Outsiders may be new employees, current employees assigned to an existing work group, or consultants or advisors hired on a temporary basis. Of course, this action can also provoke resentment from insiders who feel they were qualified for the position. The Beecham Group, a British company, once hired an executive from the United States for its CEO position, expressly to change how the company did business. His arrival brought with it new ways of doing things and a new enthusiasm for competitiveness. Unfortunately, some valued employees also chose to leave Beecham because they resented some of the changes that were made.

Changing established procedures, especially procedures that have outlived their usefulness, can also stimulate conflict. Such actions cause people to reassess how they perform their job and whether they perform it correctly. For example, one university president announced that all vacant staff positions could be filled only after written justification had received his approval. Conflict arose between the president and the department heads, who felt they had to do more paperwork than was necessary. Most requests were approved, but because department heads now had to think through their staffing needs, a few unnecessary positions were appropriately eliminated.

Controlling Conflict

One method of controlling conflict is to expand the resource base. Suppose a top manager receives two budget requests for $100,000 each. If she has only $180,000 to distribute, the stage is set for conflict because each group will believe its proposal is worth funding and will be unhappy if it is not fully funded. If both proposals are indeed worthwhile, it may be possible for the manager to come up with the extra $20,000 from some other source and thereby avoid difficulty.

As noted earlier, pooled, sequential, and reciprocal interdependence can all result in conflict. If managers use an appropriate technique for enhancing coordination, they can reduce the probability that conflict will arise. Techniques for coordination (described in Chapter 6) include making use of the managerial hierarchy, relying on rules and procedures, enlisting liaison people, forming task forces, and integrating departments. At the JCPenney store mentioned earlier, the conflict was addressed by providing salespeople with clearer forms on which to specify the merchandise they needed and in what sequence. If one coordination technique does not have the desired effect, a manager might shift to another one.

Competing goals can also be a source of conflict among individuals and groups. Managers can sometimes focus employee attention on higher-level, or superordinate, goals as a way of eliminating lower-level conflict. When labor unions like the United Auto Workers make wage concessions to ensure survival of the automobile industry, they are responding to a superordinate goal. Their immediate goal may be higher wages for members, but they realize that, without the automobile industry, their members would not even have jobs.

Finally, managers should try to match the personalities and work habits of employees so as to avoid conflict between individuals. For instance, two valuable subordinates, one a chain smoker and the other a vehement antismoker, probably should not be required to work together in an enclosed space. If conflict does arise between incompatible individuals, a manager might seek an equitable transfer for one or both of them to other units.

Resolving and Eliminating Conflict

Despite everyone's best intentions, conflict sometimes flares up. If it is disrupting the workplace, creating too much hostility and tension, or otherwise harming the organization, attempts must be made to resolve it. Some managers who are uncomfortable dealing with conflict choose to avoid the conflict and hope it will go away. Avoidance may sometimes be effective in the short run for some kinds of interpersonal disagreements, but it does little to resolve long-run or chronic conflicts. Even more unadvisable, though, is "smoothing"—minimizing the conflict and telling everyone that things will "get better." Often the conflict only worsens as people continue to brood over it.

Compromise is striking a middle-range position between two extremes. This approach can work if it is used with care, but in most compromise situations, someone wins and someone loses. Budget problems are one of the few areas amenable to compromise because of their objective nature. Assume, for example, that additional resources are not available to the manager mentioned earlier. She has $180,000 to divide, and each of two groups claims to need $100,000. If the manager believes that both projects warrant funding, she can allocate $90,000 to each. The fact that the two groups have at least been treated equally may minimize the potential conflict.

The confrontational approach to conflict resolution—also called *interpersonal problem solving*—consists of bringing the parties together to confront the conflict. The parties discuss the nature of their conflict and attempt to reach an agreement or a solution. Confrontation requires a reasonable degree of maturity on the part of the participants, and the manager must structure the situation carefully. If handled well, this approach can be an effective means of resolving conflict. In recent years, many organizations have experimented with a technique called *alternative dispute resolution*, using a team of employees to arbitrate conflict in this way.[36]

Regardless of the approach, organizations and their managers should realize that conflict must be addressed if it is to serve constructive purposes and be prevented from bringing about destructive consequences. Conflict is inevitable in organizations, but its effects can be constrained with proper attention. For example, Union

Carbide sent 200 of its managers to a three-day workshop on conflict management. The managers engaged in a variety of exercises and discussions to learn with whom they were most likely to come in conflict and how they should try to resolve it. As a result, managers at the firm later reported that hostility and resentment in the organization had been greatly diminished and that people in the firm reported more pleasant working relationships.[37]

Summary of Key Points

1. Define and identify types of groups and teams in organizations, discuss reasons why people join groups and teams, and list the stages of group and team development.
   - A group is two or more people who interact regularly to accomplish a common purpose or goal.
   - General kinds of groups in organizations are
     - functional groups
     - informal or interest groups
     - task groups and teams
   - A team is a group of workers that functions as a unit, often with little or no supervision, to carry out work-related tasks, functions, and activities.

2. Identify and discuss four essential characteristics of groups and teams.
   - People join functional groups and teams to pursue a career.
   - Their reasons for joining informal or interest groups include interpersonal attraction, group activities, group goals, need satisfaction, and potential instrumental benefits.
   - The stages of team development include forming, storming, norming, and performing.
   - Four important characteristics of teams are role structures, behavioral norms, cohesiveness, and informal leadership.
     - Role structures define task and socioemotional specialists and may be disrupted by role ambiguity, role conflict, or role overload.

   - Norms are standards of behavior for group members.
   - Cohesiveness is the extent to which members are loyal and committed to the team and to one another.
   - Informal leaders are those leaders whom the group members themselves choose to follow.

3. Discuss interpersonal and intergroup conflict in organizations.
   - Conflict is a disagreement between two or more people, groups, or organizations.
   - Too little or too much conflict may hurt performance, but an optimal level of conflict may improve performance.
   - Interpersonal and intergroup conflict in organizations may be caused by personality differences or by particular organizational strategies and practices.
   - Organizations may encounter conflict with one another and with various elements of the environment.

4. Describe how organizations manage conflict.
   - Three methods of managing conflict are
     - to stimulate it
     - to control it
     - to resolve and eliminate it

Discussion Questions

Questions for Review

1. What is a group? Describe the several different types of groups and indicate the similarities and differences between them. What is the difference between a group and a team?

2. What are the stages of group development? Do all teams develop through all the stages discussed in this chapter? Why or why not? How might the

management of a mature team differ from the management of teams that are not yet mature?

3. Describe the development of a role within a group. Tell how each role leads to the next.

4. Identify two examples of informal leaders. Can a person be a formal and an informal leader at the same time?

5. Describe the causes of conflict in organizations. What can a manager do to control conflict? To resolve and eliminate conflict?

Questions for Analysis

1. Individuals join groups for a variety of reasons. Most groups contain members who joined for different reasons. What is likely to be the result when members join a group for different reasons? What can a group leader do to reduce the negative impact of a conflict in reasons for joining the group?

2. Consider the case of a developed group, where all members have been socialized. What are the benefits to the individuals of norm conformity? What are the benefits of not conforming to the group's norms? What are the benefits to an organization of conformity? What are the benefits to an organization of nonconformity?

3. Do you think teams are a valuable new management technique that will endure, or are they just a fad that will be replaced with something else in the near future?

4. Think of several groups of which you have been a member. Why did you join each? Did each group progress through the stages of development discussed in this chapter? If not, why do you think it did not?

5. Describe a case of interpersonal conflict that you have observed in an organization. Describe a case of intergroup conflict that you have observed. (If you have not observed any, interview a worker or manager to obtain examples.) In each case, was the conflict beneficial or harmful to the organization, and why?

Building Effective Decision-Making Skills

Exercise Overview

Decision-making skills include the manager's ability to recognize and define situations correctly and to select courses of action. This exercise helps to build your decision-making skills by giving you practice in selecting members for a cross-functional team.

Exercise Background

Assume that you are the vice president of marketing and customer support for a medium-sized firm that creates and sells accounting software to businesses. Most of your clients are service firms with annual sales of $1 million to $10 million. Your company is preparing to launch a new product, an add-on to your current software that will allow customers to use your system to manage their human resources expenses and scheduling.

Your company's new-product release team is being formed now. The team will work autonomously with only minor oversight from you. The team's responsibilities will include preparing a marketing campaign to inform current and potential customers about the new product,

answering customer questions about how to use the product, and shipping the product to purchasers. Thus far, the team includes one member who helped to write the software code, one finance person, and one member from the logistics department, who is in charge of distribution of the finished product. While each of these members performs an important function on the team, you believe that the two members still to be chosen—those representing marketing and customer service—will be the most crucial factors in the creation of a positive group experience.

Your task is to choose two additional members to complete the team—one from marketing and one from customer service. As you choose members, you have four goals in mind. First, you want the new-product launch to be effective and meet sales targets. Second, you want the group's tasks to be performed quickly and efficiently. Third, you want the group to function smoothly as a team, with cohesiveness and not too much conflict. Fourth, you anticipate that your company will soon have more new-product launches, so you want to use this launch as an opportunity to train and develop workers for the future.

Exercise Task

Examine the list below. Select one person to fulfill the marketing role and one to fulfill the customer service role for the new product launch team. After you have made your selections, answer the follow-up questions.

DINEITHA WASHINGTON is 36 years old, with a degree in public relations. She began working for your company about six years ago, after her attempt to start her own PR firm failed. She is your creative marketing superstar. Every one of her advertising campaigns has been highly successful and she even won a local Chamber of Commerce award a year ago, a first for your company. She excels at ad concepts and design, but her leadership skills are weaker. She usually chooses to communicate by email or phone and is very uncomfortable speaking in front of a group. She works from home two days each week, explaining that she needs peace and quiet to "work the magic." She is emotionally mature and is often the person that other employees turn to when they are having personal problems. She has helped to resolve more than one work conflict simply by listening to each person and offering suggestions. Dineitha has expressed her interest in designing the marketing campaign for the launch team, but not the other tasks.

ERICA HUDSON, a 30-year-old with a high school diploma, is part of your customer service group. A single mother, she is ambitious and has worked hard to move up from a clerical position in your firm to a higher-paying, professional one. She is intensely loyal to your company and is also a conscientious worker, reliably completing every task well and on time. Unfortunately, her relationship with her supervisor, Sandra Williams, is not very good right now. Sandra had asked Erica to shift her work schedule into the evening hours and Erica refused, saying that her family time came first. On the whole, however, Erica is well liked by her coworkers. Because she's so efficient, she often has time to help others complete their tasks. In your opinion, Erica is invaluable to the customer service group. Erica is eager to work on the launch team in order to expand her skills.

JOEL GOLDMAN, at 24 years old, is the youngest member of the team. He is a natural computer whiz who began working as a programmer for your company while still in high school. However, when he began college, he realized that he had a passion for working with others and switched majors from computers to marketing. He finished his B.B.A. and joined the marketing department two years ago. In your opinion, Joel is the most intelligent candidate and has the best technical skills. His performance in the marketing department has been above average and other marketing staff have begun to turn to him for advice. Joel is enthusiastic, ambitious, and positive, yet he is often not very tactful with others who are not as clever or skilled as he is. You fear that Joel may not stay with your company for long because you saw an email on his computer from a headhunter, offering a salary increase. When you asked Joel if he wanted to be on the team, he said it sounded "cool," but Joel says that about most tasks.

ROBERT LAWRENCE is a 45-year-old in charge of marketing communications with customers. He has a bachelor's degree in English. He worked for a decade for your firm in customer service, where he was an average performer, before moving into marketing 10 years ago. Of all your marketing staff, Robert has the most experience with and knowledge of customers. He is extremely outgoing and positive. He can often be found in the employee lounge, telling jokes or chatting about sports. He is friends with everyone in the company and volunteers to arrange employee social events. His Christmas parties and his picnics are always well attended and enjoyable. In your opinion, Robert's performance is just barely average. He is one of the least productive workers, although everyone enjoys working with him. As a result of his work friendships, he often is asked to do less than his coworkers. Even so, his work is often of good quality. Robert has enjoyed working on cross-functional teams in the past because it allows him to visit with friends he otherwise doesn't see much.

SANDIP RAJGOPAL is an M.B.A. with 40 years' experience in customer service in the IT industry. At 61, he is the oldest candidate for the team. Sandip has never married and his career has been the most important part of his life. He joined your company five years ago, following the acquisition of his previous employer and the subsequent closing of their operations. At his previous job, he was head of the customer service group of a much larger company. He makes many innovative suggestions for improving customer service at your firm, including a recent reorganization of the department that saved the company thousands of dollars. Sandip resents working for someone like Sandra Williams who has less business-related education and experience than he does. In your opinion, his customer service knowledge is extensive and his job performance is far above average. He works longer hours and engages in more professional activities outside of work hours than anyone else at your company. Sandip has asked to work on the launch team and has already mentioned that you should name him as head of the team.

HORTENSIA GARZA, a 28-year-old, is the newest hire in the marketing department. She is attending night school while finishing her undergraduate marketing degree. She came to your company one year ago as a summer intern and did so well that she was offered a full-time job. She still has a lot to learn about marketing, but she is bright and determined. Prior to working for you company, Hortensia was a sales associate in a department store, where she learned customer service skills and developed an interest in marketing. Outside of work, she is active in a community organization that supports adult immigrants in learning English. Her fluency in Spanish is an asset in dealing with your Spanish-speaking customers. Thus far, her work has been average but you believe she will improve with further education and experience. She is cooperative and willing to try anything that she is asked to do, but she is hesitant to put forth her own ideas. She lacks confidence and seems to just "go along" with whatever others say. When you spoke to Hortensia about the team, she replied, "It sounds like a good opportunity for me, but I don't know that I'll have anything valuable to contribute."

SANDRA WILLIAMS is a 53-year-old Ph.D. holder in computer science. She is the most senior candidate, with 24 years with the company. She has been with the company since it was founded and is a personal friend of many of the senior staff. After beginning her career in the technology group, she allowed her programming skills to become out of date. She moved into customer support about 10 years ago, where she has become friendly with many of the customers. Her performance as head of customer support, in your opinion, has been average. She gets along well with everyone, but she allows her employees to get away with sloppy, slow work. Sandra is extroverted and agreeable and she hates to say "No." She is often is overly optimistic about how much she can do and takes on too many tasks. Sandra assumes that, due to her position, she has a right to a place on the launch team.

1. What qualities were most important for you as you made your choices? Did you look for the same qualities for both positions? Explain.

2. How did you cope with making choices guided by four differing goals? For example, were you forced to make trade-offs?

3. Are you satisfied that the group will meet your four goals? Explain why or why not.

4. What did you learn about the importance of group composition? How could managers benefit from what you learned?

Building Effective Conceptual Skills

Exercise Overview

Conceptual skills reflect the manager's ability to think in the abstract. Groups and teams are becoming ever more important in organizations. This exercise will give you an opportunity to practice your conceptual skills as they apply to work teams in organizations.

Exercise Background

Several highly effective groups exist outside the boundaries of typical business organizations. For example, a basketball team, a military squadron, a government policy group such as the president's Cabinet, a student committee, and the leadership of a church or religious organization are all teams.

Exercise Task

1. Use the Internet to identify an example of a real team. Choose one that (a) is not part of a normal for-profit business and (b) you can argue is highly effective.

2. Determine the reasons for the team's effectiveness. (*Hint:* You might look for websites sponsored by that group, look at online news sources for current

articles, or enter the group's name in a search engine.) Consider team characteristics and activities, such as role structure, norms, cohesiveness, and conflict management.

3. What can a manager learn from this particular team? How can the factors that account for its success be used in a business setting?

Building Effective Communication Skills

Exercise Overview

Communication skills enhance teamwork, because team members must be able to communicate effectively in order to form a cohesive team and in order to perform well on group tasks.

Exercise Background

This game requires you to share personal information with your "team members" in a light-hearted way. Honest and open communication can help to build team cohesion and so can having fun! On the other hand, please don't treat this as a group therapy session. Comments should not be too personal or make the other team members uncomfortable.

Exercise Task

1. Your class will divide up into small groups of five to six students each by counting off around the room. Get up and move to a place where your small group can sit together facing each other. Select one group member to be the recorder.

2. Your group task is to find ten things that the group members have in common with all of the members. Do not mention overly obvious answers—everyone has one head, everyone is a student at your institution. Consider these items and think of some of your own too.
   - Favorite vacation spot/restaurant/sport/hobby/ television program
   - Favorite ice cream/candy/sandwich/beverage
   - A movie/book/song everyone loves
   - Desired future profession
   - Your typical fast-food order
   - The neighborhood where you live

3. Discuss the follow-up questions with your group and/ or the class.
   - How did you feel when you first sat down with your new team? How did what you felt affect your verbal and nonverbal communication?
   - How did you feel by the end of the exercise? Did your verbal and nonverbal communication change, and if so, how?
   - What lessons does this exercise demonstrate about the process by which teams are created? What actions could a business manager take to use some of those lessons to strengthen his or her organization?

Skills Self-Assessment Instrument

Using Teams

Introduction: The use of groups and teams is becoming more common in organizations throughout the world. The following assessment surveys your beliefs about the effective use of teams in work organizations.

Instructions: You will agree with some of the statements and disagree with others. In some cases you may find making a decision difficult, but you should force yourself to make a choice. Record your answers next to each statement according to the following scale:

Rating Scale

4 Strongly agree

3 Somewhat agree

2 Somewhat disagree

1 Strongly disagree

_____ 1. Each individual in a work team should have a clear assignment so that individual accountability can be maintained.

_____ 2. For a team to function effectively, the team must be given complete authority over all aspects of the task.

_____ 3. One way to get teams to work is simply to assemble a group of people, tell them in general what needs to be done, and let them work out the details.

_____ 4. Once a team gets going, management can turn its attention to other matters.

_____ 5. To ensure that a team develops into a cohesive working unit, managers should be especially careful not to intervene in any way during the initial startup period.

_____ 6. Training is not critical to a team because the team will develop any needed skills on its own.

_____ 7. It's easy to provide teams with the support they need because they are basically self-motivating.

_____ 8. Teams need little or no structure to function effectively.

_____ 9. Teams should set their own direction, with managers determining the means to the selected end.

_____ 10. Teams can be used in any organization.

Source: Test: adapted from J. Richard Hackman, ed., *Groups That Work (and Those That Don't)*, San Francisco: Jossey-Bass Publishers, 1990, pp. 493–504. For interpretation, see Interpretations of Skills Self-Assessment Instruments in the appendix near the end of this text.

Experiential Exercise

Team Size and Performance

Purpose: Choosing the number of members in a team is an important decision that will affect team processes and outcomes. A team with too few members will have low performance because they are not receiving all of the benefits of effective teamwork. A team that is too large won't be able to develop strong cohesion and again, performance will suffer. The best team size in a particular situation depends on the members themselves, the tasks they will perform, and the nature of the interaction between them.

Instructions:

Step 1: In a small class, the class will be divided into groups of four by the instructor. In a larger class, four students may be asked to volunteer to demonstrate in front of the whole group.

Step 2: Each group will receive a regular deck of 52 playing cards from the instructor. One group member is chosen to be the "sorter." The cards should be shuffled thoroughly and placed in a stack on the desk in front of the sorter. Another group member is the timer.

Step 3: At a signal from the instructor, the sorter or sorters pick up the cards. The timer notes the starting time. They must place the cards into four stacks by suit, arranging each stack from lowest to highest card. Aces are considered to be high. The task is done when the cards are in the four stacks. The timer records the elapsed time.

Step 4: After thoroughly shuffling the cards, repeat Step 3. This time, however, the sorter will have a helper. The help may take any form—advice, encouragement, moving the cards, or anything else. After a brief discussion of the actions the helper will take to aid the sorter, begin timing and start the task. At the end, the timer notes the elapsed time.

Step 5: After thoroughly shuffling the cards, repeat Step 3. This time, however, the sorter will have three helpers. The help may take any form—advice, encouragement, moving the cards, or anything else. After a brief discussion of the actions the helpers will take to aid the sorter, begin timing and start the task. At the end, the timer notes the elapsed time.

Follow-up Questions

1. Which of the three trials was the fastest? The slowest? Which seemed to go the most smoothly for the sorter? Which seemed to be the most challenging for the sorter? Explain.

2. What was the impact of the help? Were three helpers better than one?

3. What types of help were effective or ineffective?

4. In what ways is this exercise similar to the situation in a business organization? In what ways is it dissimilar? What lessons might managers learn from this exercise?

CHAPTER CLOSING CASE

WHO CAN HEAD TEAM NIKE?

Successful entrepreneurs become so attached to their organizations, so identified with its people and products, that it can be almost impossible for them to let someone else take over. One journalist refers to this pattern as "The Return of the Founder." The latest star of the drama is Nike, where founder Phil Knight forced out CEO William Perez just 13 months after picking him. Perez had valuable experience, yet according to Knight, failed to understand and effectively deploy Nike's management teams.

From the company's founding in 1971, Nike's organization culture has been legendary. Athlete culture reigns and top managers are all competitive athletes. "Nike's early management meetings were rowdy, drunken affairs," writes journalist Daniel Roth. "When fights broke out . . . Knight would rarely interrupt. He liked to see the passion." The culture today remains intense and competitive. Knight is emotional too, and has cried "countless times" at athletic events.

A few superstars are brought in from outside, yet Nike's managerial talent is mostly homegrown. Executives rotate through various departments to broaden their experience. Thus, for any job, several people in the company can help the current jobholder. A matrix organization means everyone answers to multiple bosses, increasing information sharing. The promote-from-within mentality, strong cross-training and horizontal communications create a management team that is highly cohesive.

Knight hires bright, ambitious managers who love sports and then

gives them a tremendous amount of freedom. He does and says very little, allowing executives to interpret his silences. For example, when a top manager started a new division, Knight's only instructions were to "sell shoes." "He is less likely to sit down and break it down for you. He believes you can figure it out," says former Nike manager Liz Dolan. "He focuses more on talking to you one-on-one to get the best out of you."

Managers look to him as an inspiration, visionary, and father figure, but in fact, he meets rarely and cares little for details. Knight does not take a stand on most issues and often says, "I reserve the right to change my mind tomorrow." Executives make their own decisions. "It's been 40 years that the company has grown around my idiosyncrasies," says Knight. "They don't even know that they're idiosyncrasies anymore, and of course neither do I."

Perez, formerly CEO of consumer products company S.C. Johnson, was shy and introspective, as is Knight, but was a novice in the industry. Perez's knowledge of consumer products and diverse product lines was desirable at Nike, which was expanding its offerings in athletic wear and equipment. Perez also oversaw many acquisitions at S.C. Johnson and seemed well equipped to help Nike grow.

Perez ruffled feathers immediately. "Perez started asking questions of 20- to 30-year veterans that have never been asked before," says one manager. Perez claims that Knight interfered with his decisions. "From virtually the day I arrived, Phil was as engaged in the company as he ever

was. He was talking to my direct reports. It was confusing for the people and frustrating for me," Perez relates.

Perez questioned Nike's award-winning ads, irking many marketing executives. "He relied more on the spreadsheet, analytical approach as opposed to having a good creative marketing sense," says a marketing manager. In fact, Perez battled with numerous executives, including Mark Parker and Charlie Denson, two Nike lifers who also competed for the CEO position.

Knight blames Perez, saying, "I think the failure to really kind of get his arms around this company and this industry led to confusion on behalf of the management team." Perez blames Nike insiders, who he claims are resistant to change. Knight, for example, is making his third leadership flip-flop. "It's almost like a death wish, coming into that company from outside," says Stephanie Joseph, a corporate board expert. Observers blame the board of directors for not being able to envision the company without its founder. "The core challenge of corporate governance is getting past the concept of the imperial CEO," says governance expert Ric Marshall.

After Perez's departure, Parker and Denson became president and CEO. However, the 67-year-old Knight continues to age. Nike needs succession planning and could benefit from new ideas too. Yet Knight may not be able to let go. The board can ease the transition by making lines of responsibility clear and finding something interesting for Knight to do. Managers, even those passed over for the job, must support the new leader or step aside. Stephen Mader, an executive headhunter, sums up the dilemma. "The message about filling shoes is that you can't. You've got to design new shoes."

CASE QUESTIONS

1. List some of the norms held by work teams at Nike. How much norm conformity seems to exist at the firm?

2. What are some of the likely positive consequences of the highly cohesive Nike teams? What are some of the likely negative consequences?

3. Outsider William Perez experienced interpersonal and intergroup conflict while CEO of Nike. In your opinion, was there too much conflict, the appropriate amount of conflict, or too little conflict? Was the conflict handled correctly? Explain your answers.

CASE REFERENCES

Stanley Holmes, "Nike: Can Perez Fill Knight's Shoes?" *BusinessWeek*, November 19, 2004, www.businessweek.com on May 20, 2006; Stanley Holmes, "Inside the Coup at Nike," *BusinessWeek*, February 6, 2006, www.businessweek.com on May 20, 2006; Stanley Holmes, "Nike's CEO Gets the Boot," *BusinessWeek*, January 24, 2006, www.businessweek.com on May 20, 2006; Daniel Roth, "Can Nike Still Do It Without Phil Knight?" *Fortune*, April 4, 2005, www.fortune.com on May 20, 2006.

YOU MAKE THE CALL

Teamwork for the Tampa Bay Devil Rays

1. How would working for a sports team be similar to and different from working in a more traditional business setting?
2. Would you have an interest in working in sports management? Why or why not?
3. How might someone interested in sports management best prepare themselves for such a career?
4. In what ways might managing in one type of sports league (e.g., baseball) be similar to and different from another league (e.g., basketball)?
5. If you were going to work in sports management, what would be the relative advantages and disadvantages of working for a strong and established franchise (such as the New York Yankees or the Dallas Cowboys) versus working for a relatively new and emerging franchise (such as the Tampa Bay Devil Rays or the Houston Texans)?
6. If you owned a professional sports franchise and needed an executive team, what would be relative advantages and disadvantages of bringing in managers from outside the sports industry versus bringing in managers already working in the industry?

Test Prepper

college.hmco.com/pic/griffinfund5e

You've read the chapter, studied the key terms, and the exam is any day now. Think you're ready to ace it? Take this sample test to gauge your comprehension of chapter material. You can check your answers at the back of the book. Want more test questions? Visit the student website at http://college.hmco.com/pic/griffinfund5e/ and take the ACE quizzes for more practice.

1. T F A norm is the part that an individual plays in a group in order to help the group reach its goals. The person may take on a task specialist norm or a socioemotional norm.

2. T F Jim, the informal leader of the work team, seems to get away with behavior that others cannot. This is due to norm variation.

3. T F A high level of cohesiveness in a group is always a good thing.

4. T F When finance and operations departments disagree on issues, it is called intergroup conflict.

5. T F When unions agree to fewer benefits in order to save the company and hence their jobs, they are responding to a supraordinate goal.

6. _____ teams are the most popular type of team. They are knowledge workers who respond to a challenge and then disband.
   a. Problem-solving
   b. Quality circle
   c. Management
   d. Work
   e. Virtual

7. Tonisha joined a country club because she thinks it will help her make contacts that will support her career. Which reason best describes why she joined the club?
   a. To satisfy a need for affiliation
   b. Because the group's activities appeal to her
   c. Because of the goals of the group

   d. Because of instrumental benefits
   e. To be sure she gets enough exercise

8. A team is given a challenge to sell lemonade for one day in New York City. Around noon time, one member of one group takes a lunch break, which is viewed by most of the group as unacceptable. The group is in which stage of development?
   a. Norming
   b. Storming
   c. Forming
   d. Performing
   e. None of the above

9. The last stage of role development is which of the following?
   a. Enacted role
   b. Expected role
   c. Task specialist role
   d. Perceived role
   e. Sent role

10. All of the following are possible ways to control conflict in organizations EXCEPT
    a. expanding the resource base.
    b. setting supraordinate goals.
    c. increasing competition among individuals and teams.
    d. matching employees in terms of personalities and work habits.
    e. enhancing coordination of interdependence.

Meeting of the Minds

Part Four: Managing in the Soft-Drink Industry

This segment of the running case addresses issues raised in Part Four of the text, covering Chapters 9 through 13.

Individual Behavior

The Coca-Cola Company has a number of traits that it values in its employees. To find out more, visit the company's home page. Click on "Careers," then on "Meet Our People." In this section, browse through some of the workers' profiles to observe what values, qualities, and skills they share.

View PepsiCo's "Careers" page, clickable from its home page, and click on "Taste the Success" for details about the qualities that Pepsi prefers. Pepsi provides corporate fitness centers to help workers reduce stress. In return, Pepsi gains a workforce that is healthier and more loyal, while also reducing healthcare and other costs.

Motivation

Decision making is centralized at Coke, which might reduce motivation if lower-level employees feel they have no control over goals.

Pepsi's culture is decentralized. This can be motivating to employees and may be more effective and efficient.

Overall, both the Coca-Cola Company and PepsiCo pay their corporate executives and workers at a market rate. However, Coke, which has greater investments in foreign manufacturing facilities, is criticized more often for underpaying workers in developing countries.

In 2006, Coke's CEO, Neville Isdell, earned nearly $21 million, which includes salary, stock and options, and cash incentives. He also received executive perks and other benefits not included in that amount.

Pepsi's CEO, Indra Nooyi, earned over $8 million in 2006. Again, this includes base pay, stock and options, and cash incentives, but not perks and benefits.

Leadership

CEOs

Sixty-one-year-old Coke CEO Isdell is the ultimate Coca-Cola insider. He was born in Ireland and educated in South Africa. He headed operations in South Africa, Australia, the Philippines, and Europe and was responsible for opening many new markets, including India and the USSR. He was passed over for CEO twice, but after a three-year leave, he became CEO in 2004. Isdell will have to manage political behavior among the company's leaders, including his own feud with long-time and powerful director Donald Keough.

As CEO of PepsiCo, Nooyi is the first woman of color to head a *Fortune* 50 corporation. She grew up in India and was a bit unconventional, playing cricket and joining a rock band. She joined PepsiCo in 1994, serving as CFO for five years while overseeing the restaurant spin-off and the acquisition of Tropicana and Quaker Oats. Nooyi is a 51-year-old married mother of two whose husband works. She is a deeply religious Hindu, who sometimes walks around headquarters barefoot or sings out loud. "Behind my cool logic lies a very emotional person," she says.

Top Management Teams

Coke's team is very international: regional managers are typically native to that region. View the company's top management team by clicking on "Our Company," then "Leadership," then "Executive Leadership Team."

In spite of the company's diversity accomplishments at the middle-management level, Pepsi's top team is not particularly diverse. View a list of the company's management team by clicking on "Company," then "Officers and Directors." The list of names gives some indication about diversity.

Boards of Directors

Coke's board is far less diverse than its executive team. View the company's board of directors by clicking on "Our Company," then "Leadership," then "Board of Directors."

While Pepsi's board of directors is not especially diverse, it is more so than Coke's. View the company's board by accessing "Company" and then "Officers and Directors."

Leadership Initiatives

Coca-Cola is experiencing a top-management exodus in the face of layoffs and political behavior. Isdell has made executive recruiting and development one of his top priorities. Coke, which promotes primarily from within, has no clear management succession plans at the highest level. There are no obvious internal candidates who would be capable and welcomed in the CEO position.

PepsiCo is focused on identifying and mentoring minority candidates for middle- and senior-management positions. Beginning in 2001, Pepsi's new program for middle managers emphasized the ability to develop employees to their highest potential. Today, the company uses 360-degree performance feedback to evaluate development efforts. Middle managers' performance evaluations and compensation are tied to their ability to develop workers.

Communication

Coca-Cola recently named a new director of communications, Tom Mattia, who is likely to bring greater emphasis on global communications and electronic media. In 2006, Coke began using a company-wide blog for employees.

PepsiCo employees respond to a frequent "Organizational Health" survey about career development, diversity, and so on. Survey results are shared with employees and acted upon. A daily e-newsletter lets workers ask questions of the CEO and top managers. Pepsi sponsors a "Speak Up" hotline that employees can use to anonymously report illegal or unethical activities.

Teamwork

Neither Coke nor Pepsi has a reputation for outstanding teamwork. At Coca-Cola, one barrier to effective teamwork is a high level of centralization, which reduces the ability of teams to work autonomously. Another barrier is Coke's relatively formal and hierarchical culture. Coke's management style has been referred to as "genteel" and compared to a traditional Southern culture, with its class-consciousness and conservatism. Coke's culture stifles the spirit of equality that enables effective team-member participation.

At PepsiCo, one barrier to effective teamwork is too much decentralization. Decentralization can encourage participation; however, the downside is a lack of unity and coordination. Pepsi has recently begun to increase coordination and teamwork, citing teamwork as a key to innovation. Pepsi's "brash" organization culture may also be more supportive of teamwork than Coke's genteel one. An emphasis on results, not on hierarchy or seniority, supports effective teamwork and encourages broad participation in teams.

Online Resources for Further Research

Please look at the list of online resources for Parts One and Two for further suggestions.

1. Coca-Cola's home page at www.thecoca-colacompany.com.
2. PepsiCo's home page at www.pepsico.com.

Case Discussion Questions

Each of the case questions should be answered briefly, that is, in no more than a paragraph or two for each question.

1. The Coca-Cola Company and PepsiCo tend to hire workers with quite different personalities. How do your company's preferences for different personality types affect other parts of the organization? Consider for example, the effect on social responsibility, decision-making processes, strategy, and motivation techniques.

2. Consider both the amount and types of executive compensation paid to your company's CEO. In your opinion, how could your firm improve its executive pay plan? (For comparison purposes, the average CEO of a U.S. firm with more than $1 billion in annual sales earned almost $11 million in 2006. Pepsi's revenues were $35 billion in 2006 and Coke's were $24 billion.)

3. Describe the leadership strengths of your company's CEO, top management team, and board of directors. What are your company's leadership weaknesses?

4. How does your company's culture affect its ability to use teams? What characteristics should an effective team possess in order to fit into your company's culture?

Basic Elements of Control

chapter 14

FIRST THINGS FIRST

Effective Controls at McDonald's Boost Performance

"Ten years ago we saw every customer as a transaction count, not as a person who needed to use the restaurant in a different way."

—FRED HUEBNER, FRANCHISE OWNER, MCDONALD'S

McDonald's is the undisputed king of fast food. It serves 50 million meals daily in 118 countries. Combined sales are three times that of any competitor. For decades the company expanded by adding locations, as many as one every 4.5 hours. However, by 2002 McDonald's was reaching saturation. Profits declined for the first time. Company executives were spending one-third of their time on real estate matters. While their attention was turned elsewhere, quality, efficiency, and customer service all deteriorated.

The top three managers developed a back-to-basics approach called "Plan to Win." Now-CEO James Skinner remembers, "We knew we had to deliver a better experience for our customers. . . . We had lost our focus." After two other

McDonald's is looking for every opportunity to improve its performance. One of the firm's recent innovations is the introduction of "Premium Roast" coffee.

LEARNING OBJECTIVES

After studying this chapter, you should be able to:

- Explain the purpose of control, identify different types of control, and describe the steps in the control process.
- Identify and explain the three forms of operations control.
- Describe budgets and other tools for financial control.
- Identify and distinguish between two opposing forms of structural control.
- Discuss the relationship between strategy and control, including international strategic control.
- Identify characteristics of effective control, why people resist control, and how managers can overcome this resistance.

managers died suddenly, Skinner succeeded to the top spot in November 2004 and assumed responsibility for McDonald's turnaround efforts. The Plan's theme is "Better, not Bigger." Skinner says, "We want more customers in our existing restaurants, rather than more restaurants for our customers." The Plan set high financial and operational targets, then developed a number of controls to oversee progress.

The most important goal is to increase customer focus. McDonald's noted that Americans eat five restaurant meals per week. While lunch is the most popular time for eating out, the breakfast business is the growing faster. Increasingly, customers want meals at all hours. Breakfast, with less expensive ingredients, is a moneymaker, accounting for a quarter of revenues but half of profits. To tap into this trend, more than 90 percent of restaurants are now open extended hours and 40 percent run nonstop.

Store operations support better customer service. In testing is kitchen equipment that can accommodate breakfast and lunch simultaneously and an upgraded air-handling system to remove food odors. Redesigned stores feature popular music, glass display cases for pastries, flat-screen TVs, and even leather chairs in order to compete against upscale rivals. New electronic systems speed up transactions, from drive-thru ordering to payment processing to food preparation. At one typical restaurant, for example, new systems support a lunch-rush pace of 90 cars an hour, up from 77 two years ago. The faster pace allows McDonald's to serve 27 million daily customers today, 1 million more each year since 2003.

New and innovative products tempt customers too. After realizing that more than 50 percent of meals are ordered from the drive-thru and consumed in the car, McDonald's targeted new-product efforts toward easy-to-eat items. Their Snack Wrap is a midday take-away food and its low cost encourages sales. Another popular new favorite is premium coffee, a direct attack on Starbucks. Other new offerings include smoothies, bagels, and muffins. Their new-product pipeline contains many surprises: an Angus beef burger, specialty coffee drinks, cinnamon buns, and a Southern fried chicken biscuit.

McDonald's extensively tests new products from offices in Illinois, Hong Kong, and Paris, to analyze worldwide customers' reactions. For example, when the Snack Wrap was created, every detail was considered. The Wrap uses ranch dressing (salsa drips) and a large tortilla (small ones become slippery). The size is just right for one hand or a car's cup holder. Product design, sales, costs, cooking time, and ease of preparation are assessed in initial testing. The last is a necessity when annual turnover among cooks is greater than 100 percent. A final test consisting of hundreds of locations confirms results. Only then is a new product adopted companywide.

The changes are working. In February 2007, McDonald's reported its forty-fifth consecutive month of sales increases. Same-store sales rose over 5 percent in 2006, and corporate profits increased by over 20 percent. Skinner attributes his successful plan to his personal experience, gained as he worked his way up from crew member and then management trainee. "It's important to understand what our crews and crew managers are trying to do on a daily basis," he says.

"No one can do that better than someone who actually worked in a restaurant." Fred Huebner, a franchise owner, agrees with Skinner. He saw his revenues climb 5 percent after adopting the new Plan. Huebner says, "Ten years ago we saw every customer as a transaction count, not as a person who needed to use the restaurant in a different way."[1]

Managers at McDonald's have revived the firm's performance by relying on some of the most fundamental of management concepts. Improved efficiencies, new methods for serving customers faster, and more responsiveness to customer preferences are just a few of things the firm is using to spur growth. Moreover, each of these concepts is part of the control function. In a nutshell, effective control helps managers decide where they want their business to go, point it in that direction, and monitor results to keep it on track. Ineffective control, on the other hand, can result in a lack of focus, weak direction, and poor overall performance.

As we discussed in Chapter 1, control is one of the four basic managerial functions that provide the organizing framework for this book. This is the first of two chapters devoted to this important area. In the first section of the chapter we explain the purpose of control. We then look at types of control and the steps in the control process. The rest of the chapter examines the four levels of control that most organizations must employ to remain effective: operations, financial, structural, and strategic control. We conclude by discussing the characteristics of effective control, noting why some people resist control and describing what organizations can do to overcome this resistance. The remaining chapter in this part focuses on managing operations and managing information.

The Nature of Control

Control is the regulation of organizational activities so that some targeted element of performance remains within acceptable limits. Without this regulation, organizations have no indication of how well they are performing in relation to their goals. Control, like a ship's rudder, keeps the organization moving in the proper direction. At any point in time, it compares where the organization is in terms of performance (financial, productive, or otherwise) to where it is supposed to be. Like a rudder, control provides an organization with a mechanism for adjusting its course if performance falls outside of acceptable boundaries. For example, FedEx has a performance goal of delivering 99.8 percent of its packages on time. If on-time deliveries fall to 99.5 percent, control systems will signal the problem to managers so that they can make necessary adjustments in operations to regain the target level of performance.[2] An organization without effective control procedures is not likely to reach its goals—or, if it does reach them, to know that it has!

> **control**
> The regulation of organizational activities in such a way as to facilitate goal attainment

The Purpose of Control

As Figure 14.1 illustrates, control provides an organization with ways to adapt to environmental change, to limit the accumulation of error, to cope with organizational complexity, and to minimize costs. These four functions of control are worth a closer look.

Figure 14.1

THE PURPOSE OF CONTROL

Control is one of the four basic management functions in organizations. The control function, in turn, has four basic purposes. Properly designed control systems can fulfill each of these purposes.

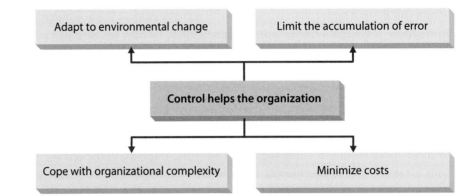

Adapting to Environmental Change In today's complex and turbulent business environment, all organizations must contend with change.[3] If managers could establish goals and achieve them instantaneously, control would not be needed. But between the time a goal is established and the time it is reached, many things can happen in the organization and its environment to disrupt movement toward the goal—or even to change the goal itself. A properly designed control system can help managers anticipate, monitor, and respond to changing circumstances.[4] In contrast, an improperly designed system can result in organizational performance that falls far below acceptable levels.

For example, Michigan-based Metalloy, a 46-year-old, family-run metal-casting company, signed a contract to make engine-seal castings for NOK, a big Japanese auto-parts maker. Metalloy was satisfied when its first 5,000-unit production run yielded 4,985 acceptable castings and only 15 defective ones. NOK, however, was quite unhappy with this performance and insisted that Metalloy raise its standards. In short, global quality standards in most industries are such that customers demand near-perfection from their suppliers. A properly designed control system can help managers like those at Metalloy stay better attuned to rising standards.

Limiting the Accumulation of Error Small mistakes and errors do not often seriously damage the financial health of an organization. Over time, however, small errors may accumulate and become very serious. For example, Whistler Corporation, a large radar detector manufacturer, was once faced with such rapidly escalating demand that quality essentially became irrelevant. The defect rate rose from 4 percent to 9 percent to 15 percent and eventually reached 25 percent. One day, a manager realized that 100 of the firm's 250 employees were spending all their time fixing defective units and that $2 million worth of inventory was awaiting repair. Had the company adequately controlled quality as it responded to increased demand, the problem would never have reached such proportions. Similarly, Fleetwood Enterprises, a large manufacturer of recreational vehicles, suffered because its managers did not adequately address several small accounting and production problems years ago. As these small problems grew into large ones, the firm struggled with how to correct them.[5]

Coping with Organizational Complexity When a firm purchases only one raw material, produces one product, has a simple organization design, and enjoys constant demand for its product, its managers can maintain control with a very basic and simple system. But a business that produces many products from myriad raw materials and has a large market area, a complicated organization design, and many competitors needs a sophisticated system to maintain adequate control. When large firms merge, the short-term results are often disappointing. The typical reason for this is that the new enterprise is so large and complex that the existing control systems are simply inadequate. Hewlett-Packard and Compaq Computer faced just this problem when HP acquired Compaq and had to address myriad issues to transform the two firms into one.

Minimizing Costs   When it is practiced effectively, control can also help reduce costs and boost output. For example, Georgia-Pacific Corporation, a large wood products company, learned of a new technology that could be used to make thinner blades for its saws. The firm's control system was used to calculate the amount of wood that could be saved from each cut made by the thinner blades relative to the costs used to replace the existing blades. The results have been impressive—the wood that is saved by the new blades each year fills 800 rail cars. As Georgia-Pacific discovered, effective control systems can eliminate waste, lower labor costs, and improve output per unit of input. In their bid to further reduce costs, businesses are cutting back on everything from health insurance coverage to overnight shipping to business lunches for clients.[6]

Types of Control

The examples of control given thus far have illustrated the regulation of several organizational activities, from producing quality products to coordinating complex organizations. Organizations practice control in a number of different areas and at different levels, and the responsibility for managing control is widespread.

Areas of Control   Control can focus on any area of an organization. Most organizations define areas of control in terms of the four basic types of resources they use: physical, human, information, and financial.[7] Control of physical resources includes inventory management (stocking neither too few nor too many units in inventory), quality control (maintaining appropriate levels of output quality), and equipment control (supplying the necessary facilities and machinery). Control of human resources includes selection and placement, training and development, performance appraisal, and compensation. Control of information resources includes sales and marketing forecasting, environmental analysis, public relations, production scheduling, and economic forecasting.[8] Financial control involves managing the organization's debt so that it does not become excessive, ensuring that the firm always has enough cash on hand to meet its obligations but does not have excess cash in a checking account, and ensuring that receivables are collected and bills are paid on a timely basis.

In many ways, the control of financial resources is the most important area, because financial resources are related to the control of all the other resources in an organization. Too much inventory leads to storage costs; poor selection of personnel leads to termination and rehiring expenses; inaccurate sales forecasts lead to disruptions in cash flows and other financial effects. Financial issues tend to pervade most control-related activities.

The crisis in the U.S. airline industry precipitated by the terrorist attacks on September 11, an economic downturn that reduced business travel, and rising fuel costs can be fundamentally traced back to financial issues. Essentially, airline revenues dropped while their costs increased. Because of high labor costs and other expenses, the airlines have faced major problems in making appropriate adjustments.[9] United Airlines, for instance, spends over half of its revenues on labor; in contrast, JetBlue spends only 25 percent of its revenues on labor.[10]

Levels of Control   Just as control can be broken down by area, Figure 14.2 shows that it can also be broken down by level within the organizational system. ***Operations control*** focuses on the processes the organization uses to transform resources into products or services.[11] Quality control is one type of operations control. ***Financial control*** is concerned with the organization's financial resources. Monitoring receivables to make sure customers are paying their bills on time is an example of financial control. ***Structural control*** is concerned with how the elements of the organization's structure are serving their intended purpose. Monitoring the administrative ratio to make sure staff expenses do not become excessive is an example of structural control. Finally, ***strategic control*** focuses on how effectively the organization's corporate, business, and functional strategies are succeeding in helping the organization meet its goals. For example, if a corporation has been unsuccessful in implementing its strategy of related diversification, its managers need to identify the reasons and either change the strategy or renew their efforts to implement it. We discuss these four levels of control more fully later in this chapter.

Responsibilities for Control   Traditionally, managers have been responsible for overseeing the wide array of control systems and concerns in organizations. They decide which types of control the organization will use, and they implement control systems and take actions based on the information provided by control systems. Thus ultimate responsibility for control rests with all managers throughout an organization.

Most larger organizations also have one or more specialized managerial positions called *controller*. A ***controller*** is responsible for helping line managers with their control activities, for coordinating the organization's overall control system, and for gathering and assimilating relevant information. Many businesses that use an H-form or M-form organization design have several controllers: one for the corporation and one for each division. The job of controller is especially important in organizations where control systems are complex.[12]

In addition, many organizations are also beginning to use operating employees to help maintain effective control. Indeed, employee participation is often used as a vehicle for allowing operating employees an opportunity to help facilitate organizational effectiveness. For example, Whistler Corporation increased employee

---

operations control
Focuses on the processes the organization uses to transform resources into products or services

---

financial control
Concerned with the organization's financial resources

---

structural control
Concerned with how the elements of the organization's structure are serving their intended purpose

---

strategic control
Focuses on how effectively the organization's strategies are succeeding in helping the organization meet its goals

---

controller
A position in organizations that helps line managers with their control activities

---

Figure 14.2
LEVELS OF CONTROL

Managers use control at several different levels. The most basic levels of control in organizations are strategic, structural, operations, and financial control. Each level must be managed properly if control is to be most effective.

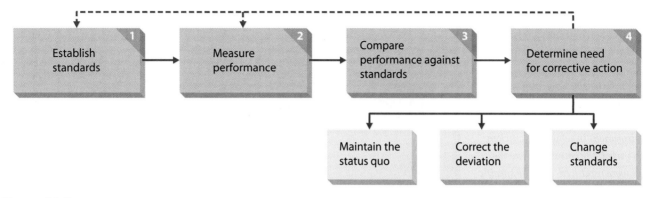

Figure 14.3
STEPS IN THE CONTROL PROCESS

Having an effective control system can help ensure that an organization achieves its goals. Implementing a control system, however, is a systematic process that generally proceeds through four interrelated steps.

participation in an effort to turn its quality problems around. As a starting point, the quality control unit, formerly responsible for checking product quality at the end of the assembly process, was eliminated. Next, all operating employees were encouraged to check their own work and told that they would be responsible for correcting their own errors. As a result, Whistler has eliminated its quality problems and is once again highly profitable.

Steps in the Control Process

Regardless of the type or levels of control systems an organization needs, there are four fundamental steps in any control process.[13] These are illustrated in Figure 14.3.

Establishing Standards   The first step in the control process is establishing standards. A ***control standard*** is a target against which subsequent performance will be compared.[14] Employees at a Taco Bell fast-food restaurant, for example, work toward the following service standards:

1. A minimum of 95 percent of all customers will be greeted within 3 minutes of their arrival.

2. Preheated tortilla chips will not sit in the warmer more than 30 minutes before they are served to customers or discarded.

3. Empty tables will be cleaned within 5 minutes after being vacated.

> *control standard*
> A target against which subsequent performance will be compared

Standards established for control purposes should be expressed in measurable terms. Note that standard 1 above has a time limit of 3 minutes and an objective target of 95 percent of all customers. In standard 3, the objective target of "all" empty tables is implied.

Control standards should also be consistent with the organization's goals. Taco Bell has organizational goals involving customer service, food quality, and restaurant cleanliness. A control standard for a retailer like Home Depot should be consistent with its goal of increasing its annual sales volume by 25 percent within five years. A hospital trying to shorten the average hospital stay for a patient will have control standards that reflect current averages. A university reaffirming its commitment to academics might adopt a standard of graduating 80 percent of its student athletes within five years of their enrollment. Control standards can be

Establishing standards, measuring performance, and correcting deviations are parts of the control process. In the European Union, all eggs must now be electronically marked for identification. This marking system provides information about the environment in which the chicken was raised, the country where the eggs were produced, and the specific producer who brought the eggs to market. This information, in turn, will be useful to monitor quality and to aid in eliminating any public health hazards that might arise.

as narrow or as broad as the level of activity to which they apply and must follow logically from organizational goals and objectives.

A final aspect of establishing standards is to identify performance indicators. Performance indicators are measures of performance that provide information that is directly relevant to what is being controlled. For example, suppose an organization is following a tight schedule in building a new plant. Relevant performance indicators could be buying a site, selecting a building contractor, and ordering equipment. Monthly sales increases are not, however, directly relevant. On the other hand, if control is being focused on revenue, monthly sales increases are relevant, whereas buying land for a new plant is less relevant.

Measuring Performance The second step in the control process is measuring performance. Performance measurement is a constant, ongoing activity for most organizations. For control to be effective, performance measures must be valid. Daily, weekly, and monthly sales figures measure sales performance, and production performance may be expressed in terms of unit cost, product quality, or volume produced. Employees' performance is often measured in terms of quality or quantity of output, but for many jobs measuring performance is not so straightforward.

A research and development scientist at Merck, for example, may spend years working on a single project before achieving a breakthrough. A manager who takes over a business on the brink of failure may need months or even years to turn things around. Valid performance measurement, however difficult to obtain, is nevertheless vital in maintaining effective control, and performance indicators usually can be developed. The scientist's progress, for example, may be partially assessed by peer review, and the manager's success may be evaluated by her ability to convince creditors that she will eventually be able to restore profitability.

Comparing Performance Against Standards   The third step in the control process is comparing measured performance against established standards. Performance may be higher than, lower than, or identical to the standard. In some cases comparison is easy. The goal of each product manager at General Electric is to make the product either number one or number two (on the basis of total sales) in its market. Because this standard is clear and total sales are easy to calculate, it is relatively simple to determine whether this standard has been met. Sometimes, however, comparisons are less clear-cut. If performance is lower than expected, the question is how much deviation from standards to allow before taking remedial action. For example, is increasing sales by 7.9 percent when the standard was 8 percent close enough?

The timetable for comparing performance to standards depends on a variety of factors, including the importance and complexity of what is being controlled. For longer-run and higher-level standards, annual comparisons may be appropriate. In other circumstances, more frequent comparisons are necessary. For example, a business with a severe cash shortage may need to monitor its on-hand cash reserves daily.

Considering Corrective Action   The final step in the control process is determining the need for corrective action. Decisions regarding corrective action draw heavily on a manager's analytic and diagnostic skills. For example, as healthcare costs have risen, many firms have sought ways to keep their own expenses in check. Some have reduced benefits; others have opted to pass on higher costs to their employees.[15]

After comparing performance against control standards, one of three actions is appropriate: maintain the status quo (do nothing), correct the deviation, or change the standards. Maintaining the status quo is preferable when performance essentially matches the standards, but it is more likely that some action will be needed to correct a deviation from the standards.

Sometimes, performance that is higher than expected may also cause problems for organizations. For example, when DaimlerChrysler first introduced its PT Cruiser, demand was so strong that customers were placed on waiting lists, and many customers were willing to pay more than the suggested retail price to obtain a car. The company was reluctant to increase production, primarily because it knew demand would eventually drop. At the same time, however, it did not want to alienate potential customers. Consequently, the firm decided to simply reduce its advertising. This curtailed demand a bit and limited customer frustration.

Changing an established standard usually is necessary if it was set too high or too low at the outset. This is apparent if large numbers of employees routinely beat the standard by a wide margin or if no employees ever meet the standard. Also, standards that seemed perfectly appropriate when they were established may need to be adjusted because circumstances have since changed.

Operations Control

One of the four levels of control practiced by most organizations, operations control, is concerned with the processes the organization uses to transform resources into products or services. As Figure 14.4 shows, the three forms of operations control—preliminary, screening, and postaction—occur at different points in relation to the transformation processes used by the organization.

Figure 14.4
FORMS OF OPERATIONS CONTROL

Most organizations develop multiple control systems that incorporate all three basic forms of control. For example, the publishing company that produced this book screens inputs by hiring only qualified employees, typesetters, and printers (preliminary control). In addition, quality is checked during the transformation process, such as after the manuscript is typeset (screening control), and the outputs—printed and bound books—are checked before they are shipped from the bindery (postaction control).

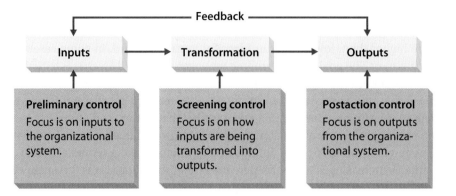

preliminary control
Attempts to monitor the quality or quantity of financial, physical, human, and information resources before they actually become part of the system

screening control
Relies heavily on feedback processes during the transformation process

postaction control
Monitors the outputs or results of the organization after the transformation process is complete

Preliminary Control

Preliminary control concentrates on the resources—financial, material, human, and information—the organization brings in from the environment. Preliminary control attempts to monitor the quality or quantity of these resources before they enter the organization. Firms like PepsiCo and General Mills hire only college graduates for their management training programs, and even then only after applicants satisfy several interviewers and selection criteria. In this way, they control the quality of the human resources entering the organization. When Sears orders merchandise to be manufactured under its own brand name, it specifies rigid standards of quality, thereby controlling physical inputs. Organizations also control financial and information resources. For example, privately held companies like UPS and Mars limit the extent to which outsiders can buy their stock, and television networks verify the accuracy of news stories before they are broadcast.

Screening Control

Screening control focuses on meeting standards for product or service quality or quantity during the actual transformation process itself. Screening control relies heavily on feedback processes. For example, in a Dell Computer assembly factory, computer system components are checked periodically as each unit is being assembled. This is done to ensure that all the components that have been assembled up to that point are working properly. The periodic quality checks provide feedback to workers so that they know what, if any, corrective actions to take. Because they are useful in identifying the cause of problems, screening controls tend to be used more often than other forms of control.

More and more companies are adopting screening controls because they are an effective way to promote employee participation and catch problems early in the overall transformation process. For example, Corning adopted screening controls for use in manufacturing television glass. In the past, finished television screens were inspected only after they were finished. Unfortunately, over 4 percent of them were later returned by customers because of defects. Now the glass screens are inspected at each step in the production process, rather than at the end, and the return rate from customers has dropped to .03 percent.

Postaction Control

Postaction control focuses on the outputs of the organization after the transformation process is complete. Corning's old system was postaction control—final inspection after the product was completed. Although Corning abandoned its postaction control system, this still may be an effective method of control, primarily if a product can be manufactured in only one or two steps or if the service is fairly simple and routine. Although postaction control alone may not be as effective as preliminary or screening control, it can provide management with information for future planning. For example, if a quality check of finished goods indicates an unacceptably high defect rate, the production manager knows that he or she must identify the causes and take steps to eliminate them. Postaction control also provides a basis for rewarding employees. Recognizing that an employee has exceeded personal sales goals by a wide margin, for example, may alert the manager that a bonus or promotion is in order.

Most organizations use more than one form of operations control. For example, Honda's preliminary control includes hiring only qualified employees and specifying strict quality standards when ordering parts from other manufacturers. Honda uses numerous screening controls in checking the quality of components during assembly of cars. A final inspection and test drive as each car rolls off the assembly line is part of the company's postaction control.[16] Indeed, most successful organizations employ a wide variety of techniques to facilitate operations control.

Financial Control

Financial control is the control of financial resources as they flow into the organization (revenues, shareholder investments), are held by the organization (working capital, retained earnings), and flow out of the organization (pay, expenses). Businesses must manage their finances so that revenues are sufficient to cover costs and still return a profit to the firm's owners. Not-for-profit organizations such as universities have the same concerns: their revenues (from tax dollars or tuition) must cover operating expenses and overhead. U.S. auto makers Ford and General Motors have realized that they have to reduce the costs of paying employees they do not need but whom they are obligated to keep as a result of longstanding labor agreements. Ford has offered to cover the full costs of a college education for certain of its employees if they will resign; GM, for its part, has offered lump-sum payments of varying amounts to some of its workers in return for their resignations.[17] A complete discussion of financial management is beyond the scope of this book, but we will examine the control provided by budgets and other financial control tools.

financial control
Concerned with the organization's financial resources

Budgetary Control

A ***budget*** is a plan expressed in numerical terms.[18] Organizations establish budgets for work groups, departments, divisions, and the whole organization. The usual time period for a budget is one year, although breakdowns of budgets by the quarter or month are also common. Budgets are generally expressed in financial terms, but they may occasionally be expressed in units of output, time, or other quantifiable factors. When Disney launches the production of a new animated cartoon feature, it creates a budget for how much the movie should cost. Several years ago, when movies like *The Lion King* were raking in hundreds of millions of dollars, Disney executives were fairly flexible about budget overruns. But, on the heels of

budget
A plan expressed in numerical terms

several animated flops, such as *Atlantis: The Lost Empire* and *Treasure Planet,* the company had to take a much harder line on budget overruns.[19]

Because of their quantitative nature, budgets provide yardsticks for measuring performance and facilitate comparisons across departments, between levels in the organization, and from one time period to another. Budgets serve four primary purposes. They help managers coordinate resources and projects (because they use a common denominator, usually dollars). They help define the established standards for control. They provide guidelines about the organization's resources and expectations. Finally, budgets enable the organization to evaluate the performance of managers and organizational units.

Types of Budgets   Most organizations develop and make use of three different kinds of budgets—financial, operating, and nonmonetary. Table 14.1 summarizes the characteristics of each of these.

A *financial budget* indicates where the organization expects to get its cash for the coming time period and how it plans to use it. Because financial resources are critically important, the organization needs to know where those resources will be coming from and how they are to be used. The financial budget provides answers to both these questions. Usual sources of cash include sales revenue, short- and long-term loans, the sale of assets, and the issuance of new stock.

For years Exxon was very conservative in its capital budgeting. As a result, the firm amassed a huge financial reserve but was being overtaken in sales by Royal Dutch/Shell. But executives at Exxon were then able to use their reserves to help finance the firm's merger with Mobil, creating ExxonMobil, and to regain the number-one sales position. Since that time, the firm has become more aggressive in capital budgeting to stay ahead of its European rival.

An *operating budget* is concerned with planned operations within the organization. It outlines what quantities of products or services the organization intends to create and what resources will be used to create them. Dell uses an operating budget

Table 14.1
DEVELOPING BUDGETS IN ORGANIZATIONS

Organizations use various types of budgets to help manage their control functions. The three major categories of budgets are financial, operating, and nonmonetary. There are several different types of budgets in each category. To be most effective, each budget must be carefully matched with the specific function being controlled.

Types of Budget	What Budget Shows
Financial Budget	*Sources and Uses of Cash*
Cash-flow or cash budget	All sources of cash income and cash expenditures in monthly, weekly, or daily periods
Capital expenditures budget	Costs of major assets such as a new plant, machinery, or land
Balance sheet budget	Forecast of the organization's assets and liabilities in the event all other budgets are met
Operating Budget	*Planned Operations in Financial Terms*
Sales or revenue budget	Income the organization expects to receive from normal operations
Expense budget	Anticipated expenses for the organization during the coming time period
Profit budget	Anticipated differences between sales or revenues and expenses
Nonmonetary Budget	*Planned Operations in Nonfinancial Terms*
Labor budget	Hours of direct labor available for use
Space budget	Square feet or meters of space available for various functions
Production budget	Number of units to be produced during the coming time period

to specify how many of each model of its personal computer will be produced each quarter.

A *nonmonetary budget* is simply a budget expressed in nonfinancial terms, such as units of output, hours of direct labor, machine hours, or square-foot allocations. Nonmonetary budgets are most commonly used by managers at the lower levels of an organization. For example, a plant manager can schedule work more effectively knowing that he or she has 8,000 labor hours to allocate in a week, rather than trying to determine how to best spend $86,451 in wages in a week.

Developing Budgets   Traditionally, budgets were developed by top management and the controller and then imposed on lower-level managers. Although some organizations still follow this pattern, many contemporary organizations now allow all managers to participate in the budget process. As a starting point, top management generally issues a call for budget requests, accompanied by an indication of overall patterns the budgets may take. For example, if sales are expected to drop in the next year, managers may be told up front to prepare for cuts in operating budgets.

As Figure 14.5 shows, the heads of each operating unit typically submit budget requests to the head of their division. An operating unit head might be a department manager in a manufacturing or wholesaling firm or a program director in a social service agency. The division heads might include plant managers, regional sales managers, or college deans. The division head integrates and consolidates the budget requests from operating unit heads into one overall division budget request. A great deal of interaction among managers usually takes place at this stage, as the division head coordinates the budgetary needs of the various departments.

Division budget requests are then forwarded to a budget committee. The budget committee is usually composed of top managers. The committee reviews budget requests from several divisions, and once again, duplications and inconsistencies are corrected. Finally, the budget committee, the controller, and the

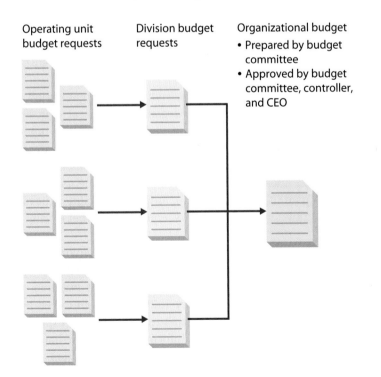

Operating unit budget requests

Division budget requests

Organizational budget
• Prepared by budget committee
• Approved by budget committee, controller, and CEO

Figure 14.5
DEVELOPING BUDGETS IN ORGANIZATIONS

Most organizations use the same basic process to develop budgets. Operating units are requested to submit their budget requests to divisions. These divisions, in turn, compile unit budgets and submit their own budgets to the organization. An organizational budget is then compiled for approval by the budget committee, controller, and CEO.

CEO review and agree on the overall budget for the organization, as well as specific budgets for each operating unit. These decisions are then communicated back to each manager.

Strengths and Weaknesses of Budgeting   Budgets offer a number of advantages, but they also have weaknesses. On the plus side, budgets facilitate effective control. Placing dollar values on operations enables managers to monitor operations better and pinpoint problem areas. Budgets also facilitate coordination and communication between departments because they express diverse activities in a common denominator (dollars). Budgets help maintain records of organizational performance and are a logical complement to planning. In other words, as managers develop plans, they should simultaneously consider control measures to accompany them. Organizations can use budgets to link plans and control by first developing budgets as part of the plan and then using those budgets as part of control.

On the other hand, some managers apply budgets too rigidly. Budgets are intended to serve as frameworks, but managers sometimes fail to recognize that changing circumstances may warrant budget adjustments. The process of developing budgets can also be very time consuming. Finally, budgets may limit innovation and change. When all available funds are allocated to specific operating budgets, it may be impossible to procure additional funds to take advantage of an unexpected opportunity. Indeed, for these very reasons, some organizations are working to scale back their budgeting systems. Although most organizations are likely to continue to use budgets, the goal is to make them less confining and rigid.

Other Tools for Financial Control

Although budgets are the most common means of financial control, other useful tools are financial statements, ratio analysis, and financial audits.

Financial Statements   A ***financial statement*** is a profile of some aspect of an organization's financial circumstances. There are commonly accepted and required ways that financial statements must be prepared and presented.[20] The two most basic financial statements prepared and used by virtually all organizations are a balance sheet and an income statement.

The ***balance sheet*** lists the assets and liabilities of the organization at a specific point in time, usually the last day of an organization's fiscal year. For example, the balance sheet may summarize the financial condition of an organization on December 31, 2008. Most balance sheets are divided into current assets (assets that are relatively liquid, or easily convertible into cash), fixed assets (assets that are longer term in nature and less liquid), current liabilities (debts and other obligations that must be paid in the near future), long-term liabilities (payable over an extended period of time), and stockholders' equity (the owners' claim against the assets).

Whereas the balance sheet reflects a snapshot profile of an organization's financial position at a single point in time, the ***income statement*** summarizes financial performance over a period of time, usually one year. For example, the income statement might be for the period January 1, 2008, through December 31, 2008. The income statement summarizes the firm's revenues less its expenses to report net income (profit or loss) for the period. Information from the balance sheet and income statement is used in computing important financial ratios.

financial statement
A profile of some aspect of an organization's financial circumstances

balance sheet
List of assets and liabilities of an organization at a specific point in time

income statement
A summary of financial performance over a period of time

Ratio Analysis   Financial ratios compare different elements of a balance sheet or income statement to one another. *Ratio analysis* is the calculation of one or more financial ratios to assess some aspect of the financial health of an organization. Organizations use a variety of different financial ratios as part of financial control. For example, *liquidity ratios* indicate how liquid (easily converted into cash) an organization's assets are. *Debt ratios* reflect ability to meet long-term financial obligations. *Return ratios* show managers and investors how much return the organization is generating relative to its assets. *Coverage ratios* help estimate the organization's ability to cover interest expenses on borrowed capital. *Operating ratios* indicate the effectiveness of specific functional areas rather than of the total organization. Walt Disney is an example of a company that relies heavily on financial ratios to keep its financial operations on track.[21]

> **ratio analysis**
> The calculation of one or more financial ratios to assess some aspect of the organization's financial health

Financial Audits   *Audits* are independent appraisals of an organization's accounting, financial, and operational systems. The two major types of financial audits are the external audit and the internal audit.

> **audit**
> An independent appraisal of an organization's accounting, financial, and operational systems

External audits are financial appraisals conducted by experts who are not employees of the organization.[22] External audits are typically concerned with determining that the organization's accounting procedures and financial statements are compiled in an objective and verifiable fashion. The organization contracts with a certified public accountant (CPA) for this service. The CPA's main objective is to verify for stockholders, the IRS, and other interested parties that the methods by which the organization's financial managers and accountants prepare documents and reports are legal and proper. External audits are so important that publicly held corporations are required by law to have external audits regularly, as assurance to investors that the financial reports are reliable.

Unfortunately, flaws in the auditing process played a major role in the downfall of Enron and several other major firms. The problem can be traced back partially to the auditing groups' problems with conflicts of interest and eventual loss of objectivity. For instance, Enron was such an important client for its auditing firm, Arthur Andersen, that the auditors started letting the firm take liberties with its accounting systems for fear that if they were too strict, Enron might take its business to another auditing firm. In the aftermath of the resulting scandal, Arthur Andersen was forced to close its doors, Enron is a shell of its former self, indictments continue to be handed down, and the accounting profession is being redefined.[23]

Some organizations are also starting to employ external auditors to review other aspects of their financial operations. For example, some auditing firms now specialize in checking corporate legal bills. An auditor for the Fireman's Fund Insurance Company uncovered several thousands of dollars in legal fee errors. Other auditors are beginning to specialize in real estate, employee benefits, and pension plan investments.

Whereas external audits are conducted by external accountants, an *internal audit* is handled by employees of the organization. Its objective is the same as that of an external audit—to verify the accuracy of financial and accounting procedures used by the organization. Internal audits also examine the efficiency and appropriateness of financial and accounting procedures. Because the staff members who conduct them are a permanent part of the organization, internal audits tend to be more expensive than external audits. But employees, who are more familiar with the organization's practices, may also focus on significant aspects of the accounting system besides its technical correctness. Large organizations like Halliburton and Ford have an internal auditing staff that spends all its time conducting audits of different divisions and functional areas of the organization. Smaller organizations may assign accountants to an internal audit group on a temporary or rotating basis.

The findings of an internal auditor led to the recent financial scandal at WorldCom. The firm's new CEO asked an internal auditor to spot-check various records related to capital expenditures. She subsequently discovered that the firm's chief financial officer was misapplying major expenses: instead of treating them as current expenses, he was treating them as capital expenditures. This treatment, in turn, made the firm look much more profitable than it really was. The CFO was fired, but it will take WorldCom a long time to sort out the $3.8 billion it has so far found to have been handled improperly.[24]

Structural Control

Organizations can create designs for themselves that result in very different approaches to control. Two major forms of structural control, bureaucratic control and decentralized control, represent opposite ends of a continuum, as shown in Figure 14.6.[25] The six dimensions shown in the figure represent perspectives adopted by the two extreme types of structural control. In other words, they have different goals, degrees of formality, performance expectations, organization designs, reward systems, and levels of participation. Although a few organizations

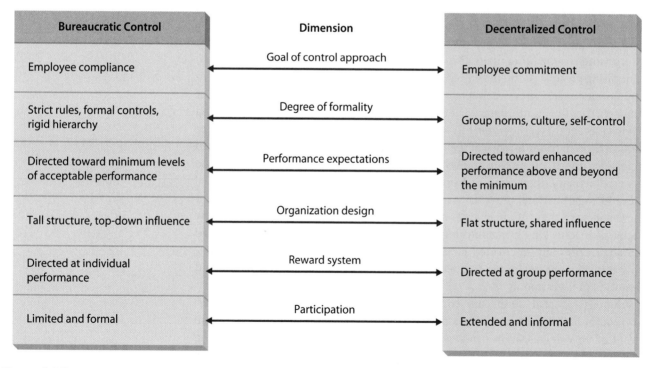

Figure 14.6
ORGANIZATIONAL CONTROL

Organizational control generally falls somewhere between the two extremes of bureaucratic and decentralized control. NBC television uses bureaucratic control, whereas Levi Strauss uses decentralized control.

fall precisely at one extreme or the other, most tend toward one end but may have specific characteristics of either.

Bureaucratic Control

Bureaucratic control is an approach to organization design characterized by formal and mechanistic structural arrangements. As the term suggests, it follows the bureaucratic model. The goal of bureaucratic control is employee compliance. Organizations that use it rely on strict rules and a rigid hierarchy, insist that employees meet minimally acceptable levels of performance, and often have a tall structure. They focus their rewards on individual performance and allow only limited and formal employee participation.

NBC television applies structural controls that reflect many elements of bureaucracy. The organization relies on numerous rules to regulate employee travel, expense accounts, and other expenses. A new performance appraisal system precisely specifies minimally acceptable levels of performance for everyone. The organization's structure is considerably taller than those of the other major networks, and rewards are based on individual contributions. Perhaps most significantly, many NBC employees have argued that they have too small a voice in how the organization is managed.

In another example, a large oil company recently made the decision to allow employees to wear casual attire to work. But a committee then spent weeks developing a 20-page set of guidelines on what was and was not acceptable. For example, denim pants are not allowed. Similarly, athletic shoes may be worn as long as they are not white. And all shirts must have a collar. Nordstrom, the department store chain, is also moving toward bureaucratic control as it works to centralize all of its purchasing in an effort to lower costs.[26] Similarly, Home Depot is moving more toward bureaucratic control to cut its costs and more effectively compete with its hard-charging rival, Lowe's.[27]

> **bureaucratic control**
> A form of organizational control characterized by formal and mechanistic structural arrangements

Decentralized Control

Decentralized control, in contrast, is an approach to organizational control characterized by informal and organic structural arrangements. As Figure 14.6 shows, its goal is employee commitment to the organization. Accordingly, it relies heavily on group norms and a strong corporate culture, and gives employees the responsibility for controlling themselves. Employees are encouraged to perform beyond minimally acceptable levels. Organizations using this approach are usually relatively flat. They direct rewards at group performance and favor widespread employee participation.

Levi Strauss practices decentralized control. The firm's managers use groups as the basis for work and have created a culture wherein group norms help facilitate high performance. Rewards are subsequently provided to the higher-performing groups and teams. The company's culture also reinforces contributions to the overall team effort, and employees have a strong sense of loyalty to the organization. Levi's has a flat structure, and power is widely shared. Employee participation is encouraged in all areas of operation.[28] Another company that uses this approach is Southwest Airlines. When Southwest made the decision to "go casual," the firm resisted the temptation to develop dress guidelines. Instead, managers decided to allow employees to exercise discretion over their attire and to deal with clearly inappropriate situations on a case-by-case basis.

> **decentralized control**
> An approach to organizational control based on informal and organic structural arrangements

Managing in Times of Change

Bringing Accountability to Toys "R" Us

Whose fault is it when a company falters? As the company slid toward bankruptcy, managers at Toys "R" Us blamed discount chains Wal-Mart and Target. In March 2006, Gerald Storch, formerly of Target, became CEO and began by asking employees to take responsibility. Pointing the finger at competitors isn't productive, according to Storch. "In every segment . . . dedicated specialty retailers are succeeding against Wal-Mart and Target," he says. Storch mentions Bed Bath & Beyond, Walgreen's, and Lowe's as success stories.

Storch is tackling problems at every level. He replaced half of the top team with outsiders from other retailers. He also corrects grammar in memos and orders stores to wax their floors more often. A formidable number cruncher, he gets more excited about spreadsheets than about toys. That may be exactly what Toys "R" Us needs.

Updating stores is one priority. The company discontinued renovations and maintenance when profits fell, feeding a vicious cycle of decay. Stores are now relocating to suburban shopping centers.

The split between the Toys "R" Us and Babies "R" Us stores backfired too. Toy shoppers buy once a year; babies' parents buy monthly. When the stores split, traffic fell. Storch's fix is a "side-by-side" design to locate the two stores next to each other. The CEO is also increasing traffic by creating more buying occasions. He's started a push for sales at Halloween, back-to-school, and other low demand times.

Storch focuses on creating fads, not following them. Toys "R" Us cannot always compete on price, but it can differentiate itself by offering exclusive items. Toy makers support this because it provides an alternative to the cost-conscious discounters, which control more than one-third of all U.S. toy sales.

Most importantly, he's increasing accountability for all employees, from the top team to store associates. Now when managers complain, Storch asks bluntly, "So what are you going to do about it?"

By focusing on the big picture and the details, Storch intends to keep Toys "R" Us from the fate of KB Toys and FAO Schwarz, which are now bankrupt. Stealing customers back from Wal-Mart and Target will be a tough fight, but if he can create accountability at all levels, he may succeed.

References: "About Toys "R" Us, Inc.," Toys "R" Us website, www.toysrus.com on March 7, 2007; Michael Barbaro, "No Playtime on Recovery Road," *New York Times*, November 19, 2006, pp. BU1, 8, 9; Anne D'Innocenzio, "As Parents Buy, Makers Push Pricier Toys," *BusinessWeek*, February 8, 2007, www.businessweek.com on March 7, 2007.

Strategic Control

Given the obvious importance of an organization's strategy, it is also important that the organization assess how effective that strategy is in helping the organization meet its goals.[29] To do this requires that the organization integrate its strategy and control systems. This is especially true for the global organization.

Integrating Strategy and Control

strategic control
Control aimed at ensuring that the organization is maintaining an effective alignment with its environment and moving toward achieving its strategic goals

Strategic control generally focuses on five aspects of organizations—structure, leadership, technology, human resources, and information and operational control systems. For example, an organization should periodically examine its structure to determine whether it is facilitating the attainment of the strategic goals being sought. Suppose a firm using a functional (U-form) design has an established goal of achieving sales growth of 20 percent per year. However, performance indicators show that it is currently growing at a rate of only 10 percent per year. Detailed analysis might reveal that the current structure is inhibiting growth in some way (for example, by slowing decision making and inhibiting innovation) and that a divisional (M-form) design is more likely to bring about the desired growth (by speeding decision making and promoting innovation).

Integrating strategy and control is an important responsibility for managers. As part of its strategy for improving flood control in New Orleans, the Army Corps of Engineers has designed a new system of pumps and floodgates. This engineer is monitoring a controlled release of water through the floodgates to test their effectiveness. Hence, the strategy (designing new pumps and floodgates) is being integrated with control (testing the efficiency of the new system as it is being constructed).

In this way, strategic control focuses on the extent to which implemented strategy achieves the organization's strategic goals. If, as outlined above, one or more avenues of implementation are inhibiting the attainment of goals, that avenue should be changed. Consequently, the firm might find it necessary to alter its structure, replace key leaders, adopt new technology, modify its human resources, or change its information and operational control systems.

Kohl's department stores essentially redefined how to compete effectively in the midtier retailing market and were on trajectory to leave competitors like Sears and Dillard's in its dust. But then the firm inexplicably stopped doing many of the very things that had led to its success—such as keeping abreast of current styles, maintaining low inventories, and keeping its stores neat and clean—and began to stumble. Now, managers are struggling to rejuvenate Kohl's strategic focus and get it back on track.[30]

International Strategic Control

Because of both their relatively large size and the increased complexity associated with international business, global organizations must take an especially pronounced strategic view of their control systems. One very basic question that has to be addressed is whether to manage control from a centralized or a decentralized perspective.[31] Under a centralized system, each organizational unit around the world is responsible for frequently reporting the results of its performance to headquarters. Managers from the home office often visit foreign branches to observe firsthand how the units are functioning.

BP, Unilever, Procter & Gamble, and Sony all use this approach. They believe centralized control is effective because it allows the home office to keep better informed of the performance of foreign units and to maintain more control over how decisions are made. For example, BP discovered that its Australian subsidiary was not billing its customers for charges as quickly as were its competitors. By shortening the billing cycle, BP now receives customer payments five days faster than before.

Managers believe that they discovered this oversight only because of a centralized financial control system.

Organizations that use a decentralized control system require foreign branches to report less frequently and in less detail. For example, each unit may submit summary performance statements on a quarterly basis and provide full statements only once a year. Similarly, visits from the home office are less frequent and less concerned with monitoring and assessing performance. IBM, Ford, and Shell all use this approach. Because Ford practices decentralized control of its design function, European designers have developed several innovative automobile design features. Managers believe that if they had been more centralized, designers would not have had the freedom to develop their new ideas.

Managing Control in Organizations

Effective control, whether at the operations, financial, structural, or strategic level, successfully regulates and monitors organizational activities. To use the control process, managers must recognize the characteristics of effective control and understand how to identify and overcome occasional resistance to control.[32]

Characteristics of Effective Control

Control systems tend to be most effective when they are integrated with planning and when they are flexible, accurate, timely, and objective.

Integration with Planning   Control should be linked with planning. The more explicit and precise this linkage, the more effective the control system is. The best way to integrate planning and control is to account for control as plans develop. In other words, as goals are set during the planning process, attention should be paid to developing standards that will reflect how well the plan is realized. Managers at Champion Spark Plug Company decided to broaden their product line to include a full range of automotive accessories—a total of 21 new products. As part of this plan, managers decided in advance what level of sales they wanted to realize from each product for each of the next five years. They established these sales goals as standards against which actual sales would be compared. Thus, by accounting for their control system as they developed their plan, managers at Champion did an excellent job of integrating planning and control.

Flexibility   The control system itself must be flexible enough to accommodate change. Consider, for example, an organization whose diverse product line requires 75 different raw materials. The company's inventory control system must be able to manage and monitor current levels of inventory for all 75 materials. When a change in product line changes the number of raw materials needed, or when the required quantities of the existing materials change, the control system should be flexible enough to handle the revised requirements. The alternative—designing and implementing a new control system—is an avoidable expense. Champion's control system included a mechanism that automatically shipped products to major customers to keep their inventories at predetermined levels. The firm had to adjust this system when one of its biggest customers decided not to stock the full line of Champion products. Because its control system was flexible, though, modifying it for the customer was relatively simple.

Accuracy Managers make a surprisingly large number of decisions based on inaccurate information. Field representatives may hedge their sales estimates to make themselves look better. Production managers may hide costs to meet their productivity targets. Human resources managers may overestimate their minority recruiting prospects to meet affirmative action goals. In each case, the information that other managers receive is inaccurate, and the results of inaccurate information may be quite dramatic. If sales projections are inflated, a manager might cut advertising (thinking it is no longer needed) or increase advertising (to further build momentum). Similarly, a sales manager unaware of hidden costs may quote a sales price much lower than desirable. Or a human resources manager may speak out publicly on the effectiveness of the company's minority recruiting, only to find out later that these prospects have been overestimated. In each case, the result of inaccurate information is inappropriate managerial action.

Timeliness Timeliness does not necessarily mean quickness. Rather, it describes a control system that provides information as often as is necessary. Because Champion has a wealth of historical data on its sparkplug sales, it does not need information on sparkplugs as frequently as it needs sales feedback for its newer products. Retail organizations usually need sales results daily so that they can manage cash flow and adjust advertising and promotion. In contrast, they may require information about physical inventory only quarterly or annually. In general, the more uncertain and unstable the circumstances, the more frequently measurement is needed.

Objectivity The control system should provide information that is as objective as possible. To appreciate this, imagine the task of a manager responsible for control of his organization's human resources. He asks two plant managers to submit reports. One manager notes that morale at his plant is "okay," that grievances are "about where they should be," and that turnover is "under control." The other reports that absenteeism at her plant is running at 4 percent, that 16 grievances have been filed this year (compared with 24 last year), and that turnover is 12 percent. The second report will almost always be more useful than the first. Of course, managers also need to look beyond the numbers when assessing performance. For example, a plant manager may be boosting productivity and profit margins by putting too much pressure on workers and using poor-quality materials. As a result, impressive short-run gains may be overshadowed by longer-run increases in employee turnover and customer complaints.

Resistance to Control

Managers sometimes make the mistake of assuming that the value of an effective control system is self-evident to employees. This is not always so, however. Many employees resist control, especially if they feel overcontrolled, if they think control is inappropriately focused or rewards inefficiency, or if they are uncomfortable with accountability.

Overcontrol Occasionally, organizations try to control too many things. This becomes especially problematic when the control directly affects employee behavior. An organization that instructs its employees when to come to work, where to park, when to have morning coffee, and when to leave for the day exerts considerable control over people's daily activities. Yet many organizations attempt to control not only these but other aspects of work behavior as well. Of particular relevance in recent years are some companies' efforts to control their employees' access to private email and the Internet during work hours. Some companies have no policies governing these activities, some attempt to limit it, and some attempt to forbid it altogether.[33]

Troubles arise when employees perceive these attempts to limit their behavior as being unreasonable. A company that tells its employees how to dress, how to arrange their desks, and how to wear their hair may meet with more resistance. Employees at Chrysler who drove non-Chrysler vehicles used to complain because they were forced to park in a distant parking lot. People felt that these efforts to control their personal behavior (what kind of car to drive) were excessive. Managers eventually removed these controls and now allow open parking. Some employees at Abercrombie & Fitch argue that the firm is guilty of overcontrol because of its strict dress and grooming requirements—for example, no necklaces or facial hair for men and only natural nail polish and earrings no larger than a dime for women. Likewise, Enterprise Rent-A-Car has a set of 30 dress-code rules for women and 26 rules for men. The firm was recently sued by one former employee who was fired because of the color of her hair.[34]

Inappropriate Focus   The control system may be too narrow, or it may focus too much on quantifiable variables and leave no room for analysis or interpretation. A sales standard that encourages high-pressure tactics to maximize short-run sales may do so at the expense of goodwill from long-term customers. Such a standard is too narrow. A university reward system that encourages faculty members to publish large numbers of articles but fails to consider the quality of the work is also inappropriately focused. Employees resist the intent of the control system by focusing their efforts only at the performance indicators being used. The cartoon features another example of inappropriately focused control.

In recent years, many organizations have sought ways to manage the size of their workforce more effectively, often through workforce reductions. Eliminating unnecessary or redundant jobs is indeed an effective strategy. But businesses sometimes go too far, eliminating jobs with a detrimental impact on the company. One executive noted that his firm had eliminated the fat but then cut out some muscle too! The manager shown here may also have fallen prey to that same mistake—cutting their sales force so much that their revenues have declined significantly.

"The dip in sales seems to coincide with the decision to eliminate the sales staff."

© The New Yorker Collection 2002 Leo Cullum from cartoonbank.com. All Rights Reserved.

Rewards for Inefficiency   Imagine two operating departments that are approaching the end of their fiscal years. Department 1 expects to have $25,000 of its budget left over; department 2 is already $10,000 in the red. As a result, department 1 is likely to have its budget cut for the next year ("They had money left, so they obviously got too much to begin with"), and department 2 is likely to get a budget increase ("They obviously haven't been getting enough money"). Thus department 1 is punished for being efficient, and department 2 is rewarded for being inefficient. (No wonder departments commonly hasten to deplete their budgets as the end of the year approaches!) As with inappropriate focus, people resist the intent of this control and behave in ways that run counter to the organization's objective.

Too Much Accountability   Effective controls allow managers to determine whether employees successfully discharge their responsibilities. If standards are properly set and performance accurately measured, managers know when problems arise and which departments and individuals are responsible. People who do not want to be answerable for their mistakes or who do not want to work as hard as their boss might like therefore resist control. For example, American Express has a system that provides daily information on how many calls each of its customer service representatives handles. If one representative has typically worked at a slower pace and handled fewer calls than other representatives, that individual's deficient performance can now more easily be pinpointed.

Overcoming Resistance to Control

Perhaps the best way to overcome resistance to control is to create effective control from the outset. If control systems are properly integrated with organizational planning and if the controls are flexible, accurate, timely, and objective, the organization will be less likely to overcontrol, to focus on inappropriate standards, or to reward inefficiency. Two other ways to overcome resistance are encouraging employee participation and developing verification procedures.

Encourage Employee Participation   Chapter 7 notes that participation can help overcome resistance to change. By the same token, when employees are involved with planning and implementing the control system, they are less likely to resist it. For instance, employee participation in planning, decision making, and quality control at the Chevrolet Gear and Axle plant in Detroit has resulted in increased employee concern for quality and a greater commitment to meeting standards.

Develop Verification Procedures   Multiple standards and information systems provide checks and balances in control and allow the organization to verify the accuracy of performance indicators. Suppose a production manager argues that she failed to meet a certain cost standard because of increased prices of raw materials. A properly designed inventory control system will either support or contradict her explanation. Suppose that an employee who was fired for excessive absences argues that he was not absent "for a long time." An effective human resource control system should have records that support the termination. Resistance to control declines because these verification procedures protect both employees and management. If the production manager's claim about the rising cost of raw materials is supported by the inventory control records, she will not be held solely accountable for failing to meet the cost standard, and some action probably will be taken to lower the cost of raw materials.

Summary of Key Points

1. Explain the purpose of control, identify different types of control, and describe the steps in the control process.
   - Control is the regulation of organizational activities so that some targeted element of performance remains within acceptable limits.
   - Control provides ways to adapt to environmental change, to limit the accumulation of errors, to cope with organizational complexity, and to minimize costs.
   - Control can focus on financial, physical, information, and human resources and includes operations, financial, structural, and strategic levels.
   - Control is the function of managers, the controller, and, increasingly, of operating employees.
   - Steps in the control process are
     - to establish standards of expected performance
     - to measure actual performance
     - to compare performance to the standards
     - to evaluate the comparison and take appropriate action

2. Identify and explain the three forms of operations control.
   - Operations control focuses on the processes the organization uses to transform resources into products or services.
   - Preliminary control is concerned with the resources that serve as inputs to the system.
   - Screening control is concerned with the transformation processes used by the organization.
   - Postaction control is concerned with the outputs of the organization.
   - Most organizations need multiple control systems because no one system can provide adequate control.

3. Describe budgets and other tools for financial control.
   - Financial control focuses on controlling the organization's financial resources.
   - The foundation of financial control is budgets, which are plans expressed in numerical terms.
   - Most organizations rely on financial, operating, and nonmonetary budgets.
   - Financial statements, various kinds of ratios, and external and internal audits are also important tools organizations use as part of financial control.

4. Identify and distinguish between two opposing forms of structural control.
   - Structural control addresses how well an organization's structural elements serve their intended purpose.
   - Two basic forms of structural control are bureaucratic and decentralized control.
     - Bureaucratic control is relatively formal and mechanistic.
     - Decentralized control is informal and organic.
   - Most organizations use a form of organizational control somewhere between total bureaucratic and total decentralized control.

5. Discuss the relationship between strategy and control, including international strategic control.
   - Strategic control focuses on how effectively the organization's strategies are succeeding in helping the organization meet its goals.
   - The integration of strategy and control is generally achieved through organization structure, leadership, technology, human resources, and information and operational control systems.
   - International strategic control is also important for multinational organizations.
   - The foundation of international strategic control is whether to practice centralized or decentralized control.

6. Identify characteristics of effective control, why people resist control, and how managers can overcome this resistance.
   - One way to increase the effectiveness of control is to fully integrate planning and control.
   - The control system should also be as flexible, accurate, timely, and objective as possible.
   - Employees may resist organizational controls because of overcontrol, inappropriate focus, rewards for inefficiency, and a desire to avoid accountability.
   - Managers can overcome this resistance by improving the effectiveness of controls and by allowing employee participation and developing verification procedures.

Discussion Questions

Questions for Review

1. What is the purpose of organizational control? Why is it important?

2. What are the different levels of control? What are the relationships between the different levels?

3. Describe how a budget is created in most organizations. How does a budget help a manager with financial control?

4. Describe the differences between bureaucratic and decentralized control. What are the advantages and disadvantages of each?

5. Why do some people resist control? How can managers help overcome this resistance?

Questions for Analysis

1. How can a manager determine whether his or her firm needs improvement in control? If improvement is needed, how can the manager tell what type of control needs improvement (operations, financial, structural, or strategic)? Describe some steps a manager can take to improve each of these types of control.

2. One company uses strict performance standards. Another has standards that are more flexible. What are the advantages and disadvantages of each system?

3. Are the differences in bureaucratic control and decentralized control related to differences in organization structure? If so, how? If not, why not? (The terms do sound similar to those used to discuss the organizing process.)

4. Many organizations today are involving lower-level employees in control. Give at least two examples of specific actions that a lower-level worker could take to help his or her organization better adapt to environmental change. Then do the same for limiting the accumulation of error, coping with organizational complexity, and minimizing costs.

5. Describe ways that the top-management team, midlevel managers, and operating employees can participate in each step of the control process. Do all participate equally in each step, or are some steps better suited for personnel at one level? Explain your answer.

Building Effective Time-Management Skills

Exercise Overview

Time-management skills—a manager's ability to prioritize work, to work efficiently, and to delegate appropriately—play a major role in the control function. That is, a manager can use time-management skills to control his or her own work more effectively. This exercise will help demonstrate the relationship between time-management skills and control.

Exercise Background

You are a middle manager in a small manufacturing plant. Today is Monday, and you have just returned from a week of vacation. The first thing you discover is that your assistant will not be in today. His aunt died, and he is out of town at the funeral. He did, however, leave you the following note:

Dear Boss:

Sorry about not being here today. I will be back tomorrow. In the meantime, here are some things you need to know:

1. Ms. Glinski [your boss] wants to see you today at 4:00.

2. The shop steward wants to see you as soon as possible about a labor problem.

3. Mr. Bateman [one of your big customers] has a complaint about a recent shipment.

4. Ms. Ferris [one of your major suppliers] wants to discuss a change in delivery schedules.

5. Mr. Prescott from the Chamber of Commerce wants you to attend a breakfast meeting on Wednesday to discuss our expansion plans.

6. The legal office wants to discuss our upcoming OSHA inspection.

7. Human resources wants to know when you can interview someone for the new supervisor's position.

8. Jack Williams, the machinist you fired last month, has been hanging around the parking lot, and his presence is making some employees uncomfortable.

Exercise Task

With the information above as context, do the following:

1. Prioritize the work that needs to be done by sorting the information in your assistant's list into three categories: very timely, moderately timely, and less timely.

2. Are importance and timeliness the same thing?

3. What additional information must you acquire before you can begin to prioritize this work?

4. How would your approach differ if your assistant were in?

Building Effective Decision-Making and Diagnostic Skills

Exercise Overview

Decision-making skills reflect the manager's ability to recognize and respond to problems and opportunities, whereas diagnostic skills focus on the visualization of appropriate responses. This exercise asks you to examine one component of an organization's control system, to diagnose any weaknesses in the system, and to develop a plan for strengthening control in that part of the system.

Exercise Background

Organizations use a wide variety of methods for control. One control system is the corporate board of directors. This group of individuals is often chosen by the firm's CEO or by other directors. Boards of directors are especially important in strategic control. They have the responsibility of ensuring that the corporation is achieving its strategic goals while acting ethically, of overseeing the performance of the CEO and other members of the top-management team, and of looking out for the interests of shareholders. Yet the recent corporate scandals at Enron, WorldCom, and other firms have shown that some boards provide inadequate control.

The U.S. Securities and Exchange Commission (SEC) has put forth proposals for a number of reforms that it hopes will enhance the control power of boards. Some of its recommendations focus on board composition. If boards do not contain the right number and kind of directors, the SEC claims, they are less likely to be effective. The SEC recommends that firms apply the following guidelines:

- Keep the size of the board to one dozen or fewer directors, so that each has a more personal stake in the process.

- Choose outside directors for the most part, to increase their objectivity. (Outside directors are not employees of the firm, are not related to any employees, and are not involved in significant business dealings with the CEO or the firm.)

- Require directors to hold significant amounts of company stock, to align their interests more closely with those of stockholders.

- Choose several experts in corporate accounting or finance, especially on the audit and compensation committees.

- Ensure that directors do not serve on more than three boards altogether, to ensure that they have sufficient time for this board.

Exercise Task

Choose an organization that interests you. Use the Internet to research its board of directors. (*Hint:* company websites contain much of this information. Also search the Web for biographies of the individual directors.)

1. Use information from the Internet to see how this board of directors measures up on the criteria listed above (board size, outside directors, stock ownership, financial expertise, and board service). Assess as many of the items as you can for each board member.

2. In which of the five areas is your firm's board of directors acceptable? In which of the five areas is your firm's board not acceptable?

3. What are some probable consequences for organizational control? Consider both positive and negative consequences.

4. What can your organization do to increase the effectiveness of its board?

Building Effective Technical Skills

Exercise Overview

Technical skills are the skills necessary to accomplish or understand the specific kind of work being done in an organization. This exercise gives you practice in applying technical skills related to building a budget and evaluating the effectiveness of a budget.

Exercise Background

Although corporate budgets are much more complicated, the steps in creating a personal budget and creating a corporate budget are much the same. Both begin with estimates of inflow and outflow. Then both compare actual results with estimated results. And both end with the development of a plan for corrective action.

Exercise Task

1. Prepare your estimated expenditures and income for one month. This is a budgeted amount, not the amount you actually spent. Instead, it should represent a typical month or a reasonable minimum. For example, is $200 a reasonable amount to spend on groceries? Estimate your necessary monthly expenses for tuition, rent, car payments, child care, food, utilities, and so on. Then estimate your income from all sources, such as wages, allowance, loans, and funds borrowed on credit cards. Calculate the totals.

2. Write down all of your actual expenses over the last month. Then write down all of your actual income.

   If you do not have exact figures, estimate as closely as you can. Calculate the totals.

3. Compare your estimates to your actual expenses and actual income. Are there any discrepancies? What caused the discrepancies, if any?

4. Did you expect to have a surplus or a deficit for the month? Did you actually have a deficit or a surplus? What are your plans for making up any deficit or managing any surplus?

5. Do you regularly use a personal budget? Is a personal budget likely to be helpful to you? Why or why not?

Skills Self-Assessment Instrument

Understanding Control

Introduction: Control systems must be carefully constructed for all organizations, regardless of their specific goals. The following assessment surveys your ideas about and approaches to control.

Instructions: You will agree with some of the statements and disagree with others. In some cases, making a decision may be difficult, but you should force yourself to make a choice. Record your answers next to each statement according to the following scale.

Rating Scale

4 Strongly agree

3 Slightly agree

2 Somewhat disagree

1 Strongly disagree

_____ 1. Effective controls must be unbending if they are to be used consistently.

_____ 2. The most objective form of control is one that uses measures such as stock prices and rate of return on investment (ROI).

_____ 3. Control is restrictive and should be avoided if at all possible.

_____ 4. Controlling through rules, procedures, and budgets should not be used unless measurable standards are difficult or expensive to develop.

_____ 5. Overreliance on measurable control standards is seldom a problem for business organizations.

_____ 6. Organizations should encourage the development of individual self-control.

_____ 7. Organizations tend to try to establish behavioral controls as the first type of control to be used.

_____ 8. The easiest and least costly form of control is output or quantity control.

_____ 9. Short-run efficiency and long-run effectiveness result from the use of similar control standards.

_____ 10. Controlling by taking into account return on investment (ROI) and using stock prices in making control decisions are ways of ensuring that a business organization is responding to its external market.

_____ 11. Self-control should be relied on to replace other forms of control.

_____ 12. Controls such as return on investment (ROI) are more appropriate for corporations and business units than for small groups or individuals.

_____ 13. Control is unnecessary in a well-managed organization.

_____ 14. The use of output or quantity controls can lead to unintended or unfortunate consequences.

_____ 15. Standards of control do not depend on which constituency is being considered.

_____ 16. Controlling through the use of rules, procedures, and budgets can lead to rigidity and to a loss of creativity in an organization.

_____ 17. Different forms of control cannot be used at the same time. An organization must decide how it is going to control and stick to that method.

_____ 18. Setting across-the-board output or quantity targets for divisions within a company can lead to destructive results.

_____ 19. Control through rules, procedures, and budgets is generally not very costly.

_____ 20. Reliance on individual self-control can lead to problems with integration and communication.

Source: Exercise adapted from Chapter 12, pp. 380–395 in Charles W. Hill and Gareth R. Jones, *Strategic Management*, Fourth Edition. Copyright © 1998 by Houghton Mifflin Company. Used by permission.
For interpretation, see Interpretations of Skills Self-Assessment Instruments in the appendix near the end of this text.

Experiential Exercise

Control Systems at State U.

Purpose: This exercise offers you an opportunity to practice analyzing an organization's need for controls. You also will describe likely challenges to implementation and list ways to overcome resistance to control.

Introduction: The case in this exercise represents an organization with seriously deficient control systems, which is rather unrealistic. However, most organizations do suffer from one or more control efforts that are lacking or ineffective. In addition, implementing controls is usually more difficult than simply diagnosing the need for controls, especially when organization members resist the control.

Instructions:

Step 1: The instructor will divide the class into small groups. Read the University Control Problem.

The University Control Problem

You are on a committee appointed by the State University Student Council to help the new president deal with a number of problems that have plagued the campus for years. For example, the university regularly runs out of funds before the academic year ends, causing major disruptions of student services. In fact, some departments seem to have no knowledge of how much money they need or how much they have spent. Students are upset because tuition fees are constantly being changed in an effort to match the university's varying demands for money. Department chairs have no idea how many students are being admitted, so they never schedule the appropriate number of courses. Some buildings are in bad physical shape. Classrooms are assigned to departments, and some classrooms seem to sit empty while others are overcrowded. There seems to be an oversupply of research equipment but a shortage of computer equipment for students. Some schools, such as the business school, don't have enough faculty to teach their classes, while some departments in liberal arts have surplus faculty with no students to teach.

Step 2: As a small group, reach consensus about how to complete the University Control Matrix, below. Identify the different controls that might be established for each of the four resources—physical, financial, human, and information—and remember to consider each type of control. Preliminary controls control inputs into the university. Screening controls act upon the university's transformation processes. Postaction controls control the university's outputs.

Step 3: As a small group, develop responses to the discussion questions, below. Discuss your responses with the class.

The University Control Matrix

System Stages	Physical Resources	Financial Resources	Human Resources	Information Resources
Preliminary Controls				
Screening Controls				
Postaction Controls				

Discussion Questions

1. Which of the recommended controls may be the hardest to implement? To manage?

2. Will the controls receive some form of resistance? If so, describe which organization members are likely to resist and the likely form of that resistance.

Source: Adapted from Morable, *Exercises in Management*, to accompany Griffin, *Management*, 8th edition.

CHAPTER CLOSING CASE

IS TOO MUCH CONTROL HURTING DELL?

Michael Dell "broke the paradigm about how to run a computer business," says professor David Yoffie. Among Dell's innovations: direct selling to customers to avoid payments to retailers, flexible manufacturing for customization at a low cost, and just-in-time inventory to keep expenses low. It's clear that Dell's phenomenal success over the last two decades was due to its tightly disciplined operations and relentless controls.

However, the future looks less promising. Customers are flocking to retail stores for the latest electronic gear, which Dell does not carry. The PC maker's customer satisfaction ratings have fallen and complaints are up. Cutthroat competition in desktop PCs, which account for over half of Dell's sales, has squeezed profit margins to a thin 3.8 percent. In February 2006, Dell announced that expected sales growth for the following quarter would be around 7 percent, a drastic drop from the previous year's 16 percent. Is too much control hurting Dell?

On the positive side, Dell's "value-priced" business model means the firm has done a good job of controlling costs. Dell's North Carolina plant, opened in October 2005, can produce PCs 40 percent faster with 30 percent less downtime. Unlike older factories, where equipment must be retooled for different types of computers, the new plant can build any of Dell's forty computer models at any time. Factory designer Richard Komm says, "Other factories have a process-driven flow. [This plant] is focused on one thing: How do we get it to the customer in the shortest amount of time?"

Automated robots are not as efficient as humans in certain tasks, such as packing small, delicate items. Instead, robots perform the heavy lifting, such as placing finished machines in shipping boxes. Automating the heavier tasks lowers the injury rate, reducing claims for workers' compensation.

Excellent quality control also reduces costs. Teams of three workers help to build a PC. Each individual has a specialized set of tasks, which eases training, speeds assembly, and reduces errors by 30 percent. Each team includes a tester who performs a quick check when every machine is finished to see that it's wired correctly and will boot. Machines that pass inspection will undergo more extensive testing, but the quick test allows rapid spotting of gross defects. Most defects are now caught in four minutes rather than 60 and the overall defect rate is lower. "The faster you get feedback to the operator, the fewer defects," says Komm.

On the negative side, some feel that Dell has gone too far in its quest for control. Home users, who make up the majority of Dell customers but are half as profitable as business users, are dissatisfied. They complain that much of Dell's customer support staff is located in India, making communications difficult at times. Very long wait times are another concern. "Consumers want to have their cake and eat it too," says Stephen Dukker, CEO of PC maker emachines, Inc. "They want that $300 PC but expect the same support that came with a machine that 10 years ago cost $2,500." Given today's industry environment, that desire is unrealistic. Dell's least expensive desktop model retails for $299, which would yield a mere $12 in profits, not enough to support much customer service.

In order to control costs, Dell introduced different levels of customer service to those who pay for pricier models. A buyer of the top-of-the-line XPS model typically waits less than five minutes for phone service, while buyers of $299 models may be put on hold for one to two hours. Dell also plans to sell varying levels of service contracts at various prices. Some standard features will disappear. For example, in the future "free shipping" on low-end models will include only delivery to a local post office, according to one Dell plan. Home delivery will cost extra.

An even bigger concern is Dell's lack of innovation. The company has always assumed that price is paramount, leading to an emphasis on inexpensive, commodity-like products. However, buyers today want tablet PCs, portable music and video players, digital photography, and more. Dell spends less on R&D than rival Apple Computers, despite being four times larger.

David Yoffie said, "Michael broke the paradigm," but went on to add, "They haven't been so great at finding the next paradigm." With competitors imitating Dell's best tactics, gaining on Dell in price and productivity, industry expert Mark Stahlman says, "Dell is singing the same old song. It's time for them to change."

Perhaps Dell could afford to give up a little control in exchange for a little more creativity, flexibility, and customer service. Perhaps they can't afford not to.

CASE QUESTIONS

1. What advantages does Dell gain from its tight control system? What disadvantages does the company experience?

2. Which types of operations controls are mentioned in this article? Give examples of each type.

3. Are Dell's control systems effective? In your opinion, what could Dell do to make its control systems more effective? Explain your responses.

CASE REFERENCES

Amanda Cantrell, "Dell to Get Served by AMD," *Money*, May 18, 2006, www.cnnmoney.com on May 23, 2006; Louise Lee, "Hanging Up on Dell?" *BusinessWeek*, October 10, 2005, www.businessweek.com on May 7, 2006; Louise Lee, "It's Dell vs. The Dell Way," *BusinessWeek*, March 6, 2006, pp. 61–62; Christopher Null, "Dude, You're Getting a Dell—Every Five Seconds," *Business 2.0*, December 1, 2005, www.money.cnn.com on May 15, 2006.

YOU MAKE THE CALL

Effective Controls at McDonald's Boost Performance

1. Have you eaten at an updated McDonald's restaurant? If you haven't, would you like to? What did you (or would you) like and not like about the experience?

2. McDonald's is under fire these days due to its "unhealthy" foods. In your opinion, will the kind of changes discussed in the opening case help or hurt McDonald's as they deal with these issues?

3. The change to 24-hour service sound promising for customers and owners, but what do you think its impact will be on employees? What actions can McDonald's take to minimize the negative impacts on workers?

4. Some people claim that McDonald's is guilty of creating the trend towards convenience dining and away from family meals. Do you agree or disagree? Explain.

Test Prepper

college.hmco.com/pic/griffinfund5e

You've read the chapter, studied the key terms, and the exam is any day now. Think you're ready to ace it? Take this sample test to gauge your comprehension of chapter material. You can check your answers at the back of the book. Want more test questions? Visit the student website at http://college.hmco.com/pic/griffinfund5e/ and take the ACE quizzes for more practice.

1. T F Strategic control is focused on monitoring how well various elements of the organization's structure are serving their intended purpose.

2. T F When H&R Block checks a completed tax file for client signature, it is using a form of postaction control.

3. T F Organizations that use decentralized control are less formal than organizations that use bureaucratic control.

4. T F Control should be integrated with planning from the very beginning.

5. T F Strict adherence to control is essential for control effectiveness.

6. Which of the following is NOT one of the purposes of a control system?

    a. Limit the accumulation of error

    b. Cope with complexity

    c. Minimize revenue

    d. Adapt to change

    e. Minimize costs

7. In the course of reaffirming its commitment to academics, a university sets the goal that, within a five-year time span, 90 percent of the students who enter with each class will graduate. This is an example of a(n)

    a. operating control.

    b. control standard.

    c. financial control.

    d. labor control.

    e. controller standard.

8. When DaimlerChrysler decided to reduce its advertising for the PT Cruiser because demand was greater than production capability, Daimler-Chrysler was acting at which step in the control process?

    a. Compare performance against standards.

    b. Establish standards.

    c. Determine any need for corrective action.

    d. Measure performance.

    e. Maintain the status quo.

9. The hours of work needed to create a website are found in a(n) _____ budget.

    a. labor

    b. space

    c. production

    d. capital expenditure

    e. operating

10. A(n) _____ is a forecast of assets and liabilities in the event that all other budgets are met.

    a. balance sheet

    b. income statement

    c. cash-flow statement

    d. financial statement

    e. capital expenditure budget

Managing Operations, Quality, and Productivity

chapter 15

FIRST THINGS FIRST

Competing Through Operations

"The point is to move the whole product line . . . to a more competitive performance position . . . rather than lower the price to be competitive."

—GORDON MOORE, FOUNDER OF INTEL AND CREATOR OF

MOORE'S LAW

In 1965, when color televisions were rare and slide rules prevailed, engineer Gordon Moore predicted, "Integrated circuits will lead to such wonders as home computers, automatic controls for automobiles, and personal portable communications equipment." Moore also noted that the number of transistors (roughly equivalent to processing capacity) on a semiconductor chip was doubling each year. This statement was interpreted by others to mean that capacity *must* double yearly

Intel relies on effective operations management to stay at the forefront of its industry.

LEARNING OBJECTIVES

After studying this chapter, you should be able to:

- Describe and explain the nature of operations management.
- Identify and discuss the components involved in designing effective operations systems.
- Discuss organizational technologies and their role in operations management.
- Identify and discuss the components involved in implementing operations systems through supply chain management.
- Explain the meaning and importance of managing quality and total quality management.
- Explain the meaning and importance of managing productivity, productivity trends, and ways to improve productivity.

and it became known as "Moore's Law." (Today, the doubling time is actually closer to two years.) Moore went on to found Intel, the semiconductor chip maker that successfully applied his law to its design and manufacturing operations.

Even though Moore never intended his observation to become a "law," former Intel CEO Craig Barrett used it to goad his employees to higher performance. "Every time we don't live up to Moore's Law, somebody else does," Barrett told his researchers. "We don't adhere to Moore's Law for the hell of it," Barrett adds. "We dangle Moore's Law in front of the new young minds . . . and say, 'Hey, your predecessors were smart enough to figure this out for the past 20 or 30 years—why aren't you?'" Former vice president of technology Sunlin Chou thinks that the law is "a self-fulfilling prophecy." He states, "In the end, Moore's Law is a philosophy as well as a strategy. It gives us the confidence to believe in the future."

Intel's faith in Moore's Law has led it to take risks in the development of innovative new products. In Ireland, the firm built its largest-ever fabrication plant, a $2.5 billion facility to produce the Itanium chips. In 2006 that plant doubled in size. Three additional multibillion-dollar plants in Israel, Arizona, and New Mexico will come on line in 2007 and 2008. Former CEO Andy Grove claims that "capacity is strategy." Worldwide, 80 percent of PCs contain Intel microprocessors, trouncing number-two Advanced Micro Devices (AMD). Intel's advantage lies in its superior design—its Pentium 4 processor has speeds of up to 3 gigahertz, whereas AMD's best efforts still fall short of 2 gigahertz. Barrett believes that Intel can build enough capacity to drive rivals out of the industry. Some, like analyst Jonathon Joseph, worry that Intel may be overbuilding. "Intel has a phobia about capacity," Joseph claims. "They're very concerned that they'll miss the next upturn [in demand for chips]. . . . They aimed forward to hit the duck, and the duck isn't there." Intel plans to shut down older plants as it opens new ones to keep capacity at a sustainable level.

The state-of-the-art factory employs flexible manufacturing to ensure that the plant can produce the next generation of chips. Intel's new facilities will "copy exactly" the design of the first, a cornerstone of the chip maker's innovation strategy. Chou explains, "Once we come up with a manufacturing process, we don't let the chip design team tinker with it." The copy-exactly technique ensures that new facilities become productive immediately and that they do not introduce any new errors into the exacting process of chip fabrication. Moore emphasizes the importance of "copy exactly," saying, "it takes a couple of years out of the life span of a generation of products. That in turn allows us to set a faster pace of innovation for our competitors to keep up with."

Another key piece of Intel's operations strategy is constant innovation, even if that means cannibalizing sales of older products. The new Itanium, for example, will replace the Pentium. During the transition, Pentium chips will be cheaper, but as Itanium production increases, Intel will cease manufacturing Pentiums. Moore says, "The point is to move the whole product line, not just a single part, to a more competitive performance position . . . rather than lower the price to be competitive."

Even as the first factory is nearing completion, Intel's R&D teams have begun work on the next-generation processors. The manufacturer is also bringing the efficiencies of Moore's Law to the manufacture of communications chips. These chips are currently made in small batches to meet each assembler's unique requirements. Intel is working to place standardized wireless and computing technology on the same chip. The semiconductors create a national wireless communications network that provides wireless connectivity to any device, anywhere in the United States.

It is a foregone conclusion that Intel will dominate chip design and manufacture for the foreseeable future. However, much of the demand for high-tech chips is now in telecommunications and flash memory, markets dominated by Samsung and other Asian firms. Intel has mastered the art of high-tech manufacturing. Can it master the challenge of expanding those skills into new markets?[1]

Intel has been highly successful in using operations management techniques and concepts to spur manufacturing and innovation. In this chapter we explore operations management, quality, and productivity. We first introduce operations management and discuss its role in general management and organizational strategy. The next three sections discuss the design of operations systems, organizational technologies, and implementing operations systems. We then introduce and discuss various issues in managing for quality and total quality. Finally, we discuss productivity, which is closely related to quality.

The Nature of Operations Management

Operations management is at the core of what organizations do as they add value and create products and services. But what exactly are operations? And how are they managed? **Operations management** is the set of managerial activities used by an organization to transform resource inputs into products and services. When Dell Computer buys electronic components, assembles them into PCs, and then ships them to customers, it is engaging in operations management. When a Pizza Hut employee orders food and paper products and then combines dough, cheese, and tomato paste to create a pizza, he or she is engaging in operations management.

operations management
The total set of managerial activities used by an organization to transform resource inputs into products, services, or both

The Importance of Operations

Operations is an important functional concern for organizations because efficient and effective management of operations goes a long way toward ensuring competitiveness and overall organizational performance, as well as quality and productivity. Inefficient or ineffective operations management, on the other hand, will almost inevitably lead to poorer performance and lower levels of both quality and productivity.

In an economic sense, operations management creates value and utility of one type or another, depending on the nature of the firm's products or services. If the product is a physical good, such as a Harley-Davidson motorcycle, operations creates value and provides form utility by combining many dissimilar inputs (sheet metal, rubber, paint, combustion engines, and human skills) to make something (a motorcycle) that is more valuable than the actual cost of the inputs used to create it. The inputs are converted from their incoming form into a new physical form. This conversion is typical of manufacturing operations and essentially reflects the organization's technology.

In contrast, the operations activities of American Airlines create value and provide time and place utility through its services. The airline transports passengers and freight according to agreed-upon departure and arrival places and times. Other service operations, such as a Coors beer distributorship or a Gap retail store, create value and provide place and possession utility by bringing together the customer and products made by others. Although the organizations in these examples produce different kinds of products or services, their operations processes share many important features.[2]

Manufacturing and Production Operations

manufacturing
A form of business that combines and transforms resource inputs into tangible outcomes

Because manufacturing once dominated U.S. industry, the entire area of operations management used to be called "production management." **Manufacturing** is a form of business that combines and transforms resources into tangible outcomes that are then sold to others. The Goodyear Tire & Rubber Company is a manufacturer because it combines rubber and chemical compounds and uses blending equipment and molding machines to create tires. Broyhill is a manufacturer because it buys wood and metal components, pads, and fabric and then combines them into furniture.

During the 1970s, manufacturing entered a long period of decline in the United States, primarily because of foreign competition. U.S. firms had grown lax and sluggish, and new foreign competitors came onto the scene with better equipment and much higher levels of efficiency. For example, steel companies in the Far East were able to produce high-quality steel for much lower prices than were U.S. companies like Bethlehem Steel and U.S. Steel (now USX Corporation). Faced with a battle for survival, many companies underwent a long and difficult period of change by eliminating waste and transforming themselves into leaner and more efficient and responsive entities. They reduced their workforces dramatically, closed antiquated or unnecessary plants, and modernized their remaining plants. In the last decade, their efforts have started to pay dividends, as U.S. businesses have regained their competitive positions in many different industries. Although manufacturers from other parts of the world are still formidable competitors and U.S. firms may never again be competitive in some markets, the overall picture is much better than it was just a few years ago. And prospects continue to look bright.[3]

Service Operations

service organization
An organization that transforms resources into an intangible output and creates time or place utility for its customers

During the decline of the manufacturing sector, a tremendous growth in the service sector kept the U.S. economy from declining at the same rate. A **service organization** is one that transforms resources into an intangible output and creates time or place utility for its customers. For example, Merrill Lynch makes stock transactions for its customers, Avis leases cars to its customers, and local hairdressers cut clients' hair. In 1947 the service sector was responsible for less than half of the U.S. gross national product (GNP). By 1975, however, this figure reached 65 percent, and by 2006 it was over 80 percent.[4] The service sector has been responsible for almost 90 percent of all new jobs created in the United States during the 1990s. Managers have come to see that many of the tools, techniques, and methods that are used in a factory are also useful to a service firm. For example, managers of automobile plants and hair salons both have to decide how to design their facilities, identify the best locations for them, determine optimal capacities, make decisions about inventory storage, set procedures for purchasing raw materials, and set standards for productivity and quality.

The Role of Operations in Organizational Strategy

It should be clear by this point that operations management is very important to organizations. Beyond its direct impact on such factors as competitiveness, quality, and productivity, it also directly influences the organization's overall level of effectiveness. For example, the deceptively simple strategic decision of whether to stress high quality regardless of cost, lowest possible cost regardless of quality, or some combination of the two has numerous important implications. A highest-possible-quality strategy will dictate state-of-the-art technology and rigorous control of product design and materials specifications. A combination strategy might call for lower-grade technology and less concern about product design and materials specifications. Just as strategy affects operations management, so, too, does operations management affect strategy. Suppose that a firm decides to upgrade the quality of its products or services. The organization's ability to implement the decision is dependent in part on current production capabilities and other resources. If existing technology will not permit higher-quality work, and if the organization lacks the resources to replace its technology, increasing quality to the desired new standards will be difficult.

Designing Operations Systems

The problems, challenges, and opportunities faced by operations managers revolve around the acquisition and utilization of resources for conversion. Their goals include both efficiency and effectiveness. A number of issues and decisions must

Facilities decisions can play a key role in the effectiveness of a firm's operations management systems. This company, Camden International, imports cocoa beans from West Africa. Because the firm has placed its warehouse near ship terminals and has designed the facility for efficient operation, a forklift operator can quickly move a load of beans from the dock receiving area into temporary storage inside the warehouse—or even move it directly through the facility and load it onto a truck.

be addressed as operations systems are designed. The most basic ones are product-service mix, capacity, and facilities.

Determining Product-Service Mix

product-service mix
How many and what kinds of products or services (or both) to offer

A natural starting point in designing operations systems is determining the **product-service mix.** This decision flows from corporate, business, and marketing strategies. Managers have to make a number of decisions about their products and services, starting with how many and what kinds to offer.[5] Procter & Gamble, for example, makes regular, tartar-control, gel, and various other formulas of Crest toothpaste and packages them in several different sizes of tubes, pumps, and other dispensers. Similarly, workers at Subway sandwich shops can combine different breads, vegetables, meats, and condiments to create hundreds of different kinds of sandwiches. Decisions also have to be made regarding the level of quality desired, the optimal cost of each product or service, and exactly how each is to be designed. GE recently reduced the number of parts in its industrial circuit breakers from 28,000 to 1,275. This whole process was achieved by carefully analyzing product design and production methods.

Capacity Decisions

capacity
The amount of products, services, or both that can be produced by an organization

The **capacity** decision involves choosing the amount of products, services, or both that can be produced by the organization. Determining whether to build a factory capable of making 5,000 or 8,000 units per day is a capacity decision. So, too, is deciding whether to build a restaurant with 100 or 150 seats, or a bank with 5 or 10 teller stations. The capacity decision is truly a high-risk one because of the uncertainties of future product demand and the large monetary stakes involved. An organization that builds capacity exceeding its needs may commit resources (capital investment) that will never be recovered. Alternatively, an organization can build a facility with a smaller capacity than expected demand. Doing so may result in lost market opportunities, but it may also free capital resources for use elsewhere in the organization.

A major consideration in determining capacity is demand. A company operating with fairly constant monthly demand might build a plant capable of producing an amount each month roughly equivalent to its demand. But if its market is characterized by seasonal fluctuations, building a smaller plant to meet normal demand and then adding extra shifts staffed with temporary workers or paying permanent workers extra to work more hours during peak periods might be the most effective choice. Likewise, a restaurant that needs 150 seats for Saturday night but never needs more than 100 at any other time during the week would probably be foolish to expand to 150 seats. During the rest of the week, it must still pay to light, heat, cool, and clean the excess capacity. Many customer service departments have tried to improve their capacity to deal with customers while also lowering costs by using automated voice prompts to direct callers to the right representative.

Facilities Decisions

facilities
The physical locations where products or services are created, stored, and distributed

Facilities are the physical locations where products or services are created, stored, and distributed. Major decisions pertain to facilities location and facilities layout.

Location   **Location** is the physical positioning or geographic site of facilities; it must be determined by the needs and requirements of the organization. A company that relies heavily on railroads for transportation needs to be located close to rail facilities. GE decided that it did not need six plants to make circuit breakers, so it invested heavily in automating one plant and closed the other five. Different organizations in the same industry may have different facilities requirements. Benetton uses only one distribution center for the entire world, whereas Wal-Mart has several distribution centers in the United States alone. A retail business must choose its location very carefully to be convenient for consumers.

Layout The choice of physical configuration, or the *layout*, of facilities is closely related to other operations decisions. The three entirely different layout alternatives shown in Figure 15.1 help demonstrate the importance of the layout decision. A *product layout* is appropriate when large quantities of a single product are needed. It makes sense to custom-design a straight-line flow of work for a product when a specific task is performed at each workstation as each unit flows past. Most assembly lines use this format. For example, Dell's personal computer factories use a product layout.

Process layouts are used in operations settings that create or process a variety of products. Auto repair shops and healthcare clinics are good examples. Each car and each person is a separate "product." The needs of each incoming job are diagnosed as it enters the operations system, and the job is routed through the unique sequence of workstations needed to create the desired finished product. In a process layout, each type of conversion task is centralized in a single workstation or department. All welding is done in one designated shop location, and any car that requires welding is moved to that area. This setup is in contrast to the product layout, in which several different workstations may perform welding operations if

location	The physical positioning or geographic site of facilities

layout	The physical configuration of facilities, the arrangement of equipment within facilities, or both

product layout	A physical configuration of facilities arranged around the product; used when large quantities of a single product are needed

process layout	A physical configuration of facilities arranged around the process; used in facilities that create or process a variety of products

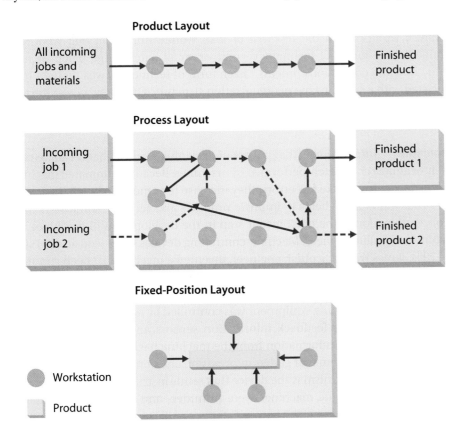

Product Layout

Process Layout

Fixed-Position Layout

● Workstation

▢ Product

Figure 15.1

APPROACHES TO FACILITIES LAYOUT

When a manufacturer produces large quantities of a product (such as cars or computers), it may arrange its facilities in an assembly line (product layout). In a process layout, the work (such as patients in a hospital or custom pieces of furniture) moves through various workstations. Locomotives and bridges are both manufactured in a fixed-position layout.

the conversion task sequence so dictates. Similarly, in a hospital, all X-rays are done in one location, all surgeries in another, and all physical therapy in yet another. Patients are moved from location to location to get the services they need.

The ***fixed-position layout*** is used when the organization is creating a few very large and complex products. Aircraft manufacturers like Boeing and shipbuilders like Newport News use this method. An assembly line capable of moving one of Boeing's new 787 aircraft would require an enormous plant, so instead the airplane itself remains stationary, and people and machines move around it as it is assembled.

The cellular layout is a relatively new approach to facilities design. ***Cellular layouts*** are used when families of products can follow similar flow paths. A clothing manufacturer, for example, might create a cell, or designated area, dedicated to making a family of pockets, such as pockets for shirts, coats, blouses, and slacks. Although each kind of pocket is unique, the same basic equipment and methods are used to make all of them. Hence, all pockets might be made in the same area and then delivered directly to different product layout assembly areas where the shirts, coats, blouses, and slacks are actually being assembled.

Organizational Technologies

One central element of effective operations management is technology. In Chapter 6 we defined ***technology*** as the set of processes and systems used by organizations to convert resources into products or services.

Manufacturing Technology

Numerous forms of manufacturing technology are used in organizations. In Chapter 6 we discussed the research of Joan Woodward. Recall that Woodward identified three forms of technology—unit or small batch, large batch or mass production, and continuous process.[6] Each form of technology was thought to be associated with a specific type of organization structure. Of course, newer forms of technology not considered by Woodward also warrant attention. Two of these are automation and computer-assisted manufacturing.

Automation   ***Automation*** is the process of designing work so that it can be completely or almost completely performed by machines. Because automated machines operate quickly and make few errors, they increase the amount of work that can be done. Thus automation helps to improve products and services, and fosters innovation. Automation is the most recent step in the development of machines and machine-controlling devices. Machine-controlling devices have been around since the 1700s. James Watt, a Scottish engineer, invented a mechanical speed control to regulate the speed of steam engines in 1787. The Jacquard loom, developed by a French inventor, was controlled by paper cards with holes punched in them. Early accounting and computing equipment was controlled by similar punched cards.

Automation relies on feedback, information, sensors, and a control mechanism. Feedback is the flow of information from the machine back to the sensor. Sensors are the parts of the system that gather information and compare it to preset standards. The control mechanism is the device that sends instructions to the automatic machine. Early automatic machines were primitive, and the use of automation was relatively slow to develop. These elements are illustrated by the example in

---

fixed-position layout
A physical configuration of facilities arranged around a single work area; used for the manufacture of large and complex products such as airplanes

cellular layout
A physical configuration of facilities used when families of products can follow similar flow paths

technology
The set of processes and systems used by organizations to convert resources into products or services

automation
The process of designing work so that it can be completely or almost completely performed by machines

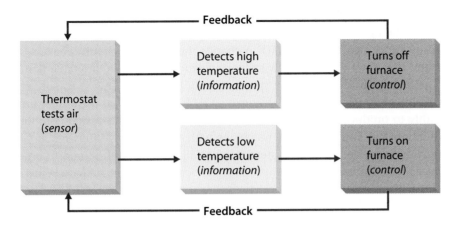

Figure 15.2

A SIMPLE AUTOMATIC CONTROL MECHANISM

All automation includes feedback, information, sensors, and a control mechanism. A simple thermostat is an example of automation. Another example is Benetton's distribution center in Italy. Orders are received, items pulled from stock and packaged for shipment, and invoices prepared and transmitted, with no human intervention.

Figure 15.2. A thermostat has sensors that monitor air temperature and compare it to a preset low value. If the air temperature falls below the preset value, the thermostat sends an electrical signal to the furnace, turning it on. The furnace heats the air. When the sensors detect that the air temperature has reached a value higher than the low preset value, the thermostat stops the furnace. The last step (shutting off the furnace) is known as *feedback*, a critical component of any automated operation.

The big move to automate factories began during World War II. The shortage of skilled workers and the development of high-speed computers combined to bring about a tremendous interest in automation. Programmable automation (the use of computers to control machines) was introduced during this era, far outstripping conventional automation (the use of mechanical or electromechanical devices to control machines). The automobile industry began to use automatic machines for a variety of jobs. In fact, the term *automation* came into use in the 1950s in the automobile industry. The chemical and oil-refining industries also began to use computers to regulate production. During the 1990s, automation became a major element in the manufacture of computers and computer components, such as electronic chips and circuits. It is this computerized, or programmable, automation that presents the greatest opportunities and challenges for management today.

The impact of automation on people in the workplace is complex. In the short term, people whose jobs are automated may find themselves without a job. In the long term, however, more jobs are created than are lost. Nevertheless, not all companies are able to help displaced workers find new jobs, so the human costs are sometimes high. In the coal industry, for instance, automation has been used primarily in mining. The output per miner has risen dramatically from the 1950s on. The demand for coal, however, has decreased, and productivity gains resulting from automation have lessened the need for miners. Consequently, many workers have lost their jobs, and the industry has not been able to absorb them. In contrast, in the electronics industry, the rising demand for products has led to increasing employment opportunities despite the use of automation.[7]

Computer-Assisted Manufacturing Current extensions of automation generally revolve around computer-assisted manufacturing. ***Computer-assisted manufacturing*** is technology that relies on computers to design or manufacture products. One type of computer-assisted manufacturing is *computer-aided design (CAD)*—the use of computers to design parts and complete products and to simulate performance

computer-assisted manufacturing
A technology that relies on computers to design or manufacture products

so that prototypes need not be constructed. Boeing uses CAD technology to study hydraulic tubing in its commercial aircraft. Japan's automotive industry uses it to speed up car design. GE used CAD to change the design of circuit breakers, and Benetton uses CAD to design new styles and products. Oneida, the table flatware firm, used CAD to design a new spoon in only two days.[8] CAD is usually combined with *computer-aided manufacturing (CAM)* to ensure that the design moves smoothly to production. The production computer shares the design computer's information and is able to have machines with the proper settings ready when production is needed. A CAM system is especially useful when reorders come in because the computer can quickly produce the desired product, prepare labels and copies of orders, and send the product out to where it is wanted.

Closely aligned with this approach is *computer-integrated manufacturing (CIM)*. In CIM, CAD and CAM are linked together, and computer networks automatically adjust machine placements and settings to enhance both the complexity and the flexibility of scheduling. In settings that use these technologies, all manufacturing activities are controlled by the computer network. Because the network can access the company's other information systems, CIM is both a powerful and a complex management control tool.

Flexible manufacturing systems (FMS) usually have robotic work units or workstations, assembly lines, and robotic carts or some other form of computer-controlled transport system to move material as needed from one part of the system to another. FMS like the one at IBM's manufacturing facility in Lexington, Kentucky, rely on computers to coordinate and integrate automated production and materials-handling facilities. And Ford Motor Company used FMS to transform an English factory producing low-cost Ford products into a Jaguar plant making Jaguar luxury cars. Using traditional methods, the plant would have been closed, its workers laid off, and the facility virtually rebuilt from the ground up. But by using FMS, Ford was able to keep the plant open and running continuously while new equipment was being installed and its workers were being retrained in small groups.[9]

These systems are not without disadvantages, however. For example, because they represent fundamental change, they also generate resistance. Additionally, because of their tremendous complexity, CAD systems are not always reliable. CIM systems are so expensive that they raise the break-even point for firms using them. This means that the firm must operate at high levels of production and sales to be able to afford the systems.

Robotics   Another trend in manufacturing technology is computerized robotics. A **robot** is any artificial device that is able to perform functions ordinarily thought to be appropriate for human beings. Robotics refers to the science and technology of the construction, maintenance, and use of robots. The use of industrial robots has steadily increased since 1980 and is expected to continue to increase slowly as more companies recognize the benefits that accrue to users of industrial robots.[10]

Welding was one of the first applications for robots, and it continues to be the area for most applications. A close second is materials handling. Other applications include machine loading and unloading, painting and finishing, assembly, casting, and such machining applications as cutting, grinding, polishing, drilling, sanding, buffing, and deburring. DaimlerChrysler, for instance, replaced about 200 welders with 50 robots on an assembly line and increased productivity about 20 percent. The use of robots in inspection work is increasing. They can check for

robot
Any artificial device that is able to perform functions ordinarily thought to be appropriate for human beings

cracks and holes, and they can be equipped with vision systems to perform visual inspections.

Robots are also beginning to move from the factory floor to all manner of other applications. The Dallas police used a robot to apprehend a suspect who had barricaded himself in an apartment building. The robot smashed a window and reached with its mechanical arm into the building. The suspect panicked and ran outside. At the Long Beach Memorial Hospital in California, brain surgeons are assisted by a robot arm that drills into the patient's skull with excellent precision. Some newer applications involve remote work. For example, the use of robot submersibles controlled from the surface can help divers in remote locations. Surveillance robots fitted with microwave sensors can do things that a human guard cannot do, such as "seeing" through nonmetallic walls and in the dark. In other applications, automated farming (called "agrimation") uses robot harvesters to pick fruit from a variety of trees.

Robots are also used by small manufacturers. One robot slices carpeting to fit the inside of custom vans in an upholstery shop. Another stretches balloons flat so that they can be spray-painted with slogans at a novelties company. At a jewelry company, a robot holds class rings while they are engraved by a laser. These robots are lighter, faster, stronger, and more intelligent than those used in heavy manufacturing and are the types that more and more organizations will be using in the future.

Service Technology

Service technology is also changing rapidly. And it, too, is moving more and more toward automated systems and procedures. In banking, for example, new technological breakthroughs led to automated teller machines and made it much easier to move funds between accounts or between different banks. Many people now have their paycheck deposited directly into a checking account from which many of their bills are then automatically paid. And credit card transactions by Visa customers are recorded and billed electronically.

Hotels use increasingly sophisticated technology to accept and record room reservations. Universities use new technologies to electronically store and provide access to books, scientific journals, government reports, and articles. Hospitals and other healthcare organizations use new forms of service technology to manage patient records, dispatch ambulances and EMTs, and monitor patients' vital signs. Restaurants use technology to record and fill customer orders, order food and supplies, and prepare food. Given the increased role that service organizations are playing in today's economy, even more technological innovations are certain to be developed in the years to come.[11]

Implementing Operations Systems Through Supply Chain Management

After operations systems have been properly designed and technologies developed, they must then be put into use by the organization. Their basic functional purpose is to control transformation processes to ensure that relevant goals are achieved in such areas as quality and costs. Operations management has a number of special purposes within this control framework, including purchasing and inventory management. Indeed, this area of management has become so important in recent years that a new term—*supply chain management*—has been coined. Specifically, **supply chain management** can be defined as the process of managing operations control, resource acquisition and purchasing, and inventory so as to improve overall efficiency and effectiveness.[12]

supply chain management
The process of managing operations control, resource acquisition, and inventory so as to improve overall efficiency and effectiveness

Operations Management as Control

One way of using operations management as control is to coordinate it with other functions. Monsanto Company, for example, established a consumer products division that produces and distributes fertilizers and lawn chemicals. To facilitate control, the operations function was organized as an autonomous profit center. Monsanto finds this effective because its manufacturing division is given the authority to determine not only the costs of creating the product but also the product price and the marketing program.

In terms of overall organizational control, a division like the one used by Monsanto should be held accountable only for the activities over which it has decision-making authority. It would be inappropriate, of course, to make operations accountable for profitability in an organization that stresses sales and market share over quality and productivity. Misplaced accountability results in ineffective organizational control, to say nothing of hostility and conflict. Depending on the strategic role of operations, then, operations managers are accountable for different kinds of results. For example, in an organization using bureaucratic control, accountability will be spelled out in rules and regulations. In a decentralized system, it is likely to be understood and accepted by everyone.

Within operations, managerial control ensures that resources and activities achieve primary goals such as a high percentage of on-time deliveries, low unit-production cost, or high product reliability. Any control system should focus on the elements that are most crucial to goal attainment. For example, firms in which product quality is a major concern (as it is at Rolex) might adopt a screening control system to monitor the product as it is being created. If quantity is a higher priority (as it is at Timex), a postaction system might be used to identify defects at the end of the system without disrupting the manufacturing process itself.

Purchasing Management

purchasing management
Buying materials and resources needed to create products and services

Purchasing management, also called *procurement,* is concerned with buying the materials and resources needed to create products and services. In many ways, purchasing is at the very heart of effective supply chain management. The purchasing manager for a retailer like Sears, Roebuck is responsible for buying the merchandise the store will sell. The purchasing manager for a manufacturer buys raw materials, parts, and machines needed by the organization. Large companies like GE, IBM, and Siemens have large purchasing departments.[13] The manager responsible for purchasing must balance a number of constraints. Buying too much ties up capital and increases storage costs. Buying too little might lead to shortages and high reordering costs. The manager must also make sure that the quality of what is purchased meets the organization's needs, that the supplier is reliable, and that the best financial terms are negotiated.

Many firms have recently changed their approaches to purchasing as a means to lower costs and improve quality and productivity. In particular, rather than relying on hundreds or even thousands of suppliers, many companies are reducing their number of suppliers and negotiating special production-delivery arrangements.[14] For example, the Honda plant in Marysville, Ohio, found a local business owner looking for a new opportunity. They negotiated an agreement whereby he would start a new company to mount car stereo speakers into plastic moldings. He delivers finished goods to the plant three times a day, and Honda buys all he can manufacture. Thus he has a stable sales base, Honda has a local and reliable supplier, and both companies benefit.

Inventory Management

Inventory control, also called *materials control*, is essential for effective operations management. The four basic kinds of inventories are *raw materials, work-in-process, finished-goods*, and *in-transit* inventories. As shown in Table 15.1, the sources of control over these inventories are as different as their purposes. Work-in-process inventories, for example, are made up of partially completed products that need further processing; they are controlled by the shop-floor system. In contrast, the quantities and costs of finished-goods inventories are under the control of the overall production scheduling system, which is determined by high-level planning decisions. In-transit inventories are controlled by the transportation and distribution systems.

Like most other areas of operations management, inventory management changed notably in recent years. One particularly important breakthrough is the ***just-in-time (JIT) method***. First popularized by the Japanese, the JIT system reduces the organization's investment in storage space for raw materials and in the materials themselves. Historically, manufacturers built large storage areas and filled them with materials, parts, and supplies that would be needed days, weeks, and even months in the future. A manager using the JIT approach orders materials and parts more often and in smaller quantities, thereby reducing investment in both storage space and actual inventory. The ideal arrangement is for materials to arrive just as they are needed—or just in time.[15]

Recall our example about the small firm that assembles stereo speakers for Honda and delivers them three times a day, making it unnecessary for Honda to carry large

> **inventory control**
> Managing the organization's raw materials, work in process, finished goods, and products in transit

> **just-in-time (JIT) method**
> An inventory system that has necessary materials arriving as soon as they are needed (just in time) so that the production process is not interrupted

Type	Purpose	Source of Control
Raw materials	Provide the materials needed to make the product	Purchasing models and systems
Work in process	Enable overall production to be divided into stages of manageable size	Shop-floor control systems
Finished goods	Provide ready supply of products on customer demand and enable long, efficient production runs	High-level production scheduling systems in conjunction with marketing
In transit (pipeline)	Distribute products to customers	Transportation and distribution control systems

Table 15.1

INVENTORY TYPES, PURPOSES, AND SOURCES OF CONTROL

JIT is a recent breakthrough in inventory management. With JIT inventory systems, materials arrive just as they are needed. JIT therefore helps an organization control its raw materials inventory by reducing the amount of space it must devote to storage.

quantities of the speakers in inventory. In an even more striking example, Johnson Controls makes automobile seats for DaimlerChrysler and ships them by small truckloads to a DaimlerChrysler plant 75 miles away. Each shipment is scheduled to arrive two hours before it is needed. Clearly, the JIT approach requires high levels of coordination and cooperation between the company and its suppliers. If shipments arrive too early, DaimlerChrysler has no place to store them. If they arrive too late, the entire assembly line may have to be shut down, resulting in enormous expense. When properly designed and used, the JIT method controls inventory very effectively.

Managing Total Quality

Quality and productivity have become major determinants of business success or failure today and are central issues in managing organizations.[16] But, as we will see, achieving higher levels of quality is not an easy accomplishment. Simply ordering that quality be improved is about as effective as waving a magic wand.[17] The catalyst for its emergence as a mainstream management concern was foreign business, especially Japanese. And nowhere was it more visible than in the auto industry. During a major gasoline shortage in the late 1970s, many people bought Toyotas, Hondas, and Nissans because they were more fuel-efficient than U.S. cars. Consumers soon found, however, that not only were the Japanese cars more fuel-efficient, they were also of higher quality than U.S. cars. Parts fit together better, the trim work was neater, and the cars were more reliable. Thus, after the energy crisis subsided, Japanese cars remained formidable competitors because of their reputation for quality.

The Meaning of Quality

quality
The totality of features and characteristics of a product or service that bear on its ability to satisfy stated or implied needs

The American Society for Quality Control defines **quality** as the totality of features and characteristics of a product or service that bear on its ability to satisfy stated or implied needs.[18] Quality has several different attributes. Table 15.2 lists eight basic dimensions that determine the quality of a particular product or service. For example, a product that has durability and is reliable is of higher quality than a product with less durability and reliability.

Quality is also relative. For example, a Lincoln is a higher-grade car than a Mercury Marquis, which, in turn, is a higher-grade car than a Ford Focus.

Table 15.2
EIGHT DIMENSIONS OF QUALITY

These eight dimensions generally capture the meaning of quality, which is a critically important ingredient to organizational success today. Understanding the basic meaning of quality is a good first step to managing it more effectively.

Source: Reprinted by permission of *Harvard Business Review.* Exhibit from "Competing on the Eight Dimensions of Quality," by David A. Garvin, November/ December 1987. Copyright © 1987 by the Harvard Business School Publishing Corporation; all rights reserved.

1. *Performance.* A product's primary operating characteristic; examples are an automobile's acceleration and a television's picture clarity
2. *Features.* Supplements to a product's basic functioning characteristics, such as power windows on a car
3. *Reliability.* A probability of not malfunctioning during a specified period
4. *Conformance.* The degree to which a product's design and operating characteristics meet established standards
5. *Durability.* A measure of product life
6. *Serviceability.* The speed and ease of repair
7. *Aesthetics.* How a product looks, feels, tastes, and smells
8. *Perceived quality.* As seen by a customer

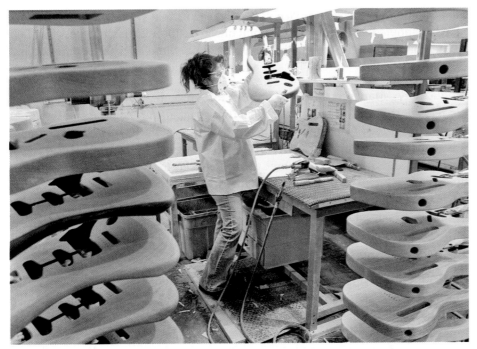

Quality is the hallmark of many successful businesses. Take the venerable Fender guitar, for example. Managers at Fender Musical Instruments go to great lengths to acquire just the right materials, meld them into just the right shapes and designs, and then painstakingly turn them into truly fine musical instruments. Rosa Aguilar is shown here hand sanding a guitar body at the Fender plant in Corona, California. While some other musical instrument manufacturers have automated many of their processes, Fender still relies on skilled hand work to turn out its guitars.

The difference in quality stems from differences in design and other features. The Focus, however, is considered a high-quality car relative to its engineering specifications and price. Likewise, the Marquis and Lincoln may also be high-quality cars, given their standards and prices. Thus quality is both an absolute and a relative concept.

Quality is relevant for both products and services. Although its importance for products like cars and computers was perhaps recognized first, service firms ranging from airlines to restaurants have also come to see that quality is a vitally important determinant of their success or failure. Service quality, as we will discuss later in this chapter, has thus also become a major competitive issue in U.S. industry today.[19]

The Importance of Quality

To help underscore the importance of quality, the U.S. government created the **Malcolm Baldrige Award**, named after the former secretary of commerce who championed quality in U.S. industry. The award, administered by an agency of the Commerce Department, is given annually to firms that achieve major improvements in the quality of their products or services. In other words, the award is based on changes in quality, as opposed to absolute quality. In addition, numerous other quality awards have been created. For example, the Rochester Institute of Technology and *USA Today* award their Quality Cup award not to entire organizations but to individual teams of workers within organizations. Quality is also an important concern for individual managers and organizations for three very specific reasons: competition, productivity, and costs.[20]

Malcolm Baldrige Award
Named after a former secretary of commerce, this prestigious award is given to firms that achieve major quality improvements

Competition Quality has become one of the most competitive points in business today. Ford, DaimlerChrysler, General Motors, and Toyota, for example, each implies that its cars and trucks are higher in quality than the cars and trucks of the others. And American, United, and Continental Airlines each claims that it provides the best and most reliable service. Indeed, it seems that virtually every U.S. business has adopted quality as a major point of competition. Thus a business that fails to keep pace may find itself falling behind not only foreign competition but also other U.S. firms.[21]

Productivity   Managers have also come to recognize that quality and productivity are related. In the past, many managers thought that they could increase output (productivity) only by decreasing quality. Managers today have learned the hard way that such an assumption is almost always wrong. If a firm installs a meaningful quality enhancement program, three things are likely to result. First, the number of defects is likely to decrease, causing fewer returns from customers. Second, because the number of defects goes down, resources (materials and people) dedicated to reworking flawed output will be decreased. Third, because making employees responsible for quality reduces the need for quality inspectors, the organization is able to produce more units with fewer resources.

Costs   Improved quality also lowers costs. Poor quality results in higher returns from customers, high warranty costs, and lawsuits from customers injured by faulty products. Future sales are lost because of disgruntled customers. An organization with quality problems often has to increase inspection expenses just to catch defective products. We noted in Chapter 14, for example, how at one point Whistler Corporation was using 40 percent of its workforce just to fix poorly assembled radar detectors made by the other 60 percent.[22]

Total Quality Management

Once an organization makes a decision to enhance the quality of its products and services, it must then decide how to implement this decision. The most pervasive approach to managing quality has been called ***total quality management***, or ***TQM*** (sometimes called ***quality assurance***)—a real and meaningful effort by an organization to change its whole approach to business in order to make quality a guiding factor in everything the organization does.[23]

Figure 15.3 highlights the major ingredients in TQM.

Strategic Commitment   The starting point for TQM is a strategic commitment by top management. Such commitment is important for several reasons. First, the organizational culture must change to recognize that quality is not just an ideal but an objective goal that must be pursued.[24] Second, a decision to pursue the goal of quality carries with it some real costs—for expenditures such as new

total quality management (TQM) (quality assurance) A strategic commitment by top management to change its whole approach to business in order to make quality a guiding factor in everything it does

Figure 15.3
TOTAL QUALITY MANAGEMENT

Quality is one of the most important issues facing organizations today. Total quality management, or TQM, is a comprehensive effort to enhance an organization's product or service quality. TQM involves the five basic dimensions shown here. Each is important and must be addressed effectively if the organization expects to truly increase quality.

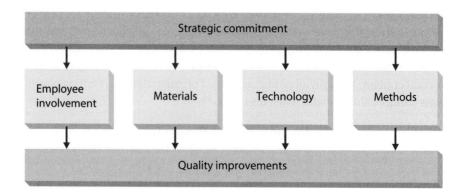

equipment and facilities. Thus, without a commitment from top management, quality improvement will prove to be just a slogan or gimmick, with little or no real change. Just a few years ago Porsche had the lowest reliability of any automobile maker in the world. But a major commitment from top management helped turn the company around. By paying more attention to consumer preferences and using the other methods described in this section, Porsche shot to the top of global automobile reliability.[25]

Employee Involvement   Employee involvement is another critical ingredient in TQM. Virtually all successful quality enhancement programs entail making the person responsible for doing the job responsible for making sure it is done right.[26] By definition, then, employee involvement is a critical component in improving quality. Work teams, discussed in Chapter 13, are common vehicles for increasing employee involvement.

Technology   New forms of technology are also useful in TQM programs. Automation and robots, for example, can often make products with higher precision and better consistency than can people. Investing in higher-grade machines capable of doing jobs more precisely and reliably often improves quality. For example, Nokia has achieved notable improvements in product quality by replacing many of its machines with new equipment. Similarly, most U.S. auto and electronics firms make regular investments in new technology to help boost quality.

Materials   Another important part of TQM is improving the quality of the materials that organizations use. Suppose that a company that assembles stereos buys chips and circuits from another company. If the chips have a high failure rate, consumers will return defective stereos to the company whose nameplate appears on them, not to the company that made the chips. The stereo firm then loses in two ways: refunds to customers and damage to its reputation. As a result, many firms have increased the quality requirements they impose on their suppliers as a way of improving the quality of their own products.

Methods   Improved methods can improve product and service quality. Methods are operating systems used by the organization during the actual transformation process. American Express Company, for example, has found ways to cut its approval time for new credit cards from 22 to only 2 days. This results in improved service quality.

TQM Tools and Techniques

Beyond the strategic context of quality, managers can rely also on several specific tools and techniques for improving quality. Among the most popular today are value-added analysis, benchmarking, outsourcing, reducing cycle times, ISO 9000:2000 and ISO 14000, statistical quality control, and Six Sigma.

Value-Added Analysis   *Value-added analysis* is the comprehensive evaluation of all work activities, materials flows, and paperwork to determine the value that they add for customers. Such an analysis often reveals wasteful or unnecessary activities that can be eliminated without jeopardizing customer service. For example, during a value-added analysis, Hewlett-Packard determined that its contracts were unnecessarily long, confusing, and hard to understand. The firm subsequently cut

value-added analysis
The comprehensive evaluation of all work activities, materials flows, and paperwork to determine the value that they add for customers

Effective total quality management requires major commitments from an organization. Thorough and rigorous quality checks and inspections are often a fundamental part of quality management. But managers who pay only lip service to inspections, such as the managers illustrated here checking water quality, should not be surprised later when they discover major quality problems throughout their organization. Only by using objective and rigorous statistical quality control measures can the firm be assured of bringing high-quality products and services to the marketplace.

INSPECTION-ON-A-SHOESTRING

Looks pretty clean!

Seems A·OK to me!

I don't have a problem with it!

© 2007 Ros Chast from cartoonbank.com. All Rights Reserved.

its standard contract form down from 20 to 2 pages and experienced an 18 percent increase in its computer sales.

benchmarking
The process of learning how other firms do things in an exceptionally high-quality manner

Benchmarking *Benchmarking* is the process of learning how other firms do things in an exceptionally high-quality manner. Some approaches to benchmarking are simple and straightforward. For example, Xerox routinely buys copiers made by other firms and takes them apart to see how they work. This enables the firm to stay abreast of improvements and changes its competitors are using. When Ford was planning the newest version of the Taurus, it identified the 400 features customers identified as being most important to them. It then found the competing cars that did the best job on each feature. Ford's goal was to equal or surpass each of its competitors on those 400 features. Other benchmarking strategies are more indirect. For example, many firms study how L.L. Bean manages its mail-order business, how Disney recruits and trains employees, and how FedEx tracks packages for applications they can employ in their own businesses.[27]

outsourcing
Subcontracting services and operations to other firms that can perform them more cheaply or better

Outsourcing Another innovation for improving quality is outsourcing. *Outsourcing* is the process of subcontracting services and operations to other firms that can perform them more cheaply or better. If a business performs each and every one of its own administrative and business services and operations, it is almost certain to be doing at least some of them in an inefficient or low-quality manner. If those areas can be identified and outsourced, the firm will save money and realize a higher-quality

Eye on Management

Outsourcing

This set of three videos discusses the possibility of outsourcing technical support for a software company. A manager listens and asks questions of two of her subordinates. One of the subordinates is in favor of outsourcing. He cites lower costs, more hours of support, and the fact that the company's competitors are using outsourced support. The other subordinate is in not in favor of outsourcing. To support her position, she cites concerns about lower morale and higher turnover if jobs are cut in tech support. She feels that using the people they already have in a more effective fashion would lower costs too.

For her part, the manager is concerned that the technical support personnel are not very productive, that they aren't staffed in a way that meets customer peak demand times, and that they are not keeping their skills up to date. She believes that effectiveness is more important than cost efficiency and doesn't want service quality to suffer.

View the first video. This six-minute clip presents viewpoints but does not resolve the outsourcing issue. Then answer the following questions individually or as a class.

1. Do you agree with the reasons given by the workers in support of outsourcing and against outsourcing? Explain.

2. Have the three individuals mentioned all of the important aspects, both positive and negative, of outsourcing? Are there benefits or disadvantages that they have overlooked?

3. In your opinion, should the company use outsourcing? Justify your answer.

The second video, a four-minute clip, follows up on the first video. It presents the outcome that results when the company chooses to outsource technical support. The third video, a five-minute clip, presents an alternate follow up to the first video. It presents the outcome that results when the company chooses *not* to outsource technical support. View these two videos and then answer the following questions individually or as a class.

4. Do you think that the situations presented in these two videos are likely responses to a company that begins to use outsourcing (second video) or rejects the use of outsourcing (third video)? Explain why or why not.

5. There is no final answer to the concerns presented in these videos. Yet it's important to look ahead. What is your immediate recommendation for this company? What is the likely outcome of your recommendation?

6. What actions do you see the company taking in the midterm, for example over the next three to five years?

---

service or operation.[28] For example, until recently Eastman Kodak handled all of its own computing operations. Now, however, those operations are subcontracted to IBM, which handles all of Kodak's computing. The result is higher-quality computing systems and operations at Kodak for less money than it was spending before. Firms must be careful in their outsourcing decisions, though, because service or delivery problems can lead to major complications. Boeing's new 787 aircraft, for example, has been running several months behind schedule because the firms to which Boeing has outsourced some of its production have been running late.[29]

Reducing Cycle Time Another popular TQM technique is reducing cycle time. *Cycle time* is the time needed by the organization to develop, make, and distribute products or services.[30] If a business can reduce its cycle time, quality will often improve. A good illustration of the power of cycle time reduction comes from General Electric. At one point the firm needed six plants and three weeks to produce and deliver custom-made industrial circuit breaker boxes. By analyzing and

> **cycle time**
> The time needed by the organization to accomplish activities such as developing, making, and distributing products or services

Table 15.3

GUIDELINES FOR INCREASING THE
SPEED OF OPERATIONS

*Many organizations today are using
speed for competitive advantage.
Listed in the table are six common
guidelines that organizations follow
when they want to shorten the time
they need to get things accomplished.
Although not every manager can do
each of these things, most managers
can do at least some of them.*

Source: From *Fortune*, February 13,
1989. Copyright © 1989 Time, Inc.
All rights reserved.

1. *Start from scratch.* It is usually easier than trying to do what the organization does now faster.

2. *Minimize the number of approvals needed to do something.* The fewer people who have to approve something, the faster approval will get done.

3. *Use work teams as a basis for organization.* Teamwork and cooperation work better than individual effort and conflict.

4. *Develop and adhere to a schedule.* A properly designed schedule can greatly increase speed.

5. *Do not ignore distribution.* Making something faster is only part of the battle.

6. *Integrate speed into the organization's culture.* If everyone understands the importance of speed, things will naturally get done more quickly.

reducing cycle time, the same product can now be delivered in three days, and only a single plant is involved. Table 15.3 identifies a number of basic suggestions that have helped companies reduce the cycle time of their operations. For example, GE found it better to start from scratch with a remodeled plant. GE also wiped out the need for approvals by eliminating most managerial positions and set up teams as a basis for organizing work. Stressing the importance of the schedule helped Motorola build a new plant and start production of a new product in only 18 months. Nokia used to need 12 to 18 months to design new cell phone models, but can do it now in six months.[31]

ISO 9000:2000
A set of quality standards created
by the International Organization
for Standardization and revised
in 2000

ISO 9000:2000 and ISO 14000   Still another useful technique for improving quality is ISO 9000. ***ISO 9000:2000*** refers to a set of quality standards created by the International Organization for Standardization; the standards were revised and updated in 2000. These standards cover such areas as product testing, employee training, record keeping, supplier relations, and repair polices and procedures. Firms that want to meet these standards apply for certification and are audited by a firm chosen by the organization's domestic affiliate (in the United States, this is the American National Standards Institute). These auditors review every aspect of the firm's business operations in relation to the standards. Many firms report that merely preparing for an ISO 9000 audit has been helpful. Many firms today, including General Electric, DuPont, Eastman Kodak, British Telecom, and Philips Electronics are urging—or in some cases requiring—that their suppliers achieve ISO 9000 certification.[32] All told, more than 140 countries have adopted ISO 9000 as a national standard, and more than 400,000 certificates of compliance have been issued. ***ISO 14000*** is an extension of the same concept to environmental performance. Specifically, ISO 14000 requires that firms document how they are using raw materials more efficiently, managing pollution, and reducing their impact on the environment.

ISO 14000
A set of standards for
environmental performance

**statistical quality control
(SQC)**
A set of specific statistical
techniques that can be used
to monitor quality; includes
acceptance sampling and in-
process sampling

Statistical Quality Control   Another quality control technique is ***statistical quality control (SQC)***. As the term suggests, SQC is concerned primarily with managing quality.[33] Moreover, it is a set of specific statistical techniques that can be used to monitor quality. *Acceptance sampling* involves sampling finished goods to ensure that quality standards have been met. Acceptance sampling is effective only when the correct percentage of products that should be tested (for example, 2, 5, or 25 percent) is determined. This decision is especially important when the test renders the product useless. Batteries, wine, and collapsible steering wheels, for example, are consumed or destroyed during testing. Another SQC method is *in-process* *sampling.* In-process sampling involves evaluating products during production so that needed changes can be made. The painting department of a furniture company might periodically check the tint of the paint it is using. The company can then adjust the color as necessary to conform to customer standards. The advantage of in-process sampling is that it allows problems to be detected before they accumulate.

Six Sigma   Six Sigma was developed in the 1980s for Motorola. The tool can be used by manufacturing or service organizations. The Six Sigma method tries to eliminate mistakes. Although firms rarely obtain Six Sigma quality, it does provide a challenging target. *Sigma* refers to a standard deviation, so a Six Sigma defect rate is 6 standard deviations above the mean rate; 1 sigma quality would produce 690,000 errors per million items. Three sigmas is challenging—66,000 errors per million. Six Sigma is obtained when a firm produces a mere 3.4 mistakes per million. Implementing Six Sigma requires making corrections until errors virtually disappear. At GE, the technique has saved the firm $8 billion in three years. GE is now teaching its customers, including Wal-Mart and Dell, about the approach.

Managing Productivity

Although the current focus on quality by U.S. companies is a relatively recent phenomenon, managers have been aware of the importance of productivity for several years. The stimulus for this attention was a recognition that the gap between productivity in the United States and productivity in other industrialized countries was narrowing. This section describes the meaning of productivity and underscores its importance. After summarizing recent productivity trends, we suggest ways that organizations can increase their productivity.

The Meaning of Productivity

In a general sense, ***productivity*** is an economic measure of efficiency that summarizes the value of outputs relative to the value of the inputs used to create them.[34] Productivity can be and often is assessed at different levels of analysis and in different forms.

> **productivity**
> An economic measure of efficiency that summarizes the value of what is produced relative to the resources used to produce it

Levels of Productivity   By level of productivity we mean the units of analysis used to calculate or define productivity. For example, *aggregate productivity* is the total level of productivity achieved by a country. *Industry productivity* is the total productivity achieved by all the firms in a particular industry. *Company productivity*, just as the term suggests, is the level of productivity achieved by an individual company. *Unit and individual productivity* refer to the productivity achieved by a unit or department within an organization and the level of productivity attained by a single person.

Forms of Productivity   There are many different forms of productivity. *Total factor productivity* is defined by the following formula:

$$\text{Productivity} = \frac{\text{Outputs}}{\text{Inputs}}$$

Total factor productivity is an overall indicator of how well an organization uses all of its resources, such as labor, capital, materials, and energy, to create all of its products and services. The biggest problem with total factor productivity is that all the ingredients must be expressed in the same terms—dollars (it is difficult to add hours of labor to number of units of a raw material in a meaningful way). Total factor productivity also gives little insight into how things can be changed to improve productivity. Consequently, most organizations find it more useful to calculate a partial productivity ratio. Such a ratio uses only one category of resource. For example, labor productivity could be calculated by this simple formula:

$$\text{Labor Productivity} = \frac{\text{Outputs}}{\text{Direct Labor}}$$

This method has two advantages. First, it is not necessary to transform the units of input into some other unit. Second, this method provides managers with specific insights into how changing different resource inputs affects productivity. Suppose that an organization can manufacture 100 units of a particular product with 20 hours of direct labor. The organization's labor productivity index is 100/20, or 5 (5 units per labor hour). Now suppose that worker efficiency is increased (through one of the ways to be discussed later in this chapter) so that the same 20 hours of labor result in the manufacture of 120 units of the product. The labor productivity index increases to 120/20, or 6 (6 units per labor hour), and the firm can see the direct results of a specific managerial action.

The Importance of Productivity

Managers consider it important that their firm maintains high levels of productivity for a variety of reasons. Firm productivity is a primary determinant of an organization's level of profitability and, ultimately, of its ability to survive. If one organization is more productive than another, it will have more products to sell at lower prices and have more profits to reinvest in other areas. Productivity also partially determines people's standard of living within a particular country. At an economic level, businesses consume resources and produce goods and services. The goods and services created within a country can be used by that country's own citizens or exported for sale in other countries. The more goods and services the businesses within a country can produce, the more goods and services the country's citizens will have. Even goods that are exported result in financial resources flowing back into the home country. Thus the citizens of a highly productive country are likely to have a notably higher standard of living than are the citizens of a country with low productivity.

Productivity Trends

The United States has one of the highest levels of productivity in the world. Sparked by gains made in other countries, however, U.S. business has begun to focus more attention on productivity.[35] Indeed, this was a primary factor in the decisions made by U.S. businesses to retrench, retool, and become more competitive in the world marketplace. For example, General Electric's dishwasher plant in Louisville cut its inventory requirements by 50 percent, reduced labor costs from 15 percent to only 10 percent of total manufacturing costs, and cut product development time in half. As a result of these kinds of efforts, productivity trends have now leveled out, and U.S. workers are generally maintaining their lead in most industries.[36]

One important factor that has hurt U.S. productivity indices has been the tremendous growth of the service sector in the United States. Although this sector

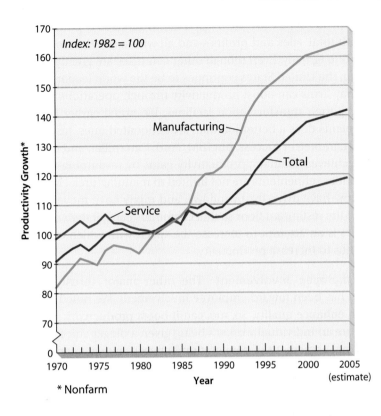

Figure 15.4

MANUFACTURING AND SERVICE PRODUCTIVITY GROWTH TRENDS

Both manufacturing productivity and service productivity in the United States continue to grow, although manufacturing productivity is growing at a faster pace. Total productivity, therefore, also continues to grow.

Source: U.S. Bureau of Labor Statistics.

grew, its productivity levels did not. One part of this problem relates to measurement. For example, it is fairly easy to calculate the number of tons of steel produced at a steel mill and divide it by the number of labor hours used; it is more difficult to determine the output of an attorney or a certified public accountant. Still, virtually everyone agrees that improving service sector productivity is the next major hurdle facing U.S. business.[37]

Figure 15.4 illustrates manufacturing productivity growth since 1970 in terms of annual average percentage of increase. As you can see, that growth slowed during the 1970s but began to rise again in the late 1980s. Some experts believe that productivity in both the United States and abroad will continue to improve at even more impressive rates. Their confidence rests on technology's potential ability to improve operations.

Improving Productivity

How does a business or industry improve its productivity? Numerous specific suggestions made by experts generally fall into two broad categories: improving operations and increasing employee involvement.

Improving Operations   One way that firms can improve operations is by spending more on research and development. Research and development (R&D) spending helps identify new products, new uses for existing products, and new methods for making products. Each of these contributes to productivity. For example, Bausch & Lomb almost missed the boat on extended-wear contact lenses because the company had neglected R&D. When it became apparent that its major competitors were almost a year ahead of Bausch & Lomb in developing the new lenses, management made R&D a top priority. As a result, the company made several scientific breakthroughs, shortened the time needed to introduce new products, and greatly enhanced both total sales and profits—and all with a smaller workforce than the company used to employ. Even though other countries are greatly increasing their R&D spending, the United States continues to be the world leader in this area.

Another way firms can boost productivity through operations is by reassessing and revamping their transformation facilities. We noted earlier how one of GE's modernized plants does a better job than six antiquated ones. Just building a new factory is no guarantee of success, but IBM, Ford, Caterpillar, and many other businesses have achieved dramatic productivity gains by revamping their production facilities. Facilities refinements are not limited to manufacturers. Most McDonald's restaurants now have drive-thru windows, and many have moved soft-drink dispensers out to the restaurant floor so that customers can get their own drinks. Each of these moves is an attempt to increase the speed with which customers can be served, and thus to increase productivity.

Increasing Employee Involvement The other major thrust in productivity enhancement has been toward employee involvement. We noted earlier that participation can enhance quality. So, too, can it boost productivity. Examples of this involvement are an individual worker's being given a bigger voice in how she does her job, a formal agreement of cooperation between management and labor, and total involvement throughout the organization. GE eliminated most of the supervisors at its one new circuit breaker plant and put control in the hands of workers.

Another method popular in the United States is increasing the flexibility of an organization's workforce by training employees to perform a number of different jobs. Such cross-training allows the firm to function with fewer workers because workers can be transferred easily to areas where they are most needed. For example, at one Motorola plant, 397 of 400 employees have learned at least two skills under a similar program.

Rewards are essential to making employee involvement work. Firms must reward people for learning new skills and using them proficiently. At Motorola, for example, workers who master a new skill are assigned for five days to a job requiring them to use that skill. If they perform with no defects, they are moved to a higher pay grade, and then they move back and forth between jobs as they are needed. If there is a performance problem, they receive more training and practice. This approach is fairly new, but preliminary indicators suggest that it can increase productivity significantly. Many unions resist such programs because they threaten job security and reduce a person's identification with one skill or craft.

Summary of Key Points

1. Describe and explain the nature of operations management.
   - Operations management is the set of managerial activities that organizations use in creating their products and services.
   - Operations management is important to both manufacturing and service organizations.
   - It plays an important role in an organization's strategy.

2. Identify and discuss the components involved in designing effective operations systems.
   - The starting point in using operations management is designing appropriate operations systems.
   - Key decisions that must be made as part of operations systems design relate to product and service mix, capacity, and facilities.

3. Discuss organizational technologies and their role in operations management.

- Technology plays an important role in quality.
- Automation is especially important today.
- Numerous computer-aided manufacturing techniques are widely practiced.
- Robotics is also a growing area.
- Technology is as relevant to service organizations as to manufacturing organizations.

4. Identify and discuss the components involved in implementing operations systems through supply chain management.
   - After an operations system has been designed and put in place, it must then be implemented.
   - Major areas of interest during the use of operations systems are purchasing and inventory management.
   - Supply chain management is a comprehensive view of managing all of these activities in a more efficient manner.

5. Explain the meaning and importance of managing quality and total quality management.
   - Quality is a major consideration for all managers today.
   - Quality is important because it affects competition, productivity, and costs.
   - Total quality management is a comprehensive, organization-wide effort to enhance quality through a variety of avenues.

6. Explain the meaning and importance of managing productivity, productivity trends, and ways to improve productivity.
   - Productivity is a major concern to managers.
   - Productivity is a measure of how efficiently an organization is using its resources to create products or services.
   - The United States is a world leader in individual productivity, but firms still work to achieve productivity gains.

Discussion Questions

Questions for Review

1. What is the relationship of operations management to overall organizational strategy? Where do productivity and quality fit into that relationship?

2. Describe three basic decisions that must be addressed in the design of operations systems. For each decision, what information do managers need to make that decision?

3. What are some approaches to facilities layout? How do they differ from one another? How are they similar?

4. What is total quality management? What are the major characteristics of TQM?

5. What is productivity? Identify various levels and forms of productivity.

Questions for Analysis

6. Is operations management linked most closely to corporate-level, business-level, or functional strategies? Why or in what way?

7. "Automation is bad for the economy because machines will eventually replace almost all human workers, creating high unemployment and poverty." Do you agree or disagree? Explain your answer.

8. Some quality gurus claim that high-quality products or services are those that are error free. Others claim that high quality exists when customers' needs are satisfied. Still others claim that high-quality products or services must be innovative. Do you subscribe to one of these views? If not, how would you define quality? Explain how the choice of a quality definition affects managers' behavior.

9. How can a service organization use techniques from operations management? Give specific examples from your college or university (a provider of educational services).

10. Think of a firm that, in your opinion, provides a high-quality service or product. What attributes of the product or service give you the perception of high quality? Do you think that everyone would agree with your judgment? Why or why not?

Building Effective Communication Skills

Exercise Overview

Communication skills reflect a manager's ability to convey ideas and information to others and to receive ideas and information from others. This exercise develops your communication skills in addressing issues of quality.

Exercise Background

Assume that you are a customer service manager of a large auto parts distributor. The general manager of ABC Auto Sales, a large auto dealer and one of your best customers, wrote the following letter. It will be your task to write a letter in response.

Dear Customer Service Manager:

On the first of last month, ABC Autos submitted a purchase order to your firm. Attached to this letter is a copy of the order. Unfortunately, the parts shipment that we received from you did not contain every item on the order. Further, that fact was not noted on the packing slip that accompanied your

shipment, and ABC was charged for the full amount of the order. To resolve the problem, please send the missing items immediately. If you are unable to do so by the end of the week, please cancel the remaining items and refund the overpayment. In the future, if you ship a partial order, please notify us at that time and do not bill for items not shipped.

I look forward to your reply and a resolution to my problem.

Sincerely,

A. N. Owner, ABC Auto Sales Attachment: Purchase Order 00001

Exercise Task

1. Write an answer to this letter, assuming that you now have the parts available.

2. How would your answer differ if ABC Auto Sales were *not* a valued customer?

3. How would your answer differ if you found out that the parts were in the original shipment but had been stolen by one of your delivery personnel?

4. How would your answer differ if you found out that the owner of ABC Auto Sales made a mistake and that, in fact, the order was filled correctly by your workers?

5. Referring to your answers to the questions above, list the important components of responding effectively to a customer's quality complaint—the tone of the letter, expressing an apology, suggesting a solution, and so on. Explain how you incorporated these components into your response.

Building Effective Diagnostic Skills

Exercise Overview

As noted in the chapter, the quality of a product or service is relative to price and expectations. A manager's diagnostic skills—the ability to visualize responses to a situation—can be useful in helping to position quality relative to price and expectations.

Exercise Background

Think of a recent occasion when you purchased a tangible product—for example, clothing, electronic equipment, luggage, or professional supplies—that you subsequently came to feel was of especially high quality. Now recall another product that you evaluated as having appropriate or adequate quality, and a third that you felt had low or poor quality. Next, recall parallel experiences involving the purchase of services. Examples might include an airline, train, or bus trip; a haircut; laundry services; or an oil change for your car.

Finally, recall three experiences in which both products and services were involved. Examples might include having questions answered by someone about a product you were buying, or returning a defective or broken product for a refund or warranty repair. It might also include a meal in a restaurant or shopping for any product where you required extensive help from the sales staff. Try to recall instances in which there was a disparity between the quality of the product and that of the service (for instance, a poor-quality product accompanied by outstanding service or a high-quality product accompanied by mediocre service).

Exercise Task

Using the nine examples identified above, do the following:

1. Assess the extent to which the quality you associated with each was a function of price and of your expectations.

2. Could the quality of each be improved without greatly affecting price? If so, how?

3. Can high-quality service offset only adequate or even poor product quality? Can outstanding product quality offset only adequate or even poor-quality service?

Building Effective Conceptual Skills

Exercise Overview

A manager's conceptual skills reflect his or her ability to think in the abstract. This exercise asks you to investigate the relationship between quality and financial performance.

Exercise Background

Is there a relationship between quality and performance? Among those who believe that such as relationship exists, some think that high-quality products lead to high earnings, whereas others believe that only firms with high performance can afford to offer high quality. A third group believes that there is no relationship.

Exercise Task

1. View a list of recent winners of the Malcolm Baldrige Award for quality. (One good place to find the list is at the National Institute of Standards and Technology, at http://www.quality.nist.gov/.) Choose three firms from the list and investigate the recent financial performance of their parent company, using earnings per share (EPS) as the measure of performance.

2. Have the winners demonstrated high performance—for example, did their EPS rise?

3. If any of the winners show high performance, did the high performance come before or after the award (or both before and after)?

4. What conclusions do you make about the relationship between high performance and quality?

Skills Self-Assessment Instrument

Defining Quality and Productivity

Introduction: *Quality* is a complex term whose meaning has no doubt changed over time. The following assessment surveys your ideas about and approaches to quality.

Instructions: You will agree with some of the statements and disagree with others. In some cases, making a decision may be difficult, but you should force yourself to make a choice. Record your answers next to each statement according to the following rating scale:

Rating Scale

4 Strongly agree

3 Slightly agree

2 Somewhat disagree

1 Strongly disagree

_____ 1. Quality refers to a product's or service's ability to fulfill its primary operating characteristics, such as providing a sharp picture for a television set.

_____ 2. Quality is an absolute, measurable aspect of a product or service.

_____ 3. The concept of quality includes supplemental aspects of a product or service, such as the remote control for a television set.

_____ 4. Productivity and quality are inversely related, so that, to get one, you must sacrifice the other.

_____ 5. The concept of quality refers to the extent to which a product's design and operating characteristics conform to certain set standards.

_____ 6. Productivity refers to what is created relative to what it takes to create it.

_____ 7. Quality means that a product will not malfunction during a specified period of time.

_____ 8. Quality refers only to products; it is immeasurable for services.

_____ 9. The length of time that a product or service will function is what is known as quality.

_____ 10. Everyone uses exactly the same definition of quality.

_____ 11. Quality refers to the repair ease and speed of a product or service.

_____ 12. Being treated courteously has nothing to do with the quality of anything.

_____ 13. How a product looks, feels, tastes, or smells is what is meant by quality.

_____ 14. Price, not quality, is what determines the ultimate value of service.

_____ 15. Quality refers to what customers think of a product or service.

_____ 16. Productivity and quality cannot both increase at the same time.

Source: Adapted from Chapter 21, especially pages 473–474, in David D. Van Fleet and Tim O. Peterson, *Contemporary Management*, 3rd ed. Copyright © 1994 by Houghton Mifflin Company.
For interpretation, see Interpretations of Skills Self-Assessment Instruments in the appendix near the end of this text.

Experiential Exercise

Preparing the Fishbone Chart

Purpose: The fishbone chart is an excellent procedure for identifying possible causes of a problem. It provides you with knowledge that you can use to improve the operations of any organization. This skill exercise focuses on the *administrative management model.* It helps you develop the *monitor role* of the administrative management model. One of the skills of the monitor is the ability to analyze problems.

Introduction: Kaoru Ishikawa developed this technique in the 1960s and it is now considered to be one of the fundamental tools of quality management. Quality circles often use the fishbone "cause-and-effect" graphical technique to initiate the resolution of a group work problem. Quite often the causes are clustered in categories such as materials, methods, people, and machines.

The fishbone technique is usually accomplished in the following six steps:

1. Write the problem in the "head" of the fish (the large block).

2. Brainstorm the major causes of the problem and list them on the fish "bones."

3. Analyze each main cause and write in minor subcauses on bone subbranches.

4. Reach consensus on one or two of the major causes of the problem.

5. Explore ways to correct or remove the major causes.

6. Prepare a report or presentation explaining the proposed change.

Instructions: Your instructor will provide you with further instructions.

Source: Adapted from Burton, Gene E., *Exercises in Management,* 5th Ed. Copyright © 1996 by Houghton Mifflin Company. Used with permission.

The fishbone will look something like this:

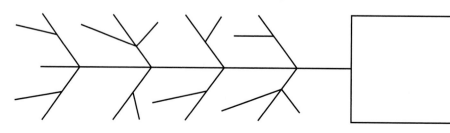

CHAPTER CLOSING CASE

E-TAILING AT AMAZON.COM

Online retailing, or e-tailing, is Amazon.com's entire business. The firm, unlike online rivals Barnes&Noble.com or Walmart.com, has no bricks-and-mortar presence. Customers interact by website, email, or phone. Yet behind the website is one of the world's largest direct-to-consumer distribution operations.

Amazon, founded in 1995 as a bookseller, has gone through many ups and downs. Early investors believed that the promise of online business outweighed the risks associated with a new type of venture, the e-tailer. Giddy expectation soon turned to disappointment because spending soared as rapidly as sales, causing profits to be nonexistent. Amazon diversified into a wide range of products, including toys, music, electronics and software, and household goods. Expansion ate into profits. Huge investments in infrastructure and IT were required before the company went into the black in 2002.

Amazon's business model, although fairly commonplace for online companies today, was revolutionary for its time. Without the need to build numerous stores in high-rent shopping areas, the company chose locations based on cost, as well as convenience to cities and airports. The company's seven distribution centers stock thousands of popular items but many of the goods are in fact "drop-shipped" directly from the manufacturer. This allows Amazon to carry a multitude of products without high inventory expense. It also can speed delivery times, eliminating one step in the distribution process.

Within Amazon's warehouses, much of the work is automated. Workers use simple, menu-driven computer programs to access and monitor customer orders. Goods are picked from the shelves and placed in a vast system of automated chutes and bins that bundles items appropriately. In the past, Amazon tried to minimize shipping expense by bundling all items for one address into one package. Now, however, they use a more effective sorting algorithm that calculates optimal package size, both to protect items and reduce costs. Automated scanners track the progress of every order. Automated boxers and labelers prepare the goods for shipping.

Software is an increasingly important part of Amazon's operations because better systems enable labor cost reductions, increase accuracy and speed, enhance the customer experience, and support effective planning. Supply chain software uses a complex formula to choose which books should be carried in the warehouse and which should be drop-shipped. Another algorithm constantly recalculates item popularity ratings, to choose which books to place in the most-frequented sections of the warehouse.

In addition, Amazon was a pioneer in the development of each of the following operations technologies.

- "One-click" purchasing allows customers to buy products with a single mouse click. Amazon patented this process and licenses it to other companies, for a fee.
- Amazon was one of the first companies to allow customers to post online product reviews. These boost sales and create a sense of community for users.
- Amazon's customers can see a customer order history, create wish lists and favorites lists, share information with friends, get personalized recommendations, receive gift-giving reminders, and tag items with customized category data.

Amazon's software is so popular with other firms that the company has launched a feature called "Amazon Web Services." Through the Internet, independent programmers and merchants gain access to Amazon's library of software, adapting it for their own use. Amazon receives no payment unless the company wants to sell through Amazon.com, in which case they collect a 15 percent commission on each sale. This service has proven so popular that 22 percent of Amazon's sales are made by other merchants.

Some companies rely on Amazon's expertise for management of their websites. Target and Office Depot contract out their online presence to Amazon. Amazon's zshops, which link business websites to Amazon's, are popular. Another initiative is "Amazon Marketplace," an online auction space for used items. The Marketplace is Amazon's attempt to catch up to online auction house eBay.

Sales grew by 34 percent in 2006, and R&D spending grew by $45 million. One of Amazon's latest products is Your Media Library, a download service that offers video, music, e-books, and software. This puts Amazon in direct competition with iTunes and other online content providers. Amazon's new technologies are young and not yet profitable, and the company may be spreading itself too thin with too many projects. But watch out! At this rate, Amazon will become the company to beat in many online industries.

CASE QUESTIONS

1. What types of decisions common to manufacturing firms are made at Amazon? What types of decisions common to service firms are made there?

2. Describe Amazon's entire supply chain. Where in the supply chain does Amazon make money? Where in the supply chain do they outsource or contract to outsiders?

3. Give example of ways in which Amazon's operations allow it to offer a high-quality shop-ping experience to customers. Give examples of ways in which operations contribute to high productivity.

CASE REFERENCES

"Amazon.com," Amazon website, www.amazon.com on May 24, 2006; Robert Hof, "Amazon's Brighter Horizon?" *BusinessWeek*, April 26, 2006, www.businessweek.com on May 24, 2006; Robert Hof, "Amazon's Costly Bells and Whistles," *BusinessWeek*, February 3, 2006, www.businessweek.com on May 24, 2006; Paul R. La Monica, "Consumers Keep on Clicking," *Money*, July 26, 2005, www.cnnmoney.com on May 24, 2006.

YOU MAKE THE CALL

Competing Through Operations

1. In your opinion, could Intel's use of Moore's Law backfire? That is, could it result in lower productivity and morale?

2. At work or at school, have you found that high expectations create motivation for you? Or do they have some other effect?

3. In your opinion, how does constant innovation benefit Intel? How does it benefit Intel's customers?

4. Would you like working at Intel? Why or why not?

Test Prepper

college.hmco.com/pic/griffinfund5e

You've read the chapter, studied the key terms, and the exam is any day now. Think you're ready to ace it? Take this sample test to gauge your comprehension of chapter material. You can check your answers at the back of the book. Want more test questions? Visit the student website at http://college.hmco.com/pic/griffinfund5e/ and take the ACE quizzes for more practice.

1. T F Because manufacturing once dominated U.S. industry, the entire area of operations management used to be called production management.

2. T F An example of a capacity decision made by the Girl Scouts is how many troops an area can support.

3. T F Oneida could use a cellular layout to manufacture forks, knives, and spoons in a similar flow path.

4. T F Computer-aided manufacturing systems use robots to move materials from one part of the system to another and convert the system as needed.

5. T F It takes more time to replace the battery on a Volvo than to replace the battery on a Ford. This is an example of reliability.

6. A manufacturing organization creates which kind of utility?

    a. Time

    b. Form

    c. Tangible

    d. Place

    e. All of the above

7. A hospital represents which type of facilities layout?

    a. Process

    b. Fixed-position

    c. Product

    d. Cellular

    e. Automation

8. When you order a pizza from the Pizza Barn, the person who takes your order uses your phone number to review your ordering history and asks whether you would like any of the toppings you have ordered in the past. This is an example of

    a. outsourcing.

    b. benchmarking.

    c. ISO 9000:2000.

    d. service technology.

    e. statistical quality control.

9. What does JIT stand for?

    a. The job-in-trouble method

    b. The just-in-time method

    c. The job-in-transit method

    d. The just-in-transit method

    e. The job-in-time method

10. Output equals $1,000, input equals $200, and direct labor equals 100 hours. Calculate the labor productivity.

    a. 5

    b. $10/hour

    c. $3.33/hour

    d. $2/hour

    e. $1,000

Part Five: Managing in the Soft-Drink Industry

This segment of the running case addresses issues raised in Part Five of the text, covering Chapters 14 and 15.

Control

Control is a challenge for both The Coca-Cola Company and PepsiCo, due to the large, complex, international nature of their businesses. The soft-drink industry is difficult because of the relationships between companies and independent bottlers. In some cases, the company owns its overseas facilities outright. Other units are joint ventures with local partners or involve partial ownership of a foreign company. Other arrangements are with completely independent firms. To further complicate matters, in some regions there is competition between bottlers working for the same manufacturer. Relationships with bottlers create control problems for the soft-drink companies because they make it difficult to monitor resources, processes, information, and quality.

Here are some of the control challenges for Coca-Cola:

- In 2006, Coca-Cola agreed to buy out Kerry Beverages, its joint venture partner in China, when the two companies could not agree on their strategy. While Kerry was more interested in developing its other businesses, Coke wanted to fund an aggressive expansion into China, a large and promising market.
- In India, Coke hired local contractor agencies to screen, employ, and compensate factory workers. Coke now faces lawsuits from workers who claim that they were underpaid, discriminated against, and denied benefits. Coke places the blame on the contractors, while the contractors point to Coke's own stated policies regarding local workers.
- Panamerican Beverages, Inc. and Bebidas y Alimentos, two independent bottlers of Coca-Cola in Columbia, are facing criminal charges alleging that their managers hired paramilitary groups to intimidate and discourage union leaders. Charges against Coke were dismissed because the company had no involvement in local union activities. In the early 1980s, Coke prevailed against similar charges in Guatemala.

Here are some of the control challenges PepsiCo has experienced:

- PepsiCo is facing allegations of poor product quality in China, where the company entered into seven joint ventures. Each of the ventures has varying levels of involvement and ownership from Pepsi, but none are wholly owned.
- After an eight-year partnership, PepsiCo ended a cooperative arrangement with Sichuan Pepsi of China in 2002. As Pepsi became more popular, the local partners demanded a greater share of profits than was specified in the original agreement. Pepsi wanted more management control and more influence over operations and strategy.

Operations

Today, The Coca-Cola Company has arrangements with more than two dozen bottlers from the U.S. to Japan. At these facilities, Coke creates more than 2,400 products bearing over 400 brand names. The number of items produced by Coke is substantially greater when packaging variations are considered. From 2005 to 2007, the number of SKUs ("stock keeping unit," unique to each product/package combination) owned by Coke doubled. In addition to Coke products, some bottlers also produce Dr Pepper or other brands belonging to Coke competitors.

Coca-Cola intends to increase capacity in the future, based on growth possibilities. Right now, only 62 percent of beverages consumed in the U.S. are nonalcoholic ready-to-drink, compared to just 40 percent in emerging markets.

Compared to Coca-Cola, PepsiCo relies more heavily on independent bottlers, who also may bottle beverages for competitors, but Pepsi does have some company-owned facilities. In all of their factories, PepsiCo is working to receive ISO 14000 certification for excellent environmental management. For example, the factories are reducing their energy and water use and recovering reusable waste products.

Both Coke and Pepsi manage their supply chain operations in a similar way. However, in 2007, Pepsi began an innovative approach to packaging. Rather than relying on standard package design to help customers recognize and trust the product, Pepsi is introducing new can designs every few weeks. The company hopes to counteract falling sales by appealing to soda drinkers' desire for novelty and their short attention spans. Thus, Pepsi will use its cans for both packaging and advertising. The new approach will require a more flexible manufacturing system that can accommodate frequent changes.

Quality

Typically, The Coca-Cola Company and PepsiCo produce beverages that are safe and tasty. However, the companies are always at risk for mistakes or problems, particularly in regions where they use independent bottlers. For example, Coke has a very high need for water, about 500,000 gallons a day in each facility. In many emerging nations, water depletion is a problem. As the water table drops lower, contamination becomes more likely. Coke is now adding extra water filtration in some plants.

Pepsi faces quality concerns in India. A nonprofit organization there claims it found pesticide residues in Pepsi soft drinks, as well as in Coke products. Pepsi responded by asking the Indian government to establish quality standards and testing. However, both companies' products are now banned in some areas of the country, due to product safety concerns.

On the more intangible measures of quality, the two companies maintain an intense rivalry. Head-to-head taste tests have led to mixed results. For an intriguing science-based view of the Pepsi Challenge, visit Brandchannel.com's website and view the article titled "The Science of Branding," by Edwin Colyer. The article is found at www.brandchannel.com/features_effect.asp?pf_id=201.

Online Resources for Further Research

Please look at the list of online resources for Parts One through Three for further suggestions.

1. Coca-Cola's home page at www.thecoca-colacompany.com.
2. PepsiCo's home page at www.pepsico.com.

Case Discussion Questions

Each of the case questions should be answered briefly, that is, in no more than a paragraph or two for each question.

1. Visit your company's home page and find the company's most recent annual review or annual report. There, examine the firm's financial results. Using a year-to-year comparison, in which areas has your company's performance improved, stayed about the same, or declined? What control measures could your company use to improve its financial control?

2. Which facility layout would be most appropriate for your company's factories? What are the advantages and disadvantages of the layout you chose?

3. Consider the complicated concept of quality as presented in the text and in the article "The Science of Branding." In your opinion, what are the most important dimensions of quality for purchasers of soft drinks? Explain.

4. How does your company convey its quality message to consumers? Do you believe that your company produces high-quality products? Why or why not?

Interpretations of Skills Self-Assessment Instruments

Chapter 1: Self-Awareness

Total your scores for each skill area.

Skill Area	Items	Score
Self-disclosure and openness to feedback from others	1, 2, 3, 9, 11	_____
Awareness of own values, cognitive style, change orientation, and interpersonal orientation	4, 5, 6, 7, 8, 10	_____
Now total your score:		_____

To assess how well you scored on this instrument, compare your scores to three comparison standards.

1. Compare your scores with the maximum possible (66).
2. Compare your scores with the scores of other students in your class.
3. Compare your scores to a norm group consisting of five hundred business school students. In comparison to the norm group, if you scored:

   55 or above, you are in the top quartile

   52 to 54, you are in the second quartile

   48 to 51, you are in the third quartile

   47 or below, you are in the bottom quartile

Your total numerical score suggests your perceptions of your possession of the skills of effective managers—the lower the total score, the lower the level of skills. You should examine your individual item scores for lower numbers and then try to use your educational experiences to develop more skill in the areas identified.

Chapter 2: Global Awareness

All the statements are true. See explanations below.

Your score should be close to 40. The closer your score is to 40, the better you understand the global context of organizational environments. The closer your score is to 10, the less you understand the global context.

1. Slurping your soup or noodles is good manners in both public and private settings. It shows enjoyment and appreciation of the quality.

2. Korean managers use "divide-and-rule" to encourage competition among subordinates. They maintain maximum control and subordinates report directly to them, ensuring the managers know more than their subordinates.

3. Public discussions of business dealings are considered inappropriate. Many American firms have been shut out of deals with Chinese firms due to discussing negotiations in the press or with other firms.

4. Public displays of affection between men and women are unacceptable, although men often walk in public holding hands as a sign of friendship.

5. Touching one another during business encounters is common practice in much of Latin America. This is true for both same-sex and opposite-sex touches and is definitely *not* considered to be sexual in nature.

6. Whereas in the U.S. being late is frowned upon, being quite late is not only accepted but expected in some South American countries. Promptness may be considered rude.

7. Public praise is embarrassing because modesty is an important cultural value. This is also true in Japan and many other Asian countries. A common Japanese saying is, "A nail that sticks up gets hammered down," meaning that workers should strive *not* to stand out from the crowd.

8. Friendship, especially of old family friends, is more important than task competence in Iran. A wise manager will carefully investigate the work-related web of family and friendship ties when working in most Middle Eastern countries.

9. Private space is considered so important in Germany that partitions are erected to separate people from one another. Privacy screens and walled gardens are the norm.

10. Whereas in the U.S., leaders are often selected for their ability to inspire, in Germany, charisma is viewed with suspicion, and leaders are typically selected for their superior job performance.

For developmental purposes, you should note any particular items for which you had a low score and concentrate on improving your knowledge of those areas.

Chapter 3: Your Work Life Strengths and Weaknesses

Consider your lists of strengths and skills. Clearly, the more strengths you possess and the fewer weaknesses, the better your chances of obtaining a satisfactory career. For further enhancement of your understanding of your work life strengths and weaknesses, do one or more of the following.

1. Rate each strength and weakness as A—a powerful strength or a significant weakness, B—a moderately important strength or weakness, or C—a nice strength to have but not essential or only a minor drawback. Assign ratings based on the qualities that are judged important in your specific career area. Following the rating, examine the results. The more "A" strengths you have the better, while "C" weaknesses are preferred.

2. Re-evaluate your lists of strengths and weaknesses relative to the job opportunities and threats to individuals in your chosen career field. For example, if your chosen field is rapidly growing and hiring many entry-level workers, the

fact that you have little work experience may not be a significant handicap. If a credential such as CPA is essential in your field, your obtaining that credential adds significantly to your employment options. If you're unaware of events and trends in your career specialty, conduct research by interviewing professors, reading trade publications, or attending professional association meetings and viewing their websites. Your school's Career Center may also have helpful information.

3. Develop a "strategic plan" to manage your career. Think about actions that might work to strengthen strengths or might help to overcome or minimize weaknesses. The more specific you are in your assessment of strengths and weaknesses, the more specific your action plan can be. For example, if you list "shy" as one your weaknesses, it's not clear what actions can be taken to offset that. On the other hand, if you list "nervous about public speaking" as one of your weaknesses, many solutions come to mind, including a communications course, participation in Toastmasters, or volunteering to give tours to prospective students. Again, as you search for solutions, professors, career placement staff, and friends can be helpful sources of information.

Chapter 4: Decision-Making Styles

Generally there are three decision-making styles: reflexive, consistent, and reflective. To determine your style, add up your score by totaling the numbers assigned to each response. The total will be between 10 and 30. A score from 10 to 16 indicates a reflexive style, a score from 17 to 23 indicates a consistent style, and a score from 24 to 30 indicates a reflective style.

Reflexive Style: A reflexive decision maker likes to make quick decisions (to shoot from the hip) without taking the time to get all the information that may be needed and without considering all alternatives. On the positive side, reflexive decision makers are decisive; they do not procrastinate. On the negative side, making quick decisions can lead to waste and duplication when the best possible alternative is overlooked. Employees may see a decision maker as a poor supervisor if he or she consistently makes bad decisions. If you use a reflexive style, you may want to slow down and spend more time gathering information and analyzing alternatives.

Reflective Style: A reflective decision maker likes to take plenty of time to make decisions, gathering considerable information and analyzing several alternatives. On the positive side, the reflective type does not make hasty decisions. On the negative side, he or she may procrastinate and waste valuable time and other resources. The reflective decision maker may be viewed as wishy-washy and indecisive. If you use a reflective style, you may want to speed up your decision making. As Andrew Jackson once said, "Take time to deliberate; but when the time for action arrives, stop thinking and go on."

Consistent Style: Consistent decision makers tend to make decisions without either rushing or wasting time. They know when they have enough information and alternatives to make a sound decision. Consistent decision makers tend to have the best record for making good decisions.

Chapter 5: An Entrepreneurial Quiz

If most of your marks are in the first column, you probably have what it takes to run a business. If most of your marks are in the second column, you are likely to have more trouble than you can handle by yourself. You should look for a partner who is strong on the points on which you are weak. If most of your marks are in the third column, not even a good partner will be able to shore you up. Now go back and answer the first question on the self-assessment.

Chapter 6: Delegation Aptitude Survey

Calculate the sum of your responses to the twenty statements. Your score represents your delegation aptitude. The higher your score, the more likely you are to prefer delegation. A person with a lower score is less likely to choose delegation.

The maximum score is 100 and the minimum is 20. No score is right or wrong, and most individuals fall somewhere in the middle of the scale.

Report your total score to your instructor and view the range of scores. You will probably note that scores vary considerably. Differences in individual scores might result from a number of factors, including business/work experience, age, religion, gender, culture, and other environmental factors.

Look at your responses to the twenty statements. Are there any items that you scored much lower than your average rating? The low-scored statements may reveal aspects of the delegation process that are the most troubling or controversial for you. Share your insights or concerns with the class and discuss.

Optimal use of delegation varies by situation. Effective managers understand that delegation can be a helpful tool at times and are comfortable using it. The survey results can make you more aware of your attitudes and behavioral tendencies. Awareness can then help you to overcome difficulties you may experience with particular aspects of the delegation process.

Chapter 7: Innovation and Learning Styles

According to Kolb, Accommodators learn and work by doing, Divergers learn and work through imagination, Convergers learn and work by problem solving, and Assimilators learn and work using inductive reasoning. Each of these types, then, has a specific role to play in innovation.

Accommodators would be best at innovation tasks such as designing and building prototypes or testing product features and functions. They would excel as product champions because they are energetic and enthusiastic.

Divergers would be best at brainstorming and generating new products. They would excel as inventors, whether of an entirely new product or of an improvement to an existing product.

Convergers would be best at testing products through experimentation or at developing additional features or enhancements to existing products. They would excel as technical advisors to the innovation process.

Assimilators would be best at thought experiments. They would excel at observing users and then generalizing from the specific observations to more general principles or ideas. They would excel as champions, because they enjoy organizing people and information toward a practical outcome.

For more information about Kolb's styles and their implications for learning and work, look online. One interesting site is http://www.businessballs.com/kolblearningstyles.htm.

Chapter 8: What Do Students Want from Their Jobs?

This survey was administered to a large group and the average results are below. Responses to this survey vary quite a bit.

If your individual scores fit the pattern of a typical student, then you will likely have an easy time explaining your job values to potential employers.

If your individual scores vary in one or more significant ways, this is not a cause for concern. Many employers seek students with job values that match those of their organizations, which can vary considerably. However, you should plan ahead about ways to effectively communicate with potential employers. Without your self-knowledge and ability to communicate your unique job values, employers would likely assume that you are typical, resulting in a poor understanding of your needs and possibly a poor person-job fit. On the other hand, good self-knowledge and communication skills can result in a superior person-job fit.

The second column of the table demonstrates that recruiters are not able to perfectly predict the relative importance of various job values to potential recruits. Again, self-knowledge and communication are the keys to finding a good person-job fit.

Job Values Survey		
Job Value	**Student Average**	**Employer Perceptions**
Working Conditions	12	–
Work with People	7	–
Employee Benefits	11	–
Challenge	2	–
Location of Job	13	–
Self-Development	3	–
Type of Work	4	–
Job Title	14	–
Training Program	9	+
Advancement	1	+
Salary	6	–
Company Reputation	10	+
Job Security	8	–
Autonomy on the Job	5	–

Chapter 9: Personality Types at Work

Conclude by addressing the following questions:

1. Do you feel that the online test accurately assessed your personality?

2. Is it easy to measure personality? What are some problems or limitations with personality assessments?

3. Share your assessment results and your answers with the class. Are the personality types equally represented in your class? If some types are over- or underrepresented, why do you think that is so?

For more information about Myers-Briggs personality types in the workplace visit http://www.myersbriggs.org/my-mbti-personality-type/mbti-basics/the-16-mbti-types.asp; http://www.teamtechnology.co.uk/tt/t-articl/mb-simpl.htm; http://www.mbtitoday.org/typechars.html; and http://www.bbc.co.uk/science/humanbody/mind/surveys/whatamilike/index.shtml. There are a host of others available online.

While none of these sites is scientifically validated and should not be used to replace the advice of a professional, they can provide you some interesting ideas and insights.

Chapter 10: Assessing Your Needs

This set of needs was developed in 1938 by H. A. Murray, a psychologist, and operationalized by another psychologist, I. W. Atkinson. Known as Murray's Manifest Needs because they are visible through behavior, they are:

1. Achievement
2. Affiliation
3. Aggression
4. Autonomy
5. Exhibition
6. Impulsivity
7. Nurturance
8. Order
9. Power
10. Understanding

To score your results, look at each question individually—the needs correspond one-to-one to the items on the assessment questionnaire.

Although little research has evaluated Murray's theory, the different needs have been investigated. People seem to have a different profile of needs underlying their motivations at different ages. The more any one or more of these needs are descriptive of you, the more you see that particular need as being active in your motivational makeup.

For more information, see H. A. Murray, *Explorations in Personality* (New York: Oxford University Press, 1938) and J. W. Atkinson, *An Introduction to Motivation* (Princeton, NJ: Van Nostrand, 1964).

Chapter 11: Managerial Leader Behavior Questionnaire

These statements represent twenty-three behavior categories that research has identified as descriptive of managerial leadership. Not all twenty-three are important in any given situation. Typically, fewer than half of these behaviors are associated with effective performance in particular situations; thus there is no "right" or "wrong" set of responses on this questionnaire. The behavior categories are

1. Emphasizing performance
2. Showing consideration
3. Providing career counseling
4. Inspiring subordinates
5. Providing praise and recognition
6. Structuring reward contingencies
7. Clarifying work roles
8. Setting goals
9. Training-coaching
10. Disseminating information
11. Encouraging participation in decisions
12. Delegating
13. Planning
14. Innovating
15. Problem solving
16. Facilitating the work
17. Monitoring operations
18. Monitoring the environment
19. Representing the unit
20. Facilitating cooperation and teamwork
21. Managing conflict
22. Providing criticism
23. Administering discipline

In military organizations at war, inspiring subordinates, emphasizing performance, clarifying work roles, problem solving, and planning seem most important. In military organizations during peacetime, inspiring subordinates, emphasizing performance, clarifying work roles, showing consideration, providing criticism, and administering discipline seem most important. In business organizations, emphasizing performance, monitoring the environment, clarifying work roles, setting goals, and sometimes innovating seem to be most important. In each of these instances, however, the level of organization, type of technology, environmental conditions, and objectives sought help determine the exact mix of behaviors that will lead to effectiveness. You should analyze your particular situation to determine which subset of these behavior categories is most likely to be important and then should strive to develop that subset.

Chapter 12: Sex Talk Quiz

1. **False**—According to studies, there is no truth to the myth that women are more intuitive than men. However, research has shown that women pay greater

attention to "detail." Linguist Robin Lakoff, in her classic book *Language and Woman's Place* (Harper Colophon, 1975), confirms this and states that women tend to use finer descriptions of colors.

2. **True**—Men are listened to more often than women. In "Sex Differences in Listening Comprehension," Kenneth Gruber and Jacqueline Gaehelein (*Sex Roles*, Vol. 5, 1979) found that both male and female audiences tended to listen more attentively to male speakers than to female speakers.

3. **False**—Contrary to popular stereotype, it is men—not women—who talk more. Studies like the one done by linguist Lynnette Hirshman showed that men far outtalk women ("Analysis of Supportive and Assertive Behavior in Conversations." Paper presented at the Linguists Society of America, July 1974).

4. **False**—Although several studies show that women talk more rapidly than men, women don't necessarily talk extremely fast.

5. **False**—Numerous studies show that women, not men, tend to maintain more eye contact and facial pleasantries. Dr. Nancy Henley, in the chapter "Power, Sex, and Non-Verbal Communication" in *Language and Sex: Difference and Dominance* (Newbury House Publishers, 1975), shows that women exhibit more friendly behavior (such as smiles, facial pleasantries, and head nods) than men.

6. **True**—Studies show that women are more open in their praise and give more "nods of approval" than men. They also use more complimentary terms throughout their speech, according to Peter Falk in his book *Word-Play: What Happens When People Talk* (Knopf, 1973).

7. **True**—Donald Zimmerman and Candace West showed that 75 percent to 93 percent of the interruptions were made by men. ("Sex Roles, Interruptions and Silences in Conversation," in *Language and Sex: Difference and Dominance*, edited by B. Thorne and N. Henley, Newbury House Publishers, 1975.)

8. **False**—Men use more command terms or imperatives, which makes them sound more demanding. In essence, several researchers have concluded that women tend to be more polite in their speech.

9. **False**—Men and women definitely differ in their sense of humor. Women are more likely to tell jokes when there is a small, same-sex group, and men are more likely to tell jokes in a larger, mixed-sex group.

10. **False**—In a survey conducted for the Playboy Channel, people were asked what they wanted to hear when making love. In general, women wanted to be told they were beautiful and loved, and men wanted to hear how good they were in bed and how much they pleased their women.

11. **True**—Deborah Tannen in her book *You Just Don't Understand: Women and Men in Conversation* (William Morrow, 1990) found that men usually will not solicit help by asking for directions, whereas women will.

12. **False**—Several surveys and numerous psychotherapists' observations have indicated that women tend to be more self-critical and more apt to blame themselves than men. Deborah Tannen's findings (see item 11) confirm this. She states that in their conversations, women also tend to use more "apologetic phrases," such as, "I'm sorry," "I didn't mean to," or "Excuse me."

13. **True**—Naturalist Charles Darwin stated that making oneself appear smaller by bowing the head to take up less space can inhibit human aggression. Other researchers found that women tend to make themselves smaller by crossing their legs at the ankles or knees or keeping their elbows to their sides.

14. **False**—As mentioned earlier, women tend to be more detailed and more descriptive than men in what they say and in how they explain things. As Robin Lakoff's research shows (see item 1), women tend to use more description in word choices.

15. **False**—Men tend to touch more than females. According to several researchers, women are more likely to be physically touched by men who guide them through the door, assist them with jackets and coats, and help them into cars.

16. **False**—Women, not men, appear to be more attentive when listening. Studies consistently show that women exhibit greater eye contact and express approval by smiling and head nodding as a form of attentiveness and agreement.

17. **True**—Men and women are equally emotional when they speak. However, according to researchers such as Robin Lakoff (see item 1), women sound more emotional because they use more psychological-state verbs: I *feel*, I *hope*, and I *wish*.

18. **False**—In general, men tend to bring up less personal topics than women. Women tend to discuss people, relationships, children, self-improvement, and how certain experiences have affected them. Men, on the other hand, tend to be more "outer-directed" as they originate discussions about events, news, sports, and topics related to more concrete physical tasks.

19. **False**—Even though men do not bring up as many subjects of conversation as women, men interrupt more, which ultimately gives them control of even the topics that are raised by women.

20. **False**—Even though there are many progressive and socially enlightened parents in the modern world, parents still treat their male children differently than their female children. They tend to communicate differently with their children according to their sex, which, in turn, induces sex-stereotyped behaviors.

21. **True**—Even though men make more direct statements, a recent survey indicated that women tend to confront and bring up a problem more often than men. Even though women bring up a problem more often, they tend to be more indirect and polite, as Deborah Tannen relates in her book (see item 11).

22. **False**—In several studies, it was determined that women are more animated and livelier speakers than men. Studies also show that women make more eye contact, use more body movement, use more intonation, have a more varied pitch range, and use more emotionally laden words and phrases.

23. **False**—Just as women bring up more topics of conversation, they also ask more questions. According to researchers, this is usually done to facilitate the conversation.

24. **False**—Men and women usually talk about different things. Studies indicate that women enjoy talking about diet, personal relationships, personal appearance, clothes, self-improvement, children, marriages, personalities of others, actions of others, relationships at work, and emotionally charged issues that have a personal component. Men, on the other hand, enjoy discussing sports,

what they did at work, where they went, news events, mechanical gadgets, the latest technology, cars, vehicles, and music.

25. **True**—A recent Gallup poll survey commissioned for Lillian Glass, *He Says, She Says,* found that women rather than men were more likely to introduce the topics of AIDS testing and safe sex.

Chapter 13: Using Teams

Judging on the basis of research conducted by J. Richard Hackman and others, all the statements are false.

1. An emphasis on individual accountability essentially undermines any effort to develop a team.

2. Complete authority is likely to lead to anarchy. Limits should be set.

3. Teams should be kept small, should have clear boundaries, and should have an enabling structure that ensures member motivation.

4. Teams need coaching, counseling, and support at certain intervals during their functioning.

5. The start-up period is critical, which is why managers must spend time and energy coaching and counseling the team during this period. Once the team gets going, the manager should pull back until it reaches a natural break or completes a performance cycle.

6. Training is absolutely critical and should be done before the team is assembled or shortly thereafter. If the needed skills and knowledge change, management should be ready to assist in training to help the team learn the new skills and acquire the new knowledge quickly.

7. Providing support for teams is difficult. A reward system must recognize and reinforce team performance, an educational system must provide needed skills and knowledge, an information system must provide necessary information, and physical and fiscal resources must be available as needed.

8. Teams need some structure to work effectively.

9. The opposite is true. Managers should set the direction and establish wide limits on constraints, whereas the means to the end should be determined by the team.

10. Teams cannot effectively be used in organizations that have strong individualistic cultures.

Chapter 14: Understanding Control

The odd-numbered items are all false, and the even-numbered ones are all true. Thus you should have positive responses for the even-numbered items and negative responses for the odd-numbered items. If you agreed strongly with all of the even-numbered items and disagreed strongly with all of the odd-numbered items, your total score would be zero.

Examine your responses to see which items you responded to incorrectly. Focus on learning why the answers are what they are.

Chapter 15: Defining Quality and Productivity

The odd-numbered items are all true; they refer to eight dimensions of quality (see Table 15.2). Those eight dimensions are performance, features, reliability, conformance, durability, serviceability, aesthetics, and perceived quality. The even-numbered statements are all false. Thus you should have positive responses for the odd-numbered items and negative responses for the even-numbered items. If you agree strongly with all of the odd-numbered items and disagree strongly with all of the even-numbered items, your total score is zero.

Examine your responses to see which items you responded to incorrectly. Focus on learning why the answers are what they are. Remember that the American Society for Quality Control defines quality as the totality of features and characteristics of a product or service that bear on its ability to satisfy stated or implied needs of customers.

Answers to Test Preppers

Chapter 1
1. F
2. F
3. T
4. F
5. T
6. d
7. b
8. c
9. a
10. a

Chapter 2
1. F
2. T
3. F
4. T
5. F
6. a
7. b
8. c
9. d
10. e

Chapter 3
1. F
2. T
3. T
4. F
5. F
6. d
7. d
8. a
9. b
10. c

Chapter 4
1. F
2. T
3. T
4. F
5. T
6. b
7. b
8. e

9. a
10. b

Chapter 5
1. T
2. T
3. T
4. F
5. F
6. b
7. d
8. e
9. d
10. d

Chapter 6
1. F
2. T
3. F
4. T
5. F
6. a
7. c
8. a
9. d
10. b

Chapter 7
1. T
2. F
3. T
4. F
5. T
6. a
7. d
8. e
9. e
10. e

Chapter 8
1. F
2. F
3. T
4. T
5. T

6. a
7. a
8. d
9. d
10. a

Chapter 9
1. F
2. T
3. T
4. T
5. F
6. a
7. f
8. e
9. d
10. e

Chapter 10
1. F
2. F
3. F
4. F
5. F
6. e
7. c
8. b
9. c
10. a

Chapter 11
1. F
2. T
3. F
4. F
5. T
6. a
7. a
8. c
9. b
10. c

Chapter 12
1. T
2. F

3. F
4. T
5. T
6. e
7. d
8. a
9. e
10. b

Chapter 13
1. F
2. T
3. F
4. T
5. T
6. a
7. d
8. c
9. a
10. c

Chapter 14
1. F
2. T
3. T
4. F
5. F
6. c
7. b
8. c
9. a
10. a

Chapter 15
1. T
2. T
3. T
4. F
5. F
6. b
7. a
8. d
9. b
10. b

Chapter Notes

CHAPTER 1

First Things First: Michael V. Copeland, "The League of Extraordinary Young Executives," *Business 2.0*, money.cnn.com on January 12, 2006; Ben Elgin, "Google's Search for Simplicity," *BusinessWeek*, October 3, 2005, www.businessweek.com on January 6, 2006; Ben Elgin, "Managing Google's Idea Factory," *BusinessWeek*, October 3, 2005, www.businessweek.com on January 6, 2006; "Corporate Information," "Marissa Mayer," Google website, www.google.com on January 12, 2006; Roben Farzad and Ben Elgin, "Googling for Gold," *BusinessWeek*, December 5, 2005, www.businessweek.com on January 6, 2006; "Google's Internet Doctor," *Red Herring*, June 6, 2005, www.redherring.com on January 12, 2006; Linda Tischler, "The Beauty of Simplicity," *Fast Company*, November 2005, www.fastcompany.com on January 6, 2006; "In Search of the Real Google," *Time*, February 20, 2006, pp. 36–49.

1. Fred Luthans, "Successful vs. Effective Real Managers," *Academy of Management Executive*, May 1988, pp. 127–132. See also "The Best Performers," *BusinessWeek*, March 26, 2007, pp. 58–92.

2. See "The Best (& Worst) Managers of the Year," *BusinessWeek*, January 10, 2005, pp. 55–86.

3. See "Executive Pay," *BusinessWeek*, April 15, 2002, pp. 80–100. See also Jim Collins, "The Ten Greatest CEO's of All Times," *Fortune*, July 21, 2003, pp. 54–68.

4. Rosemary Stewart, "Middle Managers: Their Jobs and Behaviors," in Jay W. Lorsch (ed.), *Handbook of Organizational Behavior* (Englewood Cliffs, N.J.: Prentice-Hall, 1987), pp. 385–391. See also Rosabeth Moss Kanter, "The Middle Manager as Innovator," *Harvard Business Review*, July–August 2004, pp. 150–161.

5. John P. Kotter, "What Effective General Managers Really Do," *Harvard Business Review*, March–April 1999, pp. 145–155. See also Peter Drucker, "What Makes an Effective Executive," *Harvard Business Review*, June 2004, pp. 58–68.

6. See Robert L. Katz, "The Skills of an Effective Administrator," *Harvard Business Review*, September–October 1974, pp. 90–102, for a classic discussion of several of these skills.

7. See "The Real Reasons You're Working so Hard . . . And What You Can Do About It," *BusinessWeek*, October 3, 2005, pp. 60–68; "I'm Late, I'm Late, I'm Late," *USA Today*, November 26, 2002, pp. 1B, 2B.

8. For a thorough discussion of the importance of time-management skills, see David Barry, Catherine Durnell Cramton, and Stephen J. Carroll, "Navigating the Garbage Can: How Agendas Help Managers Cope with Job Realities," *Academy of Management Executive*, May 1997, pp. 26–42.

9. Gary Hamel and C. K. Prahalad, "Competing for the Future," *Harvard Business Review*, July–August 1994, pp. 122–128.

10. James Waldroop and Timothy Butler, "The Executive as Coach," *Harvard Business Review*, November–December 1996, pp. 111–117.

11. Terence Mitchell and Lawrence James, "Building Better Theory: Time and the Specification of When Things Happen," *Academy of Management Review*, 2001, vol. 26, no. 4, pp. 530–547. See also Clayton Christensen and Michael Raynor, "Why Hard-Nosed Executives Should Care About Management Theory," *Harvard Business Review*, September 2003, pp. 67–75.

12. Peter F. Drucker, "The Theory of the Business," *Harvard Business Review*, September–October 1994, pp. 95–104. See also Clayton Christensen and Michael Raynor, "Why Hard-Nosed Executives Should Care About Management Theory," *Harvard Business Review*, September 2003, pp. 67–75.

13. "Why Business History?" *Audacity*, Fall 1992, pp. 7–15. See also Alan L. Wilkins and Nigel J. Bristow, "For Successful Organization Culture, Honor Your Past," *Academy of Management Executive*, August 1987, pp. 221–227.

14. Daniel Wren, *The Evolution of Management Theory*, 4th ed. (New York: Wiley, 1994); Page Smith, *The Rise of Industrial America* (New York: McGraw-Hill, 1984).

15. Martha I. Finney, "Books That Changed Careers," *HRMagazine*, June 1997, pp. 141–145.

16. See Harriet Rubin, *The Princessa: Machiavelli for Women* (New York: Doubleday/Currency, 1997). See also Nanette Fondas, "Feminization Unveiled: Management Qualities in Contemporary Writings," *Academy of Management Review*, January 1997, pp. 257–282.

17. Alan M. Kantrow (ed.), "Why History Matters to Managers," *Harvard Business Review*, January–February 1986, pp. 81–88.

18. Wren, *The Evolution of Management Theory*.

19. Ibid.

20. Frederick W. Taylor, *Principles of Scientific Management* (New York: Harper and Brothers, 1911).

21. Charles D. Wrege and Amedeo G. Perroni, "Taylor's Pig-Tale: A Historical Analysis of Frederick W. Taylor's Pig-Iron Experiment," *Academy of Management Journal*, March 1974, pp. 6–27; Charles D. Wrege and Ann Marie Stoka, "Cooke Creates a Classic: The Story Behind Taylor's Principles of Scientific Management," *Academy of Management Review*, October 1978, pp. 736–749.

22. Robert Kanigel, *The One Best Way* (New York: Viking, 1997); Oliver E. Allen, "'This Great Mental Revolution,'" *Audacity*, Summer 1996, pp. 52–61; Jill Hough and Margaret White, "Using Stories to Create Change: The Object Lesson of Frederick Taylor's 'Pig-Tale,'" *Journal of Management*, 2001, vol. 27, pp. 585–601.

23. Henri Fayol, *General and Industrial Management*, trans. J. A. Coubrough (Geneva: International Management Institute, 1930).

24. Max Weber, *Theory of Social and Economic Organizations*, trans. T. Parsons (New York: Free Press, 1947); Richard M. Weis, "Weber on Bureaucracy: Management Consultant or Political Theorist?" *Academy of Management Review*, April 1983, pp. 242–248.

25. Hugo Munsterberg, *Psychology and Industrial Efficiency* (Boston: Houghton Mifflin, 1913).

26. Wren, *The Evolution of Management Theory*, pp. 255–264.

27. Elton Mayo, *The Human Problems of an Industrial Civilization* (New York: Macmillan, 1933); Fritz J. Roethlisberger and William J. Dickson, *Management and the Worker* (Cambridge, Mass.: Harvard University Press, 1939).

28. Abraham Maslow, "A Theory of Human Motivation," *Psychological Review*, July 1943, pp. 370–396.

29. Douglas McGregor, *The Human Side of Enterprise* (New York: McGraw-Hill, 1960).

30. Sara L. Rynes and Christine Quinn Trank, "Behavioral Science in the Business School Curriculum: Teaching in a Changing Institutional Environment," *Academy of Management Review*, 1999, vol. 24, no. 4, pp. 808–824.

31. See Ricky W. Griffin and Gregory Moorhead, *Organizational Behavior*, 8th ed. (Boston: Houghton Mifflin, 2007), for a recent review of current developments in the field of organizational behavior.

32. Wren, *The Evolution of Management Thought*, Chapter 21.

33. "Math Will Rock Your World," *BusinessWeek*, January 23, 2006, pp. 54–61.

34. "Quantitative Analysis Offers Tools to Predict Likely Terrorist Moves," *Wall Street Journal*, February 17, 2006, p. B1.

35. For more information on systems theory in general, see Ludwig von Bertalanffy, C. G. Hempel, R. E. Bass, and H. Jonas, "General Systems Theory: A New Approach to Unity of Science," I–VI *Human Biology*, vol. 23, 1951, pp. 302–361. For systems theory as applied to organizations, see Fremont E. Kast and James E. Rosenzweig, "General Systems Theory: Applications for Organizations and Management," *Academy of Management Journal*, December 1972, pp. 447–465. For a recent update, see Donde P. Ashmos and George P. Huber, "The Systems Paradigm in Organization Theory: Correcting the Record and Suggesting the Future," *Academy of Management Review*, October 1987, pp. 607–621.

36. "Gillette's New Edge," *BusinessWeek*, February 6, 2006, p. 44.

37. Kathleen M. Eisenhardt and D. Charles Galunic, "Coevolving—At Last, a Way to Make Synergies Work," *Harvard Business Review*, January–February 2000, pp. 91–103.

38. Fremont E. Kast and James E. Rosenzweig, *Contingency Views of Organization and Management* (Chicago: Science Research Associates, 1973).

39. "Welch Memoirs Fetch $7.1M," *USA Today*, July 14, 2000, p. 1B.

40. "The BusinessWeek Best-Seller List," *BusinessWeek*, November 4, 2002, p. 26.

CHAPTER 2

First Things First: Amanda Cantrell, "Lenovo Makes Splash," *CNN Money*, April 12, 2006, www.cnnmoney.com on January 14, 2007; Bruce Einhorn, Steve Hamm and Dexter Roberts, "China's First Global Capitalist," *BusinessWeek*, December 11, 2006, pp. 52–58; David Kirkpatrick, "This American Wants You to Buy Chinese," *CNN Money*, May 22, 2006, www.cnnmoney.com on January 14, 2007 (quote); Walter S. Mossberg, "H-P and Lenovo Offer New Wave of

Laptops: Small and Affordable," *The Wall Street Journal*, May 16, 2006, p. B1.

1. See Jay B. Barney and William G. Ouchi (eds.), *Organizational Economics* (San Francisco: Jossey-Bass, 1986), for a detailed analysis of linkages between economics and organizations.

2. "How Prosperity Is Reshaping the American Economy," *BusinessWeek*, February 14, 2000, pp. 100–110.

3. See "Firms Brace for a Worker Shortage," *Time*, May 6, 2002, p. 44.

4. For example, see Susanne G. Scott and Vicki R. Lane, "A Stakeholder Approach to Organizational Identity," *Academy of Management Review*, 2000, vol. 25, no. 1, pp. 43–62.

5. Richard N. Osborn and John Hagedoorn, "The Institutionalization and Evolutionary Dynamics of Interorganizational Alliances and Networks," *Academy of Management Journal*, April 1997, pp. 261–278. See also "More Companies Cut Risk by Collaborating with Their 'Enemies,'" *Wall Street Journal*, January 31, 2000, pp. A1, A10.

6. "The Best & Worst Boards," *BusinessWeek*, October 7, 2002, pp. 104–114. See also Amy Hillman and Thomas Dalziel, "Boards of Directors and Firm Performance: Integrating Agency and Resource Dependence Perspectives," *Academy of Management Review*, 2003, vol. 23, no. 3, pp. 383–396.

7. "The Wild New Workforce," *BusinessWeek*, December 6, 1999, pp. 38–44.

8. "Temporary Workers Getting Short Shrift," *USA Today*, April 11, 1997, pp. 1B, 2B.

9. "Curves Ahead," *Wall Street Journal*, March 10, 1999, pp. B1, B10.

10. See Norman Barry, *Business Ethics* (West Lafayette, IN: Purdue University Press, 1999).

11. "Howard Gardner, "The Ethical Mind," *Harvard Business Review*, March 2007, pp. 51–56.

12. Thomas Donaldson and Thomas W. Dunfee, "Toward a Unified Conception of Business Ethics: An Integrative Social Contracts Theory," *Academy of Management Review*, vol. 19, no. 2, 1994, pp. 252–284.

13. "Drug Companies Face Assault on Prices," *Wall Street Journal*, May 11, 2000, pp. B1, B4.

14. Jeremy Kahn, "Presto Chango! Sales Are Huge," *Fortune*, March 20, 2000, pp. 90–96; "More Firms Falsify Revenue to Boost Stocks," *USA Today*, March 29, 2000, p. 1B.

15. William Dill, "Beyond Codes and Courses," *Selections*, Fall 2002, pp. 21–23.

16. See "Restoring Trust in Corporate America," *BusinessWeek*, June 24, 2002, pp. 30–35.

17. "How to Fix Corporate Governance," *BusinessWeek*, May 6, 2002, pp. 68–78. See also Catherine Daily, Dan Dalton, and Albert Cannella, "Corporate Governance: Decades of Dialogue and Data," *Academy of Management Review*, 2003, vol. 28, no. 3, pp. 371–382.

18. "Is It Rainforest Crunch Time?" *BusinessWeek*, July 15, 1996, pp. 70–71; "Yo, Ben! Yo, Jerry! It's Just Ice Cream," *Fortune*, April 28, 1997, p. 374.

19. Andrew Singer, "Can a Company Be Too Ethical?" *Across the Board*, April 1993, pp. 17–22.

20. Jonathan Lash and Fred Wellington, "Competitive Advantage on a Warming Planet," *Harvard Business Review*, March 2007, pp. 94–103 and "Green Is Good," *Fortune*, April 2, 2007, pp. 42–50.

21. "Legal but Lousy," *Fortune*, September 2, 2002, p. 192.

22. Lynn Sharp Paine, "Managing for Organizational Integrity," *Harvard Business Review*, March–April 1994, pp. 106–115.

23. "Battling 'Donor Dropsy,'" *Wall Street Journal*, July 19, 2002, pp. B1, B4.

24. "A New Way of Giving," *Time*, July 24, 2000, pp. 48–51. See also Michael Porter and Mark Kramwe, "The Competitive Advantage of Corporate Philanthropy," *Harvard Business Review*, December 2002, pp. 57–66.

25. David M. Messick and Max H. Bazerman, "Ethical Leadership and the Psychology of Decision Making," *Sloan Management Review*, Winter 1996, pp. 9–22

26. "Ethics in Action: Getting It Right," *Selections*, Fall 2002, pp. 24–27.

27. See Janet P. Near and Marcia P. Miceli, "Whistle-Blowing: Myth and Reality," *Journal of Management*, 1996, vol. 22, no. 3, pp. 507–526, for a recent review of the literature on whistle-blowing. See also Michael Gundlach, Scott Douglas, and Mark Martinko, "The Decision to Blow the Whistle: A Social Information Processing Framework," *Academy of Management Review*, 2003, vol. 28, no.1, pp. 107–123.

28. For instance, see "The Complex Goals and Unseen Costs of Whistle-Blowing," *Wall Street Journal*, November 25, 2002, pp. A1, A10.

29. "A Whistle-Blower Rocks an Industry," *BusinessWeek*, June 24, 2002, pp. 126–130.

30. "The *Fortune* Global 5 Hundred—World's Largest Corporations," *Fortune*, July 25, 2005, pp. 97–140.

31. "The *Fortune* Global 5 Hundred Ranked Within Industries," *Fortune*, July 25, 2005, pp. 125–135.

32. *Hoover's Handbook of American Business 2007* (Austin, TX: Hoover's Business Press, 2007), pp. 196–198, 579–581.

33. See "Spanning the Globe," *USA Today*, April 30, 2002, pp. 1C, 2C.

34. "Creating a Worldwide Yen for Japanese Beer," *Financial Times*, October 7, 1994, p. 20.

35. Kenichi Ohmae, "The Global Logic of Strategic Alliances," *Harvard Business Review*, March–April 1989, pp. 143–154.

36. "Finally, Coke Gets It Right," *BusinessWeek*, February 10, 2003, p. 47.

37. "What If There Weren't Any Clocks to Watch?" *Newsweek*, June 30, 1997, p. 14.

38. For an excellent discussion of the effects of NAFTA, see "In the Wake of Nafta, a Family Firm Sees Business Go South," *Wall Street Journal*, February 23, 1999, pp. A1, A10.

39. Terrence E. Deal and Allan A. Kennedy, *Corporate Cultures: The Rights and Rituals of Corporate Life* (Reading, MA: Addison-Wesley, 1982). See also Tamara Erickson and Lynda Gratton, "What it Means to Work Here," *Harvard Business Review*, March 2007, pp. 104–112.

40. Jay B. Barney, "Organizational Culture: Can It Be a Source of Sustained Competitive Advantage?" *Academy of Management Review*, July 1986, pp. 656–665.

41. For example, see Carol J. Loomis, "Sam Would Be Proud," *Fortune*, April 17, 2000, pp. 131–144.

42. "Why Wells Fargo Is Circling the Wagons," *Wall Street Journal*, June 9, 1997, pp. 92–93.

CHAPTER 3

1. Ken Belson, "In Sony's Stumble, The Ghost of Betamax," *New York Times*, February 26, 2006, pp. BU1, 4; James Brightman, "Gamemaker Acclaim Betting on Its Brand," *BusinessWeek*, April 7, 2006, www.businessweek.com on April 8, 2006 (quote); Burt Helm, "A Radical New Game Plan," *BusinessWeek*, March 20, 2006, pp. 54–56; David Kiley, "Rated M for Mad Ave," *BusinessWeek*, February 27, 2006, pp. 76–77.

2. See Peter J. Brews and Michelle R. Hunt, "Learning to Plan and Planning to Learn: Resolving the Planning School/Learning School Debate," *Strategic Management Journal*, 1999, vol. 20, pp. 889–913.

3. Max D. Richards, *Setting Strategic Goals and Objectives*, 2nd ed. (St. Paul: West, 1986).

4. Jim Collins, "Turning Goals into Results: The Power of Catalytic Mechanisms," *Harvard Business Review*, July–August 1999, pp. 71–81.

5. "GE, No. 2 in Appliances, Is Agitating to Grab Share from Whirlpool," *Wall Street Journal*, July 2, 1997, pp. A1, A6. See also "A Talk with Jeff Immelt," *BusinessWeek*, January 28, 2002, pp. 102–104.

6. "Bean Counter," *Forbes*, February 28, 2005, pp. 79–80.

7. Kenneth R. Thompson, Wayne A. Hochwarter, and Nicholas J. Mathys, "Stretch Targets: What Makes Them Effective?" *Academy of Management Executive*, August 1997, pp. 48–58.

8. "A Methodical Man," *Forbes*, August 11, 1997, pp. 70–72.

9. John A. Pearce II and Fred David, "Corporate Mission Statements: The Bottom Line," *Academy of Management Executive*, May 1987, p. 109.

10. See Charles Hill and Gareth Jones, *Strategic Management*, 7th ed. (Boston: Houghton Mifflin, 2007).

11. For early discussions of strategic management, see Kenneth Andrews, *The Concept of Corporate Strategy*, rev. ed. (Homewood, Ill.: Dow Jones–Irwin, 1980); and Igor Ansoff, *Corporate Strategy* (New York: McGraw-Hill, 1965). For more recent perspectives, see Michael E. Porter, "What Is Strategy?" *Harvard Business Review*, November–December 1996, pp. 61–78; Kathleen M. Eisenhardt, "Strategy as Strategic Decision Making," *Sloan Management Review*, Spring 1999, pp. 65–74; Sarah Kaplan and Eric Beinhocker, "The Real Value of Strategic Planning," *Sloan Management Review*, Winter 2003, pp. 71–80.

12. Hoover's *Handbook of American Business 2007* (Austin, Tex.: Hoover's Business Press, 2007), pp. 519–520.

13. For a discussion of the distinction between business- and corporate-level strategies, see Hill and Jones, *Strategic Management*.

14. "If It's on the Fritz, Take It to Jane," *BusinessWeek*, January 27, 1997, pp. 74–75.

15. Jay Barney, "Firm Resources and Sustained Competitive Advantage," *Journal of Management*, June 1991, pp. 99–120.

16. Porter, *Competitive Strategy*. See also Colin Campbell-Hunt, "What Have We Learned About Generic Competitive Strategy? A Meta-Analysis," *Strategic Management Journal*, 2000, vol. 21, pp. 127–154.

17. Ian C. MacMillan and Rita Gunther McGrath, "Discovering New Points of Differentiation," *Harvard Business Review*, July–August 1997, pp. 133–136.

18. "In a Water Fight, Coke and Pepsi Try Opposite Tacks," *Wall Street Journal*, April 18, 2002, pp. A1, A8.

19. Alfred Chandler, *Strategy and Structure: Chapters in the History of the American Industrial Enterprise* (Cambridge, MA: MIT Press, 1962); Richard Rumelt, *Strategy, Structure, and Economic Performance* (Cambridge, MA: Division of Research, Graduate School of Business Administration, Harvard University, 1974); Oliver Williamson, *Markets and Hierarchies* (New York: Free Press, 1975).

20. "Not the Flavor of the Month," *BusinessWeek*, March 20, 2000, p. 128.

21. K. L. Stimpert and Irene M. Duhaime, "Seeing the Big Picture: The Influence of Industry, Diversification, and Business Strategy on Performance," *Academy of Management Journal*, 1997, vol. 40, no. 3, pp. 560–583.

22. See Chandler, *Strategy and Structure*; Yakov Amihud and Baruch Lev, "Risk Reduction as a Managerial Motive for Conglomerate Mergers," *Bell Journal of Economics*, 1981, pp. 605–617.

23. Chandler, *Strategy and Structure*; Williamson, *Markets and Hierarchies*.

24. "Did Somebody Say McBurrito?" *BusinessWeek*, April 10, 2000, pp. 166–170.

25. For a discussion of the limitations of unrelated diversification, see Jay Barney and William G. Ouchi, *Organizational Economics* (San Francisco: Jossey-Bass, 1986).

26. See Barry Hedley, "A Fundamental Approach to Strategy Development," *Long Range Planning*, December 1976, pp. 2–11; Bruce Henderson, "The Experience Curve-Reviewed. IV: The Growth Share Matrix of the Product Portfolio," *Perspectives*, no. 135 (Boston: Boston Consulting Group, 1973).

27. "BMW: Unloading Rover May Not Win the Race," *BusinessWeek*, April 3, 2000, p. 59.

28. Michael G. Allen, "Diagramming G.E.'s Planning for What's WATT," in Robert J. Allio and Malcolm W. Pennington (eds.), *Corporate Planning: Techniques and Applications* (New York: AMACOM, 1979). Limits of this approach are discussed in R. A. Bettis and W. K. Hall, "The Business Portfolio Approach: Where It Falls Down in Practice," *Long Range Planning*, March 1983, pp. 95–105.

29. "Unilever to Sell Specialty-Chemical Unit to ICI of the U.K. for About $8 Billion," *Wall Street Journal*, May 7, 1997, pp. A3, A12; "For Unilever, It's Sweetness and Light," *Wall Street Journal*, April 13, 2000, pp. B1, B4.

30. James Brian Quinn, Henry Mintzberg, and Robert M. James, *The Strategy Process* (Englewood Cliffs, NJ: Prentice-Hall, 1988).

31. Vasudevan Ramanujam and N. Venkatraman, "Planning System Characteristics and Planning Effectiveness," *Strategic Management Journal*, 1987, vol. 8, no. 2, pp. 453–468.

32. "Coca-Cola May Need to Slash Its Growth Targets," *Wall Street Journal*, January 28, 2000, p. B2. See also "Pepsi and Coke Roll Out Flavors to Boost Sales," *Wall Street Journal*, May 7, 2002, pp. B1, B4.

33. "Finally, Coke Gets It Right," *BusinessWeek*, February 10, 2003, p. 47.

34. K. A. Froot, D. S. Scharfstein, and J. C. Stein, "A Framework for Risk Management," *Harvard Business Review*, November–December 1994, pp. 91–102.

35. "How the Fixers Fended Off Big Disasters," *Wall Street Journal*, December 23, 1999, pp. B1, B4.

36. "At Wal-Mart, Emergency Plan Has Big Payoff," *Wall Street Journal*, September 12, 2005, pp. B1, B3.

37. "Next Time," *USA Today*, October 4, 2005, pp. 1B, 2B.

38. Michael Watkins and Max Bazerman, "Predictable Surprises: The Disasters You Should Have Seen Coming," Harvard *Business Review*, March 2003, pp. 72–81.

CHAPTER 4

1. Robert Berner, "My Year at Wal-Mart," *BusinessWeek*, February 12, 2007, www.businessweek.com on February 10, 2007 (quote); Jon Birger, "The Unending Woes of Lee Scott," *Fortune*, January 22, 2007, pp. 118–122; Marcus Kabel, "Wal-Mart Strategy to Emerge Over Time," *BusinessWeek*, February 2, 2007, www.businessweek.com on February 10, 2007; David Kravets, "Court Says Wal-Mart Must Face Bias Trial," *BusinessWeek*, February 6, 2007, www.businessweek.com on February 10, 2007.

2. Richard Priem, "Executive Judgment, Organizational Congruence, and Firm Performance," *Organization Science*, August 1994, pp. 421–432. See also R. Duane Ireland and C. Chet Miller, "Decision-Making and Firm Success," *Academy of Management Executive*, 2004, vol. 18, no. 4, pp. 8–12.

3. "Disney-Pixar: It's a Wrap," *BusinessWeek*, January 24, 2006, pp. 56–59.

4. Paul Nutt, "The Formulation Processes and Tactics Used in Organizational Decision Making," *Organization Science*, May 1993, pp. 226–240.

5. For a review of decision making, see E. Frank Harrison, *The Managerial Decision Making Process*, 5th ed. (Boston: Houghton Mifflin, 1999).

6. "Kodak Moment Came Early for CEO Fisher, Who Takes a Stumble," *Wall Street Journal*, July 25, 1997, pp. A1, A6.

7. George P. Huber, *Managerial Decision Making* (Glenview, IL: Scott, Foresman, 1980).

8. For an example, see Paul D. Collins, Lori V. Ryan, and Sharon F. Matusik, "Programmable Automation and the Locus of Decision-Making Power," *Journal of Management*, 1999, vol. 25, pp. 29–53.

9. Huber, *Managerial Decision Making*. See also David W. Miller and Martin K. Starr, *The Structure of Human Decisions* (Englewood Cliffs, NJ: Prentice-Hall, 1976); Alvar Elbing, *Behavioral Decisions in Organizations*, 2nd ed. (Glenview, IL: Scott, Foresman, 1978).

10. See Alex Taylor III, "Porsche's Risky Recipe," *Fortune*, February 17, 2003, pp. 90–94; "This SUV Can Tow an Entire Carmaker," *BusinessWeek*, January 19, 2004, pp. 40–41. See also "Porsche's Road to Growth Has Real Hazards," *Wall Street Journal*, December 8, 2005, pp. B1, B2.

11. Gerard P. Hodgkinson, Nicola J. Bown, A. John Maule, Keith W. Glaister, and Alan D. Pearman, "Breaking the Frame: An Analysis of Strategic Cognition and Decision

Making Under Uncertainty," *Strategic Management Journal*, 1999, vol. 20, pp. 977–985.

12. "Andersen's Fall from Grace Is a Tale of Greed and Miscues," *Wall Street Journal*, June 7, 2002, pp. A1, A6.

13. Glen Whyte, "Decision Failures: Why They Occur and How to Prevent Them," *Academy of Management Executive*, August 1991, pp. 23–31. See also Jerry Useem, "Decisions, Decisions," *Fortune*, June 27, 2005, pp. 55–154.

14. Jerry Useem, "Boeing vs. Boeing," *Fortune*, October 2, 2000, pp. 148–160; "Airbus Prepares to 'Bet the Company' as It Builds a Huge New Jet," *Wall Street Journal*, November 3, 1999, pp. A1, A10.

15. Paul Nutt, "Expanding the Search for Alternatives During Strategic Decision-Making," *Academy of Management Executive*, 2004, vol. 18, no. 4, pp. 13–22.

16. See Paul J. H. Schoemaker and Robert E. Gunther, "The Wisdom of Deliberate Mistakes," *Harvard Business Review*, June 2006, pp. 108–115.

17. "Accommodating the A380," *Wall Street Journal*, November 29, 2005, p. B1; "Boeing Roars Ahead," *BusinessWeek*, November 7, 2005, pp. 44–45; "Boeing's New Tailwind," *Newsweek*, December 5, 2005, p. 45.

18. "The Wisdom of Solomon," *Newsweek*, August 17, 1987, pp. 62–63.

19. "Making Decisions in Real Time," *Fortune*, June 26, 2000, pp. 332–334. See also Eugene Sadler-Smith and Erella Shefy, "The Intuitive Executive: Understanding and Applying 'Gut Feel' in Decision-Making," *Academy of Management Executive*, 2004, vol. 18, no. 4, pp. 76–91.

20. Herbert A. Simon, *Administrative Behavior* (New York: Free Press, 1945). Simon's ideas have been refined and updated in Herbert A. Simon, *Administrative Behavior*, 3rd ed. (New York: Free Press, 1976), and Herbert A. Simon, "Making Management Decisions: The Role of Intuition and Emotion," *Academy of Management Executive*, February 1987, pp. 57–63.

21. Patricia Corner, Angelo Kinicki, and Barbara Keats, "Integrating Organizational and Individual Information Processing Perspectives on Choice," *Organization Science*, August 1994, pp. 294–302.

22. Kimberly D. Elsbach and Greg Elofson, "How the Packaging of Decision Explanations Affects Perceptions of Trustworthiness," *Academy of Management Journal*, 2000, vol. 43, pp. 80–89.

23. Kenneth Brousseau, Michael Driver, Gary Hourihan, and Rikard Larsson, "The Seasoned Executive's Decision-Making Style," *Harvard Business Review*, February 2006, pp. 111–112.

24. Charles P. Wallace, "Adidas—Back in the Game," *Fortune*, August 18, 1997, pp. 176–182.

25. Barry M. Staw and Jerry Ross, "Good Money After Bad," *Psychology Today*, February 1988, pp. 30–33; D. Ramona Bobocel and John Meyer, "Escalating Commitment to a Failing Course of Action: Separating the Roles of Choice and Justification," *Journal of Applied Psychology*, 1994, vol. 79, pp. 360–363.

26. Mark Keil and Ramiro Montealegre, "Cutting Your Losses: Extricating Your Organization When a Big Project Goes Awry," *Sloan Management Review*, Spring 2000, pp. 55–64.

27. Gerry McNamara and Philip Bromiley, "Risk and Return in Organizational Decision Making," *Academy of Management Journal*, 1999, vol. 42, pp. 330–339.

28. For an example, see Brian O'Reilly, "What It Takes to Start a Startup," *Fortune*, June 7, 1999, pp. 135–140.

29. Martha I. Finney, "The Catbert Dilemma—The Human Side of Tough Decisions," *HRMagazine*, February 1997, pp. 70–78.

30. Edwin A. Locke, David M. Schweiger, and Gary P. Latham, "Participation in Decision Making: When Should It Be Used?" *Organizational Dynamics*, Winter 1986, pp. 65–79; Nicholas Baloff and Elizabeth M. Doherty, "Potential Pitfalls in Employee Participation," *Organizational Dynamics*, Winter 1989, pp. 51–62.

31. "The Art of Brainstorming," *BusinessWeek*, August 26, 2002, pp. 168–169.

32. Andre L. Delbecq, Andrew H. Van de Ven, and David H. Gustafson, *Group Techniques for Program Planning* (Glenview, IL: Scott, Foresman, 1975); Michael J. Prietula and Herbert A. Simon, "The Experts in Your Midst," *Harvard Business Review*, January–February 1989, pp. 120–124.

33. Norman P. R. Maier, "Assets and Liabilities in Group Problem Solving: The Need for an Integrative Function," in J. Richard Hackman, Edward E. Lawler III, and Lyman W. Porter (eds.), *Perspectives on Business in Organizations*, 2nd ed. (New York: McGraw-Hill, 1983), pp. 385–392.

34. Anthony L. Iaquinto and James W. Fredrickson, "Top Management Team Agreement About the Strategic Decision Process: A Test of Some of Its Determinants and Consequences," *Strategic Management Journal*, 1997, vol. 18, pp. 63–75.

35. Tony Simons, Lisa Hope Pelled, and Ken A. Smith, "Making Use of Difference: Diversity, Debate, and Decision Comprehensiveness in Top Management Teams," *Academy of Management Journal*, 1999, vol. 42, pp. 662–673.

36. Richard A. Cosier and Charles R. Schwenk, "Agreement and Thinking Alike: Ingredients for Poor Decisions," *Academy of Management Executive*, February 1990, pp. 69–78.

37. Irving L. Janis, *Groupthink*, 2nd ed. (Boston: Houghton Mifflin, 1982).

38. Ibid.

CHAPTER 5

First Things First: Michelle Conlin, "You Are What You Post," *BusinessWeek*, March 27, 2006, pp. 52–53; David Kushner, "The Web's Hottest Site: Facebook.com," *Rolling Stone*, April 7, 2006, www.rollingstone.com on April 15, 2006 (quote); Sarah Michalos, "Facebook Aids in Arrest After Incident," *The Exponent* (Purdue, Indiana), www.purdueexponent.com, Matt Nagowski, "The Face Behind thefacebook.com," *Current Magazine*, November 30, 2004, www.msnbc.msn.com on February 3, 2006; Steve Rosenbush, "Facebook's on the Block," *BusinessWeek*, March 28, 2006, www.businessweek.com on March 28, 2006.

1. Bro Uttal, "Inside the Deal That Made Bill Gates $350,000,000," *Fortune*, July 21, 1986, pp. 23–33.

2. "The 400 Richest People in America," *Forbes*, October 16, 2006, p. 219.

3. Murray B. Low and Ian MacMillan, "Entrepreneurship: Past Research and Future Challenges," *Journal of Management*, June 1988, pp. 139–159.

4. U.S. Bureau of the Census, *Statistical Abstract of the United States*, 2005 (Washington, DC: Government Printing Office, 2005).

5. "Small Business 'Vital Statistics,'" www.sba.gov/aboutsba on May 24, 2000.

6. Ibid.

7. "Workforce Shifts to Big Companies," *USA Today*, March 19, 2002, p. 1B.

8. "Small Business 'Vital Statistics.'"

9. "A Five-Year Journey to a Better Mousetrap," *New York Times*, May 24, 1998, p. 8.

10. "The Top Entrepreneurs," *BusinessWeek*, January 10, 2000, pp. 80–82.

11. "New Entrepreneur, Old Economy," *Wall Street Journal*, May 22, 2000, p. R10.

12. Amar Bhide, "How Entrepreneurs Craft Strategies That Work," *Harvard Business Review*, March–April 1994, pp. 150–163.

13. "Three Men and a Baby Bell," *Forbes*, March 6, 2000, pp. 134–135.

14. *Hoover's Handbook of American Business 2007* (Austin, Tex.: Hoover's Business Press, 2007), pp. 925–926; Wendy Zellner, "Peace, Love, and the Bottom Line," *BusinessWeek*, December 7, 1998, pp. 79–82.

15. "Giving Birth to a Web Business," *New York Times*, October 15, 1998, p. G5.

16. Nancy J. Lyons, "Moonlight over Indiana," *Inc.*, January 2000, pp. 71–74.

17. F. M. Scherer, *Industrial Market Structure and Economic Performance*, 2nd ed. (Boston: Houghton Mifflin, 1980).

18. "Three Biker-Entrepreneurs Take on Mighty Harley," *New York Times*, August 20, 1999, p. F1.

19. The importance of discovering niches is emphasized in Charles Hill and Gareth Jones, *Strategic Management: An Integrative Approach*, 7th ed. (Boston: Houghton Mifflin, 2007).

20. Gregory Patterson, "An American in . . . Siberia?" *Fortune*, August 4, 1997, p. 63; "Crazy for Crunchies," *Newsweek*, April 28, 1997, p. 49.

21. "'Ship Those Boxes; Check the Euro!'" *Wall Street Journal*, February 7, 2003, pp. C1, C7.

22. Thea Singer, "Brandapalooza," *Inc. 500*, 1999, pp. 69–72.

23. "Cheap Tricks," *Forbes*, February 21, 2000, p. 116.

24. U.S. Bureau of the Census, *Statistical Abstract of the United States*, 2005 (Washington, DC: Government Printing Office, 2005). See also "Too Much Ventured, Nothing Gained," *Fortune*, November 25, 2002, pp. 135–144.

25. Susan Greco, "get$$$now.com," *Inc.*, September 1999, pp. 35–38.

26. "Internet Industry Surges 'Startling' 62%," *USA Today*, June 6, 2000, p. 1B.

27. "Up-and-Comers," *BusinessWeek*, May 15, 2000, pp. EB70–EB72.

28. Andy Serwer, "There's Something About Cisco," *Fortune*, May 15, 2000, pp. 114–138.

29. "High-Tech Advances Push C.I.A. into New Company," *New York Times*, September 29, 1999, p. A14.

30. "The Courtship of Black Consumers," *New York Times*, August 16, 1998, pp. D1, D5. See also Diane Sullivan, "Minority Entrepreneurs: More Likely to Try, But Less Likely to Succeed?" *Academy of Management Perspectives*, February 2007, pp. 78–79.

31. See *The Wall Street Journal Almanac 1999*, pp. 179, 182.

32. "Women Entrepreneurs Attract New Financing," *New York Times*, July 26, 1998, p. 10.

33. "Women Increase Standing as Business Owners," *USA Today*, June 29, 1999, p. 1B.

34. Norman M. Scarborough and Thomas W. Zimmerer, *Effective Small Business Management: An Entrepreneurial Approach*, 6th ed. (Upper Saddle River, NJ: Prentice Hall, 2000), pp. 412–413.

35. "Expert Entrepreneur Got Her Show on the Road at an Early Age," *USA Today*, May 24, 2000, p. 5B.

CHAPTER 6

1. Taffy Akner, "How to Be a Late-Night TV Joke Writer," Avant Guild website, www.mediabistro.com on April 12, 2006; "David Letterman, Host," CBS website, www.cbs.com on April 12, 2006; Brian Doben, "Who Ever Said Comedy Had to Be Fun?" *Fast Company*, May 2003, www.fastcompany.com on April 12, 2006 (quote).

2. See Gareth Jones, *Organization Theory*, 5th ed. (Upper Saddle River, NJ: Prentice-Hall, 2007).

3. Ricky W. Griffin, *Task Design* (Glenview, IL: Scott Foresman, 1982).

4. Anne S. Miner, "Idiosyncratic Jobs in Formal Organizations," *Administrative Science Quarterly*, September 1987, pp. 327–351.

5. M. D. Kilbridge, "Reduced Costs Through Job Enrichment: A Case," *Journal of Business*, vol. 33, 1960, pp. 357–362.

6. Ricky W. Griffin and Gary C. McMahan, "Motivation Through Job Enrichment," in *Organizational Behavior: State of the Science*, ed. Jerald Greenberg (New York: Lawrence Erlbaumand Associates, 1994), pp. 23–44.

7. Kilbridge, "Reduced Costs Through Job Enrichment: A Case."

8. Frederick Herzberg, *Work and the Nature of Man* (Cleveland: World Press, 1966).

9. J. Richard Hackman and Greg R. Oldham, *Work Redesign* (Reading, MA: Addison-Wesley, 1980).

10. Jerry Useem, "What's That Spell? Teamwork!" *Fortune*, June 12, 2006, pp. 64–66.

11. Richard L. Daft, *Organization Theory and Design*, 9th ed. (Cincinnati: South-Western, 2007).

12. David D. Van Fleet and Arthur G. Bedeian, "A History of the Span of Management," *Academy of Management Review*, 1977, pp. 356–372.

13. James C. Worthy, "Factors Influencing Employee Morale," *Harvard Business Review*, January 1950, pp. 61–73.

14. Dan R. Dalton, William D. Todor, Michael J. Spendolini, Gordon J. Fielding, and Lyman W. Porter, "Organization Structure and Performance: A Critical Review," *Academy of Management Review*, January 1980, pp. 49–64.

15. See Jerry Useem, "Welcome to the New Company Town," *Fortune*, January 10, 2000, pp. 62–70, for a related

discussion. See also "Wherever You Go, You're on the Job," *BusinessWeek*, June 20, 2005, pp. 87–90.

16. See Daft, *Organization Theory and Design*.

17. William Kahn and Kathy Kram, "Authority at Work: Internal Models and Their Organizational Consequences," *Academy of Management Review*, 1994, vol. 19, no. 1, pp. 17–50.

18. Carrie R. Leana, "Predictors and Consequences of Delegation," *Academy of Management Journal*, December 1986, pp. 754–774.

19. Jerry Useem, "In Corporate America It's Cleanup Time," *Fortune*, September 16, 2002, pp. 62–70.

20. Kevin Crowston, "A Coordination Theory Approach to Organizational Process Design," *Organization Science*, March–April 1997, pp. 157–166.

21. James Thompson, *Organizations in Action* (New York: McGraw-Hill, 1967). For a recent discussion, see Bart Victor and Richard S. Blackburn, "Interdependence: An Alternative Conceptualization," *Academy of Management Review*, July 1987, pp. 486–498.

22. Jay R. Galbraith, *Designing Complex Organizations* (Reading, MA: Addison-Wesley, 1973) and *Organizational Design* (Reading, MA: Addison-Wesley, 1977).

23. Paul R. Lawrence and Jay W. Lorsch, "Differentiation and Integration in Complex Organizations," *Administrative Science Quarterly*, March 1967, pp. 1–47.

24. Max Weber, *Theory of Social and Economic Organizations*, trans. T. Parsons (New York: Free Press, 1947).

25. Paul Jarley, Jack Fiorito, and John Thomas Delany, "A Structural Contingency Approach to Bureaucracy and Democracy in U.S. National Unions," *Academy of Management Journal*, 1997, vol. 40, no. 4, pp. 831–861.

26. Joan Woodward, *Industrial Organization: Theory and Practice* (London: Oxford University Press, 1965).

27. Joan Woodward, *Management and Technology, Problems of Progress Industry*, no. 3 (London: Her Majesty's Stationery Office, 1958).

28. For example, see Michael Russo and Niran Harrison, "Organizational Design and Environmental Performance: Clues from the Electronics Industry," *Academy of Management Journal*, 2005, vol. 48, no. 4, pp. 582–593.

29. Tom Burns and G. M. Stalker, *The Management of Innovation* (London: Tavistock, 1961).

30. Paul R. Lawrence and Jay W. Lorsch, *Organization and Environment* (Homewood, IL: Irwin, 1967).

31. Edward E. Lawler III, "Rethinking Organization Size," *Organizational Dynamics*, Autumn 1997, pp. 24–33. See also Tom Brown, "How Big Is Too Big?" *Across the Board*, July–August 1999, pp. 14–20.

32. Derek S. Pugh and David J. Hickson, *Organization Structure in Its Context: The Aston Program I* (Lexington, Mass.: D. C. Heath, 1976).

33. "Can Wal-Mart Get Any Bigger?" *Time*, January 13, 2003, pp. 38–43.

34. Robert H. Miles and Associates, *The Organizational Life Cycle* (San Francisco: Jossey-Bass, 1980). See also "Is Your Company Too Big?" *BusinessWeek*, March 27, 1989, pp. 84–94.

35. Douglas Baker and John Cullen, "Administrative Reorganization and Configurational Context: The Contingent Effects of Age, Size, and Change in Size," *Academy of Management Journal*, 1993, vol. 36, no. 6, pp. 1251–1277. See also Kevin Crowston, "A Coordination Theory Approach to Organizational Process Design," *Organization Science*, March–April 1997, pp. 157–168.

36. Oliver E. Williamson, *Markets and Hierarchies* (New York: Free Press, 1975).

37. Ibid.

38. Michael E. Porter, "From Competitive Advantage to Corporate Strategy," *Harvard Business Review*, May–June 1987, pp. 43–59.

39. Williamson, *Markets and Hierarchies*.

40. Jay B. Barney and William G. Ouchi (eds.), *Organizational Economics* (San Francisco: Jossey-Bass, 1986); Robert E. Hoskisson, "Multidivisional Structure and Performance: The Contingency of Diversification Strategy," *Academy of Management Journal*, December 1987, pp. 625–644. See also Bruce Lamont, Robert Williams, and James Hoffman, "Performance During 'M-Form' Reorganization and Recovery Time: The Effects of Prior Strategy and Implementation Speed," *Academy of Management Journal*, 1994, vol. 37, no. 1, pp. 153–166.

41. Stanley M. Davis and Paul R. Lawrence, *Matrix* (Reading, Mass.: Addison-Wesley, 1977).

42. "Martha, Inc.," *BusinessWeek*, January 17, 2000, pp. 63–72.

43. Davis and Lawrence, *Matrix*.

44. See Lawton Burns and Douglas Wholey, "Adoption and Abandonment of Matrix Management Programs: Effects of Organizational Characteristics and Interorganizational Networks," *Academy of Management Journal*, 1993, vol. 36, no. 1, pp. 106–138.

45. See Michael Hammer and Steven Stanton, "How Process Enterprises Really Work," *Harvard Business Review*, November–December 1999, pp. 108–118.

46. Raymond E. Miles, Charles C. Snow, John A. Mathews, Grant Miles, and Henry J. Coleman, Jr., "Organizing in the Knowledge Age: Anticipating the Cellular Form," *Academy of Management Executive*, November 1997, pp. 7–24.

47. "The Horizontal Corporation," *BusinessWeek*, December 20, 1993, pp. 76–81; Shawn Tully, "The Modular Corporation," *Fortune*, February 8, 1993, pp. 106–114.

48. "Management by Web," *BusinessWeek*, August 28, 2000, pp. 84–96.

49. Peter Senge, *The Fifth Discipline* (New York: Free Press, 1993). See also David Lei, John W. Slocum, and Robert A. Pitts, "Designing Organizations for Competitive Advantage: The Power of Unlearning and Learning," *Organizational Dynamics*, Winter 1999, pp. 24–35.

CHAPTER 7

1. Kerry Capell, "Ikea," *BusinessWeek*, November 14, 2005, www.businessweek.com on February 2, 2006 (quote); Cora Daniels, "Create Ikea, Make Billions, Take Bus," *Fortune*, May 3, 2004, www.cnnmoney.com on April 15, 2006; "Facts & Figures," Ikea website, www.ikea.com on February 20, 2007; John Leland, "How the Disposable Sofa Conquered America," *New York Times*, December 1, 2002, www.nytimes.com on April 15, 2006; Gianfranco Zaccai,

"What Ikea Could Teach Alitalia," *BusinessWeek*, January 19, 2006, www.businessweek.com on February 2, 2006.

2. For an excellent review of this area, see Achilles A. Armenakis and Arthur G. Bedeian, "Organizational Change: A Review of Theory and Research in the 1990s," *Journal of Management*, 1999, vol. 25, no. 3, pp. 293–315.

3. For additional insights into how technological change affects other parts of the organization, see P. Robert Duimering, Frank Safayeni, and Lyn Purdy, "Integrated Manufacturing: Redesign the Organization Before Implementing Flexible Technology," *Sloan Management Review*, Summer 1993, pp. 47–56.

4. Joel Cutcher-Gershenfeld, Ellen Ernst Kossek, and Heidi Sandling, "Managing Concurrent Change Initiatives," *Organizational Dynamics*, Winter 1997, pp. 21–38.

5. Michael A. Hitt, "The New Frontier: Transformation of Management for the New Millennium," *Organizational Dynamics*, Winter 2000, pp. 7–15. See also Michael Beer and Nitin Nohria, "Cracking the Code of Change," *Harvard Business Review*, May–June 2000, pp. 133–144; and Clark Gilbert, "The Disruption Opportunity," *MIT Sloan Management Review*, Summer 2003, pp. 27–32.

6. See Warren Boeker, "Strategic Change: The Influence of Managerial Characteristics and Organizational Growth," *Academy of Management Journal*, 1997, vol. 40, no. 1, pp. 152–170.

7. Alan L. Frohman, "Igniting Organizational Change from Below: The Power of Personal Initiative," *Organizational Dynamics*, Winter 1997, pp. 39–53.

8. Nandini Rajagopalan and Gretchen M. Spreitzer, "Toward a Theory of Strategic Change: A Multi-Lens Perspective and Integrative Framework," *Academy of Management Review*, 1997, vol. 22, no. 1, pp. 48–79.

9. Anne Fisher, "Danger Zone," *Fortune*, September 8, 1997, pp. 165–167.

10. "Kodak to Cut Staff up to 21% Amid Digital Push," *Wall Street Journal*, January 22, 2005, pp. A1, A7.

11. John P. Kotter and Leonard A. Schlesinger, "Choosing Strategies for Change," *Harvard Business Review*, March–April 1979, p. 106.

12. Clayton M. Christensen and Michael Overdorf, "Meeting the Challenge of Disruptive Change," *Harvard Business Review*, March–April 2000, pp. 67–77.

13. "To Maintain Success, Managers Must Learn How to Direct Change," *Wall Street Journal*, August 13, 2002, p. B1.

14. See Eric Abrahamson, "Change Without Pain," *Harvard Business Review*, July–August 2000, pp. 75–85. See also Gib Akin and Ian Palmer, "Putting Metaphors to Work for Change in Organizations," *Organizational Dynamics*, Winter 2000, pp. 67–76.

15. Erik Brynjolfsson, Amy Austin Renshaw, and Marshall Van Alstyne, "The Matrix of Change," *Sloan Management Review*, Winter 1997, pp. 37–54.

16. Kurt Lewin, "Frontiers in Group Dynamics: Concept, Method, and Reality in Social Science," *Human Relations*, June 1947, pp. 5–41.

17. Michael Roberto and Lynne Levesque, "The Art of Making Change Initiatives Stick," *MIT Sloan Management Review*, Summer 2005, pp. 53–62.

18. "Time for a Turnaround," *Fast Company*, January 2003, pp. 55–61.

19. See Connie J. G. Gersick, "Revolutionary Change Theories: A Multilevel Exploration of the Punctuated Equilibrium Paradigm," *Academy of Management Review*, January 1991, pp. 10–36.

20. For a good illustration of how resistance emerges, see Gerald Andrews, "Mistrust, the Hidden Obstacle to Empowerment," *HRMagazine*, November 1994, pp. 66–74.

21. See Clark Gilbert and Joseph Bower, "Disruptive Change," *Harvard Business Review*, May 2002, pp. 95–104.

22. "RJR Employees Fight Distraction amid Buy-out Talks," *Wall Street Journal*, November 1, 1988, p. A8.

23. Arnon E. Reichers, John P. Wanous, and James T. Austin, "Understanding and Managing Cynicism About Organizational Change," *Academy of Management Executive*, February 1997, pp. 48–59.

24. For a classic discussion, see Paul R. Lawrence, "How to Deal with Resistance to Change," *Harvard Business Review*, January–February 1969, pp. 4–12, 166–176.

25. Lester Coch and John R. P. French, Jr., "Overcoming Resistance to Change," *Human Relations*, August 1948, pp. 512–532.

26. Eric von Hippel, Stefan Thomke, and Mary Sonnack, "Creating Breakthroughs at 3M," *Harvard Business Review*, September–October 1999, pp. 47–54. See also Jerry Useem, "Tape + Light Bulbs = ?" *Fortune*, August 12, 2002, pp. 127–132.

27. Benjamin Schneider, Arthur P. Brief, and Richard A. Guzzo, "Creating a Climate and Culture for Sustainable Organizational Change," *Organizational Dynamics*, Spring 1996, pp. 7–19.

28. "Troubled GM Plans Major Tuneup," *USA Today*, June 6, 2005, pp. 1B, 2B.

29. Paul Bate, Raza Khan, and Annie Pye, "Towards a Culturally Sensitive Approach to Organization Structuring: Where Organization Design Meets Organization Development," *Organization Science*, March–April 2000, pp. 197–211.

30. David Kirkpatrick, "The New Player," *Fortune*, April 17, 2000, pp. 162–168.

31. "Mr. Ryder Rewrites the Musty Old Book at *Reader's Digest*," *Wall Street Journal*, April 18, 2000, pp. A1, A10.

32. "Struggling Saks Tries Alterations in Management," *Wall Street Journal*, January 10, 2006, pp. B1, B2.

33. Thomas A. Stewart, "Reengineering—The Hot New Managing Tool," *Fortune*, August 23, 1993, pp. 41–48.

34. "Old Company Learns New Tricks," *USA Today*, April 10, 2000, pp. 1B, 2B.

35. Richard Beckhard, *Organization Development: Strategies and Models* (Reading, Mass.: Addison-Wesley, 1969), p. 9.

36. W. Warner Burke, "The New Agenda for Organization Development," *Organizational Dynamics*, Summer 1997, pp. 7–20.

37. Wendell L. French and Cecil H. Bell, Jr., *Organization Development: Behavioral Science Interventions for Organization Improvement*, 2nd ed. (Englewood Cliffs, NJ: Prentice-Hall, 1978).

38. "Memo to the Team: This Needs Salt!" *Wall Street Journal*, April 4, 2000, pp. B1, B14.

39. Roger J. Hower, Mark G. Mindell, and Donna L. Simmons, "Introducing Innovation Through OD," *Management Review*, February 1978, pp. 52–56.

40. "Is Organization Development Catching On? A Personnel Symposium," *Personnel*, November–December 1977, pp. 10–22.

41. For a classic discussion on the effectiveness of various OD techniques in different organizations, see John M. Nicholas, "The Comparative Impact of Organization Development Interventions on Hard Criteria Measures," *Academy of Management Review*, October 1982, pp. 531–542.

42. Constantinos Markides, "Strategic Innovation," *Sloan Management Review*, Spring 1997, pp. 9–24. See also James Brian Quinn, "Outsourcing Innovation: The New Engine of Growth," *Sloan Management Review*, Summer 2000, pp. 13–21.

43. L. B. Mohr, "Determinants of Innovation in Organizations," *American Political Science Review*, 1969, pp. 111–126; G. A. Steiner, *The Creative Organization* (Chicago: University of Chicago Press, 1965); R. Duncan and A. Weiss, "Organizational Learning: Implications for Organizational Design," in B. M. Staw (ed.), *Research in Organizational Behavior*, vol. 1 (Greenwich, Conn.: JAI Press, 1979), pp. 75–123; J. E. Ettlie, "Adequacy of Stage Models for Decisions on Adoption of Innovation," *Psychological Reports*, 1980, pp. 991–995.

44. See Alan Patz, "Managing Innovation in High Technology Industries," *New Management*, September 1986, pp. 54–59.

45. "Flops," *BusinessWeek*, August 16, 1993, pp. 76–82.

46. "Apple Can't Keep up with Demand for Newest iMac," *USA Today*, August 26, 2002, p. 3B.

47. See Willow A. Sheremata, "Centrifugal and Centripetal Forces in Radical New Product Development Under Time Pressure," *Academy of Management Review*, 2000, vol. 25, no. 2, pp. 389–408. See also Richard Leifer, Gina Colarelli O'Connor, and Mark Rice, "Implementing Radical Innovation in Mature Firms: The Role of Hubs," *Academy of Management Executive*, 2001, vol. 15, no. 3, pp. 102–113.

48. See "Amid Japan's Gloom, Corporate Overhauls Offer Hints of Revival," *Wall Street Journal*, February 21, 2002, pp. A1, A11.

49. Dorothy Leonard and Jeffrey F. Rayport, "Spark Innovation Through Empathic Design," *Harvard Business Review*, November–December 1997, pp. 102–115.

50. See Steven P. Feldman, "How Organizational Culture Can Affect Innovation," *Organizational Dynamics*, Summer 1988, pp. 57–68.

51. Geoffrey Moore, "Innovating Within Established Enterprises," *Harvard Business Review*, July–August 2004, pp. 87–96.

52. See Gifford Pinchot III, *Intrapreneuring* (New York: Harper & Row, 1985).

CHAPTER 8

1. Matthew Boyle, "Best Buy's Giant Gamble," *Fortune*, April 3, 2006, pp. 68–75; Matthew Boyle, "Best Buy's Transformative CEO," *Fortune*, March 23, 2006,
www.fortune.com on February 1, 2007; Michelle Conlin, "Smashing the Clock," *BusinessWeek*, December 11, 2006, pp. 60–68 (quote); Danielle Sacks, "What's the Biggest Change Facing Business in the Next 10 Years?" *Fast Company*, March 2006, www.fastcompany.com on February 1, 2007.

2. For a complete review of human resources management, see Angelo S. DeNisi and Ricky W. Griffin, *Human Resource Management*, 3rd ed. (Boston: Houghton Mifflin, 2008).

3. Patrick Wright and Gary McMahan, "Strategic Human Resources Management: A Review of the Literature," *Journal of Management*, June 1992, pp. 280–319.

4. Augustine Lado and Mary Wilson, "Human Resource Systems and Sustained Competitive Advantage: A Competency-Based Perspective," *Academy of Management Review*, 1994, vol. 19, no. 4, pp. 699–727.

5. David Lepak and Scott Snell, "Examining the Human Resource Architecture: The Relationships Among Human Capital, Employment, and Human Resource Configurations," *Journal of Management*, 2002, vol. 28, no. 4, pp. 517–543.

6. "Maryland First to OK 'Wal-Mart Bill,'" *USA Today*, January 13, 2006, p. 1B.

7. "Is Butter Flavoring Ruining Popcorn Workers' Lungs?" *USA Today*, June 20, 2002, pp. 1A, 8A.

8. "While Hiring at Most Firms Chills, Wal-Mart's Heats Up," *USA Today*, August 26, 2002, p. 1B.

9. John Beeson, "Succession Planning," *Across the Board*, February 2000, pp. 38–41.

10. "Star Search," *BusinessWeek*, October 10, 2005, pp. 66–78.

11. James A. Breaugh and Mary Starke, "Research on Employee Recruiting: So Many Studies, So Many Remaining Questions," *Journal of Management*, 2000, vol. 26, no. 3, pp. 405–434.

12. "Pumping Up Your Past," *Time*, June 10, 2002, p. 96.

13. Frank L. Schmidt and John E. Hunter, "Employment Testing: Old Theories and New Research Findings," *American Psychologist*, October 1981, pp. 1128–1137.

14. Robert Liden, Christopher Martin, and Charles Parsons, "Interviewer and Applicant Behaviors in Employment Interviews," *Academy of Management Journal*, 1993, vol. 36, no. 2, pp. 372–386.

15. Paul R. Sackett, "Assessment Centers and Content Validity: Some Neglected Issues," *Personnel Psychology*, 1987, vol. 40, pp. 13–25.

16. Renee DeRouin, Barbara Fritzsche, and Eduardo Salas, "E-Learning in Organizations," *Journal of Management*, 2005, vol. 31, no. 6, pp. 920–940.

17. "'Boeing U': Flying by the Book," *USA Today*, October 6, 1997, pp. 1B, 2B. See also "Is Your Airline Pilot Ready for Surprises?" *Time*, October 14, 2002, p. 72.

18. See Paul Levy and Jane Williams, "The Social Context of Performance Appraisal: A Review and Framework for the Future," *Journal of Management*, 2004, vol. 30, no. 6, pp. 881–905.

19. See Angelo S. DeNisi and Avraham N. Kluger, "Feedback Effectiveness: Can 360-Degree Appraisals Be Improved?" *Academy of Management Executive*, 2000, vol. 14, no. 1, pp. 129–139.

20. Barry R. Nathan, Allan Mohrman, and John Milliman, "Interpersonal Relations as a Context for the Effects of Appraisal Interviews on Performance and Satisfaction: A Longitudinal Study," *Academy of Management Journal*, June 1991, pp. 352–369.

21. "Goodyear to Stop Labeling 10% of Its Workers as Worst," *USA Today*, September 12, 2002, p. 1B.

22. Stephanie Armour, "Show Me the Money, More Workers Say," *USA Today*, June 6, 2000, p. 1B.

23. "To Each According to His Needs: Flexible Benefits Plans Gain Favor," *Wall Street Journal*, September 16, 1986, p. 29.

24. For an example, see "A Female Executive Tells Furniture Maker What Women Want," *Wall Street Journal*, June 25, 1999, pp. A1, A11.

25. Patricia L. Nemetz and Sandra L. Christensen, "The Challenge of Cultural Diversity: Harnessing a Diversity of Views to Understand Multiculturalism," *Academy of Management Review*, 1996, vol. 21, no. 2, pp. 434–462. See also "Generational Warfare," *Forbes*, March 22, 1999, pp. 62–66.

26. Christine M. Riordan and Lynn McFarlane Shores, "Demographic Diversity and Employee Attitudes: An Empirical Examination of Relational Demography Within Work Units," *Journal of Applied Psychology*, 1997, vol. 82, no. 3, pp. 342–358.

27. Sara Rynes and Benson Rosen, "What Makes Diversity Programs Work?" *HR Magazine*, October 1994, pp. 67–75.

28. Karen Hildebrand, "Use Leadership Training to Increase Diversity," *HR Magazine*, August 1996, pp. 53–59.

29. Barbara Presley Nobel, "Reinventing Labor," *Harvard Business Review*, July–August 1993, pp. 115–125.

30. John A. Fossum, "Labor Relations: Research and Practice in Transition," *Journal of Management*, Summer 1987, pp. 281–300.

31. "How Wal-Mart Keeps Unions at Bay," *BusinessWeek*, October 28, 2002, pp. 94–96.

32. Max Boisot, *Knowledge Assets* (Oxford, UK: Oxford University Press, 1998).

33. Thomas Stewart, "In Search of Elusive Tech Workers," *Fortune*, February 16, 1998, pp. 171–172.

34. "FBI Taps Retiree Experience for Temporary Jobs," *USA Today*, October 3, 2002, p. 1A.

35. "When Is a Temp Not a Temp?" *BusinessWeek*, December 7, 1998, pp. 90–92.

CHAPTER 9

1. "About Gore," "Corporate Culture," Gore website, www.gore.com on February 12, 2007; Alan Deutschman, "The Fabric of Creativity," *Fast Company*, November 1, 2005, www.fastcompany.com on May 16, 2006 (quote); Paul Kaihla, "Best-Kept Secrets of the World's Best Companies," *Business 2.0*, March 16, 2006, www.money.cnn.com on February 12, 2007; Jena McGregor, "How Failure Breeds Success," *BusinessWeek*, July 10, 2006, www.businessweek.com on February 12, 2007.

2. Lynn McGarlane Shore and Lois Tetrick, "The Psychological Contract as an Explanatory Framework in the Employment Relationship," in C. L. Cooper and D. M. Rousseau (eds.), *Trends in Organizational Behavior* (London: Wiley, 1994). See also Jacqueline Coyle-Shapiro and Neil Conway, "Exchange Relationships: Examining Psychological Contracts and Perceived Organizational Support," *Journal of Applied Psychology*, 2005, vol. 90, no. 4, pp. 774–781.

3. Elizabeth Wolfe Morrison and Sandra L. Robinson, "When Employees Feel Betrayed: A Model of How Psychological Contract Violation Develops," *Academy of Management Review*, January 1997, pp. 226–256.

4. Lawrence Pervin, "Personality" in Mark Rosenzweig and Lyman Porter (eds.), *Annual Review of Psychology*, vol. 36 (Palo Alto, CA: Annual Reviews, 1985), pp. 83–114; S. R. Maddi, *Personality Theories: A Comparative Analysis*, 4th ed. (Homewood, IL: Dorsey, 1980).

5. L. R. Goldberg, "An Alternative 'Description of Personality': The Big Five Factor Structure," *Journal of Personality and Social Psychology*, 1990, vol. 59, pp. 1216–1221.

6. Michael K. Mount, Murray R. Barrick, and J. Perkins Strauss, "Validity of Observer Ratings of the Big Five Personality Factors," *Journal of Applied Psychology*, 1994, vol. 79, no. 2, pp. 272–280; Timothy A. Judge, Joseph J. Martocchio, and Carl J. Thoreson, "Five-Factor Model of Personality and Employee Absence," *Journal of Applied Psychology*, 1997, vol. 82, no. 5, pp. 745–755.

7. J. B. Rotter, "Generalized Expectancies for Internal vs. External Control of Reinforcement," *Psychological Monographs*, 1966, vol. 80, pp. 1–28. See also Simon S. K. Lam and John Schaubroeck, "The Role of Locus of Control in Reactions to Being Promoted and to Being Passed Over: A Quasi Experiment," *Academy of Management Journal*, 2000, vol. 43, no. 1, pp. 66–78.

8. Marilyn E. Gist and Terence R. Mitchell, "Self-Efficacy: A Theoretical Analysis of Its Determinants and Malleability," *Academy of Management Review*, April 1992, pp. 183–211.

9. T. W. Adorno, E. Frenkel-Brunswick, D. J. Levinson, and R. N. Sanford, *The Authoritarian Personality* (New York: Harper & Row, 1950).

10. "The Rise and Fall of Dennis Kozlowski," *BusinessWeek*, December 23, 2002, pp. 64–77.

11. Jon L. Pierce, Donald G. Gardner, and Larry L. Cummings, "Organization-Based Self-Esteem: Construct Definition, Measurement, and Validation," *Academy of Management Journal*, 1989, vol. 32, pp. 622–648.

12. Michael Harris Bond and Peter B. Smith, "Cross-Cultural Social and Organizational Psychology," in Janet Spence (ed.), *Annual Review of Psychology*, vol. 47 (Palo Alto, CA: Annual Reviews, 1996), pp. 205–235.

13. See Daniel Goleman, *Emotional Intelligence: Why It Can Matter More Than IQ* (New York: Bantam, 1995).

14. Daniel Goleman, "Leadership That Gets Results," *Harvard Business Review*, March–April 2000, pp. 78–90. See also Kenneth Law, Chi-Sum Wong, and Lynda Song, "The Construct and Criterion Validity of Emotional Intelligence and Its Potential Utility for Management Studies," *Journal of Applied Psychology*, 2004, vol. 87, no. 3, pp. 483–496.

15. Leon Festinger, *A Theory of Cognitive Dissonance* (Palo Alto, CA: Stanford University Press, 1957).

16. See John J. Clancy, "Is Loyalty Really Dead?" *Across the Board*, June 1999, pp. 15–115.

17. Patricia C. Smith, L. M. Kendall, and Charles Hulin, *The Measurement of Satisfaction in Work and Behavior* (Chicago: Rand-McNally, 1969). See also Steven Currall, Annette Towler, Tomothy Judge, and Laura Kohn, "Pay Satisfaction and Organizational Outcomes," *Personnel Psychology*, 2005, vol. 58, pp. 613–640.

18. "Companies Are Finding Real Payoffs in Aiding Employee Satisfaction," *Wall Street Journal*, October 11, 2000, p. B1.

19. James R. Lincoln, "Employee Work Attitudes and Management Practice in the U.S. and Japan: Evidence from a Large Comparative Study," *California Management Review*, Fall 1989, pp. 89–106.

20. Ibid.

21. Richard M. Steers, "Antecedents and Outcomes of Organizational Commitment," *Administrative Science Quarterly*, 1977, vol. 22, pp. 46–56.

22. For research work in this area, see Jennifer M. George and Gareth R. Jones, "The Experience of Mood and Turnover Intentions: Interactive Effects of Value Attainment, Job Satisfaction, and Positive Mood," *Journal of Applied Psychology*, 1996, vol. 81, no. 3, pp. 318–325; Larry J. Williams, Mark B. Gavin, and Margaret Williams, "Measurement and Nonmeasurement Processes with Negative Affectivity and Employee Attitudes," *Journal of Applied Psychology*, 1996, vol. 81, no. 1, pp. 88–101.

23. Sigal Barsade and Donald Gibson, "Why Does Affect Matter in Organizations?" *Academy of Management Perspectives*, February 2007, pp. 36-59.

24. Kathleen Sutcliffe, "What Executives Notice: Accurate Perceptions in Top Management Teams," *Academy of Management Journal*, 1994, vol. 37, no. 5, pp. 1360–1378.

25. For a classic treatment of attribution, see H. H. Kelley, *Attribution in Social Interaction* (Morristown, N.J.: General Learning Press, 1971).

26. For a recent overview of the stress literature, see Frank Landy, James Campbell Quick, and Stanislav Kasl, "Work, Stress, and Well-Being," *International Journal of Stress Management*, 1994, vol. 1, no. 1, pp. 33–73.

27. Hans Selye, *The Stress of Life* (New York: McGraw-Hill, 1976).

28. M. Friedman and R. H. Rosenman, *Type A Behavior and Your Heart* (New York: Knopf, 1974).

29. "Work & Family," *BusinessWeek*, June 28, 1993, pp. 80–88.

30. Richard S. DeFrank, Robert Konopaske, and John M. Ivancevich, "Executive Travel Stress: Perils of the Road Warrior," *Academy of Management Executive*, 2000, vol. 14, no. 2, pp. 58–67.

31. Steven Rogelberg, Desmond Leach, Peter Warr, and Jennifer Burnfield, "'Not Another Meeting!' Are Meeting Time Demands Related to Employee Well Being?" *Journal of Applied Psychology*, 2006, vol. 91, no. 1, pp. 86–96.

32. "Breaking Point," *Newsweek*, March 6, 1995, pp. 56–62. See also "Rising Job Stress Could Affect Bottom Line," *USA Today*, July 28, 2003, p. 18.

33. John M. Kelly, "Get a Grip on Stress," *HRMagazine*, February 1997, pp. 51–58.

34. "Nice Work If You Can Get It," *BusinessWeek*, January 9, 2006, pp. 56–57.

35. See Richard W. Woodman, John E. Sawyer, and Ricky W. Griffin, "Toward a Theory of Organizational Creativity," *Academy of Management Review*, April 1993, pp. 293–321.

36. "In Secret Hideaway, Bill Gates Ponders Microsoft's Future," *Wall Street Journal*, March 28, 2005, pp. A1, A13.

37. John Simons, "The $10 Billion Pill," *Fortune*, January 20, 2003, pp. 58–68.

38. Christina E. Shalley, Lucy L. Gilson, and Terry C. Blum, "Matching Creativity Requirements and the Work Environment: Effects on Satisfaction and Intentions to Leave," *Academy of Management Journal*, 2000, vol. 43, no. 2, pp. 215–223. See also Filiz Tabak, "Employee Creative Performance: What Makes It Happen?" *Academy of Management Executive*, 1997, vol. 11, no. 1, pp. 119–122.

39. "That's It, I'm Outa Here," *BusinessWeek*, October 3, 2000, pp. 96–98.

40. For recent findings regarding this behavior, see Philip M. Podsakoff, Scott B. MacKenzie, Julie Beth Paine, and Daniel G. G. Bacharah, "Organizational Citizenship Behaviors: A Critical Review of the Theoretical and Empirical Literature and Suggestions for Future Research," *Journal of Management*, 2000, vol. 26, no. 3, pp. 513–563.

41. Dennis W. Organ "Personality and Organizational Citizenship Behavior," *Journal of Management*, 1994, vol. 20, no. 2, pp. 465–478; Mary Konovsky and S. Douglas Pugh, "Citizenship Behavior and Social Exchange," *Academy of Management Journal*, 1994, vol. 37, no. 3, pp. 656–669; and Jacqueline A-M. Coyle-Shapiro, "A Psychological Contract Perspective on Organizational Citizenship," *Journal of Organizational Behavior*, 2002, vol. 23, pp. 927–946.

42. See Anne O'Leary-Kelly, Ricky W. Griffin, and David J. Glew, "Organization-Motivated Aggression: A Research Framework," *Academy of Management Review*, January 1996, pp. 225–253. See also Ricky Griffin and Yvette Lopez, "'Bad Behavior' in Organizations: A Review and Typology for Future Research," *Journal of Management*, 2005, vol. 31, no. 6, pp. 988–1005.

CHAPTER 10

1. "2005 Financial Report," "Beyond the Headlines," "What Is Doctors Without Borders?" Doctors Without Borders website, www.doctorswithoutborders.org on January 23, 2006; "About DNDI," Drugs for Neglected Diseases Initiative website, www.dndi.org on January 20, 2006; Nicolas de Torrenté, "The Professionalization and Bureaucratization of Humanitarian Action," Social Sciences Research Institute website, March 23, 2005, www.ssrc.org on January 20, 2006; Carlotta Gall, "Afghan Aid Killings: Suspect, No Arrests," *New York Times*, April 10, 2005, www.nytimes.com on January 20, 2006; Karin Moorhouse and Wei Cheng, *No One Can Stop the Rain*, Insomniac Press, April 2005; Cynthia M. Piccolo, "Across Careers and Continents," MedHunters website, www.medhunters.com on January 20, 2006; Kristin Rothwell, Nurse Zone website, www.nursezone.com on January 20, 2006 (quote); Nayana Somaiah, "Keep Up the Fight, Nigerians!" MedHunters website, www.medhunters.com on January 20, 2006; Stephanie Strom, "As Disaster Follows Disaster, Relief Groups Feel the Strain," *New York Times*, October 13, 2005, www.nytimes.com on January 20, 2006.

2. Richard M. Steers, Gregory A. Bigley, and Lyman W. Porter, *Motivation and Leadership at Work*, 6th ed. (New York: McGraw-Hill, 1996). See also Maureen L. Ambrose and Carol T. Kulik, "Old Friends, New

Faces: Motivation Research in the 1990s," *Journal of Management*, 1999, vol. 25, no. 3, pp. 231–292; and Edwin Locke and Gary Lartham, "What Should We Do About Motivation Theory? Six Recommendations for the Twenty-First Century," *Academy of Management Review*, 2004, vol. 29, no. 3, pp. 388-403.

3. See Nigel Nicholson, "How to Motivate Your Problem People," *Harvard Business Review*, January 2003, pp. 57–67. See also Hugo Kehr, "Integrating Implicit Motives, Explicit Motives, and Perceived Abilities: The Compensatory Model of Work Motivation and Volition," *Academy of Management Review*, 2004, vol. 29, no. 3, pp. 479–499.

4. See Jeffrey Pfeffer, *The Human Equation* (Cambridge, Mass.: Harvard Business School Press, 1998).

5. For a recent discussion of these questions, see Eryn Brown, "So Rich So Young—But Are They Really Happy?" *Fortune*, September 18, 2000, pp. 99–110.

6. Abraham H. Maslow, "A Theory of Human Motivation," *Psychological Review*, 1943, vol. 50, pp. 370–396; Abraham H. Maslow, *Motivation and Personality* (New York: Harper & Row, 1954). Maslow's most recent work is Abraham H. Maslow and Richard Lowry, *Toward a Psychology of Being* (New York: Wiley, 1999).

7. For a review, see Craig Pinder, *Work Motivation in Organizational Behavior* (Upper Saddle River, NJ: Prentice-Hall, 1998).

8. Frederick Herzberg, Bernard Mausner, and Barbara Snyderman, *The Motivation to Work* (New York: Wiley, 1959); Frederick Herzberg, "One More Time: How Do You Motivate Employees?" *Harvard Business Review*, January–February 1987, pp. 109–120 (reprinted in *Harvard Business Review*, January 2003, pp. 87–98).

9. Robert J. House and Lawrence A. Wigdor, "Herzberg's Dual-Factor Theory of Job Satisfaction and Motivation: A Review of the Evidence and a Criticism," *Personnel Psychology*, Winter 1967, pp. 369–389; Victor H. Vroom, *Work and Motivation* (New York: Wiley, 1964). See also Pinder, *Work Motivation in Organizational Behavior*.

10. David C. McClelland, *The Achieving Society* (Princeton, N.J.: Van Nostrand, 1961); David C. McClelland, *Power: The Inner Experience* (New York: Irvington, 1975).

11. "Best Friends Good for Business," *USA Today*, December 1, 2004, pp. 1B, 2B.

12. David McClelland and David H. Burnham, "Power Is the Great Motivator," *Harvard Business Review*, March–April 1976, pp. 100–110 (reprinted in *Harvard Business Review*, January 2003, pp. 117–127).

13. See "The Rise and Fall of Dennis Kozlowski," *BusinessWeek*, December 23, 2002, pp. 64–77.

14. Vroom, *Work and Motivation*.

15. "Starbucks' Secret Weapon," *Fortune*, September 29, 1997, p. 268.

16. Lyman W. Porter and Edward E. Lawler III, *Managerial Attitudes and Performance* (Homewood, Ill.: Dorsey, 1968).

17. J. Stacy Adams, "Towards an Understanding of Inequity," *Journal of Abnormal and Social Psychology*, November 1963, pp. 422–436.

18. See Edwin A. Locke, "Toward a Theory of Task Performance and Incentives," *Organizational Behavior and Human Performance*, 1968, vol. 3, pp. 157–189.

19. Gary P. Latham and J. J. Baldes, "The Practical Significance of Locke's Theory of Goal Setting," *Journal of Applied Psychology*, 1975, vol. 60, pp. 187–191.

20. For a recent extension of goal-setting theory, see Yitzhak Fried and Linda Haynes Slowik, "Enriching Goal-Setting Theory with Time: An Integrated Approach," *Academy of Management Review*, 2004, vol. 29, no. 3, pp. 404–422.

21. B. F. Skinner, *Beyond Freedom and Dignity* (New York: Knopf, 1971).

22. Fred Luthans and Robert Kreitner, *Organizational Behavior Modification and Beyond: An Operant and Social Learning Approach* (Glenview, Ill.: Scott, Foresman, 1985).

23. Ibid.; W. Clay Hamner and Ellen P. Hamner, "Behavior Modification on the Bottom Line," *Organizational Dynamics*, Spring 1976, pp. 2–21.

24. "At Emery Air Freight: Positive Reinforcement Boosts Performance," *Organizational Dynamics*, Winter 1973, pp. 41–50; for a recent update, see Alexander D. Stajkovic and Fred Luthans, "A Meta-Analysis of the Effects of Organizational Behavior Modification on Task Performance, 1975–95," *Academy of Management Journal*, 1997, vol. 40, no. 5, pp. 1122–1149.

25. David J. Glew, Anne M. O'Leary-Kelly, Ricky W. Griffin, and David D. Van Fleet, "Participation in Organizations: A Preview of the Issues and Proposed Framework for Future Analysis," *Journal of Management*, 1995, vol. 21, no. 3, pp. 395–421.

26. Baxter W. Graham, "The Business Argument for Flexibility," *HRMagazine*, May 1996, pp. 104–110.

27. A. R. Cohen and H. Gadon, *Alternative Work Schedules: Integrating Individual and Organizational Needs* (Reading, Mass.: Addison Wesley, 1978).

28. "The Easiest Commute of All," *BusinessWeek*, December 12, 2005, pp. 78–80.

29. Daniel Wren, *The Evolution of Management Theory*, 4th ed. (New York: Wiley, 1994).

30. C. Wiley, "Incentive Plan Pushes Production," *Personnel Journal*, August 1993, p. 91.

31. "When Money Isn't Enough," *Forbes*, November 18, 1996, pp. 164–169.

32. Jacquelyn DeMatteo, Lillian Eby, and Eric Sundstrom, "Team-Based Rewards: Current Empirical Evidence and Directions for Future Research," in L. L. Cummings and Barry Staw (eds.), *Research in Organizational Behavior*, vol. 20 (Greenwich, CT.: JAI, 1998), pp. 141–183.

33. Theresa M. Welbourne and Luis R. Gomez-Mejia, "Gainsharing: A Critical Review and a Future Research Agenda," *Journal of Management*, 1995, vol. 21, no. 3, pp. 559–609.

34. Harry Barkema and Luis Gomez-Mejia, "Managerial Compensation and Firm Performance: A General Research Framework," *Academy of Management Journal*, 1998, vol. 41, no. 2, pp. 135–145.

35. Rajiv D. Banker, Seok-Young Lee, Gordon Potter, and Dhinu Srinivasan, "Contextual Analysis of Performance Impacts of Outcome-Based Incentive Compensation," *Academy of Management Journal*, 1996, vol. 39, no. 4, pp. 920–948.

36. M. Blair, "CEO Pay: Why Such a Contentious Issue?" *The Brookings Review*, Winter 1994, pp. 23–27.

37. Steve Kerr, "The Best-Laid Incentive Plans," *Harvard Business Review*, January 2003, pp. 27–40.

38. "Now It's Getting Personal," *BusinessWeek*, December 16, 2002, pp. 90–92.

CHAPTER 11

1. Adrienne Carter, "Miller Brewing: It's Norman Time," *BusinessWeek*, May 29, 2006, www.businessweek.com on May 20, 2006 (quote); Emily Fredrix, "Miller to Launch Mexican-Style Beer," *BusinessWeek*, February 5, 2007, www.businessweek.com on February 23, 2007; Emily Fredrix, "Miller to Push Miller Lite," *BusinessWeek*, February 23, 2007, www.businessweek.com on February 23, 2007; Lorne Manly, "BrewTube," *The New York Times Magazine*, February 4, 2007, pp. 50–55; "SABMiller—Senior Appointments," SABMiller website, www.sabmiller.com on February 23, 2007; Patricia Sellers, "SAB Brews Up Big Trouble for Bud," *Fortune*, August 22, 2005, www.fortune.com on February 23, 2007.

2. See Ronald A. Heifetz and Donald L. Laurie, "The Work of Leadership," *Harvard Business Review*, January–February 1997, pp. 124–134. See also Arthur G. Jago, "Leadership: Perspectives in Theory and Research," *Management Science*, March 1982, pp. 315–336, and "The New Leadership," *BusinessWeek*, August 28, 2000, pp. 100–187.

3. Gary A. Yukl, *Leadership in Organizations*, 3rd ed. (Englewood Cliffs, N.J.: Prentice-Hall, 1994), p. 5. See also Gregory G. Dess and Joseph C. Pickens, "Changing Roles: Leadership in the 21st Century," *Organizational Dynamics*, Winter 2000, pp. 18–28.

4. John P. Kotter, "What Leaders Really Do," *Harvard Business Review*, May–June 1990, pp. 103–111 (reprinted in *Harvard Business Review*, December 2001, pp. 85–93). See also Daniel Goleman, "Leadership That Gets Results," *Harvard Business Review*, March–April 2000, pp. 78–88; and Keith Grints, *The Arts of Leadership* (Oxford, UK: Oxford University Press, 2000).

5. John R. P. French and Bertram Raven, "The Bases of Social Power," in Dorwin Cartwright (ed.), *Studies in Social Power* (Ann Arbor: University of Michigan Press, 1959), pp. 150–167.

6. Hugh D. Menzies, "The Ten Toughest Bosses," *Fortune*, April 21, 1980, pp. 62–73.

7. Bennett J. Tepper, "Consequences of Abusive Supervision," *Academy of Management Journal*, 2000, vol. 43, no. 2, pp. 178–190.

8. Bernard M. Bass, *Bass & Stogdill's Handbook of Leadership*, 3rd ed. (Riverside, N.J.: Free Press, 1990).

9. Shelley A. Kirkpatrick and Edwin A. Locke, "Leadership: Do Traits Matter?" *Academy of Management Executive*, May 1991, pp. 48–60. See also Robert J. Sternberg, "Managerial Intelligence: Why IQ Isn't Enough," *Journal of Management*, 1997, vol. 23, no. 3, pp. 475–493.

10. Timothy Judge, Amy Colbert, and Remus Ilies, "Intelligence and Leadership: A Quantitative Review and Test of Theoretical Propositions," *Journal of Applied Psychology*, 2004, vol. 89, no. 3, pp. 542–552.

11. Rensis Likert, *New Patterns of Management* (New York: McGraw-Hill, 1961); Rensis Likert, *The Human Organization* (New York: McGraw-Hill, 1967).

12. The Ohio State studies stimulated many articles, monographs, and books. A good overall reference is Ralph M. Stogdill and A. E. Coons, eds., *Leader Behavior: Its Description and Measurement* (Columbus: Bureau of Business Research, Ohio State University, 1957).

13. Edwin A. Fleishman, E. F. Harris, and H. E. Burt, *Leadership and Supervision in Industry* (Columbus: Bureau of Business Research, Ohio State University, 1955).

14. See Timothy Judge, Ronald Piccolo, and Remus Ilies, "The Forgotten One? The Validity of Consideration and Initiating Structure in Leadership Research," *Journal of Applied Psychology*, 2004, vol. 89, no. 1, pp. 36–51.

15. Robert R. Blake and Jane S. Mouton, *The Managerial Grid* (Houston: Gulf Publishing, 1964); Robert R. Blake and Jane S. Mouton, *The Versatile Manager: A Grid Profile* (Homewood, Ill.: Dow Jones-Irwin, 1981).

16. Fred E. Fiedler, *A Theory of Leadership Effectiveness* (New York: McGraw-Hill, 1967).

17. Chester A. Schriesheim, Bennett J. Tepper, and Linda A. Tetrault, "Least Preferred Co-Worker Score, Situational Control, and Leadership Effectiveness: A Meta-Analysis of Contingency Model Performance Predictions," *Journal of Applied Psychology*, 1994, vol. 79, no. 4, pp. 561–573.

18. Fiedler, *A Theory of Leadership Effectiveness*; Fred E. Fiedler and M. M. Chemers, *Leadership and Effective Management* (Glenview, Ill.: Scott, Foresman, 1974).

19. For recent reviews and updates, see Lawrence H. Peters, Darrell D. Hartke, and John T. Pohlmann, "Fiedler's Contingency Theory of Leadership: An Application of the Meta-Analysis Procedures of Schmidt and Hunter," *Psychological Bulletin*, vol. 97, pp. 274–285; and Fred E. Fiedler, "When to Lead, When to Stand Back," *Psychology Today*, September 1987, pp. 26–27.

20. Martin G. Evans, "The Effects of Supervisory Behavior on the Path-Goal Relationship," *Organizational Behavior and Human Performance*, May 1970, pp. 277–298; Robert J. House and Terence R. Mitchell, "Path-Goal Theory of Leadership," *Journal of Contemporary Business*, Autumn 1974, pp. 81–98. See also Yukl, *Leadership in Organizations*.

21. For a recent review, see J. C. Wofford and Laurie Z. Liska, "Path-Goal Theories of Leadership: A Meta-Analysis," *Journal of Management*, 1993, vol. 19, no. 4, pp. 857–876.

22. See Victor H. Vroom and Philip H. Yetton, *Leadership and Decision Making* (Pittsburgh: University of Pittsburgh Press, 1973); and Victor H. Vroom and Arthur G. Jago, *The New Leadership* (Englewood Cliffs, NJ: Prentice-Hall, 1988).

23. Victor Vroom, "Leadership and the Decision-Making Process," *Organizational Dynamics*, 2000, vol. 28, no. 4, pp. 82–94.

24. Vroom and Jago, *The New Leadership*.

25. Ibid.

26. See Madeline E. Heilman, Harvey A. Hornstein, Jack H. Cage, and Judith K. Herschlag, "Reaction to Prescribed Leader Behavior as a Function of Role Perspective: The Case of the Vroom-Yetton Model," *Journal of Applied Psychology*, February 1984, pp. 50–60; R. H. George Field, "A Test of the Vroom-Yetton Normative Model of Leadership," *Journal of Applied Psychology*, February 1982, pp. 523–532.

27. George Graen and J. F. Cashman, "A Role-Making Model of Leadership in Formal Organizations: A Developmental

Approach," in J. G. Hunt and L. L. Larson (eds.), *Leadership Frontiers* (Kent, Ohio: Kent State University Press, 1975), pp. 143–165; Fred Dansereau, George Graen, and W. J. Haga, "A Vertical Dyad Linkage Approach to Leadership Within Formal Organizations: A Longitudinal Investigation of the Role-Making Process," *Organizational Behavior and Human Performance*, 1975, vol. 15, pp. 46–78.

28. See Kathryn Sherony and Stephen Green, "Coworker Exchange: Relationships Between Coworkers, Leader-Member Exchange, and Work Attitudes," *Journal of Applied Psychology*, 2002, vol. 87, no. 3, pp. 542–548.

29. Steven Kerr and John M. Jermier, "Substitutes for Leadership: Their Meaning and Measurement," *Organizational Behavior and Human Performance*, December 1978, pp. 375–403.

30. See Charles C. Manz and Henry P. Sims, Jr., "Leading Workers to Lead Themselves: The External Leadership of Self-Managing Work Teams," *Administrative Science Quarterly*, March 1987, pp. 106–129. See also "Living Without a Leader," *Fortune*, March 20, 2000, pp. 218–219.

31. See Robert J. House, "A 1976 Theory of Charismatic Leadership," in J. G. Hunt and L. L. Larson (eds.), *Leadership: The Cutting Edge* (Carbondale, Ill.: Southern Illinois University Press, 1977), pp. 189–207. See also Jay A. Conger and Rabindra N. Kanungo, "Toward a Behavioral Theory of Charismatic Leadership in Organizational Settings," *Academy of Management Review*, October 1987, pp. 637–647.

32. Stratford P. Sherman, "Donald Trump Just Won't Die," *Fortune*, August 13, 1990, pp. 75–79.

33. David A. Nadler and Michael L. Tushman, "Beyond the Charismatic Leader: Leadership and Organizational Change," *California Management Review*, Winter 1990, pp. 77–97.

34. Jane Howell and Boas Shamir, "The Role of Followers in the Charismatic Leadership Process: Relationships and Their Consequences," *Academy of Management Review*, 2005, vol. 30, no. 1, pp. 96–112.

35. James MacGregor Burns, *Leadership* (New York: Harper & Row, 1978). See also Rajnandini Pillai, Chester A. Schriesheim, and Eric J. Williams, "Fairness Perceptions and Trust as Mediators for Transformational and Transactional Leadership: A Two-Sample Study," *Journal of Management*, 1999, vol. 25, no. 6, pp. 897–933.

36. Robert Rubin, David Munz, and William Bommer, "Leading from Within: The Effects of Emotion Recognition and Personality on Transformational Leadership Behaviors," *Academy of Management Journal*, 2005, vol. 48, no. 5, pp. 845–858.

37. Kenneth Labich, "The Seven Keys to Business Leadership," *Fortune*, October 24, 1988, pp. 55-61.

38. Jerry Useem, "Tape + Light Bulbs = ?" *Fortune*, August 12, 2002, pp. 127–132.

39. Dusya Vera and Mary Crossan, "Strategic Leadership and Organizational Learning," *Academy of Management Review*, 2004, vol. 29, no. 2, pp. 222–240.

40. "The Best & Worst Managers of the Year," *BusinessWeek*, January 19, 2005, pp. 55–84.

41. See Kurt Dirks and Donald Ferrin, "Trust in Leadership," *Journal of Applied Psychology*, 2002, vol. 87, no. 4, pp. 611–628.

42. Jeffrey Pfeffer, *Power in Organizations* (Marshfield, MA: Pitman, 1981), p. 7.

43. Timothy Judge and Robert Bretz, "Political Influence Behavior and Career Success," *Journal of Management*, 1994, vol. 20, no. 1, pp. 43–65.

44. Victor Murray and Jeffrey Gandz, "Games Executives Play: Politics at Work," *Business Horizons*, December 1980, pp. 11–23; Jeffrey Gandz and Victor Murray, "The Experience of Workplace Politics," *Academy of Management Journal*, June 1980, pp. 237–251.

45. Don R. Beeman and Thomas W. Sharkey, "The Use and Abuse of Corporate Power," *Business Horizons*, March–April 1987, pp. 26–30.

46. "How Ebbers Kept the Board in His Pocket," *BusinessWeek*, October 14, 2002, pp. 138–139.

47. See William L. Gardner, "Lessons in Organizational Dramaturgy: The Art of Impression Management," *Organizational Dynamics*, Summer 1992, pp. 51–63; Elizabeth Wolf Morrison and Robert J. Bies, "Impression Management in the Feedback-Seeking Process: A Literature Review and Research Agenda," *Academy of Management Review*, July 1991, pp. 522–541.

48. See Chad Higgins, Timothy Judge, and Gerald Ferris, "Influence Tactics and Work Outcomes: A Meta-Analysis," *Journal of Organizational Behavior*, 2003, vol. 24, pp. 89–106.

49. Murray and Gandz, "Games Executives Play."

50. Beeman and Sharkey, "The Use and Abuse of Corporate Power."

51. Stefanie Ann Lenway and Kathleen Rehbein, "Leaders, Followers, and Free Riders: An Empirical Test of Variation in Corporate Political Involvement," *Academy of Management Journal*, December 1991, pp. 893–905.

CHAPTER 12

1. Howard Bloom, "The King of All Sports Media," *Sports Business News*, December 20, 2006, www.sportsbusinessnews.com on February 28, 2007; "Corporate Information," ESPN website, www.espnmediazone.com on February 27, 2007; Bryan Curtis, "Adrift on the Sea of ESPN.com," *Play* (supplement to *The New York Times*), June 2006, pp. 42–44; David Kirkpatrick, "Active.com and the Morphing of Media," *Fortune*, March 2, 2007, www.fortune.com on February 28, 2007; Tom Lowry, "ESPN.com: Guys and Dollars," *BusinessWeek*, October 17, 2005, www.businessweek.com on February 28, 2007; Tom Lowry, "In the Zone," *BusinessWeek*, October 17, 2005, www.businessweek.com on February 28, 2007 (quote).

2. Henry Mintzberg, *The Nature of Managerial Work* (New York: Harper & Row, 1973).

3. See Michael H. Zack, "Managing Codified Knowledge," *Sloan Management Review*, Summer 1999, pp. 45–58.

4. Edward W. Desmond, "How Your Data May Soon Seek You Out," *Fortune*, September 1997, pp. 149–154.

5. Bruce Barry and Ingrid Fulmer, "The Medium and the Message: The Adaptive Use of Communication Media in Dyadic Influence," *Academy of Management Review*, 2004, vol. 29, no. 2, pp. 272–292.

6. Mintzberg, *The Nature of Managerial Work*.

7. Reid Buckley, "When You Have to Put It to Them," *Across the Board*, October 1999, pp. 44–48.

8. "'Did I Just Say That?!' How to Recover from Foot-in-Mouth," *Wall Street Journal*, June 19, 2002, p. B1.

9. "Executives Who Dread Public Speaking Learn to Keep Their Cool in the Spotlight," *Wall Street Journal*, May 4, 1990, pp. B1, B6.

10. Mintzberg, *The Nature of Managerial Work*.

11. Buckley, "When You Have to Put It to Them."

12. See "Watch What You Put in That Office Email," *BusinessWeek*, September 30, 2002, pp. 114–115.

13. Nicholas Varchaver, "The Perils of E-mail," *Fortune*, February 17, 2003, pp. 96–102; "How a String of E-Mail Came to Haunt CSFB and Star Banker," *Wall Street Journal*, February 28, 2003, pp. A1, A6; "How Morgan Stanley Botched a Big Case by Fumbling Emails," *Wall Street Journal*, May 16, 2005, pp. A1, A10.

14. A. Vavelas, "Communication Patterns in Task-Oriented Groups," *Journal of the Accoustical Society of America*, 1950, vol. 22, pp. 725–730; Jerry Wofford, Edwin Gerloff, and Robert Cummins, *Organizational Communication* (New York: McGraw-Hill, 1977).

15. Nelson Phillips and John Brown, "Analyzing Communications in and Around Organizations: A Critical Hermeneutic Approach," *Academy of Management Journal*, 1993, vol. 36, no. 6, pp. 1547–1576.

16. Walter Kiechel III, "Breaking Bad News to the Boss," *Fortune*, April 9, 1990, pp. 111–112.

17. Mary Young and James Post, "How Leading Companies Communicate with Employees," *Organizational Dynamics*, Summer 1993, pp. 31–43.

18. For one example, see Kimberly D. Elsbach and Greg Elofson, "How the Packaging of Decision Explanations Affects Perceptions of Trustworthiness," *Academy of Management Journal*, 2000, vol. 43, no. 1, pp. 80–89.

19. Keith Davis, "Management Communication and the Grapevine," *Harvard Business Review*, September–October 1953, pp. 43–49.

20. "Spread the Word: Gossip Is Good," *Wall Street Journal*, October 4, 1988, p. B1.

21. See David M. Schweiger and Angelo S. DeNisi, "Communication with Employees Following a Merger: A Longitudinal Field Experiment," *Academy of Management Journal*, March 1991, pp. 110–135.

22. Nancy B. Kurland and Lisa Hope Pelled, "Passing the Word: Toward a Model of Gossip and Power in the Workplace," *Academy of Management Review*, 2000, vol. 25, no. 2, pp. 428–438.

23. See Tom Peters and Nancy Austin, *A Passion for Excellence* (New York: Random House, 1985).

24. Albert Mehrabian, *Non-verbal Communication* (Chicago: Aldine, 1972).

25. Michael B. McCaskey, "The Hidden Messages Managers Send," *Harvard Business Review*, November–December 1979, pp. 135–148.

26. David Givens, "What Body Language Can Tell You That Words Cannot," *U.S. News & World Report*, November 19, 1984, p. 100.

27. Edward J. Hall, *The Hidden Dimension* (New York: Doubleday, 1966).

28. For a detailed discussion of improving communication effectiveness, see Courtland L. Bovee, John V. Thill, and Barbara E. Schatzman, *Business Communication Today*, 7th ed. (Upper Saddle River, N.J.: Prentice Hall, 2003).

29. See Otis W. Baskin and Craig E. Aronoff, *Interpersonal Communication in Organizations* (Glenview, Ill.: Scott, Foresman, 1980).

30. See "You Have (Too Much) E-Mail," *USA Today*, March 12, 1999, p. 3B.

31. Justin Fox, "The Triumph of English," *Fortune*, September 18, 2000, pp. 209–212.

32. Joseph Allen and Bennett P. Lientz, *Effective Business Communication* (Santa Monica, Calif.: Goodyear, 1979).

33. See "Making Silence Your Ally," *Across the Board*, October 1999, p. 11.

34. Boyd A. Vander Houwen, "Less Talking, More Listening," *HRMagazine*, April 1997, pp. 53–58.

35. For a discussion of these and related issues, see Eric M. Eisenberg and Marsha G. Witten, "Reconsidering Openness in Organizational Communication," *Academy of Management Review*, July 1987, pp. 418–426.

36. For a recent illustration, see Barbara Kellerman, "When Should a Leader Apologize—and When Not?" *Harvard Business Review*, April 2006, pp. 72–81.

CHAPTER 13

1. Bill Chastain, "Q&A with Stuart Sternberg," Devil Rays website, October 6, 2005, tampabay.devilrays.mlb.com on May 4, 2006; Mark Hyman, "Baseball: Money Can't Buy Me Wins," *BusinessWeek*, October 4, 2005, www.businessweek.com on May 4, 2006; Chris Isidore, "Baseball Spending Spree Ahead," *Money*, October 7, 2005, www.cnnmoney.com on May 4, 2006; Landon Thomas, Jr., "Case Study: Fix a Baseball Team," *New York Times*, April 2, 2006, pp. BU1, 9 (quote).

2. For a review of definitions of groups, see Gregory Moorhead and Ricky W. Griffin, *Organizational Behavior*, 8th ed. (Boston: Houghton Mifflin, 2007).

3. Dorwin Cartwright and Alvin Zander, eds., *Group Dynamics: Research and Theory*, 3rd ed. (New York: Harper & Row, 1968).

4. Rob Cross, Nitin Nohria, and Andrew Parker, "Six Myths About Informal Networks—And How to Overcome Them," *Sloan Management Review*, Spring 2002, pp. 67–77.

5. Robert Schrank, *Ten Thousand Working Days* (Cambridge, Mass.: MIT Press, 1978); Bill Watson, "Counter Planning on the Shop Floor," in Peter Frost, Vance Mitchell, and Walter Nord (eds.), *Organizational Reality*, 2nd ed. (Glenview, Ill.: Scott, Foresman, 1982), pp. 286–294.

6. "After Layoffs, More Workers Band Together," *Wall Street Journal*, February 26, 2002, p. B1.

7. Bradley L. Kirkman and Benson Rosen, "Powering Up Teams," *Organizational Dynamics*, Winter 2000, pp. 48–58.

8. Brian Dumaine, "Payoff from the New Management," *Fortune*, December 13, 1993, pp. 103–110.

9. Arvind Malhotra, Ann Majchrzak, and Benson Rosen, "Leading Virtual Teams," *Academy of Management Perspectives*, February 2007, pp. 60–70.

10. "Why Teams Fail," *USA Today*, February 25, 1997, pp. 1B, 2B.

11. Brian Dumaine, "The Trouble with Teams," *Fortune*, September 5, 1994, pp. 86–92. See also Susan G. Cohen

and Diane E. Bailey, "What Makes Teams Work: Group Effectiveness Research from the Shop Floor to the Executive Suite," *Journal of Management*, 1997, vol. 23, no. 3, pp. 239–290; and John Mathieu, Lucy Gilson, and Thomas Ruddy, "Empowerment and Team Effectiveness: An Empirical Test of an Integrated Model," *Journal of Applied Psychology*, 2006, vol. 91, no. 1, pp. 97–108.

12. Marvin E. Shaw, *Group Dynamics: The Psychology of Small Group Behavior*, 4th ed. (New York: McGraw-Hill, 1985).

13. "How to Avoid Hiring the Prima Donnas Who Hate Teamwork," *Wall Street Journal*, February 15, 2000, p. B1.

14. See Connie Gersick, "Marking Time: Predictable Transitions in Task Groups," *Academy of Management Journal*, June 1989, pp. 274–309. See also Avan R. Jassawalla and Hemant C. Sashittal, "Building Collaborative Cross-Functional New Product Teams," *Academy of Management Review*, 1999, vol. 13, no. 3, pp. 50–60.

15. See Gilad Chen, "Newcomer Adaptation in Teams: Multilevel Antecedents and Outcomes," *Academy of Management Journal*, 2005, vol. 48, no. 1, pp. 101–116.

16. For a review of other team characteristics, see Michael Campion, Gina Medsker, and A. Catherine Higgs, "Relations Between Work Group Characteristics and Effectiveness: Implications for Designing Effective Work Groups," *Personnel Psychology*, Winter 1993, pp. 823–850.

17. David Katz and Robert L. Kahn, *The Social Psychology of Organizations*, 2nd ed. (New York: Wiley, 1978), pp. 187–221. See also Greg L. Stewart and Murray R. Barrick, "Team Structure and Performance: Assessing the Mediating Role of Intrateam Process and the Moderating Role of Task Type," *Academy of Management Journal*, 2000, vol. 43, no. 2, pp. 135–148; and Michael G. Pratt and Peter O. Foreman, "Classifying Managerial Responses to Multiple Organizational Identities," *Academy of Management Review*, 2000, vol. 25, no. 1, pp. 18–42.

18. See Travis C. Tubre and Judith M. Collins, "Jackson and Schuler (1985) Revisited: A Meta-Analysis of the Relationships Between Role Ambiguity, Role Conflict, and Job Performance," *Journal of Management*, 2000, vol. 26, no. 1, pp. 155–169.

19. Robert L. Kahn, D. M. Wolfe, R. P. Quinn, J. D. Snoek, and R. A. Rosenthal, *Organizational Stress: Studies in Role Conflict and Role Ambiguity* (New York: Wiley, 1964).

20. Daniel C. Feldman, "The Development and Enforcement of Group Norms," *Academy of Management Review*, January 1984, pp. 47–53.

21. "Companies Turn to Peer Pressure to Cut Injuries as Psychologists Join the Battle," *Wall Street Journal*, March 29, 1991, pp. B1, B3.

22. James Wallace Bishop and K. Dow Scott, "How Commitment Affects Team Performance," *HRMagazine*, February 1997, pp. 107–115.

23. Anne O'Leary-Kelly, Joseph Martocchio, and Dwight Frink, "A Review of the Influence of Group Goals on Group Performance," *Academy of Management Journal*, 1994, vol. 37, no. 5, pp. 1285–1301.

24. Philip M. Podsakoff, Michael Ahearne, and Scott B. MacKenzie, "Organizational Citizenship Behavior and the Quantity and Quality of Work Group Performance, *Journal of Applied Psychology*, 1997, vol. 82, no. 2, pp. 262–270.

25. Suzy Wetlaufer, "Common Sense and Conflict," *Harvard Business Review*, January–February 2000, pp. 115–125.

26. Kathleen M. Eisenhardt, Jean L. Kahwajy, and L. J. Bourgeois III, "How Management Teams Can Have a Good Fight," *Harvard Business Review*, July–August 1997, pp. 77–89.

27. Thomas Bergmann and Roger Volkema, "Issues, Behavioral Responses and Consequences in Interpersonal Conflicts," *Journal of Organizational Behavior*, 1994, vol. 15, pp. 467–471.

28. Robin Pinkley and Gregory Northcraft, "Conflict Frames of Reference: Implications for Dispute Processes and Outcomes," *Academy of Management Journal*, 1994, vol. 37, no. 1, pp. 193–205.

29. "How 2 Computer Nuts Transformed Industry Before Messy Breakup," *Wall Street Journal*, August 27, 1996, pp. A1, A10.

30. Bruce Barry and Greg L. Stewart, "Composition, Process, and Performance in Self-Managed Groups: The Role of Personality," *Journal of Applied Psychology*, 1997, vol. 82, no. 1, pp. 62–78.

31. "Delta CEO Resigns After Clashes with Board," *USA Today*, May 13, 1997, p. B1.

32. "Why Boeing's Culture Breeds Turmoil," *BusinessWeek*, March 21, 2005, pp. 34–36.

33. "A 'Blood War' in the Jeans Trade," *BusinessWeek*, November 13, 1999, pp. 74–81.

34. Peter Elkind, "Blood Feud," *Fortune*, April 14, 1997, pp. 90–102.

35. See Patrick Nugent, "Managing Conflict: Third-Party Interventions for Managers," *Academy of Management Executive*, 2002, vol. 16, no. 1, pp. 139–148.

36. "Solving Conflicts in the Workplace Without Making Losers," *Wall Street Journal*, May 27, 1997, p. B1.

37. "Teaching Business How to Cope with Workplace Conflicts," *BusinessWeek*, February 18, 1990, pp. 136, 139.

CHAPTER 14

1. Michael Arndt, "McDonald's 24/7," *BusinessWeek*, February 5, 2007, www.businessweek.com on March 2, 2007 (quote); Michael Arndt, "Skinner's Winning McDonald's Recipe," *BusinessWeek*, February 5, 2007, www.businessweek.com on March 2, 2007; Dave Carpenter, "McDonald's May Add Smoothies, New Drinks," *BusinessWeek*, February 28, 2007, www.businessweek.com on March 6, 2007; "McDonald's Reports Sales Jump," *Money*, March 8, 2007, www.cnnmoney.com on March 6, 2007; "McDonald's Tests a Bigger Burger, Report Says," *Money*, March 7, 2007, www.cnnmoney.com on March 6, 2007.

2. For a complete discussion of how FedEx uses control in its operations, see "The FedEx Edge," *Fortune*, April 3, 2006, pp. 77–84.

3. Thomas A. Stewart, "Welcome to the Revolution," *Fortune*, December 13, 1993, pp. 66–77.

4. William Taylor, "Control in an Age of Chaos," *Harvard Business Review*, November–December 1994, pp. 64–70.

5. "Fleetwood: Not a Happy Camper Company," *BusinessWeek*, October 9, 2000, pp. 88–90.

6. "An Apple a Day," *BusinessWeek*, October 14, 2002, pp. 122–125; "More Business People Say: Let's Not Do

Lunch," *USA Today*, December 24, 2002, p. 1B; David Stires, "The Breaking Point," *Fortune*, March 3, 2003, pp. 107–114.

7. Mark Kroll, Peter Wright, Leslie Toombs, and Hadley Leavell, "Form of Control: A Critical Determinant of Acquisition Performance and CEO Rewards," *Strategic Management Journal*, 1997, vol. 18, no. 2, pp. 85–96.

8. See Karynne Turner and Mona Makhija, "The Role of Organizational Controls in Managing Knowledge," *Academy of Management Review*, 2006, vol. 31, no. 1, pp. 197–217.

9. "It's Showtime for the Airlines," *BusinessWeek*, September 2, 2002, pp. 36–37.

10. "United's Bid to Cut Labor Costs Could Force Rivals to Follow," *Wall Street Journal*, February 25, 2003, pp. A1, A6.

11. Sim Sitkin, Kathleen Sutcliffe, and Roger Schroeder, "Distinguishing Control from Learning in Total Quality Management: A Contingency Perspective," *Academy of Management Review*, 1994, vol. 19, no. 3, pp. 537–564.

12. Robert Lusch and Michael Harvey, "The Case for an Off-Balance-Sheet Controller," *Sloan Management Review*, Winter 1994, pp. 101–110.

13. Edward E. Lawler III and John G. Rhode, *Information and Control in Organizations* (Pacific Palisades, Calif.: Goodyear, 1976).

14. Charles W. L. Hill, "Establishing a Standard: Competitive Strategy and Technological Standards in Winner-Take-All Industries," *Academy of Management Executive*, 1997, vol. 11, no. 2, pp. 7–16.

15. "Shifting Burden Helps Employers Cut Health Costs," *Wall Street Journal*, December 8, 2005, pp. B1, B2.

16. "An Efficiency Guru Refits Honda to Fight Auto Giants," *Wall Street Journal*, September 15, 1999, p. B1.

17. See "To Shed Idled Workers, Ford Offers to Foot Bill for College," *Wall Street Journal*, January 18, 2006, pp. B1, B3; "GM's Employees Buyout Offer," *Fast Company*, May 2006, p. 58.

18. See Belverd E. Needles, Jr., Henry R. Anderson, and James C. Caldwell, *Principles of Accounting*, 2002 ed. (Boston: Houghton Mifflin, 2002).

19. "At Disney, String of Weak Cartoons Leads to Cost Cuts," *Wall Street Journal*, June 18, 2002, pp. A1, A6.

20. Needles, Anderson, and Caldwell, *Principles of Accounting*.

21. "Mickey Mouse, CPA," *Forbes*, March 10, 1997, pp. 42–43.

22. Needles, Anderson, and Caldwell, *Principles of Accounting*.

23. Jeremy Kahn, "Do Accountants Have a Future?" *Fortune*, March 3, 2003, pp. 115–117.

24. "Inside WorldCom's Unearthing of a Vast Accounting Scandal," *Wall Street Journal*, June 27, 2002, pp. A1, A12.

25. William G. Ouchi, "The Transmission of Control Through Organizational Hierarchy," *Academy of Management Journal*, June 1978, pp. 173–192; Richard E. Walton, "From Control to Commitment in the Workplace," *Harvard Business Review*, March–April 1985, pp. 76–84.

26. "Nordstrom Cleans Out Its Closets," *BusinessWeek*, May 22, 2000, pp. 105–108.

27. "Best Managed Companies in America," *Forbes*, January 9, 2006, p. 118.

28. See "In Bow to Retailers' New Clout, Levi Strauss Makes Alterations," *Wall Street Journal*, June 17, 2005, pp. A1, A15.

29. Peter Lorange, Michael F. Scott Morton, and Sumantra Ghoshal, *Strategic Control* (St. Paul, Minn.: West, 1986). See also Joseph C. Picken and Gregory G. Dess, "Out of (Strategic) Control," *Organizational Dynamics*, Summer 1997, pp. 35–45.

30. "Kohl's Works to Refill Consumers' Bags," *USA Today*, April 8, 2005, pp. B1, B1.

31. See Hans Mjoen and Stephen Tallman, "Control and Performance in International Joint Ventures," *Organization Science*, May–June 1997, pp. 257–265.

32. For a recent study of effective control, see Diana Robertson and Erin Anderson, "Control System and Task Environment Effects on Ethical Judgment: An Exploratory Study of Industrial Salespeople," *Organization Science*, November 1993, pp. 617–629.

33. "Workers, Surf at Your Own Risk," *BusinessWeek*, June 12, 2000, pp. 105–106.

34. "Enterprise Takes Idea of Dressed for Success to a New Extreme," *Wall Street Journal*, November 20, 2002, p. B1.

CHAPTER 15

1. Cliff Edwards, "A Weaker David to Intel's Goliath," *BusinessWeek*, October 21, 2002, p. 48; Michael Kanellos, "Intel to Expand Irish Manufacturing Facilities," *CNet News*, May 19, 2004, www.news.com on February 12, 2006; Tom Krazit, "Intels Plans New 300mm Manufacturing Plant for Arizona," *InfoWorld*, July 25, 2005, www.infoworld.com on February 12, 2006; John Markoff and Steve Lohr, "Intel's Huge Bet Turns Iffy," *New York Times*, September 29, 2002, pp. BU1, 12, 13; Brent Schlender, "How Intel Took Moore's Law from Idea to Ideology," *Fortune*, October 27, 2002, www.fortune.com on February 17, 2003 (quote); Brent Schlender, "Intel's $10 Billion Gamble," *Fortune*, November 11, 2002, pp. 90–102.

2. Paul M. Swamidass, "Empirical Science: New Frontier in Operations Management Research," *Academy of Management Review*, October 1991, pp. 793–814.

3. See Anil Khurana, "Managing Complex Production Processes," *Sloan Management Review*, Winter 1999, pp. 85–98.

4. "Service Sector Grows," *USA Today*, March 3, 2006, p. 1B.

5. For an example, see Robin Cooper and Regine Slagmulder, "Develop Profitable New Products with Target Costing," *Sloan Management Review*, Summer 1999, pp. 23–34.

6. Joan Woodward, *Industrial Organization: Theory and Practice* (London: Oxford University Press, 1965).

7. See "Tight Labor? Tech to the Rescue," *BusinessWeek*, March 20, 2000, pp. 36–37.

8. "Computers Speed the Design of More Workaday Products," *Wall Street Journal*, January 18, 1985, p. 25.

9. "New Plant Gets Jaguar in Gear," *USA Today*, November 27, 2000, p. 4B.

10. "Thinking Machines," *BusinessWeek*, August 7, 2000, pp. 78–86.

11. James Brian Quinn and Martin Neil Baily, "Information Technology: Increasing Productivity in Services," *Academy of Management Executive*, 1994, vol. 8, no. 3, pp. 28–37.

12. See Charles J. Corbett, Joseph D. Blackburn, and Luk N. Van Wassenhove, "Partnerships to Improve Supply Chains," *Sloan Management Review*, Summer 1999, pp. 71–82; Jeffrey K. Liker and Yen-Chun Wu, "Japanese Automakers, U.S. Suppliers, and Supply-Chain Superiority," *Sloan Management Review*, Fall 2000, pp. 81–93. See also Gabriel Bitran, Suri Gurumurthi, and Shiou Lin Sam, "Supply Chain Governance," *MIT Sloan Management Review*, Spring 2007, pp. 30-37.

13. See "Siemens Climbs Back," *BusinessWeek*, June 5, 2000, pp. 79–82.

14. See M. Bensaou, "Portfolios of Buyer-Supplier Relationships," *Sloan Management Review*, Summer 1999, pp. 35–44.

15. "Just-in-Time Manufacturing Is Working Overtime," *BusinessWeek*, November 8, 1999, pp. 36–37.

16. "Quality—How to Make It Pay," *BusinessWeek*, August 8, 1994, pp. 54–59.

17. Rhonda Reger, Loren Gustafson, Samuel DeMarie, and John Mullane, "Reframing the Organization: Why Implementing Total Quality Is Easier Said Than Done," *Academy of Management Review*, 1994, vol. 19, no. 3, pp. 565–584.

18. Ross Johnson and William O. Winchell, *Management and Quality* (Milwaukee: American Society for Quality Control, 1989). See also Carol Reeves and David Bednar, "Defining Quality: Alternatives and Implications," *Academy of Management Review*, 1994, vol. 19, no. 3, pp. 419–445; C. K. Prahalad and M. S. Krishnan, "The New Meaning of Quality in the Information Age," *Harvard Business Review*, September–October 1999, pp. 109–120.

19. "Quality Isn't Just for Widgets," *BusinessWeek*, July 22, 2002, pp. 72–73.

20. W. Edwards Deming, *Out of the Crisis* (Cambridge, MA: MIT Press, 1986).

21. David Waldman, "The Contributions of Total Quality Management to a Theory of Work Performance," *Academy of Management Review*, 1994, vol. 19, no. 3, pp. 510–536.

22. Joel Dreyfuss, "Victories in the Quality Crusade," *Fortune*, October 10, 1988, pp. 80–88.

23. Thomas Y. Choi and Orlando C. Behling, "Top Managers and TQM Success: One More Look After All These Years," *Academy of Management Executive*, 1997, vol. 11, no. 1, pp. 37–48.

24. James Dean and David Bowen, "Management Theory and Total Quality: Improving Research and Practice Through Theory Development," *Academy of Management Review*, 1994, vol. 19, no. 3, pp. 392–418.

25. See "Porsche Figures Out What Americans Want," *USA Today*, June 28, 2006, p. 4B.

26. Edward E. Lawler, "Total Quality Management and Employee Involvement: Are They Compatible?" *Academy of Management Executive*, 1994, vol. 8, no. 1, pp. 68–79.

27. Jeremy Main, "How to Steal the Best Ideas Around," *Fortune*, October 19, 1992, pp. 102–106.

28. See James Brian Quinn, "Strategic Outsourcing: Leveraging Knowledge Capabilities," *Sloan Management Review*, Summer 1999, pp. 8–22.

29. "Global Gamble," *Forbes*, April 17, 2006, pp. 78–82.

30. Thomas Robertson, "How to Reduce Market Penetration Cycle Times," *Sloan Management Review*, Fall 1993, pp. 87–96.

31. "Speed Demons," *BusinessWeek*, March 27, 2006, pp. 68–76.

32. Ronald Henkoff, "The Hot New Seal of Quality," *Fortune*, June 28, 1993, pp. 116–120. See also Mustafa V. Uzumeri, "ISO 9000 and Other Metastandards: Principles for Management Practice?" *Academy of Management Executive*, 1997, vol. 11, no. 1, pp. 21–28.

33. Paula C. Morrow, "The Measurement of TQM Principles and Work-Related Outcomes," *Journal of Organizational Behavior*, July 1997, pp. 363–376.

34. John W. Kendrick, *Understanding Productivity: An Introduction to the Dynamics of Productivity Change* (Baltimore: Johns Hopkins University Press, 1977).

35. "Study: USA Losing Competitive Edge," *USA Today*, April 25, 1997, p. 9D.

36. "Why the Productivity Revolution Will Spread," *BusinessWeek*, February 14, 2000, pp. 112–118. See also "Productivity Grows in Spite of Recession," *USA Today*, July 29, 2002, pp. 1B, 2B; "Productivity's Second Wind," *BusinessWeek*, February 17, 2003, pp. 36–37.

37. Michael van Biema and Bruce Greenwald, "Managing Our Way to Higher Service-Sector Productivity," *Harvard Business Review*, July–August 1997, pp. 87–98.

Name Index

Organization and Product Index

Subject Index

Photo Credits

Chapter 1
Page 1: Torsten Silz/AFP/Getty Images; page 14: Courtesy of AT&T Archives and History Center; page 20: © Carsten Rehder/dpa/Corbis.

Chapter 2
Page 31: Mike Clarke/AFP/Getty Images; page 38: AP Images; page 43: AP Images.

Chapter 3
Page 61: AP Images; page 69: AP Images; page 80: AP Images.

Chapter 4
Page 95: Tim Boyle/Getty Images News; page 97: Steve Liss/Getty Images; page 105: AP Images.

Chapter 5
Page 121: AP Images; page 129: David L. Ryan/Globe Photos; page 135: AP Images.

Chapter 6
Page 157: AP Images; page 160: AP Images; page 178: Mike Kepka/San Francisco Chronicle/Corbis.

Chapter 7
Page 189: Pascal Le Segretain/Getty Images; page 191: Dennis MacDonald/PhotoEdit, Inc.; page 198: Bill Pugliano/Getty Images.

Chapter 8
Page 221: Tim Boyle/Getty Images; page 229: Amy Etra/PhotoEdit; page 242: AP Images.

Chapter 9
Page 259: David Young-Wolff/PhotoEdit, Inc.; page 265: AP Images; page 277: Michael Lewis.

Chapter 10
Page 291: AP Images; page 297: AP Images; page 304: AP Images.

Chapter 11
Page 323: AP Images; page 327: Fernando Medina/NBAE via Getty Images; page 342: AP Images.

Chapter 12
Page 355: AP Images; page 364: Koichi Kamoshida/Getty Images; page 371: David Deal.

Chapter 13
Page 383: AP Images; page 388: AP Images; page 399: AP Images.

Chapter 14
Page 415: Tim Boyle/Getty Images; page 422: AP Images; page 433: AP Images.

Chapter 15
Page 447: AFP/Getty Images; page 451: AP Images; page 461: AP Images.